S. R.

Irkutsk L. BAYKAL

Ulan
Bator

MONGOLIA

INNER MONGOLIA

BI

I   N   A

Lanchow

YANGTZE

Chungking

Kunming

Hanoi

AOS

O   11

AILAND   VIETNAM

gkok

CAMBODIA

Saigon

9

ALAYA

Singapore   I   N   D   O   N   E   S   I   A

HOKKAIDO

Harbin

MANCHURIA

YALU

Mukden

KOREA

Peking   Seoul   16

YELLOW
SEA

Nanking   Shanghai

EAST
CHINA
SEA

Taipei

TAIWAN

Canton   12

Hong
Kong

SOUTH CHINA SEA

Manila

PHILIPPINES

13   Sulu Arch.

BRUNEI   NORTH
BORNEO

SARAWAK   BORNEO

18

SEA OF JAPAN

JAPAN
Tokyo

RYUKUS   15

PACIFIC   OCEAN

PACIFIC

Communist China

Communist China

Harold C. Hinton

The George Washington University
Institute for Defense Analyses

in World Politics

HOUGHTON MIFFLIN COMPANY · BOSTON

NEW YORK · ATLANTA · GENEVA, ILL. · DALLAS · PALO ALTO

Under the editorship of

DAYTON D. McKEAN

UNIVERSITY OF COLORADO

To the memory of my father

Preface

The list of serious books on Communist China published in the Western world is not so remarkable for length or quality that any special apology is needed for adding a new item to it. Nor do I agree with the widespread belief that "we know" so little about Communist China that no useful work of a comprehensive character can be written on it. Those who feel ignorant have mainly themselves to blame, since more usable material is available in a variety of languages than any one person can possibly find time to read.

This book represents an effort to understand and communicate as much as possible of what is significant about the important, interesting, and complex subject that is the foreign policy and relations of Communist China. China's size and population, its potential power, and its impact on the world are enough to establish the importance and interest. As for the complexity, this is also undeniable, but much of it is not intrinsic to the subject but rather extrinsic, or in other words in the mind of the observer. Most of those who have devoted serious study to Communist China have brought with them an established competence in some other field, usually the study of traditional or modern China, of some other Asian country, of the Soviet Union or international Communism, or of some conventional academic discipline without reference to area. Each of these may be helpful, but each is inadequate and may even be misleading. For Communist China is a vast field of study in its own right, which abuts on those just mentioned and on others beside but is far from coinciding with them, and which displays some similarities with them but also many significant differences.

My own background is mainly in the study of modern Chinese history, but during the past decade I have made an earnest effort to study Communist China without being influenced by any more of this background than was genuinely applicable. Whether I have been successful, and whether whatever success I may have had is reflected in this book, is of course not for me to say. I have also made a strenuous effort to preserve as much objectivity as possible in my analysis of Communist Chinese foreign policy, and to save my own views for the last chapter. My values, insofar as they relate to the subject of the book, may be stated very briefly. My attitude toward

Communism and the leadership and present policies of Communist China is the same as that of Calvin Coolidge's preacher toward sin: I am against them. I believe that the freedom and progress of individuals and communities are best promoted in an open, pluralistic political environment, such as the extreme right and extreme left do their best to prevent or eliminate.

This book presupposes some basic familiarity with China, with Communism, and with Communist China. Those who may lack such a familiarity would do well to consult the Bibliographical Note, where suggestions for background reading will be found.

On the other hand, it must be admitted that this book contains some inferences and interpretations that are at variance with what may be found in the suggested reading or in most of the sources cited in the text. Some of my views, whether right, wrong, or partly right and partly wrong, I believe to be original in the sense that they have not previously appeared in print. Some of them will, I presume, be controversial. I have neither sought nor avoided controversiality for its own sake; my concern has been to present, to the best of my ability, Communist China's foreign policy *wie es eigentlich gewesen*.

I proceed on the basis of no general theory of social or political action; I find most such theories vague and pretentious. In any case, general political theory has little that is useful to say about the twentieth century states that, for lack of a better word, we call totalitarian. In general, political scientists have been too preoccupied with trying to define totalitarianism to give much attention to studying it. Nor do I employ any unique or complex method based on some such general theoretical point of departure. I prefer history, in the sense of observed data and inferences from them, to what may be called science fiction, or the imposition of theory on data. I believe that what is sometimes called kremlinology, demonology, or the study of esoteric communication is essential to an understanding of Communist China as well as of any other Communist regime. This includes such skills as an understanding of what range of current meanings may be attached to familiar terminology, some appreciation of the limitations on the extent to which theory determines political action, a feeling for what has been omitted from a document as well as for what has been said, a grasp of the possibilities for devious historical and chronological allusions, and the like. There is no royal road to such understanding; it must be gained through years of hard work. If there is a master key, it is context and educated intuition.

In saying this, I have presumably made it clear that I have drawn extensively on official Communist Chinese sources in various forms. This would be a much shorter and much weaker book, however, if I had relied exclusively on such official sources, for they specialize in the art of masterly omission and tendentious distortion. It is possible to write intelligently on a totalitarian regime largely on the basis of official and semiofficial sources, as Leonard Schapiro's masterly *The Communist Party of the Soviet Union* shows. There are, however, all too few Leonard Schapiros, and most efforts of this kind have verged on the deplorable; out of professional courtesy I shall refrain from becoming more specific. Communist Chinese official documents are if anything more monolithic and tendentious than Soviet documents, except for those dating from the apogee of Joseph Stalin's reign. I have therefore made extensive, but I hope selective and critical use, of secondary sources, including not only scholarly writings but newspapers. On the latter point, I have generally found that any one trying to do serious work on some obscure episode in the past will consult the best available newspapers for the period; I fail to see why the same procedure should not be applied to the present and the recent past. This is all the more true because of the enormous information-gathering facilities that are available to the world press, and to the American press in particular. Furthermore, trained correspondents are by no means to be despised as interpreters of the events about which they write. In short, the public record is a valid and in fact indispensable basis for writing a book of this kind.

In the text the abbreviation CPR is employed for the Chinese People's Republic (Communist China), and CPC for the Communist Party of China. There is an important distinction between these terms. They correspond respectively to the state and party aspects of the phenomenon under consideration, and these two aspects should not be confused even though they have many points of mutual contact. Having said this, I must now admit that there are places in the text where I use the two abbreviations somewhat indiscriminately, for the sake of variety, as well as probably more numerous places where I use the one rather than the other abbreviation for a particular reason. I believe there will be no confusion on this account; context will provide the clue.

Chinese, Japanese, Korean, and Vietnamese personal names are given in the text (not necessarily in citations in the notes) with the family name first, except for those of Syngman Rhee and John M. Chang. It is becoming conventional in the West, however, to use the last element of most Vietnamese names (except that of Ho Chi Minh, which is really a Chinese name) as though it were the family name ("President Diem").

This book was written over a period of approximately two years, during which the Institute for Defense Analyses freed me from participation in its normal work, which consists of contract research for government agencies on problems relating to national security, in order to further its program for the professional advancement of its staff members and, hopefully, to make possible a contribution to public enlightenment. I am of course grateful for this support. In particular I am indebted to James E. King, Jr., who while Director of the International Studies Division (now the Economic and Political Studies Division) authorized and encouraged the writing of the book. I am also indebted, for a variety of reasons and to various degrees, to the following members or former members of the division: John B. Cary,

James E. Cross, Sidney F. Giffin, Bernard K. Gordon, Paul Guinn, Donald B. Keesing, Maury Lisann, William A. Niskanen, Roger Pineau, William H. Street, and John R. Thomas. In addition, I naturally owe a vast debt of gratitude to scholars who have labored in the same or in adjoining vineyards. This debt, I believe, is adequately reflected in the notes to the text, without specific acknowledgment here. Any list of names would be incomplete, and it would be invidious to refer to some while omitting others. There is a third category of individuals to whom I owe a debt of gratitude; these are persons who have contributed over the past decade to my knowledge and understanding of the problems touched on in this book in other ways than through published writings, but whom I do not feel free to name. I say this not to lend the book any mysterious aura of authority, but in order that if any of these individuals should read it he will know that he has not been forgotten. There are also some individuals who have contributed to my understanding of particular points and whose names are given in the notes to the appropriate portions of the text. I must add that neither the Institute for Defense Analyses, nor any department or agency of the United States government, nor any of the individuals named or referred to above bears any responsibility for the conclusions drawn and views expressed, which are solely mine.

Thanks are also due to Virginia Walker for typing, and to Richard N. Clark for editing, the manuscript.

Harold C. Hinton

Washington, D.C.
February 10, 1965

Contents

■ PART THREE / Communist China as an Asian Power

CONTENTS

CONTENTS

PART ONE

Background

□ 1

The Roots of Communist China's Foreign Policy

To say that the Chinese Communist revolution is a non-Western revolution is more than a truism. That revolution has been primarily directed, not like the French Revolution against indigenous tradition, but against alien Western influences that approached the level of domination and drastically altered China's traditional relationship with the world. Hence the Chinese Communist attitude toward China's traditional past is selectively critical, but by no means totally hostile. The Chinese Communist revolution, and the foreign policy of the regime to which it has given rise, have several roots, each of which is imbedded in the past more deeply than one would tend to expect of a movement seemingly so convulsive.

■ THE CHINESE TRADITION

Being the easternmost of the primary civilizations that arose in the Old World, traditional China was probably the most isolated, although not necessarily the most nearly unique, of those civilizations.[1] Its contacts with other primary civilizations, although not with its immediate environs, tended furthermore to diminish with the passage of time.[2]

---

[1] I would maintain that, among the primary civilizations, India developed in the most nearly unique direction, by virtue of the interaction between the Dravidian and Indo-Iranian cultures after about 1500 B.C.

[2] One reason for this was the spread of Islam across much of Central Asia, beginning in the mid-eighth century. The Chinese also tended to isolate themselves, from about the ninth century, by means of a growing xenophobia. (Edwin O. Reischauer and John K. Fairbank, *East Asia: The Great Tradition*, Boston: Houghton Mifflin, 1960, pp. 183ff.)

Within its own somewhat limited horizons, traditional China was pre-eminent for its power and its cultural attainments. China to its inhabitants was the Middle Kingdom, the center of a world order in which status was proportional to the varying degrees of acceptance of Chinese ethics, culture, and agricultural practices.[3] Since numerous other Asian rulers found it advisable or advantageous, or both, to accommodate themselves to the Chinese view, traditional China at its times of greatest power was the center of a large but rather loose system of tributary states.[4]

The Chinese superiority complex institutionalized in this tributary system was justified by any standards less advanced or efficient than those of the modern West. China developed an elaborate and effective political system resting on a remarkable cultural unity, the latter in turn being due mainly to the general acceptance of a common, although difficult, written language and a common set of ethical and social values, known as Confucianism.[5] At the base of the entire culture lay a uniquely productive traditional agriculture that combined with increasing efficiency the elements of rice culture, water control, and the maintenance of soil fertility.[6]

Traditional China to a great extent was undone by its own success. Its superiority complex, however justified by its own standards, deprived it of the flexibility and willingness to learn that might have enabled it to adjust, and that did enable Japan to adjust, to the impact of a wholly different type of culture, that of the modern West. Even apart from that, Chinese agriculture and the resulting high levels of nutrition set in motion a process of demographic growth that has made the Chinese for centuries the most numerous single people on earth. For many centuries there was room for expansion, mainly in South China and usually at the expense of less advanced peoples.[7] By the beginning of the nineteenth century, however, even before the Western powers began to detach China's tributary states and otherwise impinge upon its expansion and development, most of the available cultivable land had been occupied, and mountain and desert barriers made further expansion difficult. The factors that were bound to produce a crisis sooner or later in China's traditional culture were therefore internal as well as external in origin.

---

[3] This order, in the full sense, included only Korea, Japan, and Vietnam (or Annam). The Central Asian nomadic peoples were not included, except at times as tributaries.

[4] Cf. John K. Fairbank and S. Y. Teng, "On the Ch'ing Tributary System," *Harvard Journal of Asiatic Studies*, vol. vi (1941), pp. 135–246.

[5] Although China was conquered in the seventeenth century by the non-Chinese Manchus, they adopted enough of traditional Chinese culture to make possible a reasonable preservation of its continuity. The already considerable disunity within traditional India, on the other hand, was worsened by the conquest of most of it by the Moslem Moguls in the sixteenth century.

[6] F. H. King, *Farmers of Forty Centuries, or Permanent Agriculture in China, Korea and Japan,* London: Jonathan Cape, 1927.

[7] Herold J. Wiens, *China's March Toward the Tropics,* Hamden, Conn.: The Shoe String Press, 1954.

The main common thread linking this complex traditional past with current Communist Chinese foreign policy is the concept of Chinese superiority.[8] Communist, like traditional, China believes that it is the repository of unique values that ought to be accepted by all mankind and that this acceptance should create a willingness to acknowledge Chinese political leadership even in remote areas where China's power cannot reach, and still more in Asia where it can. There are important differences, of course. Traditional China tended to be aggressive as a state but relatively passive as an ideological force; it often invaded the territory of other peoples but did not ordinarily try to spread its culture in this way. For a number of reasons that include the risks of the nuclear age, Communist China tends to behave in just the opposite manner. As a state it has not been especially aggressive, at least in its overt behavior, but it propagates its ideology outside its borders with vigor and sometimes with violence. Another important difference is the fact that whereas the values of traditional China were almost entirely indigenous, those of Chinese Communism are, to a significant extent, Marxist-Leninist and therefore essentially of European origin. For this the Chinese Communists seem to consider themselves more than compensated, however, by a belief that in accepting Marxism-Leninism they are marching with the forces of human progress, which will eventually restore to China the position of preeminence in the world that it once occupied in the eyes of its own tradition.

■ MODERN CHINESE HISTORY

Traditional China had neither the knowledge nor the power that would have been necessary to cope with the superior science, technology, economic organization, and military force that an expanding West brought to bear on it, beginning in the eighteenth century. From the middle of the nineteenth, the tributary states fell one by one under the control of Britain, France, Russia, or Japan. At the end of the nineteenth century the most productive parts of China itself, except for the inland province of Szechuan, were carved up into commercial and to some extent political spheres of influence by the same powers, plus Germany. Without becoming a colony, China lost, or failed to acquire, many attributes of sovereignty. It had many of the disadvantages of colonial status, and few of the advantages. In this it resembled the Arab world, and nowhere has anti-Western nationalism burned more fiercely in the twentieth century than among the Arabs and the Chinese. In the Chinese case, the general sense of national weakness and humiliation was rendered still keener by a unique phenomenon, the modernization of Japan

---

[8] Cf. the opening passage in Mao Tse-tung, *The Chinese Revolution and the Chinese Communist Party* (December, 1939), in *Selected Works of Mao Tse-tung*, New York: International Publishers, 5 vols. to date, 1954–63, vol. 3, pp. 72–74.

and its rise to great power status. Japan's success threw China's failure into sharp relief.[9]

The Japanese performance contributed to the discrediting and collapse of China's imperial system, but it did little to make things easier for the latter's successor. The Republic (1912–1928) was never able to achieve territorial and national unity in the face of bad communications and the widespread diffusion of modern arms throughout the country. Lacking internal authority, it did not carry much weight in its foreign relations. As it floundered, there arose two more radical political forces, the relatively powerful Kuomintang of Sun Yat-sen and Chiang Kai-shek, and the younger and weaker Communist Party of China (CPC). With indispensable support, down to 1927, from the CPC and from the Third International, the Kuomintang achieved sufficient success by 1928 so that it felt justified in proclaiming a new government, controlled by itself, for the whole of China.[10]

For a time the Kuomintang made a valiant effort to tackle China's numerous and colossal problems, including those that had ruined its predecessor — poor communications and the wide diffusion of arms. It also took a strongly anti-Western line in its foreign relations, with some success. By 1935 it had reduced the once influential CPC, now in revolt against it, to the level of a seemingly manageable nuisance.

It is impossible to say whether the Kuomintang's regime would ultimately have proven viable and successful if it had not been ruined by an external enemy, as the Republic had been by its internal opponents. The behavior of that enemy, imperial Japan, suggests an estimate on its part that the Kuomintang was in fact making significant progress toward national unification and development. The more the Japanese exerted preemptive pressures on China, however, the more its people tended to look on the Kuomintang as the only force that could prevent China from being dominated by Japan.

When a large-scale Sino-Japanese war broke out in 1937, the Kuomintang immediately suffered major military defeats and lost control of eastern China. Confined to the backward interior and almost cut off from the outside world, it was saved from total futility or defeat only by Japan's suicidal decision to attack the United States and overrun Southeast Asia. But military rescue from Japan brought no significant improvement in the Kuomintang's domestic performance in the political and economic fields, which tended if anything to get worse.

Clearly the pre-Communist history of modern China has been essentially one of weakness, humiliation, and failure. This is the atmosphere in which the present leadership of the CPC grew up. The result has been a strong

---

[9] Cf. Ssu-yü Teng and John K. Fairbank, *China's Response to the West: A Documentary Survey, 1839–1923*, Harvard University Press, 1954, p. 150.

[10] Cf. Conrad Brandt, *Stalin's Failure in China, 1924–1927*, Harvard University Press, 1958.

determination on the part of that leadership to eliminate foreign influence within China, to modernize their country, and to eliminate Western (including ultimately Soviet) influence from eastern Asia.[11]

■ UNDERDEVELOPMENT AND SOCIAL CHANGE

During the late nineteenth and early twentieth centuries, enclaves of modern industry appeared in some of China's cities. Much of this was owned by foreign nationals and therefore not fully under Chinese control. Still less under Chinese control was the major heavy industrial base that the Japanese constructed in Manchuria after they seized it in 1931. Far more than it was energized by these two modern sectors, the Chinese economy was held back by the massive poverty and overpopulation of its third sector, the vast traditional, rural hinterland.[12] The modern sectors had some effect on the traditional one, but the effect was disruptive as well as constructive. Still more disruptive was the impact of the Japanese invasion of eastern China in 1937, which displaced millions of people into the interior and greatly accelerated social changes that had previously been only in their early stages. One of the most important of these changes was a strong tendency toward the breakup of the traditional extended family into its nuclear components and the erosion of the traditional solidarity even among members of the nuclear family.

China was changing and even developing, but its overwhelming marks were still poverty and weakness. During their rise to power the Chinese Communists, like most politically conscious Chinese, were aware of these conditions and anxious to eliminate them. Mao Tse-tung's famous work *On New Democracy*, published in 1940, envisaged a mixed economy under Communist control, such as had existed in the Soviet Union during the period of the New Economic Policy.[13] The stress was more upon social transformation, social justice, and public ownership of the "commanding heights" of the economy than upon development. By 1945, Mao was talking more unequivocally about development, still within the framework of a mixed

---

[11] Cf. ". . . the Chinese revolution will affect neighboring countries — large colonies like India, Indo-China, Java, and Korea — arousing the teeming masses of those oppressed nations to political struggle; it will fundamentally shake the foundations of imperialist Japan and England and deal a heavy blow to capitalism in the U.S.A." (Political Resolution of the Sixth National Congress of the CPC, September, 1928, in Conrad Brandt, Benjamin Schwartz, and John K. Fairbank, *A Documentary History of Chinese Communism*, Harvard University Press, 1952, p. 130). The statement about the Soviet Union is frankly an inference; by 1964, however, the CPC was demanding that the Soviet Union be refused representation at the forthcoming Second Asian-African Conference, on the ground that it was not properly an Asian state.

[12] Cf. Alexander Eckstein in Howard L. Boorman and others, *Moscow-Peking Axis: Strengths and Strains*, New York: Harper, 1957, pp. 55–60.

[13] *Selected Works*, vol. 3, pp. 122–123.

economy under Communist control, and stressing the need for more heavy industry; presumably he had been impressed by the role of heavy industry in determining the outcome of the Second World War. He said that the necessary capital would come mainly from "the accumulated wealth of the Chinese people" but added that China would welcome foreign aid and even private foreign investment, under nonexploitative conditions.[14]

For a number of reasons, the CPC attempted to preserve at least the flavor of this relatively moderate program as it approached and gained power. Apart from the natural desire to maintain at least the semblance of consistency, there was the need to avoid alienating too much Chinese public support. Among the reasons for this, in turn, was the fact that such support would be essential to the regime if Stalin treated it as he had treated Tito. Furthermore, the CPC was extremely anxious to avoid encouraging Stalin to think of Communist China as being on the same footing with Eastern Europe, which he mercilessly oppressed after his break with Tito. Accordingly, the CPC not only refused to accept for itself the term "people's democracy," which Stalin coined for Eastern Europe and applied to the Communist regime in China as well, but continued to use the term "new democracy" not only for itself but even for the East European countries.[15]

On the other hand, there were limits to the CPC's ability and desire to assert its independence from Stalin. The fate of Tito served as an ominous warning. The CPC thought it necessary to conciliate Stalin in order to mitigate his pressures on Manchuria and Sinkiang.[16] There was an assumed need for military protection from the United States. Furthermore, temporary compliance with Stalin's wishes, where these did not impinge intolerably on Chinese freedom of action, might enable the CPC to acquire the industrial aid that would enable it in time to assert a more nearly complete independence.[17] Even if the politically distasteful West were willing to provide such aid, it would be difficult to receive it since two of China's major ports, Shanghai and Canton, were under Nationalist blockade.[18] In any case, Stalin's veto of the East European desire to participate in the Marshall Plan in 1947 made it very unlikely that he would tolerate acceptance of Western aid by Communist China even if it were available.

But there were also limits to Stalin's freedom to maneuver against the

---

[14] This does not appear in the edited version in the *Selected Works;* for the original version see *Mao Tse-tung hsuan-chi* (Selected Works of Mao Tse-tung), Manchuria Publishing House, 1948, p. 336, and Stuart Gelder, *The Chinese Communists*, London: Gollancz, 1946, p. 46.

[15] Cf. Benjamin I. Schwartz in *Moscow-Peking Axis, op. cit.,* pp. 125–132.

[16] On these pressures see the United States Department of State's statement of January 26, 1950 (quoted in Max Beloff, *Soviet Policy in the Far East, 1944–1951,* Oxford University Press, 1953, p. 72).

[17] Note the expectation of Soviet aid expressed by the Third Plenary Session (Plenum) of the CPC's Seventh Central Committee, in March, 1949 (*Documentary History, op. cit.,* p. 445).

[18] Tientsin was not blockaded, but it is a poor port and had been badly battered during its capture from the Nationalist garrison.

CPC. He was almost certainly anxious to avoid another rupture like the one with Tito. For political reasons as well as considerations of Soviet security, he could not take lightly the possibility that the CPC might either fail massively in its domestic program or suffer a serious defeat at the hands of an external opponent. Still more important, by the spring of 1949 he evidently felt an urgent need to compensate himself for the colossal setback in Europe represented by the failure of the Berlin Blockade and the formation of NATO. For this purpose the Chinese Communists, even before they had formally proclaimed themselves to be in power, appeared the best available instrument, although far from an ideal one.[19] Accordingly in April, 1949, as Chinese Communist armies began to capture the cities of the Yangtze Valley, Soviet pronouncements on the CPC took on a much more respectful and enthusiastic tone. In May Stalin ended his implicit support, or at least acceptance, of the possibility of a division of the mainland of China between the Communists and the Nationalists, in the manner of Germany or Korea, by at last withdrawing his ambassador from the Nationalist capital, which was then Canton.[20] On June 7-9, *Pravda* reprinted an important work by Liu Shao-ch'i, *On Internationalism and Nationalism*, originally published seven months earlier, which gave a somewhat qualified support to Stalin as against Tito and an unqualified support to the Soviet Union as against the United States.[21] In the same month, an important meeting of Soviet orientalists endorsed Maoism as the basic strategy for revolutionizing the underdeveloped areas.[22] In July, Stalin made a major trade agreement with the Chinese Communist regional government of Manchuria.[23]

Clearly a far-reaching accommodation was in the making by the middle of 1949. On the Chinese side, it found its major public formulation in Mao Tse-tung's celebrated work, *On the People's Democratic Dictatorship*, published on July 1. In this document Mao announced the CPC's rejection of any possibility of aid from the West, proclaimed his party's alignment with the "socialist camp" in the Cold War and its rejection of neutralism for China or any other country ("a third road does not exist"), and indicated his acceptance of a basically Stalinist domestic program: a party-controlled police state, the development of state-owned heavy industry, and the "step-by-step" socialization of agriculture.[24] The CPC continued to

---

[19] At the end of 1949 the Soviet press referred to the CPC's victory in the Chinese civil war as the most important event of the year, even more so than the Soviet Union's first nuclear test.

[20] Beloff, *op. cit.*, p. 65.

[21] English summary of the original in *China Digest* (Hong Kong), December 14, 1948.

[22] John H. Kautsky, *Moscow and the Communist Party of India*, New York: John Wiley, 1956, p. 91.

[23] Beloff, *op. cit.*, pp. 69-70.

[24] Abridged translation of the original in *Documentary History, op. cit.*, pp. 449-461. The famous denunciation of neutralism (*ibid.*, pp. 453-454) has been deleted from the recent official translation (*Selected Works of Mao Tse-tung*, Peking: Foreign

insist, however, that the adoption of this program did not represent a repudiation of "new democracy."

It is clear, then, that even before officially coming to power, the CPC adopted for a variety of reasons a domestic program that was as nearly Stalinist as Chinese conditions, including the state of Chinese public opinion and a felt need for a degree of consistency with earlier pronouncements by Mao on economic policy, would allow. The adoption of this program, and the redirection of China's external trade toward the Soviet Union and Eastern Europe to which it gave rise, were intensified but not caused by the imposition of strategic trade controls against Communist China (the CPR) as a result of its intervention in the Korean War late in 1950. On the other hand, neither did the CPC merely imitate Stalin's program and throw itself into his arms. In the economic as in other fields, the decision to "lean to one side" was a calculated one in which ideology played the part of a necessary but not a sufficient cause.

■ MARXISM-LENINISM AND THE SOVIET UNION

Marx and Engels regarded traditional China as unique among early non-Western civilizations because of the prevalence of private landholding. They considered the China trade, as it existed during their own lifetimes, to be essential to the survival of capitalism in Europe. Thus they hoped that a reduction of this trade due to Chinese national resistance to European penetration, such as they interpreted the Taiping Rebellion to be, might bring about the overthrow of capitalism in Europe. Their high estimate of China's potential as a world revolutionary force later helped to commend their thinking to radical Chinese intellectuals, after that thinking had been dramatically called to the latter's attention by the October Revolution in Russia.[25]

Even before 1917, Lenin saw nationalism in China, as well as in the colonial countries, as a valuable potential ally against "imperialism" and identified Sun Yat-sen as the most promising Chinese nationalist leader. In July, 1919, when Chinese opinion was extremely hostile to the West and Japan, Lenin's revolutionary regime announced its repudiation of all the special privileges extorted from China by the tsarist regime, which had already been lost in any case. The powerful impact of this renunciation on Chinese opinion was not entirely obliterated by the fact that the Soviet

Languages Press, 1961, vol. iv, p. 415; note that vol. iv of this edition, whose first three volumes have not yet been published, covers 1945–49 and is not identical with vol. 4 of the London and New York editions, which cover the years up to 1949 in five volumes).

[25] Maurice Meissner, "The Despotism of Concepts: Wittfogel and Marx on China," *The China Quarterly*, no. 16 (October–December, 1963), pp. 99–111.

government shortly began to seek to regain control of the strategic Chinese Eastern Railway across Manchuria.[26]

On the other hand, the assertion of Soviet national interests has often tended to impede the realization of international and local Communist revolutionary aims, in China and elsewhere. Another impediment has been a frequent Soviet tendency, since Lenin's time, to identify as progressive and even revolutionary leaders and movements of "national bourgeois" origin who have then shown themselves quite capable of turning on their Communist allies and rending them, so as not to be subverted by them. At the Second World Congress of the Comintern in 1920, Lenin rightly disagreed with the Indian Communist M. N. Roy and insisted that the proletariat in any underdeveloped country was too weak to allow a Communist-led revolution at that time. On the other hand, Lenin accepted Roy's distinction between the revolutionary segment of the "national bourgeoisie," which could be trusted, and the reformist section, which could not.[27] Lenin was probably justified, from the Communist viewpoint, in trusting Sun Yat-sen, but Stalin was certainly wrong, after the death of both men, in according a comparable degree of trust to Chiang Kai-shek. Since the ensuing catastrophe the leadership of the CPC has never forgotten the distinction that Roy had urged on Lenin and has always regarded Chiang as not even a reformist but a reactionary. In recent years the CPC has explicitly urged the importance of the distinction between the revolutionary and nonrevolutionary segments of the "national bourgeoisie" on Khrushchev, who they are convinced tended to ignore it. The CPC also harks back to Roy, without mentioning him, in stressing the desirability of revolutions being led by "proletarian" (Communist) rather than by "national bourgeois" parties.[28]

Although from the ideological standpoint China was perhaps a less attractive target than India to Lenin and the early Comintern, it was more accessible and more advantageous from the standpoint of the Soviet national interest. China was remarkable for its size, its population, and its potential importance in world politics. If not a colony, it was the classic example of a "semicolony"; the Comintern could strike at all the "imperialist" powers by undermining their position in China. The Chinese proletariat was small, but it was in a militant mood and was situated in and near the major enclaves of "imperialist" influence. The entire country was in an advanced state of political turmoil. Sun Yat-sen and his Kuomintang seemed a promising ally. Finally, in such a chaotic situation there was always the possibility that Japan, a power much feared by the Bolsheviks, might establish a strong position in China and thus threaten the security of Soviet Asia. Conversely, a revolu-

[26] Allen S. Whiting, *Soviet Policies in China, 1917–1924*, Columbia University Press, 1954, Chapter II.

[27] John P. Haithcox, "The Roy-Lenin Debate on Colonial Policy: a New Interpretation," *The Journal of Asian Studies*, vol. xxiii, no. 1 (November, 1963), pp. 93–101.

[28] Wang Chia-hsiang, "The International Significance of the Chinese People's Victory," in *Ten Glorious Years*, Peking: Foreign Languages Press, 1960, pp. 271–282.

tionary China aligned with the Comintern would be a valuable counterweight to Japan.

The appeal of Marxism-Leninism, the October Revolution, and the Comintern encountered considerable receptivity on the part of Chinese intellectuals. It is sometimes said that this was due in part to some aspects of the Chinese cultural tradition, but such a theory has little to recommend it. Most of that tradition had already been discredited and undermined by its failure to cope with the challenge of the West, and in any case it was among the modern-minded, not the traditionally oriented, sections of Chinese society that the impact of Marxism-Leninism was felt. It was not only Chinese tradition that had become discredited; so to a large extent had its Western liberal alternative, by virtue of the failure of parliamentary institutions in China under the Republic and the high-handed behavior toward China of Japan and the Allied powers at the time of the Versailles Conference.[29] Under these circumstances, Marxism-Leninism, the October Revolution, and the Comintern, and in particular Lenin's support for a worldwide struggle against "imperialism," had a considerable appeal.

Since China was not a Western colony, its intelligentsia was not introduced to Marxism before 1917, as Indonesia's was. Chinese students and intellectuals did not have large-scale contact with European opposite numbers until the years immediately following the First World War, when many lived and studied in Europe. It is not surprising that Marxist groups and then Communist Party branches soon emerged among the Chinese student communities in several European cities, notably Paris.[30] A parallel process in China resulted in the formation of the CPC in 1921.

China's first Communists were impressed and attracted by Marxism-Leninism's claim to scientific infallibility, by the dramatic spectacle of the October Revolution in what had been the most backward of the "imperialist" nations, by the vision of a worldwide revolution against "imperialism" supported by the new Soviet government and the Comintern, and by the possibilities of Leninism as a technique of political action in China. Later the Stalinist techniques of nation-building also exercised some attraction.

More immediately, the CPC was faced with Stalin's increasing control of the Soviet party and of the Comintern. This process had passed the point of no return by the time that Sun Yat-sen's death (1925) brought to the surface the latent tensions between the center and the right of the Kuomintang, on the one hand, and the left Kuomintang, the Comintern and Soviet agents in China, and the CPC on the other. Stalin was caught in a dilemma. He could not abandon his alliance with the Kuomintang or give up his efforts to

---

[29] Cf. Benjamin I. Schwartz, *Chinese Communism and the Rise of Mao,* Harvard University Press, 1951, pp. 13, 21.

[30] Cf. Conrad Brandt, "The French-Returned Elite in the Chinese Communist Party," in E. F. Szczepanik, ed., *Symposium on Economic and Social Problems of the Far East,* Hong Kong University Press, 1962, pp. 229–238.

impart a leftist flavor to its behavior because of Trotsky, who continually criticized his China policy as not revolutionary enough. He could not take too leftist a line, however, because of the danger of arousing the right Kuomintang and the "imperialist" powers, Britain and Japan in particular; by the spring of 1927, when the tensions within the Kuomintang-Communist alliance were coming to a head, there was serious apprehension in the Soviet Union of a war with Britain. Stalin's resulting vacillations, translated into contradictory Comintern directives to the CPC and reflecting also conflicting advice from his representatives in China,[31] left the CPC unprepared to protect itself when Chiang Kai-shek turned his army against it in April, 1927.[32]

In spite of this catastrophe, Stalin and the Comintern retained their control of the central apparatus of the CPC, which gravitated to Shanghai, where it could maintain contact with Comintern agents and receive subsidies from the Comintern. A series of arrests of Comintern agents by British police in various parts of Asia in 1930–31 largely interrupted contact between the Comintern and the CPC for the time being and contributed to the rise within the latter of a more indigenous-minded leadership under Mao Tse-tung. After the CPC established its main base in Northwest China in 1935, increased contact occurred through Sinkiang, which was then controlled by a warlord who was under Soviet influence.[33] Stalin never regained the influence on the CPC that he had exerted before 1931, although there is reason to think that after the outbreak of the Sino-Japanese War he wanted his confidant Wang Ming to take leadership of the CPC away from Mao Tse-tung and steer the party into a path of sincere collaboration with the Kuomintang against Japan.[34] Stalin dissolved the Comintern in May, 1943, just before the end of the Trident Conference in Washington, at which plans were made for an Allied landing in North China, in addition to the already projected landings in Sicily, Italy, and France.[35] Such a landing might produce complications between Allied and Communist troops, and Stalin presumably did not want to be involved. Soon afterward he made some deprecating remarks about the CPC, to the effect that its members were not Communists at all.[36] When the Kuomintang intensified its military pressures on the CPC at the same time, however, the Soviet press responded with

---

[31] Robert C. North and Xenia J. Eudin, *M. N. Roy's Mission to China: The Communist-Kuomintang Split of 1927*, University of California Press, 1963, p. 59.

[32] Brandt, *op. cit.*, Chapters IV–V.

[33] Cf. Allen S. Whiting and General Sheng Shih-ts'ai, *Sinkiang: Pawn or Pivot?*, Michigan State University Press, 1958.

[34] Charles B. McLane, *Soviet Policy and the Chinese Communists, 1931–1946*, Columbia University Press, 1958, pp. 119–123.

[35] On the Trident Conference see Maurice Matloff, *Strategic Planning for Coalition Warfare, 1943–1944*, Washington: Department of the Army, 1959, Chapter VI.

[36] Tang Tsou, *America's Failure in China, 1941–50*, University of Chicago Press, p. 163.

some rebukes that seem to have contributed, together with American pressures, to moderating the Kuomintang's behavior toward the CPC.[37]

Beginning in 1943, and most notably at Yalta and Potsdam in 1945 and the Foreign Ministers Conferences of 1945 and 1947, Stalin attempted to secure the agreement of the United States, without the participation of either the Chinese Nationalists or the Chinese Communists, to a situation in postwar China acceptable to him. His main objectives were the removal of American forces from China and (by his own forces) of Japanese heavy industrial installations from Manchuria, both of which he regarded as threats to Soviet security. He also put himself in a position to deny access to Port Arthur, Dairen, and the important railway lines leading northward from them, to any hostile power. He denounced American military and even economic aid to the Nationalists but is not known to have given anything resembling equivalent aid to the Communists. He denied the latter the right formally to accept Japanese surrenders at the end of the war and apparently wanted them to establish their main base in Manchuria, where they could be controlled. They were to enter into a political and military coalition of some kind with the Nationalists, rather than fighting an all-out civil war against them, in the hope that they would eventually come to power by primarily political means that would not induce American intervention.[38]

Notwithstanding Stalin's consistent subordination of the interests of the CPC, as well as of other Communist Parties, to the requirements of Soviet national security and policy, he retains a high place in the CPC's regard, even though one sometimes suspects that the CPC prefers him dead to alive. As the CPC has made abundantly clear since Stalin began to be publicly attacked in the Soviet Union in 1956, the CPC regards him as a legitimate "continuator" of Marxism-Leninism and as a major statesman who displayed both greater resolution and greater restraint in action in the struggle against "imperialism" than his successors have displayed.[39] As the CPC was later to urge Khrushchev to be, Stalin was strategically bold and tactically cautious.

■ **THE RISE OF THE COMMUNIST MOVEMENT**[40]

After Chiang Kai-shek broke with it in 1927, the CPC found itself in a bad way. It had no armed forces or territorial bases of its own. It had no program or strategy other than that of Stalin, who from the Sixth World Congress of the Comintern in 1928 to the Seventh in 1935 insisted, largely because of the disaster he had suffered in China in 1927, that Communist

---

[37] McLane, *op. cit.*, pp. 166–169.
[38] Cf. *ibid.*, pp. 177ff.; Beloff, *op. cit.*, pp. 20ff.
[39] Cf. Lewis S. Feuer, "Marxisms . . . How Many?" *Problems of Communism*, vol. xiii, no. 2 (March–April, 1964), p. 50.
[40] Probably the best short history in English is Wan Yah-kang, *The Rise of Communism in China (1920–1950)*, Hong Kong: Chung Shu Publishing Company, 1952.

Parties everywhere must promote world revolution in a time of depression, and the security of the Soviet Union, by waging all-out political war against the indigenous bourgeoisie. The CPC was ridden with factionalism; the successful effort to replace this situation with one of relative "bolshevization" (a Communist euphemism for monolithic, imposed unity) was ultimately to be made, not by Stalin, but by Mao Tse-tung. The CPC had no significant domestic allies. Worst of all, it had no historic opportunities until after 1937, when it was able to take advantage of several presented by policy errors attributable to the Japanese and the Kuomintang. These handicaps were progressively overcome during the two decades following the disaster of 1927, and the result was victory.

Parallel with the Comintern-dominated central apparatus of the CPC in Shanghai, there arose a half dozen Communist-led base areas, each with a guerrilla army, in Central and South China. These bases existed mainly by virtue of the efforts of the local Communist leadership to satisfy the serious economic and social grievances of the local peasants, often violently, through such means as redistribution of land at the expense of landlords and the reduction of interest rates at the expense of moneylenders.[41] Of these base areas, or soviets, the most important was the one led by Mao Tse-tung and centered in southeastern Kiangsi. Accordingly, Mao was elected chairman of a Central Soviet Government, supposedly controlling all the Communist base areas, in November, 1931.

The relations between these base areas and the party headquarters in Shanghai were touchy. The former alone disposed, on a limited scale, of armed force and revenues derived from the power to tax, whereas the latter was dependent on the support of the Comintern. The virtual interruption of contact with, or at least subsidies from, the Comintern in 1931, plus mounting Kuomintang police pressures, dealt a severe blow to the central apparatus in Shanghai, then under the control of a Moscow-oriented group known as the Returned Students.

The latter had no choice but to move to Mao's soviet in Kiangsi, with results that have been variously interpreted. On the one hand, it has been asserted that Mao then established control over the Returned Students and the central machinery of the party.[42] On the other hand, the official Maoist version, published after 1943, is that the Returned Students succeeded in some unexplained way in taking control of the Central Soviet Government, and more particularly of the Red Army, away from Mao.[43] Actually, neither explanation appears accurate, and it seems that a "collective leadership," a state of controlled tensions between Mao and his rivals, existed in which Mao

---

41 Cf. Mao Tse-tung, *Why Can China's Red Political Power Exist?*, *Selected Works*, vol. 1, pp. 63–70.
42 Wan, *op. cit.*, pp. 34–35; Schwartz, *op. cit.*, p. 185.
43 Hu Chiao-mu, *Thirty Years of the Communist Party of China*, Peking: Foreign Languages Press, 1954, pp. 35–36.

was an important but not a dominating figure.[44] The fiction of Returned Student dominance was very probably invented much later in order to relieve Mao of blame for the military disaster soon suffered by the CPC and to fasten it on the Returned Students.[45]

During 1934 Chiang Kai-shek succeeded in surrounding the Kiangsi Soviet with an enormous army and exerting unendurable pressure on it. In mid-October, however, most of the surrounded Communists succeeded in breaking out and set off on their famous Long March, whose original destination was apparently Szechuan, in Southwest China.

According to the CPC's official, post-1943 version of its own history, Mao upset the "Left opportunist" Returned Students, without purging them, and assumed the "leading position in the whole Party" at a conference held at Tsunyi, in Kweichow, in January, 1935.[46] There are strong reasons for doubting this version. The timing again suggests a desire to blame the Returned Students for military disaster, this time during the early stages of the Long March. For Mao to have assumed formal leadership of the CPC at that time would have brought him into undesirably direct contact with the Comintern and would have imposed the necessity either to obey Stalin's directives or defy him openly. Mao preferred to circumvent Stalin, a process that has been aptly described as "emancipation by conspiracy." The situation in the party apparatus seems rather to have remained a "collective leadership" whose main components were Mao, Chou En-lai and the Returned Students, and Chang Kuo-t'ao.[47] On the whole, Mao gained power within the party in gradual stages and did not choose to complete the process until he had effective control of the Red Army and, largely through it, of the base areas that had been created by the CPC. Mao's rise seems to have been due not to Moscow's favor but to his intelligence, his skill at intra-party maneuvering, and his high qualifications as a political and military strategist.

In the summer of 1935, Mao debated with Chang Kuo-t'ao the important question of the destination of the Long March and therefore of the future

---

[44] Mao made the principal speech (omitted from the *Selected Works;* for a summary see Tso-liang Hsiao, *Power Relations within the Chinese Communist Movement, 1930–1934: A Study of Documents,* University of Washington Press, 1961, p. 270–273) and was reelected Chairman of the Central Soviet Government (*ibid.,* pp. 280–281) at a congress of soviets held in January, 1934.

[45] One indication is that whereas sources connected with the Returned Students listed six Kuomintang campaigns against the soviet districts, Maoist sources have consistently given five. Hu, *op. cit.,* p. 36, gives 1933, which is too late, as the date for the Returned Students' move to Kiangsi, probably in order to emphasize their connection with the last stage of the military operations in Kiangsi. There were differences of outlook, as well as something of a power contest, between Mao and the Returned Students; the latter appear to have been more doctrinaire, urban, and Moscow-oriented.

[46] *Ibid.,* p. 37.

[47] This is strongly suggested by the composition of the CPC's delegation to the Executive Committee of the Comintern elected at the latter's Seventh World Congress in 1935: Wang Ming, Mao Tse-tung, Chou En-lai, and Chang Kuo-t'ao (McLane, *op. cit.,* p. 61, n. 31).

main base of the Chinese Communist movement. Szechuan had become militarily untenable. Chang apparently advocated going to Sinkiang, then under the control of a pro-Soviet warlord.[48] Mao objected, evidently on the ground that a Chinese revolutionary movement must be based in China Proper, and perhaps also on the ground that a movement based in Sinkiang would be too easily dominated by Stalin. On the other hand, northern Shensi offered many advantages: an existing Communist base, immunity from being surrounded by central government forces, sufficient nearness to the Soviet Union to permit communication (via Sinkiang) and yet enough remoteness to prevent direct domination, and access to the strategic areas of Shansi and the North China Plain. After Chang's forces suffered serious defeats in 1936 that fatally weakened his power position within the party, he had no choice but to join Mao in Shensi. He was expelled from the party in 1938, ostensibly for advocating sincere collaboration with the Kuomintang in a common struggle against Japan, rather than the more devious strategy favored by Mao.

The CPC had no hope of coming to power solely, or even primarily, through armed force until at least as late as 1937, and by 1935 its armies had been seriously weakened by prolonged fighting with stronger opponents. It was clearly necessary to supplement "armed struggle" with "political struggle." This meant a search for support against the hard core of the Kuomintang from one or more other elements of the population. But this search inevitably encountered a dilemma. Potential allies among the Establishment, such as regional warlords, dissident elements of the Kuomintang, and businessmen, as well as intellectuals and students, tended to respond best to nationalist appeals. Peasants and workers, on the other hand, and peasants in particular, tended to be relatively indifferent to such appeals but to respond readily to others based on class struggle and social revolution — land redistribution, rent and interest reduction, strikes, and the like.[49] Clearly the CPC could not have it both ways by maximizing its appeal to both groups simultaneously. The problem, as usual in politics, was to find some formula representing an optimal combination of the two types of appeal for a given historical situation. But this truth was not immediately apparent to the CPC.

Initially, after the break with the Kuomintang in 1927, the emphasis was heavily on class struggle, and this line in any case conformed with that of the Comintern between its Sixth and Seventh World Congresses. The Japanese Army's invasion of Manchuria in 1931, however, and still more the Japanese Navy's attack on Shanghai early in 1932, opened up another perspective. If

---

[48] There is some confusion on this point because Chang subsequently wintered in Sikang, in eastern Tibet. He made for Sinkiang in 1936, however, only to suffer severe defeats en route.

[49] For an excellent case study focused on Shansi see Donald G. Gillin, " 'Peasant Nationalism' in the History of Chinese Communism," *The Journal of Asian Studies*, vol. xxiii, no. 2 (February, 1964), pp. 269–289.

the natural tendency of the Japanese armed forces to flesh their swords on the Kuomintang's armies could be inflamed to the point of invasion, and the Chinese Red Army kept largely out of the way, perhaps the Japanese would destroy the Kuomintang, or make it possible for the CPC to do so later. Mao for one predicted, at least as early as 1936, that Japan would become involved in a war with the Western powers over Southeast Asia, and perhaps with the Soviet Union as well. This he expected to lead in turn to Japan's defeat and communization.[50] It was in this context of Japanese defeat of the Kuomintang, followed by Japan's collapse in a major war, that Mao evidently expected his party to triumph in China. If so, it was an essentially accurate prognosis. Accordingly, the Central Soviet Government declared war on Japan in the spring of 1932 and thereafter lost few opportunities to incite anti-Japanese demonstrations and conduct military maneuvers bound to lend credibility to the Japanese Army's assertion that China was faced with a Communist menace from which only Japan could rescue it.

This anti-Japanese line was increasingly acceptable to the Chinese Establishment, apart from the leadership of the Kuomintang, which tried to appease Japan until 1936, and to Stalin, especially after 1935. Since it made little appeal as yet to the masses, however, the CPC also pursued a policy of class struggle, apparently without fully realizing the degree of incompatibility between the two. After the Seventh World Congress of the Comintern in 1935 various Comintern representatives, and in particular Wang Ming, then the chief representative of the CPC in Moscow, began to point this incompatibility out. The clear preference of Stalin and the Comintern, and of the Chinese Establishment and Chinese public opinion in general (apart from the peasants), for an anti-Japanese line over a class struggle line was progressively borne in on the CPC by a series of events during 1936 culminating in the famous Sian Incident, involving the kidnaping of Chiang Kai-shek by some of his own generals, in December.

Accordingly, the CPC made a pretense in 1936–37 of dropping class struggle and even of accepting the leadership of Chiang Kai-shek and the Kuomintang, to whom Stalin shortly began to send military aid, in a common struggle against Japan. To have adopted such a policy in reality, however, as Mao evidently realized, would have been to accept futility and probably defeat. The reason was that the CPC had no effective way of ensuring its own security against the Japanese and the Nationalists, let alone

---

[50] Cf. Edgar Snow, *Red Star Over China*, New York: Random House, 1944, pp. 93–96; and the concluding sentences from the original version of Mao's *Strategic Problems of China's Revolutionary War*, published in December, 1936 (*Hsuan-chi*, p. 646; this passage has been omitted from *Selected Works*, vol. 1, p. 253): "In the whole world, furthermore, there will be a great, destructive war; the First Imperialist Great War has already seriously risked its [i.e., imperialism's] destruction, but this is not enough to [make] it take warning from the growing revolutionary insurrections and revolutionary wars. Among insurrections and wars of this kind, the important ones rely on attacking and destroying their opponent and solving their problems [in this way]."

of improving its revolutionary position, other than guerrilla warfare. This required peasant support, which in turn required class struggle. The strategy adopted was a skillful one of dosage: the continuation of a subdued form of class struggle in the countryside sufficient to gain peasant support and yet not enough to arouse the Kuomintang, Stalin, or the world at large unduly;[51] the use of anti-Japanese slogans as a safe cover and as a means of peasant mobilization that became particularly effective after the Japanese Army initiated widespread terrorism in 1939–40 against peasants in the areas where the Red Army was operating;[52] and relatively unpublicized military and territorial expansion at the expense of both the Japanese and the Kuomintang, as opportunity offered, by means of guerrilla warfare and political activity. Growing understanding of this strategy on the part of the Kuomintang brought a sharp deterioration in its relations with the CPC after 1938. The Kuomintang was unable to compete with the CPC at its own game, however. Furthermore, the trend of the war in the Pacific caused the Japanese forces in China to withdraw more than ever into the towns after 1943, and the Communists were able to occupy many of the areas that the Japanese had evacuated. Thus the Communists emerged from the war in 1945 in a far stronger position than when they had entered it, whereas the Nationalists were in reality so weakened by the strains of the war as to be far weaker relative to the CPC than they had been in 1937.

For reasons already suggested, Stalin seems to have regarded this growth of the CPC's power, and the prospect of contact whether friendly or hostile between it and American forces in North China, with serious reservations. Furthermore, at least as early as 1943 he decided to invade Manchuria and perhaps even North China as far as Peiping (Peking) and Kalgan.[53] These expectations probably contributed to his decision to dissolve the Comintern (May 1943), which tended to relieve him of responsibility for the CPC's actions and also of the suspicion of planning an invasion of North China in order to give direct support to the CPC.

Whatever Stalin's motives in dissolving the Comintern, the action seems to have given Mao the opportunity to complete the consolidation of his leadership of the CPC. In addition, Mao probably felt that the expected incursion by the Soviet Army into Manchuria might threaten his own party with a satellitization far more effective than the one that he had contributed to throwing off, unless the CPC were firmly unified under his own leadership and all Stalinist party figures were brought under strict discipline.

Impelled by growing Japanese pressures after 1939 and taking advantage of Stalin's deep involvement in the war with Germany, Mao had already

---

[51] For implementation of this in Shansi, see Gillin, *loc. cit.*, pp. 281–289.

[52] Chalmers A. Johnson, *Peasant Nationalism and Communist Power: The Emergence of Revolutionary China, 1937–1945*, Stanford University Press, 1962, pp. 49ff.

[53] Cf. Herbert Feis, *The China Tangle: The American Effort in China from Pearl Harbor to the Marshall Mission*, Princeton University Press, 1953, p. 230.

begun a "rectification" (*cheng-feng*) campaign within the CPC.[54] Among its principal targets were the remaining Returned Student Leaders, Wang Ming in particular. Li Li-san, who had led the CPC from 1928 to 1930, was in Moscow and beyond Mao's reach. He returned to North China in 1945 and then went to Manchuria but soon seems to have been brought under control by the CPC.[55]

Shortly after the dissolution of the Comintern, Mao was elected Chairman of the Central Committee and of its Politburo; these were new titles clearly designed to legitimate and complete Mao's ascent to power within the party and to distinguish his position from that of General Secretary, which had traditionally been held by a Comintern-oriented figure and was now in abeyance. At the Seventh National Congress of the CPC, held in the spring of 1945, Mao was given the additional title of Chairman of the Secretariat, which was still intended to be distinct from that of General Secretary, and Liu Shao-ch'i emerged as actually, although not yet formally, the second ranking figure in the party.[56] Mao followed up his triumph of 1943 with a substantial purge,[57] and by the end of the year he had begun to impose his own interpretation of the party's history on his colleagues.[58]

The collapse of Japan in August, 1945, confronted the CPC both with great opportunities and serious problems. There is little doubt that the CPC and the Kuomintang both planned to resume their struggle for control of China and that each expected to win, the Kuomintang in a short war and the CPC in a long one. Both faced the difficulty that the Chinese public, the United States, and the Soviet Union all opposed a renewal of civil war, and that there were American troops in China Proper and Soviet troops in Manchuria. Under these conditions both sides went through the motions of negotiating with each other. The CPC was also faced for a short time with the difficult problem of having no real or imaginary foreign enemy against whom to mobilize popular feeling, since Japan had surrendered and it was not yet safe or feasible to treat the United States as its successor. In clear oppo-

---

[54] For some early (1939) documents see *Documentary History, op. cit.*, pp. 318–351. On the movement in general, see Boyd Compton, *Mao's China: Party Reform Documents, 1942–1944*, University of Washington Press, 1952. On the cultural aspect see *Selected Works*, vol. 4, pp. 46–93; Merle Goldman, "Writers' Criticism of the Party in 1942," *The China Quarterly*, no. 17 (January–March, 1964), pp. 205–228. Liu Shao-ch'i's key tract, *On the Intra-Party Struggle* (excerpts in *Documentary History, op. cit.*, pp. 356–372) was published on July 2, 1941, almost immediately after the German invasion of the Soviet Union.

[55] Li Li-san made an interesting but obviously incomplete "confession" before the CPC's Eighth National Congress, in which he said cryptically that he first "came across" (or was shown?) some of Mao Tse-tung's writings, and in particular those relating to the "rectification" campaign, when he was in Harbin (Manchuria) in early 1946 (*People's Daily*, September 24, 1956).

[56] Cf. Howard L. Boorman, "Teng Hsiao-p'ing: A Political Profile," *The China Quarterly*, no. 21 (January–March, 1965), p. 119.

[57] Wan, *op. cit.*, p. 69; cf. *Selected Works*, vol. 4, pp. 111–117.

[58] Cf. *Selected Works*, vol. 4, pp. 157–170.

sition to the concept of a more or less genuine coalition government favored by the Chinese public, the United States, and the Soviet Union, the CPC put forward as the only alternative to civil war acceptable to it a demand for what amounted to a bogus coalition government. The CPC would retain control of its own armed forces and territorial bases, would have freedom of political action in the Kuomintang-controlled areas, and (together with friendly minor parties) have a veto over any major actions by the nominal coalition government.[59] This proposal naturally failed to gain acceptance by the Kuomintang, and the result was deadlock. The United States deprived itself by demobilizing, and specifically by deactivating its China Theater in May, 1946, of its most effective means of influencing the situation. The Soviet Union did the same, at about the same time, by withdrawing its forces from Manchuria. Full-scale war promptly broke out between Nationalist and Communist armies in Manchuria, which both sides regarded as the decisive theater of operations.[60] The CPC also began to denounce the United States for its support of the Kuomintang and for its alleged role as leader of the "imperialist" camp.

The Kuomintang lost the ensuing civil war fully as much as the Communists won it. Already weakened by the long war against Japan, it allowed political and economic conditions to disintegrate rapidly. Shunting qualified field commanders aside, it entrusted control of operations to politically influential generals of outstanding incompetence.[61] In these and other respects the Communist performance was relatively efficient. The result was an almost unbroken string of Communist military victories, under the impact of which the CPC's energetic but of course illegal political activity in the Kuomintang areas grew increasingly effective. It is unlikely that anything the United States could have done, except perhaps committing its own ground forces (if they had existed) to action against the CPC and compelling the Kuomintang to undertake drastic political and economic reforms, would have sufficed to reverse the trend. By the end of 1947, Mao Tse-tung felt able to announce a transition from predominantly guerrilla

[59] For the first major statement of this demand see Mao Tse-tung, *On Coalition Government*, April 24, 1945 (in *Selected Works*, vol. 4, pp. 244–315). For a summary of the complex CPC-Kuomintang negotiations, under United States mediation, see *United States Relations With China With Special Reference to the Period 1944–1949*, Washington: Department of State, 1949, pp. 73–112, 127–220. The resemblance between the CPC's proposals and the arrangement for the "neutralization" of Laos in 1962 is obvious although not perfect. The outcome in China, had the CPC's demands been accepted, would probably have resembled what is happening in Laos.

[60] Cf. Ray Huang, "Some Observations on Manchuria in the Balance Early 1946," *Pacific Historical Review*, vol. xxvii, no. 2 (May, 1958), pp. 159–169. While in Manchuria, Soviet forces had facilitated the occupation of large areas and the acquisition of stocks of Japanese weapons by CPC forces, in addition to removing much capital equipment installed by the Japanese (Tsou, *op. cit.*, pp. 330–332).

[61] Cf. A. Doak Barnett, *China on the Eve of Communist Takeover*, New York: Praeger, 1963; *United States Relations With China, op. cit.*, Chapter VI.

warfare to regular, mobile warfare.[62] By this time, the CPC had also intensified the class struggle in the areas under its control; after some interruptions, this trend culminated in a virtually nationwide land redistribution campaign in 1950–52.

Once overall military superiority had passed to the CPC, as it did in 1947, the end of the war came with surprising speed. In addition to all the obvious reasons for wanting to win as soon as possible, the CPC was probably motivated by an important extrinsic consideration. Stalin cracked down very hard on the European satellites after his break with Tito, and it was important that the CPC consolidate its own position as rapidly and fully as possible before he turned his attention to it. Stalin's preoccupation with Eastern Europe and the Berlin Blockade provided a respite from Soviet pressures. Accordingly, the CPC launched major, successful offensives in Manchuria and Central China in the autumn of 1948; took Peking in January, 1949, and prepared to establish its capital there; made its victory virtually irreversible by capturing the major Yangtze valley cities in the spring of 1949, as Stalin was lifting the Berlin Blockade; and proclaimed the Chinese People's Republic on October 1, 1949, even before the Kuomintang had been forced to transfer its own headquarters from the mainland to Taiwan.[63]

---

[62] *Selected Works*, vol. iv, pp. 157–176.

[63] General L.-M. Chassin, *La conquête de la Chine par Mao Tse-tung* (1945–1949), Paris: Payot, 1952. As late as October, 1948, Mao apparently expected the war to last into 1951 (*Selected Works*, vol. iv, p. 272), but the success of the offensives was so great that by November he was predicting that the war would be over in "only another year or so" (*ibid.*, vol. iv, p. 288).

□ **2**

Fifteen Years of Communist China's Foreign Policy

The purpose of this chapter is to provide a chronological summary of the evolution of Communist Chinese foreign policy, as an aid to understanding. More detailed treatment and documentation of the major individual topics or episodes discussed may be found in other chapters.

■ **INITIAL STEPS**

The CPC was presented with an interesting opportunity in April, 1949, when Nationalist Acting President Li Tsung-jen proposed a negotiated settlement of the civil war. Had the CPC accepted, it might have been able to form a unified coalition government, dominated by itself, whose claim to international status might have been considerably better than has in fact been the case. The CPC was in no mood for compromise, however, and in any case Chiang Kai-shek, although nominally retired from the presidency, was already installed on Taiwan. Li was therefore presented with a virtual ultimatum to surrender, which he rejected, and the opportunity passed.[1]

By the end of 1949 mopping up operations on the mainland, except for the "liberation" of Tibet, were substantially complete. These operations, however, drove perhaps forty thousand Nationalist soldiers across the frontier into Burma and Vietnam, where they subsequently caused international complications. The CPC feared that these troops might take part, together with the main Nationalist forces on Taiwan aided perhaps by the

---

[1] I owe this interesting idea to Professor Michael Lindsay of the American University.

United States, in an attempt to invade the mainland before it could be consolidated under Communist control.

When the CPR was formally proclaimed on October 1, 1949, it announced that it would "examine" all treaties that had been concluded by the Nationalist government and "recognize, abrogate, revise, or re-negotiate them according to their respective contents."[2] In reality, most of them lapsed.

The CPR promptly began to claim the right to control China's permanent seat on the United Nations Security Council. It also appealed for general diplomatic recognition, with the explicit proviso that it would enter into diplomatic relations only with "governments which have severed relations with the Kuomintang reactionary clique and which adopt a friendly attitude towards the People's Republic of China."[3] On this basis, recognition was received, promptly or within the next few months, from all Communist countries (including Yugoslavia), from six Asian neutrals (Burma, India, Pakistan, Afghanistan, Ceylon, and Indonesia), from Israel, from all the Scandinavian countries, from the United Kingdom, from the Netherlands, and from Switzerland.[4] All these recognitions were reciprocated except for that of Yugoslavia, which was ignored for five years. In several other cases, however, diplomatic relations were not actually established for several years.[5] The CPR has never established diplomatic relations with Israel.

The CPR did not molest Hong Kong, which Britain had annexed in 1842, in part because exports to it are the CPR's largest single earner of non-Communist foreign exchange. After the CPR's intervention in the Korean War, however, it seized virtually all private foreign investments and holdings on the mainland and drove most private foreign residents out of the country. This applied to the property and nationals of countries that had recognized the CPR, such as India and Britain, as well as to others. The CPC drew down the Bamboo Curtain between itself and the non-Communist world. It nearly isolated Chinese intellectuals and Christian communities from contact with the West. The CPR began to shift its external trade toward the Communist bloc even before its intervention in the Korean War, which accelerated the trend.

The establishment of working relations with the Soviet Union began

---

[2] Common Program, Article 55.

[3] Common Program, Article 56.

[4] The United Kingdom recognized the CPR not only because it was the de facto government of the mainland of China but in order to protect Hong Kong and as much as possible of British trade with and investments in China, to avoid if possible driving the CPR further into the arms of the Soviet Union, and perhaps most important of all to please Nehru (who was very insistent on recognition of the CPR) and keep India in the Commonwealth.

[5] Albania, Afghanistan, Ceylon, the United Kingdom. For details see "Diplomatic Relations of Communist China," *Current Background*, Hong Kong: American Consulate General, no. 440, March 12, 1957.

with Mao's visit to Moscow from December, 1949, to February, 1950. Mao discussed with Stalin many subjects of common interest, including some relating to the expansion of Communism in Asia.[6] After much hard bargaining, Stalin agreed without publicity to begin a program of limited military aid to the CPR. He also signed an alliance with it, valid for thirty years and directed against Japan or any power allied with it, directly or indirectly (meaning the United States). The right of the Soviet Union, acquired under a treaty of 1945 with Nationalist China, to use and virtually to control the major Manchurian ports and railways was confirmed until the conclusion of a peace treaty with Japan or until the end of 1952, whichever came sooner. Nothing was specified about the status of Outer Mongolia or Sinkiang. The Soviet Union extended a credit to the CPR of $300 million, to be repaid with one percent interest in ten annual installments, beginning at the end of 1954.[7] On March 27, 1950, a Sino-Soviet agreement was reached to establish four joint stock companies. Like their East European counterparts, these were largely for Soviet benefit and largely Soviet-controlled, especially since the Chinese had almost no capital equipment to contribute to them. Two, an oil company and a company for extracting nonferrous minerals (probably including uranium) were to operate in western Sinkiang, where Soviet influence had been strong for about two decades. A third was to be an airline between the two countries. The fourth was to be a shipyard at Dairen, in Manchuria.

■ "ARMED STRUGGLE" (1948–51)

The CPC leadership believed that the turning of the tide in its civil war with the Nationalists in 1947 foreshadowed an expansion of Chinese Communist influence in Asia, much as the turning of the tide at Stalingrad had foreshadowed a great extension of Soviet influence in Eastern Europe. Accordingly, the CPC began to recommend to other Asian Communist movements "the way of Mao Tse-tung," with emphasis on armed struggle. These exhortations, and the CPC's own example, probably helped to precipitate armed risings in Burma, Malaya, Indonesia, and the Philippines in 1948. The CPC was not in a position to give much aid to these risings, even after it came to power in 1949. It did, however, play a critical role in a more important and more accessible Communist revolutionary war, the one in Vietnam.

It seems likely that coordination of strategies among the major Communist Parties of Asia, and in particular those of China, Korea, and Vietnam,

---

[6] The affairs of the Japanese, Korean, Vietnamese, and Indian Communist movements were certainly discussed.

[7] Text of treaty and agreements in O. B. van der Sprenkel, ed., *New China: Three Views*, New York: John Day, 1951, pp. 227–235.

began at a conference convened in Peking by the World Federation of Trade Unions in November, 1949, before Mao's trip to Moscow. Mao probably undertook to secure Stalin's consent and logistical support, and did so. One aspect of the coordinated strategy was evidently an offensive by the Vietnamese Communists against the French, which began in the autumn of 1950 but was largely unsuccessful. Another was a Chinese Communist attempt to take Taiwan, which also ran into difficulties and was finally stopped by the extension of American protection to the island on June 27, 1950. A third was the North Korean invasion of South Korea.

When unexpected American intervention in the Korean War, beginning on June 27, 1950, first slowed and then stopped the North Korean offensive, the Communist side was confronted with a serious problem. Both the Soviet Union and the CPR made diplomatic gestures aimed at a political settlement, which to the CPR meant its own admission to the United Nations and the withdrawal of American protection from Taiwan, as well as of American troops from Korea. When the United States indicated in mid-August a determination to invade North Korea, the CPR began to make preparations for intervention if necessary. As United Nations forces approached the 38th parallel at the end of September, the CPR began to utter warnings and threats. When these proved to be of no avail, Chinese forces began to cross the Yalu River into North Korea in mid-October. Undoubtedly with Soviet approval and perhaps at Soviet insistence, they were called volunteers so as to minimize the chances of direct American retaliation against China. After a month of limited and ambiguous action presumably designed to bring about a United Nations withdrawal without a major fight, the Chinese felt their hand to be forced by General MacArthur's "home by Christmas" offensive.

The primary Chinese motive in intervening was almost certainly to protect the security of Manchuria. Other probable motives were to rescue North Korea and to avoid the creation of a situation in which Stalin might feel compelled either to intervene openly or (more probably) to abandon North Korea, and perhaps China, to their fate.

An initially successful Chinese offensive was halted and rolled back roughly to the 38th parallel in the early months of 1951. Sensing imminent international agreement on a truce that would leave its major demands unsatisfied, the CPR launched two powerful but unsuccessful offensives, in April and May. Truce talks then began, at Soviet initiative, along the lines that the CPR had feared.

The introduction into the truce talks by the United Nations Command, at the beginning of 1952, of the politically explosive issue of the disposition of prisoners who did not want to be repatriated raised the level of tension dramatically. Subsequent events kept the level high, until early in 1953 a threat by the Eisenhower administration to expand the war to the mainland of China and use nuclear weapons, Stalin's death, and the unwarlike attitude of his successors compelled the CPR to capitulate on the prisoner issue and sign an armistice, with its major demands still unfulfilled.

■ THE SEARCH FOR AN ALTERNATE POLICY (1951–55)

Apart from the rewarding investment in Vietnam, Communist insurrection in South and Southeast Asia did not pay well. The Soviet Union clearly objected to the concept of "the way of Mao Tse-tung," with its overtones of Chinese leadership in Asia. Chinese defeats in Korea in the spring of 1951 also contributed to a downward revision by the CPC of its estimate of the safety and effectiveness of armed force as a means of expanding Communism and Chinese influence in Asia, at any rate as long as the Communist bloc lacked the ability to deter the United States from escalating a local war, such as the Korean conflict.

Accordingly, in 1952 the CPC began to de-emphasize armed struggle and to soften its line toward the leaders and governments of the newly independent Asian countries, whom it had earlier denounced as "running dogs of imperialism" but whose neutrality it was now beginning to appreciate. Soviet and Chinese wooing of the neutrals was intensified after 1953 by the Dulles policy of chilliness toward the neutrals combined with efforts to sway some of them into alignment with the West. It was and remains important to the Communist powers to deny the neutrals to the West, politically speaking, and if possible to render them neutral "in favor of" the Communist bloc on the issues of the Cold War.

The first major overt sign of the CPR's effort to take some of the tension out of its external relations was not the Korean armistice, which was forced on the CPR by circumstances beyond its control. The first such sign was rather the willingness of the CPR as well as the Soviet Union to accept a settlement of the Indochina crisis on terms substantially short of the maximum demands of the Vietnamese Communists. The latter were playing a winning military hand, and there was no need for the CPR to involve itself in the hostilities beyond sending weapons and technicians to the Communists. Nor, in all probability, would the CPR have considered it advisable to do so, except perhaps in case of a collapse of the Communists and an "imperialist" threat to the Chinese frontier, in view of the growing American military involvement on the French side. As usual in such affairs, the Chinese problem was to achieve substantial political and military gains without incurring serious American escalation of the conflict. In this case the problem was solved, although as indicated not on a basis fully acceptable to the Vietnamese Communists.

The Indochina crisis produced several important diplomatic consequences. One was the formation under American leadership of the Southeast Asia Treaty Organization (SEATO), with the aim of stopping the further expansion of North Vietnamese arms and Communist Chinese arms or influence in Southeast Asia. Another was a tendency toward growing Sino-Soviet rivalry in Asia. At the Geneva Conference, which ended the hostilities in Indochina, the Soviet Union had given clear signs of continuing to assign first priority to European affairs, for the sake of its own security. Considerations of national interest also led the Soviet Union, after the conference, into increased economic and political wooing of India, the leading Asian neutral and a country that the CPR seems always to have regarded as at once its own rival, target, and sphere of influence. The Indochina settlement also led to informal contacts between the CPR and France and to the raising of the hitherto ambiguous relations between the CPR and Britain to the diplomatic, although not to the ambassadorial, level.

Another important indication of the Chinese search for a new policy was a Sino-Indian agreement of April 29, 1954, whose most important features were that it recognized the Chinese claim to Tibet (described throughout the agreement as "the Tibet region of China"), incorporated the platitudinous "Five Principles of Peaceful Coexistence," and by common agreement omitted any definition of the Sino-Indian frontier. It was apparently at this time that the Indian government first realized that there was a genuine and serious disagreement as to the location of the frontier in some areas. Accordingly, both sides increased their patrolling in the frontier region and there were some incidents during the next few years, minor as compared with what was to come later.

The CPR's relations with its neutral neighbors were further improved by visits of Chou En-lai to New Delhi and Rangoon in June, 1954, and subsequent visits of Nehru and Nu to Peiping. The essence of the understanding reached at that time was that India and Burma promised to continue to observe strict neutrality in the Cold War and to foster friendly relations with China; in return, Peking promised not to commit aggression and to negotiate on the thorny question of the citizenship of the overseas Chinese. The CPC evidently expected this arrangement, which it did not intend to preclude it from exerting covert, revolutionary pressures on the countries involved, to serve as the basis for its relations with other neutral Asian states.

In February, 1953, in a psychological maneuver intended to contribute to an armistice in Korea, the Eisenhower administration had "unleashed Chiang Kai-shek," or in other words removed the overt prohibition on Nationalist offensive operations against the mainland. In 1954, the United States began to impart some substance to this gesture by increasing its military aid to the Nationalists and encouraging them to occupy the offshore islands in force. These developments, plus some threatening statements by high Nationalist officials, evidently convinced the CPR that the Nationalists were contemplating an attack — the spring of 1954 was a time of crisis in the CPR owing to the purging of Kao Kang — and needed to be taught a lesson. It would have been too dangerous to do so, however, while the Indochina war remained unsettled.

Almost immediately after the signing of the Geneva Agreement on July 21, the CPR launched a major propaganda campaign for the "liberation" of Taiwan. On September 3, Communist artillery began shelling Quemoy, the largest of the offshore islands.

Such was the situation when a Soviet delegation, led by Khrushchev but not including Premier Malenkov or Foreign Minister Molotov, arrived in Peking at the end of September. Khrushchev's main aim was probably to gain at least tacit Chinese support for his approaching effort to unseat Malenkov as premier and replace him with Bulganin, who accompanied Khrushchev to Peking. The Chinese were evidently agreeable, since they preferred Khrushchev's stress on heavy industry and his relatively activist approach to foreign policy to Malenkov's emphasis on consumer goods and his tendency to conciliate the West. To gain Chinese support Khrushchev was prepared to make important concessions, provided they did not endanger Soviet security. He did not, for example, make any overt commitment on the Taiwan issue, and only routine mention of it was made in the joint communiqué, issued on October 11.[8] That document provided for a second Soviet credit (this time of $130 million) to the CPR; for a joint, allegedly peaceful, approach to international problems, especially those of Asia; for a willingness to establish "normal" relations with Japan, conservative and pro-American though its government was; for a Soviet withdrawal from Port Arthur (in Manchuria) in the spring of 1955; for transfer of the joint stock companies, with compensation to the Soviet Union, to Chinese ownership at the beginning of 1955; for Soviet scientific and technical aid to the CPR, including as it turned out assistance in basic nuclear research; and the completion of new rail connections, already begun, between the two countries via Sinkiang and Outer Mongolia.

The unsettled crisis in the Taiwan Strait continued to mount in intensity. In November, 1954, the CPR tried and sentenced thirteen American prisoners, presumably to increase its leverage on the United States. At the end of the year the United States signed a treaty of alliance with the Republic of China, and in January, 1955, the United States Congress passed the "Formosa Resolution," authorizing the President to commit American forces to the defense of the offshore islands if he judged a Communist attack on them to be part of an attack on Taiwan itself. On March 8, 1955, Secretary Dulles threatened Communist China with tactical nuclear weapons in the event of "open armed aggresison." The Soviet Union, then preoccupied with European problems and the negotiation of the Warsaw Pact, failed to respond to this threat. Left to its own devices and anxious to appear in the best possible light at the forthcoming Bandung Conference of Afro-Asian

---

[8] Text in *The New York Times*, October 12, 1954.

countries, the CPR eased its pressure on the offshore islands in April, 1955, and the United States for its part tried unsuccessfully to persuade the Nationalists to evacuate the offshore islands.

A situation of at least temporary stability having been attained with respect to the three major crisis areas along the CPR's periphery — Korea, Indochina, and Taiwan and the offshore islands — the CPR now felt it both possible and advisable to concentrate on improving its relations with the Afro-Asian neutrals along the lines that it had been exploring since about 1952.

■ THE BANDUNG PHASE (1955–57)

Chou En-lai went to the Asian-African Conference (held at Bandung, Java, in April, 1955) prepared to be conciliatory. When he encountered unexpectedly severe criticism from neutral leaders of the CPR's antireligious domestic policies and of its pressures on Southeast Asia, he became even more conciliatory. He went so far as to offer to negotiate with the United States on the Taiwan question. All in all, he made a very good impression, broadened the CPR's contacts greatly, and probably learned much about the Afro-Asian leaders. The Bandung Conference can be taken as marking the beginning of the CPR's transition from the status of an almost purely Asian power to that of an Afro-Asian power.[9]

Several important results for the CPR followed from the Bandung Conference. By this time the CPC had decided that for the sake of its other interests it must abandon, overtly at least, its claim on the citizenship and political support of the overseas Chinese, whom in any case it could not effectively protect. The governments of the host countries were reluctant, however, to grant citizenship and therefore nondiscriminatory treatment to their active and prosperous Chinese communities. An apparent exception was Indonesia. During the Bandung Conference, Chou En-lai signed with the left neutralist Sastroamidjojo government a treaty providing for local Chinese to give up dual citizenship by opting for either Chinese or Indonesian citizenship. The terms of the treaty were drawn substantially as the Indonesian government desired and tended to minimize rather than maximize the number of Chinese who would acquire Indonesian citizenship. Nevertheless, the treaty became a political issue in Indonesia, which did not ratify it until the end of 1957. Even then, the treaty did not go into effect because the Indonesian government did not agree to an exchange of ratifications.[10]

---

[9] Cf. *China and the Asian-African Conference (Documents)*, Peking: Foreign Languages Press, 1955; George McT. Kahin, *The Asian-African Conference: Bandung, Indonesia, April 1955*, Cornell University Press, 1956.

[10] Cf. Donald E. Willmott, *The National Status of the Chinese in Indonesia*, rev. ed., Cornell University: Modern Indonesia Project, 1961, Chapters III–IV.

At Bandung Chou En-lai made contact with Nasser, with the result that Egypt accorded diplomatic recognition to the CPR a year later. The CPR established a major political base in Cairo and took an active part in the First Afro-Asian People's Solidarity Conference, which was held there at the end of 1957. Africa and the Middle East tended to supplant Asia as the most promising field for revolutionary activity, while Chinese Asian policy remained largely committed for the time being to the cultivation of good relations with neutral governments.

Partly as a result of Chou's offer at Bandung, ambassadorial talks between the United States and the CPR got under way at Geneva in August, 1955, and lasted until July, 1958. The main Chinese purpose in maintaining this contact, tenuous and intermittent though it was, apart from gaining some propaganda advantage, was probably to keep in touch with the American mood and minimize the chances both of an American attack on China and of some sort of Soviet-American deal at Chinese expense.

The Geneva Agreements had provided that elections should be held throughout the whole of Vietnam. These were expected to deliver South Vietnam into Communist control, sooner or later, and thus to compensate the North Vietnamese for the incompleteness of their triumph in 1954. Exactly for that reason, President Diem's South Vietnamese government refused to allow the elections to be held. As the two-year deadline approached and passed, there was a feeling of tension in Indochina, in expectation of some drastic move by the North Vietnamese. Both Cambodia and Laos looked to Peking for support and, whether for that reason or not, there was no crisis. Following a visit by Prince Sihanouk to Peking in February, 1956, the CPR made an economic aid agreement with Cambodia in June. It rapidly established a political presence there as well, even in the absence (until 1958) of diplomatic relations. Sihanouk has claimed that the CPR agreed to restrain North Vietnamese pressures on Cambodia and seems to believe that it has actually done so. In Laos, Premier Souvanna Phouma succeeded in getting a nonaggression pledge, in addition apparently to Chinese acquiescence in his efforts to bring the Communist-controlled Pathet Lao into a coalition government, in 1956.

Between mid-November, 1956, and early February, 1957, Chou En-lai visited eight Asian countries.[11] Apart from specific issues, the main purposes of the trip were apparently to counter the impact of the Hungarian crisis and to capitalize on the impact of the Suez crisis. The underlying coolness of Sino-Indian relations, intensified by the border dispute, unrest in Tibet, Soviet economic aid and political support for the Nehru government, and the CPR's insistence on maintaining neutrality on the Kashmir dispute, appeared in the fact that only in New Delhi did Chou's visit fail to produce a joint communiqué.

---

[11] North Vietnam, Cambodia, India, Burma, Pakistan, Afghanistan, Nepal, Ceylon.

The Bandung phase of Communist Chinese foreign policy, coming as it did after a military operation in the Taiwan Strait that had ended in a virtual stalemate, was marked by a propaganda campaign for a "peaceful liberation" of Taiwan by means of an agreement with the Nationalists. The CPC was careful, however, not to yield to the American insistence that it formally renounce the use of force with respect to the recovery of Taiwan. It also demanded a "pact of collective peace" in Asia and the Pacific, presumably in order to inhibit any American use of force in defense of Taiwan. Individual Nationalist personnel were offered amnesty, jobs on the mainland, the right to revisit their original homes, and even the right to return to Taiwan.[12] By early 1957, the thirtieth anniversary of the beginning of hostilities between the CPC and the Kuomintang, the CPC seemed to have some hope that its overtures were having an effect.[13]

The CPC's distrust of Khrushchev, which had probably been aroused early in 1955, was confirmed by the Soviet party's Twentieth Congress in February, 1956. In his public report, Khrushchev took virtually a peace-at-any-price line toward the Cold War, seemed to repudiate Soviet responsibility for the fate of other Communist Parties, and urged them to explore the possibility of a "peaceful" path to power while implying a desire for continued Soviet influence over them.[14] Worse still, in his Secret Speech he attacked Stalin for his own political purposes.[15] A few days after its own delegation returned from Moscow, the CPC published what it regarded as a more balanced appraisal of Stalin, in an unmistakable rebuke to Khrushchev.[16] Nevertheless, the Soviet Union made a new economic aid commitment, including a pledge to help build a nuclear reactor but not including a credit, a few days afterward.

The Twentieth Congress and the Secret Speech brought to a head in the East European countries the popular hatred of the Stalinist regimes that still held power there, if no longer in the Soviet Union. For the most part, the CPC approved of the loosening of Soviet controls and the removal of Stalinist holdovers in Eastern Europe but could not swallow Nagy, who tried

[12] See Chou En-lai's report to the Chinese People's Political Consultative Conference, January 30, 1956 (New China News Agency dispatch, same date).

[13] The original version of Mao Tse-tung's speech on "contradictions" of February 27, 1957 (but not the edited version published on June 18, 1957), is believed to have said that relations with the Nationalists might be brought within the "nonantagonistic" category. When Soviet Chairman Voroshilov visited the CPR in April, 1957, CPR leaders made several public references to the possibility of friendly relations with the Nationalists, to one of which Voroshilov replied, "Co-operate permanently."

[14] This was roughly what had happened in Czechoslovakia, the example of a "peaceful" seizure of power cited at the congress.

[15] Khrushchev attacked Stalin mainly for his crimes against those who had helped him to power and for his military errors. Khrushchev was implicitly pleading for political support from the rank and file of the CPSU and from the armed forces and promising them that he would not behave toward them as Stalin had behaved after 1934.

[16] "On the Historical Experience Concerning the Dictatorship of the Proletariat," People's Daily, April 5, 1956.

to dissolve the Communist dictatorship in Hungary and take it out of the Warsaw Pact. The CPC then supported, and may even have urged, the Soviet military intervention in Hungary. In addition to rebuking Tito for his ambivalent stand on the crisis, reaffirming its positive evaluation of Stalin, and trying to sketch an ideological credo on which all Communists could and should agree,[17] the CPC sent Chou En-lai to the Soviet Union, Poland, Czechoslovakia, and Hungary for ten days in January, 1957. The CPC's position was essentially that the East European countries must recognize Soviet leadership, but within a confederative framework that permitted national autonomy.[18] Until November, 1957, the CPC continued to be regarded in Eastern Europe as an ally against Soviet pressures. While in Moscow Chou signed with his Soviet opposite number, Bulganin, a joint declaration affirming their joint support of "peaceful coexistence" and denouncing alleged "imperialist" offenses against it, such as the Suez and Hungarian crises and the Eisenhower Doctrine.[19]

■ "THE EAST WIND HAS PREVAILED OVER THE WEST WIND" (1957–59)

In May and June, 1957, the CPC suffered an immense domestic political catastrophe with international repercussions. The "Hundred Flowers" campaign for free discussion of public issues, personally sponsored by Mao Tse-tung, erupted in a flurry of unexpected recriminations by people in various walks of life against the CPC and its policies. The CPC, after serious internal debate, concluded that it had no choice but to silence and "remould" its critics through an "antirightist struggle," which continued into 1958. The episode was all the more painful for the CPC because of the contrast with the political fortunes of Khrushchev, who unhorsed the "antiparty group" in June, 1957, and was able to announce a successful ICBM test (August 26) and the orbiting of the first earth satellite (October 4).[20]

This disaster led to an agonizing reappraisal of the CPC's domestic and foreign policies, beginning in the summer of 1957.[21] There was a tendency for radical policies, and presumably radical individuals, to come to the fore.[22] The sense of being an old man in a hurry, which seems to have begun to afflict Mao after his illness at the beginning of 1954, now apparently haunted him more than ever.

[17] In "More on the Historical Experience Concerning the Dictatorship of the Proletariat," *People's Daily*, December 29, 1956.

[18] Donald S. Zagoria, *The Sino-Soviet Conflict, 1956–1961*, Princeton University Press, 1962, pp. 61–62.

[19] Text in *The New York Times*, January 19, 1957.

[20] Furthermore, Khrushchev, in a television interview with American correspondents on May 28, 1957, had denied that "contradictions," the theoretical basis of the Hundred Flowers campaign, existed in the Soviet Union.

[21] Mao, who was apparently greatly shaken, spent the summer at Tsingtao, a coastal resort.

[22] Cf. Zagoria, *op. cit.*, Chapter 2.

It would be an oversimplification, however, to infer that this crisis produced an immediate change in the relatively tolerant attitude that the CPC had displayed toward the Afro-Asian neutrals during the Bandung phase of its foreign policy. On the contrary, in a time of crisis the friendship of the neutrals, if it could be retained without the sacrifice of any of the CPR's essential national or revolutionary objectives, was a valuable asset, because of its restraining effect on the real or assumed aggressive tendencies of the "imperialists" toward the CPR. The neutrals, furthermore, had reacted unfavorably to a major recent American initiative, the Eisenhower Doctrine. As late as February, 1958, we find Chou En-lai referring publicly and favorably to Nehru and to "Our great neighbor India."[23] This tone rapidly disappeared when Nehru announced on April 8 that he would soon visit Lhasa in order to make good an earlier promise to the Dalai Lama to try to moderate the CPC's Tibetan policy. The CPC evidently took this announcement, which came at a time of growing revolt in eastern Tibet, as a form of interference in the CPR's internal affairs. In July the visit was cancelled at Chinese insistence,[24] and the CPR published a map restating its version of the Sino-Indian frontier and showing a Chinese military highway recently built across part of the disputed territory, shown on Indian maps as being in Ladakh.[25] By the time that the CPC published a collection of Mao's writings on "imperialism," entitled *Imperialists and All Reactionaries Are Paper Tigers*, at the end of October,[26] the CPC evidently meant to include Nehru, and perhaps other Afro-Asian neutrals, among the "reactionaries."

Nor was this the only indigenous trend in the Afro-Asian world that disturbed the CPC during 1958. Serious opposition to the elected Communist government of the state of Kerala, in India, began in the summer of 1958. Worse still, there was a series of military coups and revolts in Afro-Asian countries — Algeria (by the Secret Army), the Sudan, Pakistan, Burma, Thailand, and Indonesia — during 1958. The most serious in the eyes of the CPC was evidently the Moslem and military revolt in Indonesia, in which the CPC claimed to see the hand of "imperialism," against growing Communist influence on Sukarno's government. On May 15, incidentally after the worst of the fighting was over, the CPR offered the Indonesian government whatever aid it might require, including "volunteers" if necessary.

Another situation almost certainly disturbing to the CPR was the unreliability of Soviet military aid and protection, at a time of mounting

---

[23] Chou En-lai, report to National People's Congress, February 10, 1958 (New China News Agency dispatch, same date).

[24] Cf. George N. Patterson, *Peking Versus Delhi*, New York: Praeger, 1963, pp. 159–160.

[25] In *China Pictorial*, no. 95 (July, 1958), pp. 20–21. Cf. Indian protests in White Paper I, pp. 26–27, 46.

[26] *People's Daily*, October 31, 1958.

tension in the Taiwan Strait and in spite of Soviet successes in the missile and space fields. Early in 1958 Khrushchev began to show signs of regretting his recent commitment to help the CPR with the production of nuclear weapons, for example by proclaiming a unilateral cessation of nuclear testing. It may have been at this time that the Soviet Union made what the CPR later interpreted as a demand for Soviet control over the CPR's armed forces, meaning perhaps Soviet control of any surface-to-surface missiles and nuclear warheads stationed in the CPR and joint control of all naval forces in the China Sea. In such a seemingly dangerous situation, the CPR may well have reflected that the United States might be best distracted from the Far East, to the advantage of the CPR, by a Chinese policy of encouraging and aiding anti-"imperialist" revolutions in as many underdeveloped countries as possible.

All this probably seemed to indicate to the CPC that its reservations about the Soviet "peaceful path" had been right all the time, and that "bourgeois reactionaries" would always use or try to use force to prevent political developments adverse to their interests. The CPC's answer was to reassert the validity of Maoist guerrilla warfare, although not as loudly and blatantly as in 1948–52.[27] It was in this spirit that the CPR became the only power to grant prompt recognition to the Algerian provisional government proclaimed by the FLN in the autumn of 1958; the CPR also extended economic and military aid to it.

It was obvious, however, that economic and military limitations would prevent the CPR from doing anything spectacular for the "national revolutionary movement" and against "imperialism" in the underdeveloped areas, except perhaps in the immediate vicinity of the CPR. The major supporting role could be played only by the Soviet Union. A similar consideration apparently influenced the CPR's thinking on the paramount question of the "liberation" of Taiwan, a "peaceful liberation" by means of an agreement with the Kuomintang having been rendered all but out of the question by the crisis on the mainland in 1957. Now a "liberation" would probably have to use force, and only the Soviet Union disposed of adequate force.

To the CPC, the Soviet ICBM test and earth satellite apparently removed any basis for Soviet fears of an American surprise or even retaliatory attack. Although the CPR's press emphasized the military importance of these developments,[28] it seems to have considered their main significance to be psychological. As Mao put it in a meaningfully nonmaterial metaphor, "the East wind has prevailed over the West wind." In other words, the sense of disarray in the United States, symbolized by the phrase "missile gap," was the main thing. Since the United States would soon launch an ICBM

---

[27] Cf. Ch'en Po-ta, "Under the Banner of Comrade Mao Tse-tung," *Red Flag*, July 16, 1958.

[28] Alice Langley Hsieh, *Communist China's Strategy in the Nuclear Era*, Englewood Cliffs, N.J.: Prentice-Hall, 1962, pp. 76ff.

and an earth satellite of its own, the opportunity was likely to be short. The Soviet Union must make good use of it, while the American sense of confusion and the American economic recession persisted.

The first major opportunity presented itself in Syria, where a leftist government became involved in a crisis with the United States and Turkey in August, 1957. The CPR began to express concern on August 22, the Soviet Union not until September 8. A Soviet threat to take military action against Turkey was withheld until September 11, the day after Secretary Dulles had indicated that American action under the Eisenhower Doctrine would probably not be required. In October Khrushchev briefly stirred up a patently synthetic second round of the crisis, in order to capitalize on the psychological impact of Sputnik I and almost certainly also in order to cover the dismissal of Marshal Zhukov, with whom he had been having a serious dispute.[29] Perhaps the main result of this serio-comic affair was the formation of the United Arab Republic, which brought Syria under Egyptian control and prevented it from drifting further to the left, on February 1, 1958. The CPR recognized the new state slightly later than did the other powers — on February 23, Soviet Army Day. Khrushchev had scarcely acquitted himself as the CPC would have liked.

Nor was Khrushchev doing very much to help the CPR to implement its decision to become a nuclear power, which it had evidently taken in 1956, and its decision to catch up with Britain in gross heavy industrial output by 1972, which Liu Shao-ch'i announced on December 2, 1957. The Soviet commitment of October 15, 1957, to help the CPR construct its own nuclear weapons was evidently little more than a token one, and Chinese statements in the spring of 1958 suggested that it would be a long time before the CPR possessed operational nuclear weapons.[30] Soviet economic credits, although not aid uncovered by credits, ceased to flow in 1957. Britain conducted a series of hydrogen bomb tests in the Pacific during 1957 and appeared to hope that it would thereby secure greater collaboration in nuclear matters from the United States.[31] General de Gaulle told Secretary Dulles in July, 1958, not only that France intended to become a nuclear power but that it hoped for American cooperation in the process. Khrushchev, who had been angling for a summit conference since October, 1957, approached the problem of nuclear sharing in roughly the opposite of the way that the CPC would have liked. One of his first acts after taking over the premiership from Bulganin was to announce, on March 31, 1958, a unilateral cessation of nuclear testing, with the express purpose of preventing nuclear diffusion.[32]

---

[29] Maury Lisann, *The Syrian Crisis of 1957*, unpublished manuscript.
[30] Hsieh, *op. cit.*, pp. 107ff.
[31] Such at least appeared to be the implication of the Declaration of Interdependence, issued by President Eisenhower and Prime Minister Macmillan on October 25, 1957.
[32] Cf. Hsieh, *op. cit.*, p. 107.

The United States also proceeded to create problems for the CPR, during the spring of 1958, by reducing its representation at the Sino-American talks in Geneva below the ambassadorial level, something that the CPR considered unacceptable. In March, a meeting of the SEATO Council concerned itself largely with "indirect aggression," meaning Communist subversion, clearly a major instrumentality of the CPR and those Asian Communist Parties closest to it.

The CPR's greater-than-usual irritation at Soviet and American policy contributed to its political and propaganda offensives in May against Tito, who in any case had become increasingly active in the underdeveloped areas, and the pro-American Kishi government in Japan, the pretext in the latter case being an insult to the CPR's flag by some Japanese.

The Middle Eastern crisis in the summer of 1958, marked by the Kassem revolution in Iraq on July 14, an American landing in Lebanon, and fears in Moscow and Peking that the United States might also move against Kassem, gave the CPR a superb opportunity to beat the propaganda drums on behalf of Arab nationalism and to urge the Soviet Union to counter-intervene, at least with "volunteers," against the "imperialists."[33] Far from complying, Khrushchev began to demand a conference on the question at which India and the Arab countries, as well as the permanent members of the United Nations Security Council except for the Republic of China, would be represented. At one time he even seemed willing to accept a Western counterproposal that representation be limited to the permanent Security Council members, including the Republic of China. Neither conference seems to have been acceptable to the CPR, not only because it disapproved on principle of Khrushchev's recourse to diplomacy rather than pressures, but because it would be represented at neither conference and disliked the idea of either the Republic of China or India being present. Probably under the influence of the CPR's objections, Khrushchev dropped his own proposal and, after a hasty visit to Peking at the end of July, also rejected the West's proposal in favor of a demand for a special session of the United Nations General Assembly. He also reiterated the demand that the CPR be admitted to the United Nations. At no time did he give any serious sign of an intent to take forceful action over the crisis. This attitude reflected not only a continuing respect for American military power but also a realization, from fairly early in the crisis, that that power would not actually be used against the new Iraqi regime. To the CPC, Khrushchev had failed in his responsibilities once more and had invited further acts of "imperialistic aggression" against the "oppressed nations."[34]

---

[33] Cf. Yü Chao-li, "A New Upsurge in National Liberation," *Red Flag*, August 1, 1958 (Chinese Red Army Day). This was the first appearance in the CPC press of the pseudonymous Yü Chao-li.

[34] Cf. Zagoria, *op. cit.*, pp. 195–199.

A probable specific reason why the CPR wanted the Soviet Union to take a strong line in the Middle East was an assumed need to divert American attention from the Taiwan Strait, where another crisis seemed to be building up. As in 1954, the Naitonalist armed forces had been receiving a large injection of American aid, and a major operation against the mainland, at a time when it was disrupted by the Great Leap Forward, seemed to be a strong possibility. The easing of the Middle Eastern crisis seems to have added the further consideration in the CPC's eyes that Khrushchev needed to be taught an object lesson in how to deal with "imperialism."

Despite obvious Soviet lack of enthusiasm, the CPR accordingly launched a propaganda offensive over the Taiwan question. A month later it began trying to blockade Quemoy by means of artillery fire and air action. The attempt barely failed, because the United States helped to keep the island resupplied under bombardment. Faced with a possibility of Nationalist and even American retaliation against the mainland, the CPR began to ease its pressures on Quemoy on September 6 and proposed a resumption of Sino-American ambassadorial talks, which occurred on September 15. Only after the CPR made this conciliatory gesture and the United States had accepted it did Khrushchev, on September 7, make a threatening statement in support of the CPR. On October 23, Secretary Dulles and President Chiang Kai-shek issued a joint statement strongly implying that the Nationalists would not try to invade the mainland unless the Communist regime collapsed from internal weakness.[35] As in 1955, the situation in the Taiwan Strait was stalemated.

The Soviet Union had been basically hostile to the Great Leap Forward, not only because of the CPC's implicit claims that it was "building communism" and not merely "socialism," and that the "people's communes" were a universally applicable model, but also because of a certain nervousness that the CPR's phenomenal exertions might in fact attain the goals at which they were aimed. Soviet annoyance and the actual shortcomings of the Great Leap Forward were such that the CPC modified its ideological claims for it in December, 1958. In return Khrushchev, at the Soviet party's Twenty-first Congress in January, 1959, admitted an implicit obligation to aid the CPR by saying that all "socialist" states would attain "communism" "more or less simultaneously." Shortly afterward he conceded the CPR another increment of industrial aid, uncovered by a credit.[36]

The Chinese seem to have been more impressed than the Russians by Castro's coming to power at the beginning of 1959, even though the CPC realized that he was not formally a Communist. Likewise, the CPC was annoyed at Khrushchev for his support of Kassem, in 1959, against the threat of a Communist coup, which the CPC evidently favored. The CPC

---

[35] Cf. *ibid.*, pp. 200–217.
[36] *Ibid.*, Chapter 3.

also went further than Moscow in its propaganda attacks on Nasser, who was bearing down hard on his own Communists.[37]

From January, 1959, following a visit to Peking by Ho Chi Minh, the CPR showed increasing concern over the pro-Western and anti-Communist orientation of the Laotian government, and in particular over its effort to absorb the remaining armed forces of the Communist-led Pathet Lao movement into its own army and so render them harmless.[38]

Although apparently alarmed by West Germany's rejection of the Polish Rapacki Plan for an atom-free zone in Central Europe, Khrushchev waited until the Taiwan Strait had quieted down before coming to grips with this problem, which seriously affected Soviet interests in Europe. On November 27, 1958, the Soviet government demanded an acceptable Berlin settlement within six months, the aim apparently being to eliminate Berlin as a possible cause of war. After the resignation and death of Secretary Dulles in the spring of 1959, however, Khrushchev showed less interest in pressing the West on Berlin than in seeking a détente with the United States. For this purpose, according to the CPC, he terminated on June 20 the program of nuclear aid to the CPR that he had begun in 1957.[39] It is hardly surprising that the CPC showed the opposite of enthusiasm for Khrushchev's visit to the United States in the second half of September.[40]

The growing unrest in Tibet erupted on March 10, 1959, in fighting in the streets of Lhasa, followed by the flight of the Dalai Lama to India, where he was warmly received. To the CPC both the domestic and the international aspects of this humiliating affair appeared extremely serious.[41] At home, the episode seems to have led to an intensification of the Great Leap Forward[42] and may have contributed to the "election" of the CPC's leading doctrinaire, Liu Shao-ch'i, to succeed Mao as Chairman of the CPR in April.

The crisis in Tibet, the growing tension with India, the excesses of the Great Leap Forward and their impact on the armed forces, and the implications of the increasing Sino-Soviet friction for future Soviet military aid to and protection of the CPR were evidently too much for Defense Minister P'eng Te-huai. During a visit to Eastern Europe in the spring of 1959 he held talks with Soviet leaders, probably including Khrushchev, and apparently found them in agreement with him. On his return to the CPR he tried to get the policies to which he objected reversed, only to be outvoted at the

---

[37] *Ibid.*, pp. 258–262.

[38] Cf. *Concerning the Situation in Laos*, Peking: Foreign Languages Press, 1959.

[39] CPR government statement of August 15, 1963 (New China News Agency dispatch, same date).

[40] Zagoria, *op. cit.*, Chapter 9.

[41] Cf. *Concerning the Question of Tibet*, Peking: Foreign Languages Press, 1959.

[42] Cf. directive by the General Political Department of the People's Liberation Army General Staff, March 13, 1959, ordering military personnel to perform up to two months of labor per year in support of the Great Leap Forward.

Eighth Plenary Session of the CPC Central Committee (held at Lushan, in Kiangsi, August 2–16) and then purged.[43] His replacement as Defense Minister by Marshal Lin Piao was announced on September 17.

The Tibetan crisis led to further forward movements by Chinese and Indian troops into the disputed regions along the Sino-Indian frontier. The Chinese were afraid that dissident Tibetans who had escaped to Nepal and India might acquire arms somehow and reenter Tibet unless the frontier were effectively sealed. The result was some skirmishes between Chinese and Indian border patrols, whose significance was more political than military, interspersed with an exchange of notes between Nehru and Chou En-lai. On September 9, 1959, a Soviet statement expressed a pained neutrality with respect to the dispute, an attitude that the CPC interpreted as one of thinly veiled hostility toward itself.[44] On November 7, a few days after it was announced that President Eisenhower would visit India, the CPR proposed talks between Nehru and Chou on the dispute.

In mid-1959 the CPR was seriously embarrassed by a series of Indonesian ordinances aimed at alien (meaning Chinese) retail traders in rural areas. Since the Indonesian government had not agreed to exchange ratifications of the 1955 treaty, it was difficult for such persons to acquire Indonesian citizenship and thus escape discriminatory treatment. Through a campaign of intense diplomatic and political pressures, the CPR succeeded in bringing the Indonesian government on January 20, 1960, to an exchange of ratifications. This led to a considerable easing of the crisis.

When Khrushchev visited China at the beginning of October after his trip to the United States, his reception was a chilly one, and he lectured the Chinese publicly on the need not to "test by force the stability of the capitalist system." In a speech to his own Supreme Soviet at the end of October, he went even further. He warned against the use of force in several parts of Asia, including Taiwan and the Sino-Indian border, and by implication equated Chinese foreign policy with Trotsky's heretical slogan, "neither peace nor war." He also insisted on the necessity for improving relations with the West.[45]

By this time the CPC had evidently concluded that there was very little hope of bringing Khrushchev to accept and act on the implications of its assertion that "the East wind has prevailed over the West wind," unless perhaps the "imperialists" committed some outrage sufficient to bring him to his senses. For its part the CPC took advantage of the eightieth anniversary

---

[43] David A. Charles, "The Dismissal of Marshal P'eng Teh-huai," *The China Quarterly*, no. 8 (October–December, 1961), pp. 63–76 (an interesting but not entirely reliable account).

[44] The CPC waited more than three years before describing this statement as the first occasion when Sino-Soviet differences were brought into the open ("Whence the Differences?" *People's Daily*, February 27, 1963).

[45] Zagoria, *op. cit.*, Chapter 11.

of Stalin's birth (December 21, 1959) to remind Khrushchev and the world pointedly that Stalin had been "an uncompromising enemy of imperialism."[46]

■ THE CAMPAIGN AGAINST KHRUSHCHEV (1960–63)

While preparing to intensify its political pressures on Khrushchev, the CPC moved to tidy up its relations with the Asian neutrals, which had been seriously strained by the tough Chinese line during the preceding period, and in particular by the crisis in Tibet and the fighting along the Sino-Indian border. The desirability of doing so was emphasized by an announcement at the beginning of 1960 that Khrushchev would shortly visit India, Burma, and Indonesia. The virtually complete failure of talks between Chou En-lai and Nehru in April, however, confirmed the CPR's conviction that India must be regarded as essentially hostile. At the end of January, on the other hand, the CPR signed a fairly reasonable settlement of its boundary dispute, and a treaty of friendship and nonaggression, with Burma, followed in the spring by a similar settlement with Nepal. One purpose of these agreements was to isolate India from the signatories and head off if possible an increase of Soviet influence in neutral Asia.[47]

Again as a form of protection for its flank while it prepared to focus its main attention on Khrushchev and the international Communist movement, the CPC vociferously welcomed the turbulent demonstrations in Japan, in the spring of 1960, against ratification of the revised security treaty with the United States.[48] The CPC also launched a propaganda tirade against President Eisenhower's visit to the Far East in June, which spanned the tenth anniversary of the beginning of the Korean War.[49]

The CPC opened a bitter and militant propaganda attack on Khrushchev, which however stopped short of naming him, on the occasion of the ninetieth anniversary of Lenin's birth (April 22, 1960). The attack was clearly designed, among other things, to embarrass and hamper Khrushchev when he went to the Paris summit conference in May. By that time, however, Khrushchev seems already to have become convinced, through several tough statements by Western leaders, that he had no chance of getting a German settlement on his terms. He was therefore looking for a way out. The fortuitous downing of an American U-2 on May 1, and the refusal of President Eisenhower to apologize for such flights, gave Khrushchev the pretext

---

[46] Ai Ssu-ch'i, "In Commemoration of the Eightieth Birthday of Stalin," *People's Daily*, December 21, 1959.

[47] Cf. A. M. Halpern, "The Chinese Communist Line on Neutralism," *The China Quarterly*, no. 5 (January–March, 1961), pp. 90–115.

[48] Cf. *Support the Just Struggle of the Japanese People Against the Japan-U.S. Treaty of Military Alliance*, Peking: Foreign Languages Press, 1960.

[49] Cf. *Drive U.S. Imperialism out of Asia!* Peking: Foreign Languages Press, 1960.

he wanted to break off the conference.[50] Unfortunately for him, the entire episode, as well as later developments in the Congo and Laos, seemed by Communist standards to confirm the harsher Chinese analysis of "imperialism" (and of the United Nations) rather than his own.

In June the Sino-Soviet dispute began to be extended into the international front organizations and congresses of other Communist Parties. The CPC developed some support from certain of the Asian parties and from Albania. After some inconclusive preparatory meetings in September and October, a conference of eighty-one Communist Parties convened in Moscow in November to discuss and if possible compose the differences between the Soviet and Chinese parties. The ensuing bitter confrontation was indecisive, mainly because of Chinese insistence on a unanimous vote (or veto) rather than majority rule, and the Moscow statement issued by the conference was essentially an evasion of most of the major issues.

During the next several months Soviet-Albanian relations worsened, and Sino-Albanian relations grew correspondingly closer. When Khrushchev took the momentous step of denouncing the Albanians publicly at his party's Twenty-second Congress (October, 1961), the CPC stood by its Balkan ally despite its own economic weakness.

Meanwhile the Indochinese situation had worsened, following a neutralist seizure of power in Vientiane in August, 1960. In December, anti-Communist forces under General Phoumi Nosavan drove the neutralist forces out of Vientiane and virtually into alliance with the Pathet Lao. At the request of neutralist Premier Souvanna Phouma, the Soviet Union began to airlift arms at the end of the year to the neutralist forces under Kong Le, and incidentally also to the Pathet Lao. Perhaps because of the latter aspect, the CPR cooperated in this airlift, which passed over its territory, even though the airlift gave the Soviet Union considerable influence on the Pathet Lao until it ended early in 1962. During this period the CPR began quietly to turn the adjacent Laotian province of Phong Saly into a virtual Chinese sphere of influence, and therefore also into a buffer. The CPR took an active part, apparently in fairly close cooperation with the Soviet Union, in the Geneva Conference on Laos (May, 1961–July, 1962), which resulted in a nominal neutralization of the country and a weak coalition government presided over by Souvanna Phouma.

An intensification of American military aid to the government of South Vietnam at the end of 1961, on the other hand, evoked little overt response from the CPR beyond an increase in its own program of military

---

[50] The U-2 affair also gave Khrushchev a chance to increase the prestige of the Soviet rocket forces, which he favored as a relatively cheap minimum deterrent to American attack (cf. John R. Thomas, "The Role of Missile Defense in Soviet Strategy," *Military Review*, vol. xliv, no. 5 [May, 1964], p. 49), and to continue with his effort to cut Soviet ground forces, about which the CPC evidently had reservations (cf. A. L. Hsieh, *The Significance of Chinese Communist Treatment of Khrushchev's January 14 Speech on Strategy*, RAND corporation, RM 2534, February 19, 1960).

aid to North Vietnam and an endorsement (early in 1962) of the idea of a neutral South Vietnam, along the lines of the settlement in Laos.

In the spring of 1962, as already indicated, the CPR found itself confronted with not one but several threats to its security. The economy was at its lowest ebb. The Republic of China seemed to be preparing for an invasion of the mainland, possibly with American support. It was announced on May 15 that in view of an outburst of fighting in Laos, the United States would send troops to Thailand. The Soviet Union was beginning to intrigue with dissident minorities in Sinkiang. The Indian Army was pushing outposts forward closer and closer to the Chinese military highway first revealed to the Indians in 1958, and considered by them as passing across their territory (in Ladakh).

On the whole, the threats dissipated without a crisis. The CPC massed troops opposite Taiwan, and the Nationalists did not attempt an invasion. The United States gave an assurance (on June 23, in Warsaw) that it would not support a Nationalist invasion if one should occur and began to withdraw its troops from Thailand a few weeks after they arrived. The Soviet Union was apparently not ready for serious border trouble with the CPR and in any case was preoccupied after July with the shipment of weapons, ultimately including surface-to-surface missiles, to Cuba. The evaporation of the threats from the other quarters left the CPR free to deal with the Indians.

Annoyed by Chinese pressures on its outposts during the summer, the Indian government announced in mid-October that it would soon launch an offensive to clear all Chinese troops off all territory claimed by India. Concerned by this development, which threatened to put the Indian army in a position from which it could give aid to Tibetan insurgents if it chose, the Chinese struck first, on October 20. After four days of successful fighting, the CPR proposed a ceasefire and a border settlement on a compromise basis similar to that of a proposal it had made in 1959. Only after the new proposal was formally rejected, in mid-November, did the CPR resume offensive operations, again with success. By this time, however, a number of political and military considerations, including indications of a sizeable American military aid program to India, rendered moderation advisable. On November 21 the CPR announced a unilateral ceasefire, to be followed by a withdrawal to the proposed de facto border indicated in the earlier ceasefire offer. The CPR had won a military and to some extent a political victory, but it was not able to bring India to the conference table in a compliant mood. Prolonged wrangling over the terms of a settlement, accompanied by an effort at mediation by certain Afro-Asian powers, ensued. The one thing that seemed fairly clear was that the CPR was unlikely, unless offered strong provocation by the Indians, to launch another major offensive.

The CPR seems to have watched the buildup of Soviet arms in Cuba with cautious approval, because it seemed to commit the Soviet Union to defend the Castro regime—as the CPR could not—and because it promised to disrupt an apparent trend toward a Soviet-American détente. These hopes were dissipated, of course, by Khrushchev's decision (between October 26 and October 28) to withdraw his missiles and bombers from Cuba even without a formal no-invasion pledge by the United States. On November 5, therefore, the CPR made its celebrated accusation that Khrushchev was trying to "play the Munich scheme against the Cuban people."

The infuriated Khrushchev struck back with the equally exaggerated charge that the CPC had been trying to incite a world war over Cuba. He then organized anti-CPC demonstrations at congresses of several European Communist Parties, and the CPC replied with bitter editorial denunciations. By June, Kozlov had been eliminated from the Soviet political scene, allegedly by a stroke, and Khrushchev had begun to ease the jamming of the Voice of America and show an interest in President Kennedy's proposal for a ban on nuclear tests, other than underground. On June 14 the CPC sent Khrushchev what amounted to an ultimatum to cease and desist or face an open split in the international Communist movement. The Soviet party rejected the ultimatum in a long open letter on July 14, issued while inconclusive talks between representatives of the Soviet and Chinese Central Committees were still in progress, and initialed the test ban treaty on July 25.

The CPR's most important expressed objections, and probable but unexpressed objections, to the test ban treaty are roughly as follows. The treaty promotes an atmosphere of détente ("an illusion of peace") and opens the way to further similar steps. It distracts attention from the CPR's demand for general nuclear disarmament. It implies a willingness on the part of the Soviet Union to resign itself to more or less permanent strategic inferiority to the United States and therefore to a continuing inability to inflict major politico-military setbacks on the United States. It reduces the already slight chance of a resumption of Soviet aid to the CPR in the development of nuclear weapons. It conveys the idea that the Soviet Union alone among the "socialist" countries has the right to possess nuclear weapons and makes it politically more embarrassing for the CPR to test its own nuclear weapons when they have been developed.

■ **THE "THIRD WORLD" POLICY (1963–)**

At least as early as 1962, the CPC defined the enemies of its foreign policy, and allegedly of human progress as well, as "the imperialists, the reactionaries of various countries and the modern revisionists."[51] Khrush-

---

[51] Communiqué of the Tenth Plenary Session of the CPC Central Committee (New China News Agency dispatch, September 28, 1962).

chev's signature of the test ban treaty confirmed his place among the "modern revisionists" and the place of the "modern revisionists" among the enemy. The CPC has had somewhat more difficulty in formulating its concept of its friends, in large part because of an important distinction between those whom it feels able to acknowledge (these may be termed its de jure friends) and those whom it wants but does not feel free to acknowledge in a formal way (these may be termed its de facto friends). The de jure friends it has defined as "the fraternal socialist countries, the fraternal parties [i.e., in both cases, those that the CPC has not written off as irrevocably committed to Moscow], the Marxist-Leninists [i.e., acceptable leftists whether Communist or non-Communist], and the revolutionary [i.e., anti-"imperialist"] people of all countries."[52] This conglomeration being predominantly nonwhite, the CPC often resorts to virulent antiwhite propaganda.

The de facto friends have been named only in informal Chinese statements, which refer to them plus the CPR as the "third world." These are the major non-Communist industrial countries, except for the United States, including their impeccably bourgeois governments: France, West Germany, Great Britain, Japan, and in some versions Italy.[53] It is obvious that, except perhaps for France, active cooperation between these countries and the CPR is far more desired (by the Chinese) than actual. It is also obvious that the CPC is unable, especially in view of its vulnerability to Soviet propaganda charges, to name these countries publicly and authoritatively as its would-be friends. The purpose of these Chinese approaches to the "third world" are presumably to encourage trade, perhaps to receive eventual economic and even military aid, to split the other countries from the United States, and to compete with Soviet approaches to the non-Communist world.

In essence, the CPC seems to have given up all hope for the time being of splitting the United States and the Soviet Union and of preventing a détente between them. Instead, the CPC is trying to make itself the leader, and only common member, of two disparate coalitions: its leftist de jure friends, whom its Communist opponents accuse it of trying to weld into a "Fourth International," and its bourgeois hoped-for de facto

---

[52] "The Leaders of the CPSU Are the Greatest Splitters of Our Times," *People's Daily* and *Red Flag*, February 4, 1964. The latter category includes, in Asia, Africa, and Latin America, "extremely broad sections of the population [who] refuse to be slaves of imperialism. They include not only the workers, peasants, intellectuals, and petty bourgeoisie, but also the patriotic national bourgeoisie and even certain kings, princes and aristocrats who are patriotic" (CPC Central Committee letter of June 14, 1963, to CPSU Central Committee).

[53] Mao recently said to a visiting French delegation, "France herself, Germany [clearly West Germany], England on the condition that she ceases to be the courtier of America, Japan, and we ourselves — there is your third world" (quoted in *The New York Times*, February 21, 1964). Soviet and Yugoslav sources have included Italy in this list.

friends, the "third world." At present the CPC's chances of welding and leading either coalition, and using it affectively in its own interest in opposition to the United States, the Soviet Union, and their respective friends, appear no better than fair, and probably slight. Nevertheless, the CPC can presumably expect to make limited gains for its revolutionary objectives, mainly by working with its de jure friends, and for its national objectives, mainly by working with its de facto friends, as a result of its present policy.

Soon after expressing its objections to the test ban treaty, the CPC inaugurated a series of joint editorials in the *People's Daily* and *Red Flag* in reply to the Soviet party's Central Committee's open letter of July 14, 1963. The first in this series, published on September 6,[54] was the first public statement by the CPC to name Khrushchev as the main object of its wrath. A separate CPC statement published on December 26, 1963 (Mao's seventieth birthday) indicated an intent to split those Communist Parties whose leadership could not be captured and recognize the pro-CPC fragments as "Marxist-Leninist" parties.[55] While the CPC continued, during 1964, to try with some success to implement this policy, it also strove to fend off another general international Communist conference, on which Khrushchev had apparently decided when the series of replies to his open letter began in September, 1963. The latest (as of mid-1964) in this series announced in threatening language that it was time "to repudiate and liquidate Khrushchev's revisionism."[56]

The main triumph of the CPR's "third world" policy to date has of course been its establishment of diplomatic relations with France at the end of January, 1964. This is a complicated episode in itself that can only be summarized here. The main common interest that has drawn France and the CPR together, in spite of an incompatibility of ideology and domestic orientation that is publicly admitted on both sides, is de Gaulle's and Mao's analogous but not identical objections to Soviet-American détente and to the test ban treaty, to which neither France nor the CPR adhered. There are also other interests, less important because (except for an interest in increased trade) they are not held in common. These include such things as de Gaulle's desire to participate in working out a political settlement in Indochina, presumably on the basis of something less than the full Communist demands; and the CPR's interest in a major increment of international prestige, a major political base in Western Europe, and a flying start on its "third world" policy.

---

[54] "The Origin and Development of the Differences Between the Leadership of the CPSU and Ourselves," *People's Daily* and *Red Flag*, September 6, 1963.

[55] Statement by Chou Yang, a leading CPC propagandist, on October 26, 1963 (not released until two months later).

[56] "The Proletarian Revolution and Khrushchev's Revisionism," *People's Daily* and *Red Flag*, March 31, 1964.

Since inaugurating that policy the CPR has continued to conduct revolutionary activity in the Afro-Asian world, in Zanzibar for example. It has also made one major effort to broaden its contacts with non-Communist "revolutionary people" and "oppressed nations." This was Chou En-lai's visit (December 13, 1963–February 5, 1964) to ten African countries (the United Arab Republic, Algeria, Morocco, Tunisia, Ghana, Mali, Guinea, the Sudan, Ethiopia, Somalia),[57] to Albania, and to three Asian countries (Burma, Pakistan, Ceylon). Chou evidently also wanted to visit France but was not invited. Apart from Albania, where Chou was on specifically Communist business, the main general purpose of the trip was to combat Indian influence and specifically the proposal for a second conference of nonaligned countries (the first having been held at Belgrade, in September, 1961) and to promote instead the alternative, favored by Indonesia and the CPR, of another Asian-African Conference. The latter alternative had the advantage in Chinese eyes that the CPR would be represented and the Soviet Union would not (or at least it had not been at the first Asian-African Conference). While making some anti-American, anti-Soviet, and anti-Indian propaganda, Chou in general was mild and conciliatory in his tone. Ethnic propaganda was somewhat muted. He talked of aid and trade. He indicated that the CPC regards Algeria as the major regional revolutionary center for Africa, as it does Cuba for Latin America. He indicated support for the goals of African and Arab unity. He reiterated the Chinese line that the CPR protects the interests of small countries (such as Yemen and Albania) against the major powers.

Chou's trip was a fair success, although he aroused little enthusiasm and encountered some hostile criticism of Chinese policies and behavior. Tunisia recognized the CPR on January 10, before France did, apparently not due to Chou's visit but probably as an indirect result of de Gaulle's known decision to recognize the CPR. In February the Republic of Congo, or Congo Brazzaville (the former French, not Belgian, Congo), also recognized the CPR, presumably as a result of de Gaulle's move. The other French-speaking African countries seemed in no hurry to follow de Gaulle's example, however, nor is there any convincing evidence that France urged them to do so.

Another major development was an intensification of the crisis in Indochina. The downfall of the Diem regime in South Vietnam on November 1, 1963, was followed by increased insurgency and political pressures for a neutral South Vietnam in which Communists or pro-Communists would take part in a coalition government, as in Laos. The United States also

---

[57] Chou was originally scheduled to visit Tanganyika, Kenya, and Uganda as well, but it was announced on February 4, 1964, at whose initiative is not clear, that these visits would be "postponed." The probable reason is the leftist revolution in Zanzibar in January. During the trip Chou also received invitations to visit Zanzibar and Burundi at a later date, which he accepted. See W. A. C. Adie, "Chou En-lai on Safari," *The China Quarterly*, no. 18 (April–June, 1964), pp. 174–194.

increased its involvement in the struggle. In Laos itself, the increasing futility of its coalition government led to an anti-Communist coup in Vientiane on April 19, 1964. This was followed in turn by an intensification of military activity by the Pathet Lao and (in June) by American air action in support of Souvanna Phouma's neutralist government.

There is a widespread belief that the CPR is somehow responsible for, or in control of, Communist activities in Laos and South Vietnam. This is an oversimplification of a very complex situation, which may be summarized as follows. The CPR wants to increase its influence on North Vietnam and has been fairly successful in recent years in doing so. This influence does not amount to control, however, and is due largely to the CPR's being somewhat more militant than the Soviet Union in its approach to Indochinese problems. The CPR does not want to become embroiled in a military conflict with the United States in Indochina, however, still less to suffer direct American retaliation. Hence it does not want the North Vietnamese to incur American retaliation, which might either set a process of escalation in motion or force the CPR to back down. The North Vietnamese seem to believe that they have reason to feel uncertain of Chinese support in such a case. The CPR does not want direct American involvement in Laos and has uttered some vague threats in order to deter it.

Both the Chinese and the North Vietnamese appear to think, however, that these contingencies are fairly remote, and that by resolution and skilfull maneuvering the United States can be prevented from making good its various threats. This being the case, the Chinese and North Vietnamese both seem to believe that victory can be won in South Vietnam and Laos after a fairly long struggle, of which the United States will grow weary. There is no doubt that the CPR wants North Vietnam to take over South Vietnam by means of military and political pressures and has increased its military aid to the North Vietnamese and their irregular forces in South Vietnam. In Laos the situation is more obscure; the CPR as well as North Vietnam aids, supports, and influences the Pathet Lao. It is not certain, in other words, that the CPR has assigned Laos to the North Vietnamese sphere as it has South Vietnam.[58]

Although Indochina does not seem generally to have been a subject of serious Sino-Soviet disagreement, some signs of such disagreement have appeared during the recent crisis. As might be expected, the Soviet Union has taken a more conciliatory line toward the West in the crisis than has the CPR, even while agreeing to additional arms shipments to Indonesia in support of its "confrontation" with Britain and Malaysia. On June 27,

[58] See the excellent analysis, "Hanoi Foresees Victory in South Vietnam — But Only After Long Guerrilla War," *Special Information Notes* (Washington), no. 39 (April 7, 1964). The CPC held a "working conference," followed by a "military review," in June, evidently as part of the war of nerves over Indochina.

1964, the CPR forbade unauthorized movement by "foreign nonmilitary vessels" through the strait between the island of Hainan and the South China mainland. The regulations were presumably aimed at Soviet arms shipments to North Vietnam, and possibly to Indonesia as well.[59]

At the time the CPR celebrated its fifteenth birthday on October 1, 1964, it was involved not only in a confrontation with the United States over Indochina but in one with Khrushchev. He had decided to read the CPC out of the international Communist movement, and he had pushed Sino-Soviet relations in the state field fairly close to war because of his anger at the CPR's unyielding position on the Sino-Soviet border dispute and his concern over the imminence of the first Chinese nuclear test.

---

[59] New China News Agency dispatch, June 27, 1964. Although supposedly adopted on June 5, the regulations were not published until two days after an announcement of additional Soviet military aid for Indonesia. The strait is relatively secure from the United States Seventh Fleet.

PART TWO

Communist China on the World Stage

- ☐ Maoism
- ☐ Objectives and Instrumentalities of Foreign Policy
- ☐ The Sino-Soviet Alliance and the West
- ☐ China and International Communism
- ☐ Communist China's Policy Toward the Middle East, Africa, and Latin America

□ 3

Maoism[1]

By Maoism, or the "thought of Mao Tse-tung" as the CPC would put it, is meant here the entire evolving complex of patterns of official thought and behavior that the CPC has developed while under Mao's leadership. It is of course difficult to disentangle Mao's individual contribution from that of others, but it can be safely assumed to have been very great. It is also difficult to separate the pre-1949 and post-1949 aspects and the domestic from the international aspects.

■ **GENERAL CHARACTERISTICS[2]**

The first basic characteristic of Maoism is a deep and sincere nationalism that has been so merged with the strictly Communist elements as to resemble a chemical compound, in which the original components can no longer be separated. Closely related to nationalism is a strong strain of populism, so that the CPC sees itself not merely as the "vanguard" of the proletariat, or even of the proletariat plus the peasantry plus the "progressive" sections of the bourgeoisie, but of "the people" (the others are "reactionaries" and hence not "people") who are defined in effect as those who oppose the "three big mountains" ("imperialism, feudalism, and bureaucratic capitalism") and accept at least passively the "leadership" of the CPC. Thirdly, Maoism even more than Leninism recognizes the decisive importance in history of conscious, voluntary activity and of subjective

---

[1] General sources on Maoism: *Selected Works; Chinese Communist World Outlook,* Washington: Department of State, 1962; Stuart R. Schram, *The Political Thought of Mao Tse-tung,* New York: Praeger, 1963.

[2] Benjamin I. Schwartz, *Communist Ideology in China,* Santa Barbara, California: General Electric Company, RM 62TMP-90, December, 1962.

forces, as opposed to deterministic, objective forces. Fourthly, Maoism stresses "contradictions" and struggle, or what might be called the power of negative thinking, to the point where it invents foreign and domestic enemies, while describing them as few in number and as essentially weak "paper tigers." Through this runs, as with all Communists, a deep-seated mystique of the Party as the vessel and vanguard of history and progress.

■ AS A TECHNIQUE OF POLITICAL LEADERSHIP[3]

Under this heading Maoism connotes an effort to identify the CPC with major forces and trends, such as Chinese nationalism and peasant land hunger. This enables the CPC, in theory at least, to maximize the number of its friends and minimize the number of its enemies, who can therefore be isolated and discredited before being destroyed or neutralized. The leadership cultivates an image of reasonableness and lack of interest in personal power. On the other hand, Mao has long tried to create for himself a unique aura as a revolutionary and a statesman, comparable in recent times only to that of Stalin.[4] Within the party, Mao has generally employed the technique of the iron fist in the velvet glove. Factionalism has generally been held down to a manageable level. Nevertheless two general tendencies, which may be termed adventurous and moderate, have existed in Chinese Communist domestic and foreign policy, especially since 1949. While it is possible to identify these, tentatively at least, with particular individuals, with Mao serving as the balance wheel, the relationship between them has not seemed to be one of hostility but rather one of complementarity.[5] Disgraced leaders have generally not been purged, but kept at work and sometimes even partially rehabilitated.[6] The one unpardonable offense seems to be to have, or seek to develop, unusually close Soviet connections and to try to use them in a power struggle or policy debate.[7]

In general, it can be said that the CPC learned before 1949 to make effective use, and still makes effective use, of the standard controls employed by modern totalitarian regimes: ideology; organization, with an important innovation in the extensive use of small groups; propaganda, with important

---

[3] John Wilson Lewis, *Leadership in Communist China*, Cornell University Press, 1963; John Wilson Lewis, *Chinese Communist Party Leadership and the Succession to Mao Tse-tung: An Appraisal of Tensions*, Washington: Department of State, January, 1964.

[4] This point is developed more fully below, in the section on Maoism "As an Approach to Relations Among Communist Parties and States."

[5] A tempting, if not necessarily accurate, analogy is the concept of nonantagonistic dualism (*yin* and *yang*) in traditional Chinese philosophy. The adventurous tendency has been generally in the ascendant since at least as long ago as the spring of 1958.

[6] For example, Li Li-san has recently been identified as a secretary of the North China Bureau of the CPC Central Committee.

[7] This appears to have been a major cause for the purging of Kao Kang (1954) and P'eng Te-huai (1959).

innovations in the form of "coercive persuasion" ("brainwashing") of individuals, "rectification" campaigns among selected groups, and "mass campaigns" among the populace at large; and terror, with important innovations in the widespread use of volunteer as well as paid informers and of highly coercive "struggle meetings" against selected victims.

■ AS A VARIANT OF MARXISM-LENINISM[8]

It has already been suggested that Maoism differs significantly in spirit from orthodox, or Soviet, Marxism-Leninism, and it will be shown later that Maoism has introduced major innovations in the fields of "socialist revolution" and "socialist construction." Here the aim is to consider Maoism, primarily and briefly, as a theoretical system.

The CPC claims, with little validity, that Mao has made a major contribution to the theory of dialectical materialism in two published works, *On Practice* and *On Contradiction*, both allegedly written in 1937 but more probably put into their present form between 1950 and 1952. These essays actually contribute nothing of importance to this tedious subject.

The CPC also claims that Mao has made a major contribution to the theory, as well as the practice, of revolution. It maintained his originality in this respect even during the years immediately following 1949, when it was anxious to depict Mao as a "comrade-in-arms" and "disciple" of Stalin. Mao never advanced as a theoretical proposition the idea that a proletarian (Communist) party can exist without a proletarian (urban) base, and his theory of a "democratic" anti-imperialist revolution in a peasant country followed by a "socialist" revolution does not vary significantly from Lenin's formulations except in one respect. Whereas Lenin, at least as interpreted by Stalin, was prepared to accept bourgeois leadership of the revolution throughout the "democratic" stage, Mao would accept only bourgeois participation and insisted on Communist leadership, under the rubric of "new democracy," from as early as possible in the "democratic" stage, or in other words before the Communist assumption of state power.[9]

For the period after the Communist seizure of power, Maoism envisages not a "proletarian dictatorship" but a "people's democratic dictatorship" in which "the people," including all the "revolutionary classes," exercise dictatorship over the "reactionaries" but are themselves led in a "democratic" fashion by the Communist Party. Non-Communist parties also exist and, like the nonproletarian "revolutionary classes," supposedly participate in the exercise of the dictatorship. Such is the Royal Lie of Communist China.

---

[8] Arthur A. Cohen, "How Original is Maoism?" *Problems of Communism*, vol. x, no. 6 (November–December, 1961), pp. 34–42.

[9] Richard Lowenthal in Kurt London, ed., *New Nations in a Divided World: The International Relations of the Afro-Asian States*, New York: Praeger, 1963, p. 59.

The main theoretical task of the "people's democratic dictatorship" is to effect the "transition to socialism" from the "new democratic" stage. When this transition officially began in 1953, it was suddenly and confusingly stated to have been actually in effect since 1949. The reason for this was apparently a deep-seated conviction that Maoist revolutionary strategy makes possible the elimination of all effective organized opposition before the Communist assumption of state power. Hence the way is open for the "people" to begin immediately a "basically peaceful transition to socialism" during which the bourgeoisie will be deprived first of its economic base and then of its ideology by manipulation and persuasion, rather than force. The concept of a peaceful "ideological remoulding" of the bourgeoisie is original with Mao. In 1958, in the early phases of the "Great Leap Forward," the CPC introduced a further complication into its theoretical timetable by strongly implying, even before it had officially claimed to have attained "socialism," that it was already in the next stage, that of "building communism." This claim was quickly withdrawn in the face of Soviet objections, however.

In 1956, in the wake of de-Stalinization, the CPC began to assert that "nonantagonistic contradictions" (i.e., differences of opinion and conflicts of interest capable of being compromised) would persist in a "socialist" and even in a "communist" society. Mao then used this unorthodox and original theory, which specifically included an affirmation of the existence of "contradictions" between the leaders and the led, as the basis for his celebrated Hundred Flowers campaign. This ultimately backfired in the spring of 1957 by evoking unexpectedly sharp criticisms of the regime from many non-Communist and even from some Communists.

Thus Mao can claim to have made some genuine if not sweeping ideological contributions to Marxism-Leninism. It is doubtful that these contributions are sufficient to rank Mao in the eyes of Communists in general as a major "continuator" of Marxism-Leninism. Soviet leaders and writers have generally avoided conceding any major contributions by Mao to the theory of "building socialism" and have confined their tributes to Mao to his accomplishments as a revolutionary strategist, as a virtuoso in the seizure of power. Even there, the Soviet Union has tended to stress Mao's practical rather than his theoretical innovations.

■ AS A STRATEGY FOR THE SEIZURE OF POWER[10]

The authoritative and usual summary of Maoism as a revolutionary strategy is that the Communist Party leads the "new democratic" revolution

[10] *Selected Works*, especially vol. 2; Brigadier General Samuel B. Griffith, *Mao Tse-tung on Guerrilla Warfare*, New York: Praeger, 1962; Edward L. Katzenbach, Jr., and Gene Z. Hanrahan, "The Revolutionary Strategy of Mao Tse-tung," *Political Science Quarterly*, vol. 70, no. 3 (September, 1955), pp. 321–340; "The Sino-Soviet Dispute in

against "imperialism, feudalism, and bureaucratic capitalism" and uses as its primary tactics "armed struggle" (organized warfare) and "political struggle," often subsumed under the rubric "united front."[11]

On the party, despite its central importance, little need be said here.[12] Theoretically, it is a "monolithic" Leninist "vanguard" party of essentially classless professional revolutionaries masquerading as a proletarian party. Although much if not most of its revolutionary activity must be conducted in rural areas, it cannot therefore become a peasant party. It claims to represent the peasantry as well as the proletariat and tolerates no other party that claims to represent either, but it does not permit its policies to be dictated by the interests of either of these two "revolutionary" classes. It will, however, collaborate under conditions of its own choosing with bourgeois parties. The party need not restrict its membership to the conspiratorial elite visualized by Lenin for a party still seeking power. On the contrary, during the mid-1920s and again after 1937 the CPC acquired a mass membership, mainly in order to facilitate its own control of territorial bases, military units, mass organizations, and the like, but also perhaps to increase its bargaining power in dealing with Stalin and the Comintern.

As for "armed struggle,"[13] Maoism naturally does not preach the resort to warfare by Communist Parties under suicidal conditions, but it does insist that warfare under viable conditions is the most satisfactory, in fact the only thoroughly satisfactory, method of establishing a Communist Party firmly in power.[14] It is only in such a way that a party can create a fully "homegrown" totalitarian regime. Otherwise, it must either be a "derivative" party dependent on the Soviet Union and installed in power, if at all,

Chinese Perspective," *Current Scene* (Hong Kong), vol. 2, no. 17 (July 15, 1963). A classic early statement is Liu Shao-ch'i's speech to the Trade Union Conference of Asian and Australasian Countries, Peking, November 16, 1949 (New China News Agency dispatch, November 23, 1949). An important recent statement is "The Proletarian Revolution and Khrushchev's Revisionism," *People's Daily* and *Red Flag*, March 31, 1964.

[11] Cf. *Selected Works*, vol. 3, p. 65.

[12] The 1945 constitution of the CPC, drafted largely by Liu Shao-ch'i, is translated in *Documentary History, op. cit.*, pp. 419–439. For an analysis of Liu's official commentary on the constitution see H. Arthur Steiner, "Lui Shao-ch'i, *On the Party:* A Review Article," *The Far Eastern Quarterly*, vol. xi, no. 1 (November, 1951), pp. 79–84. The 1956 constitution may be found in Peter S. H. Tang, *Communist China Today*, 2 vols., New York: Praeger, 1957–58, vol. 2, pp. 112–113. The official commentary is by Teng Hsiao-p'ing (New China News Agency dispatch, September 16, 1956). The CPC has never adopted a party program, and the CPSU has recently criticized it for this ("On Certain Aspects of Party Life in the CPC," *Pravda*, April 28, 1964).

[13] Arthur Cohen (*loc. cit.*, p. 38) rightly points out that Chu Teh and other Red Army leaders undoubtedly made major but unacknowledged contributions to Mao's military thought. Other contributors, such as the ancient Chinese author Sun Tzu and T. E. Lawrence, could also be mentioned.

[14] "The Proletarian Revolution and Khrushchev's Revisionism," *loc. cit.* This article even insists that the Communist seizure of power in Czechoslovakia, long pictured by the CPSU as an example of a "peaceful" path to power, was achieved mainly through indigenous armed struggle.

by the Soviet Army,[15] or it must seek power primarily by peaceful means and thus be at the mercy of the bourgeoisie. In particular, it is desirable that a Communist Party capture its own capital city, rather than receiving it from the hands of the Soviet Army.[16]

Organized warfare requires base areas, which at least in a peasant country and in the early stages of the revolution must be rural. In time, the party can "encircle the cities from the countryside." It is not desirable that the base areas be "active sanctuaries"[17] on foreign soil nor is it necessary that they all be next to an international boundary or otherwise unassailable by the enemy. On the other hand, location of some of the bases near a friendly international boundary, as in northern Manchuria after 1945, may be helpful by providing a secure rear and a source of supply, as long as such a relationship does not threaten the autonomy of the movement. In particular, the central headquarters must be located so as to be secure both from the enemy and from overly powerful foreign allies.

Normally such a war will be a protracted one waged against an initially stronger enemy and falling into three stages. In the first, that of the strategic defensive, mobile warfare waged by regular units will be the primary strategy. In the second phase, that of strategic stalemate, guerrilla warfare waged by both regular and irregular units will be primary. The third stage, that of the strategic offensive, will require organizational regularization and technical modernization of the Red Army and will be waged primarily by regular units fighting mobile warfare. Positional warfare will be required at the end to take cities. Thus, in addition to the three stages of the war there are three types of warfare (positional, mobile, and guerrilla) and three types of forces (regulars, guerrillas, and militia); a unit of one type can be trained and then promoted to a higher category (militia to guerrillas, or guerrillas to regulars). Especially in guerrilla warfare, which the CPC of course developed into a fine art and which it regards as auxiliary to and not independent of the regular operations of the Red Army, tactics consist essentially of avoiding combat except when it is possible to achieve surprise and local numerical superiority.

Warfare as waged by the CPC before 1949 always had a strong guerrilla character, and it is axiomatic that any guerrilla war is a highly politicized war.[18] Accordingly, Mao and other CPC spokesmen have insisted time and again, even since the advent of the nuclear age, that men are more im-

---

[15] Cf. Richard Lowenthal, "The Rise and Decline of International Communism," *Problems of Communism*, vol. xii, no. 2 (March–April, 1963), pp. 21ff.

[16] Apart from the hitherto unique case of Cuba, the only Communist countries whose capitals were not "liberated" by the Soviet Army are Albania, the CPR, and North Vietnam. This fact and the historical conditions that it symbolized help to account for the exceptional closeness of the CPC to the Albanian and North Vietnamese regimes.

[17] The phrase is Bernard Fall's (cf. his *Street Without Joy: Indochina at War, 1946–54*, Harrisburg, Pa.: Military Service Publishing Company, 1961, especially p. 294).

[18] Cf. the excellent article by Chalmers A. Johnson, "Civilian Loyalties and Guerrilla Conflict," *World Politics*, vol. xiv, no. 4 (July, 1962), pp. 646–661.

portant in war than are weapons. This platitude should be interpreted as implying little more than the CPC's insistence on the primacy of political factors in war, and as an effort at psychological self-compensation for the fact that the CPC has generally been weaker in weaponry than its main actual or potential opponent. Actually, the CPC has never passed up a chance to improve its weaponry. It was happy to acquire Japanese arms in Manchuria in 1945–46, with the cooperation of the Soviet Army, and to capture American weapons from the Nationalists during the ensuing years. Since 1950 it has created impressive conventional forces, again with Soviet aid, and since 1956 has begun to acquire a nuclear capability of its own.

In the politicized type of warfare envisaged by Mao, the army has three types of political relationships: with the party, with the people, and with the enemy. The CPC implements the famous principle that "the Party commands the gun, and the gun will never be allowed to command the Party"[19] by selecting trustworthy and capable unit commanders, checking them with a system of political officers ("commissars") and party committees, maintaining the proportion of CPC members in the armed forces at roughly one-third, indoctrinating the troops intensively through the political departments of the various units, and maintaining a network of informers and police agents in the armed forces. Good relations with the populace, and especially the peasantry, are essential for a number of reasons, the most urgent of which is to make it possible to use them as a source of supplies, of intelligence, of shelter (by day) and hence of mobility (by night), and thus of surprise. This requires above all respecting the peasant's property, or at least paying for whatever is taken, and leaving his women alone. The peasantry also serves as the prime source of recruits; down to 1954, manpower was acquired through a highly organized and semicoercive process known as "joining the army" (ts'an-chün).[20] Land, or the promise of land, can be used to induce peasant families to provide recruits. As for the enemy, the CPC has always stressed the use of propaganda to induce defections and promote defeat or surrender. Prisoners are subjected to intensive and often successful reindoctrination.[21]

As the CPC has recently said, "Armed struggle was the chief form [of struggle] in the Chinese revolution, but the revolution could not have been victorious without the use of other forms of struggle."[22] The point is not merely that a degree of popular, or at least peasant, support is essential to the

---

[19] *Selected Works*, vol. 2, p. 272.

[20] Chin Ta-k'ai and Chang Ta-chün, *Chung Kung chün-shih p'ou-shih* (An Analysis of Chinese Communist Military Affairs), Hong Kong: Independent Press, 1954, pp. 76ff.

[21] During World War II the CPC organized, with the help of the Japanese Communist leader Nozaka Sanzo, a remarkably effective program of reindoctrinating Japanese prisoners (cf. Rodger Swearingen and Paul Langer, *Red Flag in Japan: International Communism in Action 1919–1951*, Harvard University Press, 1952, pp. 75–79).

[22] "The Proletarian Revolution and Khrushchev's Revisionism," *loc. cit.*

Maoist way of defeating the enemy's forces. The point is rather that the main object of the war is not simply the defeat of those forces, but rather a revolutionary seizure of political power throughout the entire country. This requires among other things intensive political activity in the cities before their "liberation" from the enemy and the working out and propagation of a political program likely to appeal to a significant portion of the urban population.

As already indicated, the Maoist political program stresses nationalistic opposition to the "three big mountains" of "imperialism, feudalism, and bureaucratic capitalism."[23] While the emphasis is normally on nationalism and social revolution (or class war), the CPC is not above trying to exploit racialism (as in its current contests with the United States and the Soviet Union), or communalism and tribalism.[24] The CPC has traditionally employed not only agitation, propaganda, and organization, but also espionage, subversion, and even overt terror as techniques of political action. These can be directed against friend or foe alike, the criterion being one of political advantage or opportunism. In fact, the spirit of the Maoist approach to the CPC's allies in the revolutionary coalition or "united front," centering theoretically on the proletariat, the peasants, the petty bourgeoisie, and the "patriotic" segments of the national bourgeoisie, that the CPC leads to power is a highly ambivalent one. In its policy toward the bourgeois components of the united front, Maoism admits the need to "combine union with struggle,"[25] with the main aim of strengthening the CPC's leadership of the united front. Thus, although Maoism resembles the classic "right" strategy of international Communism in its broad anti-"imperialist" appeal, it resembles the "left" strategy in that it operates on its allies "from below" rather than "from above." In other words, the CPC does not cooperate at all with other proletarian or peasant parties (of which there have been none in China in any case) and only in name with bourgeois parties. In reality, it seeks to isolate and manipulate the latter even if they remain friendly, or to undermine and destroy them if they do not.[26] This aspect of the CPC's policy has been directed since the mid-1930s by the United Front Work Department of its Central Committee.

The essence of the Maoist revolutionary strategy is the idea of the convergence of two processes: one, the defeat of "imperialism, feudalism, and

---

23 By "bureaucratic capitalism" is meant a corrupt form of state capitalism that permits high officials to acquire private fortunes and thus strengthen further their political positions.

24 In addition to numerous recent examples of the latter, it might be mentioned that the CPC was successful, during the Long March period, in dealing with primitive peoples of Southwest China, notably the Lolos. On the other hand, it has been much less successful, then and later, in dealing with more highly evolved minorities, such as the Moslems of Northwest China and the Tibetans.

25 Cf. *Selected Works*, vol. 3, p. 59.

26 Cf. Harold C. Hinton, "The 'Democratic Parties': End of an Experiment?" *Problems of Communism*, vol. vii, no. 3 (May–June, 1958), pp. 39–46.

bureaucratic capitalism" by the revolutionary "new democratic united front" led by the Communist Party; the other, the consolidation of the party's control over its nominal allies in the united front. It is expected that both processes will be punctuated, and indeed facilitated, by crises some of which may take the form of "imperialist" intervention; the Japanese invasion of China is of course the classic example. Such crises not only give the Communist Party the opportunity to increase its power at the expense of both its enemies and its nominal friends; they also have a profound educational effect, in a negative way at least, on the people. The result of this convergence of processes is expected to be a genuinely "homegrown" totalitarian regime that is neither dependent on foreign allies to support its domestic power nor vulnerable any longer to attack by domestic enemies. It may, of course, still be vulnerable to attack by "imperialism," as the Soviet regime was in its early years.

The Maoist strategy does not require the party implementing it to refrain from aiding "fraternal" parties in other countries in their quest for power; on the contrary, such aid where feasible is regarded as an obligation. But it must be kept as covert and limited as possible, not only to minimize the risk of "imperialist" retaliation against the giver of aid but also to preserve the essentially "homegrown" character of the recipient party.

It would be rash to conclude that the advent of nuclear weapons, intercontinental warfare, and the "balance of terror" have rendered the Maoist revolutionary strategy obsolete. Nuclear warfare will be waged, if at all, between states, whereas Maoism envisages a struggle conducted by a revolutionary party that is so entangled with the civilian population as to be relatively immune to threats of mass destruction. Thus in South Vietnam the immediate and apparent enemy of the government is the local Viet Cong, not the North Vietnamese state which controls the Viet Cong. The political obstacles and drawbacks to military retaliation against North Vietnam for the acts of the Viet Cong are considerable. It can be argued that in an era when general nuclear war seems "unthinkable" and limited nuclear war and conventional war (except when both belligerents are nonnuclear) seem improbable, unconventional or subconventional war is the most likely kind. History since the end of the Korean War seems to bear this out. And if so, Maoism as a proven approach to unconventional war cannot be regarded as obsolete.

■ AS A FORMULA FOR "SOCIALIST CONSTRUCTION"[27]

As we have seen, Mao's original domestic program, as he elaborated it in 1949 in *On the People's Democratic Dictatorship*, was essentially Stalinist

---

[27] *Communist China 1955–1959: Policy Documents with Analysis*, Harvard University Press, 1962; Ygael Gluckstein, *Mao's China: Economic and Political Survey*, Boston: Beacon Press, 1957.

in that it envisaged a party-controlled police state, heavy industrialization, and socialization of agriculture, with some sugarcoating dictated by a desire to appear consistent with earlier pronouncements and to retain as much public support as possible. It might be described as a formula for building socialism in almost all of one country, since Taiwan remained to be "liberated" and China was thus still in a state of civil war. Yet Mao did not have a complete ready-made formula for nation-building in 1949, and the regime has necessarily elaborated a great deal on his original rough blueprint as it went along. In addition, the CPC has managed to avoid, consciously in all probability, some of Stalin's mistakes and excesses, such as his extreme use of police terror, his brutal and almost disastrous approach to the collectivization of agriculture,[28] and the decline in real wages and productivity of capital and labor during the Soviet First Five Year Plan.[29]

A necessarily brief summary of the main stages of Communist China's domestic development may be helpful. The first stage (1949–52)[30] was essentially one of the elimination of organized opposition and the inauguration of "democratic reforms" such as "agrarian reform" and "marriage reform," and of economic rehabilitation. The second stage (1953–55)[31] was one of political centralization and consolidation and the launching of industrialization and of a rather cautious socialization of agriculture. At the end of July, 1955, Mao Tse-tung personally and suddenly inaugurated the third stage (1955–56),[32] which was a "socialist upsurge" involving a drastic acceleration of the socialization of agriculture, handicrafts, and commerce and a sharp increase in industrial investment, accompanied by certain political concessions such as the "Hundred Flowers" campaign to encourage the public, particularly the non-Communist intellectuals, to speak their minds. A brief retrenchment of industrial investment and a barrage of severe criticism of the regime by the intellectuals and others, both in early 1957,

---

[28] Cf. Donald S. Zagoria in A. Doak Barnett, ed., *Communist Strategies in Asia: A Comparative Analysis of Governments and Parties*, New York: Praeger, 1963, pp. 22, 24–26.

[29] Cf. Richard Moorsteen, "Economic Prospects for Communist China," *World Politics*, vol. ix, no. 2 (January, 1959), pp. 196–197, 209.

[30] Basic document: the Common Program of the Chinese People's Political Consultative Conference, September 29, 1949 (text in O. B. van der Sprenkel ed., *New China: Three Views*, New York: John Day, 1951, pp. 199–216).

[31] Basic documents: constitution of the CPR (text in Tang, *op. cit.*, vol. 2, pp. 91–110); Li Fu-ch'un, *Report on the First Five Year Plan for Development of the National Economy of the People's Republic of China 1953–1957*, July 5–6, 1955 (text in *Communist China 1955–59, op. cit.*, pp. 43–91).

[32] Basic documents: Mao Tse-tung, *The Question of Agricultural Cooperation*, July 31, 1955 (text in *Communist China 1955–1959, op. cit.*, pp. 94–105); Lu Ting-yi, *Let a Hundred Flowers Bloom, Let a Hundred Schools of Thought Contend*, May 26, 1956 (text in *Communist China 1955–1959, op. cit.*, pp. 151–163); Liu Shao-ch'i, *Political Report of the Central Committee of the Communist Party of China*, September 15, 1956 (text in *Communist China 1955–1959, op. cit.*, pp. 165–203); Mao Tse-tung, *On the Correct Handling of Contradictions among the People*, February 27, 1957 (text in *Communist China 1955–1959, op. cit.*, pp. 273–294).

inaugurated the fourth stage (1957–58),[33] one of political crisis and a "recti-fication campaign" followed by debate and an initial decision to mobilize peasant labor on a huge scale during the winter of 1957–58 and to decentralize the economy so as to achieve growth without the strains of the "socialist upsurge," if possible. The results of this program, which were considered favorable, as well as other considerations of an economic, political, and military nature, decided the CPC after heated debate to launch the fifth stage, that of the "Great Leap Forward" (1958–60).[34] This involved an extensive use of slogans and ideological incentives, and an unprecedented mobilization and exploitation of labor, throughout the economy and in agriculture in particular. The main innovation was the rural "people's communes," which were accompanied by a local industry ("backyard steel") campaign and a huge enlargement of the militia. Although after the initial "upsurge" the Great Leap was modified several times, generally in a more moderate direction, it disrupted the entire economy and brought it by 1960 to the brink of disaster. In the autumn of 1960, accordingly, the CPC suddenly launched the sixth stage (1960–63),[35] one of substantial although not complete retreat. The subordination of heavy industry to agriculture and light industry was openly proclaimed, and important concessions were made to the peasants. The result was a modest but real recovery. Emboldened by this trend and evidently pervaded by a sense of external crisis, the CPC launched the seventh stage,[36] one of militarization, at the beginning of 1964. The slogan has been "learning from the People's Liberation Army"; in practice, this seems to have meant an introduction of more or less military discipline into all public organizations, and in particular the institution of political officers, like those in the armed forces, to supervise the responsible heads of those organizations. In addition, it has been officially predicted that after the CPR finishes repaying its debt to the Soviet Union in 1965 it will launch another industrialization drive.[37]

As has already been implied, not all these frequent and drastic oscillations in domestic policy can be explained by purely domestic considera-

[33] Basic document: Teng Hsiao-p'ing, *Report on the Rectification Campaign*, September 23, 1957 (text in *Communist China 1955–1959, op. cit.*, pp. 343–363).

[34] Basic documents: Liu Shao-ch'i, *The Present Situation, the Party's General Line for Socialist Construction and Its Future Tasks*, May 5, 1958 (text in *Communist China 1955–1959, op. cit.*, pp. 417–438); Resolution of the Central Committee on the Establishment of People's Communes in the Rural Areas, August 29, 1958 (text in *Communist China 1955–1959, op. cit.*, pp. 454–456); Communiqué of the Sixth Plenary Session of the Central Committee, December 10, 1958 (text in *Communist China 1955–1959, op. cit.*, pp. 484–487); Communiqué of the Eighth Plenary Session of the Central Committee, August 26, 1959 (text in *Communist China 1955–1959, op. cit.*, pp. 533–536); *Ten Glorious Years*, Peking: Foreign Languages Press, 1959.

[35] Basic document: Communiqué of the Ninth Plenary Session of the Central Committee, New China News Agency dispatch, January 20, 1961.

[36] Basic document: "Political Work is the Lifeline of All Work," *Red Flag*, March 31, 1964 (text in *Current Scene: Supplement*, vol. i, no. 1, no date).

[37] *The New York Times*, February 7, 1964, citing Po I-po.

tions. The swings in a moderate direction can largely be so explained, to be sure; as will be argued at greater length later, however, the swings in a radical direction (1955–1958, 1964) occurred in an atmosphere of real or fancied international crisis or external danger. A regime that regards socialization and industrialization as the twin keys to national power, as the CPC clearly does, would naturally tend to accelerate these processes when it thought itself threatened.

It might be thought that the CPC would manufacture an atmosphere of external crises whenever it wanted to launch an economic offensive at home. At times there have been elements of this in its behavior, as when shortly before it published the First Five Year Plan in 1955 it announced the purging of Kao Kang and Jao Shu-shih and accused them of having objectively been "agents of imperialism and the bourgeoisie within our Party."[38] It is also true that Stalin used to exaggerate the danger to his own regime from alleged collaboration between his foreign and domestic opponents and take advantage of the atmosphere of tension to strengthen his own position and push ahead with his programs. On the other hand, Stalin was genuinely afraid of a combination between the "Trotskyites" and the "imperialists" (Britain in 1927, Japan after 1931, and Germany after 1933), even though not until about 1938, a decade after the launching of collectivization and industrialization, was any external enemy in a position to launch a really serious attack against the Soviet Union. There can be little doubt that this sense of danger and fear had a great deal to do with Stalin's decision to inaugurate the First Five Year Plan and collectivization.[39]

If Stalin had genuine fears and some reason for them, the CPC has probably more reason for fear. The Republic of China still exists on Taiwan, and President Chiang Kai-shek has repeatedly vowed to "return to the mainland" whenever the political and military situation permits. Since June, 1950, the Nationalists have been under American protection, and since the beginning of 1955 they have been formally allied with the United States,

---

[38] "National Conference of Communist Party of China, March 21–31, 1955," *Current Background* (Hong Kong: American Consulate General), no. 324, April 5, 1955. The charge was most unfair; Kao's external connections were Soviet, not American. The first indications that he was in political trouble came on December 24, 1953 (see Communiqué of the Fourth Plenary Session of the Central Committee, *People's Daily*, February 18, 1954), the day that Beria's execution was announced in the Soviet Union. Kao received his last warning some six weeks later (at the Fourth Plenary Session of the Central Committee) and died, allegedly a suicide, soon after that. Announcement of the affair was withheld until about eight weeks after the resignation of Malenkov, Beria's erstwhile ally in the post-Stalin power struggle, as premier (February 8, 1955).

[39] Cf. *History of the Communist Party of the Soviet Union (Bolsheviks)*, Moscow: Foreign Languages Publishing House, 1949, pp. 348–349, 371–373. This point was explicitly made by Stalin in a famous speech in February, 1931 (text in J. Stalin, *Problems of Leninism*, Moscow: Foreign Languages Publishing House, 1947, pp. 350–358). For a convincing interpretation of the Great Purges that stresses Stalin's genuine and not unjustified fear of a combination between his domestic and foreign enemies see Geoffrey Bailey (pseud.), *The Conspirators*, New York: Harper, 1960, Part Two.

a thermonuclear superpower and the main external enemy of Communist China in the eyes of the latter's rulers. This creates in the mind of the CPC a situation of real if not always acute danger as well as a certain primacy of foreign policy over domestic policy, in the sense that the mandate for survival and the assumed external threat, which has occasionally risen to crisis proportions, have exerted a strong influence on internal developments.

In the political and social fields, the CPC moved rapidly after 1949 to eliminate remaining rival power centers, such as vestigial warlordism and the rural landlord class. Meanwhile it was setting up a Communist dictatorship, with a democratic façade behind which non-Communists were progressively eliminated from all but advisory or decorative posts. There was also an imposing "cult of personality" focused on Mao Tse-tung, which increased if anything after his retirement from the post of Chairman of the CPR, or head of state, in 1958–59.[40] The party grew rapidly in size (to an estimated 18.5 million by 1964) and remained the prime mover. The police were of course in existence and freely used, but they were not allowed to get out of hand or terrorize the party apparatus as occurred in the Soviet Union under Stalin. The armed forces were pruned by half from their swollen strength of five million (in 1950), centralized, and modernized to a considerable extent. The Soviet Union made this process possible with capital equipment and weapons from late 1950 until the virtual termination of Soviet economic and military aid to the CPR in 1960. At no time, however, did the Soviet Union turn over major, operational, offensive weapons or systems, such as heavy or medium bombers, surface-to-surface missiles, nuclear weapons, aircraft carriers, or battleships. The state system, including of course the bureaucracy, was elaborately designed to combine the reality of centralized administration under party control with an appearance of popular participation and even democracy.

The problem of the ethnic minorities, who make up only about five per cent of the total population but include some warlike communities who live in strategic border areas, has been handled in a similar way. As in the Soviet Union, they have been granted an illusory political and cultural autonomy under the cover of which their lands are being steadily taken over by settlers belonging to the dominant race, but in the CPR the principal minorities do not enjoy even a theoretical right to secede, as they do in the Soviet Union. Religion is handled similarly: under a clever cloak of religious freedom that applies particularly to the Moslems and Buddhists, all religions are controlled and squeezed by a combination of hostile propaganda (especially among the youth), organizational manipulation, and oc-

---

[40] Mao of course remained as head of the CPC. Since his retirement as Chairman of the CPR in favor of Liu Shao-ch'i, he has ranked ahead of Liu even at state (as distinct from party) functions and has often been referred to as "the great leader of all the nationalities" (i.e., not only the Han, or ethnic Chinese, but of the "national minorities" as well).

casional outright persecution. Finally, the CPC has tried with fair success, for both ideological and economic reasons, to prevent the emergence of an entrenched and well paid "New Class" of managers and technicians, such as has come to exist in the Soviet Union.[41]

In the economic field, the CPR starts of course from a markedly unfavorable relationship, by twentieth century standards, between population and resources, food in particular. For ideological reasons,[42] and also because of a typical totalitarian belief in a large population as a source and symbol of national power, the CPC has found it difficult to understand and grapple with this problem. Nevertheless, one of the fairly numerous indications that it is more flexible in reality than it often appears is the fact that the CPC has on two occasions (in the mid-1950s and again since 1961) adopted a program of population control.[43] The CPC's formula for both the state and consumer sectors of the Chinese economy is of course one of revolutionary modernization via socialization and industrialization. The overall timetable, worked out in the early 1950s and laid down in the First Five Year Plan, calls for three years (1950–52) of recovery, the creation of a fully socialist economy with a self-sufficient industrial system after three Five Year Plans (1953–67), and the attainment of the status of a major industrial power by about the end of the twentieth century. Since this process must operate on a very narrow margin, the CPR has experimented with what may be called a cut-rate approach to science, technology, and capital construction, which has had only fair success but certainly holds potential interest for other underdeveloped countries. Agriculture has not been neglected to the same degree as in the Soviet Union under Stalin, but investments in it have been largely in the form of unbudgeted (because unpaid) inputs of local labor. Public works have been carried on in the same way. Agriculture has been exploited as a source of investment funds more indirectly than under Stalin; the main immediate source of such funds has been the profits of government-owned light industrial enterprises, which buy most of their raw materials from the peasants at low prices and sell their products to the public at relatively high prices.[44]

Down to 1960, the CPR received about $2 billion in long-term credits from the Soviet Union[45] and conducted about three-fourths of its foreign

41 Cf. T. H. Rigby in Kurt London, ed., *Unity and Contradiction: Major Aspects of Sino-Soviet Relations,* New York: Praeger, 1962, pp. 19–36.

42 Marxism holds that labor is the only source of wealth; obviously, the more people the more labor.

43 It might be noted that for understandable reasons, including political ones, no country has yet contemplated adopting the only kind of population control program that seems likely to be effective under twentieth century conditions in halting population growth: mass sterilization, presumably compulsory, after, say, three children.

44 Franz Schurmann, "China's 'New Economic Policy' — Transition or Beginning?" *The China Quarterly,* no. 17 (January–March, 1964), p. 68.

45 Soviet sources give 1.816 billion new roubles (one new rouble equals $1.11, at the official rate, in international transactions).

trade with the Communist Bloc, mainly the Soviet Union. From the Bloc, the CPR imported industrial and military equipment (including advanced machine tools), technical assistance, and industrial raw materials. From the non-Communist world it imported mainly industrial raw materials; the Afro-Asian countries, including Japan, tended to grow in importance as trading partners at the expense of the West.[46]

This pattern of relationships, which was not mainly the result of trade controls imposed against the CPR by non-Communist countries,[47] created a degree of dependence on the Soviet Union that proved increasingly galling. Politically, it made the CPR more vulnerable to Soviet pressures than it would otherwise have been and tended to make the Soviet Union take the CPR for granted, so that Moscow came increasingly to aid neutral countries more than it did its Chinese ally. Economically the Soviet Union's superior bargaining power enabled it to impose (at least until 1958) an exchange rate between the rouble and the yuan unfavorable to the latter.[48] Furthermore, the prices of Soviet goods were increased by inordinately high transport costs resulting from the fact that most were carried long distances by rail.[49] Finally, the CPR found it necessary to resist Soviet efforts after 1957, sweetened by a new rouble-yuan exchange rate more favorable to the yuan than the old one had been, to draw the CPR at least partly into the Soviet-dominated Bloc economic organization, the Council for Mutual Economic Aid (CEMA). One of the drawbacks, for any Communist country, of membership in this organization is that it has to pay a higher price for an import from another member country than it would for the same commodity if imported from a non-Communist country.[50]

Since the economic disaster of 1960, which was accompanied and probably worsened by a virtual termination of Soviet economic and military aid, Communist China now preaches a policy of national self-reliance. This means in practice less emphasis, at least for the time being, on most sectors of heavy industry and more emphasis on agriculture and light industry, diversification of trading partners, and the acquisition of modern weapons (in particular, nuclear weapons and delivery systems) to supplement China's conventional military capability.

Sino-Soviet trade has dropped off sharply (roughly from $2 billion in 1959 to $675 million in 1962). The fall would have been even more abrupt

---

[46] A. Doak Barnett, *Communist Economic Strategy: The Rise of Mainland China*, Washington: National Planning Association, 1959, Chapters 8–9.

[47] These controls did however make it difficult for the CPR to acquire sufficient petroleum and copper wire; the latter commodity is needed in vast quantities for the CPR's huge electrification projects.

[48] Kang Chao and Feng-hwa Mah, "A Study of the Rouble-Yuan Exchange Rate," *The China Quarterly*, no. 17 (January–March, 1964), pp. 192–204.

[49] Feng-hwa Mah, "The Terms of Sino-Soviet Trade," *The China Quarterly*, no. 17 (January–March, 1964), pp. 174–191.

[50] *Ibid.*, pp. 174–175; Oleg Hoeffding in London, *Unity and Contradiction, op. cit.*, pp. 296–298.

except for the fact that China has continued to pay off its accumulated debt to the Soviet Union by running an export surplus.[51] The Chinese say, and there is reason to believe, that by the end of 1965 this repayment process will have been completed.

This situation has not so far produced any great increase in the total volume of trade between China and the non-Communist world, which reached $1.4 billion in 1958 and has hovered in that neighborhood ever since. What has changed has been mainly the composition of the trade and the level of expectations on the non-Communist side. Instead of running an export surplus with the non-Communist world, as China usually did in the past in order to help repay its debt to the Soviet Union, it now runs an import surplus, mainly because of large grain imports (approximately 15 million tons in 1961–1963). The Chinese have also bought some light industrial equipment in Japan and some machine tools in Western Europe. These imports have been financed through exports (including an increased export of nongrain foodstuffs to Hong Kong), sales of silver, the drawing down of foreign exchange reserves, encouragement of increased remittances by overseas Chinese, and credits.[52]

In addition to certain economic advantages to trading with non-Communist countries, there are some important political and psychological ones. The Chinese apparently feel that non-Communist trade carries fewer "strings" than does Communist trade, except in the vague sense that the non-Communist countries may hope to promote an ultimate "mellowing" of the Communist Chinese regime by economic means, among others.

■ **AS A MODEL FOR THE UNDERDEVELOPED AREAS[53]**

It is doubtful whether the CPC would ever have come to power if it had complied with Stalin's wishes, which in the mid-1920s and again from 1935 to 1945 or 1946 were that the CPC concede the primary place in Chinese political life to the Kuomintang, for the sake of Soviet national interests as Stalin saw them. At least as early as the disaster of 1927, this situation must have raised in the minds of some Chinese Communists the question whether the Soviet Union was too Western to direct the revolution in the underdeveloped areas (the "colonial and semicolonial countries," "the East"), or even to understand its prerequisites. If so, why should not China, the most populous of the underdeveloped countries and almost the only one that had had dealings with all the "imperialist" countries, assume this leading role?

---

[51] China's export surplus with the Soviet Union was $184 million in 1961.
[52] Cf. "The China Market: 1962," *Current Scene* (Hong Kong), vol. ii, no. 14 (June 1, 1963).
[53] Cf. A. M. Halpern, "The Foreign Policy Uses of the Chinese Revolutionary Model," *The China Quarterly*, no. 7 (July–September, 1961), pp. 1–16.

Accordingly, we find Mao Tse-tung writing as early as December, 1936, that the Chinese revolution would "exert a far-reaching influence on the revolution in the East as well as in the whole world."[54] As we have seen, the essence of the Maoist formula was to take an anti-"imperialist," or at least an anti-Japanese, stand more obvious than the Soviet Union's,[55] to insist on Communist rather than on bourgeois leadership of the anti-"imperialist" revolution from the earliest possible time, and to rely on prolonged, politicized guerrilla warfare waged from rural bases.

In the spring of 1946, Liu Shao-ch'i told the sympathetic American journalist Anna Louise Strong that "Mao Tse-tung's great accomplishment has been to change Marxism from a European to an Asiatic form. . . . He has created a Chinese or Asiatic form of Marxism. . . . There are similar conditions [to those in China] in other lands of southeast Asia. The courses chosen by China will influence them all."[56] Two years later, in a message to the Communist-dominated Southeast Asia Youth Conference at Calcutta, the CPC praised what it portrayed as burgeoning "armed struggle" in Southeast Asia and boasted that "in this respect the people of China have set forth extremely valuable experience for the peoples of the Eastern countries."[57]

After the formal assumption of power by the CPC, its advertising of its own revolutionary model grew even more blatant. As already mentioned, the Soviet Union, which had suffered serious setbacks in the West and apparently had no very clear message of its own for the Communists of "the East" except for a vague call to anti-Western militancy, endorsed the CPC's model, while insisting that it was based on Soviet experience. In November, 1949, Liu Shao-ch'i proclaimed that "The path taken by the Chinese people in defeating imperialism and its lackeys and in founding the People's Republic of China is the path that should be taken by the peoples of the various colonial and semicolonial countries in their fight for national independence and people's democracy."[58]

---

[54] *Selected Works*, vol. 1, p. 191. Mao made a similar statement in December, 1947 (*Selected Works*, vol. iv, p. 158).

[55] The CPC softened its tone toward Nazi Germany during the lifetime of the Hitler-Stalin pact, but there is no reason to think that its behavior toward Japan was similarly moderated. On the contrary, the CPC launched its largest operation of the war, the so-called Hundred Regiments Offensive, in August, 1940 (Johnson, *op. cit.*, pp. 56–58). There is reason to think that the CPC was distressed by the Soviet-Japanese neutrality pact of April, 1941, signed at a time when the Japanese army was pressing the CPC very hard in North China, even though the pact contributed to Japan's attack on the Western powers.

[56] Quoted in Donald S. Zagoria, *The Sino-Soviet Conflict, 1956–1961*, Princeton University Press, 1962, pp. 14–15.

[57] "Congratulations on the Opening of the Southeast Asia Youth Conference," New China News Agency dispatch, North Shensi radio, February 16, 1948 (excerpts in *Chinese Communist World Outlook*, Washington: Department of State, 1962, p. 6).

[58] Liu Shao-ch'i, speech at Trade Union Conference of Asian and Australasian Countries, *loc. cit.* (excerpts in *Chinese Communist World Outlook, op. cit.*, pp. 6–7).

Probably the high-water mark of propaganda for the Chinese revolutionary model occurred on July 1, 1951, at a time when the celebration of the thirtieth anniversary of the founding of the CPC[59] outweighed, at least on the surface, defeats suffered in Korea. On that date a leading CPC spokesman, Lu Ting-yi, described the Chinese revolution as "the greatest event in world history since the October Revolution" and as the "prototype of the revolutions in colonial and semicolonial countries."[60] This and other strident claims evoked a Soviet denial that the Chinese revolution could serve as a "stereotype" for the rest of Asia. During 1952, in view of this Soviet attitude, the need for Soviet support because of the growing tension in Korea, and the failure of the Communist insurrections in Southeast Asia except in Vietnam, the CPC dropped its calls to "armed struggle" against "imperialism" in Asia and moderated its claims for its own revolutionary model. The Soviets in return conceded that the Chinese revolution furnished valuable lessons, but not a unique or exclusive model, for other Asian Communists.[61]

As the CPR's shift to a primarily diplomatic rather than a primarily revolutionary foreign policy gained momentum from such events as the end of the Korean War, the Indochinese settlement at Geneva (1954), and the Bandung Conference (1955), the concept of a Chinese revolutionary model remained correspondingly in the background. It was by no means forgotten, however.[62] Its reassertion was prevented for a time not only by the considerations already mentioned but, at first, by the need to shore up Soviet prestige in Communist circles after the Hungarian crisis of October–November, 1956, and then by the hope that the CPC could cajole the Soviet Union into a vigorous exploitation, on behalf of the CPR as well as of Communism in general, of the temporary and essentially psychological advantage over the West conferred by the Soviet Union's first intercontinental ballistic missile test and earth satellite in 1957. Thus at the end of 1956 the CPC adumbrated what it called "the path of the October Revolution" and said that all countries must follow it, with essentially minor adaptations to local conditions.[63] This model, to be sure, was so generalized that the CPC felt

---

[59] In reality, the First National Congress of the CPC seems to have convened on July 20, 1921 (Chen Kung-po, *The Communist Movement in China*, ed. by C. Martin Wilbur, Columbia University: East Asian Institute, 1960, p. 81), but for some reason the CPC celebrates July 1 as the anniversary.

[60] Lu Ting-yi, "The World Significance of the Chinese Revolution," *People's China*, July 1, 1951 (excerpts in *Chinese Communist World Outlook, op. cit.*, pp. 7, 83). Lu was good enough to add that the October Revolution was the prototype for the "imperialist" countries.

[61] Zagoria in Barnett, *Communist Strategies, op. cit.*, pp. 17–18.

[62] Cf. "The Chinese revolution is the major sector of the revolution in the East," (Chen Yun, "In Memory of J. V. Stalin," *People's China*, March 16, 1954, quoted in *Chinese Communist World Outlook, op. cit.*, p. 7).

[63] "More on the Historical Experience Concerning the Dictatorship of the Proletariat," *People's Daily*, December 29, 1956 (text in *Communist China 1955–1959, op. cit.*, pp. 257–272).

able to claim that "The Chinese people have followed the path of the October Revolution"[64] and that "The Chinese revolution is a continuation of the October Revolution."[65]

By 1958, however, Khrushchev had shown that he had no intention of designing his foreign policy along the lines desired by the CPC. The latter, in any event and in part for that reason, altered its own foreign policy somewhat in a more revolutionary and less diplomatic direction and launched the "Great Leap Forward," accompanied by a clearly implicit claim that China was "building communism," and not merely socialism. Along with this went a revival of the concept of a Chinese model, with the emphasis this time more on the phase of "socialist construction" than on the phase of "socialist revolution."[66] The stress on the latter was revived in 1959, however.[67]

Soon afterward the talk of a Chinese revolutionary model began to die away. Even the idea that anti-"imperialist" revolutions must always be Communist-led began to wither away, except occasionally in the context of the effort to discredit Khrushchev in Communist circles as nonrevolutionary.[68] Like Khrushchev, the CPC was aware that nearly all revolutionary movements then in progress in the underdeveloped areas, with the notable exceptions of Laos and Vietnam, were led not by Communists but by non-Communist nationalists who showed little if any interest in copying foreign revolutionary models. Of these non-Communist revolutionary leaders, only the one (Castro) in the country most exposed to "imperialist" pressures, Cuba, went so far as to declare, at the end of 1961, that he was a Marxist-Leninist. The main object was apparently to get Soviet aid and protection without necessarily accepting the requirements for internal and international discipline implied by the term Communist. Both the Soviet Union and the CPR have felt it advisable to acquiesce in this, and in 1963 both conceded that Cuba was a member of the "socialist camp."[69]

Broadly speaking, Khrushchev's answer to this increasingly complex situation had been to seek at least a temporary détente with the West, cultivate a wide range of friendships, often sweetened by economic aid, with non-Communist leaders in the underdeveloped areas, including many who

---

64 "Long Live the October Revolution! Long Live Socialism!" *People's Daily*, November 6, 1957.

65 Lin Po-ch'ü, speech of November 6, 1958 (New China News Agency dispatch, same date).

66 Ch'en Po-ta, "Under the Banner of Comrade Mao Tse-tung," *Red Flag*, July 16, 1958.

67 Wang Chia-hsiang, "The International Significance of the Chinese People's Victory," in *Ten Glorious Years, op. cit.*, pp. 271–282.

68 E.g., "Long Live Leninism!" *Red Flag*, April 16, 1960 (text in *Long Live Leninism*, Peking: Foreign Languages Press, 1960, pp. 1–55).

69 The Soviet Union for the first time in its May Day slogans for 1963 (*Pravda*, April 8, 1963); the CPC for the first time in its letter of June 14, 1963, to the CPSU's Central Committee.

were not actively struggling against Western "imperialism" as well as many who were; and to begin building up local Communist Parties in those under-developed countries, notably in Africa, where they were either nonexistent or very weak. The latter step can of course be interpreted as preparation for ultimate Communist seizures of power; the main opportunity that it pre-sents in the short run, however, is for the Soviet Union to increase the num-ber of parties that support it in its contest with the CPC within the inter-national Communist movement. In fact, the Soviet Union appears willing and even anxious to postpone formal Communist seizures of power in most of the underdeveloped countries until those countries have had time to achieve some degree of economic development and therefore, presumably, a state of mind that will cause them to look to Moscow rather than Peking for any external guidance they may be willing to accept.

This Soviet approach to the common dilemma is naturally anathema to the CPC. The latter rejects détente, with the United States at any rate, and preaches Cold War up to, but not over, the brink of general hot war. The CPC virtually excludes from the circle of its chosen friends all those nation-alist leaders in the underdeveloped areas whom it does not consider to be struggling actively against "imperialism and its lackeys." On the other hand, if a leader is so struggling he can be of any class origin at all, even a "feudal element" like the kings of Nepal and Morocco, and he can pursue almost any internal policy including even the proscription of the local Communist Party, such as is in effect in every Middle Eastern and North African coun-try except Israel. On the other hand, the CPC seems to hope that in a coun-try that is struggling against "imperialism, colonialism, and neocolonialism," and against the United States in particular, crises will occur that will bring the local Communist Party to power in a period substantially shorter than the one envisaged by Khrushchev.[70] This would mean that the country would be still poor, if not devastated, and presumably in a mood to accept guidance from Peking. In the meantime, a "Marxist-Leninist" regime like that of Castro is acceptable as at least an interim situation.[71] The CPC has tried to protect itself in advance from excessive demands for aid from new Communist regimes by preaching that such regimes must rely largely on their own resources.

It is obvious that the CPC is projecting its image of its own rise to power on the underdeveloped areas. By the same token, it may believe that it will take some two decades for the independent non-Communist regimes in the underdeveloped countries to collapse, in favor of Communist regimes, from a combination of "imperialist" pressures, domestic failures, and Com-munist attacks. The CPC failed to capture control of the Kuomintang and

---

[70] Cf. "The Proletarian Revolution and Khrushchev's Revisionism," *loc. cit.*; "Apologists of Neocolonialism," *People's Daily* and *Red Flag*, October 21, 1963.

[71] Cf. remark by Chou En-lai quoted in Benjamin I. Schwartz, "The Polemics Seen by a Non-Polemicist," *Problems of Communism*, vol. xiii, no. 2 (March–April, 1964), p. 106.

of the Chinese revolution in the mid-1920s, but it succeeded in driving the Kuomintang off the mainland of China and seizing power twenty years later.

What is left of the Maoist revolutionary strategy as a model for the underdeveloped areas? Clearly the requirement for Communist leadership so insistently maintained in the "new democracy" concept has been diluted and postponed, although it is still of course preferred. Militant opposition to "imperialism," and especially to the United States, not only by "political struggle" but by "armed struggle" when feasible and necessary, is still mandatory, and in fact the key requirement. This revolutionary model, although currently acceptable to the CPC, is apparently not regarded as identical with the Chinese model; the latter is still advocated, but less loudly and to more carefully selected audiences.

Changing circumstances have modified the CPC's model for "socialist construction" as well as its model for "socialist revolution." Probably the main factor has been the collapse of the Great Leap Forward, which the CPC has tried unconvincingly to blame on bad weather, and the consequent necessity to suspend heavy industrialization and import food. This has reduced the vigor with which the Chinese model for "socialist construction" is extolled, although it is still advocated to audiences that are presumed to be receptive.[72] The realization that Communist seizures of power are not imminent in most of the newly independent countries has led the CPC to drop its insistence that its model of "socialist construction" can be implemented only by a Communist Party; it now calls merely for "a party armed with the theory of Marxism-Leninism."[73]

It has been suggested that one of the main lessons that the CPC has to teach the emerging countries, and that the latter might be willing to learn from it, is the secret of how to achieve stable and effective leadership at the top and eliminate factionalism and instability.[74] This argument seems unconvincing. The subject of leadership at the top is too sensitive for the CPC to discuss it openly, much less to recommend its own experience as an example. Stability has been bought at the price of a growing tendency toward rigidity and ossification. The CPC's top leadership is now the second oldest in the world, the oldest being that of the Vatican Curia, and its passing is obviously imminent. Nor can any one predict with confidence what will happen after Mao's death, still less affirm that the transition will be smooth. Furthermore, leadership as exercised in the CPR contains a much higher element of coercion and less charismatic appeal to the people (one hesitates to say voters) than is to be found in most of the emerging countries.

---

[72] E.g., Chou En-lai's speech at Algerian cadres meeting, December 25, 1963.

[73] In the speech just cited, Chou quotes a passage to this effect from the revised version of Mao's *On the People's Democratic Dictatorship* (Selected Works, vol. iv, p. 422); the original (*Documentary History, op. cit.,* p. 460) specifies a party "armed with the theories of Marx, Engels, Lenin, and Stalin. . . ."

[74] Roderick MacFarquhar in London, *New Nations, op. cit.,* pp. 222–235.

In this respect, as in others, the concept of a foreign model has little appeal to the developing countries, unless and until their current experiments with indigenous formulae fail much more dramatically than they have to date.

One important principle that the CPC does preach to the newly independent nations is the maintenance of armed forces, allegedly for the main purpose of protecting themselves against "imperialism, colonialism, and neo-colonialism." The CPC has occasionally expressed fear that Soviet disarmament maneuvers might tend to strip the emerging countries of their conventional forces. On one occasion, Foreign Minister Chen Yi went so far as to imply that as many non-"imperialist" countries as possible should acquire nuclear weapons, so as to maximise the chances of attaining the complete nuclear disarmament (without conventional disarmament) that the CPC claims to want.[75]

The CPC of course rejects any suggestion that the Soviet Union (or for that matter the United States, India, or Yugoslavia) offers any kind of model for the developing countries.[76]

■ AS A STRATEGY FOR CHINESE HEGEMONY IN ASIA[77]

Probably no serious student of Communist China's foreign policy doubts that it aims at ultimate hegemony in Asia, somewhat along the lines of the traditional Chinese empire. But what kind of hegemony, and over how much of Asia? It is difficult to say. On the first point, there is no convincing evidence that the CPC intends to conquer, annex or colonize other Asian countries, although it has explicitly reserved the right, in case it is attacked, to do what the Soviet Union did in Eastern Europe: to pursue the beaten enemy onto foreign soil and to take part in the creation of local Communist regimes.[78] The CPC realizes, of course, that the Soviet satelliti-

---

[75] "The more nuclear powers there are, the better will be the conditions to eliminate nuclear weapons ultimately" (Tokyo *Asahi*, November 10, 1962).

[76] This view was implicit in many of the statements made by Chou En-lai during his foreign tour at the end of 1963.

[77] Useful introductions are Robert C. North, "Peking's Drive for Empire: The New Expansionism," *Problems of Communism*, vol. ix, no. 1 (January–February, 1960), pp. 23–30; Yuan-li Wu, "Peking's Drive for Empire: The Weapon of Trade," *Problems of Communism*, vol. ix, no. 1 (January–February, 1960), pp. 31–39; Robert A. Scalapino, "Tradition and Transition in the Asian Policy of Communist China," in Edward F. Szczepanik, ed., *Symposium on Economic and Social Problems of the Far East*, Hong Kong University Press, 1962, pp. 262–277; A. Doak Barnett, *Communist China and Asia: Challenge to American Policy*, New York: Harper, 1960.

[78] "When a socialist country, in the face of imperialist attack, is compelled to wage a defensive war and launch counterattacks, is it justified in going beyond its own border to pursue and eliminate its enemies from abroad, as the Soviet Union did in the war against Hitler? Certainly it is completely justified, absolutely necessary and entirely just. In accordance with the strict principles of communists, such operations by the socialist countries must absolutely be limited to the time when imperialism launches a war of aggression against them. Socialist countries never permit themselves to send,

zation of Eastern Europe was made possible by a world war and at least a degree of consent from the Soviet Union's allies, circumstances that are not likely to be repeated in the CPR's case. On the whole, the CPC seems to prefer, in Asia as elsewhere, an indigenous Communist seizure of power which will result in a regime disposed to follow the Chinese lead but not a satellite in the full sense. In Asia, the process is presumably intended to be accomplished with more Chinese aid and support, and to convey a higher degree of Chinese influence, than elsewhere. Obviously North Vietnam is the only regime in Asia to date that approximates this ideal. As to the second point, it is unlikely that the CPC intends its claim to hegemony to coincide with the traditional Chinese cultural orbit (Korea, Japan, and Vietnam), or with those countries that contain a significant Chinese community (i.e., Southeast Asia), or with the former tributaries of the Chinese empire (a fluctuating group of mainland and insular states around the Chinese periphery). My own view, to be developed more fully later, is that CPC hopes to dominate, in the somewhat indirect manner already indicated, the entire mainland of Asia south of the Soviet border,[79] but that it concedes the right to an autonomous existence, and even to spheres of influence of their own, to Japan and Indonesia, which are effectively beyond its reach.

It is clear that there are many military and political obstacles in the way of the attainment of any such goal. Among these may be mentioned the CPR's failure to "liberate" Taiwan; the existence of a Nationalist army on Taiwan as a partial deterrent to Chinese Communist military adventures elsewhere; the American policy of containing the CPR, which although certainly not completely successful has been more effective than is often realized; and the CPC's tendency to avoid unambiguously aggressive military action for political as well as military reasons.[80]

It has been aptly said, with reference to the CPR, that "In the period of its ascendancy, a major power seeks first to define and defend its boundaries;

---

never should and never will send their troops across their borders unless they are subjected to aggression from a foreign enemy. Since the armed forces of the socialist countries fight for justice, when these forces have to go beyond their borders to counterattack a foreign enemy, it is only natural that they should exert an influence and have an effect wherever they go; but even then, the emergence of people's revolutions and the establishment of the socialist system in those places and countries where they go will still have to depend on the will of the masses of the people there" (*Long Live Leninism, op. cit.,* p. 34).

[79] The CPC has probably written off Soviet Asia, although it is contesting what it regards as Soviet alterations of the boundary at its expense and is certainly aware of the possibility that the Soviet Union might resume the major pressures, short of annexation, on China's border territories that it has exerted from time to time since the late nineteenth century. See the interesting analysis in *Chrisian Science Monitor,* June 4, 1964.

[80] This latter fact largely invalidates the otherwise inevitable comparison between Japanese and Communist Chinese expansionism. The Chinese offensive in the Himalayas of October–November, 1962, was a complex affair that does not constitute a clearcut exception to this generalization.

secondly, to acquire some type of buffer system that gives security in depth; and finally, to exercise some degree of hegemony over the general region with which it has primary contact."[81]

The CPR has signed boundary treaties since 1960, generally on reasonable terms, with most of those countries with which it has had border disputes and has indicated a willingness to negotiate with the other two, India (in 1959)[82] and the Soviet Union (in 1963 or 1964).[83] In the process of negotiation, the CPR has undoubtedly used the frontier issue as a means of extracting concessions from weaker neighbors. Nor does the signing of a boundary treaty put an end to overt and covert Chinese pressures on the country concerned.

The CPR often refers to its neighbors, and in particular Korea, Vietnam, and Burma, as its lips: "When the lips are gone, the teeth will feel the cold." If the lips are to protect the teeth effectively, the main requirement is that they should harbor no American bases, and no American ground forces above all. In fact, the CPC seems to be highly allergic to the idea of American forces anywhere on the Asian mainland, even more so than to the actual basing of far greater American striking power in the islands and seas of the Western Pacific. An American military presence in South Korea and South Vietnam is tolerated because North Korea and North Vietnam are still in existence as Communist-controlled buffers, and because intolerance would be dangerous. With three of its non-Communist neighbors—Burma, Afghanistan, and Cambodia — the CPR signed in 1960 "treaties of friendship and mutual nonaggression," which specify that neither shall enter into an alliance against the other; this means that the non-Chinese party is obligated not to ally itself with the United States or allow American bases on its soil.[84] With Nepal the CPR has merely a treaty of "peace and friendship" (1960), which does not specifically rule out such an alliance.[85] The same applies to a treaty of "friendship" with Indonesia (1961).[86]

As for hegemony, all major Chinese revolutions of the twentieth century have had an impact on Asia. That of 1949 has had the greatest impact of all, since it has given rise to the first strong government that China has had since the late eighteenth century. The CPR intends ultimately to ex-

---

[81] Scalapino, loc. cit., p. 266.

[82] Note of Chou En-lai to Nehru (Indian White Paper I, pp. 52–54); the basis proposed was the status quo, which would have left the CPR in possession of most of the disputed area in the west and India in possession of the disputed area in the east, known as the Northeast Frontier Agency.

[83] Cf. Chou En-lai's interview of January 23, 1964, with Edgar Snow (The Washington Post and Times Herald, February 3, 1964).

[84] Cf. Article III of the Sino-Burmese treaty (A Victory for the Five Principles of Peaceful Co-Existence, Peking: Foreign Languages Press, 1960, p. 31).

[85] Text in New Development in Friendly Relations Between China and Nepal, Peking: Foreign Languages Press, 1960, pp. 29–31.

[86] New China News Agency dispatch, June 14, 1961. The CPR also has treaties of "friendship" with Yemen (1958 and 1964), Guinea (1960), Ghana (1961), Mali (1964), and Congo Brazzaville (1965).

clude the Soviet Union,[87] as well as the United States, from Asia; if there ever was a Sino-Soviet agreement on the division of Asia into spheres of influence, which is doubtful, it certainly has been invalid since the mid-1950s. The Chinese find opposition to "imperialism" a useful common ground, real or imaginary, in dealing with Asian states and trying to influence them. By the same token, at least a brave show of anti-"imperialism," such as Prince Sihanouk has made, is normally a prerequisite for friendly relations with the CPR.[88] The CPR tries to encourage not only hostility to "imperialism" but fear of itself. This it has been largely successful in doing except in Japan and Indonesia, which are relatively invulnerable to any threat from the CPR. In addition to the CPR's real or assumed potential for ultimate glacial expansion over the mainland of Asia, the CPR has inspired fear by the hardships to which it has subjected its own people, especially during the Great Leap Forward.

The CPR's disarmament policy, if it could be implemented, would tend to promote both Chinese security and Chinese hegemony in Asia. The adoption of complete nuclear disarmament, without conventional disarmament, would leave the CPR the strongest military power on the mainland of Asia south of the Soviet border. The CPR has also suggested, more deviously, on at least one occasion that only Asian countries should be allowed to base nuclear weapons in Asia; this might leave the CPR sooner or later the only nuclear power in the area and thus greatly increase its influence.[89]

So far this discussion has dealt mainly with the state or national aspect of the CPR's aspirations for Asian hegemony. There is also an important party or revolutionary aspect centering on the CPC's relations with the Communist Parties of Asia, whether in power or not.[90]

The way for the CPC's rise as a revolutionary influence on Asian Communist Parties was paved to a degree by the Soviet party's poor success, during the early postwar years, in playing the same role. Soviet geographical and cultural remoteness, as well as the perennial primacy of Soviet national

[87] Note the apparently successful Chinese effort to exclude the Soviet Union from the Second Asian-African (Bandung) Conference, to be held in 1965.

[88] This is not true of Pakistan as yet, but Pakistan and the CPR have an overriding common interest in hostility to India.

[89] "The conference [i.e., the Afro-Asian People's Solidarity Conference at Cairo, December, 1957] . . . held that Asia and Africa should be a peace zone in which no *foreign* country should deploy nuclear and rocket weapons" (Chou En-lai, report to the National People's Congress on foreign affairs, February 10, 1958, New China News Agency dispatch, same date; emphasis added). The resolution of the conference, which had Soviet and widespread neutral support, had merely specified an atom-free zone, without such a qualification.

[90] Cf. "Appendix: Peking and the Communist Parties of Asia," in Barnett, *Communist China and Asia, op. cit.*, pp. 476–501; Robert A. Scalapino, "Moscow, Peking and the Communist Parties of Asia," *Foreign Affairs*, vol. 41, no. 2 (January, 1963), pp. 323–343; A. M. Halpern, "The Emergence of an Asian Communist Coalition," *The Annals of the American Academy of Political and Social Science*, vol. 349 (September, 1963), pp. 117–129.

policy toward Western Europe, complicated the problem of establishing a satisfactory base from which to influence the Asian Communist Parties. Soviet preoccupation with splitting France from the other Western powers prevented the Soviet Union from giving more than verbal support to the cause of the Vietnamese Communists, the most militant and successful Communist Party in Asia apart from China.[91] The Soviet Union approved of the Indonesian nationalist revolution against the Dutch and evidently hoped to establish a regional revolutionary base in Indonesia. Stalin was evidently disillusioned, however, by the Indonesian Republic's inability to fight the Dutch on equal terms, by its consequent tendency to compromise with them, a trend that began with the Renville Agreement of January, 1948, and by the coming to power of the relatively conservative Hatta government immediately thereafter.[92] The Soviet Union then tried to establish a regional revolutionary base of sorts in India, an even more unlikely place because Stalin had always despised the Congress Party and the Nehru government for having accepted what he regarded as a spurious and deceptive independence from the British without waging "armed struggle." After the Calcutta Conference of February, 1948, the Indian Communist Party went into armed revolt, not necessarily in accordance with Stalin's actual wishes, only to be promptly crushed by the Government of India except in those rural areas where it employed a strategy of the Maoist type.[93] The Communist insurrections that broke out in Burma, Malaya, the Philippines, and Indonesia in 1948 were almost equally unsuccessful.[94] In any event, Stalin's attention was largely distracted from the Far East for a crucial year by major developments in Europe, notably the coup in Czechoslovakia, the break with Tito, and the Berlin Blockade. During this period the CPC achieved, apparently contrary to Stalin's expectations, an irreversible superiority in its

[91] Cf. Joseph Frankel in Max Beloff, *Soviet Policy in the Far East, 1944–1951*, Oxford University Press, 1953, pp. 224–225. Stalin's seeming tendency toward disillusionment with a strategy based largely on local Communist Parties, in favor of one based more on the Soviet and later the Communist Chinese states, may have been significantly strengthened by the fact that on March 19, 1948, the Communist Minister of the Interior in Finland warned the Chief of Staff of an impending Communist coup (James H. Billington in Cyril E. Black and Thomas P. Thornton, eds., *Communism and Revolution: The Strategic Uses of Political Violence*, Princeton University Press, 1964, p. 129).

[92] Ruth T. McVey, *The Soviet View of the Indonesian Revolution*, Cornell University: Modren Indonesia Project, 1957, especially pp. 38ff. The Southeast Asia Youth Conference, originally scheduled to be held in Indonesia, was shifted to Calcutta in mid-1947.

[93] Barnett, *Communist China and Asia, op. cit.*, pp. 499–501.

[94] Cf. Ruth T. McVey in Black and Thornton, *op. cit.*, pp. 145–184. The exact extent of Soviet responsibility for these risings remains obscure. It may have been less than is usually supposed. In May, 1948, Stalin displayed his characteristic Machiavellianism by sending an ambassador to the right-wing military government of Pibul Songgram in Thailand and by trying to maneuver the Hatta government in Indonesia into establishing consular relations (Beloff, *op. cit.*, p. 239; McVey, *The Soviet View, op. cit.*, pp. 47–51).

civil war with the Kuomintang, and as we have seen the Soviet Union thought it best to give an explicit although somewhat qualified endorsement to the Maoist strategy as a model for Asia.

On the other hand, by the beginning of 1951 the CPC too was encountering serious setbacks in its effort to give encouragement and support to, and increase its influence over, the Asian Communist Parties. The two most important of the latter, those of Vietnam and Indonesia, were in danger, one from a major French counteroffensive, and the other from Moslem and other anti-Communist elements of the Indonesian political scene. Both crises were surmounted, but in very different ways and with differing effects on the prospect for enhanced Chinese influence. The Vietnamese Communists, probably on Chinese advice, formed themselves into a new party, the Lao Dong, in February and renewed and intensified their military operations with increased Chinese logistical support;[95] the inevitable result was a tendency toward greater Chinese influence. In Indonesia, a new leadership under D. N. Aidit took control of the Indonesian Communist Party (PKI) beginning in January, 1951. By 1953 this leadership had evolved a flexible and effective strategy involving the repudiation of "armed struggle,"[96] the retention of the Maoist concept of a "united front" led by the proletariat and including "patriotic" elements of the bourgeoisie, opposition to "imperialism" and wooing of Sukarno as the main symbol of Indonesian nationalism, energetic and successful efforts to gain popular and electoral support, and the elimination of overseas Chinese from positions of leadership in the party.[97] The inevitable result was a decrease in Chinese influence on the PKI.

In India, a shift in Communist policy similar to the one in Indonesia occurred under the direct supervision of the Soviet Union and the Cominform. In the first half of 1951 the Indian Communist Party (CPI), emboldened by the Korean War, the Chinese Communist "liberation" of Tibet, and the existence of famine conditions in India, evolved a highly militant program. It envisaged urban as well as rural violence and specifically repudiated the idea that Chinese experience could serve as a sufficient model for the CPI. Suddenly, in the middle of the year, Soviet policy apparently changed, probably as the result of the beginning of truce talks in Korea, the Government of India's success in dealing with Communist violence, Nehru's continued demonstrations of independence of the West in such important matters as the Korean War and the Japanese peace treaty, and the approach of the first general elections in independent India at the end of the year. In

---

[95] Bernard B. Fall, *The Two Viet-Nams: A Political and Military Analysis*, New York: Praeger, 1963, pp. 179–180.

[96] Especially after August, 1951, when the Sukiman government conducted mass arrests of PKI members following a wave of labor unrest.

[97] Herbert Feith, *The Wilopo Cabinet, 1952–1953: a Turning Point in Post-Revolutionary Indonesia*, Cornell University: Modern Indonesia Project, 1958, pp. 83–102; Barnett, *Communist China and Asia, op. cit.,* p. 495.

October a new leadership under A. K. Ghosh took control of the CPI. On a platform hostile to the Nehru government, the CPI emerged from the elections as the strongest opposition party in parliament. The result was a decline in what had been strong Chinese influence on the central leadership of the CPI, although such influence persisted in several of the state party organizations.[98]

From these trends the CPC apparently inferred that neither the revolutionary situation nor the quality of the local Communist Parties (except in Vietnam) was mature enough to offer any hope of Communist seizures of power in the near future. The Malayan Communist Party, which was probably under stronger Chinese influence than any other, admitted to itself during 1951 that it had reached a dead end in its guerrilla war against the British and attempted to shift to a more political and less military strategy.[99] In the Philippines, Magsaysay turned the tide against the Communist insurrectionaries at about the same time by an effective combination of political and military tactics.

During 1952 the CPR, like the Soviet Union three or four years earlier, became preoccupied with events closer to home, tacitly admitted the failure of its strategy in Southeast Asia (again except for Vietnam), and moderated its formulations of that strategy along lines then in favor in Moscow. The events were mainly the Japanese peace treaty, the ensuing mutual defense agreement between the United States and Japan, and rising tension in Korea; impressive Soviet commitments to the CPR at the state level, including a large increment of military aid, were secured to counter these developments, but such commitments had little relevance to the CPR's standing as a source of revolutionary influence in Southeast Asia, except for Vietnam. The CPC's new outlook was expressed at a "Peace Conference of the Asian and Pacific Regions" held at Peking in October, 1952, at which much was said about the American threat to peace in Asia but not much (in public, at any rate) about the need for Communist revolutions in Asia.[100]

Beginning in 1951, both the Soviet Union and the CPR softened their public statements on the neutral Asian leaders and governments, partly no doubt in order to encourage them not to exert too much pressure on the

[98] Cf. M. R. Masani, *The Communist Party of India: A Short History*, New York: Macmillan, 1954, pp. 115–164. The Soviet Union and the CPR both shipped some grain to India in 1951 as famine relief.

[99] Gene Z. Hanrahan, *The Communist Struggle in Malaya*, New York: Institute of Pacific Relations, 1954, pp. 70, 73–74.

[100] Materials in *People's China*, September 1–November 16, 1952. The CPR sent out the invitation to the conference on March 21, 1952 ("A Call for the Convocation of a Peace Conference for Asia and the Pacific Regions," supplement to *People's China*, May 16, 1952). By this time the CPC had become impressed with the anti-American potential of Asian nationalist neutralism as a result of such developments as India's rejection of the Japanese peace treaty, the fall of the Sukiman cabinet in Indonesia in 1952, and the rejection by Indonesia of aid "with strings" from the United States under the terms of the Mutual Security Act of 1951 (on the latter see Feith, *op. cit.*, pp. 57–66).

local Communist Parties, as well as to assist in cultivating their anti-Western tendencies. This approach turned into outright courtship of Asian neutralism after the coming to power of the Eisenhower administration and the death of Stalin in 1953. The minimum aim was to guard against the slight chance that the neutrals might be lured into the Western camp, and the maximum aim was to exploit the dislike of the neutrals for John Foster Dulles's policies. Although Moscow and Peking moved along roughly parallel lines, the rivalry between their Asian interests that had been implicit from the beginning soon came to the surface. In this rivalry, which will be discussed more fully later, the CPR had the obvious and important advantage of being a genuinely Asian power, a fact symbolized by China's presence at and the Soviet Union's absence from the Bandung Conference in 1955.

Parallel with the overt wooing of neutralism went a relatively covert process of building up and maturing the Asian Communist Parties against the time when they might again make a bid for power, by whatever means, with greater chances of success. Here again the Chinese had a significant advantage by virtue of geography and culture.[101] There was also an important strategic difference. The CPC, with its long standing preference for a political approach operating "from below," found it difficult to accept and advocate the idea of electoral alliances and what later came to be known as the "parliamentary path" to power (in essence, the Aidit formula), whereas the Soviet Union, in view of its long history of operating "from above," found it easy to endorse the electoral approach. The Philippine Communists, faced with increasingly effective governmental counteraction, split on this issue in 1954.[102] The Malayan Communists, faced with a somewhat similar situation, tried to persuade the new Malayan government to grant them legality at the end of 1955, but the negotiations broke down because the MCP refused to surrender its arms to the government.[103] In 1954 and 1955 political violence caused by leftist Chinese in Singapore, presumably with the CPC's approval if not actually at its instigation, assumed the proportions of a major crisis before being curbed in 1956.[104]

The Indonesian general elections in late 1955, in which the PKI won one-sixth of the popular vote only to be excluded from the cabinet in spite of Sukarno's wish to bring it in, demonstrated both the potentialities and the limitations of the Aidit approach. Khrushchev's response was to continue essentially as before: in other words, to cultivate neutral governments and hope that this would help the political fortunes of the local Communist Parties, which were otherwise to be left to their own devices and to find

---

[101] For a good summary of Chinese relations with the Asian Communist Parties during this period, see U. Alexis Johnson in C. Grove Haines ed., *The Threat of Soviet Imperialism*, Baltimore: Johns Hopkins University Press, 1954, p. 360.

[102] McVey in Black and Thornton, *op. cit.*, p. 182.

[103] Barnett, *Communist China and Asia, op. cit.*, p. 487.

[104] Robert S. Elegant, *The Dragon's Seed: Peking and the Overseas Chinese*, New York: St. Martin's Press, 1959, pp. 145–183.

their way to power, or at least to prepare the way for an assumption of power, primarily via the ballot box.[105] Khrushchev conferred formal sanction on the "parliamentary path to power" at his party's Twentieth Congress in February, 1956.[106]

This formulation was essentially unacceptable to the CPC, which did not endorse it except in the most perfunctory way and has recently indicated that it and the denunciation of Stalin were the two features of the Twentieth Congress to which it most objected from the beginning.[107] The CPC continued to cultivate Asian neutralism, especially as a means of countering American policy in Asia, and references to "armed struggle" disappeared from its pronouncements until about 1958. Nevertheless, it refused to go as far as the Russians in endorsing the idea of a Communist path to power that would be essentially peaceful and even parliamentary, at any rate until the final stage. Implicitly rather than explicitly, the major Chinese policy pronouncements of 1965, such as the two statements on the Stalin question and the proceedings of the CPC's Eighth National Congress, rejected the "parliamentary path" in favor of "revolutionary struggle" outside the electoral process.[108]

Khrushchev's preference for the "parliamentary path," like several other aspects of his foreign policy, was dictated primarily by his fear of the escalation of local confrontations with the United States into nuclear war. The psychological climate created throughout the world by Soviet achievements in military and space technology during 1957 seemed to the CPC to make this fear unreal. Accordingly, it urged a widespread revision of Khrushchev's policies, including his preference for the "parliamentary path," on him at a conference of Communist Parties at Moscow in Novem-

---

[105] This approach came out clearly during Bulganin's and Khrushchev's visit to India at the end of 1955 (they also visited Burma and Afghanistan). In the spring of 1957, Voroshilov toured portions of Java in the company of Sukarno and contributed thereby to an impressive showing by the PKI in the ensuing local elections. The Communist electoral victory in the Indian state of Kerala (April, 1957) was the greatest triumph for the "parliamentary path" to date.

[106] ". . . the working class . . . is in a position to defeat the reactionary forces opposed to the popular interest, to capture a stable majority in parliament, and transform the latter from an organ of bourgeois democracy into a genuine instrument of the people's will" (Tass, February 14, 1956). The CPSU's emphasis on the "peaceful transition" or "parliamentary path" to power has not led it to deny the possibility of violent seizures of power.

[107] "The Origin and Development of the Differences Between the Leadership of the CPSU and Ourselves," *People's Daily* and *Red Flag*, September 6, 1963.

[108] Recently the CPC has stated, in refutation of the "parliamentary path" concept, that "Until the time arrives for seizing state power, the fundamental and most important task for the proletarian party is to concentrate on the painstaking work of accumulating revolutionary strength. . . . The proletarian party should use the various forms of day-to-day struggle to raise the political consciousness of the proletariat and the masses of the people, to train its own class forces, to temper its fighting capacity, and to prepare for revolution ideologically, politically, organizationally, and militarily ("The Proletarian Revolution and Khrushchev's Revisionism," *loc. cit.*).

ber, 1957, but with little success.[109] The Soviet Union made it clear, by about the end of 1958, that whatever major military and political pressures it might feel able to bring to bear on the United States would be exerted in the West, not in Asia. The CPR was obviously in no position to exert any comparable pressures on its own account or on that of other Asian Communist Parties.

The CPC evidently concluded, and still believes, that it will be a long time before truly revolutionary situations appear in most non-Communist Asian countries. When and if such situations materialize, they will presumably result from the convergence of domestic crises, flowing from the failure of non-Communist governments to solve pressing internal problems, and external crises produced by "imperialist" blunders. Since the CPR is not strong enough yet to manage such crises or give decisive support to Asian Communist Parties involved in them, unless perhaps the area involved is close to the Chinese border, the CPR must be wary of fomenting them.

During the rather long period of preparation that seems to lie ahead, the CPR apparently intends to work with and count on the rising generation of Asian Communists, more than the present leaderships. Where those leaderships have committed themselves to follow the Soviet lead, as in India, Ceylon, and Outer Mongolia, the CPC has tried to split them, successfully in the first two cases. In general, however, the CPC bids for support within the Asian parties but is careful not to exert undue pressure or behave in too domineering a way. It has formed some Asian regional organizations of Communist fronts, but not of Communist Parties. Above all, it does not prod parties into assuming unwise revolutionary risks from whose results it might then be called on to rescue them.

Against this background, some relevant events of the past several years make reasonable sense. Certain events of 1959, such as Nehru's ouster of the Communist government in Kerala and Sukarno's indefinite postponement of general elections in Indonesia, and 1960, such as the successful rigging of the Laotian election of April 24 by the right wing government, augured badly for the future of the "parliamentary path." It is hardly surprising that the CPC included an explicit rejection of that path as a general principle, apparently for the first time in public, in the general propaganda offensive that it opened against Khrushchev in April, 1960, and denied his right to prevent other parties from launching violent revolutions.[110]

---

[109] "The Origin and Development of the Differences," loc. cit. The CPC's frustration was reflected in part in its attack on Tito beginning in May, 1958 (cf. In Refutation of Modern Revisionism, Peking: Foreign Languages Press, 1958).

[110] "It can thus be seen that the proletariat is compelled to resort to the means of armed revolution. . . . Whether the transition will be carried out through armed uprising or by peaceful means is a question that is fundamentally different from that of peaceful coexistence between the socialist and capitalist countries; it is an internal affair of each country, one to be determined only by the relative strength of class forces in that country in a given period, a matter of policy to be decided only by the Communists of that country themselves" (Long Live Leninism, op. cit., pp. 42–44).

On the other hand, it did not follow that the CPC issued any general exhortation to the Asian parties to resort to violence. As usual, an exception must be made for North Vietnam, which raised the level of its guerrilla activities in Laos and South Vietnam in 1959 following an effort by the Laotian government to dissolve the Pathet Lao's legal armed forces.[111] The CPR's image, in Asia as elsewhere, was harmed during this period by its brutalities in Tibet, mounting tension on the Sino-Indian frontier, and the excesses of the Great Leap Forward, for which only the North Korean party showed any enthusiasm.

Chinese Communist influence is predominant at present, virtually to the exclusion of Soviet influence, on two categories of Asian Communist Parties: those (notably the Malaysian) that are strongly Chinese in their ethnic composition, and those (such as the Burmese and Thai) that are so weak as to stand in absolute need of external support such as only the CPC is able and willing to provide. The Japanese party supports the CPC for essentially these reasons, except that in the first case the bond is a cultural rather than an ethnic one. The North Koreans have made what appears to be an autonomous decision to support the Chinese, largely because of a preference for Peking's international strategy over Moscow's; the Soviet Union's proximity makes a shift of allegiance possible whenever it might come to seem desirable. Chinese influence is somewhat less strong, although still greater than Soviet influence, on the Indonesian Communist Party, which the CPC is not in a position either to support or coerce effectively, but which feels much closer to Peking than to Moscow on such basic issues as Stalin, Albania, "modern revisionism" (communism of the Khrushchev-Tito-Togliatti variety), the Sino-Indian border dispute, the need for militant "confrontation" with "imperialism," and the like. The same applies to the most militant and successful (at the polls) of the regional machines within the Indian Communist Party, those of Andhra, Kerala, West Bengal, and East Punjab. The Vietnam Labor (actually, Communist) Party of Ho Chi Minh has a complex and ambiguous relationship with the CPC that cannot be equated with that of any other party. For obvious reasons of geography and superior Chinese power, the Vietnamese party can never defy the CPC completely and side with the Soviet Union, or for that matter with any one else; the frequently suggested potential analogy with Tito is unconvincing, since Yugoslavia lacks a common frontier with the Soviet Union such as North Vietnam has with the CPR and has never had such bad relations with the West as North Vietnam has. Furthermore, the North Vietnamese party needs Chinese support in various forms. On the other hand, the Vietnamese have long feared the Chinese and have struggled, successfully on the whole, to fend off domination by them; there is every reason to think that this attitude still prevails. Furthermore, the North Vietnamese

---

[111] Cf. A. M. Halpern and H. B. Fredman, *Communist Strategy in Laos*, the RAND Corporation, RM-2561, June 14, 1960; Fall, *The Two Viet-Nams, op. cit.*, pp. 351ff.

seem to be impelled to maintain a certain reserve toward the Chinese, even while endorsing most of their arguments against the Russians, by the thought that too much closeness might lead to satellitization, and that the Soviet Union is too far away to render effective help.

In general, then, several of those Asian Comunist Parties that have committed themselves to the Chinese rather than to the Soviet side have done so with some reservations; for one thing, they do not intend to reject domination by Soviet power merely in order to accept domination by Chinese numbers. Furthermore, it is not clear that the Chinese any more than the Russians intend to expose themselves to serious risks on behalf of the Asian Communist Parties. The Soviet Union apparently understands these reservations and in general refrains from attacking these parties openly, as it has the Chinese. In some cases, notably those of North Korea and North Vietnam, it has tried to woo them back onto its side with offers of aid and support.

Among the few Communist movements of eastern Asia that support the Soviet rather than the Chinese side, that of Ceylon is not important enough to deserve explicit consideration. The weak central leadership of the Indian Communist Party supports Moscow partly at least because of its objections to the strategy and tactics of the militant regional organizations already mentioned, which support the CPC. The Outer Mongolian party supports the Soviet Union virtually without reservations, because of the traditional Mongol fear of Chinese domination, the role of Russia (white or red) in modern times as a protector of the Mongols against the Chinese (white or red), the crucial role of the Soviet Army in the creation of the Communist regime in Outer Mongolia, and the fact that Outer Mongolia has had a defensive alliance with the Soviet Union since 1936 under whose terms the Soviet Union is entitled to keep troops on Mongolian soil.

■ AS AN APPROACH TO RELATIONS AMONG COMMUNIST PARTIES AND STATES

Sino-Soviet relations during Stalin's lifetime and after the beginning of Mao's ascendancy reflected two conflicting attitudes on the part of the CPC. On the one hand, it tried with increasing success to use the Soviet party and state as a ladder on which to climb to greater power and influence; whether the CPC intended at that time to kick the rungs out later is uncertain. On the other hand, the CPC was afraid of domination or satellitization and therefore concerned with establishing its autonomy from Soviet interference in its internal affairs. Both these tendencies emerged in the Sino-Soviet alliance of February 14, 1950, which pledges the Soviet Union not only to protect the CPR from attack by Japan or any ally of Japan's (meaning the United States), but also to behave "in conformity with the principles of equality, mutual benefit and mutual respect for the national sovereignty and territorial integrity and noninterference in the internal affairs" of the CPR.[112] The reference to territorial integrity, a phrase consciously or unconsciously borrowed from the Open Door doctrine, was almost certainly aimed at Stalin's pressures on Manchuria and Chinese Central Asia.

The CPC has displayed a cautious attitude toward Soviet pressures in the party as well as in the state field and a desire to uphold its autonomy and dignity. Mao has never attended a Soviet party congress, either during Stalin's lifetime or since.[113] His first visit to Moscow was made in December, 1949–February, 1950, when for the first time he could go as the leader of a Communist state as well as of a Communist party, and thus with greater bargaining power.

There can be no serious doubt that Mao recognized Stalin as the leader not only of the Soviet party and state, but also (after the Second World War) of the "socialist camp" and (even after the dissolution of the Comintern in 1943) of the international Communist movement. This recognition was limited both in outward expression and in practice, however, by some important considerations. One was a desire not to risk undesirable complications with the Kuomintang, with Chinese public opinion, and with the Western powers during the war against Japan and the ensuing civil war. Another was a desire to safeguard the autonomy of the CPC, even if it was to be an autonomy within the framework of Stalin's suzerainty. A third was the desire to stake out a Chinese claim to leadership of Communist revolution in Asia under the rubric of "Asian Marxism."[114]

After 1949 public acknowledgment of the leadership of Stalin and the Soviet Union became both safer and, more important, desirable for opportunistic reasons. Mao began to be described as Stalin's "disciple and comrade-in-arms."[115] Apart from the opportunistic reasons for such talk, there were some real ones. The man who had led the Soviet Union in the war against Nazi Germany and then in the Cold War against the United States could hardly be considered soft on "imperialism."

After Stalin's death in 1953, Mao's initial response was to emphasize his

---

[112] Article V (in van der Sprenkel, *op. cit.*, pp. 228–229).

[113] This fact was evidently so embarrassing to the CPSU at the time of its Nineteenth Congress that *Pravda* (October 9, 1952) made an almost certainly conscious error by referring to Liu Shao-ch'i, the leader of the CPC delegation, as General Secretary of the CPC Central Committee.

[114] For Mao's comments on the dissolution of the Comintern see Gelder, *op. cit.*, pp. 169–173.

[115] E.g., in Ch'en Po-ta, *Stalin and the Chinese Revolution*, Peking: Foreign Languages Press, 1953, p. 28; the original version was published by New China News Agency, December 19, 1949 (just before Stalin's seventieth birthday). Both this document and the *Selected Works* (vol. 3, pp. 102–103) attribute certain laudatory statements about Stalin to Mao on the occasion of Stalin's sixtieth birthday (December 21, 1939) that I have been unable to find in a pre-1949 source (e.g., *Hsuan-chi*). There is a reference to, but no quotation from, Mao's greeting to Stalin on that occasion on p. 4 of *Pravda*, December 23, 1939, below the text of greetings from individuals then regarded in Moscow as more important, including Hitler and Chiang Kai-shek.

own personal seniority within the international Communist movement[116] but to continue to acknowledge the leading position of the Soviet party among the parties of that movement and of the Soviet Union in the "socialist camp."[117] Within eighteen months the CPC, disgusted by the internecine quarrels and external policies of Stalin's successors and seeing in them an opportunity to enhance its own position, had implicitly withdrawn its endorsement of Soviet party leadership and had begun to claim de facto, although not yet de jure, coleadership of the "socialist camp" for the CPR.[118] Khrushchev's concessions to Chinese pretensions, which he made at least partly in order to secure the CPC's acquiescence in his own bid to unseat Malenkov, were criticized by his conservative opponents as having in effect acknowledged this coleadership.[119] By 1956, after Khrushchev's attack on Stalin, the CPC was implying strongly that the Soviet party's position as the "center" (a term somewhat weaker than "head") of the international Communist movement then rested on nothing but the historical accident that it was the first Communist Party to seize state power, and furthermore in the largest country on earth.[120] This formulation strongly implied an obliga-

---

[116] Neither Mao nor Liu Shao-ch'i attended Stalin's funeral.

[117] "The Communist Party of the Soviet Union . . . has been our model in the past, is our model now and will remain our model in the future. . . . There is not the slightest doubt that the world camp of peace, democracy and Socialism headed by the Soviet Union will be still more united and become still more powerful" (Mao Tse-tung, "The Greatest Friendship," *People's China*, March 16, 1953).

[118] In September–October, 1954, Khrushchev led a delegation to the CPR, the first time that important Sino-Soviet negotiations had taken place in Peking rather than in Moscow. The nominal occasion was a state rather than a party one (the fifth anniversary of the founding of the CPR), and the Soviet delegation was publicly referred to as a state one even though it was led by the party First Secretary and did not include the Premier (Malenkov) or the Foreign Minister (Molotov). Compare Tito's insistence, the following spring, on treating Khrushchev's pilgrimage to Belgrade, accompanied this time by the Premier (now Bulganin), as a state rather than a party occasion. The Sino-Soviet joint communiqué (text in *The New York Times*, October 12, 1954) gave the names of the Chinese but not of the Soviet negotiators, presumably in order not to emphasize the confusion surrounding the character of the Soviet delegation.

[119] Molotov, in a speech of February 8, 1955, to the Supreme Soviet, referred to the "socialist camp" as being led by the Soviet Union and the CPR. Kaganovich did the same at the CPSU's Twentieth Congress. Note that at that time Khrushchev was still trying to conciliate the CPC, to the point of scheduling the opening day of the congress on February 14, 1956, the anniversary of the signing of the Sino-Soviet alliance in 1950, in spite of the fact that he enunciated at the congress several propositions that were unacceptable to the CPC.

[120] "More on the Historical Experience Concerning the Dictatorship of the Proletariat," *loc. cit.*, refers to the Soviet Union (not the CPSU) as the center of the international Communist movement. An earlier similar statement ("On the Historical Experience Concerning the Dictatorship of the Proletariat," *People's Daily*, April 5, 1956 [text in *Communist China 1955–1959, op. cit.*, pp. 144–151]) implies the same thing. Khrushchev had opened the way to this by his concept of the "socialist commonwealth" (see Kurt L. London, "The 'Socialist Commonwealth of Nations': Pattern for Communist World Organization," *Orbis*, vol. 3, no. 4 [winter, 1960], pp. 424–442), first authoritatively promulgated in an important Soviet government statement of October 30, 1956, which the CPC now claims to have inspired ("The Origin and Development of the Differences," *loc. cit.*).

tion on the part of the Soviet Union to make the fruits of its experience available to other "socialist" countries, in the form of aid and support.

Khrushchev's formulation was almost exactly the opposite. Since the "socialist" states formed a "commonwealth," the Soviet Union could not play the role of "head" and therefore had no moral obligation, over and above specific commitments, to aid, support, or defend them, except where it was in the Soviet interest to do so. On the other hand, Krushchev still wanted to be able to give as much guidance as possible, through party channels, to the international Communist movement.[121] Aware of the difference between his own concept and the Chinese, he tried at the end of 1956 and in early 1957 to find some common ground by praising Stalin as a staunch foe of "imperialism," a point of great importance to the CPC since it implied a determination to continue the struggle that Stalin had waged. This concession was not enough to bridge the gap, and it was therefore quietly dropped.[122]

By this time the CPC had grown so annoyed with Krushchev, and in particular with his desire for influence without responsibility, that it would probably have welcomed his displacement by the opposition.[123] Not only did Khrushchev trounce the opposition (in June, 1957), however, but he also succeeded in ousting the troublesome Marshal Zhukov (in October) and in gaining prestige for the Soviet state (not necessarily for the party) by testing an ICBM (in August) and launching a successful earth satellite (on October 4). From the Chinese point of view, these achievements underlined all the more the ability and the duty of the Soviet state to render aid and support to the other members of the "socialist camp" and the international Communist movement.

The outcome was a seemingly authoritative, but actually curious and unstable, compromise in which each side in effect conceded the other's point, for the time being as it turned out. The occasion was the fortieth anniversary of the October Revolution (November 7, 1957).[124] The com-

---

[121] In his report to the Twentieth Congress, Khrushchev did not refer to the Soviet leadership of the "socialist camp," but he clearly intended to give doctrinal and strategic guidance to the entire international Communist movement.

[122] The long-delayed official biography of Stalin (in *The Large Soviet Encyclopedia*, vol. 40, pp. 419–424, signed to press on November 20, 1957) does not stress his role as a fighter against "imperialism."

[123] Zagoria, *The Sino-Soviet Conflict, op. cit.*, points out that the CPC's comment on Khrushchev's victory over the "antiparty group" led by Malenkov and Molotov in June, 1957, was "the least enthusiastic of the entire Bloc."

[124] The so-called Twelve Party Declaration (Tass, November 22, 1957), issued by those Communist Parties (other than that of Yugoslavia) that exercised state power, but allegedly not binding on parties not in power, formulated the compromise. Soviet state leadership was endorsed ("the invincible camp of socialist countries headed by the Soviet Union . . . the first and mightiest socialist power"). On the other hand, it was stated that "The historic decisions of the Twentieth Congress of the CPSU . . . have opened a new stage in the world communist movement. . . ." For explicit Chinese endorsements of Soviet party leadership at this time, see Mao's speech of November

promise soon broke down, mainly it would seem because Khrushchev launched a campaign of summit diplomacy and displayed more concern for improving his relations with the West than for maintaining the delicate equilibrium so recently attained in his relations wth the CPR. On March 31, 1958, in one of his first acts after assuming the premiership, he proclaimed a unilateral suspension of nuclear testing, with the announced purpose of minimizing the chances of nuclear diffusion (to West Germany by the United States, and by implication to the CPR by the Soviet Union).[125]

By this time the CPC had decided that Khrushchev was guilty of "modern revisionism," a term apparently used in public for the first time in the Twelve Party Declaration, although for the time being it confined its explicit application of the term to Tito.[126] Khrushchev proceeded to confirm his "modern revisionist" tendencies in the eyes of the CPC by a long series of further acts, among which may be mentioned the publication of a major theoretical work embodying his views[127] and an explicit repudiation[128] of Soviet leadership of the "socialist camp." This repudiation, although implicit in his behavior for several years past, was probably precipitated by an announcement by the United States government that it considered the Soviet Union to bear "partial responsibility" for the acts of the CPR.[129] Worst of all was the test ban treaty of 1963, which the CPC regarded as virtually the ultimate in Soviet shirking of its responsibility to the other members of the "socialist camp."

After that the CPC began to elaborate publicly a position on the Soviet Union whose essentials are as follows.[130] In the party sphere, just as the German party betrayed Marxism, so the Soviet leadership has betrayed Leninism (or Marxism-Leninism) and adopted "modern revisionism." The CPC does not comment publicly on the obvious possibility that it may some day betray Maoism. Thus as long as the Soviet party remained under Khrushchev's leadership it could be regarded as having "split" with Marxism-Leninism and all true Marxist-Leninists, who included not only "good" Communists but also many likeminded non-Communists. Obviously Marxist-Leninists are not obligated to take orders from the Soviet party or consider

17, 1957, in Moscow (*People's Daily*, November 20, 1957; quoted in Zagoria, *The Sino-Soviet Conflict, op. cit.*, p. 146), and Friedrich Ebert's account of Mao's remarks at the Twelve Party Conference (*Neues Deutschland*, November 30, 1957).

[125] Cf. Alice Langley Hsieh, *Communist China's Strategy in the Nuclear Era*, Englewood Cliffs, N.J.: Prentice-Hall, 1962, p. 107.

[126] Cf. *In Refutation of Modern Revisionism, op. cit.*

[127] *The Fundamentals of Marxism-Leninism*, Moscow: Foreign Languages Publishing House, 1960. For commentary see Zagoria, *The Sino-Soviet Conflict, op. cit.*, Chapter 8.

[128] At the time of the Moscow Conference of November-December, 1960, and in his celebrated speech of January 6, 1961.

[129] Speech by Under Secretary of State Douglas Dillon, October 7, 1959 (text in *The New York Times*, October 8, 1959).

[130] The most important statement is "The Leaders of the CPSU are the Greatest Splitters of Our Times," *People's Daily* and *Red Flag*, February 4, 1964.

its proceedings, such as its Twentieth and Twenty-second Congresses and its Party Program of 1961, as having any binding force on them. In the state sphere, the CPR evidently regards Sino-Soviet relations as having been reduced to a more or less minimal level by the Soviet repudiation of leadership and responsibility,[131] with the important qualification that the CPR often expresses the hope, phrased as a certainty, that in case of a major war the two would stand side by side.

Although the most important, the Soviet party is obviously not the only other Communist Party with which the CPC has had relations bearing an ideological significance. Other cases can be found in Eastern Europe.

For several years prior to 1949 one of the CPC's leading foreign friends, the American Anna Louise Strong, had been in Europe trying to convey the CPC's viewpoint to Communist Parties on both sides of the Iron Curtain, including the Soviet party itself. In February, 1949, she was arrested as a "secret agent" in the Soviet Union while on her way back to the CPR and expelled in a westerly direction shortly afterward.[132] Meanwhile, on November 1, 1948, Liu Shao-ch'i's authoritative commentary on the Stalin-Tito controversy and on the broad subject of relations among Communist states, entitled *On Internationalism and Nationalism*, had been published.[133] The CPC's interest in this subject had almost certainly been greatly increased by the recent fall of Mukden and the realization that it would soon be in power. In this document Liu insists that any federation of states, especially Communist states, and of "nations" (nationalities or minorities) within states must be entirely free and voluntary. This was almost certainly aimed at Tito's effort to take advantage of divisions within the Albanian leadership to make Albania the first state to join the projected Yugoslav-dominated Balkan federation.[134] If so, one may trace back to this episode both the first promulgation by the CPC of the proposition that a "socialist" state must not annex or directly dominate another, and the beginnings of the seemingly

---

[131] Somewhat similarly, the CPC announced in 1958 its intention to maintain minimal diplomatic relations with Yugoslavia while severing all party ties, which were tenuous in any case (*In Refutation of Modern Revisionism, op. cit.*, p. 31).

[132] R. Conquest, *Power and Policy in the U.S.S.R.: The Study of Soviet Dynastics,* New York: St. Martin's Press, 1961, pp. 102–103, attributes Miss Strong's arrest to her Titoist sympathies, but it is doubtful whether this was the sole cause. A more probable reason was the publication or forthcoming publication of her books, *Tomorrow's China,* New York: Committee for a Democratic Far Eastern Policy, December, 1948 (published in Bombay as *Dawn Over China*); and *The Chinese Conquer China,* New York: Doubleday, 1949, and Stalin's suspicions as to what she might do if allowed to return to China. The charges against her were publicly withdrawn on March 4, 1955 (Conquest, *op. cit.*, p. 261).

[133] Semiofficial English condensation in *China Digest* (Hong Kong), December 14, 1948.

[134] On this episode see Milovan Djilas, *Conversations with Stalin,* New York: Harcourt, Brace, 1962, pp. 133ff.; William E. Griffith, *Albania and the Sino-Soviet Rift,* Cambridge: The M.I.T. Press, 1963, pp. 19–20. Stalin objected strongly to this approach to the Balkan federation project, of which he claimed to approve in principle (provided his own tame Bulgarian regime had at least an equal voice in it with Yugoslavia).

incongruous friendship between the Communist regimes of China and Albania. On the other hand, the CPC also seems to have had reservations about the high-handed way in which Stalin was treating Tito.[135]

The crucial question of what constituted a "socialist" country, raised by Tito himself through the "revisionist" domestic policies and the quasi-neutral foreign policy that he adopted after his break with Stalin, came to a head at the time of the Polish and Hungarian crises of 1956. The CPC seems to have encouraged the Poles beforehand to assert their autonomy from Moscow[136] and to have supported Gomulka's successful assertion of such autonomy.[137] At the time when the first version of an important Chinese statement on the East European situation was broadcast on November 1, the CPC still regarded Nagy's program for Hungary as being in the same category.[138] Three hours later, a revised version was broadcast, and then published in the *People's Daily*, in which the CPC's support for Nagy was implicitly withdrawn.[139] In the interval, Budapest radio had announced the dissolution of the Communist dictatorship in Hungary, Hungarian withdrawal from the Warsaw Pact, and the adoption of a neutral foreign policy to be guaranteed by the United Nations. Like Tito, Nagy had abandoned "socialism." The CPC now claims[140] to have prodded a reluctant Khrushchev into using force against the Hungarians, and in any case it certainly approved of the Soviet intervention even while regretting the alleged necessity for it. Thus, according to the CPC, a "socialist" state need not submit to domination by another, but if it breaks with the "socialist camp" it may be coerced into rejoining it.

Tito reacted rather differently to the Hungarian affair. In his speech at Pula on November 11, 1956, he attributed it to vestiges of Stalinism and said that such vestiges were present in other Communist regimes as well. He added that Stalinism was "the product of a system" rather than the defect of an individual and implied that the best alternative to it was his own system.[141] This was too much for the CPC; after pondering his remarks for

---

[135] Cf. "On the Historical Experience Concerning the Dictatorship of the Proletariat," *loc. cit.*

[136] Zagoria, *The Sino-Soviet Conflict, op. cit.*, pp. 55–56.

[137] The CPC now implicitly claims to have restrained Khrushchev from crushing the Poles by force ("The Origin and Development of the Differences," *loc. cit.*).

[138] "The Government of the People's Republic of China notes that the people of Poland and Hungary in the recent happenings have raised demands that democracy, independence, and equality be strengthened. . . . These demands are completely proper" (New China News Agency dispatch, November 1, 1956).

[139] In the revised version, the words "and Hungary" were deleted from the following sentences of the original (although the passage quoted in the foregoing note was not changed): "As a result of these misunderstandings and estrangement, a tense situation has sometimes occurred which otherwise would not have occurred. The handling of the 1948–1949 Yugoslav situation and the recent happenings in Poland and Hungary are enough to illustrate this."

[140] "The Origin and Development of the Differences," *loc. cit.*

[141] Excerpts in *The New York Times*, November 17, 1956.

several weeks, it concluded that for the second time in eight years he needed a public lecture. This appeared in the form of a major editorial, said to be based on discussions at a meeting of the CPC's Politburo. In this document Tito's points were rebutted, and the editorial went on to lecture him, Communists in general, and by implication Khrushchev in particular, on Stalin's merits and the essentials of the "way of the October Revolution."[142]

Tito remained unrepentant, refused to rejoin the "socialist camp" as the CPC urged him to do,[143] and continued to design his domestic and foreign policies to suit himself. Mainly because of his objections to the concept of Soviet leadership of the "socialist camp" that the CPC was advocating, he refused to adhere to the Twelve Party Declaration of November, 1957. In March, 1958, his party published a "draft program" that embodied his "revisionist" stand. Already infuriated with Tito, and angry with Khrushchev for his own policies and for his failure to criticize Tito except in mild tones, the CPC evidently decided to force the issue. Beginning on May 5, the 140th anniversary of the birth of Karl Marx and the day on which the CPC convened the party congress that launched the Great Leap Forward, the CPC began a propaganda assault on Tito. There is reason to think that this assault forced Khrushchev to adopt a less tolerant attitude toward Tito, raised the level of tension in Eastern Europe, and contributed to the execution of Nagy on June 16. The CPC spoke of Tito as having inspired and sheltered Nagy, and as being no better than Nagy. Presumably, Tito deserved Nagy's fate.[144] Nevertheless, as it predicted, the CPC maintained minimal, correct diplomatic and economic relations with Yugoslavia, as Stalin had done a decade before. Since the trend toward rapprochement between Tito and Khrushchev began in 1961, the CPC has continued to maintain that Yugoslavia is not a "socialist" country and therefore cannot belong to the "socialist camp."[145] Frol Kozlov evidently tended to agree with the CPC, but Khrushchev did not, and after what appears to have been a struggle between the two men Yugoslavia was formally listed as belonging to the "socialist camp" in the Soviet May Day slogans for 1963. Kozlov does not seem to have been a factor in Soviet politics since that time.[146]

---

142 "More on the Historical Experience Concerning the Dictatorship of the Proletariat," loc. cit.

143 For example, during the visit of a delegation from the CPR's National People's Congress to Yugoslavia in late January, 1957.

144 Cf. Harold C. Hinton, "East Wind, West Wind," The New Republic, July 21, 1958, pp. 9–12; Peter Wiles, "China im Kräftespiel der Ostblockstaaten," Osteuropa, January, 1959, pp. 31–38. In his interesting article Mr. Wiles has assembled much information bearing on the CPC's toughened foreign policy at this time and in particular on its relations with Eastern Europe, but he frequently misinterprets his material, for example by assuming that all manifestations of Soviet foreign policy at this time represented a continuum equally affected by Chinese policy.

145 "Is Yugoslavia a Socialist Country?" People's Daily and Red Flag, September 26, 1963.

146 The original version of the Soviet May Day slogans for 1963 was published in Pravda on April 8; it referred to Yugoslavia in a friendly way but did not list it as a

Probably one of the main reasons why the CPC openly attacked Tito in the spring of 1958 was the hope of bringing Khrushchev to break with him also, and a belief that only such a break could prevent Yugoslavia from swallowing Albania, much as Stalin's break with Tito earlier had saved Albania then. The CPC's feeling of affinity for the Albanian regime stemmed not only from a liking for the Stalinist posture in which that regime was locked by its hatred of Tito and its fear of a Soviet-Yugoslav rapprochement, but also by a desire to needle and pressure Tito and Khrushchev and by solid economic considerations; Albania is a major exporter among other things of chrome, large quantities of which are needed in making steels of the types used in nuclear weapons programs.[147]

As the CPC failed to disrupt significantly the improving relations between Tito and Khrushchev, it extended increasing countervailing support to the Albanians. Hence when the CPC launched its attacks on Khrushchev in 1960, the Albanians supported it. This in turn contributed to a rapid worsening of Soviet-Albanian relations, which led to a withdrawal of Soviet aid to Albania in the spring of 1961, as well as unsuccessful Soviet efforts to overthrow the Albanian regime. The CPC participated in the dispute by getting a condemnation of Yugoslav "revisionism" inserted in the so-called Moscow Statement of December, 1960, and more significantly by beginning a substantial aid program to Albania in 1961. This in turn helped to worsen Sino-Soviet relations. Khrushchev took the unprecedented step of attacking the Albanian regime publicly at his party's Twenty-second Congress in October, 1961, probably in the belief that the CPC, which was then in serious economic trouble, might abandon the Albanians. It did not; in his speech to the congress, Chou En-lai politely but firmly rebuked Khrushchev for his attack on the Albanians and left Moscow before the end of the congress.[148] The CPC had not only upheld its principle that small "socialist" countries had the right of autonomy from large ones, but had gained a badly needed ally within the "socialist camp" in its burgeoning struggle with Khrushchev and the other "modern revisionists."

Asia also presents some interesting case studies in the theory and practice of the CPC's approach to other Communist Parties and states.

Before coming up to power the CPC occasionally evinced an interest, although one less blatant than the Kuomintang's, in the eventual recovery of

---

member of the "socialist camp" ("building socialism"). Khrushchev was then vacationing, and Kozlov was in charge in Moscow. On April 11, *Pravda* published an unprecedented correction which promoted Yugoslavia to membership in the "socialist camp." Soon afterward it was announced that Kozlov was ill, and he was scarcely heard of again until his death in January, 1965.

[147] For background see Griffith, *op. cit.*; Stavro Skendi, "Albania and the Sino-Soviet Conflict," *Foreign Affairs*, vol. 40, no. 3 (April, 1962), pp. 471–478; Daniel Tretiak, "The Founding of the Sino-Albanian Entente," *The China Quarterly*, no. 10 (April–June, 1962), pp. 123–143.

[148] Zagoria, *The Sino-Soviet Conflict, op. cit.*, Chapter 16.

Outer Mongolia, which had formed part of the Manchu empire.[149] Caution was dictated, however, by the fact that Outer Mongolia was a nominally independent Soviet satellite state, with which Stalin had concluded a military alliance in March, 1936. That alliance, incidentally, is still in effect, something that helps greatly to account for the fact that Outer Mongolia has felt able to give total endorsement to Khrushchev's position as against the CPR, which the Mongols greatly fear. When Outer Mongolia offered the CPR diplomatic recognition on October 6, 1949, the CPR reciprocated only after an unusual delay of ten days.[150] It is equally obvious that the CPR realized that recognition would tend to cancel its claim to Outer Mongolia,[151] and that the CPR saw no realistic alternative to recognition.

In 1936, Mao Tse-tung articulated an interesting differentiation among those former Chinese territories and dependencies that had been lost or were about to be lost to Japan, as contrasted with Outer Mongolia which had been lost to the Soviet Union. Manchuria, being almost entirely Chinese in population, must be "regained." Inner Mongolia, "which is populated by both Chinese and Mongolians," was to be "autonomous," although presumably under Chinese sovereignty. Korea and Taiwan, whose inhabitants Mao apparently did not consider Chinese, were to be independent of both Japan and China, and "we will extend them our enthusiastic help in their struggle for independence."[152] It is clear that this formula has been applied since, with one very important exception: the CPC has since laid claim to Taiwan, which was promised to China by the Cairo Declaration of 1943.[153] The same declaration promised Korea its independence "in due course," and the installation of a "socialist" regime in the northern half of the country under the auspices of the Soviet Army after 1945 apparently confirmed the CPC's view that Korea's formal independence must be respected. Although the CPR greatly increased its influence over the North Korean regime during the Korean War, it did not attempt to annex North Korea or convert it into a full-fledged Chinese satellite. A significant practical consideration is that North Korea's main geopolitical usefulness to the CPR is as a buffer, and it could not play that role if it were formally incorporated into the CPR.

A discussion of the relationship that the CPC envisages for itself with the international Communist movement as a whole can well begin with a

---

149 "When the people's revolution has been victorious in China the Outer Mongolian republic will automatically become a part of the Chinese federation, at their own will" (Mao Tse-tung, as quoted in Edgar Snow, *Red Star Over China*, New York: Modern Library, 1944, p. 96 n.).

150 "Diplomatic Relations of Communist China," *Current Background* (Hong Kong: American Consulate General), no. 440, March 12, 1957.

151 On the other hand, the Republic of China recognized the independence of Outer Mongolia in 1946 but subsequently withdrew that recognition.

152 Snow, *op. cit.*, p. 96. A sentence similar to the one quoted appears in the original of a work written by Mao in May, 1938 (*Hsuan-chi*, p. 701) but has been deleted from the revised version (*Selected Works*, vol. 2, p. 188).

153 Text in *United States Relations With China, op. cit.*, p. 519.

consideration of the personal position of Mao Tse-tung. He is the "banner-bearer" who "creatively applied" the "universal truth of Marxism-Leninism" and integrated it "with the practice of the Chinese revolution."[154] This clearly implies that the CPC is claiming for Mao the lofty status of a "continuator" of Maxism-Leninism in the same category as Marx, Engels, Lenin, and Stalin. The concept of "continuator" in effect originated with Stalin, who used it to buttress his power with the myth of an ideological authority derived directly from Lenin. Lenin did not need such a concept to reinforce his authority. One could say that Lenin's essential method of dealing with opponents within the party was to shout at them, whereas Stalin's was to shoot at them. The concept of a "continuator" has lapsed in the Soviet party since the death of Stalin. Khrushchev did not know Lenin and repudiated Stalin; furthermore, he had neither the objective qualifications nor the subjective liking for such a role, which he probably considered a manifestation of the "cult of personality."

In the Maoist tradition, the concept of "continuator" seems to have undergone a more subtle change. Mao never knew Lenin and in fact was never in the Soviet Union during Lenin's lifetime. Hence any alleged tie between Mao and Lenin can hardly involve a directly transferred authority. Much the same applies to Stalin. Mao was not put in charge of the CPC by Stalin, did not meet him until 1949, and did not attend his funeral. Mao's status as a "continuator" is therefore essentially self-generated; it derived its inspiration, but not its authority, from Moscow.

Mao's stature derives fundamentally from his claim to have originated an "Asian Marxism" to deal with "special conditions unknown to the European countries."[155] Mao's authority as a "continuator" was validated, not by any laying on of hands in Moscow, but by the victory of 1949, just as Leninism was validated by the October Revolution. Thus there were not one but two "continuators," Stalin and Mao, from 1949 to 1953. Mao's concept of his own role could be described as separate though junior. Since Stalin's death and the failure of his party to produce, or even to claim to have produced, another "continuator," Mao's claim to that title remains unique, if not necessarily widely accepted outside his own party. There are many indications of Mao's continuing respect for Stalin as a "continuator," combined however with a desire not to base his authority on Stalin and a claim to roughly equal status. One of the most interesting is a statement by Mao in 1961 implying that he wished to die at the same age (73) as Stalin.[156]

The essential attribute of the only living "continuator" of Marxism-Leninism, such as Mao evidently considers himself to be, is the authority to

---

[154] Ch'en Po-ta, "Under the Banner of Comrade Mao Tse-tung," *loc. cit.*

[155] The latter phrase is quoted in *ibid.* from an obscure passage in Lenin.

[156] "He himself [i.e., Mao] had no wish to go on living after seventy-three. . . ." (Field-Marshal Viscount Montgomery, "China on the Move," *The Sunday Times Magazine Section* [London], October 15, 1961).

define what is and what is not Marxism-Leninism, and therefore who are and who are not Marxist-Leninists. This is a formidable claim, even though lacking Stalin's power Mao must try to enforce it primarily through maneuver and invective. Whether Mao expects and intends that the CPC should produce another "continuator" after his death is uncertain. Both the logic of the situation and the recent efforts to increase Liu Shao-ch'i's international as well as national stature, however, suggest that the answer to the question is yes.[157]

The CPC's attitude toward its own collective relationship, as distinct from Mao's personal relationship, to the "socialist camp" and the international Communist movement has evolved against a long historic backdrop marked by the decline of organizational ties and pressures as a major binding force in world communism. Among the major landmarks in this decline were the dissolution of the Comintern (1943), Mao's success in effecting an "emancipation by conspiracy" of the CPC from Stalin's control, and Stalin's death (1953). The decline of organization has left ideology, for what it is worth, as the principal remaining binding force. Hence, to a large extent, the CPC's stress on "safeguarding the purity of Marxism-Leninism."

Among the major landmarks in the evolution of the CPC's current position on its own relationship to the rest of the Communist world have been the great crisis in Eastern Europe (1956); the CPC's failure to gain more than nominal acceptance by Khrushchev of its ideological and strategic views at the time of the Moscow conference of 1957; Mao's retirement as Chairman of the CPR (but not as Chairman of the CPC Central Committee) in the spring of 1959, with the announced purpose among other things of devoting more time to "Marxist-Leninist theoretical work";[158] the eruption of open Sino-Soviet debate in 1960 and the ensuing Moscow conference; and Khrushchev's denunciation of the Albanian regime at the Soviet Twenty-second Congress and his subsequent severance of diplomatic relations with it.[159]

In 1957, the CPC reverted to recognition of the Soviet party, and not merely of the Soviet state, as the "center" of the international Communist

---

[157] For example, Liu has never attended a Soviet party congress since Stalin's death; on the other hand, he led the CPC delegation to the second (1960) international Communist conference in Moscow since Stalin's death, Mao having led the CPC delegation to the first (in 1957).

[158] CPC Central Committee announcement of December 10, 1958 (text in *Communist China 1955–1959, op. cit.*, pp. 487–488).

[159] "The Twenty-second CPSU Congress in October, 1961, marked a new low in the CPSU leadership's efforts to oppose Marxism-Leninism and split the socialist camp and the international Communist movement. . . . Disregarding everything, the leadership of the CPSU broke off diplomatic relations with socialist Albania, an unprecedented step in the history of relations between fraternal parties and countries" ("The Origin and Development of the Differences," *loc. cit.*). Stalin did not break off diplomatic relations with Yugoslavia in 1948.

movement and continued to refer to the Soviet state as the "head of the socialist camp" down to the Moscow conference of 1960, at which Khrushchev repudiated this role.[160] Shortly before the conference, the CPC proposed to the Soviet party a formula whereby the two parties shared the major responsibility for the welfare of the international Communist movement, with the CPC evidently accepting a junior role.[161] When this was not included in the Moscow statement, the CPC included it, with itself apparently in the senior role, in an editorial, together with some further comments on the Soviet position that seem to represent a compromise between the Chinese and Soviet views.[162]

After the Twenty-second Congress, the tenuous compromise reached at Moscow in 1960 became untenable. A series of events served to emphasize and harden the differences between the Chinese and Soviet positions. Shortly after Kozlov's disappearance from the Soviet political scene, the CPC served a last warning on Khrushchev to mend his ways, and by implication not sign a test ban treaty, or face an organizational split in the international Communist movement whose foundations the CPC was already laying. In this document the CPC enunciated once more the concept of coresponsibility for the "socialist camp" and the international Communist movement, with itself apparently in the senior position.[163] A month later, on the eve of the beginning of the test ban treaty negotiations and while ideological talks between delegations of the Soviet and Chinese parties' Central Committees were still in progress, the CPSU issued a long,

---

[160] The Moscow Statement refers to the Soviet party as the "universally recognized vanguard" of the international Communist movement but says nothing about the Soviet state's leadership of the "socialist camp" (text in *The New York Times*, December 7, 1960). The last CPC document in which I have found a reference to the Soviet Union's leadership of the "socialist camp" is "Hold High the Red Banner of the October Revolution, March from Victory to Victory," *People's Daily*, November 7, 1960. Cf. William E. Griffith, "The November 1960 Moscow Meeting: A Preliminary Reconstruction," *The China Quarterly*, no. 11 (July-September, 1962), p. 51.

[161] "Both the Soviet Union and China, and both the Soviet and Chinese parties, bear great responsibilities regarding the international situation and toward the international communist movement" ("The Origin and Development of the Differences," *loc. cit.*).

[162] "China and the Soviet Union are the two biggest countries in the socialist camp and the Communist parties of China and the Soviet Union are the two biggest parties in the international communist movement. The solidarity and unity between these two parties and countries is of the greatest significance to the solidarity and unity of the whole socialist camp and the entire international communist movement. The great Soviet Union is not only the most advanced and powerful country in the socialist camp. The great Communist Party of the Soviet Union is the acknowledged vanguard with the longest history in the international communist movement and the most experience. The statement of the meeting correctly points out the position of prime importance of the great Soviet Union in the whole socialist camp and of the great CPSU in the entire international communist movement" ("The Banner of Victory, the Banner of Unity," *People's Daily*, December 7, 1960).

[163] "The Chinese and Soviet parties bear a heavier responsibility for the unity of the entire socialist camp and the international communist movement and should, of course, make commensurately greater efforts" (CPC Central Committee letter of June 14, 1963, to CPSU Central Committee).

public rejection.[164] This act, followed by the initialing of the test ban treaty on July 25, seems to have represented a point of no return in Sino-Soviet relations.

The CPC's current position on its own relationship to the "socialist camp" and the international Communist movement may perhaps best be clarified by an analysis of the significance that it appears to attach to three key terms — unity, solidarity (or cohesion), and leadership. These are old Marxist-Leninist cliches with frequently ambiguous meanings, but the CPC has made its own understanding of them reasonably precise and clear in recent years.

Unity is an ideological, not an organizational, condition. "True" unity can be attained only on the basis of Marxism-Leninism, as interpreted of course by the CPC. "Modern revisionism" can serve as the basis only of "sham" unity.[165] Hence unity can be achieved not only among Communist Parties of the "socialist camp" and the international Communist movement (the "world proletariat"), but among all Marxist-Leninists (including many non-Communists) and even to a degree among the "people" of the world (who are by definition anti-"imperialist" and are represented by the Marxist-Leninists).[166] Khrushchev's "modern revisionism" has captured the leadership of the Soviet party, but allegedly not yet the entire party, and is disrupting the Sino-Soviet unity that the CPC has been struggling to preserve. The Soviet and Chinese peoples still enjoy unity with each other, whatever the relations between the parties may be. It is the "modern revisionists," not the Marxist-Leninists, who are "splitting" the international Communist movement by failing to maintain unity. The Marxist-Leninists of course continue to preserve unity among themselves.

How, specifically, can unity be achieved and maintained? The Chinese formula is "unanimity through consultation." This means that the CPC recognizes the ideological authority, apart from its own, only of general international Communist conferences such as those of 1957 and 1960. The CPC denies that any one party, at such a conference or anywhere else, can impose its will on the other parties. Nor did the CPC accept Khrushchev's demand for majority rule at international conferences. The CPC's insistence on unanimity, which so far has neither been officially endorsed nor officially

---

164 Open letter of July 14, 1963 (text in *The New York Times*, July 15, 1963).

165 "Are the ranks of the international communist movement to be united or not? Is there to be genuine unity or sham unity? On what basis is there to be unity — is there to be unity on the basis of the Moscow declaration and the Moscow statement or 'unity' on the basis of the Yugoslav revisionist program or on some other basis? In other words, are differences to be ironed out and unity strengthened, or are differences to be widened and a split created?" ("More on the Differences Between Comrade Togliatti and Us: Some Important Problems of Leninism in the Contemporary World," *Red Flag*, March 4, 1963).

166 *Long Live Leninism, op. cit.*, p. 106.

rejected by the movement as a whole,[167] obviously represents a claim to a veto for itself (and, at least in theory, for any other party) and for the right to form and lead "fractions" (combinations) within the international Communist movement.[168] Since the CPC recognizes international Communist conferences as authoritative, even though its insistence on unanimity tends to vitiate their effectiveness, it is in no hurry to see another such conference.[169]

Solidarity (or cohesion) is an organizational term applicable both to the "socialist camp" and the international Communist movement and connoting cooperation based on independence and equality.[170] Even before 1963, the CPC was almost certainly opposed to any resurrection of the Comintern, under whatever name, unless it were done under conditions that would give the CPC a veto and a preeminent voice.

Leadership means responsibility to support the legitimate interests of other Communist countries and parties; it does not convey the right to control them.[171] Khrushchev, however, violated this principle by attacking first the Chinese and then the Albanians and trying to impose his objections to them on the other parties; as the CPC has put it, "someone went so far as to wave his baton. . . ."[172]

The CPC's behavior has increasingly suggested to others, both within and outside the international Communist movement, that it aspires ultimately to lead (in the sense of control) the movement, or the "socialist camp," or both, for instance by creating an organization in which voting strength would be proportional to party membership. The CPC has loudly denied the charge, on the ground that there is no such thing as leadership of the international Communist movement.[173] The question must be left open.

---

[167] On the Moscow Statement's vagueness on this question, see Griffith, *loc. cit.*, p. 55.

[168] *Ibid.*, p. 56.

[169] "We maintain that a series of preparatory steps are necessary in order to make the international meeting of fraternal parties a success. . . . Judging by present circumstances, it may require perhaps four or five years or even longer to complete these preparations" (Letter of the CPC Central Committee to the CPSU Central Committee, May 7, 1964, New China News Agency dispatch, May 8, 1964).

[170] "International solidarity of the Communist Parties is an entirely new type of relationship in human history. . . . The Communist Parties must seek unity with each other as well as maintain their respective independence" ("More on the Historical Experience Concerning the Dictatorship of the Proletariat," *loc. cit.*).

[171] "We hold that the existence of the position of 'head' does not contradict the principle of equality among fraternal parties. It does not mean that the CPSU has any right to control other parties; what it means is that the CPSU carries greater responsibility and duties on its shoulders" ("The Leaders of the CPSU are the Greatest Splitters of Our Times," *loc. cit.*).

[172] "Whence the Differences?" *People's Daily*, February 26, 1963.

[173] "They say: 'You are trying to seize the leadership!' No, friends! It is not at all clever of you to make this slander. The way you put it, it would seem that some people are contending with you for some such thing as 'the leadership.' Is this not tantamount to shamelessly claiming that some sort of 'leadership' exists in the international communist movement, and that you have this 'leadership?' It is a very, very bad habit of yours

The CPC evidently expects to prevail in the long run over its Soviet adversary, as it intends to convey whenever it says that their differences are only temporary, but it probably does not pretend to know what form that victory or the ultimate shape of the international Communist movement will take. In political as in military war, *on s'engage, puis on voit*.

■ AS A THEORY AND PRACTICE OF INTERNATIONAL RELATIONS

Until about 1945 the CPC had little contact with, knowledge of, or interest in international developments outside the Far East and tended to follow the Soviet lead on such matters. It was very alert, however, to developments in the Far East and to Soviet policy toward them.[174] The CPC probably considered that a clear split between the democratic and fascist members of the "imperialist camp" did not develop until 1941, when Great Britain and the United States came to the aid of the Soviet Union and China following the German invasion and Pearl Harbor, respectively.

In spite of its strenuous exertions during the war against Japan, the CPC found itself in an anomalous position by the spring of 1945. The United States, Great Britain, and the Soviet Union appeared to be getting along reasonably well and had just concluded at Yalta an agreement (the details as yet unpublished) with which the CPC would have to live, for the time being at least. The war against Germany was almost over, and the Far East was obviously about to receive increased attention from the major powers. A postwar United Nations Organization was emerging in which China (meaning the recognized government controlled by the Kuomintang) ranked as one of the Big Five. The Soviet Union had not yet entered the war against Japan, although it had denounced their neutrality pact on April 5.

The CPC could do nothing but seem to ride with the tide in the hope of avoiding an international intervention while it searched for a way of settling its political and military accounts with the Kuomintang. The CPC

---

thus to put on the airs of a patriarchal party. It is entirely illegitimate. The 1957 declaration and the 1960 statement clearly state that all communist parties are independent and equal. According to this principle, the relations among fraternal parties should under no circumstances be like the relations between a leading party and the led, and much less like the relations between a patriarchal father and his son. We have always opposed any one party commanding other fraternal parties, and it has never occurred to us that we ourselves should command other fraternal parties. So the question of contending for leadership simply does not arise" ("The Origin and Development of the Differences," *loc. cit.*).

174 For example, Chou En-lai flew from Yenan to the Soviet Union on September 16, 1939, the day after Stalin signed an armistice with Japan following an undeclared war near the frontier between Outer Mongolia and Manchuria (*The New York Times*, September 17, 1939).

succeeded in gaining representation on the Chinese delegation to the San Francisco conference that launched the United Nations Organization.[175] On April 24, 1945, on the eve of the opening of the conference, Mao delivered his important report, *On Coalition Government*, to the CPC's Seventh National Congress. He referred to Great Britain, the United States, and the Soviet Union, in that order, as the "three great democracies" and the "three great powers." The same nations, plus China and France, again in that order, he described as the "five great powers," and he declared that all major international issues must be settled by them; presumably he was aware of the proposal for a great power veto in the Security Council. The approaching defeat of Japan he attributed to the efforts of the Chinese people, the participation of Great Britain, and in particular the victories of the United States in the Pacific.[176]

After the Japanese collapse in August, the CPC became increasingly enraged by the efforts of the United States to deny it the power to occupy former Japanese-controlled territory and to aid the Kuomintang in occupying such territory instead. Continuing, although limited, American support for the Kuomintang and Stalin's overt launching of his Cold War on the United States early in 1946 combined to bring the CPC to the view, or at least the line, that the United States had assumed the leadership of the "imperialist camp" and was preparing for a Third World War.[177]

In *On Coalition Government*, Mao expressed the hope that after liberating them from Japan, Great Britain, the United States, France, and the Netherlands would grant independence to their dependencies in Southeast Asia "on the basis of the attitude that the Crimea [i.e., Yalta] Conference adopted toward the liberated areas of Europe."[178] Both Mao and Stalin were evidently surprised by the decision of the British Labor Government, some two years later, to withdraw from the former Indian Empire (including Burma), as well as from Greece, Turkey, and Palestine. It is clear that Stalin regarded the independence that the British granted to India and Pakistan in 1947, and to Burma and Ceylon in 1948, as merely a fraud behind which the local bourgeoisie would accept a continuation of an essentially imperialist relationship. He regarded the neutrality proclaimed by all four

---

[175] The CPC's representative was one of its elder statesmen, Tung Pi-wu, since the Kuomintang had vetoed its first choice, Chou En-lai. An American who met Tung while he was in the United States says that he showed great interest in learning about the United States and in escaping from the attentions of the American fellow travelers who surrounded him. The CPC had long had some strong friends among American leftists, including some who used to publicize its views even when these were at variance with those of Stalin.

[176] *Hsuan-chi*, pp. 289–290. For a reasonably faithful translation see Gelder, *op. cit.*, pp. 2–4; for excerpts see *Documentary History, op. cit.*, p. 296. This passage has been drastically altered in *Selected Works*, vol. 4, pp. 245–246.

[177] Cf. *Selected Works*, vol. iv, pp. 87–88.

[178] *Hsuan-chi*, p. 342; Gelder, p. 51, altered version in *Selected Works*, vol. 4, pp. 303–304.

of the new states[179] as equally fictitious; they belonged to the "imperialist camp." Soviet approval was extended only to the Communist revolutions in China and Vietnam and the non-Communist revolution in Indonesia, where of course "armed struggle" was being waged against "imperialism." The crisis created in Stalin's mind by what he regarded as the British Labor Party's clever trick had much to do with the establishment of the Cominform (September, 1947) and the strongly anticolonial line that it took from the outset.[180]

The CPC seems to have agreed from the beginning with this analysis. In December, 1947, Mao referred to "the eastern part of the world where there is a population of more than one thousand million people — half of mankind — suffering under imperialist oppression."[181] Two months later the CPC alleged that "With regard to Burma, Ceylon, Malaya, and Singapore, the British imperialists either give them false independence or nominal self-government, or else maintain their old form of rule unchanged."[182] Even the recognition of the CPR by India, Pakistan, Burma, and Ceylon at the beginning of 1950 did not change their status; they were still denounced as "running dogs of imperialism" and false neutrals. Their leaders, including Hatta of Indonesia, were described collectively as "the Nehrus, Jinnahs, Luang Phibun Songgrams, Quirinos, Syngman Rhees, and other feebleminded bourgeoisie of the East."[183]

The proclamation of the CPR in 1949 led its leaders to demand general diplomatic recognition and control of China's permanent seat in the United Nations Security Council. The CPR's involvement in the Korean War a year later gave it an opportunity to insist with growing vehemence that it must participate in the deciding of all major international questions, Far Eastern questions in particular. These claims were made in a spirit of arrogance and remained largely unrealized. Nevertheless, the CPR's defiance of the West in Korea helped to earn it increasing sympathy from Asian neutrals, and this in turn contributed to a reappraisal of neutralism in Peking. The first finding of this reappraisal, which coincided roughly with the CPR's involvement in the Korean War (1950–53), was that neutralism was a genuine phenomenon and not a fraud. The second evidently was that neutralism could have both positive utility to the CPR, as an ally in the struggle against "imperialism," and negative utility, as a political deterrent to "imperial aggression" against the CPR. If neutralism was to play this essentially instrumental role, it needed to be reassured that it had nothing to fear from the CPR and that the only external threat stemmed from

---

179 Paskistan was neutral from 1947 to 1953.

180 Cf. McVey, *The Soviet View, op. cit.,* pp. 24–37.

181 *The Present Situation and Our Tasks* (van der Sprenkel, *op. cit.,* p. 153).

182 "Congratulations on the Opening of the Southeast Asia Youth Conference," *loc. cit.*

183 New China News Agency dispatch, North Shensi, March 21, 1949 (in *China Digest,* April 5, 1949).

"imperialism." Such has been the main purpose of the famous Five Principles of Peaceful Coexistence. These were first set forth in an agreement with India signed in April, 1954 and have become the proclaimed basis of the CPR's national (not revolutionary) policy toward the entire non-Communist world (except for the United States, as long as it continues its present policy toward the CPR). They read as follows: "Mutual respect for each other's territorial integrity and sovereignty, mutual nonaggression, mutual noninterference in each other's internal affairs, equality and mutual benefit and peaceful coexistence." These platitudes provided the main propaganda basis for the CPR's effort to win neutral support for its national policies while reserving freedom of action for its revolutionary policies.

More than the Russians, the Chinese seem to differentiate sharply between neutrals who are actively hostile to "imperialism" and neutrals who are not. It is true that for reasons of state, including the need to compete with the Soviet Union, the CPR has cultivated at various times neutrals falling in the second category. The only governments in the underdeveloped areas of which the CPR seems genuinely to approve, however, are those that have had some sort of confrontation with "imperialism, colonialism, and neocolonialism" during or since their attainment of independence: in Asia, Burma,[184] Cambodia,[185] Ceylon,[186] and Indonesia;[187] in the Middle East and North Africa, Yemen, Egypt (at least at the time of its recognition of the CPR in 1956 and the Suez Canal crisis), and Algeria; in Sub-Saharan Africa, Somalia, Zanzibar, Guinea (for a few years after 1958), Congo Brazzaville, and Mali; in Latin America, Cuba.

In recent years the CPC has elaborated, how much in earnest and how much for propaganda purposes it is difficult to say, an image of world politics substantially along the following lines.[188] On the left stands the "socialist camp," from which Yugoslavia is excluded and to which Cuba has been admitted since June, 1963. Between the "socialist camp" and its main enemy, the United States, there is a "vast intermediate zone," no part of which should be written off as irreversibly committed to the United States. The struggle between the "socialist camp" and the United States will be decided in the "oppressed nations" (underdeveloped countries) within the "vast intermediate zone," not through proletarian revolutions in the capitalist countries. "It is impossible for the working class in the European and American capitalist countries to liberate itself unless it unites with the

---

184 Note Burma's excitement in 1953 over the presence of "KMT irregulars" on its soil and its consequent termination of American aid.

185 Note Sihanouk's protest flight to Thailand in 1953.

186 Diplomatic relations between the CPR and Ceylon were established only in 1957, after the election of the leftist and neutralist Bandaranaike government (1956).

187 Note Indonesia's rejection of American military aid in 1952.

188 Based mainly on "More on the Differences Between Comrade Togliatti and Us," *loc. cit.*

oppressed nations and unless those nations are liberated."[189] There are serious "contradictions" between the United States and the other capitalist countries including West Germany and Japan, and the latter are experiencing a resurgence of militarism.

Apart from leaders who are pro-"imperialist" or otherwise reactionary, there are two major political forces at work in the "oppressed nations" — oppressed, that is, by "imperialism, colonialism, and neocolonialism." One is the (non-Communist) "national liberation movement," the other the (Communist) "people's revolutionary movement." Since both have a common immediate objective, the expulsion of "imperialism, colonialism, and neocolonialism," the two can work together for the present, although ultimate revolutionary leadership is of course expected to pass to the "people's revolutionary movement." The two are referred to collectively as the "national revolutionary movement" or the "national (and) democratic revolution," the implication being that even Communists in the "oppressed nations" are working for the present toward a "democratic" rather than a "socialist" revolution.

Some secret Chinese documents recently published add certain details to this picture without contradicting it. Direct relations between the CPR and the United States are essentially a stalemate. A resolution of the stalemate can be achieved only if the United States gives in on all the disputed issues, such as Taiwan, at one time. While the bilateral stalemate continues, the main arena of struggle is of course the underdeveloped countries, and in particular Africa and Indochina.[190]

Soviet objections to the Chinese view of the world run substantially as follows.[191] The CPC places too little stress on the positive role of the "socialist camp" in world affairs, and relatively too much on the "national revolutionary movement." By its objections to Soviet disarmament policy and the "peace movement," and by its insistence on militant struggle against American "imperialism," it increases the risk of general war. It understates the danger from West Germany. It derides both the motivation and the effectiveness of Soviet economic activity in the underdeveloped areas. Its entire policy, in fact, constitutes an insufferable claim to leadership of the "socialist camp," the international Communist movement, and the "vast intermediate zone."

Something needs to be said about the formulation and implementation of Communist Chinese foreign policy, as well as about the CPC's philosophy of international relations.

Most of the CPC's highest leaders come from inland provinces and,

---

[189] CPC Central Committee letter of June 14, 1963, to the CPSU Central Committee.

[190] Lewis, *Chinese Communist Party Leadership, op. cit.*, pp. 26–27.

[191] Based mainly on CPSU Central Committee open letter of July 14, 1963, *loc. cit.*, and Mikhail Suslov, "On the CPSU's Struggle for Cohesion of the International Communist Movement," February 14, 1964 (published on April 3, 1964).

except for a few who had fairly extensive experience abroad as students, seem to have had little knowledge of the world when they joined the Communist movement. A qualified observer has stated that down to about 1949 they "appeared to welcome foreign contacts" but were "very badly informed on world affairs."[192] Since 1949, almost the opposite has become the case. The CPC leadership values and encourages certain forms of foreign contacts, but for political purposes; it is not receptive to new ideas. On the other hand, the CPC has developed an elaborate intelligence operation, including detailed study of non-Communist periodicals and other publications. Its foreign policy operations are therefore based on information at least as good as is available to most other governments. Errors and failures seem to be attributable to ideologically caused misconceptions more often than to insufficient or incorrect factual information. The CPC's propaganda, particularly its foreign propaganda, gives only a very distorted reflection of the information available to it.

Who makes foreign policy in th CPR? For matters of major importance, the answer is the same as for other subjects: the Standing Committee of the Political Bureau (or Politburo) of the CPC Central Committee, chaired by Mao Tse-tung. Within the Standing Committee, as within the CPC since the mid-1930's, the leading specialist in foreign affairs is Chou En-lai. Born in Kiangsu, a coastal province, in 1898, into an upper-class family well educated in China and abroad, able, hard-working, flexible, tough, and charismatic, Chou is a formidable figure by any standards. There is no necessary reason to think that Chou gave up more than administrative functions when he turned the Foreign Ministry over to Chen Yi in February, 1958, while retaining the Premiership. On the other hand, although Chou continues to appear not only valuable but indispensable in foreign as well as in domestic affairs, it seems that his views are fairly moderate (by the standards prevailing within the CPC) and are not always in favor with his most influential colleagues.[193]

Liu Shao-ch'i, who succeeded Mao as Chairman of the CPR in 1959 and is apparently destined to succeed him as Chairman of the CPC Central Committee, on the other hand, has a seemingly deserved reputation for being doctrinaire and antiforeign. Nevertheless, whereas Mao has never traveled abroad except to the Soviet Union (in 1949–50 and 1957), Liu has visited not only the Soviet Union (in 1921–22, 1952–53, and 1960) but also the two Asian Communist countries (North Vietnam and North Korea)

---

[192] Michael Lindsay, *China and the Cold War: A Study in International Politics,* Melbourne University Press, 1955, p. 172.

[193] When Chou En-lai was in Rangoon late in 1956, he was interviewed by Edward R. Murrow. When Mr. Murrow telecast the interview shortly afterward in the United States, he remarked after the showing that at the end of the interview he had asked Chou a spontaneous question about the Hungarian crisis. At that point two men in Chou's entourage stood up as a signal for him to terminate the interview.

and the three Asian neutrals (Indonesia, Burma, and Cambodia) with whom the CPR has the closest relations, all in 1963.

Virtually nothing is known in detail of how the CPC leadership arrives at decisions on matters of foreign policy. It seems likely, however, that within the limits of ideology, which are probably less narrow than is generally believed, such decisions are based on the best information available and reflect "a continuing calculation of the world balance of power."[194] Once the decision is taken, implementation, if required, can be attempted through one or more of three primary channels. The first, the party channel, leads mainly via the International Liaison Department of the CPC Central Committee to the foreign Communist Parties and the foreign and international front organizations. The second, the state channel, leads mainly via the Ministry of Foreign Affairs to foreign governments, Communist and non-Communist, with which the CPR has diplomatic or quasi-diplomatic relations.[195] The third, the channel of "people's diplomacy," leads mainly via the Chinese People's Institute of Foreign Affairs to numerous foreign private individuals and organizations, mostly non-Communist. The nature of the decisions taken must be inferred mainly from the manner of their implementation, although published official statements are often helpful in reconstructing them.

It has already been pointed out that when national security so dictates, or is thought to dictate, the CPC ruthlessly subordinates the requirements of domestic policy to those of foreign policy. The same holds true at the level of propaganda and public relations whether of the state or "people's diplomacy" variety. Huge crowds are manufactured to greet visiting statesmen. Elaborate "guided tours" are organized for private foreign visitors. Foreign students in the CPR are fed and housed much better than their Chinese counterparts. There can be little doubt that all this is extremely galling to those numerous Chinese who are aware of it, especially since the CPC claims to have liberated the Chinese people from their former "semicolonial" relationship to the West.[196] It is a fair question why the Chinese people should be further impoverished in order to pay, among other things, for their leaders' grandiose and not always realizable aims in the field of foreign policy.

[194] A. M. Halpern, "The Foreign Policy Uses of the Chinese Revolutionary Model," *loc. cit.*, p. 4.

[195] Donald W. Klein, "Peking's Evolving Ministry of Foreign Affairs," *The China Quarterly*, no. 4 (October–December, 1960), p. 34, points out that the CPR generally sends its best ambassadors to non-Communist countries. An important exception is the able and experienced Wang Ping-nan, who served as Ambassador to Poland from early 1955 to the spring of 1964. During that period he conducted ambassadorial talks with the United States, first at Geneva and later at Warsaw. Informal but significant contacts between the CPR and France took place in Warsaw in the mid-1950s.

[196] Robert Loh, "Setting the Stage for Foreigners," *The Atlantic*, vol. 204, no. 6 (December, 1959), pp. 80–84; Emmanuel John Hevi, *An African Student in China*, London: Pall Mall Press, 1963.

4

Objectives and Instrumentalities
of Foreign Policy

Many of the puzzling peculiarities of Communist Chinese external behavior arise out of frustration at the considerable gap that exists between
aims and desires, on the one hand, and available means and attainable results,
on the other.

■ SECURITY

The first essential for any individual or collective entity is to survive,
and therefore to achieve a tolerable degree of security from hostile external
influences.

It might be argued that the CPR has no serious external security problem, and that this very fact permits the CPR to behave as it does in international affairs. Reasonable though this argument may appear, however, this
does not seem to be the way in which the Communist Chinese leaders
view their situation. Even apart from the tendency to fear aggression from
the "imperialist camp," the United States in particular, on ideological
grounds, it must be remembered that China is a divided country. The
Communist regimes in all four of the divided countries — the others being
Korea, Vietnam, and Germany — find the United States allied in one way
or another with the non-Communist regimes and consider it as not only an
obstacle to reunification but a threat to survival. In addition, East Germany,
as well as the other East European countries and the Soviet Union itself,
has a deep fear of West Germany's military potential, even if unsupported
by the United States. On a somewhat reduced scale, the Communist Chinese

COMMUNIST CHINA ON THE WORLD STAGE

also fear Japan's military potential, particularly if it should be developed with American support. In all four Communist regimes in the divided countries, we find internal and external policies that are harsh and militant even by Communist standards. More than the others, the Chinese considers itself as overwhelmingly superior to its domestic opponent, and therefore as prevented from achieving territorial unification almost exclusively by the United States.

In terms of logical possibilities, the greatest threat to Chinese security would of course be a strategic attack with thermonuclear weapons. For the present and the indefinite future, such an attack could come only from the United States or the Soviet Union. Either possibility is remote, but it cannot safely be regarded by the CPC as zero, except probably for the case of a totally unprovoked attack by either of the two nuclear superpowers.

It is clear that Soviet bombers and missiles in the Far East are capable of hitting Chinese territory, and it has also become clear that a Sino-Soviet war cannot be dismissed as out of the question. The political deterrents to the use of nuclear weapons against a nonnuclear power being what they are, however, the most probable utility to the Soviet Union of its own nuclear weapons in the event of hostilities with the CPR would be to deter the latter from escalating the conflict beyond a fairly low level. Against the Soviet strategic military threat the CPR has no sure defense, since it obviously cannot rely on American protection, but it can clearly count under most circumstances on its own caution and on Soviet self-restraint.

An American attack presents a different problem. Although somewhat less unlikely, whether as an act of aggression or of retaliation, than a Soviet attack, an American decision to attack the CPR would have to reckon with the Sino-Soviet alliance. The alliance has been so eroded by tensions, however, that Soviet strategic protection for the CPR is at least open to doubt.[1] Indeed, it has apparently seemed doubtful to the CPC since about 1951, and since that time it has held its external behavior down to a level at which complications were unlikely to arise that could not be managed if necessary by the CPR itself, unaided except by American belief in the validity of the Sino-Soviet alliance.[2] It seems likely, although it cannot be proven, that Soviet strategic protection or retaliation is available to the CPR only in three

---

[1] Cf. ". . . the Peking leaders from time to time still utter highsounding hypocritical phrases that 'in the stern hour of trial' the CPR and the Soviet Union will always be together. But every sober-minded person will tell them: How do you intend to insure this when a filthy anti-Soviet propaganda campaign is going in China, when the most monstrous accusations are formulated against the Soviet Union from morning to night? Is not this dangerous political game, directed toward undermining the very foundations of Sino-Soviet friendship, too risky?" (Yu. Zhukov, "The Chinese Wall," *Pravda*, June 21, 1964).

[2] Cf. "In fighting imperialist aggression and defending its security, every socialist country has to rely in the first place on its own defense capability, and then — and only then — on assistance from fraternal countries and the people of the world" (Chinese government statement, August 15, 1963, New China News Agency dispatch, same date).

extremely improbable eventualities: an unprovoked American strategic attack on the CPR, a more localized air attack against targets near the Soviet border, or the landing of substantial American combat forces in Chinese territory anywhere near the Soviet border. In other cases, including an American strategic attack that was clearly provoked — and Chinese provocation of that order is another extremely improbable contingency — it is unlikely that the Soviet Union would do more than send military equipment and "volunteers" to help the CPR, as it hinted in 1962.[3] If the CPR were to disintegrate from internal weakness, accompanied perhaps by a Nationalist invasion, it is doubtful whether the Soviet Union would feel either able or obligated to restore the situation; it might confine itself to reestablishing spheres of influence in Manchuria and Sinkiang.

A more realistically possible threat to the security of the CPR than the ones so far mentioned is a Chinese Nationalist attack, timed probably to coincide with an internal crisis on the mainland, and supported by the United States, perhaps with tactical nuclear weapons. Against such a threat, which seems to have worried the CPC a great deal at certain times, Soviet protection is of doubtful availability, and the CPC must rely on maintaining domestic control, keeping its guard up, exercising due caution, and hoping for a continuation of real or assumed American irresolution.

In addition to strategic attack and local attack or border probes, the CPR is also nervous of the possibility that, as so often during the heyday of "imperialism," a strong foreign power might entrench itself on China's border and proceed to project a preponderant influence into the nearest region of China Proper. It should be borne in mind that China's frontier regions, apart from Manchuria, are in general sparsely populated by restless minorities, backward, and poorly connected with the rest of the country. Manchuria, the traditional "cockpit of Asia" and the CPR's major heavy industrial region, is also considered vulnerable even though it is much more developed. By far the most important reason why the CPR intervened in the Korean War was the determination to prevent a powerful American army from entrenching itself on the Yalu River, with possibly serious effects on the CPR's hold on Manchuria. Similarly, the CPR was worried in 1962 by what seemed to it the overly close approach of the Indian Army to the border of restless Tibet, and the CPR would also take a very dim view of any intrusions by American ground forces into such regions bordering directly on the CPR as North Vietnam or Laos.

Another logically possible threat that worries the CPR is one from India to the security of China's Himalayan frontier and to Tibet, which

[3] Cf. M. Domogatskikh and V. Karymov, "An Instructive Lesson," *Pravda*, July 7, 1962. There were other articles to the same effect in the Soviet press at this time, which was the twenty-fifth anniversary of the Japanese attack on China. The articles recalled that the Soviet Union has sent arms and "volunteers" to China (Nationalist, not Communist, as the articles failed to mention) at that time.

is in a state of unrest. Such a threat from India would be serious, in all probability, only if it coincided by accident or design with a threat from some other quarter.

There is no doubt that the time of maximum danger to the CPR's security, to date, was the period from its intervention in the Korean War (October, 1950) to the termination of the war (July, 1953). A second period of considerable danger, or at least assumed danger, occurred in the spring of 1962. The domestic situation was bad. The Chinese Nationalists appeared to be girding for an attempt at invasion, perhaps with American support. The United States sent troops into Thailand. The Indian Army was moving into border areas claimed by the CPR. The Soviet Union was beginning to create trouble along the Sino-Soviet frontier and to collude with rebellious minorities in Sinkiang. How the CPR continued to maintain its external security during these periods, as well as others less critical, is discussed elsewhere.

There is no doubt that, in view of the unreliability and uncontrollability of Soviet protection, and in any case the undesirability of being unduly dependent on it, the CPC believes that the best way to deter or combat threats to its security would be to acquire its own nuclear weapons and delivery systems, with a regional even if not an intercontinental range. Since this situation is some years in the future, the CPC generally behaves in a way that Mao has described as strategically bold but tactically cautious.

It should not necessarily be assumed that after the CPR acquires nuclear weapons its behavior, toward Taiwan or elsewhere, will become markedly bolder. Even the Soviet Union, after all, has succeeded since the Second World War in maintaining no more than an essentially minimum deterrent posture with respect to the United States.[4] This posture has proven to be an insufficient basis on which to make major strategic gains at the expense of the United States on those few occasions when an attempt has been made to do so, notably in Cuba in 1962. The addition of a nuclear Communist China to this situation need not make a decisive difference, since the United States clearly can more than match both the Communist powers combined in nuclear weapons for the indefinite future. Thus the gain to the CPR of a nuclear capability, and hence its main reason apart from prestige for seeking it, is likely to be more defensive than offensive.

It would clearly be a gain for the CPR's security, as well as for its influence in Asia, if American sea and air bases could be removed from the Far East and the Western Pacific. The CPC considers Japan to be the main such base; this is a reasonable view, especially when one realizes that when the CPC refers to Japan in this context it means to include Okinawa, with its huge complex of American bases.[5] Since the CPR is obviously in no position

---

[4] John R. Thomas, "The Role of Missile Defense in Soviet Strategy," *Military Review*, vol. xliv, no. 5 (May, 1964), pp. 46–58.

[5] Okinawa is the military keystone of American containment of the CPR.

to remove these bases by force, it must content itself with essentially political maneuvers, such as efforts to inflame local public feeling against the bases.

The CPR denies that the United States has any right to maintain bases or forces in the Far East, but it cannot openly do the same for the Soviet Union. Nevertheless, the remote Soviet threat as well as the more immediate American threat to Chinese security would be substantially reduced if the Far East and the Western Pacific became an atom-free zone, or better still a "peace zone" in which only indigenous states were allowed to have nuclear weapons. This consideration helps to explain the support, although a rather equivocal support, that the CPR has given to the concept of an atom-free zone since 1958.[6]

POWER

Although security is essential even if one lacks power, it is obvious that power is very helpful in the search for security.

An obvious element of future Chinese power, nuclear weapons, has already been mentioned. In addition, the CPR has maintained since 1949 the most powerful armed forces of any strictly Asian state, with the possible, partial, and recent exception of Indonesia.[7] From 1950 to 1960, the Communist Chinese armed forces were progressively modernized with Soviet aid, although the Soviet Union was careful to withhold from its Chinese ally, as it usually has from its other allies, any major, operational offensive weapons. After about 1955, the emphasis in the Soviet military aid program to the CPR shifted, as the Chinese desired, from weapons deliveries to aid in the construction of Chinese defense industries.[8] The entire program soon ran

---

[6] A Chinese government statement of July 31, 1963, demanded a "nuclear weapon-free zone of the Asian and Pacific region, including the United States, the Soviet Union, China, and Japan" (New China News Agency dispatch, same date).

[7] On Communist China's armed forces see, in addition to works already cited, Lt. Col. Robert B. Rigg, *Red China's Fighting Hordes*, Harrisburg, Pa.: The Military Service Publishing Company, 1951; Hanson W. Baldwin, "China as a Military Power," *Foreign Affairs*, vol. 30, no. 1 (October, 1951), pp. 51–62; P. G. Gittins, "The Red Dragon of China: A Brief Review of Communist China as a Military Power," *Australian Army Journal*, no. 132 (May, 1960), pp. 5–18; Allan S. Nanes, "Communist China's Armed Forces," *Current Scene* (Hong Kong), vol. i, no. 16 (October 25, 1961); Harold C. Hinton, "Communist China's Military Posture," *Current History*, vol. 43, no. 253 (September, 1962), pp. 149–155. On the political aspect see Harold C. Hinton in Harry L. Coles ed., *Total War and Cold War*, Ohio State University Press, 1962, pp. 266–292; Ralph L. Powell, *Politico-Military Relationships in Communist China*, Department of State: External Research Staff, 1963; J. Chester Cheng, "Problems of Chinese Communist Leadership as Seen in the Secret Military Papers," *Asian Survey*, vol. iv, no. 6 (June, 1964), pp. 861–872.

[8] Cf. Raymond L. Garthoff, "Sino-Soviet Military Relations," *The Annals of the American Academy of Political and Social Science*, vol. 349 (September, 1963), pp. 81–93. The CPR has stated, and the Soviet Union has not denied, that the Soviet Union

afoul of growing Sino-Soviet tensions, however, and was terminated during 1960. Since that time the absence of Soviet aid and spare parts deliveries and the continued weakness of the Chinese economy seem to have resulted in a fairly rapid obsolescence of Communist China's conventional military capabilities, except perhaps for the ground forces. The effort to acquire a nuclear capability undoubtedly continues.

Clearly the extent of the CPR's national power is affected by the degree to which it maintains internal political control and is believed abroad to maintain it. In this respect the CPR has had repeated, almost continuous, difficulties in the non-Chinese border areas, especially Tibet and Sinkiang, but much less trouble in China Proper. In the latter the most serious situation to date probably occurred in the spring of 1962, when the CPC was concerned not only about the external threats already mentioned but also apparently by the possibility, however slight, that party officials in relatively well-fed areas might withhold "surplus" grain from the famine areas.[9] This crisis, if such it was, passed without a disaster, although not without lingering aftereffects. On the whole, especially in view of the size of the country and its population, the poor state of communications and technology in general, and the record of previous Chinese regimes, the CPC has been remarkably successful in acquiring and maintaining internal control. The main reason for this is the fact that it is a "homegrown" totalitarian regime, one that learned how to control and manipulate populations before coming to power over the country as a whole, rather than one that came to power suddenly as the result of some accident or of installation in power by the Soviet Union. The CPC's success in acquiring and maintaining internal control has unquestionably increased the CPR's national power to a significant degree.

Power in the modern world of course requires an economic base, communications and heavy industry in particular. Measured against the standards of the modern West (including the Soviet Union) or those of its own ambitions, the CPR is still seriously deficient in these respects. On the other hand, by comparison with pre-Communist China or with any other Asian country except Japan, its performance has been fairly impressive. The highway and to a lesser extent the rail systems are being steadily extended into the border regions and toward the frontiers, for economic reasons as well as for political and military ones, whether offensive or defensive.[10] Industrial growth, which was rapid although precarious down to

agreed on October 15, 1957, to give the CPR at least token aid in the production of nuclear weapons but terminated the program on June 20, 1959, in the interest of Soviet-American relations (Chinese government statement of August 15, 1963, *loc. cit.*).

[9] Cf. *The Washington Post and Times Herald*, June 27, 1962.

[10] Cf. Denis Warner, "China's New Roads: Where Do They Lead?" *The Reporter*, September 26, 1963; *Christian Science Monitor*, February 8, 1964. There are road, rail, and air connections with all of the CPR's Communist neighbors (the Soviet Union, North Korea, Outer Mongolia, and North Vietnam). The connection with the Soviet

1960, was reversed by the crisis of that year, which was accentuated by the withdrawal of most Soviet aid, and it has not yet recovered from this disaster."[11]

The CPR's power, in the sense of the ability to enforce its will against objections or opposition, has almost certainly declined somewhat since 1960. Furthermore, it has never had the ability to project its power across salt water — to Japan, Taiwan (since 1950), or Indonesia, in particular. Nevertheless, and although the CPR still lives in the shadow of the vastly superior power of the United States and the Soviet Union, it remains the strongest strictly indigenous regime on the mainland of Asia, far ahead of its closest rivals, North and South Korea, North Vietnam, India, and Pakistan.

An important element of power is of course the extent to which the possessor is generally believed to be willing to use it. In this respect the CPC has been remarkably successful, even if one ignores its occasional remarks implying a bullish attitude toward a Third World War.[12] By means of repeated, carefully calculated resort to force — notably in Korea, over the offshore islands in 1954–55 and 1958, and along the Sino-Indian frontier in 1962 — the CPR has succeeded among other things in keeping alive a fairly general and somewhat exaggerated idea of its willingness to take its power out of reserve and commit it to action. This willingness, real and still more assumed, must be accounted a major component of the CPR's national power.

■ **UNIFICATION**

There can be no doubt that territorial unification ranks high on the CPR's list of external objectives. There have been occasional intimations

Union (opened at the beginning of 1956) is broad gauge from the point where it begins in Inner Mongolia; this is the only case where the Soviet broad gauge has been projected outside the Soviet frontier, and was almost certainly due to the insistence of the Outer Mongols on this form of protection from Chinese infiltration. There are thus change of gauge points in Inner Mongolia, at the Soviet frontier in Manchuria, and at the North Vietnamese frontier (the North Vietnamese railways are narrow gauge). An additional Sino-Soviet rail link via Sinkiang is supposedly under construction, but it is far behind schedule. There are also external highway connections with India and Laos; connections are being constructed with Nepal, and perhaps with Afghanistan and Pakistan (cf. A. R. Field, "Strategic Development in Sinkiang," *Foreign Affairs*, vol. 39, no. 2 [January, 1961], pp. 312–318). A rail connection with Burma is projected (see *China: Provisional Atlas of Communist Administrative Units*, Washington: Central Intelligence Agency, 1959, Plate 3). There are air connections with Hong Kong, Burma, Cambodia, Pakistan, Ceylon, and Indonesia.

[11] Cf. "Plain Living and Hard Struggle: An Economic Assessment," *Current Scene* (Hong Kong), vol. ii, no. 28 (February 15, 1964).

[12] "Of course, whether or not the imperialists will unleash a war is not determined by us; we are, after all, not their chief-of-staff. . . . On the debris of imperialism, the victorious people would create very swiftly a civilization thousands of times higher than the capitalist system and a truly beautiful future for themselves" (*Long Live Leninism, op. cit.*, pp. 21–22).

in official statements[13] and textbooks designed for internal circulation[14] that this objective might apply to the whole of the former Manchu empire, or even to the traditional tributary system at its maximum extent. Such statements appear, however, to be designed mainly for political effect, internal or external.

In reality the CPR's territorial claims are much more modest, nor is there any convincing evidence, apart from bombastic propaganda, that it is willing to take any serious risks in order to realize them. This objective, like the CPR's other objectives, is evidently expected to require a great deal of time for its fulfillment. Specifically, the CPR claims as of right, in addition to China Proper, Manchuria, Inner Mongolia, Sinkiang, Tibet, Taiwan (since the Cairo Declaration of 1943, as we have seen), and the Paracel and Spratly Islands in the South China Sea.[15] The first three of these regions were in Chinese Communist hands by the time of the end of the civil war on the mainland in 1949. Tibet was "liberated," by force, in 1950–51. Taiwan remains to be "liberated." The CPR does not appear as yet to have made any serious effort to establish control of the Paracel or Spratly Islands.

It is well known that the outer frontiers of these areas are not clear or generally agreed on in all cases. In fact, the CPR has or has had a border dispute of some sort with every country, Communist or non-Communist, on which it borders, with the apparent exception of North Vietnam.[16] In every case but two — India and the Soviet Union — these disputes have been settled through a compromise of one kind or another, sometimes to be sure after a crisis in which the CPR has employed considerable pressure. In none of these settlements does the CPR seem to have insisted on its maximum demands, and the latter must therefore be regarded mainly as bargaining devices. The Indian and Soviet disputes are still unresolved, but there is reason to think that the CPR would also settle these, under conditions it considered appropriate, on the basis of something less than its maximum demands.

Territorial unification is a major objective, then, but it is not a fetish, still less a be-all and end-all to be pursued at suicidal risk.

Something further needs to be said about Taiwan, in view of its peculiar position and importance as the seat of a rival government claiming jurisdiction over the whole of China.

Both the Communist and the Nationalist regimes regard Taiwan as

---

[13] E.g., "A Comment on the Statement of the CPUSA," *People's Daily*, March 8, 1963.

[14] E.g., the one discussed in Jacques Jacquet-Francillon, "The Borders of China: Mao's Bold Challenge to Khrushchev," *The New Republic*, April 20, 1963, pp. 18–22.

[15] On the CPR's claim to the Paracels and Spratlys, which obviously have potential naval importance, see Maps 33, 34, and 36 in *Atlas of the Northern Frontier of India*, New Delhi: Ministry of External Affairs, 1960.

[16] Cf. Guy Searls, "Communist China's Border Policy: Dragon Throne Imperialism?" *Current Scene* (Hong Kong), vol. ii, no. 12 (April 15, 1963).

Chinese territory, a view that is not necessarily shared by the indigenous Taiwanese. To the Communists, the "liberation" of Taiwan would constitute the biggest single step remaining to be taken toward the unification of China. It would confer on them unquestioned sole custody of the symbols of China's sovereignty and status, including general diplomatic recognition (except perhaps for that of the United States) and China's permanent seat on the United Nations Security Council, assuming that these had not already been acquired.

On the other hand, the Chinese Communists clearly realize that a military "liberation" of Taiwan was rendered impossible by the extension of American protection to the island on June 27, 1950. For the present, this would cease to be true only if the Soviet Union were to lend active military support to a Communist attack on Taiwan.

It is equally clear that the Soviet Union has been most reluctant to become involved in the CPR's quest for the "liberation" of Taiwan and that the CPR has been determined to involve it. The CPR has consistently maintained since June, 1950, that the United States was committing aggression against the CPR by occupying, or in other words protecting, Taiwan, the clear implication being that the Soviet Union was obligated under the Sino-Soviet alliance to take whatever action might be necessary to eliminate the American presence from Taiwan and turn the island over to the control of the CPR.[17]

The situation might also change when and if the CPR acquires its own nuclear capability, but this is still some time in the future. The situation would certainly change if the United States withdrew its protection from Taiwan, but there is no sign of this despite the Communists' best efforts to erode the American military position in the Far East and the Western Pacific through political action.

Realistically speaking, there is no way at present for the Communists to "liberate" Taiwan except by means of a political arrangement with the Nationalists that would have as one of its main features a repudiation by the latter of American protection. The Communists have always been careful to keep open the possibility of such an accommodation. They have never demanded unconditional surrender — a meaningless term in the contemporary world, in any case — by the Nationalists. Rather, they have implicitly held up as a model, not the harsh terms proposed to Nationalist

---

[17] Khrushchev once stated a willingness to give military support to the CPR in connection with the "liberation" of Taiwan in an interview with Governor Averell Harriman (see *Life*, July 13, 1959, p. 36), but this was almost certainly bluster for political effect. The main purpose was probably to deter the Chinese Nationalists and the United States from threatening the mainland when the Communists were involved in Tibet and on the Himalayan frontier. A secondary purpose was probably to support Marshal P'eng Te-huai, one of whose arguments in opposition to the policies being pursued by the CPC evidently was that Soviet protection could be relied on, provided the CPC did not antagonize the Soviet Union unduly, and that the CPR therefore did not have to strain its economy further in order to produce nuclear weapons.

Acting President Li Tsung-jen in April, 1949, but the relatively moderate terms granted to General Fu Tso-yi when he surrendered Peking in January, 1949. To date, the Nationalists on Taiwan are not known to have shown serious interest in Communist efforts to persuade them to accept a subordinate if allegedly secure place in the Communist system.[18]

The problem cannot be disposed of quite so simply, however. A curious dialogue takes place across the Taiwan Strait. Each side asserts and demonstrates, from time to time, its independence of its powerful ally and patron. The Communists' demonstration of independence has been wholly convincing since 1960, when they accepted the termination of Soviet economic and military aid rather than abandon their political pressures on the Russians. The Nationalists, as the weaker party, have not yet felt it feasible to give a comparable demonstration of independence. Their closest approach to one so far has been the Black Friday riots of May 24, 1957, in Taipei, which stemmed from anger at the refusal of the United States to pay to its Chinese ally the tribute it had paid to its Japanese former enemy, that of signing a status-of-forces agreement. It is a curious fact that most of the prominent individuals[19] who have gotten into serious political difficulties on either side of the Taiwan Strait have had closer-than-average connections with the foreign patron of each one's respective regime. Each party to the dialogue across the Taiwan Strait accuses the other of subservience to its patron — the Nationalists, to be sure, have modified their charges in the light of the Sino-Soviet dispute — not so much because it believes its own charges as to discredit the other and to evoke further demonstrations of independence from it.

Certainly many obstacles stand in the way of a political accommodation between Peking and Taipei, among them the convincing demonstration by the Communists in 1957, when they silenced and persecuted their "rightist" critics, that there is no secure place in the Communist system for the dissenter. On the other hand at least two obstacles, Mao Tse-tung and Chiang Kai-shek, will presumably not be operative much longer. Furthermore, the Nationalists must face the fact that the Communist regime shows no signs of internal collapse, that their own example and appeals have failed to capture the imagination of the mainland Chinese as an alternative to the Communist regime, and that they have little prospect of conquering the mainland by force.

It appears, then, that neither side is in a position to impose its will on

---

[18] Cf. Lewis Gilbert, "Peking and Taipei," *The China Quarterly*, no. 15 (July–September, 1963), pp. 56–64. Chiang Kai-shek's memoirs, *Soviet Russia in China: A Summing-Up at Seventy*, New York: Farrar, Straus and Cudahy, 1957, represent among other things a rejection of Communist overtures, which were especially obvious in 1956, on the ground that the historical record shows that the good faith of neither the Chinese Communists nor the Soviet Union can be trusted.

[19] On the mainland: Kao Kang and P'eng Te-huai. On Taiwan: K. C. Wu, Sun Li-jen, and Lei Chen.

the other, and that the only workable alternative to the present state of suppressed war would be one that could be agreed to, tacitly at least, by both sides. One obvious possibility would be a "two Chinas situation," which would probably require among other things a Nationalist evacuation of the offshore islands, but neither side has so far given any persuasive evidence of willingness to accept such a solution. A more likely outcome, in the long run at any rate, and barring the collapse of either regime, would be reunification through some sort of accommodation.[20] If this materializes, it would be a striking vindication of General de Gaulle's belief that national identity is a more durable force than ideology.

■ INFLUENCE

The CPR's objectives under the heading of influence may be discussed fairly briefly, since for the most part they have already been treated in the previous chapter.

The first is hegemony of some sort on at least the mainland of eastern Asia. As a first major step toward this goal, the CPR would probably like its land frontiers to be ringed, insofar as possible, with buffers, which need not be satellites. As usual, it has given no evidence of an intent to force this process at the cost of incurring serious risks. The process is going ahead, nonetheless, fairly slowly and as inconspicuously as possible. The CPC would also like the greatest influence attainable, again short of unacceptable risks or political costs, on the other Asian Communist Parties.

The CPC clearly aspires to a leading role, of some kind that it may not claim to be able to foresee, in the "socialist camp" and the international Communist movement. This has been conceded by most students of Sino-Soviet relations since 1963, when the CPC began seriously trying to set up an "international" of its own in rivalry with the parties that tend to support the Soviet Union. The CPC evidently expects, or at least claims to expect, that the Soviet-led coalition will disintegrate from its internal ideological errors and political weaknesses, so that the victory will fall to the CPC almost by default.

The CPC certainly aspires to provide a "model," or example, and if possible a degree of leadership, for the whole of the underdeveloped areas (the "oppressed nations"). This implies the ultimate exclusion of Soviet as well as American influence from these regions.

The CPC apparently hopes to make China, by about the end of the

---

[20] Speaking purely hypothetically, such an accommodation might involve political, economic, and military autonomy for Taiwan, perhaps under the guise of a federation with the mainland, at least nominal participation by its leaders in a unified coalition government, and a unified representation in foreign countries and the United Nations. There is an obvious likelihood that such an arrangement would prove to be no more than temporary.

twentieth century, a superpower comparable to the United States and the Soviet Union. This implies such things as the creation of a first-class industrial economy, although not necessarily of high living standards; a nuclear and space capability; United Nations representation and control of China's seat on the Security Council; and the right to an active role in the settlement of all major international issues.

The complete satisfaction of this desire for superpower status being unlikely, the CPR might decide that the best way to compensate for its limitations without entirely giving up its ambitions is to try to play the role of balancing power between the United States and the Soviet Union. Such a role, if it were actually attempted, would presumably require a lessening of Sino-American tension sufficient to allow the CPR to assume a posture of approximate equi-distance between the United States and the Soviet Union.

Finally, the CPC claims to anticipate and probably does anticipate the eventual worldwide triumph of "communism," however that term may be defined as a concept and organized as a system at the time of its hypothetical triumph.[21] The Chinese view of this subject, at least as expressed in 1958, differs significantly from older Marxist-Leninist formulations and from Khrushchev's recent interpretation of them by implying that a country need not be economically and culturally advanced in order to be said to have attained "communism," but may be "poor and blank," like China.[22]

■ POLICY INSTRUMENTALITIES

The instrumentalities that the CPC has employed to date in pursuit of its external objectives occupy a rather wide spectrum with respect to the degree of violence involved and can be categorized conveniently as violent, semiviolent and nonviolent.

Apart from intervention in Korea, which taught the CPC a painful lesson on the disadvantages of challenging American military power too

---

21 "However many twists and turns may await us on our forward journey, humanity will eventually reach its bright destiny — communism. There is no force that can stop it." ("More on the Historical Experience Concerning the Dictatorship of the Proletariat," *People's Daily*, December 29, 1956).

22 The term "poor and blank" was first used by Mao Tse-tung ("Introducing a Cooperative," *Red Flag*, June 1, 1958) to describe the economic and cultural state of the Chinese people in 1958, when the CPC was claiming that "the attainment of communism in China is no longer a remote future event" (Decision of the Eighth Central Committee of the CPC, August 29, 1958 [New China News Agency dispatch, September 10, 1958]). Shortly afterward the time table was stretched out with the admission that "the socialist system will have to continue [in China] for a very long time" before the attainment of "communism" (resolution of the Sixth Plenary Session of the Eighth Central Committee of the CPC, December 10, 1958 [New China News Agency dispatch, December 18, 1958), but the CPC has not admitted publicly that "communism" presupposes economic and cultural abundance.

forcefully, the Chinese employment of overt violence in external relations has consisted mainly of military actions in or near the Taiwan Strait (in 1954–55 and in 1958) and armed incursions into disputed border areas (India from 1950 on, Burma intermittently from about 1952 to 1961) or demilitarized zones (Nepal briefly in 1960). In each of these cases, the CPC was trying to eliminate or head off something that it regarded as a threat to its security, and in each case it employed subterfuges of one kind or another to confuse the opposition and minimize international ill will and the chances of unwanted escalation. Similar subterfuges can be expected in similar situations in the future. The CPC, for example, can deny that the incident occurred at all, assert that only Chinese "volunteers" and not regular troops were involved, claim that the incident took place on Chinese soil or in Chinese territorial waters, charge the other side with being the intruder or aggressor, or some combination of these.

In keeping with its typically communist desire to have the fruits of war without war, the CPC makes use of a number of ambiguous or borderline instrumentalities that may be called semiviolent. These include border disputes (mainly with India and the Soviet Union), subversion, threats of military action either by regular forces or "volunteers," military demonstrations (such as the heavy redeployment near the Taiwan Strait in the spring of 1962), and military aid and advice to communist allies (North Korea and North Vietnam) and foreign left-wing movements.

At the lower end of the spectrum of violence, the CPC of course makes use of a number of nonviolent instrumentalities, some of which are potentially applicable to any other country, others only to nearby Asian countries. Among the former category, the first is diplomacy; a good example of Chinese communist diplomacy is the effort in recent years to bolster China's political position in East Asia by establishing or strengthening friendly relations with countries that are either weak neutrals incapable of rivaling China for regional leadership (such as Burma and Cambodia), the enemies of China's enemies (such as Pakistan), or the objects of Soviet wooing (such as Indonesia). A second nonviolent instrumentality is Communist China's extensive program of "people's diplomacy" (cultural relations and propaganda) directed at groups, mainly but not exclusively leftist, whose opinions Peking wishes to influence or confirm.[24]

Thirdly, China attempts both to pressure and attract other countries, especially underdeveloped ones, through trade and aid, roughly one quarter of its activity in both fields being directed outside the Communist bloc down to about 1960. Since then, the emphasis has shifted to non-bloc countries. Since 1956, when it made its first aid commitment to a non-Communist country (Cambodia), the CPR has extended (down to mid-1964) credits of

---

[24] For an excellent study of this see Herbert Passin, *China's Cultural Diplomacy*, New York: Praeger, 1963.

various kinds, often interest-free, totaling about half a billion dollars to Afro-Asian countries, as well as to Cuba. The recipients have generally drawn only a part of their credits, which of course can be used only for Chinese goods and services, and have often found these goods and services to be of inferior quality. The non-Communist Afro-Asian recipients of Chinese credits have been Burma, Laos, Cambodia, Indonesia, Ceylon, Nepal, Yemen, Algeria, Ghana, Guinea, Mali, Nigeria, Somalia, Zanzibar, Kenya, and Tanganyika. The Chinese aid program is far smaller than the American or Soviet program, with both of which it attempts to compete, and is conducted along different lines; it does not, for example, include aid in the field of heavy industry. While in Mali in January, 1964, Chou En-lai laid down "eight principles" governing the CPR's economic aid program: mutuality of benefit, "no strings," low interest or none, a goal of self-sufficiency rather than dependence, emphasis on light industry ("projects which require less investment while yielding quicker results"), valuations at international market prices (which are high when charged for generally inferior Chinese equipment), training of local personnel to operate the enterprises constructed with Chinese aid, and living standards for Chinese personnel no higher than those of corresponding personnel of the country in question.[25] To the extent that they are practiced, these principles are obviously not to be wholly condemned. On the other hand, the principles are designed to secure a maximum political return, including the fostering of the public sector in the economy of the aided country, from a modest economic outlay. In the case of industrial countries, including Japan, the CPR seeks trade (especially since 1960) not only for economic reasons but also to split the country in question from the United States, to increase the chances of diplomatic recognition, and to promote other such political objectives.

Fourthly, the CPC maintains liaison with most if not all foreign Communist Parties, by both covert and overt means. It tries to influence them in directions favorable to itself, or (since 1963) to split them and form pro-Chinese splinter parties. The CPC maintains covert party branches among overseas communities. Chou En-lai promised that they would be dissolved when he was in Southeast Asia at the end of 1956, but this does not appear to have been done.

In its dealings with nearby countries the CPC employs such special techniques as organized covert migration (to Burma), the harboring and exploitation of political exiles, the maintenance of "autonomous" minority areas near the border as a possible means of influencing kindred minorities across the frontier, and manipulation of various overseas Chinese communities within limits dictated by Chinese desire for good relations with indigenous governments and ethnic groups.

---

[25] Chou's report on his trip to the Standing Committee of the National People's Congress (excerpts released by New China News Agency, April 25, 1964).

■ THE RELATIONSHIP BETWEEN OBJECTIVES
AND INSTRUMENTALITIES

In general, the CPC has tended to reserve overt violence for the defense of its security — as interpreted of course by itself — and has attempted to enhance its influence mainly through semiviolent and nonviolent means. On the other hand, whereas the CPC has shown itself to be willing to use violence in defense of its security, including violence of a preemptive or forestalling kind, it has always (except in the spring of 1951, in Korea) shown great caution in its employment of even defensive violence. The main, but not sole, restraint has been the fear of American retaliation. The same consideration has dictated even greater restraint on any unambiguously offensive use of force. Notwithstanding all the talk about Chinese bellicosity, one looks in vain for instances in recent years of Chinese military aggression, in the sense of attacks against neighboring countries or foreign forces that were not motivated, largely at least, by fear for Chinese security.[26] Offensive action is restrained not only by fear of American retaliation or other military consequences, but also by a realization that acts of aggression would adversely affect the prospects for achieving the CPR's long-term political objectives.

The CPC is apparently convinced, however, that the United States will not retaliate for anything less than an overt Chinese resort to violence. A combination of traditional Chinese arrogance and Communist doctrinarism, therefore, has produced a recurrent Chinese tendency to overestimate the extent to which the CPC's influence objectives, especially in the underdeveloped areas and Asia in particular, could be safely and advantageously promoted by a very energetic employment of ambiguous semiviolent techniques, as well as by nonviolent ones. When such an overestimate has occurred the result has generally been a setback.

On the whole, however, the record to date of Communist Chinese foreign policy in promoting the CPR's objectives, both national and revolutionary, has been fairly impressive.

---

[26] As will be shown later, these considerations apply essentially even to the CPC's policy toward Taiwan, the offshore islands, and the Sino-Indian frontier.

5

The Sino-Soviet Alliance
and the West

During the period since 1949 as a whole, the CPC has considered its main enemy and obstacle to be what it calls "the imperialist camp headed by the United States." Generally speaking, the CPC has regarded the Sino-Soviet alliance as its main shield, and potentially at least as its main sword as well, against the "imperialist camp." But to what extent has the CPR's entangling alliance actually helped it in coping with its adversary?

■ THE ALLIANCE UNDER STALIN

In modern times China has been so vast and chaotic that no foreign power has felt fully able to understand it, let alone control it. The nearest thing to an exception was Japan, between 1937 and 1945. On the whole, and again with the partial exception of Japan, the powers' main interest in China has been to prevent it from becoming the cause of a major war.

This generalization applied to Stalin. As we have seen, during and for a short time after the Second World War he made efforts to ensure that China would not become the occasion of hostilities between the Soviet Union and the United States. When the CPC came to power in 1949, it was probably under no illusion that its policy of "leaning to one side" could prevent Stalin from pursuing his own interests in Manchuria and Sinkiang. The CPC almost certainly did hope and believe, however, that by allying itself with the Soviet Union it could insure against another deal between Stalin and the United States over China. The Cold War alone probably did not seem to the CPC to provide adequate insurance. Focused as it was on

Europe and the Middle East, it prevented an overall Soviet American settlement, but it might also have impelled Stalin, if not to make a deal over China, at least to abandon it quietly to its fate. When the alliance was signed in February, 1950, Taiwan was not yet under American protection, and the alliance probably had no genuinely offensive purpose. It was probably Stalin, rather than Mao, who preferred to name Japan instead of the United States as the power against whose alleged aggressive tendencies the alliance was explicitly directed.

The CPC was probably under no impression that it could expect much protection from the Soviet Union's infant nuclear capability, which Stalin himself made virtually no effort to exploit in his dealings with the West. The main military deterrent to "imperialist aggression" against the CPR after the signing of the Sino-Soviet alliance, as to such action against the Soviet Union, was the real or assumed Soviet ability to invade Western Europe. Practically speaking, this was a blackmail threat without any actual intent to invade, but it was certainly effective and was of course the main reason for the formation of NATO. Even after that, and certainly during the Korean War, the possibility of a Soviet invasion of Western Europe remained a powerful factor in the thinking of Western statesmen, and by the same token a restraint on military action against the CPR.

From this restraint the CPR benefited greatly after it threw down an open military challenge to "imperialism" by intervening in the Korean War in October, 1950. As a measure of deterrence against American extension of the war to Manchuria, Stalin prolonged the Soviet military presence in Port Arthur beyond 1952, when it would normally have terminated under the agreements of 1950. On the other hand, he made no threatening gestures or statements of any importance in support of the CPR, at least until near the end of the war. He forced the CPR to bear not only the human but most of the economic cost of its intervention in Korea, and there are indications that there was resentment in the CPR over this policy.[1]

The divergence between the Soviet and Chinese roles in the Korean War placed serious strains on the Sino-Soviet alliance. Participation in the war under the protecting wing of the alliance did not enable the CPR to realize its three main demands, which were for the withdrawal of American forces from Korea, the removal of American protection from Taiwan, and the CPR's admission to the United Nations. It is very likely, nevertheless, that the CPC has since come to feel that Stalin was preferable as an ally to his successors. As will be shown later (in Chapter 8), he was apparently prepared to take strong action, just before the end of the war, in order to rescue the CPR from having to sign an armistice that would prevent it from regaining control over all or most of the prisoners it had lost. Thus at

---

[1] Cf. Raymond L. Garthoff, "Sino-Soviet Military Relations," *The Annals of the American Academy of Political and Social Science*, vol. 349 (September, 1963). p. 85.

the end Stalin proved himself once more to be what the CPC has since called him, "an uncompromising enemy of imperialism."

■ **THE ALLIANCE DURING THE SOVIET SUCCESSION STRUGGLE (1953–55)**

Stalin's heirs were much less uncompromising. In fact, they left the CPR to sink or swim, or rather to sign an armistice that was unfavorable as far as the prisoner issue was concerned. Probably by design, Malenkov's announcement that the Soviet Union possessed the hydrogen bomb was not made until August 8, 1953, after the signing of the Korean armistice and the same day, incidentally, as the initialing of a mutual defense treaty between the United States and South Korea.

The year 1954 was a difficult one for the Sino-Soviet alliance. Like the Korean War a year earlier, the Indochina crisis reached a climax in the early months of 1954. Although there was a general desire for peace, except perhaps on the part of the North Vietnamese, the CPR could not rule out the possibility of an American escalation of the crisis in an effort to secure more favorable terms. As usual, the Soviet Union was preoccupied mainly with Europe, and specifically with a desire to ensure the euthanasia of the proposed European Defense Community. Probably most important of all, the United States initiated an awe-inspiring series of hydrogen bomb tests in the Pacific in March and announced at about the same time that it had developed operational tactical nuclear weapons. In January, Secretary Dulles announced the disturbing doctrine of "massive retaliation." American forces in Europe were equipped with tactical nuclear weapons a few years later. This tended to cancel the blackmail effect of the Soviet threat to invade Western Europe, and hence impaired somewhat the protective value of the Sino-Soviet alliance to the CPR. The Soviet Union soon acquired the ability to attack and probably destroy, and therefore to blackmail, Western Europe by means of bombers and then by means of medium range missiles, but for reasons that will be suggested shortly this was not a threat of comparable military credibility or political effectiveness to the earlier assumed ability to invade.

At this point, the Chinese party to the Sino-Soviet alliance was not entirely naked to its enemies, however. For one thing, the United States had been formally allied with Japan since the spring of 1952, a fact that under the wording of the Sino-Soviet alliance gave the CPR the full right to invoke Soviet protection in the event of an American attack. In the summer of 1954, when tension was building up in the Taiwan Strait, the CPR began to stress the "indivisibility of peace in Europe and Asia."[2] This

---

[2] Alice Langley Hsieh, *Communist China's Strategy in the Nuclear Era*, Englewood Cliffs, N.J.: Prentice-Hall, 1962, pp. 17–18.

presumably meant that, notwithstanding the disadvantageous strategic situation facing the Soviet Union, it should regard the protection of the CPR and the support of its major objectives, the "liberation" of Taiwan in particular, as equally important with its own interests in Europe. The CPR also probably intended to imply that the Soviet Union should be willing to exert diversionary pressures in Europe, on West Berlin for example, on behalf of the CPR.

Military developments in the Soviet Union seemed to hold some promising possibilities. As the CPC has recently reminded the world,[3] the foundations of Soviet nuclear and missile power were laid during Stalin's reign. Nevertheless, Stalin's preoccupation with land warfare and the alleged "permanently operating factors" of war seriously inhibited Soviet thinking until after his death.[4] Discussion of all aspects of military doctrine then began among Soviet military men. At the policy-making level, there occurred what amounted to a public debate on strategy between Malenkov and Khrushchev, much of it evidently precipitated by the "massive retaliation" doctrine. Malenkov regarded general war as "unthinkable," took a relatively mild line toward the West, and minimized the Soviet strategic commitment to the CPR; such an attitude was probably necessitated by his program for giving the Soviet citizen a better life, known as the New Course. Mainly no doubt in order to differentiate himself from Malenkov and bid for the political support of the Soviet armed forces, Khrushchev took a roughly opposite line: the Soviet Union should not merely avoid war, but actively deter it through a strong military posture and be ready to fight it if necessary. Clearly Khrushchev's position implied a greater willingness and ability to honor Soviet commitments to the CPR and was therefore the more acceptable of the two to the CPC.[5] This in turn paved the way for Khrushchev to receive, as he evidently did when he went to Peking in September–October, 1954, at least passive Chinese support for his bid to unseat Malenkov from the premiership, which he made soon afterward. There is no reason to think, however, that Khrushchev made any major new strategic commitments to the CPR at that time. The joint communiqué did not mention the "indivisibility of peace." The decision then announced to withdraw Soviet troops from Port Arthur (in Manchuria), although in keeping with general Soviet policy and perhaps satisfying to Chinese pride, also removed an element of deterrence against possible American attack on Manchuria. Furthermore, Khrushchev's public pronouncements on the Taiwan Strait crisis that had erupted shortly before his arrival in Peking were little more than ritualistic.

Whatever the reliability of Soviet strategic support and protection

---

[3] "On the Question of Stalin, "*People's Daily* and *Red Flag*, September 13, 1963.

[4] Cf. H. S. Dinerstein, *War and the Soviet Union*, rev. ed., New York: Praeger, 1962, pp. 33–36.

[5] Hsieh, *op. cit.*, pp. 8–9, 24–25.

for the CPR, the latter had every reason to want to improve its own military posture, with the aid of Soviet military equipment. It had begun to do this during the Korean War, which clearly demonstrated the inadequacy of the military establishment inherited from the civil war for coping with a first class opponent. The CPR therefore streamlined and modernized the organization of its armed forces during 1954 and 1955, in addition to introducing conscription. It also permitted, and probably encouraged, active discussion of strategic issues by its military leaders, much as the Soviet Union was then doing. A tendency emerged toward a division of opinion between the relatively professionally oriented officers of the "People's Liberation Army" General Staff and the relatively party-oriented officers in the newly created Defense Ministry. The former stressed the importance of modern weapons, surprise attack, and the desirability of an independent Chinese strategic capability (presumably including nuclear weapons) regardless of expense, and by implication disparaged the utility of Mao's military thought and of rigid party controls over the armed forces. The Defense Ministry officers, on the other hand, stressed the importance of men rather than weapons in modern war, the probability that even a nuclear war launched against China would be a "broken-backed" one in which China would ultimately emerge victorious, insisted that the acquisition of a Chinese strategic capability be subordinated to long-term economic development, claimed to be confident that China could rely on Soviet deterrent protection, and exalted Mao's military thought and party control over the armed forces.[6] The issue remained unresolved for the time being, probably because its resolution depended partly on external developments.

■ THE ALLIANCE DURING KHRUSHCHEV'S ASCENDANCY (1955–59)

Khrushchev's partial triumph over Malenkov, in February, 1955, was marked by Bulganin's assumption of the premiership and Zhukov's appointment as Defense Minister. Almost immediately there appeared in the Soviet military press a number of articles dealing with the role of surprise attack in modern war and strongly implying that the Soviet Union must be prepared to launch a preemptive attack in the event that it saw reason to believe that the enemy was planning a surprise attack against it.[7] The probable reason for this apocalyptic line of thinking is that by this time the Soviet bomber and missile programs had progressed to such a point that Moscow feared the United States might feel tempted to strike first and naturally wished to deter it from doing so. The Soviet stress on a preemptive attack also obviously reflected a lack of confidence in an ability

---

[6] *Ibid.*, pp. 21, 32ff.
[7] Dinerstein, *op. cit.*, pp. 184ff.

to survive an enemy first strike with enough retaliatory capacity to launch its own strike. In reality, then, the seemingly tough talk appears to have stemmed from a feeling of insecurity and vulnerability.

Khrushchev's general foreign policy at that time was compatible with such an interpretation. The emphasis was on Europe, where he took a number of conciliatory steps such as the Austrian state treaty. He made no belligerent moves or statements with respect to the Taiwan Strait crisis, which reached a peak of tension in March, 1955. The Soviet Union had been working toward a summit meeting since the autumn of 1954 and did not want to be sidetracked. On March 10, 1955, it made a new set of disarmament proposals that came far closer than any it had made previously to being acceptable to the West; these proposals showed a particular interest in safeguards against surprise attack. At the Geneva summit conference (July 18–23, 1955), no progress was made toward a German settlement and very little toward disarmament. The tone, however, was friendly. More important, however, it was the first conference of its kind in a decade, and the CPR, which was insisting that it deserved a permanent seat on the United Nations Security Council and a place at all major international conferences, was of course not represented. The spectre of some sort of deal between the Soviet Union and the West that would tend to reduce the reliability of Soviet protection of and support for the CPR must have suggested itself in Peking.

The CPC's obsession with self-strengthening, to borrow a hackneyed phrase favored by Chinese reformers of the nineteenth century, is well known. Whatever other arguments there may be in favor of socialization of the economy, and of agriculture in particular, it is unlikely that the CPC would ever have gone in for it unless it believed that socialization contributed materially, even if only in the long run, to industrialization and general self-strengthening. It is also entirely possible, under a totalitarian regime such as that of the CPR, that the elapsed time between the perception of an assumed need for increased self-strengthening and the initiation of steps to fill this need, through an acceleration of socialization, might be very short.

The first occasion on which Chinese behavior tended to bear out this hypothesis occurred in 1955. The Chinese First Five Year Plan, in the form in which it was belatedly published on July 5–6, visualized roughly one-third of all peasant households in "lower level, or semisocialist, agricultural producer cooperatives" by the end of 1957.[8] These "cooperatives" were similar (apart from the absence of machinery) to Soviet collective farms, except that they were smaller and the peasants retained nominal title to their

---

[8] *Communist China 1955–1959: Policy Documents with Analysis*, Harvard University Press, 1962, pp. 55, 65. Party policy on the rate of socialization had been oscillating for several months previously, on the basis it would appear of domestic rather than external considerations (*ibid.*, pp. 92–93).

land. In a speech delivered on July 31, not long afterward and only a few days after the Geneva summit conference, Mao raised the quota to 43 per cent by the end of 1956.[9] The speech was not published until October 16, 1955, presumably in order not to disrupt the autumn harvest, and its publication was followed by a rapid series of decisions further accelerating the process of socialization. In actual fact, 87.8 per cent of all peasant households were in "higher level, or fully socialist, agricultural producer co-operatives," or in other words collective farms minus machinery, by the end of 1956.[10] So rapid was the acceleration of the pace that it is reasonable to suppose that the final result was already envisaged at the time of Mao's speech but was only revealed to the public by installments, for political reasons. If so, the case for the hypothesis that the decision was connected with security considerations crystallized by the Geneva summit conference, and specifically with the apparent materialization of the CPR's constant bugbear, a Soviet-American détente that would further weaken the reliability of Soviet strategic protection of the CPR, is strengthened.

Since 1949, so many issues had accumulated between the CPR and the United States that, in spite of the mutual unwillingness to establish diplomatic relations, it had become worse not to talk about them than to talk about them. The United States was concerned in particular about the fate of American civilian and military personnel taken prisoner by the CPR, some of whom were known to be still in jail but others of whom were unaccounted for. Informal Sino-American talks on this question began in 1954, during the Geneva Conference on Indochina.[11] At the beginning of 1955, United Nations Secretary General Dag Hammarskjold visited Peking in an effort to secure the prisoners' release; he failed, but he conferred a welcome element of prestige on the CPR. At the same time, in the CPR's eyes, the United States complicated the situation by signing a mutual security agreement with the Republic of China providing formally for an American defense of Taiwan, and thus allegedly inaugurating a "two Chinas" policy (i.e., tending to perpetuate the division of China by preventing a Communist "liberation" of Taiwan). The Taiwan Strait crisis then in progress showed among other things that the CPR was in no position to remedy this situation by force, especially in the absence of active Soviet support. Accordingly, as we have seen, Chou En-lai at the Bandung Conference proposed Sino-American talks on the status of Taiwan, presumably in the hope of promoting by guile what could not be seized outright.

With British and Indian encouragement and mediation, Sino-American ambassadorial talks began at Geneva on August 1. The CPR released some

---

[9] *Ibid.*, pp. 95–96.

[10] Edwin Jones, "Peking's Economy: Upwards or Downwards?" *Problems of Communism*, vol. xii, no. 1 (January-February, 1963), p. 18.

[11] See the excellent survey of Sino-American ambassadorial talks in *The New York Times*, April 22, 1964.

of its American prisoners at that time and during the next few months,[12] and an "agreed announcement" issued by both negotiators on September 10 pledged the release of all nationals of either side who were held by the other.[13] The CPR continued, however, to hold some of its American prisoners and not to account for others, presumably in order to retain an element of leverage on the United States. The CPR also demanded that the United States ease its trade controls and agree to a meeting of foreign ministers, proposals for which the American side showed little enthusiasm. The CPR adamantly refused an American demand that it agree to a "renunciation of force" with respect to Taiwan, insisting that the United States had no right to prevent it from "liberating" Taiwan by any means it chose.[14] In January, 1956, immediately after the fact of a deadlock had become obvious, the CPR shifted the focus of its efforts to "liberate" Taiwan from the United States to the Nationalists.

Sufficient strains had accumulated in the Sino-Soviet alliance, as well as in other aspects of Sino-Soviet relations, to make the Twentieth Congress of the CPSU, which opened on February 14, 1956 (the anniversary of the signing of the alliance), an event of great interest to the CPC. Its delegation to the congress was led by Chu Teh, its military elder statesman; the other members were specialists in party and ideological affairs. The delegation stayed in the Soviet Union for more than a month after the close of the Congress and returned to Peking on April 2, whereupon a Politburo meeting was immediately held, and the *People's Daily* published its first editorial on the "de-Stalinization" question.[15] More important from the standpoint of the alliance, Mikoyan promptly arrived in Peking, in a visit that had presumably been arranged during Chu Teh's stay in the Soviet Union, and signed on April 7 an important economic aid agreement.[16] As it later turned out, this included a commitment to provide the CPR with a small nuclear research reactor, which was installed and put into operation in 1958.

The problems for the Sino-Soviet alliance raised by the Twentieth Congress and by Khrushchev's policies in general, however, were too serious to be resolved by such agreements or by the increasing Soviet deliveries of machine tools for the manufacture of conventional weapons. The CPC wanted to be able to stand on its own feet as much and as soon as possible, but it also wanted protection and support from its more powerful ally.

In his important opening report to the congress,[17] Khrushchev indicated, underneath clouds of optimistic verbiage, a massive fear of general

---

[12] Cf. *The New York Times*, August 2, 1955.

[13] Text in *The New York Times*, September 11, 1955.

[14] See United States statement of January 21, 1956 (in *The New York Times*, January 22, 1956).

[15] "On the Historical Experience Concerning the Dictatorship of the Proletariat," *People's Daily*, April 5, 1956.

[16] Joint communiqué released by the New China News Agency, April 7, 1956.

[17] Tass dispatch, February 14, 1956.

war masquerading as a belief in the "noninevitability" of such a war. This consideration presumably helped to explain another prominent feature of the report, an emphasis on a "peaceful" or "parliamentary" path to power for local Communist Parties; obviously such a strategy would be the least likely to create situations that might escalate into general war. Another significant innovation was an indication of a willingness to tackle the disarmament question in a way that might be fruitful, or in other words step by step rather than on a "package deal" basis. Specifically, Khrushchev stated that "Prior to agreement on the most important aspects of disarmament, we are willing to take certain partial steps — for example, to discontinue thermonuclear weapon tests. . . ."

Khrushchev had come a long way, in the wrong direction from the CPC's standpoint, from the view he had expressed while feuding with Malenkov in 1954 — that the Soviet Union could actively deter or if necessary win a general war. The CPC had approved and still clung to his earlier line. As early as October, 1955, the CPC had inaugurated a series of statements to a similar effect that was to continue for about five years.[18] The general theme was that a world war, while not to be desired or sought, was not to be feared unduly. Mankind would survive, but "imperialism" would not, and "socialism" would triumph. Such statements were only rarely[19] made in authoritative, published sources; usually they were made in oral statements to foreigners — British, Soviet, Japanese, Yugoslav, etc. The aim was almost certainly political: to stiffen Khrushchev's spine, if possible; to terrorize non-Communists into nonresistance to Communist pressures; and to convey the idea that the CPC did not intend to be deterred from pursuing its external objectives by the risk of a general war, which it regards as low. It was, in short, a debate on the likelihood of a thermonuclear war, masquerading as one on the consequences of such a war. By 1958 the CPC's various opponents, Communist and non-Communist, were beginning to quote and sometimes exaggerate its statements on thermonuclear war as an effective means of embarrassing it.[20] As will be shown later, the main Sino-Soviet difference on war has been not so much on general war as such as on local war and the chances of its escalating into general war.

As might be expected, the CPC's editorial comments on the military aspects of the Twentieth Congress were superficially favorable but also somewhat ambiguous.[21] It seems fairly clear that shortly after the Twentieth Congress the doctrinal debate that had been in progress in Chinese military circles was resolved, presumably at the highest level. In view of the un-

---

[18] Cf. Hsieh, *op. cit.*, p. 49.

[19] As in Mao Tse-tung, "On the Correct Handling of Contradictions Among the People," February 27, 1957 (released June 18, 1957); and "Long Live Leninism!" *Red Flag*, April 16, 1960.

[20] Cf. Edvard Kardelj, *Socialism and War*, Belgrade, 1960.

[21] Hsieh, *op cit.*, p. 50.

reliability of Soviet protection and the evidence of Soviet interest in reaching some kind of disarmament agreement with the West, the CPR must develop its own nuclear weapons and delivery systems. The cost of this program, as well as that of basic industrial development, was to be met in part through a cutback in the conventional military budget. On the other hand, every effort was to be made to preserve the assumed political advantages of the earlier doctrine, such as strict party control over the armed forces. The slight possibility of an American strategic attack while the CPR's nuclear program was maturing would be countered abroad by maintaining that the CPR was not afraid of nuclear war, and at home by reiteration of the old line that men are more important than weapons.[22] This policy represented a compromise between the two basic schools of thought, not a clear-cut victory for either. Defense Minister P'eng Te-huai, speaking to the CPC's Eighth National Congress on behalf of the Military Committee of the Central Committee,[23] summarized the desired military posture in the phrase, "people's armed forces handling modern weapons."[24]

Khrushchev behaved as though he believed that, if he were to ignore Mao's advice by being strategically cautious, he must also violate it by being tactically bold, in order to avoid politico-military setbacks at the hands of "imperialism." Beginning in 1956, during his visit to Britain, he launched his campaign of "rocket rattling." His threats were rarely directed against the United States; on one occasion when they were, in 1960 over Cuba, he later admitted that they had been "symbolic." Most of the threats were hurled at American allies. Perhaps his most famous threat, the one against Britain and France at the time of the Suez crisis, was not uttered until after the United States and a majority of the United Nations had indicated opposition to their behavior and an end of the fighting was imminent. All this can hardly have done much to strengthen the CPC's belief in the value of the Sino-Soviet alliance.

As we have seen, Khrushchev used the psychological advantage gained in 1957 from the Soviet ICBM test and earth satellite more to press for another summit conference than to exert politico-military pressures on the West so as to give the CPR greater protection while it was developing a nuclear capability. Khrushchev agreed in mid-October to a small program of aid to the CPR in the production of weapons. In November, a Chinese military mission led by P'eng Te-huai visited Moscow, and an agreement on scientific and technical cooperation was signed in January, 1958.[25] It seems probable that at that time the Soviet Union agreed to provide further mili-

---

[22] Cf. *ibid.*, pp. 51–52.
[23] On this body see Ralph L. Powell, "The Military Affairs Committee and Party Control of the Military in China," *Asian Survey*, vol. iii, no. 7 (July, 1963), pp. 347–356.
[24] New China News Agency dispatch, September 19, 1956.
[25] Cf. Hsieh, *op. cit.*, pp. 101–102.

tary aid, including aid in the development of some types of missiles.[26] All of this, of course, did not guarantee Soviet protection or diversionary action on behalf of the CPR. Furthermore, Khrushchev tended to undercut his aid by appearing to subscribe at the end of 1957 to an idea much favored by Afro-Asian neutrals, that of an atom-free zone in Asia, which if implemented would prevent the CPR from becoming a nuclear power while leaving the strategic power of the United States and the Soviet Union comparatively unaffected. Soon afterward, the CPR began to advocate an approach to disarmament to which it has adhered in its essentials ever since: complete, uninspected nuclear disarmament, including the destruction of nuclear stockpiles, without conventional disarmament.[27] This proposal, which is unacceptable to the United States and the Soviet Union, would if accepted leave the CPR probably the strongest military power in Asia and would virtually eliminate the need for the Sino-Soviet alliance. At the end of March, Khrushchev announced a unilateral suspension of nuclear testing, a step designed primarily to minimize the chances of American nuclear diffusion to West Germany, but also a step with possible adverse implications for Soviet military aid to and support of the CPR.

The CPC was therefore confronting a situation something like that of 1955. In addition, the United States had announced in May, 1957, that it would emplace Matador missiles, capable of hitting a part of the mainland with either conventional or nuclear warheads, on Taiwan.[28] The idea of limited nuclear war, with tactical nuclear weapons, seemed to be gaining favor in the United States.[29] Chiang Kai-shek's memoirs, published in 1957, advocated a conventional war in the Far East as the best means to defeat Communism.[30] Khrushchev's behavior must have created serious doubts in the CPC's mind as to what if anything he would do in the event of an American use of tactical nuclear weapons against the CPR in support of a Chinese Nationalist landing.

The years 1957–58 in the CPR, when the Great Leap Forward was conceived and born, have sometimes been compared to the years 1927–28 in the Soviet Union, when Stalin's First Five Year Plan and collectivization program originated. In one respect the comparison is even apter than is

---

[26] Cf. P. G. Gittins, "The Red Dragon of China: A Brief Review of Communist China as a Military Power," *Australian Army Journal*, no. 132 (May, 1960), pp. 15–18.

[27] Cf. Hsieh, *op. cit.*, pp. 104–105.

[28] *Ibid.*, p. 62.

[29] Henry A. Kissinger's influential book, *Nuclear Weapons and Foreign Policy*, New York: Harper, 1957, advocating limited nuclear war, was published at about this time.

[30] Cf. ". . . if the democracies wish to prevent the outbreak of a world war, and to save mankind from a major calamity, the only way is to substitute a local war in East Asia for an all-out world war, and to fight a war with conventional weapons instead of a war of annihilation with thermonuclear weapons" (Chiang Kai-shek, *Soviet Russia in China: A Summing-up at Seventy*, New York: Farrar, Straus and Cudahy, 1957, p. 341).

usually realized. Stalin was trying to deal not only with domestic problems, such as the withholding of grain by the peasants, but with an external crisis of sorts, marked by a major setback in China and a war scare with Britain. Similarly, the causes of the Great Leap Forward seem to have been external — specifically, the trends already mentioned — as well as domestic.

As early as 1956, at the CPC's Eighth National Congress, it had been implied that the CPR's First Five Year Plan (1953–57) had erred in following too closely the highly centralized Soviet model of economic planning and control, and that the Second (1958–62) would see an effort at more decentralized administration. Industrial decentralization actually got under way in the autumn of 1957. It involved a combination of increased industrial investment; decentralization of control in theory to local governmental, but in practice to party, authorities; and the establishment of small, local, pre-dominantly light industries.[31] Apparently it was hoped that this program would stimulate local initiative and make it possible, as Liu Shao-ch'i pre-dicted in December, for the CPR to catch up with Britain by 1972 in output of major industrial products. In the agricultural sector, the collective farms were reduced in size and it was decided (at the Third Plenary Session of the Central Committee, in September–October) that their organization would "not be altered for ten years."[32] Peasants were drafted by millions during the winter of 1957–58 to work on capital construction projects, such as irrigation systems.

All this, however, was not yet the Great Leap Forward. It is fairly clear that the latter's main features, and in particular the massive mobilization of labor through "people's communes" each controlling a dozen or so collective farms, was decided on at least tentatively between the session of the National People's Congress (the nominal legislature) in February, 1958, and the Second Session of the CPC's Eighth National Congress in May, which met in an atmosphere of great urgency and secrecy. This decision may well have reflected among other things the CPC leadership's concern over the external trends already mentioned. The definite decision to establish "people's communes" on a nationwide basis was announced to the country and the world by a party conference held from August 17 to 30, during which period the shelling of Quemoy began.[33] The conference also an-nounced an important decision with regard to industry: the steel target for the year, which had been fixed at 8.0–8.5 million tons at the end of May, was raised to 10.7 million tons. The difference, some two million tons, was to be produced by shifting the emphasis of the local industry campaign begun in the previous year from light to heavy industry, or in other words by estab-

---

[31] Franz Schurmann, "Economic Policy and Political Power in Communist China," *The Annals of the American Academy of Political and Social Science,* vol. 349 (September, 1963), pp. 54–62; *Communist China 1955–1959, op. cit.,* p. 17.

[32] Schurmann, *loc. cit.,* p. 56.

[33] Text of resolution in *Communist China 1955–1959, op. cit.,* pp. 454–456.

lishing furnaces to make "backyard steel" within the people's communes.[34] It may be relevant to note that a conference of Soviet and Western official experts had issued a communiqué on August 21 stating that an agreement on a controlled cessation of nuclear tests was possible.

It was clear from the beginning that whatever other purposes it might have served, if it had succeeded, the "backyard steel" campaign would be helpful if the major industrial installations should be knocked out by air attack.[35] Similarly, the huge militia force, whose formation paralleled the establishment of the "people's communes" and began shortly after the start of the Taiwan Strait crisis, had among its possible uses defense against a Nationalist landing. This thought tends to be confirmed by the fact that the militia campaign was particularly intense in the province of Fukien, opposite Taiwan.[36]

Another unique event in this unusual year was a conference convened by the Military Committee of the CPC Central Committee from May 27 to July 22, or in other words for virtually the whole time elapsing between the party congress and the start of the propaganda campaign for the "liberation" of Taiwan. Among other things, according to the press release on the conference, it "discussed and adopted decisions concerning the work of national defense in the light of the current international situation."[37] One of these certainly related to the Taiwan Strait.

Undoubtedly alarmed by the ensuing propaganda barrage and military movements, Khrushchev flew secretly to Peking on July 31. There he and Marshal Malinovsky, among others, discussed with the Chinese leadership a variety of party, state and military matters. The Russians almost certainly warned the Chinese against any risky moves in the Taiwan Strait, and the rather platitudinous joint communiqué failed to mention the Taiwan question or the "indivisibility of peace."[38]

The CPC has recently stated that "In 1958 [possibly during the talks just mentioned] the leadership of the CPSU put forward unreasonable demands designed to bring China under Soviet military control. These unreasonable demands were rightly and firmly rejected by the Chinese Government."[39] This may be a reference to what seems to have been a Soviet effort to create a joint Sino-Soviet Pacific naval Command, probably in order to restrain Chinese belligerency toward Taiwan.[40] According to Polish reports,

---

[34] New China News Agency dispatch, August 31, 1958.
[35] Cf. Richard Moorsteen, *An Economic Development of Strategic Significance in Communist China*, The RAND Corporation, P-1578, December 15, 1958.
[36] Cf. Ralph L. Powell, "Everyone a Soldier: The Chinese Communist Militia," *Foreign Affairs*, vol. 39, no. 1 (October, 1960), pp. 100–111; John Gittings, "China's Militia," *The China Quarterly*, no. 18 (April–June, 1964), pp. 104–106.
[37] New China News Agency dispatch, July 25, 1958.
[38] Text in *The New York Times*, August 4, 1958.
[39] "The Origin and Development of the Differences Between the Leadership of the CPSU and Ourselves," *People's Daily* and *Red Flag*, September 9, 1963.
[40] Cf. Garthoff, *loc. cit.*, p. 87.

however, the Russians did agree at the Peking talks to give the CPR additional aid with its nuclear and missile program.[41]

As we have seen, Khrushchev's threats during the crisis to come to the defense of the CPR were made after a Sino-American exchange of statements had made it clear that there would be no major war. His pressures on Berlin between November, 1958, and May, 1959, had no particular diversionary value to the CPR, since it was under no serious "imperialist" threat at that time and was in no position to take any major initiatives of its own.

Probably as a riskless way of appearing to seek security for the CPR, as well as in an attempt to gain a general propaganda advantage in Asia, Khrushchev stated in January, 1959, that "a zone of peace, above all, an atom-free zone, can and must be created in the Far East and the entire Pacific basin area." In the unlikely event of adoption, this proposal would eliminate not only American nuclear weapons but American testing sites from the Pacific. The CPC, obviously with one eye on Asian opinion, Japanese opinion in particular, endorsed this initiative, but hesitantly and ambiguously.[42]

The CPC was unquestionably angered by Khrushchev's effort to support P'eng Te-huai in his proposals to moderate the Great Leap Forward and improve Sino-Soviet relations. It was still more annoyed by Khrushchev's pursuit of détente with the United States following his failure in May to enforce his "ultimatum" on Berlin.[43] On August 3,[44] the day after the convening of the Eighth Plenary Session of the CPC Central Committee, it was announced that Khrushchev would visit the United States. On August 6, the *People's Daily* launched a massive propaganda campaign against "right opportunists," among whom it certainly meant to include P'eng Te-huai. As we have seen, P'eng was outvoted at the Plenary Session and soon purged. The Central Committee announced at that time a substantial cut in the previous economic claims for 1958 and in the targets for 1959. On the other hand, it also toughened and intensified certain features of the Great Leap Forward.[45]

---

[41] *Ibid.*, p. 89.

[42] Hsieh, *op. cit.*, pp. 155–161.

[43] Cf. "Since 1959 Khrushchev has become obsessed with summit meetings between the Soviet Union and the United States" ("Peaceful Coexistence—Two Diametrically Opposed Policies," *People's Daily* and *Red Flag*, December 12, 1963).

[44] The anniversary of the Mao-Khrushchev communiqué of 1958. It should be remembered that in June Khrushchev had terminated his aid program to the CPR in the production of nuclear weapons. On this general subject see Harold P. Ford, "Modern Weapons and the Sino-Soviet Estrangement," *The China Quarterly*, no. 18 (April–June, 1964), pp. 160–173.

[45] Communiqué of Eighth Plenary Session, in *Communist China 1955–1959*, *op. cit.*, pp. 533–536. For commentary see *ibid.*, pp. 33–36; Donald S. Zagoria, *The Sino-Soviet Conflict, 1956–1961*, Princeton University Press, 1962, pp. 137–139; David A. Charles, "The Dismissal of Marshal P'eng Teh-huai," *The China Quarterly*, no. 8 (October–December, 1961), pp. 63–69.

Khrushchev got an understandably chilly reception when he came to the CPR late in September, after visiting the United States. It was probably rendered even chillier than it would have been otherwise by the fact that he had just proposed, before the United Nations General Assembly, a plan for "general and complete disarmament" (i.e., conventional as well as nuclear) within four years. He further congealed his Chinese hosts by lecturing them publicly on the need not to "test by force the stability of the capitalist system." The enunciation of the doctrine of the Soviet Union's "partial responsibility" for the acts of the CPR by Under Secretary of State Dillon soon afterward probably represented an American effort to convince Khrushchev that, if he wanted a détente, he could not confine himself to public lectures and disclaimers of responsibility for Chinese behavior. Khrushchev's reaction, beginning with his speech of October 31 before the Supreme Soviet, was to repudiate "partial responsibility" and in fact Soviet leadership of the "socialist camp." Although his behavior had certainly called the validity of the Sino-Soviet alliance into question, he evidently wanted at least for the time being to preserve as much as possible both of the alliance and the "spirit of Camp David."

■ THE FOUNDERING OF THE ALLIANCE (1960–64)

On January 14, 1960, Khrushchev made an important speech in which he announced an impending cut (later abandoned) of one-third in the Soviet Union's ground forces, reiterated his interest in "general and complete disarmament," and stated for the first time that the Soviet Union had the ability (he did not say the intention) to use thermonuclear weapons in the defense of "other socialist countries." Chinese commentary on the speech indicated an unwillingness to interpret the latter statement as a reliable guarantee. The CPC was evidently afraid that the Soviet Union would try, in the Ten-Nation Disarmament Committee about to meet at Geneva, to bind the CPR to some sort of disarmament agreement. On January 21, the National People's Congress adopted a resolution proposed by Foreign Minister Chen Yi, to the effect that the CPR would not consider itself bound by any disarmament agreement in whose negotiation it had not participated or which it had not signed.[46]

Meanwhile, on January 19, the United States and Japan had signed a mutual security treaty that, although it embodied important concessions to Japan as compared with the preceding treaty signed in 1951, retained the right of the United States to operate military bases in Japan (including Okinawa). The signing of the treaty, to which the CPR of course objected in many ways, nevertheless gave it a welcome opportunity to remind the

[46] A. L. Hsieh, *The Significance of Chinese Communist Treatment of Khrushchev's January 14 Speech on Strategy*, The RAND Corporation, RM-2534, February 19, 1960.

Soviet Union that the United States was still allied with Japan and that the Sino-Soviet alliance therefore still applied against the United States.

The opportunity to remind the Soviet Union of this situation was all the more welcome because it fell just before the tenth anniversary of the signing of the Sino-Soviet alliance (February 14, 1960). Both partners celebrated the anniversary with correctness, and the Chinese with at least a show of hopeful enthusiasm.[47] A possible indication of Khrushchev's view of the alliance was the fact that he spent the anniversary in New Delhi, the capital of the CPR's most hated Asian rival.

The CPC's anger at Khrushchev's interest in some sort of disarmament agreement and détente with the West probably contributed to the unleashing of its propaganda and ideological offensive against him in April. This in turn may have contributed, although not decisively, to his decision to break off the Paris summit conference.

By this time the Eisenhower administration was drawing to a close. The CPC had always felt apprehensive about John Foster Dulles' doctrine of "massive retaliation" and his occasionally expressed willingness to use tactical nuclear weapons against the CPR. Probably it had breathed a good deal easier since his death in the spring of 1959, or at least it would have done so if Khrushchev had not launched his drive for a détente. The American presidential campaign of 1960 afforded the CPR a useful opportunity to gauge the views of the two major candidates on China policy. Senator Kennedy was much the less assertive of the two, although his ideas were by no means wholly acceptable to the CPC. He favored bringing the CPR into the test ban negotiations.[48] He pronounced the offshore islands nonessential and indefensible; he said that the United States should not defend them and implied that the Chinese Nationalists should evacuate them.[49] Although such an evacuation, by itself, would be unacceptable to the CPC because it would tend to create "two Chinas," the CPC may well have concluded that Senator Kennedy's China policy would be preferable to that of his opponent. In any event, the CPC felt either so concerned about the state of the Chinese economy, or so unconcerned about American China policy in the near future, that it started to abandon the Great Leap Forward at the beginning of November, a few days before the American presidential election.

The CPR selected August 1, 1960, to make its first major initiative in the disarmament field since 1958. Because of the poor state of the economy and the withdrawal of Soviet technicians, the CPR was probably engaged in stretching out its timetable for the acquisition of nuclear weapons. Furthermore, it was probably worried by the continuing negotiations on disarmament and yet anxious not to appear in a wholly negative light. Speaking at

---

[47] Cf. documents in *Sino-Soviet Alliance: Mighty Bulwark of World Peace*, Peking: Foreign Languages Press, 1960.

[48] Speech of June 14, 1960 (*The New York Times*, June 15, 1960).

[49] Speech of October 12, 1960 (*The New York Times*, October 13, 1960).

the Swiss Embassy, Chou En-lai proposed that all countries of Asia and the Pacific area, specifically including the United States, create an atom-free zone and sign a nonaggression pact.

It was clear to both parties to the Sino-Soviet alliance that President-elect Kennedy believed, although mistakenly, that the United States was in danger of losing the strategic military lead to the Soviet Union, and that he intended to remedy this situation. The fighting that broke out in Laos in December, 1960, suggested that the main problem was the extent to which the incoming American administration would be prepared to intervene in such local crises in the underdeveloped areas, to use tactical nuclear weapons, and perhaps to escalate such conflicts to the level of general war. On this question the Chinese and Soviet parties held divergent views.

On New Year's Day, 1961, *Red Flag* published a characteristically militant article by Yü Chao-li.[50] He drew the CPC's usual sharp distinction between "just" (revolutionary) and "unjust" (counterrevolutionary) wars. He affirmed flatly that "We are of the opinion that should imperialism be permitted to unleash local wars of aggression and obtain what it wants in these wars, it is likely that a world war would result." On the other hand, he stated that "it is possible to prevent counterrevolutionary wars launched by imperialism and reactionaries from turning into a world war. . . ." He did not specify how, but he presumably had in mind vigorous deterrence or counterintervention by the "socialist camp," the Soviet Union in particular.

He soon had the Russian answer. In a long and important speech delivered on January 6,[51] Khrushchev denied that the Soviet party attempted to exercise leadership over other Communist Parties and delivered himself of a major analysis of war. He discussed first the problem of world wars, which he blamed wholly on "imperialism," without saying anything new. Next he discussed local wars started by "imperialism." One of these, he said, no matter which "imperialist" power launches it, "may grow into a world thermonuclear rocket war. We must therefore combat both world wars and local wars." The specific, and the normal, example that he gave of the Soviet Union's "combating" such a local war was its behavior in the Suez crisis; this had been aimed so as to be a riskless and almost meaningless act of "combating" the "imperialists." This was almost certainly not the kind of behavior demanded by Yü Chao-li. Next Khrushchev discussed "national liberation wars," which he promised to support, but without indicating how. Finally, he discussed "popular uprisings" (evidently in industrial countries) in similar terms. It was a typical Khrushchev performance — impressive at first sight, but essentially cautious and noncommittal. He gave no clear indication of an intent to play a more than "symbolic" role, as in Cuba the

[50] "New Situation in the People's Struggle Throughout the World."
[51] Text in *Kommunist,* no. 1 (January, 1961).

previous year, in local war situations in which the United States might be involved, as it had not been in the Suez crisis.

There has been some speculation that one reason for the easing of Sino-Soviet polemics in early 1961 was a Chinese agreement to allow Khrushchev six months to take the measure of the Kennedy administration. To the CPC the first portents must have seemed encouraging: the Bay of Pigs fiasco, and the decision to neutralize Laos. The Kennedy administration's firm reaction to the Berlin Wall (August 13, 1961), however, the strengthening of American military capabilities of all types under the rubric of "flexible response," and a series of tough statements by high American officials in 1961 and 1962 on the United States' willingness to fight a nuclear war if necessary, seem to have genuinely worried the CPR, notwithstanding the American unwillingness to fight for Laos.[52]

Marshal Malinovsky's claim at the Soviet party's Twenty-second Congress (October, 1961) that "the problem of destroying rockets in flight has ... been successfully solved"[53] may have reminded the CPC that, by the time it acquired a locally significant nuclear capability, the two superpowers might have developed a workable missile defense. This might mean that the United States would be able to protect its bases and allies in the Far East from any Chinese nuclear attack, defy the Soviet Union behind the shield of its own missile defenses, and destroy the CPR at its leisure if it wished to do so. The Soviet Union, for its part, might be relieved of one of its existing disincentives to leave the CPR to its fate, the fear that an American strategic attack on the CPR might be a prelude to an attack on the Soviet Union. The CPC does not seem to have commented publicly on the Malinovsky claim, although it had commented earlier on the Soviet Union's acquisition of nuclear weapons, thermonuclear weapons, and of course the ICBM. Malinovsky gave the CPR further food for thought by saying, in January, 1962, that the Soviet Union could (not would) destroy an enemy "if he attacks us or the socialist countries friendly to us."[54] It had never before been publicly implied in such a context that a "socialist" country might not be friendly to the Soviet Union. It is unlikely that Malinovsky was thinking solely of Albania, which had been informally expelled from the Warsaw Pact by the end of 1961. Friendly or not, the CPR was not counting on Soviet support in case of war, if we may so interpret the absence of any reference to such support in some secret Chinese military documents captured in 1961.[55]

---

[52] Cf. Jen Ku-ping, "A Scrutiny of the Counterrevolutionary Grand Strategy of U. S. Imperialism," *People's Daily*, July 22, 1962.

[53] Moscow radio, October 24, 1961.

[54] *Izvestia*, January 25, 1962 (quoted in John R. Thomas, "Soviet Behavior in the Quemoy Crisis of 1958," *Orbis*, vol. vi, no. 1 [spring, 1962], p. 64).

[55] Cf. John Wilson Lewis, *Chinese Communist Party Leadership and the Succession to Mao Tse-tung: An Appraisal of Tensions*, Department of State: External Research Staff, 1964, p. 28.

Khrushchev gave the CPR only token support in its security crisis of the spring of 1962. In fact, the Soviet press implied that the most the CPR could expect would be arms and "volunteers," such as the Soviet Union had sent to Nationalist China twenty-five years earlier when it was attacked by Japan. The CPC continued to denounce Khrushchev, without naming him publicly, for his "modern revisionism." Nevertheless, the CPC probably thought it possible that the Berlin and German situations, which were tense in the summer of 1962, and still more the massive shipments of Soviet arms to Cuba after July, might have some effects beneficial to it. Soviet and American attention would probably be diverted from the Himalayas, where the CPR began in July to build up pressure on the Indian Army. More important still, Khrushchev's recurring tendency to seek détente with the West and progress toward "general and complete disarmament" might be permanently frustrated, and the Sino-Soviet alliance strengthened at least to that extent. The CPC was presumably relieved when the Soviet Union rejected a proposal by the Western powers in August, 1962, for an uninspected ban on nuclear tests other than underground.

The Sino-Indian border and Cuba missile crises originated independently if almost simultaneously, but they became intertwined as they progressed. At first the Chinese and Russians followed very similar propaganda lines and gave each other declaratory support, although the CPR's support for Castro was louder than its support for Khrushchev.[56] Not until October 27, when Khrushchev had begun to show signs of "blinking first" over Cuba, did the CPC issue what amounted to a demand that he, as well as the Indian Communists, repudiate Nehru as a "reactionary nationalist."[57]

The CPC obviously believed that Khrushchev should not have agreed so readily to pull first his missiles and then his bombers out of Cuba, without getting substantial concessions such as a formal no-invasion pledge in return. What enraged the CPC most of all, however, was Khrushchev's willingness to accept international on-site inspection — "another Munich."[58]

---

[56] New China News Agency dispatch, October 25, 1962.

[57] "More on Nehru's Philosophy in the Light of the Sino-Indian Boundary Question," *People's Daily*, October 27, 1962.

[58] "On more than one occasion we have made it clear that we neither called for the establishment of missile bases in Cuba nor obstructed the withdrawal of the so-called 'offensive weapons' from Cuba. We have never considered that it was a Marxist-Lenist attitude to brandish nuclear weapons as a way of settling international disputes. Nor have we ever considered that the avoidance of a thermo-nuclear war in the Caribbean crisis was a 'Munich.' What we did strongly oppose, still strongly oppose and will strongly oppose in the future is the sacrifice of another country's sovereignty as a means of reaching a compromise with imperialism. A compromise of this sort can only be regarded as 100 percent appeasement, a 'Munich' pure and simple" ("The Differences Between Comrade Togliatti and Us," *People's Daily*, December 31, 1962).

". . . during the Cuban events certain people first committed the error of adventurism, and then committed the error of capitulationism, wanting the Cuban people

The CPC apparently wanted the Soviet Union to run the United States naval blockade, which it denounced as piracy, and conducted a massive propaganda campaign in Cuba to obstruct, or get credit for trying to obstruct, the withdrawal of the Soviet bombers.[59] If a Polish account is correct, as seems very doubtful, a Chinese missile crew shot down the American U-2 that was lost over Cuba on October 27.[60]

Although Khrushchev seems to have been in political difficulties after the Cuban crisis,[61] he did not fall. He did not regard the CPR with greater friendliness or make additional commitments to it. On the contrary, he was enraged at its behavior during the Cuban crisis and stingingly demanded to know why it did not throw down a challenge to "imperialism" over Hong Kong and Macao.[62] In retaliation the CPC threatened to review the treaties that had fixed the Sino-Soviet border in the nineteenth century, as well as other agreements forced upon China by the "imperialists" at that time.[63]

Worst of all, perhaps, for the CPR, Khrushchev resumed his quest for a détente with the West. Indeed, whereas his previous moves in this direction had been tactical to a large extent, he seems to have been jolted by the Cuban crisis and his domestic economic troubles into an agonizing re-appraisal of his entire foreign policy. His conclusion seems to have been that he must ease his pressures on the West and the underdeveloped areas for a time and concentrate on strengthening, in all respects, the Soviet Union, the "socialist camp," and the international Communist movement.[64] Such a policy would imply an indefinite, though presumably not permanent, détente with the West. It also might imply a greater willingness to risk or even seek a break of some sort with the CPR, which Khrushchev had clearly come to regard as an element of discord, weakness, and even danger in the "socialist camp" and the international Communist movement. Any such operation would be an extremely difficult and delicate one, however. The Soviet Union would have to appear to have sufficient justification for its action; it would have to avoid conveying the impression that it could not be relied on by "friendly socialist countries"; and it would have to try not to give aid and comfort to "imperialism."

---

to accept humiliating terms which would have meant the sacrifice of the sovereignty of their country" ("More on the Differences Between Comrade Togliatti and Us," *Red Flag*, March 4, 1963).

[59] *The Washington Post and Times Herald*, December 28, 1962.

[60] *The New York Times*, November 17, 1962. On the CPR and the Cuban crisis in general, see "Communist China in the Cuban Crisis," *Current Scene* (Hong Kong), vol. ii, no. 8 (January 28, 1963).

[61] Cf. Carl Linden, "Khrushchev and the Party Battle," *Problems of Communism*, vol. xii, no. 5 (September–October, 1963), pp. 27–35.

[62] Speech of December 12, 1962 (text in *The Washington Post and Times Herald*, December 16, 1962).

[63] "A Comment on the Statement of the CPUSA," *People's Daily*, March 8, 1963.

[64] Cf. Richard Lowenthal, "The End of an Illusion," *Problems of Communism*, vol. xii, no. 1 (January–February, 1963), pp. 1–10.

Closely related to the question of Khrushchev's handling of his Chinese problem, and even more important, was his desire for a détente with the West. There were apparently two major obstacles to this, in addition to the Chinese. One was Kozlov, who seems to have been Khrushchev's main opponent and rival within the CPSU and to have been closer than he to the Chinese on party, even if not necessarily on state, questions.[65] Kozlov disappeared from the Soviet political scene, in April or May, 1963, allegedly on account of illness. The other major obstacle, Castro, was squared, apparently, by the inclusion of Cuba in the "socialist camp" (in the Soviet May Day slogans for 1963), a triumphal one-month tour of the Soviet Union, and a promise of Soviet support and additional aid.[66] The CPC got no concessions except for a talk between delegations of the two parties (July 5–20).

Progress toward an uninspected ban on nuclear tests, other than underground, which had been interrupted the previous August, resumed following an American Senatorial resolution of May 27 to this effect, and President Kennedy's speech of June 10 at American University. Soviet jamming of the Voice of America first decreased and then, on June 18, stopped.[67]

The CPC regarded Khrushchev's signature of the test ban treaty as a betrayal, among other things, of the spirit of the Sino-Soviet alliance, and therefore of the relationship between the Communist Chinese and Soviet states. For that reason the test ban treaty, unlike earlier analogous actions by Khrushchev, evoked a formal protest from the Communist Chinese government, as distinct from the party. This protest took the form of a statement addressed to all governments of the world and proposing complete cessation of nuclear testing, complete nuclear disarmament, a conference of all heads of governments, and a series of atom-free zones, among them one in "the Asian and Pacific region, including the United States, the Soviet Union, China and Japan."[68] The Soviet government's reply of course rejected the CPR's demands and implied that the Soviet Union had the right to speak on matters pertaining to nuclear weapons for the entire "socialist camp."[69] To this the CPR replied on August 15, insisting that it needed its own nuclear weapons to defend itself, but not going so far as

---

[65] The local press in Leningrad (Kozlov's bailiwick) had deleted some unfavorable references to the CPR that appeared in a Soviet article August, 1960. Kozlov had seen Chou En-lai off at the airport when he left Moscow following his rebuke to Khrushchev at the Twenty-second Congress. Kozlov's had been the only Soviet speech to the congress to be reprinted in full on the front page of the *People's Daily* (on November 3). Kozlov had been in charge in Moscow when *Pravda* (April 8, 1963) indicated in the first version of its May Day slogans for 1963 that Yugoslavia was not a full-fledged member of the "socialist camp."

[66] Cf. Soviet-Cuban joint communiqué of May 25, 1963. Nevertheless, Castro subsequently refused to sign the test ban treaty.

[67] Maury Lisann, *Soviet Suspension of VOA Jamming: Political and Propaganda Factors*, Institute for Defense Analyses, Internal Note N-142, May, 1964.

[68] New China News Agency dispatch, July 31, 1963.

[69] Statement of August 3 (Tass dispatch, same date).

to deny a need for Soviet support or protection.[70] The Soviet response (August 21) lectured the CPR on the horrors of nuclear war, stated that a nuclear weapons program would beggar the Chinese economy, and threatened to withhold sensitive military information if the CPR continued to reveal such information (as it had in its statement of August 15).[71] The CPR then (September 1) threatened the Soviet Union with the prospect of a nuclear-armed West Germany and accused Khrushchev of subscribing, by virtue of his acquiescence in the Republic of China's adherence to the test ban treaty, to a "two Chinas" policy.[72] To this the Soviet government answered (September 20) by denying the accusation about "two Chinas," charging the CPR with provocative behavior along the Sino-Soviet frontier, rebutting the Chinese line on local war ("Chinese leaders make a serious error contending that under no conditions would local conflicts lead to a universal thermo-nuclear war") and insisting that the Soviet Union still recognized its obligation to defend the CPR against unprovoked strategic attack ("if the imperialist aggressors attack the socialist camp they will receive a crushing rebuff"). On the other hand, the statement insisted that the CPR's nuclear weapons program implied that it had "some sort of special aims and interests which cannot be supported by the military force of the socialist camp." In short, as the CPR had realized long ago, the Soviet Union regarded the Sino-Soviet alliance as a strictly defensive one, not one to be invoked by the CPR in support of its effort to "liberate" Taiwan. In this statement the Soviet government was warning the CPR that its acquisition of nuclear weapons would not enable it to drag or blackmail the Soviet Union into making commitments of an offensive kind.[73]

Khrushchev's curious proposal of December 31, 1963, for a general renunciation of force in the settlement of territorial disputes, was probably an effort to shame the CPR into making such a renunciation not only with respect to Taiwan, which he mentioned, but also with respect to the rest of the Chinese frontier including its Soviet sector, which he did not. On January 23, 1964, Chou En-lai disclosed that the Soviet Union and the CPR had agreed to negotiate their differences on the border.[74] There have been repeated reports that each side has been strengthening its forces and border defenses along the common frontier.[75]

It is understandable that the CPR has regarded the Sino-Soviet alliance as existing exclusively for its own benefit. What is less understandable is

[70] New China News Agency dispatch, August 15, 1963.

[71] Tass dispatch, August 21, 1963.

[72] New China News Agency dispatch, September 1, 1963.

[73] Text in *The New York Times*, September 23, 1963.

[74] Interview with Edgar Snow (*The New York Times*, February 3, 1964).

[75] E.g., *Christian Science Monitor*, October 23, 1963; *The New York Times*, December 26, 1963. For an appreciation of the Soviet view of this problem see Malcolm Mackintosh, "Soviet Generals Look at China," *The New Statesman*, October 4, 1963 (reprinted in *Survival*, vol. 5, no. 6 [November–December, 1963], pp. 269–272).

that having seen that it could not extract offensive commitments from the Soviet Union, with respect to Taiwan in particular, it has nevertheless hoped to keep the alliance alive while exerting all sorts of party pressures on the Soviet Union. The latter, whose high cards are generally in the suit of state rather than party relations, has naturally cast doubt on the continued validity of the alliance. Indeed, just as Chinese pressures were probably a factor, although not the main factor, in Khrushchev's recurring toughness toward the West, so the overdoing of Chinese party pressures on Khrushchev was probably a factor, although not the main factor, in his intermittent quest for a détente.

It seems likely that, as suggested earlier, the Soviet Union regards itself as obligated to defend the CPR only in three highly improbable contingencies: an unprovoked American strategic attack on the CPR, a localized American attack on targets near the Soviet border, and the landing of American troops in Manchuria or North China. Whether, if this is the case, the Sino-Soviet alliance is regarded as alive or dead is a matter of interpretation. The CPC appears to regard it, if not as dead, at least as useless in any likely situation.

In the course of the public anti-Khrushchev party polemic that the CPC launched after the test ban treaty, it made an important and fairly comprehensive statement of its views on war.[76] In this it denied once more any desire for a general thermonuclear war, or for any sort of military clash between the United States and the Soviet Union. On the other hand, the "socialist camp" should not yield to "imperialist" nuclear blackmail, as Khrushchev had over Cuba. Under no circumstances must the "socialist camp" be the first to use nuclear weapons. It must not use them at all in support of "national liberation wars" or "revolutionary civil wars," because such action might bring "imperialist" nuclear retaliation against the people concerned. Nevertheless, within these limits the "socialist camp" must support all "just" (i.e., revolutionary) wars to the best of its ability.

■ **THE CHINESE RESPONSE TO THE TEST BAN TREATY (1963–64)**

The test ban treaty and the anemic state of the Sino-Soviet alliance formed only one part, although an important part, of a sea of troubles in which the CPR found itself awash in mid-1963. Among these were the continuing sluggishness of the economy; serious political discontent, especially among the youth; the generally poor state of Sino-Soviet relations; and a sense of partial international isolation. Beginning in July, there were almost continual conferences in Peking, at the highest level, for a period of

[76] "Two Different Lines on the Question of War and Peace," *People's Daily* and *Red Flag*, November 19, 1963.

several weeks.[77] From the beginning of 1964, the CPC launched a massive militarization of the economy and of Chinese society under the slogan, "Learning from the People's Liberation Army."[78] There was also an intensification of indoctrination and of party controls under the slogan, "Politics is the commander and soul."[79] The timing of this campaign suggests, however, that, although the CPC may have felt worried by external as well as domestic developments, it did not sense an external security crisis to the extent that it seems to have done in July, 1955, the late spring and summer of 1958, and the spring of 1962.

One reason for the difference may be that on the first two occasions the Sino-American ambassadorial contact had not been immediately available to the CPR as a means of forming an impression of American intentions. Now it was. On August 7, 1963, the two ambassadors held an unusually long meeting in Warsaw,[80] and this may have eased any Chinese fears on the score of immediate American intentions.

President Kennedy's assassination was greeted in the CPR by public rejoicing, and in private probably by a keen interest in his successor's China policy. The first major indication was to the effect that there would be no major change in President Kennedy's effort to find a less hostile basis for Sino-American relations, without going so far as to extend diplomatic recognition to the CPR. On December 13, Assistant Secretary of State Roger Hilsman delivered an important speech on China policy.[81] In it he expressed a temperate hope that the passage of time would bring to the top a new Chinese leadership less doctrinaire than its predecessors. He indicated, however, that no rapid or spectacular improvement in Sino-American relations was to be expected. He also warned American businessmen that there were obstacles to Sino-American trade on the Chinese as well as on the American side. The Chinese comment was brief and caustic, but of course not alarmed.[82]

The CPR took the occasion of the Panama crisis of January, 1964, to restate its line that "United States imperialism is a menace to the Soviet Union and all other socialist countries, and its ultimate object is to destroy the socialist camp."[83] In another, more important, statement[84] the CPR indicated that it was not interested in any alleged softening of American China policy or in moderating its own attitude toward the United States. This line probably represented a combination of genuine but long-term

[77] *The New York Times,* September 29, 1963.
[78] Cf. "The Whole Country Must Learn from the People's Liberation Army," *People's Daily,* February 1, 1964.
[79] From "Advance from Victory to New Victory," *People's Daily,* January 1, 1964.
[80] *The New York Times,* August 8, 1963.
[81] Excerpts in *The New York Times,* December 14, 1963.
[82] Cf. *The New York Times,* December 16, 1963.
[83] "All Anti-U.S.-Imperialist Forces in the World, Unite!" *People's Daily,* January 21, 1964.
[84] *People's Daily,* February 19, 1964.

fear of an American threat to the CPR's security, the lack of any sense of immediate danger,[85] and a self-imposed political compulsion to continue pillorying the United States as the sworn enemy of all "anti-imperialist" and "peace-loving" people in the world. This line could be readily moderated for specific tactical purposes, however. Mao Tse-tung is reported to have told some French visitors that the United States could get on friendly terms with the CPR by abandoning Taiwan.[86] In particular, the CPC seems to be afraid of a perpetuation and ultimate legitimation of a "two Chinas" situation as a result of American protection of Taiwan.

There can be no question that one of the most important consequences of the test ban treaty has been the Sino-French rapprochement. This trend, however, can be better understood if it is seen against the background of the CPR's policy toward Western Europe as a whole. The current phase of Chinese economic policy toward Western Europe dates roughly from the collapse of the Great Leap Forward, and the current phase of political policy from the emergence of serious strains between France and the rest of NATO, and in particular since the French veto of Britain's application to join the Common Market and the announcement of French opposition to the American proposal for a Multilateral Nuclear Force within NATO (January, 1963).

The CPR's policy toward Western Europe consists essentially of trying within limits to establish beneficial economic relations and split the region politically from the United States, while at the same time opposing Western European influence in the underdeveloped areas whenever Chinese revolutionary objectives seem to require it.

As in its dealings with other parts of the world, the CPR uses trade, or the hope of trade, as one means of promoting diplomatic recognition by Western European countries and presumes that recognition will lead sooner or later to a favorable vote on the issue of Chinese representation in the United Nations. It is generally true that Western European countries having diplomatic relations with Communist China have voted for it on this question; the main exceptions have been the United Kingdom, which did not shift from an adverse to a favorable vote until 1961, and the Netherlands, which presumably following the British lead shifted from an adverse vote to an abstention in 1961. From 1951 through 1960, the General Assembly had voted every year a "moratorium" on the Chinese representation question, so that it had not been formally discussed on its merits during that period. In 1961 the United States dropped its support of the moratorium, but a series of Communist and Afro-Asian (in 1963, Albania and

---

[85] For example, the CPR has repeatedly complained that American, as well as Chinese Nationalist, reconnaissance aircraft have overflown its territory (cf. *The New York Times*, March 10, 1964). It has also complained about the extension of the activities of the United States Seventh Fleet into the Indian Ocean.

[86] *The New York Times*, February 21, 1964.

Cambodia) efforts to gain representation for the CPR, either instead of the Republic of China or in conjunction with a relabeling of the latter's seat as belonging to "Taiwan," failed.[87]

The CPR objects to the Multilateral Nuclear Force on the ground that it will enable the United States and Britain to dominate the continental countries, but it approves of the independent French nuclear force and would like to see other European countries imitate France's example.[88] The CPR has welcomed the Common Market — even while depicting it as the "highest stage of capitalism" — the erstwhile de Gaulle-Adenauer axis within it, and France's veto of British membership, as evidences of sharpening "contradictions" among the "imperialists."[89] On the latter point, it is worth noting that the Chinese speak of Britain as a Trojan horse for the United States in Europe, whereas in the Far East they often treat it as a means of exerting pressure on the United States. For instance, whenever the CPR has found a Taiwan Strait crisis on its hands it has generally stirred up trouble of some sort in Hong Kong, presumably as a means of reminding the British of their vulnerability and the necessity for good behavior.

The reasons why the CPR should seek an expansion of its economic relations with West Germany are obvious. Diplomatic or political relations, although they would be in keeping with the CPR's "third world" policy, might seem to be out of the question because of the CPR's recognition of East Germany as a "fraternal socialist state." On the other hand, it might be pointed out that West Germany maintains diplomatic relations with neither of the "two Chinas" (presumably because of its own status as a divided country), so that it would have nothing to lose with respect to the Republic of China if it became feasible and desirable to establish a closer relationship with the CPR.[90] Furthermore, East German spokesmen have recently accused the CPR of seeking a rapprochement with West Germany at East Germany's expense.[91]

At the present time the CPR seems to be so fed up with the United Nations, and perhaps so convinced of its nonviability, that it shows no great interest in whether the United Nations complies with its longstanding conditions for admission: the expulsion of the Republic of China

[87] On the general question of the CPR and the United Nations, see Sheldon Appleton, *The Eternal Triangle? Communist China, the United States, and the United Nations*, Michigan State University Press, 1961.

[88] Ouyang Hsing, "Imperialist Contradictions Around the Question of Great Nuclear Power Status," *China Youth*, February 10, 1963; Hsieh Fan, "A Close Look at the Question of the Multilateral Nuclear Force," *World Culture*, March 10, 1963.

[89] Huan Hsing-i, "New Developments in Contradictions Among the Imperialists as Seen from the Disruption of the Brussels Talks," *World Culture*, February 20, 1963; Fan Ch'eng-hsiang, "Some Problems Concerning the Development of Current Contradictions of Imperialism," *Red Flag*, March 16, 1963.

[90] Soviet relations with East Germany did not prevent West Germany from establishing diplomatic relations with the Soviet Union in 1955, although this is the only such case to date.

[91] *The New York Times*, April 25 and May 15, 1964.

altogether, and the substitution of the CPR for it. In fact, the CPR seems to be trying to use the gradually increasing sentiment in favor of bringing the CPR into the United Nations, and into the disarmament talks that it sponsors, as a means of improving Peking's chances of getting control of Taiwan.

Switzerland, because of its recognition of the CPR and its unique international status, has long been a major base for Chinese activity in Western Europe. Apart from the possibility of increased trade, this continues to be its main usefulness to the CPR.[92] The Chinese would probably like to see the Swiss acquire nuclear weapons, a possibility that was kept open by a referendum held in April, 1962.[93]

Sweden has served as a comparable Chinese listening post and base of operations in northern Europe. In addition, its highly modern armed forces and its nearness to the Soviet Union make it interesting to the CPR as a possible source of military aid and support.[94]

Although Portugal has generally abstained in the United Nations on the Chinese representation question and has shown approval of the CPR's anti-Indian policies since the Indian seizure of Goa in December, 1961, there seems to be little overt interest on the Chinese side in an improvement of relations. The main probable reason is that the CPR assigns a higher priority to giving political and perhaps military support to revolutionaries in Angola and Portuguese Guinea.

The most important aspect of the CPR's current Western European policy, and probably of its response to the test ban treaty as well, is of course its relationship with France. The analogies between the positions of the CPR and France within their respective alliance systems are obvious and are the main reason for the relationship that they have established with each other. There are also important differences between their positions, however. The CPR is engaged in a direct struggle with the United States, over Taiwan and many other things, and feels that both its security and the achievement of its external objectives are therefore in danger. The trend toward détente has probably decreased the chances of a major war between the CPR and the United States markedly less than it has decreased the chances of such a war between the Soviet Union and the United States. These considerations, or their analogue, do not apply to France. There is very little direct clash of interests between France and the Soviet Union, and France would be in danger from the Soviet Union only in the context of general war or something approaching it, not in the context of a direct Soviet strike against France alone. Thus Soviet-Western détente, by diminishing the chances of general war over Europe, has had much more

---

92 For details see *The Washington Post and Times Herald,* January 26, 1964.
93 Chou En-lai selected the Swiss embassy in Peking as the place to make a major disarmament proposal (on August 1, 1960).
94 A Chinese military mission visited Sweden in the autumn of 1963.

value and brought greater freedom of maneuver to France than it has to the CPR. The French third force policy therefore has a larger element of opportunism in it, the Chinese third force policy a larger element of fear.

In a general sense, de Gaulle's recognition of Communist China forms a major part of his own third force policy, along with such other components as increased trade with the European Communist countries and expanded relations with Latin America. Probable specific considerations, in addition to those already mentioned, are France's traditionally poor relations with the Republic of China, a desire to shield Cambodia and French-speaking Africa from Communist pressures, interest in increasing pressures on the United States and more particularly on the Soviet Union, and a hope for at least moral support in defying the test ban treaty.

The Chinese, for their part, regard recognition by a third permanent member of the United Nations Security Council as a major enhancement of their international status and of their chances of entering the United Nations and gaining additional diplomatic recognitions, especially in the French-speaking countries of Africa. French recognition tends to worsen relations between the United States and Western Europe and to increase Chinese leverage on the United States, the Soviet Union, and perhaps the French Communist Party. It provides an additional important base for Chinese activity in Western Europe. It offers at least a possible way out of the tension between political necessity and military danger in Vietnam. It seems to open the way to some useful trade, including imports of French oildrilling and refining equipment and Saharan oil. It might facilitate China's defiance of the test ban treaty and its ambition to become a nuclear power.[95]

De Gaulle expressed in November, 1959, the view that there were serious differences between Communist China and the Soviet Union and strongly implied that France might take the lead in bringing the latter into a more cooperative relationship with the West.[96] Khrushchev's subsequent behavior, beginning with his wrecking of the Paris summit conference, frustrated this hope and may have suggested to de Gaulle the idea of trying to work with the other partner in the Sino-Soviet relationship. De Gaulle then turned his attention to other matters, such as the Common Market and his rapprochement with Adenauer. The Algerian settlement in early 1962 created at the least the political possibility of a Sino-French relationship. In mid-1963, de Gaulle was greatly perturbed by the test ban treaty and the prospect of a Multilateral Nuclear Force, both of which seemed to be adverse to France's position as an independent nuclear power, and the first of which seemed to constitute another effort by the "Anglo-Saxon

---

[95] Thorez has recently referred to the "de facto agreement between de Gaulle and Mao Tse-tung about the dissemination of the nuclear weapon" (quoted in *The Washington Post and Times Herald*, March 29, 1964).

[96] *The New York Times*, November 11, 1959.

powers" and the Soviet Union, like the one at Yalta, to settle matters of concern to Europe without European participation.[97] Another consideration, of lesser importance, relates to the Indochina crisis. The crisis in South Vietnam that began in August, 1963, seems to have convinced de Gaulle that the time had come for French support for neutralization of Vietnam. Such an arrangement would benefit mainly North Vietnam, but it might also allow of a French "presence" once more. Communist China had endorsed the idea of neutralization in 1962, presumably with the idea of eventually enlarging its own influence. De Gaulle, on the other hand, seems to want to reduce Chinese influence in the Indochina area; this goal, if attainable at all, evidently appears to him to be so only within the context of Sino-French diplomatic relations.

The foundation for the establishment of such relations was laid by a visit to the CPR by former French Premier Edgar Faure in October–November 1963.[98] The Hilsman speech on December 13 may have accelerated the process, by suggesting that the United States was contemplating some modifications in its China policy, even though it could not be expected to approve of French recognition of the CPR. An ambiguous arrangement was worked out at the beginning of 1964 whereby recognition would be extended and reciprocated without France's breaking relations with the Republic of China, where it had purely nominal diplomatic representation. It seems that this arrangement was differently interpreted by the two parties. The French knew that the United States was urging the Republic of China not to break relations with France and therefore hoped for a time that French recognition might pave the way for acceptance, by Peking and Taipei as well as the rest of the world, of "two Chinas."[99] The CPR, on the other hand, has always attributed the desire for "two Chinas" to the United States and some of its "lackeys," never to the Republic of China, and it correspondingly seems to have expected from the beginning that the latter would break relations with France.[100]

The CPR and France exchanged recognitions on January 27, 1964, with an indication by each side that recognition did not imply approval of the other's social system, and under an arrangement whereby ambassadors were to be exchanged within three months. Contrary to the CPR's expecta-

---

[97] See de Gaulle's statement on the treaty (in *The New York Times*, July 30, 1963).

[98] Faure had also visited the CPR in 1956 (cf. his *The Serpent and the Tortoise: Problems of the New China*, New York: St. Martin's Press, 1958). See Stephen Erasmus, "General de Gaulle's Recognition of Peking," *The China Quarterly*, no. 18 (April–June, 1964), pp. 195–200.

[99] The hope that the Republic of China would not break relations with France seems to have been conveyed to Taipei by General Zinovi Pechkoff, a former French ambassador to China, during a visit on behalf of General de Gaulle in January, 1964, but Pechkoff apparently was told that the Republic of China would break relations if France recognized the CPR (*The New York Times*, January 26, 1964).

[100] Cf. *The New York Times*, January 30, 1964.

tions, and the current French view as well, the Republic of China did not sever relations with France, and France made no move to initiate such a break. The CPR thereupon issued a pointed reminder to France and the world that the "government of the People's Republic of China" was the "sole legal government representing all the Chinese people," that "recognition of the new government of a country naturally implies ceasing to recognize the old ruling group overthrown by the people of that country," and that "The Chinese Government deems it necessary to reaffirm that Taiwan is part of China's territory and that any attempt to detach Taiwan from China or otherwise to create 'two Chinas' is absolutely unacceptable to the Chinese Government and people."[101]

This put France in an extremely embarrassing position, from which the least ungraceful way out was to maneuver the Republic of China into being the first to break relations. This was accomplished on February 10, after a statement by de Gaulle that France recognized only one China. The implication was that the Republic of China could maintain relations with France only in the capacity of the government of Taiwan, something that by now was obviously unacceptable to Taipei.[102] Only then were definite arrangements made for an exchange of chargés d'affaires between Paris and Peking. An agreement to exchange ambassadors was announced on April 27, exactly three months after recognition. The CPR's first ambassador to France was to be Huang Chen, a former ambassador to Indonesia. Huang left a post as Deputy Minister of Foreign Affairs in order to come to Paris.[103] France retained purely consular representation in Taiwan. Thus its relations with China superficially resembled those of Britain, which maintains diplomatic relations with the CPR and has consular representation on Taiwan. The British, however, have never been able to exchange ambassadors with the CPR. The reason for the difference appears to be that Britain is regarded in Peking as a "lackey" of the United States, whereas France is not.

As might have been expected, the course of the Franco-Chinese marriage of convenience has not run very smoothly. Premier Pompidou has suggested self-determination for Taiwan, an idea that is anathema to the CPR.[104] The CPR has begun to establish a major political base in France, which it evidently hopes will serve to promote not only its national objectives but also its revolutionary objectives in Africa as well as in Europe. The CPR attacked French policy toward and influence in Gabon and the former French Congo simultaneously with the latter's recognition of the CPR.[105] The French government suppressed the seventh issue of the CPC's propaganda publication *Révolution*, published in Paris (the English edition

---

101 CPR statement, New China News Agency dispatch, January 28, 1964.
102 *The New York Times*, February 11, 1964.
103 *The New York Times*, April 28, 1964.
104 *The New York Times*, April 24, 1964.
105 *The New York Times*, February 24, 1964.

is published in Switzerland). This issue demanded independence for the remaining French insular dependencies and pictured their inhabitants as living in poverty and oppression.[106] It would be surprising if further strains did not develop in the Franco-Chinese relationship, which to date has been decidedly more advantageous to the CPR than to France.

[106] *Christian Science Monitor*, March 25, 1964. On *Révolution* see *Christian Science Monitor*, March 5, 7, 1964.

☐ 6

China and International Communism

Communist China's relations with the Soviet Union and the rest of the Communist bloc and the international Communist movement have attracted worldwide attention in recent years and have received more adequate treatment in readily available published sources than has any other aspect of Chinese external relations. For this reason, and also because some aspects have been discussed in previous chapters, the treatment in this one will be kept as brief as possible.

■ SINO-SOVIET DIFFERENCES: SOURCES AND GENERAL COMMENTS[1]

In a field as vast and complex as that of Sino-Soviet differences, it is often difficult to distinguish cause from effect.

Among what I regard as the fundamental causes of Sino-Soviet differences, I would list first the sociological category, without necessarily implying that it is the most important.[2] This includes such factors as the immense differences between the essentially European, less civilized Russian tradition and the thoroughly Asian and highly sophisticated Chinese tradition.[3] It includes the serious but not overwhelming antagonisms between

---

[1] Excellent brief analyses are Leonard Schapiro in Kurt London, ed., *Unity and Contradiction: Major Aspects of Sino-Soviet Relations*, New York: Praeger, 1962, pp. 353–374; Richard Lowenthal, "Factors of Unity and Factors of Conflict," *The American Academy of Political and Social Science*, vol. 349 (September, 1963), pp. 106–116.

[2] Cf. T. H. Rigby in London, *op. cit.*, pp. 19–36.

[3] The standard treatment of this aspect is Klaus Mehnert, *Peking and Moscow*, New York: G. P. Putnam, 1963.

the Russian and Chinese states and (to a lesser extent) peoples in modern times. It includes the current, competitive nationalisms and messianisms of the two systems.

A second major source of the differences is the profound divergence between the respective historical experiences of the two parties, both before and since the seizure of power. The Soviet party came to power suddenly, almost accidentally, and it then had to extemporize its political institutions in an environment of civil war and foreign intervention. Partly because of the unavoidable immaturity of those institutions, it succumbed to a full-blown totalitarian tyranny. In its external relations it was primarily oriented toward the West. This orientation, overwhelmingly hostile, had much to do with the outbreak of the Second World War and the unleashing of the *furor teutonicus* first on Western Europe and then on the Soviet Union itself.[4] The Chinese party came to power in a much more prolonged and complex fashion. By the time it came to power, it had already developed on a regional basis political institutions that could then be extended to the entire country. Essentially, civil war and foreign intervention occurred before rather than after the seizure of power. The CPC has never permitted the emergence of terroristic police rule, under the control of one man, to any-thing like the extent that prevailed in the Soviet Union under Stalin. The CPC has been oriented toward Asia. To the extent that it has helped to precipitate a major regional war, it did so in the 1930's, by giving Japanese militarists a convenient pretext for invading China. Only once since 1949, at the beginning of 1953, has the CPR verged on being the cause, intentional or unintentional, of a major Far Eastern war. It is unlikely to precipitate a comparable crunch again.

Nevertheless, with respect to the third major cause of Sino-Soviet differences, the divergent national positions and interests of the two regimes, it is the Chinese party that is the more militant and irreconcilable. China is a poor and divided country, and the CPC feels itself threatened by "imperialism." The Soviet Union, although it has some serious internal problems (notably in agriculture) and some unsatisfied external objectives (notably with respect to Germany), is, comparatively speaking, a satiated power. It is more its ideological interests, including the need to compete with the CPC in the international Communist arena, than its national interests that tend to bring it into conflict with the West.

Finally, there was undoubtedly a personal antipathy and a state of rivalry for authority and leadership within the international Communist movement between Mao and Khrushchev. As for the personal antipathy, Mao's wife is reported recently to have told a visitor that her husband disliked Khrushchev because he had bad table manners and became malodorous when excited. There is no doubt that Mao regarded Khrushchev's

---

[4] Cf. George F. Kennan, *Russia and the West Under Lenin and Stalin,* New York: Mentor, 1962, pp. 268ff.

political style, such as his shoe-pounding at the United Nations, as boorish. The contest for authority and leadership between the two men is also a valid and important aspect of the problem,[5] although it cannot explain everything. Mao has undoubtedly considered himself the world's senior Communist since the death of Stalin and resented Khrushchev's efforts, beginning with the Twentieth Congress, to give ideological and strategic guidance to the entire international Communist movement.

One of the most important, and superficially one of the most surprising, aspects of the Sino-Soviet dispute is the tendency for ideology to become a divisive rather than a unifying factor. Actually, this tendency should not surprise any one who has studied the history of religion, in which Communism represents a recent, secularist mutation. Within an authoritarian religious or quasi-religious movement, ideology becomes an intensely divisive force whenever it is differently interpreted by two autonomous power centers. Within such a movement, the heretic is generally seen as worse than the infidel.

One of the most fundamental aspects of the differences of outlook between the Soviet and Chinese parties is the disagreement over the nature of the current historical era. The CPSU has held, since about the time of the Twentieth Congress at any rate, that the dominant characteristic of the present era is the growing strength of the "socialist camp" and the increasing influence that it is exerting, largely through the force of example, on the course of world affairs. From this proposition the Soviet leadership draws, not always explicitly, three inferences of great operational significance: The only thing that could stop or reverse this trend is a general war; such a war must therefore be avoided at virtually any cost; and the thing most likely to precipitate such a war would be excessive revolutionary pressures on the "imperialist camp." The CPC holds, on the other hand, that the dominant characteristic of the present era is the decline of "imperialism," especially in the underdeveloped areas. "Imperialism," while weakening, is still dangerous, but it is most unlikely to give way to its perpetual impulse to initiate general war because it knows or believes that to do so would be to commit suicide. It is therefore possible and necessary to apply militant pressures on "imperialism," especially in the underdeveloped areas, and these are not likely to escalate into general war.[6]

Parallel with this major difference of views goes a divergence of political styles. Being fundamentally afraid of war, the Soviet party is strategically cautious, even if tactically bold on occasion. It tends to rely on economic

---

[5] This aspect is stressed by Franz Michael; see his "Khrushchev's Disloyal Opposition: Structural Change and Power Struggle in the Communist Bloc," *Orbis,* vol. vii, no. 1 (spring, 1963), pp. 49–76; and his contribution to Kurt London, ed., *New Nations in a Divided World: The International Relations of the Afro-Asian States,* New York: Praeger, 1963, pp. 236–255, especially p. 246.

[6] Cf. Donald S. Zagoria, *The Sino-Soviet Conflict, 1956–1961,* Princeton University Press, 1962, pp. 348ff.

activity of various kinds, which is both feasible and safe and which it refers to as "peaceful economic competition with capitalism,"[7] as probably the most important single means of promoting its economic objectives.[8] To the CPC, on the other hand, general war seems less likely and local war therefore less risky. The Soviet approach appears to be a "no win" strategy. Economic activity is useful at most as a minor instrumentality, because of China's poverty and backwardness, and in any case the CPC has fairly consistently demonstrated, at home and abroad, a preference for political over economic lines of activity. This tendency was never more evident than in 1958, at the height of the Great Leap Forward, when the slogan was, "politics in command."

Much as the CPC believes in strategic boldness, so it has been generally on the strategic offensive against the Soviet party since about 1956, even if sometimes on the tactical defensive. This has been especially true in the fields of ideology and strategy, where the Soviet party's economic and military strength does it little good and where the CPC's political skill and boldness and self-proclaimed ideological orthodoxy have been fairly effective. There is no doubt that the CPC has scored remarkable gains in this bizarre contest since about 1960. Whether one considers that these gains are sufficient to justify saying that the CPC has won, or will win, the contest is a matter of interpretation. Much depends on one's estimate of the CPC's ultimate objective, and in particular on whether this objective amounts to solid leadership or even control of the international Communist movement. As indicated earlier, it seems wisest to leave this question open.

Finally, the question may be raised whether the Sino-Soviet dispute helps or harms the cause of Communism, on balance. There was once a widespread impression that there was really no dispute at all.[9] When this view became untenable after 1960, some of its proponents shifted to a slightly less unsophisticated variant whereby the Russians and Chinese were feigning a dispute in order to confuse and weaken the West. Under this interpretation, which made as little sense as it would to insist that rival popes maintained themselves at Rome and Avignon in the fourteenth century in order to confuse and weaken the Orthodox and Islamic worlds, the dispute would of course be a source of strength. An improved variant of this, now that the dispute is admitted by virtually everyone to be genuine, is that the dispute is a "nonantagonistic contradiction" within the framework of the dialectic, and therefore not a serious source of tension or weakness.[10] To

---

[7] Cf. Nikita S. Khrushchev, "On Peaceful Coexistence," *Foreign Affairs*, vol. 38, no. 1 (October, 1959), pp. 1–18.

[8] Cf. ". . . at present, we use our economic policy as the main influence toward world revolution" (S. Chervonenko, Soviet ambassador to the CPR, speech as quoted by New China News Agency, November 6, 1960).

[9] See, for example, "Bear and Dragon, What Is the Relation Between Moscow and Peking," supplement to the *National Review*, November 5, 1960.

[10] Cf. Peter S. H. Tang, "Moscow and Peking: The Question of War and Peace," *Orbis*, vol. v, no. 1 (spring, 1961), pp. 15–30.

argue in this way is to allow oneself to be captured by the Communists' way of looking at their own problems and unconsciously to accept its validity.

A more reasonable view would hold that since the Sino-Soviet dispute promotes polycentrism and devolution within world Communism, it may make Communism more attractive to prospective converts. So it may to some, but most potential intellectual Communists are people looking for total, infallible solutions, and the Sino-Soviet dispute hardly enhances Communism's aura of infallibility. Or again, it is sometimes argued that the Soviet approach may succeed in some areas, and the Chinese in others, in a way that would be impossible under a monolithic system. This may be true, but it does not follow that Communism as a whole is necessarily the stronger for it.

The most persuasive view, it seems to me, is that the Sino-Soviet dispute is a source of serious weakness, or at least potential weakness, within the Communist fold. Evidence advanced at various places in this study suggests that this proposition has been validated by experience. However true the proposition may be, its significance for the non-Communist world will obviously depend to a considerable extent on the degree to which the latter tries actively to exploit the dispute, not in a generalized hardnosed fashion but pragmatically in particular relevant situations.

■ SINO-SOVIET DIFFERENCES: THE STATE ASPECT

It has already been suggested that there are differences, and even conflicts, of national interest between the CPR and the Soviet Union.

One aspect of these is an old-fashioned rivalry for territory and spheres of influence. There is a Sino-Soviet border dispute of sorts. It is unlikely, however, that Chinese population growth will ever lead to development of the Chinese border regions sufficient to put demographic pressures on Soviet Asian territory, as was predicted by a German doctor in 1954, in a widely discussed book.[11] There is also an undeniable rivalry for influence in Asia, both on Communist Parties and regimes and on non-Communist governments and political movements.

A good example is Outer Mongolia. Here Chinese activity and influence have increased somewhat since 1952. Nevertheless, while the Mongols no longer show overt signs of being a Soviet satellite they have remained thoroughly loyal to the Soviet Union in the Sino-Soviet dispute, and Soviet influence far outweighs Chinese.[12] Despite a Sino-Mongolian boundary treaty signed at the end of 1962, the Mongols like the Russians accused

[11] Cf. John E. Tashjean, *Where China Meets Russia: An Analysis of Dr. Starlinger's Theory*, Washington: Central Asian Collectanea, ed. Rudolf Loewenthal, no. 2, 1959.

[12] Cf. Robert A. Rupen in A. Doak Barnett, ed., *Communist Strategies in Asia*, New York: Praeger, 1963, pp. 262–292; Robert A. Rupen, "Mongolia in the Sino-Soviet Dispute," *The China Quarterly*, no. 16 (October–December, 1963), pp. 75–85.

the CPC in 1963, among other things, of distributing anti-Soviet propaganda on their soil.[13] A large number of Chinese technicians and workers were expelled from Outer Mongolia shortly afterward.[14] The main probable reason for the undeviatingly pro-Soviet orientation of at least the dominant element in the Outer Mongolian leadership is the traditional Mongol fear (since traditional times) of Chinese imperialism. In addition to that, the Soviet Union has always taken care to maintain Outer Mongolia as a buffer, if not as a satellite, since 1921.[15] It is entirely possible that, under a Soviet-Mongolian alliance dating from 1936, there are Soviet troops in Outer Mongolia.

Significant Soviet political (other than revolutionary) and economic activity around the Chinese periphery began in the mid-1950s: in India about 1955, with economic aid and political support on such issues as Kashmir; in Indonesia about 1956, with economic and later military aid and political support on such issues as West Irian (Dutch New Guinea); and in Japan about 1956, with diplomatic recognition, something that the CPR was in no position to duplicate because of Japan's relations with the Republic of China. The main original purpose of this Soviet activity was almost certainly to counter American policy, such as military aid to Pakistan, and exploit neutral Asian objections to it. Soon, however, Soviet activity seems to have acquired the important additional objective of building counterweights to the CPR. The policy was perhaps most obvious in India, the only one of the three countries mentioned that has a continental rather than an insular location; most strenuous in Indonesia, where a direct confrontation with "imperialism" was in progress when Soviet and East European military aid began in 1958; and most difficult in Japan, which is probably the only major country in Asia where the Soviet Union is regarded with more fear and dislike than is the CPR. The CPC has expressed keen resentment at Soviet aid to and support of India, expecially in connection with the Sino-Indian border dispute.[16] A probable reflection of this resentment is the fact that at the end of 1962, after the Sino-Indian fighting, the CPR withdrew its ambassador, P'an Tzu-li, from New Delhi without replacing him and designated him as ambassador in Moscow, where he could presumably present or at least symbolize the Chinese case on the Sino-Indian dispute. In mid-1964, Mikoyan visited Japan, India, Indonesia, and Burma, with the obvious purpose of mending Soviet fences against Chinese influence. In Indonesia he made a new military aid commitment and may have received

---

13 Resolution of Fifth Plenary Session of the Central Committee of the Mongolian People's Revolutionary Party (not published until June 13, 1964, in *Unen*).

14 *The New York Times*, May 22, 1964.

15 Cf. William B. Ballis, "The Political Evolution of a Soviet Satellite: The Mongolian People's Republic," *The Western Political Quarterly*, vol. 9, no. 2 (June, 1956), pp. 293–328.

16 E.g., "The Truth About How the Leaders of the CPSU Have Allied Themselves with India Against China," *People's Daily*, November 1, 1963.

in exchange a pledge to work for the Soviet Union's admission, which the CPR opposes, to the forthcoming second Asian-African (Bandung) Conference.[17]

As already indicated, there are serious strains in the Sino-Soviet alliance, stemming mainly from Soviet fear of involvement in a Far Eastern war (over Taiwan, in particular), Soviet reluctance to see the CPR become a nuclear power, and Soviet moves toward détente and disarmament agreements with the West. It is also highly probable that fallout from Soviet nuclear tests has affected the CPR and caused its leadership concern.[18]

Another source of friction, and indeed the main source in the opinion of some, has been economic relations, despite the large and indispensable Soviet contribution to the Chinese industrialization program down to 1960. The CPR evidently resented the ending of Soviet long-term credits in 1957, Soviet efforts to integrate the Chinese economy into the Council of Economic Mutual Assistance, the withdrawal of Soviet technical assistance in 1960, and Soviet refusal to give the CPR what the latter regarded as due consideration in its hour of economic crisis. At that time the Soviet Union seems to have fixed a ceiling on the value of its exports to the CPR and allowed the Chinese to choose what to import within the quota. Petroleum was one of the main items that the CPR continued to import from the Soviet Union.[19] There have been some recent indications, however, that Soviet petroleum exports to the CPR have declined or ended, at whose initiative is not clear. Among these indications are Chinese dealings with such other petroleum exporters as Rumania, Iraq, and Indonesia.

Finally, it has been clear since about 1954 that there has been little effective coordination between Soviet and Communist Chinese foreign policies. The most spectacular example is probably the wide divergence between Soviet and Chinese behavior in the Sino-Indian border and Cuban crises of 1962, where there was not only lack of coordination but outright antagonism.

■ SINO-SOVIET DIFFERENCES: THE PARTY ASPECT

Broadly speaking, the relationship between the Soviet and Chinese parties has tended to shift from one of bargaining between partners[20] to one of rivalry between opponents. The transition from the one phase to the other may be considered to have occurred between 1956 and 1960. In the

---

[17] *The New York Times*, July 5, 1964.

[18] Cf. *The New York Times*, October 28, 1961.

[19] Cf. Oleg Hoeffding, "Sino-Soviet Economic Relations, 1959–1962," *The Annals of the American Academy of Political and Social Science*, vol. 349 (September, 1963), pp. 94–105.

[20] On this phase see Zbigniew Brzezinski in London, *Unity and Contradiction, op. cit.*, pp. 382–405.

earlier phase, the unity between the two parties, and the unity of the entire "socialist camp," had genuine meaning for each, although tendencies adverse to it were certainly present. During the transition phase, unity became increasingly a bargaining device or hostage, the threat of whose destruction was used, especially by the Chinese, to extract concessions from the other party. As both the seemingly more orthodox and the seemingly more willing to see unity killed rather than compromised, the CPC enjoyed important psychological advantages in this process. After 1960 unity was dead, although it still appeared possible for it to be resurrected through the death or surrender of one of the opposing leaders, and each party devoted itself to an effort to prove the other guilty of the murder. In 1963 the Russians all but destroyed what was left of the state relationship, and the Chinese all but destroyed what was left of the party relationship, so that a schism existed in fact although not quite in name. Such, roughly and in brief, have been the dynamics of the star-crossed Sino-Soviet party relationship.

On occasion, each party has intervened or tried to intervene in the internal affairs of the other, in the hope of promoting favored individuals and policies, but with little success. First Stalin and then Beria probably tried to use Kao Kang in this way. Khrushchev almost certainly tried to use P'eng Te-huai in this way. The CPC certainly played at least an indirect role in the post-Stalin succession crisis in the Soviet Union. For a time after October, 1954, it gave at least passive support to Khrushchev, specifically in his contest with Malenkov. How actively the CPC expressed its sympathy for the "anti-party group" in the crisis that led to its overthrow by Khrushchev in June, 1957, is uncertain. There is evidence, however, that the CPC had contacts with Molotov during the period (1957–60) when he was the Soviet ambassador to Outer Mongolia.[21] After that the CPC evidently pinned its hopes on Kozlov until his disappearance in the spring of 1963. Throughout the recent stages of the open debate between the parties, each has aimed its shafts explicitly at the other's leadership and thus implicitly called for a removal of that leadership from below. Even if a new leadership were not much more congenial to the opponent than the old, there might be some advantages in a turnover in the ranks of the other party.

The Sino-Soviet difference of opinion, mentioned earlier, on the nature of the present era is closely related to divergent views of "imperialism," although this divergence seems to be less pronounced than the one over the question of how to deal with it.

Leaving aside the superficially similar terms in which the Russians and Chinese discuss the nature of "imperialism," we can infer that Khrushchev considered it to be objectively more dangerous (if directly provoked), and

---

[21] One of the indications of this is the fact that Kuusinen said at the Twenty-second Congress that Molotov "decided to muddy the water so that later on he could try to catch fish in there. . . . If it is not in the domestic reservoirs, then perhaps in some foreign waters" (Moscow radio, October 27, 1961).

subjectively less aggressive, than does Mao. Probably the only element of the "imperialist camp" that seems to pose a serious threat to Soviet national interests even in the absence of direct Soviet provocation is West Germany. The United States is of course an obstacle, and in the long run perhaps an active threat, to the achievement of Soviet revolutionary objectives. The common interest of the two superpowers in the avoidance of general war seemed to Khrushchev so great that genuine negotiations and various kinds of disarmament agreements and détente were both possible and necessary. This might seemingly postpone the revolutionization of the underdeveloped areas, but to act otherwise would be to risk provoking the destruction of the "socialist camp" and thus to incur an irretrievable setback to the otherwise irresistible, if gradual, advance of world Communism.

The CPC is somewhat less concerned about the objective danger of "imperialism," in part because of the latter's preoccupation with the Soviet Union and the existence of at least a nominal Sino-Soviet alliance. Thus the CPC is less reluctant than the CPSU to become involved, by proxy at least, in local wars in which "imperialism" may be directly involved on the other side. The CPC, on the other hand, claims to be much more convinced of the incurable subjective aggressiveness of "imperialism" than the CPSU is. It is difficult to say whether this claim represents a genuine conviction or a fear that to leave the Soviet interpretation of "imperialism" unchallenged would merely invite further Soviet moves toward a détente with the West, with disadvantageous effects on Chinese interests; probably each hypothesis is partly valid. To the extent that the latter hypothesis corresponds to the Chinese view, it seems to have had some basis in fact down to the crises of 1962, in the sense that prior to that time Chinese pressures on Khrushchev probably did tend to push him on occasion into greater hostility to the West than he would otherwise have displayed. The crises of 1962, however, seem to have convinced Khrushchev that at least for the time being the military danger of yielding to Chinese pressures for a hard line toward the West outweighed the political danger of resisting those pressures. To the extent that the CPC is genuinely convinced of the "brutish" and aggressive nature of "imperialism," it can find some basis for believing that the United States is not only an obstacle but an active threat to the achievement of both the CPC's national and revolutionary objectives. The CPC holds that as long as "imperialism" exists, local (not general) war is "inevitable," "general and complete disarmament" and a genuine détente are essentially a dream, and negotiations with "imperialism" are permissible and useful only for tactical and defensive reasons (as at Warsaw), or for the propaganda purpose of "unmasking imperialism." Although this view did not prevent the CPR from playing a serious and important part in the Geneva Conferences of 1954 and 1961–62, it has clearly contributed, together with such other factors as partial diplomatic isolation, to making the CPR a far less frequent participant than the Soviet Union in negotiations and conferences with the West.

Obviously the question of "imperialism" is closely linked in Communist minds with that of war and peace. If we again leave largely to one side the confusing terminology that encrusts the dialogue, it is clear that neither side wants general war. The CPC has said so flatly in recent years, in order to counteract the politically disadvantageous opposite impression that it had seen fit to create after the Twentieth Congress.[22] Nor is there any convincing reason to doubt the genuineness of the current Chinese disavowal of desire for general war. Even if the CPR were not a primary "imperialist" target in such a war — and it can never be certain that it would not be — it could be rendered largely uninhabitable merely from the fallout produced by a thermonuclear attack on the Soviet Union. If the CPR were a primary target, the industrial installations and command and control centers that it has worked and sacrificed to build would be totally destroyed. Its population and agricultural land, which are heavily concentrated in the eastern third of the country, might well suffer fatal damage. Even if the Chinese people survived, the Chinese Communist regime probably would not. It is inconceivable that a leadership that in its actual external behavior — not necessarily in its pronouncements — generally displays a high degree of realism and tactical caution has not thought through a matter of such central importance to its own survival and that of its people. In fact, secret Chinese military papers dating from 1961 prove that the CPC has given much thought to these problems.[23]

Thus what has superficially appeared to be a Sino-Soviet debate on the effects of general war has actually been a debate on its likelihood. Even on this score the difference is more complex than it might appear. If either the Soviet or Chinese party thought that there were a serious likelihood (since 1957 at any rate) of "imperialism" launching a general thermonuclear war except under grave provocation, it would have shown much more alarm than either has in fact done. Nor would it be reasonable to suppose that the difference lies in each party's estimate of the likelihood of its own involvement in general war from an early stage. As already suggested, the CPR can feel no assurance, at least since it inaugurated its own nuclear weapons program, that it could remain on the sidelines during a thermonuclear exchange between the Soviet Union and the United States. Hence the CPR would have no incentive, even if it had the ability, to catalyze such an exchange.

The basic Sino-Soviet difference on war seems to reduce itself to a

---

[22] For an analysis generally similar to mine but differing in some respects, see Davis B. Bobrow, "Peking's Military Calculus," *World Politics*, vol. xvi, no. 2 (January, 1964), pp. 287–301.

[23] Alice Langley Hsieh, "China's Secret Military Papers: Military Doctrine and Strategy," *The China Quarterly*, no. 18 (April–June, 1964), pp. 79–97.

divergence as to the likelihood of general war growing out of local war through a process of escalation, and as to the best means of preventing such a contingency. The CPC believes, or at least insisted apparently in earnest down to about 1962, that the Soviet Union's power confers on it the ability and obligation to exert pressures on "imperialism," including intervention in local wars, of a kind that the CPR is not in a position to duplicate. Since 1962, and the Cuban missile crisis in particular, the CPC no longer seems seriously to expect Soviet intervention of this kind, and it is more concerned with denouncing the Russians for their unwillingness to intervene. The CPC must have always realized, and it was reminded in 1962, that the strategic striking power of the United States is targeted overwhelmingly on the Soviet Union, and that the Soviet Union too is aware of that fact. This situation inhibits Soviet willingness to intervene directly in local wars. On the other hand, it also creates a kind of differential threshold in favor of the CPR, which can do at relatively low risk things that it would be unsafe for the Soviet Union to do at all. A major reason for this is of course the lingering American conviction that a major war against the CPR might either produce Soviet intervention or retaliation or might at least leave the Soviet Union free to make gains elsewhere. It would therefore be "the wrong war, at the wrong place, at the wrong time, and with the wrong enemy."

A hypothetical example may make this important point clearer. In 1958 the CPR shelled Quemoy, an island garrisoned by, and recognized by the United States as belonging to, the Republic of China, with which the United States had (and has) an alliance, without creating any serious risk of a major war. If the Soviet Union took an analogous action, say by shelling a Norwegian coastal island, the danger of a major war would be very great.

In short, the CPC sees both the superpowers as hobbled by their fear of each other, and its own interests as served by trying to embroil them with one another as long as the confrontation does not escalate into general war. Such efforts are relatively safe from the Chinese standpoint, since the superpowers are obviously at least as determined as the CPR that there shall be no general war.

The concept of the differential threshold probably accounts for much of the significant difference between the Soviet and Chinese attitudes toward local war (using the term in the restricted sense of wars involving forces of an "imperialist" power and weapons up to but not beyond tactical nuclear weapons). The Soviet attitude, as suggested earlier, seems to be that overt intervention in such wars by the "socialist camp," at least if the United States is involved on the "imperialist" side, may lead to escalation of the conflict to the level of general war. The best course for the Soviet Union is to deter, or halt, such wars by threats if possible, but not to involve itself directly, except perhaps to the extent of sending arms and — less likely — "volunteers."

The CPC considers this Soviet attitude to be craven and oblivious of the distinction between "just" (revolutionary) and "unjust" (counter-revolutionary) wars. The "socialist camp," says the CPC, must "resolutely support" the "people" in all such wars, by whomever unleashed, and regardless of whether the United States is involved. The CPC generally refrains from hinting at the method; presumably it favors in principle the strongest "support" feasible in a given case without prohibitive risk, up to and including the commitment of Communist bloc forces or at least "volunteers." The CPC apparently has a lower estimate than the CPSU of the likelihood that the "imperialists" will retaliate for such action by escalating the conflict to the level of general war. This is because the CPC regards "imperialism" as irresolute, even though strong.

What should be the nationality of these forces, if they are committed? This is an important question, since the country that sends them will run the most immediate risks but also stand to make gains in the event of success. In the days of the assumed "missile gap" in favor of the Soviet Union, the CPC apparently wanted the "resolutely supporting" forces to be Soviet, since the Soviet Union could hardly be expected to run the risks inherent in deterring escalation, through a credible threat of strategic retaliation on behalf of Communist bloc forces operating on foreign soil, unless those forces were its own. Since about 1961, however, the United States has become increasingly convinced that if there is a "missile gap" it is in favor of the United States. Thus the rationale for the CPC's apparent advocacy of committing Soviet forces to local wars has largely collapsed, at least for the present.

From the political standpoint, this situation is by no means entirely disadvantageous to the CPC. In cases where the Soviet Union appears to have the power but lacks the will to intervene, the CPC may be able to discredit the Soviet Union and promote an alternative approach of its own. This places less emphasis on material and more on moral "support," and hence on guerrilla rather than on regular warfare. It also may include, however, the cautious and ambiguous commitment of non-Soviet Communist forces (primarily Chinese or North Vietnamese to date) to nearby areas when necessary, on the basis of the differential threshold concept.

Although the Soviet and Chinese parties agree on the necessity for "peaceful coexistence," they disagree strongly on the meaning and application of the latter term. The CPC asserts, with some justification, that Khrushchev has made "peaceful coexistence" into a permanent strategic principle of the Soviet Union's relations, not only with the non-"imperialist" but with the "imperialist" countries. This, the CPC asserts, amounts to "begging imperialism for peace." The CPC contends that with the "imperialist" countries "peaceful coexistence" can be no more than a temporary tactic, never a permanent strategy, nor can it be interpreted as ruling out revolutionary violence against "capitalist" governments.[24] "Peaceful co-existence," in the Chinese view, can be elevated to the dignity of a strategy only in the context of relations between the "socialist camp" and the un-committed countries. As the basis and precedent for such relations, the CPC constantly cites its own "Five Principles of Peaceful Coexistence," which are very vague, apply only to state relations, and offer no guarantee against Chinese pressures and intervention through party channels. An analogous Sino-Soviet difference exists with regard to the "peace move-ment" ("ban the bomb," etc.). Khrushchev regarded this as the "highest form of struggle" against "imperialism" in the party sphere and believed that it should be broadly based. The CPC assigns the "peace movement" a lower priority than the "national liberation movement" and believes that the former should be confined to Communist and extreme fellow travelers.

Important Sino-Soviet differences also exist with respect to the ex-pansion of Communism in the underdeveloped areas. With some exaggera-tion, but not complete inaccuracy, the CPC recently accused Khrushchev of opposing the revolutions in the "oppressed nations," and even of desir-ing to abolish those revolutions. More specifically, the CPC objected to Khrushchev's version of "peaceful coexistence" and his strategy of "peace-ful competition with capitalism," to his economic aid programs, to his approach to disarmament (which the CPC has said might tend to weaken the armed forces of the "oppressed nations"), to his reliance on the United Nations as a means to eliminate colonialism, and to his tendency to oppose "wars of national liberation."[25] In short, the CPC accused him of sub-ordinating the interests of world revolution to those of Soviet foreign policy.[26]

As might be expected, the CPSU has also hurled the last charge at the CPC, which is certainly open to it.[27] On the other hand, largely because of the differential threshold and its particular view of local war, the CPC is less prone than the CPSU to subordinate its revolutionary to its purely national objectives. The tendency toward such subordination is strongest

---

[24] "The principle of peaceful coexistence can apply only to relations between coun-tries with different social systems, not to relations between oppressed and oppressor nations, nor to relations between oppressed and oppressing classes" ("The Differences Between Comrade Togliatti and Us," *loc. cit.*). See also "Peaceful Coexistence—Two Diametrically Opposed Policies," *People's Daily* and *Red Flag*, December 12, 1963.

[25] "Apologists of Neocolonialism," *People's Daily* and *Red Flag*, October 21, 1963. Indications of Soviet reservations about "wars of national liberation" in early 1960 probably helped to precipitate the CPC's propaganda offensive against the CPSU at that time (cf. Harry Gelman, "Russia, China, and the Underdeveloped Areas," *The Annals of the American Academy of Political and Social Science*, vol. 349 [September, 1963], p. 132). On the other hand, Khrushchev showed himself willing to send large amounts of arms to the governments of "oppressed nations" (especially Egypt, Iraq, India, and Indonesia) when there seemed to be some advantage in doing so and the arms were not likely to be used against the United States.

[26] Cf. *ibid.*, p. 134, n. 9.

[27] E.g., Suslov speech of February 14, 1964 (published on April 3, 1964).

in Asia, where the risks and potential gains for Chinese national objectives are greatest. Conversely, in areas beyond Asia the tendency is less strong.

The CPC believes that the main progressive trends of the present era are the "national democratic revolutionary movement" in Asia, Africa, and Latin America, and the "international proletarian socialist revolutionary movement" (i.e., the international Communist movement plus other groups recognized as "Marxist-Leninist").[28] Obviously these movements overlap but are not identical. Thus to the CPC the future of Communism depends largely on developments in the underdeveloped areas, rather than on the growing strength of the existing "socialist camp" as Khrushchev insisted.

Whenever Chinese revolutionary influence has made itself felt in an "oppressed nation," it has operated implicitly or explicitly in competition with Soviet influence, if any. The competition has become an open one, sometimes to the point of producing factional splits in local Communist Parties, since about the beginning of the public Sino-Soviet debate on revolutionary strategy in 1959–60.[29] There is evidently considerable receptivity to the CPC's message among the extreme left in the underdeveloped areas.

What is the nature of this message? The CPC appears to believe, again with some exaggeration but by no means wholly erroneously, that a wave of nationalism, antiforeignism, and antiwhite racism is sweeping the underdeveloped areas. Negative emotions predominate, and the problem is to harness this tremendous force as a prime mover for the advance of Communism. As a relatively prosperous and essentially white power, the Soviet Union is largely irrelevant to the political and psychological aspects, which the CPC considers central, of the situation in the underdeveloped areas. As the most populous non-white country, and one furthermore that was once a "semicolony" of the West, the CPR hopes for a response that the Soviet Union cannot evoke. Obviously the CPC is not serving the cause of Communism in a selfless spirit, merely because the CPSU has its problems in dealing with the "oppressed nations." The CPC is frying its own national and revolutionary fish, often to the detriment of Soviet interests.

Deeply distrustful of the "national bourgeoisie," the CPC favors leadership of the revolution by a Communist, or at least "Marxist-Leninist," movement. This movement should be indigenously controlled, if only because of the strength of antiforeign feeling in the underdeveloped areas. Indigenous control does not, of course, rule out foreign training, advice, and arms, which the CPC sometimes provides although as inconspicuously as

---

[28] The two trends are listed in this order in the CPC Central Committee's letter of June 14, 1963, to the CPSU Central Committee, and in the opposite order in "The Proletarian Revolution and Khrushchev's Revisionism," *People's Daily* and *Red Flag*, March 31, 1964.

[29] Cf. Donald S. Zagoria, "Sino-Soviet Friction in Underdeveloped Areas," *Problems of Communism*, vol. x, no. 2 (March–April, 1961), pp. 10–12.

possible. The CPC believes that at some point the revolution will usually be resisted forcibly by the "bourgeoisie." "Imperialism" being what it is, there may also be foreign intervention. Even if there is no counterintervention by the "socialist camp," the revolution will survive and triumph, and the people will be educated through the force of negative example as to the true nature of "imperialism."[30]

If the CPC's challenge to the CPSU had been confined to the realms of national interest and strategy for dealing with the West and the underdeveloped areas, it would have been a serious and even dangerous problem for Khrushchev, but it would probably not have provoked him to such a drastic response. But it became increasingly clear after about 1956 that the CPC felt emboldened, if not compelled, by Khrushchev's espousal of what the CPC calls "modern revisionism" to challenge him for the position of primary, although not necessarily exclusive, authority and leadership in the international Communist movement. This position, if attained at all, would clearly have to be based, not upon power, but upon ideological and strategic correctness. Thus the Chinese challenges to Khrushchev over strategy and over authority and leadership were closely intertwined.

A bid, or at least the threat of a bid, for leadership was implicit in the CPC's efforts in 1956 to pronounce authoritatively on such important questions as the role of Stalin and the essentials of Marxism-Leninism.

Stalin has of course remained an issue in and a barometer of the Sino-Soviet struggle for authority and leadership ever since. He received particularly rough treatment at the Twenty-second Congress, when Khrushchev had evidently decided to challenge the Chinese as well as his domestic opponents. Stalin symbolizes in the context of the Sino-Soviet dispute, among other things, the concept of the "continuator," the militant struggle against "imperialism," and the sternly controlled domestic situation.

Another such issue and barometer has been the "antiparty group" led by Malenkov and Molotov. It appears to have symbolized Stalin's legacy to the Soviet Union, Khrushchev's remaining "conservative" opponents, and probably Chinese intrigues against Khrushchev. Like Stalin, the "antiparty group" generally had a difficult time whenever Khrushchev was especially irritated at the CPC. It is interesting that of the group Molotov, with whom the CPC is believed to have maintained some contact after 1957, was the most severely denounced. The "antiparty group" was finally expelled from the CPSU at a Central Committee Plenary session in February, 1964, following an important speech by Suslov that was devoted largely to attacking the CPC.[31]

Other important, interrelated issues and barometers are Yugoslavia and

---

[30] Cf. "The Sino-Soviet Dispute in Chinese Perspective," *Current Scene* (Hong Kong), vol. ii, no. 17 (July 15, 1963).
[31] *Christian Science Monitor*, April 7, 1964. This plenary session also adopted a resolution denouncing the CPC.

Albania. Khrushchev's relations with Albania and the CPC tended to be worst when his relations with Yugoslavia were best, and conversely. To the CPC, Tito is the original "modern revisionist," and the fact that since 1961 his economic troubles have driven him to improve his relations with the Soviet Union and toughen his domestic policy has not been enough to restore Yugoslavia to membership in the "socialist camp." Albania, on the other hand, is run along unreconstructed Stalinist lines, and the CPC therefore insists that since Albania is "building socialism" it cannot be expelled from the "socialist camp," no matter how bad its relations with the Soviet Union may become. In fact, Khrushchev did not attempt formally to expel Albania from the "socialist camp." Obviously the CPC is trying among other things to establish a principle from which it too may benefit, in view of the state of its relations with the Soviet Union. But there is a broader issue: What are the criteria for membership in the "socialist camp," and who is to have the authority to determine when they have been satisfied and when they have not? This is certainly one of the most important aspects of the contest for authority and leadership between the Soviet and Chinese parties. Actually, there are some indications that Khrushchev might have been willing at one time to concede to the Communist Chinese state at least a nominal coleadership of the "socialist camp." But the authority to determine who is a member of that "camp" belongs to the realm not of state but of party affairs, and in that realm Khrushchev showed no signs of willingness to share whatever authority he claimed with the CPC.

Since 1958, the CPC has implied that political, not economic or social, criteria determine when a country may be said to have attained "communism." Such a country may be "poor and blank," like the CPR. Khrushchev denounced this concept, in his usual colorful language, as "pantless communism."[32] He maintained at the Twenty-first Congress (January, 1959) that "communism" presupposes economic and cultural abundance, a state of affairs that he once labeled "goulash communism." The CPC has denounced Khrushchev's approach and the party program that the CPSU adopted in 1961 as "phoney communism,"[33] Obviously the power to define "communism" authoritatively and determine who has attained it and who has not is an attribute of ideological sovereignty.

As has been already suggested, it is not clear how far the CPC intends to push its bid for authority and leadership within the international Communist movement, or what it visualizes as the next step if the alignment of pro-Soviet parties does not collapse from its own internal contradictions, as the CPC appears to expect it to do. But it is clear that the CPC has thrown down a challenge to the CPSU in this vital arena, as well as in others.

[32] Interview with Gardner Cowles, April 20, 1962.
[33] "On Khrushchev's Phoney Communism and Its Historical Lessons for the World," *People's Daily* and *Red Flag*, July 14, 1964.

■ THE INTERNATIONAL FRONT ORGANIZATIONS

One of the first convincing signs that the CPC had passed from urging a different outlook and strategy on the Soviet party to challenging its authority was the initiation of anti-Soviet agitation in the international Communist front organizations, which are indispensable to the Soviet "peace movement." This process began in 1960, shortly after the beginning of the open phase of the Sino-Soviet ideological controversy and after the collapse of the Paris summit conference. The occasion was a meeting in Peking, on June 5–9, of the World Federation of Trade Unions. There the CPC's position on basic issues, such as the assertion that local wars are "inevitable" and complete disarmament is impossible while "imperialism" exists, was forcefully stated by Liu Ch'ang-sheng. Liu's remarks, which were clearly an attack on Khrushchev, startled the delegates and provoked a long and bitter debate. As might be expected, a majority of the delegates appeared to favor the CPSU, but the Chinese position received varying degrees of support from the delegations from Japan, Burma, North Vietnam, Ceylon, Zanzibar, Sudan, Somalia, Argentina, and Indonesia.[34] This episode set a precedent that was to be followed for about three years.

It would be unnecessary and impossible to give a complete account of the comparable clashes that have occurred at similar meetings since 1960, but some analytical comments seem to be in order. Even before 1963, the CPC's preoccupation with the Afro-Asian countries and the realization that most of its support was likely to come from Communists and fellow travelers in those countries led the CPC to pay particular attention to Afro-Asian international organizations, without neglecting the worldwide front organizations in which other countries were represented and Soviet influence was generally stronger. At meetings of the Afro-Asian organizations, Chinese delegates began in late 1961 to suggest that Afro-Asian countries should accept aid only from other Afro-Asian countries, a proposal that would obviously preclude aid not only from the United States but from the Soviet Union. At the meetings of the worldwide organizations, the "peace movement" was usually the main subject discussed, and Chinese delegates continued to insist that it must not be given priority over the anti-"imperialist" struggle, especially in the underdeveloped areas.

A sharp deterioration of Sino-Soviet relations of course occurred after the Cuban missile crisis, in which Khrushchev's behavior seemed to the CPC to prove to the world that Khrushchev was in fact subordinating the anti-"imperialist" struggle to the "peace movement" and that the latter was simply a front for Soviet national interests. The CPC intensified its anti-Soviet efforts in both the Afro-Asian and the general international organizations. Beginning with the Third Afro-Asian People's Solidarity Conference

---

[34] Zagoria, *op. cit.*, pp. 320–323.

at Moshi, Tanganyika (February, 1963), the CPC also tried similarly to discredit and undermine India, whose delegations tended to support their own government and the Soviet Union in their respective controversies with the CPR. With the support of the Indonesian delegation and government, the Chinese managed to dominate the First Asian-African Journalists Conference, held at Djakarta in April, 1963. The Chinese delegation succeeded in defeating a resolution of the delegation from the United Arab Republic that the Soviet observers at the conference be admitted as full delegates. This episode corresponded roughly to the beginning of an only partially successful effort by the CPC to exclude the Soviet Union from the Afro-Asian organizations and establish, if not a dominant position, at least a kind of veto power for itself in those organizations. Both in the Afro-Asian and the worldwide organizations the increasingly arrogant Chinese performance was already having the effect of making non-Communist delegates more able and willing to reject Communist leadership and determine their own behavior.[35]

As might be expected, the test ban treaty served to intensify the CPC's efforts in the international front organizations. It formed a number of new Afro-Asian organizations, which it could reasonably hope to dominate.[36] It succeeded in gaining control of an organization supervising propaganda broadcasts to Asia.[37] With Indonesian cooperation and over violent Soviet objections, it launched an attempt to split the World Federation of Trade Unions and bring the Afro-Asian unions under its own control.[38]

The initiative was not entirely in Chinese hands, however. The Soviet Union had been enraged by the CPC's blatant anti-Soviet and anti-Indian line at the Moshi Conference. With the support of the Cypriote, Indian, and other delegations, the Soviet delegation won some important victories on such issues as the test ban treaty and the Sino-Indian border dispute at a meeting of the Executive Committee of the Afro-Asian People's Solidarity Organization in Nicosia (September, 1963).[39] The CPC was similarly out-maneuvered and outvoted at a World Peace Council meeting in Warsaw (November–December, 1963).[40] It continued, however, to enjoy support not only from several Asian countries and Albania but also some others. The Fourth Afro-Asian People's Solidarity Conference (Algiers, March, 1964) seems to have been roughly a standoff between the Chinese and Rus-

---

[35] Cf. *The New York Times*, June 29, 1963.

[36] Cf. Kevin Devlin, "Boring from Within," *Problems of Communism*, vol. xiii, no. 2 (March–April, 1964), p. 38.

[37] *The New York Times*, September 21, 1963.

[38] *Christian Science Monitor*, August 20, 1963; *The New York Times*, October 29, 1963.

[39] *The Washington Post and Times Herald*, September 15, 1963; "Communist Techniques: How to Manage International Conferences—II: The AAPSO Meeting in Cyprus," *Special Information Note* (Washington), no. 23 (October 25, 1963).

[40] *The New York Times*, December 3, 1963.

sians, and many delegates were apparently weary of both.[41] By this time, in fact, leftists in some neutral countries had begun to show an interest in forming international organizations from which the Chinese and their supporters would be barred.[42] To this the CPC of course objected vigorously, as it did to a proposal made by the United Arab Republic and Ceylon in October, 1963, and favored by India, for a second conference of governments of nonaligned nations.

■ THE SINO-SOVIET DISPUTE AND THE OTHER PARTIES

It would be a serious oversimplification to think of the Communist world as divided neatly into a pro-Soviet collection of parties and splinter groups and an opposing pro-Chinese collection. The emergence of the Sino-Soviet dispute into the open in 1960 came after a period of approximately four years of growing polycentrism within the Communist world. Parties as a whole and (primarily among the parties not in power) factions within parties had begun to range themselves along a spectrum running the gamut, by Communist standards, from right through center to left. The Yugoslavs stood on the right, the Russians in the center, the Chinese on the left. Whether or not this trend has been accentuated by the Sino-Soviet dispute, it has certainly not been terminated by it.

It is clear that as long as adherence to Communism is taken to require the maintenance of political ties with fellow-adherents, there will be a strong compulsion, even apart from Soviet and Chinese pressures, for each party to take an official stand that is recognizably and admittedly closer to that of the one or the other contestant, or perhaps to remain neutral in the hope of promoting reconciliation. It has already been suggested, however, that adoption of a stand apparently closer to that of one of the contestants should not necessarily be interpreted as signifying a willingness to accept the leadership, much less the control, of that contestant. Even a complete split of the international Communist movements into two rival sets of parties and splinter groups would probably not bring them under Soviet or Chinese control, respectively. Such a possibility of course exists, and it apparently accounts for the reluctance of the less slavishly pro-Soviet East European parties — those of Hungary, Poland, and Rumania — to see a complete Sino-Soviet rupture. An analogous reluctance exists on the part of such largely but not totally pro-Chinese Asian parties as those of North Vietnam and Indonesia. Opinions such as these carry great weight with the Russians and the Chinese, each of whom is anxious that if any one becomes isolated within the international Communist movement it is their

[41] *The New York Times*, March 28, 1964.
[42] *Christian Science Monitor*, August 20, 1963.

opponent and not themselves. Thus there have been unsuccessful attempts to mediate the dispute by the North Vietnamese party (in January, 1962, and probably in February, 1964), by the Indonesian party (in August–September, 1963), by the New Zealand party (at about the same time), and by the Rumanian party (in April, 1964).

The Sino-Soviet dispute was first brought unavoidably to the attention of the other parties in the spring of 1960. It confronted them with the agreeable possibility of increased freedom of action, to the extent that a given party could remain united, but also with the disagreeable alternative of a schism in the ranks.[43] Some that were already factionally inclined, such as the Indian and Japanese parties, began to show signs of internal schism soon after the 1960 Moscow conference. The Twenty-second Congress and the Albanian issue greatly reinforced the divisive tendencies within many of the parties. The CPC promoted schism as a matter of policy after 1963, and the CPSU replied by trying to split some of the pro-Chinese parties.

The effect of the Sino-Soviet dispute on Eastern Europe, where there has been one, has been essentially to accentuate trends already in effect.[44] It has made possible, but it did not cause, Albania's defiance of the Soviet Union; the primary cause was the perennially bad state of Yugoslav-Albanian relations and the rapprochement between Tito and Khrushchev after 1955.[45] The latter trend was not caused by the Sino-Soviet dispute, although it may have been accelerated by it; if anything, the causal relationship has been the other way around.[46] Bulgaria made an effort to reproduce the Great Leap Forward, but only briefly and on a small scale.[47] Rumania has welcomed the Sino-Soviet dispute mainly as a means of defying Khrushchev's attempt to integrate its economy into the Council of Economic Mutual Assistance and so hamper its industrial development; it was probably with this in mind that Rumania agreed in December, 1963, to export petroleum to the CPR and wheat to Albania.[48] The relatively moderate Kadar regime in Hungary has objected strongly to the CPC's behavior but has used the Sino-Soviet dispute to enlarge its own freedom from Soviet interference.[49] Much the same has been true of the Gomulka regime in

---

[43] Robert A. Scalapino, "Moscow, Peking and the Communist Parties of Asia," *Foreign Affairs*, vol. 41, no. 2 (January, 1963), p. 342.

[44] Cf. William E. Griffith, "European Communism and the Sino-Soviet Schism," *The Annals of the American Academy of Political and Social Science*, vol. 349 (September, 1963), pp. 144–149.

[45] William E. Griffith, *Albania and the Sino-Soviet Rift*, Cambridge: M.I.T. Press, 1963.

[46] Cf. Robert F. Byrnes in London, *Unity and Contradiction, op. cit.*, pp. 159–184.

[47] Liliana Brisby, "Bulgaria: Leaping Forward Without Communes," *The China Quarterly*, no. 3 (July–September, 1960), pp. 80–84.

[48] "Communist Quarrels, January–February 1964," *Special Information Note* (Washington), no. 36 (April 1, 1964), p. 3, n. 2. It is conceivable that Rumania hopes to use the Sino-Soviet dispute as a means of ultimately regaining Bessarabia.

[49] Tamas Aczel, "Hungary: Glad Tidings from Nanking," *The China Quarterly*, no. 3 (July–September, 1960), pp. 89–96; Griffith, *loc. cit.*, pp. 146–147.

Poland.[50] The essentially Stalinist regime in Czechoslovakia, like those in East Germany and Bulgaria, has followed the foreign, but not domestic, lead of the nominal anti-Stalinist Khrushchev and has made no particular move to take advantage of the Sino-Soviet dispute.[51] On the surface the same is true of East Germany; on the other hand, the Ulbricht regime's problems and militancy are such that the Soviet Union's main guarantee against pro-Chinese sympathies on its part is the presence of a large Soviet occupation force in East Germany.[52] With the definite exception of Albania and the possible exception of East Germany, all the East European regimes are fundamentally opposed to the CPC's policies and behavior. The more moderate ones (Yugoslavia, Poland, and Hungary), however, have tried to use the Sino-Soviet dispute to enlarge their own autonomy. The more rigid Rumanian regime has used a similar tactic, but for basically economic rather than political reasons.

Intensive Chinese propaganda has not so far shaken the essential loyalty of the West European and Scandinavian parties to the Soviet party. At most it has produced the defection or expulsion of a few splinter groups. The reasons for the strong Soviet position among these parties vary somewhat from case to case. In general, the main ones are the absence of strong leadership, except in Italy; the traditional orientation toward Moscow; the seeming impossibility of coming to power in the Chinese way; and the general prosperity of the area.[53] The strongest and best led of these parties, the Italian, has been the only one to play an independent, creative part in the Sino-Soviet dispute; Togliatti's strongly pro-Soviet stand and his "revisionist" espousal of "structural reform" made him a special target of Chinese wrath.[54] The most important Chinese success among the West European parties to date has probably been in Belgium, where the New China News Agency has had an office since early 1963. Soon afterward a militantly pro-Chinese faction within the Belgian Communist Party, led by Jacques Grippa, was expelled and proceeded to form a new "Marxist-Leninist" party. A similar development occurred in Switzerland in 1963.[55]

There has been a small but vocal current of pro-CPC feeling within the American left wing since the early 1930's. The Sino-Soviet dispute has served to turn this feeling against Khrushchev. There are four main pro-CPC

[50] Leopold Labedz, "Poland: The Small Leap Sideways," *The China Quarterly*, no. 3 (July–September, 1960), pp. 97–103; Griffith, *loc. cit.* pp. 146–147.

[51] *Ibid.*, p. 147.

[52] Cf. *ibid.*, pp. 147–148; M. J. Esslin, "East Germany: Peking-Pankow Axis?" *The China Quarterly*, no. 3 (July–September, 1960), pp. 85–88.

[53] Griffith, *loc. cit.*, pp. 149–152; Devlin, *loc. cit.*, pp. 32–36.

[54] Cf. "The Differences Between Comrade Togliatti and Us," *People's Daily*, December 31, 1962; "More on the Differences Between Comrade Togliatti and Us: Some Important Problems of Leninism in the Contemporary World," *Red Flag*, March 4, 1963; John Ducoli, "The New Face of Italian Communism," *Problems of Communism*, vol. xiii, no. 2 (March–April, 1964), pp. 88–90.

[55] Devlin, *loc. cit.*, pp. 32–34.

publications, at various levels of sophistication, in the United States: *Hammer and Steel, Progressive Labor, Marxist-Leninist Quarterly,* and *Monthly Review.*[56]

In Latin America as in Western Europe (except for France and Italy), the Communist Parties are generally small, factional, and ineffective in spite of, or perhaps because of, the prevalence of Marxist influences in intellectual life. Unlike the European, the Latin American parties have the example of a recent, nearby revolution that has gained Communist approval without being under genuinely Communist leadership. This tends to reduce the CPC's distinctive appeal, although there is pro-Chinese factional activity in several parties. There are two countries, however, in which major gains have come the CPC's way. In Brazil, there have been two Communist Parties since 1962. One is pro-CPC and furthermore can make some claim that it is the original, legitimate party and its opponent the secessionist party. The CPC seems to have some influence on Francisco Julião, an extremist agrarian revolutionary in impoverished northeastern Brazil. In Peru, pro-CPC and pro-Castro elements gained control of the party in January, 1964, and expelled their opponents.[57]

In most of the African and middle Eastern countries, Communist Parties are either nonexistent or illegal. Where such parties exist, their leaderships generally appear to favor the CPSU's side of the Sino-Soviet dispute.

In Australasia, the Communist Party of New Zealand has sided clearly with the CPC.[58] The Australian party, after some equivocation, has sided with the CPSU, but a rival "Marxist-Leninist" party seems to be in process of formation.[59]

In Asia, as already indicated, most of the parties tend to side with the CPC, although in some cases with reservations that appear to reflect primarily a fear of Chinese domination.[60] The North Korean party in particular has swung increasingly to the Chinese side, since 1961 or 1962, mainly it would appear because it finds the CPC somewhat more sympathetic than the CPSU to its efforts to reunify the country. The Mongolian party of course seems solidly pro-Soviet.

The Indian party has contained militant and pro-CPC elements in West Bengal, Punjab, and Andhra since the late 1940's, and the less radical Kerala party seems to have sided with the CPC since its ouster from power by the Nehru government in 1959. Curiously, the militant, pro-CPC elements have done better than the others in elections. The Sino-Soviet and Sino-Indian border disputes have been a serious embarrassment to the CPI, but they have also enabled the pro-Soviet elements to strengthen their hold on the party's

---

56 *Ibid.,* pp. 30–32.
57 *Ibid.,* pp. 28–30.
58 "Communist Quarrels," *loc. cit.,* p. 4.
59 Devlin, *loc. cit.,* pp. 38–39.
60 For a good survey see *The New York Times,* January 6, 1964.

central machinery and to cooperate in police action against the pro-Chinese elements to an extent that has seemed excessive even to the Soviet party and some of its European adherents.[61] The easing of Sino-Indian tension after 1963 enabled the pro-CPC elements to recover and to increase their factional activity within the party. The outcome was the formation of a pro-Chinese "Marxist-Leninist" party in 1964.

In Ceylon, the Communist Party in August, 1963, formed a united front with the two other Marxist parties on a platform of nonviolent, parliamentary pursuit of power. Pro-CPC elements objected, seceded in November, and proceeded to form a new "Marxist-Leninist" party.[62]

It is probable that a majority of the world's Communists support the CPC; the combined membership of the CPC and PKI alone amounts to about half the world total.[63] This fact probably helps to explain why the CPC has cultivated the PKI to the point of tolerating its nonviolent program. On the other hand, it is each party rather than each Communist that theoretically has one vote at international Communist gatherings; the CPC has not tried formally to reverse this situation and therefore still insists on a veto under the rule of unanimity.[64] Undoubtedly it realized that even its friends have no desire to be submerged by its numbers.

Each of the two major contestants makes exaggerated claims as to the number of parties that support it and would presumably vote for it if another international Communist conference were held. The CPC proposed such a conference more than once in 1962; the CPSU did the same more than once in 1963, but the CPC has been urging delay and careful preparations. The subject was undoubtedly discussed during the talks between the delegations of the two Central Committees in July, 1963, but the nature of the talks is unknown and the results were evidently inconclusive. Khrushchev's efforts in the autumn to convene a conference to deal with the CPC (there is really no formal body except conceivably the "socialist camp" from which it could be expelled) were apparently restrained by the moderate East European parties.

Since that time the CPC has proposed a preparatory conference to be attended by delegations from 17 parties (Albania, Bulgaria, China, Cuba, Czechoslovakia, East Germany, Hungary, Korea, Mongolia, Poland, Rumania, the Soviet Union, Vietnam, Indonesia, Japan, Italy, and France). On the basis of current indications, this would yield a division into 6 pro-Chinese parties, 9 pro-Soviet parties, and 2 neutrals (Cuba and Rumania); the CPC's veto would of course give it protection against its opponent's

---

[61] Harry Gelman, "The Indian CP Between Moscow and Peking," *Problems of Communism*, vol. xi, no. 6 (November-December, 1962), pp. 18–27; Harry Gelman, "Indian Communism in Turmoil," *Problems of Communism*, vol. xii, no. 3 (May–June, 1963), pp. 45–48.
[62] Devlin, *loc. cit.*, pp. 36–37.
[63] Cf. *The New York Times*, April 18, 1964.
[64] Cf. CPC Central Committee letter of May 7, 1964, to CPSU Central Committee.

"mechanical majority."[65] The CPSU has proposed a preparatory conference of 26 parties (the same 17 plus West Germany, Britain, Finland, Argentina, Brazil, Syria, India, the United States and Australia), these being the ones that drafted the Moscow Statement of 1960; in this group the pro-Soviet majority would be even greater.[66]

■ **THE FUTURE OF THE SINO-SOVIET DISPUTE**

If we assume a continuation in power of both the current Soviet and Chinese Communist leadership or of like-minded successors (an assumption that is highly probable for the Russians but less so for the Chinese), the Sino-Soviet dispute is likely to proceed farther along its present course. This could mean the formation of two clear-cut, opposing groups of Communist and "Marxist-Leninist" parties, neither of them in all probability sufficiently tightly organized to be called "internationals"; and the reduction of direct Sino-Soviet relations to the purely diplomatic level, accompanied by an informal and perhaps even a formal repudiation of the Sino-Soviet alliance. Neither side is likely to surrender, compromise, or collapse of its own "internal contradictions." Whole parties might shift their allegiance from one side to the other, although the number of such transfers is not likely to be very great once an initial clear-cut choice has been made. If such a situation emerges, the CPC will then have achieved all it can reasonably expect to achieve, barring some unforeseen disaster to the Soviet Union in the party or state sphere, or both, in the way of continuing its recent advances at Soviet expense.

If there occurs a radical divergence from this prognosis, it is likely to be the result of a shift in Chinese policy toward moderation. This might occur as a result of some internal catastrophe or external defeat, but probably during the reign of Mao's presumed successor Liu Shao-ch'i rather than during that of Mao himself. After Liu's death or removal (he appears to have been born in 1898), a shift to a more conciliatory attitude toward the Soviet Union could emerge even in the absence of defeat or disaster. If so, it would probably be accompanied by a similar moderation in behavior toward the "imperialists" and "various reactionaries." The chances for such a development are imponderable, but they certainly cannot be ruled out.[67]

---

[65] CPC Central Committee letter of February 29, 1964, to CPSU Central Committee.

[66] CPSU Central Committee letter of March 7, 1964, to CPC Central Committee.

[67] For a good discussion of this subject, including some specific projections, see John R. Thomas, "Sino-Soviet Relations After Khrushchev and Mao," *Orbis*, vol. vii, no. 3 (Fall, 1963), pp. 537–549.

□ 7

Communist China's Policy Toward the Middle East, Africa, and Latin America

History and political analysis tend to be written in terms of countries and continents, and this study follows this convention. On the other hand, sea and airpower render it more and more inadequate.

■ COMMUNIST CHINA AND THE INDIAN OCEAN REGION[1]

From the standpoint of this study, it should be noted that any advances the CPR might wish to make into the Pacific are largely blocked at present by American power and influence, except in the Southwest Pacific. This is much less true, however, of the highly strategic Indian Ocean (or the Indonesian Ocean, as the Indonesians like to call it), which was formerly a British lake but is now the object of growing Soviet-American rivalry, and the countries bordering it. Relatively poor in sea and airpower, the CPR can nevertheless join in this rivalry through political, rather than military or economic, methods. Much of the CPR's policy toward South and Southeast Asia can reasonably be interpreted as the Chinese entry in the race for access to and influence in the Indian Ocean area. China was the major naval power in the Indian Ocean for a short time in the early fifteenth century.

The CPR undoubtedly views the Indian Ocean area, like other regions, first and foremost from the standpoint of its own security. The CPR re-

---

[1] See *Christian Science Monitor*, November 21, 1963.

members that for two centuries British power in India, plus British domination of the Indian Ocean, was the base from which British influence radiated into the Arab countries, Southeast Asia, and China itself. At the present time, India is of course internally weak and lacking in significant naval or air power. Nevertheless, the current trend toward closer Indian military relations with the West, as well as the strengthening of the Western military presence in the Indian Ocean area, threatens a possible long-term reversion to something resembling the earlier situation. Such a trend, at least as viewed from Peiping, could become a threat not only to China's revolutionary interests in South and Southeast Asia but even to the security of China itself, and especially to its Himalayan frontier. It seems safe to predict, therefore, that to the extent such a trend develops the CPR will oppose it, primarily by political means.

■ COMMUNIST CHINA AND THE ARAB COUNTRIES

Among the Middle Eastern countries, Turkey and Iran have not yet played a significant role in the CPR's external policy. This is obviously not true of the Arab countries, which may be divided for convenience into two groups. Most of the countries in both groups were subject in early modern times to the Ottoman Turks, the rough analogue in Middle Eastern history of the Manchus in Chinese history. The first group, the North African countries, passed under Western colonial rule, more or less, in the nineteenth or early twentieth centuries. The other group, the Near Eastern countries, remained under Turkish rule until after the First World War and then entered into a relationship with the West (meaning Britain, or in the case of Syria and Lebanon, France) that may not inaptly be describd with the Communist term "semicolonial." The result, especially in the Near Eastern countries and Egypt (the least colonial of the North African countries), has been an intense anti-Westernism not unlike that found in "semicolonial" China in modern times. An important point of difference is that, whereas Chinese cultural and political unity have generally been a reality, Arab unity has remained a dream, largely because of differing schools of Islam and the ancient rivalry between the two traditional centers of Middle Eastern civilization, Egypt (the Nile Valley) and Iraq (Mesopotamia). On the whole, a Chinese Communist political strategist looking at the Arab countries might be pardoned for concluding that there were some important analogies and opportunities, in spite of or perhaps because of the fact that there have been no significant pre-Communist cultural contacts between the two regions since the Middle Ages.

It may be useful to review some of the major recent political trends in the Arab countries that formed the background of Chinese policy. In North Africa, independence was attained relatively peacefully by Libya (1951),

Tunisia (1956), and Morocco (1956), but by Algeria only after a long and bitter war (1954–62). An important motive force was the service of many French North African soldiers in Indochina, where they were exposed to revolutionary influences. Egypt, obviously the key country linking North Africa and the Near East, was greatly humiliated, like the other Arab countries, by the resounding Israeli victory in 1948. The result was a military coup in 1952 and the emergence of a revolutionary government, headed first in fact and then also in name by Nasser, and devoted to the cause of Arab unity under Egyptian leadership and independence for all Middle Eastern and African countries. Egypt gave considerable support to the independence movements in the French North African countries. In the Arab countries of the Near East, hostility to Israel and the West, of which Israel is regarded as an agent, was and is the dominant political emotion. The Eisenhower Doctrine (1957) and the efforts of Christian Lebanese to use it to gain external support against their Moslem fellow countrymen produced a crisis in 1958 whose most important result was the overthrow of the right-wing government of Iraq by a revolutionary government under Kassem and Iraq's withdrawal from the Western-oriented Baghdad Pact (now the Central Treaty Organization).

One of the CPR's main objectives in the Middle East, as elsewhere, is the disruption of Western alliance systems through political action. The CPR does not seem to object to a formal alignment between a given government and the United States or Great Britain, as long as there is no concrete cooperation directly detrimental to Chinese interests, because such a relationship is subject to numerous stresses and may make the ally more vulnerable in some respects to Communist propaganda and political action.

Another Chinese national interest, or possible interest, in the Middle East is oil. The CPR produces only about half of its present modest requirements and is short of refining capacity. Hence the CPR is almost certainly interested in possible alternatives to the Soviet Union as sources of petroleum imports, obviously including the Arab countries as well as Indonesia, North Borneo, and Rumania, and also in possible sources of aid in the construction of additional refining capacity, notably Rumania.

The CPR maintains diplomatic relations with four Middle Eastern countries (Egypt, Syria, Iraq, and Yemen) and has had commercial and cultural contacts with a number of others as well (such as Lebanon, Jordan, and Saudi Arabia). Naturally enough, the CPR has not established diplomatic relations with any Middle Eastern country while it was allied with the West. Its relations with Iraq date from 1958, after Iraq's withdrawal from the Baghdad Pact. On the other hand, the CPR has not yet broken diplomatic relations with any Middle Eastern country on account of a change of government or external orientation.

In the Middle East, as elsewhere, the CPR's essential revolutionary interest is the promotion of ultimate seizures of power by local Communist Parties, under such circumstances that they are oriented toward the CPR and away not only from the United States but from the Soviet Union. Fortunately for the CPC, much of the residual anti-British feeling in the Middle East can be and has been redirected against the United States. Since Middle Eastern Communist Parties and other left-wing movements are generally weak and immature, the CPR must not only try to strengthen them but also take account of existing governments, most of which are (at least by Communist definition) either "feudal" or "bourgeois" in nature. In individual cases, where there is some special national or revolutionary interest to be served, the CPR will maintain friendly relations with a government of either kind, but on principle it is hostile to governments of both kinds. In general it does not like to see any of the leading "bourgeois" governments grow substantially stronger or acquire additional territories or allies; this applies most strongly to Egypt. Neutralism, of which Nasser has been a leading exponent, is obnoxious to the CPC to the extent that it tends to encourage regional groupings of nonaligned countries under the general leadership of the strongest among them. A neutral posture, without external alignments with a stronger neutral neighbor, on the part of a small, weak country is highly acceptable to the CPR on both national and revolutionary grounds; Yemen is an excellent example.

In its policy toward the Middle East, the CPR operates under serious military limitations, of which it is well aware. It lacks the weaponry and logistical capability to project its power more than a short distance beyond its borders. The economic constraints limiting Chinese activity in the Middle East are equally obvious and serious. The weak condition of the CPR's economy, and in particular its shortage of foreign exchange and of exports acceptable in the Middle East, have hitherto severely limited its economic penetration of the region. The political limitations and restraints under which the CPR operates are at least equally important, although perhaps less obvious. There are strong indications that the CPR has as much difficulty as most other outsiders in understanding the rapid and unpredictable fluctuations of Arab politics. The weakness of left-wing movements in the Middle East has already been noted, and the Chinese do not always exercise a strong influence on them where they exist.

As we have seen, the CPR exchanged recognitions with Israel in 1950 but has never established diplomatic relations with it.[2] The main reason was probably that the CPR, like the Soviet Union, soon awakened to the fact that Arab hatred of Israel and of "imperialism" was the dominant force in the Middle East and must be respected if significant gains were to be made. The CPC demonstrated its understanding of this when in January, 1951, it

[2] For many of these details on the CPR's early policy toward the Middle East I am indebted to Dr. John M. H. Lindbeck of Harvard University. I am indebted to Dr. Edwin M. Wright of the Foreign Service Institute, Department of State, for much background information on the Middle East.

named King Farouk's Egypt as one of the countries it proposed to invite to a conference to settle the Korean War. More specifically, the Communist Party of Israel was (and is) the only legal Communist Party in the Middle East, and it exchanged greetings with the CPC in 1950. Thus there was probably a party as well as a state aspect to the CPC's coolness toward the Israeli government.

Significant contacts between the CPC and Middle Eastern Communists and fellow travelers appear to have begun about the time of the Asian and Pacific Peace Conference in Peking (October, 1952), which a number of them attended. Encouraged no doubt by the turn of events in Egypt, the CPR sent messages of encouragement to various resistance leaders in North Africa in 1952. In the following year it began to try to exploit the Chinese Moslem community as a means of influencing the Arab countries by permitting pilgrimages by Chinese to Mecca. This development did not become significant until after the Bandung Conference, however.

By at least as early as 1954 the CPC had decided that Nasser was the key to the Middle East, and the CPC's approaches to him were greatly facilitated by the improvement of its relations with Nehru in the same year. In February, 1955, a delegation of Egyptian lawyers visited the CPR. On April 15, 1955, on his way to the Bandung Conference, Chou En-lai had talks at Rangoon with Nehru and Nasser, as well as with U Nu and Foreign Minister Naim of Afghanistan. These contacts were continued at the conference itself and led to diplomatic recognition of the CPR in May, 1956, a major triumph for Chou's diplomacy. Syria and Yemen recognized the CPR a few weeks later. Egyptian recognition, almost as much as the Egyptian cotton-for-arms agreement with Czechoslovakia the previous year,[3] proved to be a momentous event in Middle Eastern history. These two actions by Egypt led the United States to withdraw financial support for the Aswan High Dam (later financed by the Soviet Union), which led to Nasser's seizure of the Suez Canal and in turn (together with his raids against Israel) to the Suez crisis of October–November, 1956.

Political, economic, and cultural contacts between the CPR and the Arab countries expanded greatly after the Bandung Conference, after Egyptian recognition of the CPR, and still more after the Suez crisis, during which the CPR gave Egypt loud propaganda support, a vague offer of "volunteer" technicians, and a token grant of money. The CPR's embassy in Cairo became the base for remarkably widespread Chinese diplomatic and revolutionary activity in the Middle East and North Africa. Probably annoyed at this development and definitely annoyed at its absence from the Bandung Conference, the Soviet Union had been trying since 1955 to increase its own contacts with Asia, Africa, and the Middle East. It too

[3] It is possible that the CPR encouraged Nasser to buy arms from Czechoslovakia (Richard Lowenthal in Zbigniew Brzezinski, ed., *Africa and the Communist World*, Stanford University Press, 1963, p. 152).

realized Nasser's crucial importance. Working rather deviously through the World Peace Council, it contributed to the emergence of an Afro-Asia Solidarity Council (later the Afro-Asian People's Solidarity Organization), an unofficial body with headquarters, as was especially logical after the Suez crisis, in Cairo. Although Nasser regarded this organization with some reservations, the CPC quickly decided to take full advantage of it.[4]

The organization convened the First Afro-Asian People's Solidarity Conference at Cairo on Mao Tse-tung's birthday (December 26) in 1957. A number of developments at the conference, such as a celebrated Soviet offer of aid to the developing countries "without limit or strings" and a resolution for an atom-free zone in Asia and Africa, could not have been entirely welcome to the CPC. Nevertheless, its role in the conference was an active one and its comments on it entirely positive. One of the main Chinese reports to the conference, given by Ch'u T'u-nan, stressed the alleged traditional friendship and cultural contacts between China and the other Afro-Asian countries, which have been one Chinese answer to the Soviet economic aid program.[5] Another, by Kuo Mo-jo, stressed the Five Principles of Peaceful Coexistence, the struggle of the Afro-Asian peoples for independence, the recent Soviet technological achievements, the CPR's newly announced plan to overtake Britain in industrial production within fifteen years, and the "liberation" of Taiwan (he did not specify that it should be peaceful).[6] The major *People's Daily* editorial on the conference was much more militant than the published speeches of the Chinese delegates: "The flames of anticolonialism burn fiercely in Algeria, Oman, Yemen, Cyprus, Kenya, the Cameroons, Uganda, and Ifni despite savage armed aggression and suppression by the imperialists."[7]

After the conference the CPR continued to play an active role in the Afro-Asian People's Solidarity Organization, which it obviously regarded as a major avenue to the Middle East and Africa and as one in which it could compete on roughly equal terms with the Soviet Union. The CPR also continued to expand its diplomatic and commercial contacts, for example, by sending large exhibits to trade fairs in Tunis and Casablanca. Chinese radio broadcasts to the Middle East in Arabic, Turkish, and Persian had begun in 1957, and early in 1958 the New China News Agency opened an office in Cairo. It soon became a major source of copy for Arab newspaper editors, and Chinese radio broadcasts to the Middle East were comparable in quantity to those of the Soviet Union and clearly exceeded only by those of Radio Cairo. Limited numbers of students from Arab countries, as well as other developing countries, began to go to the CPR for advanced educa-

---

4 *Ibid.*, pp. 152–154.

5 New China News Agency dispatch, December 27, 1957; Lowenthal, *loc. cit.*, p. 156.

6 New China News Agency dispatch, December 31, 1957.

7 *People's Daily,* December 26, 1957.

tion and in some cases for political training; the CPC has always exploited, and often overexploited, the opportunity for indoctrination presented to it in this way.[8]

From the beginning the CPR had proclaimed its opposition to the Eisenhower Doctrine, which was announced early in 1957 and badly received by most of the Arab countries. The first crisis to arise under the shadow of increased American involvement that the doctrine cast over the Middle East was the Syrian crisis of the summer and autumn of 1957. As we have seen, the CPR began to denounce alleged Turkish and American pressures on Syria before the Soviet Union did, and it was undoubtedly disgusted by Khrushchev's failure to do anything more effective than bluster. The main concrete result of the crisis was the formation by Nasser and Syrian anti-Communists of the United Arab Republic (February 1, 1958). By this time the CPR had begun to cool somewhat toward Nasser on account of his anti-Communist domestic policy, his relatively good relations with Khrushchev and Tito, and probably a Chinese reluctance to see the movement toward Arab unity translated from words into action. Some of this appears to be implied in a seemingly mild remark by Chou En-lai soon after the formation of the United Arab Republic: "We . . . sincerely hope that the United Arab Republic will rely on the patriotic and democratic forces in Egypt and Syria. . . ."[9] Nevertheless, the CPR has never thought it necessary or expedient to engage in an overt political confrontation with Nasser. Instead, it has generally chosen to maintain good relations with him in minor matters and circumvent him on major ones, for example by maintaining relations with such rivals of Nasser's as the current Ba'athist government of Syria and the recent Ba'athist government of Iraq.

A desire to head off Nasser, as well as a desire to compete with a Soviet economic and military aid program and political presence dating from about 1955, probably account for the CPR's next major move in the Middle East, the establishment of closer relations with Yemen. Yemen's strategic location near the southern entrance to the Red Sea has been recognized since Roman times. Furthermore, the Imam's government was on bad terms with the British and its Arab neighbors in the mid-1950s. The CPR signed a treaty of friendship with Yemen in January, 1958, and in April agreed to build a highway between its two principal cities, Sana and Hodeida. Although a fairly modest affair, the CPR's presence in Yemen represented one of its few tangible footholds in the Arab countries and one that it has been obviously anxious to preserve. When the pro-Nasser Yemeni Arab Republic was proclaimed on September 26, 1962, following the death of the old Imam, the CPR accordingly recognized it (on October 6). In February, 1963, both countries raised their missions from legations to embassies. In

---

[8] Cf. Lowenthal, *loc. cit.*, pp. 154–160.

[9] Report to National People's Congress (New China News Agency dispatch, February 10, 1958).

June, 1964, the CPR signed a treaty of friendship with the Yemeni Arab Republic substantially the same as the one it had signed with the Imam's government six years earlier.[10] At the same time the CPC announced rather pompously that it was basing its policy toward the Arab countries on five principles: support for the Arab struggle for complete independence and against "imperialism," support for Arab neutralism, support for Arab unity, support for efforts by Arab countries to settle their disputes (with whom is not quite clear) through consultation, and opposition to external interference in Arab affairs "from any quarter."[11]

Soon after the inauguration of an active Chinese policy in Yemen, there occurred the Middle Eastern crisis of the summer of 1958. This led, among other things, to Iraq's recognition of the CPR and its withdrawal from the Baghdad Pact. As we have seen, the CPR seems to have repaid Kassem a year later by favoring and perhaps urging an attempt to seize power by the Iraqi Communists, whom Khrushchev preferred to restrain and whom Kassem promptly moved to render harmless. The CPC was certainly distressed by this episode, but while it sometimes criticized Kassem it made no overt move against him, perhaps because it was even more preoccupied with Nasser.[12] The present Ba'athist government of Iraq, formed after the violent overthrow of the Kassem government on February 8, 1963, received recognition by the CPR on February 12. There was no change in this policy when the military elements in President Aref's government expelled the Ba'athist elements in November, 1963. The CPR has occasionally criticized the Aref government's severe repression of the Iraqi Communists, but there has been nothing in Peking comparable to the demonstrations against the Iraqi embassy in Moscow. The CPR has not followed the Soviet lead in making declarations of limited support for the Kurds. It is possible that the CPR is cultivating friendly relations with the politically distasteful Aref government with an eye to getting access to Iraqi oil.[13]

Probably out of deference to the Iraqi claim to Kuwait, the CPR did not follow the example of the Soviet Union when the latter extended diplomatic recognition to Kuwait on March 11, 1963. On the other hand, the CPR had congratulated Kuwait on its attainment of independence (in June,

---

[10] Text of treaty released by New China News Agency, June 15, 1964.

[11] Joint communiqué released by New China News Agency, June 15, 1964.

[12] By this time Nasser's increasingly anti-Communist domestic orientation and independence in foreign policy had brought a brief deterioration even in his relations with Khrushchev. Going farther than Khrushchev, the CPC allowed the Syrian Communist Khalid Bakdash, while in Peking in September, 1959, to make a speech strongly attacking Nasser (Donald S. Zagoria, *The Sino-Soviet Conflict, 1956–1961*, Princeton University Press, 1962, pp. 260–262). The CPR was alleged also to have harassed the United Arab Republic's embassy in Peking (*The New York Times*, October 4, 1959).

[13] *Pravda*, June 27, 1963, carried a highly unusual article saying that the CPR and Albania had renewed their trade agreements with Iraq. This may have represented an effort to lay the groundwork for future Soviet charges of unprincipled Chinese collaboration with an anti-Communist regime, or to prepare the Soviet public for a possible Chinese effort to acquire Iraqi oil, or both.

1961) and had subsequently denounced the presence of British troops in this small sheikdom, which happens virtually to float on a sea of oil. The CPR has also denounced the British presence and British military activities in Oman and Aden.

The Syrian Arab Republic, proclaimed on September 28, 1961, requested recognition from the CPR two days later, but the latter did not respond until October 11, after the Soviet Union and the United States had extended recognition. The CPR recognized the Ba'athist government of Syria ten days after its formation on March 8, 1963, and is reported to have made its embassy in Damascus into a major center for propaganda and other forms of political activity.

The focal point of the CPR's policy toward North Africa, once its disenchantment with Nasser set in, was of course Algeria. One of the main effects of the Middle Eastern crisis of 1958 on the CPC seems to have been a strengthening of its conviction that Khrushchev was essentially non-revolutionary and that there was both a need and an opportunity to enlarge its own revolutionary activity in the area. Such a program would involve competition not only with Khrushchev but with Nasser.

The first overt contacts between the CPR and the Algerian National Liberation Front (FLN) occurred in December, 1958, when the FLN sent a small delegation to Peking, evidently to seek arms.[14] They were received by Mao and listened to a strong speech by Foreign Minister Chen Yi praising their "armed struggle" against French "imperialism."[15] More important, the CPR granted de facto diplomatic recognition to the FLN. A military mission followed in the spring of 1959 and apparently secured an unannounced credit, perhaps on the order of $10 million, for the purchase of arms and other supplies, and an agreement to provide training in guerrilla warfare. The CPC also kept silent about the outlawing of the Communist Party by the FLN and the Moroccan government. In return, the CPC asked the FLN to request Tunisia to follow the example set by Morocco in October, 1958, in granting diplomatic recognition to the CPR. Tunisia did not do so, nor did it allow more than small shipments of Chinese arms across its territory to the FLN. Morocco, on the other hand, did cooperate in this way.[16] It is possible that Albania served as a transshipment point and that this fact contributed to the steady strengthening of Sino-Albanian relations.[17]

Nor did the FLN have cause to feel grateful to the CPR solely for credits and arms. The CPR praised the Algerian revolution as a model for the Middle East and still more for colonial Africa, obviously to the dis-

[14] *The New York Times*, December 1, 1958.
[15] New China News Agency dispatch, December 7, 1958.
[16] *The New York Times*, May 21, 1959; Edmond Taylor, "The Chinese Invasion of North Africa," *The Reporter*, September 17, 1959, p. 33.
[17] Lowenthal, *loc. cit.*, p. 163.

advantage of Nasser's competitive ambitions in those regions. This tendency became particularly strong after the beginning of the semiconcealed Sino-Soviet debate on revolutionary strategy in 1959.[18]

General de Gaulle's offer of self-determination for Algeria in September, 1959, intensified this debate and produced a sharp divergence between Soviet and Chinese policies toward Algeria. With a typical Soviet priority for Europe over other areas, Khrushchev took a mild line toward de Gaulle's Algerian policy and gave the FLN little more than token support. The CPR, on the other hand, strongly denounced de Gaulle's proposal a month after it was made. Whereas Khrushchev emphasized negotiations between the French government and the FLN. The CPR emphasized continuation of the war, not because it objected to negotiations altogether but because it wanted the FLN to be able to negotiate from a military position of strength, not weakness. The problem was to provide the FLN with enough incentives and support to keep it fighting until it could attain a better military position. One answer was an offer of Chinese "volunteers," made when another FLN military mission visited the CPR in the spring of 1960. The FLN used the offer, without actually accepting it, as a means of putting pressure on France and the other Western powers.[19]

At the end of September, 1960, an FLN delegation led by Premier Ferhat Abbas arrived in the CPR after a rather cool reception in Moscow. On October 1, he stood on the reviewing stand at Mao Tse-tung's right hand to witness the National Day parade. The CPR reaffirmed its political support for the FLN and apparently promised to urge the Soviet Union to grant it diplomatic recognition.[20] Abbas' triumphal reception in the CPR, and a strong lecture on revolutionary zeal that he read to his Russian hosts while he was in Moscow again on his way back to Africa, seem to have been what led Khrushchev to grant the FLN de facto recognition, ambiguously and ungracefully, while he was in New York attending the United Nations General Assembly.[21] This meant that, although Khrushchev still did not come out as strongly as the CPC in opposition to de Gaulle's Algerian policy, the FLN was now able to claim Soviet as well as Chinese support.[22]

The CPC hailed the agreement of March, 1962, on Algerian independence as a great victory for the "revolutionary double tactics of combining armed struggle with negotiation."[23] When the new Algerian government

---

18 Cf. *ibid.*, p. 163.

19 *Ibid.*, pp. 171–173.

20 Joint communiqué released by New China News Agency, October 5, 1960.

21 Isaac Deutscher, "Uneasy Allies in Algeria," *The Reporter*, November 10, 1960, pp. 21–24.

22 Cf. *The New York Times*, October 24 and November 5, 1960. For a description of the arms, including Chinese arms, used by the FLN in the last stages of the war see *The New York Times*, April 19, 1962.

23 "The Algerian People's Great Victory," *People's Daily*, March 20, 1962.

banned the Communist Party late in 1962, the CPSU protested but the CPC did not, at least in public.[24] This tolerance, as well as propaganda of all kinds, kept the CPC's image in the minds of Algerian officials and intellectuals a fairly favorable one.[25] Algeria signed a cultural exchange agreement with the CPR before signing one with the Soviet Union.[26] In addition to the obvious political reasons for Chinese cultivation of Algerian friendship, there was at least one possible economic reason: Saharan oil.[27] This oil is under partial French control, but the establishment of diplomatic relations between the CPR and France at the beginning of 1964 and Chou En-lai's visit to Algeria soon afterward may be presumed to have made this aspect of the problem easier of solution. In any event, in February, 1964, it was reported that a Chinese delegation had arrived in Algeria to discuss oil procurement.[28]

During his recent foreign tour, Chou En-lai visited the United Arab Republic (or Egypt, December 14–21, 1963), Algeria (December 21–27), Morocco (December 21–30), and Tunisia (January 9–10, 1964).

Chou's main purpose in the United Arab Republic was evidently to project an image of reasonableness to counter Nasser's reservations about the CPR, his pro-Indian attitude as a mediator in the Sino-Indian border dispute, and the renewed closeness of his relations with the Soviet Union. When Chou arrived, Nasser was in Tunis conferring with Bourguiba, quite possibly about how to treat his Chinese visitor. Chou was taken rather pointedly to see the Aswan Dam, which of course had been built with Soviet aid and which Khrushchev was soon to visit for a ceremonial opening. Chou said, among other things, that the CPR had no objections to another conference on nonaligned countries but of course could not attend such a conference. On the whole he seems to have made a good impression, but neither Nasser nor any of the other African leaders Chou visited acknowledged in public his repeated assertions that the CPR had a special obligation to support revolutions (not necessarily Communist) in other countries.[29] Apparently in an effort to counter this line, Khrushchev gave an interview to some Afro-Asian editors in which he insisted that "peaceful coexistence" was not incompatible with the "national liberation movement," and that he did not oppose "armed struggle" on principle.[30]

In Algeria, the most leftist of the North African countries, Chou encountered one of the warmest welcomes he was to receive from any country in Africa. He reportedly offered to help Algeria build a trans-Saharan high-

---

[24] Lowenthal, *loc. cit.*, p. 192.

[25] *The Washington Post and Times Herald*, December 11, 1962; *The New York Times*, September 1, 1963.

[26] *The New York Times*, September 12, 1963.

[27] Cf. *The New York Times*, January 26, 1964.

[28] *The New York Times*, February 19, 1964.

[29] W. A. C. Adie, "Chou En-lai on Safari," *The China Quarterly*, no. 18 (April–June, 1964), pp. 182–183.

[30] *Pravda* and *Izvestia*, December 22, 1963.

way, which if actually built would certainly enhance Algeria's role south of the Sahara. On the other hand, President Ben Bella had already shown that there were limits to his admiration of the CPR by expelling Jacques Vergès, who had been in the CPR and went to Paris from Algeria to edit the violently pro-CPC and pro-Castro periodical *Révolution*. Chou's solution to the difficult problem of the Chinese as against the Algerian revolutionary model was to urge the FLN tactfully to proclaim itself a "Marxist-Leninist" party. The joint communiqué issued at the end of Chou's visit gave evidence of differences of opinion: Algeria gave only lukewarm endorsement to the idea of another Asian-African Conference and almost none to the CPR's foreign policy goals; the CPR showed some reservations about the degree to which Algeria was a "socialist" country.[31]

In Morocco, to which the CPR has been exporting green tea in exchange for cobalt, which is used in nuclear experimentation,[32] Chou's reception was less ambiguously cordial. The joint communiqué supported the CPR's claim to the Chinese seat at the United Nations and congratulated Morocco on its efforts to secure the removal of American military bases.[33]

By the time that Chou reached Tunisia, it already seemed likely that Bourguiba intended to recognize the CPR.[34] Perhaps with the idea that this gave him the right to speak frankly, he lectured Chou in no uncertain terms on the CPC's hostility not only to the West but to nonalignment.[35]

The imperfect success of Chou's visit to the four North African countries, and the CPR's obvious inability if not unwillingness to extend large-scale economic aid, should not obscure the fact that both the diplomatic and the revolutionary aspects of Chinese Middle Eastern policy have made sufficient gains to cause considerable worry in the region itself, in the West, and in the Soviet Union.[36]

■ COMMUNIST CHINA AND SUB-SAHARAN AFRICA

There being no heritage of significant pre-Communist contacts between China and Africa apart from some indirect trade, the CPR has been able to start from scratch in Sub-Saharan Africa, as in the Middle East. There are some differences between the two regions that are significant from the standpoint of the CPR's policy. One is that Sub-Saharan Africa was, or is, overwhelmingly colonial, whereas the Middle East was predominantly

31 Joint communiqué released by New China News Agency, December 28, 1963. On Chou's visit to Algeria in general see Adie, *loc. cit.*, pp. 183–185.
32 Arslan Humbaraci, "Chou's Mediterranean Tour," *Far Eastern Economic Review*, January 23, 1964, p. 154.
33 Adie, *loc. cit.*, pp. 185–186.
34 *The New York Times*, December 28, 1963.
35 Adie, *loc cit.*, pp. 186–187.
36 Cf. *Christian Science Monitor*, July 15, 1963.

"semicolonial." Thus in the former, unlike most of the latter, the possibility of "armed struggle" for independence from "imperialism" has been a theoretical possibility. It must be assumed that the CPC is disgusted at the fact that, because of "imperialism's" relatively speedy and almost voluntary withdrawal from much of Africa, not a single Sub-Saharan country that has gained its independence so far has done so primarily by means of "armed struggle." Another significant difference between Africa and the Middle East is that the former is even more immature, although not necessarily more unstable, from the political standpoint and much less homogeneous from the ethnic and cultural standpoints. The dominant emotion in Sub-Saharan Africa is not so much modern nationalism as ethnic feeling against other groups in the same country, especially if they are white, or against outsiders, especially whites. Both the desire to compensate for the lack of "armed struggle" against "imperialism" prior to independence and the effort to play on ethnic antagonisms are marked characteristics of the CPR's policy toward Sub-Saharan Africa.

One of the CPR's national objectives in Africa is undoubtedly to gain the best possible access to its important mineral and vegetable resources. It is obviously impossible for the CPR to exclude the stronger economies of the United States, Western Europe, and the Soviet Union from access to these raw materials, however. Another objective is to counteract and minimize the political influence of the countries just mentioned as well as of the United Arab Republic, Yugoslavia, and India, all of which exert some form of influence south of the Sahara. The CPR tries to reverse or nullify the tendency of most African governments to sympathize with India in the Sino-Indian border dispute. In addition, since the votes of the African countries could be decisive in determining the possession of China's seat in the United Nations, the CPR competes actively with the Republic of China for influence in the area.[37] The box score with respect to diplomatic recognitions is complicated by the wish and tentative efforts of several African countries to have relations with both regimes; three of these, Mauritania, Nigeria, and Senegal, have recognized both but have not established relations with the CPR. One (Malawi) has never recognized either. Eleven (Ghana, Guinea, Mali, Somalia, Sudan, Tanzania, Uganda, Congo Brazzaville, Burundi, Kenya, and Dahomey) have recognized the CPR and have established diplomatic relations with it. One (Ethiopia) has recognized the CPR but has not established diplomatic relations with it. One (Zambia) has indicated that it intends to recognize the CPR. The other thirteen Sub-Saharan countries have recognized the Republic of China.[38]

[37] Leon M. S. Slawecki, "The Two Chinas in Africa," *Foreign Affairs*, vol. 41, no. 2 (January, 1963), pp. 398–409; George T. Yu, "Peking Versus Taipei in the World Arena: Chinese Competition in Africa," *Asian Survey*, vol. iii, no. 9 (September, 1963), pp. 439–453.

[38] "Africa and the Two Chinas: A Summary of Known Facts (as of January 1, 1965)," *Africa Report*, January, 1965, back cover.

From the standpoint of the CPR's revolutionary objectives, Africa (including North Africa) appears to be the most promising region in the world. A secret CPC document written in 1961 stated that "When the opportunity is ripe, the wave of revolution will roll up the continent of Africa like a mat so that more than 200 million Africans will become world leaders.[39] The CPSU has a fairly long start over the CPC, in the sense that Moscow-oriented Western European Communist Parties have exercised a strong influence on leftist political and labor movements in Africa since before the Second World War. For this reason and others, however, Chinese revolutionary policy is generally more active than Soviet, and this display of energy is rendered comparatively riskless by Africa's geographical remoteness from the CPR as well as from the two thermonuclear superpowers. A Chinese embassy in an African country tends to bring with it among other things a New China News Agency office, which not only distributes large amounts of literature and films to supplement the efforts of the powerful Chinese radio transmitters beamed at Africa but also sometimes engages in direct revolutionary activity. The CPC tends to concentrate its revolutionary efforts on a few strategic areas that offer promise of an "armed struggle" against "imperialism, colonialism, and neocolonialism" (such as Cameroon and the Congo provinces of Kwilu and Kivu) or that have internal tensions, including tribal hostilities, or external antagonisms that can be exploited so as to create a Chinese political and revolutionary base (such as Guinea, Burundi, Somalia, Congo Leopoldville, and Zanzibar). In Sub-Saharan Africa at the present time, the CPC considers that "armed struggle" is in progress in Angola and Portuguese Guinea, and that active anticolonial struggles short of "armed struggle" are being waged in Gambia, Spanish Guinea, Northern and Southern Rhodesia, Malawi (formerly Nyasaland), Mozambique, Bechuanaland, Southwest Africa, Basutoland, and Swaziland.[40] The CPC can be assumed to object to the African unity movement, which it has almost no chance of capturing and which could substantially hamper Chinese activity in individual African countries. The CPC certainly has reservations about the movement known as Afro-Marxism, except where adherents to it are willing to struggle vigorously against "imperialism, colonialism, and neocolonialism." The CPC tries, contrary to the facts, to make Africans believe that the Chinese alone among non-African peoples have no racial prejudice. It is presumably with this partly in mind that the CPC often expresses "support" for American negroes, as Mao Tse-tung did in a special statement in 1963.[41]

Because of its preoccupation in its early years with other things, the CPC made a late start in Africa. The "armed struggle" phase of its policy

---

[39] Quoted in John Wilson Lewis, *Chinese Communist Party Leadership and the Succession to Mao Tse-tung: An Appraisal of Tensions*, Washington: External Research Staff, Department of State, 1964, p. 27.

[40] See map in Donald W. Klein, "Peking's Diplomats in Africa," *Current Scene* (Hong Kong), vol. ii, no. 36 (July 1, 1964), p. 2.

[41] New China News Agency dispatch, August 8, 1963.

(1948–52) did not really concern itself with Africa and seems to have aroused no significant response there, except perhaps for its stand against the West in the Korean War. It will be recalled that two of the leaders of the Mau Mau movement in Kenya, which assumed serious proportions in 1952, called themselves General China and General Korea. It is also possible that the CPC felt some interest in a violent movement that was led by indigenous intellectuals and not controlled by European Communists, that was aimed not only against "imperialist" rule but against a white settler population, that effectively gave political direction to popular and even primitive feelings, and that may have hampered the British in dealing with what they called Communist terrorism in Malaya.

As with the Middle East, significant Chinese contacts with Sub-Saharan Africa began about the time of the Bandung Conference. At that time, however, the CPR's foreign policy was emphasizing the national aspect and hence dealings with foreign governments, and none of the colonial Sub-Saharan countries had yet gained its independence. The CPR recognized the first to do so, Sudan, at the beginning of 1956, but the recognition was not reciprocated until the end of 1958, after the military coup in Sudan.[42]

Ghana became independent in March, 1957, and the CPR sent Vice Premier Nieh Jung-chen to attend its independence celebration. Diplomatic recognitions were not exchanged between Ghana and the CPR, however, until July, 1960, when Ghana became formally a republic. Ghana evidently decided that it assumed full freedom of action in international affairs only at that time, and it determined to follow the British precedent in China policy. The same has generally been true of the other former British colonies in Sub-Saharan Africa that have attained independence since 1960; in any event, none of them except Sierra Leone recognizes only the Republic of China President Nkrumah visited the CPR in August, 1961. He was given a rousing welcome and signed several agreements, including a treaty of friendship. The occasion is also of interest because it seems to have been the first on which a Chinese spokesman, in this case Liu Shao-ch'i, indicated approval for the largely Soviet-inspired concept of leftist but non-Communist "national democracy," about which the CPC had previously implied reservations.[43]

The CPC was obviously pleased when Guinea acquired complete independence in 1958, if not by "armed struggle" at least by rejecting de Gaulle's constitution for the French Community, and showed signs of

[42] When the CPR's first ambassador to Sudan arrived in 1959, he was accompanied by a staff interpreter speaking perfect Sudanese Arabic (Howard L. Boorman, "Peking in World Politics," *Pacific Affairs*, vol. xxxiv, no. 3 [Fall, 1961], p 235, n. 11). President Ibrahim Abboud of Sudan visited the CPR in May, 1964.

[43] Cf. *The Chinese People Resolutely Support the Just Struggle of the African People*, Peking: Foreign Languages Press, 1961, p. 18. On the concept see Richard Lowenthal in Kurt London, ed., *New Nations in a Divided World: The International Relations of the Afro-Asian States*, New York: Praeger, 1963, pp. 56–74. On Chinese reservations see Zagoria, *op. cit.*, pp. 362–363, p. 450, n. 17.

becoming a major base for leftist revolutionary activity. The CPR made some gifts of rice to Guinea in 1958 and 1959, and diplomatic relations were established in 1959. President Sékou Touré visited the CPR in the autumn of 1960, was given a huge ovation, signed a treaty of friendship, and received the first economic aid commitment that the CPR had made to an African country.[44] The CPC seems to have cooled somewhat toward Sékou Touré since the end of 1961. His shift toward the right in foreign policy at that time was a reaction to Soviet, more than Chinese, over-eagerness to accelerate the pace of revolution in Guinea, but he also drew closer to the United States.

In 1960 the virtual dissolution of the French Community, the approach of independence for the British Sub-Saharan dependencies, and the granting of independence to the Belgian Congo startled the CPC into the realization that a revolutionary situation in Africa might be more imminent than it had supposed. A China-African People's Friendship Association was formed in April. In the same month, at the Second Afro-Asian People's Solidarity Conference in Conakry (Guinea), the CPC took a very militant line in opposition to Western influence in Africa, and implicitly also in opposition to Soviet influence. The CPC was clearly trying to promote "armed struggle" in Africa.[45] There also began about this time a great intensification not only of Chinese propaganda in and general cultural relations with Africa but of training of African students, revolutionaries, and subversives in the CPR. There they encountered not only poor living conditions and indifferent academic standards but also racial discrimination, and many of them became intensely embittered.[46]

At first the CPC seems to have pinned great hopes on Dr. Felix-Roland Moumié, an extreme leftist from Cameroon who visited the CPR in the autumn of 1959. He in fact inaugurated an "armed struggle" along Chinese lines in his own country against its independent government and led that struggle until his mysterious death, in Switzerland, late in 1960. Even then the CPC continued to give active, covert support to his movement.[47]

The rapid breakdown of order in the Congo from July, 1960, brought on Belgian intervention and then action by the United Nations. The Soviet Union at first supported intervention by the United Nations, apparently in the belief that it could be made to work in favor of the leftist following of Patrice Lumumba. When the opposite turned out to be the case, Khrushchev inaugurated an airlift to Lumumba's forces and launched a bitter propaganda attack on Secretary General Dag Hammarskjold. He was almost certainly aware that his initial support for United Nations interven-

[44] Lowenthal in Brzezinski, op. cit., pp. 165–167, 183–184.
[45] Cf. ibid., pp. 176–177.
[46] Cf. John Hevi, An African Student in China, London: Pall Mall Press, 1963. See also The New York Times, October 4, 1962.
[47] Alexander Dallin in Brzezinski, op. cit., pp. 38–39; Lowenthal in ibid., pp. 164, 173–174, 192; Slawecki, loc. cit., p. 405.

tion had tended to lend credibility to the Chinese charge that he was lacking in revolutionary militancy. The CPC had evidently disapproved of the United Nations' involvement in the Congo crises from the beginning, not only because of its preference for independent action by leftist revolutionaries without external restraints but also because of its own absence from the United Nations and its memory of that body's role in the Korean War. Lumumba seems to have appealed to the CPR not only for arms but for "volunteers," but to have been turned down on the latter score because of the distance and the confused situation in the Congo.[48] Nevertheless, the CPR gave vociferous propaganda support to Lumumba and then to his leftist successor Gizenga, who maintained what purported to be a legal government of the Congo at Stanleyville for a short time. When the Gizenga regime collapsed in 1961, the CPR recalled its mission from the Congo and did not establish relations with the Adoula government at Leopoldville, which recognized the Republic of China. The CPC continued to speak of Gizenga as the only "patriotic" Congolese leader, whereas the Soviet Union established relations with the Adoula government at the end of 1961.[49]

Late in 1963 a Congolese leftist, Pierre Mulele, returned to the Congo after some two years in Egypt and the CPR. He made contact with a group of leftist Congolese exiles based in the former French Congo and calling themselves the National Liberation Committee. At about the time that the Brazzaville government recognized the CPR (February, 1964), Mulele began an "armed struggle" along Chinese lines in Kwilu province, not far east of Leopoldville.[50] Soon afterward Chinese involvement was reported in another rebellion sponsored by the National Liberation Committee, this one in Kivu province, which is adjacent to Uganda, Rwanda, Burundi, and Tanganyika.[51] The rebel Gbenye regime in the Congo seems to be under some Chinese influence and to be copying the Chinese revolutionary strategy to a degree.[52]

In December, 1963, the CPR established diplomatic relations with the smaller former Belgian protectorate of Burundi, which is a monarchy dominated by the Watusi tribe. The Watusi seem to be open to leftist influences, probably because they are embittered at the loss of their former ascendancy over the Bahutu tribe, which dominates the adjacent state of Rwanda. The CPC appears to have been active among the Watusi since about 1960 and to have incited and supported some attacks, so far disastrously unsuccessful, by the Watusi on the Bahutu. The CPC's object seems to be

[48] *The New York Times*, October 1, 1960.
[49] Lowenthal in Brzezinski, *op. cit.*, pp. 167, 178–182.
[50] Robert A. Scalapino, "Sino-Soviet Competition in Africa," *Foreign Affairs*, vol. 42, no. 4 (July, 1964), p. 646; *The New York Times*, May 12, 1964.
[51] *The New York Times*, June 24, 1964.
[52] Max Clos, "The Chinese Role in the Congo: Fact or Fiction," *Africa Report*, January, 1965, p. 19.

not so much to crush Rwanda as to establish a major revolutionary base in Burundi, from which it could have access to a substantial part of Eastern and Central Africa.[53] As a result of these activities, Burundi became at the end of January, 1965, the first country to break off diplomatic relations with the CPR. The latter reluctantly withdrew its embassy, with the expressed hope that Burundi would eventually agree to resume relations.[54]

Powerful Portuguese military pressures and the pro-Portuguese attitude of Premier Tshombe in Leopoldville have pushed the Angolan revolutionary movement under Holden Roberto to the left and led it to seek arms from the CPR and other Communist sources. There are indications that the CPR has agreed to provide arms, and it has certainly expressed support for the revolutionaries in Angola and Mozambique.[55]

After the overthrow of the corrupt, pro-French government of Fulbert Youlou in Congo Brazzaville in 1963, Chinese influence on the country increased rapidly. The new government of Alphonse Massemba-Debat recognized the CPR shortly after France did so. Real power in Congo Brazzaville, however, appears to be exercised not so much by the government as organized bands of revolutionary youths, on whom Chinese influence seems to be very strong. There is little doubt that the CPR hopes to make Congo Brazzaville a major base for revolutionary penetration of a much more important target, Congo Leopoldville.[56] On the other hand, attempted revolts in Niger, apparently launched with Chinese support, were crushed early in 1965.[57]

On the whole, the CPC seems to consider East Africa, where its embassies are larger than those of any other country, as its most promising revolutionary target in Africa at present. The countries of this region front on the Indian Ocean, contain white settler populations or other exploitable political situations, and in most cases have established diplomatic relations with the CPR. The highest ranking and perhaps most important Chinese representative in East Africa is Ho Ying, ambassador to Tanzania.[58] In addition to its political objectives, the CPR seems to be interested in the mineral deposits, including cobalt, of the Rhodesias and Malawi (formerly Nyasaland).[59]

By the end of 1960, when it established diplomatic relations with Somalia, the CPR had already made contact with Somali leftists. The country is strategically situated in relation to the Red Sea, poor, revolutionary,

---

[53] Claire Sterling, "Chou En-lai and the Watusi," *The Reporter*, March 12, 1964, pp. 22–24; "Sino-Soviet Interest in Africa," *Special Information Note* (Washington), no. 34 (March 9, 1964), p. 6.

[54] Text of Chinese note released by New China News Agency, January 30, 1965.

[55] Scalapino, *loc. cit.*, p. 646; *The New York Times*, January 4, 1964; William E. Griffith, "Africa," *Survey*, no. 54 (January, 1965), pp. 177–178.

[56] Cf. *Christian Science Monitor*, February 1, 1965.

[57] *Christian Science Monitor*, February 8, 1965.

[58] Cf. Klein, *loc. cit.*, pp. 5–6.

[59] *Christian Science Monitor*, March 26, 1964.

and involved in a serious territorial dispute with Ethiopia and Kenya. For these reasons the Somali government has been glad to accept economic and military aid from Communist regimes, including the CPR. It has shown a greater receptivity to Soviet than to Chinese influence, however, even though the CPR has aided and abetted Somali pressures on Ethiopia and French Somaliland.[60] Chinese influence seems to be greater on unofficial Somali revolutionaries than on the Somali government.[61]

Before the revolution in Zanzibar, the CPC had some influence with the dominant Arab community, which it seems to have gained largely through supporting its opposition to the British idea of a federation with the mainland territories.[62] There is some uncertainty and disagreement as to the extent of outside influence on the revolution of January, 1964, which installed leftists elements of the African community in power. There is at least a strong possibility that the revolution occurred with outside aid, support, and inspiration, mainly Chinese and Cuban, but it was not under outside control.[63] The new Foreign and Defense Minister, Abdul Rahman Mohammed, known as Babu, was a strong admirer of the CPR.[64] The latter for its part hailed the new regime in Zanzibar and, together with other Communist states, supplied it with economic and military aid.[65] East German and Soviet influence soon largely replaced Chinese influence, however.[66]

The CPR appears to consider Tanzania, the name given to the union formed between Tanganyika and Zanzibar in 1964, as its most important base, although not necessarily its important target, in East Africa. At any rate its embassy at Dar es Salaam is the largest in the region.[67] Although President Julius Nyerere is believed to have strong reservations about the CPR, he has come under increasing pressure from younger, more leftist colleagues who admire it, and in February, 1965, he paid a state visit to Peking.

Although the CPR has antagonized President Jomo Kenyatta of Kenya, it is on good terms with the leftist Home Minister, Oginga Odinga, who is reportedly one of the growing number of African politicians who have received secret Chinese payments amounting to bribes.[68]

---

[60] Lowenthal in Brzezinski, *op. cit.*, pp. 193–194; Robert Counts, "Chinese Footprints in Somalia," *The Reporter*, February 2, 1961, pp. 32–34; Gordon Brook-Shepherd, "Red Rivalry in the Black Continent," *The Reporter*, January 18, 1962, pp. 23–25; "Sino-Soviet Interest in Africa," *loc. cit.*, p. 6.

[61] *The Washington Post and Times Herald*, August 30, 1963.

[62] Lowenthal in Brzezinski, *op. cit.*, pp. 193–194; *The New York Times*, September 4, 1960.

[63] Cf. *The New York Times*, January 14, 1964.

[64] Cf. his remarks quoted in *The Washington Post and Times Herald*, March 15, 1964.

[65] Cf. *The New York Times*, June 15, 1964.

[66] Griffith, *loc. cit.*, p. 187.

[67] Colin Legum, "Peking's Strategic Priorities," *Africa Report*, January, 1965, p. 20.

[68] Griffith, *loc. cit.*, p. 176.

The CPR has also antagonized President Hastings Banda of Malawi, who is believed to have rejected a Chinese offer of an £18 million credit.[69]

The CPR has often indicated its support for the illegal, harassed Communist Party of South Africa, whose leadership however remains pro-Soviet, and there is no doubt that the Chinese like many Africans would be happy to see South Africa become the scene of an "armed struggle," if only one were feasible. The paradoxical and embarrassing fact that the CPR, like many other governments and regimes that denounce the South African government on political grounds, has continued to trade with it has been pointed out by Africans on more than one occasion.

Chou En-lai's first stop in Sub-Saharan Africa was Ghana (January 11–16, 1964), where his reception was a fairly enthusiastic one. Nkrumah expressed support not only for a second Bandung Conference but also for the CPC's proposal for an anti-"imperialist" conference of Latin American as well as Afro-Asian nations. On the other hand, there were also some discordant notes; for example, Chou did not endorse Nkrumah's Afro-Marxist claim to be "building socialism."[70]

In Mali (January 16–21), unlike Ghana, Chou was thanked for Chinese economic aid, and he took advantage of the opportunity to formulate eight principles supposedly governing the CPR's extension of such aid. The political passages in the joint communiqué were more cordial on both sides than those in the earlier Sino-Ghanaian joint communiqué.[71]

Chou's visit to Guinea (January 21–26) was marked by even greater security precautions than were his other African visits.[72] The joint communiqué was slightly more friendly than the Sino-Ghanaian one, slightly less so than the Sino-Malian one.[73]

Roughly the same was true in Sudan (January 27–30), where resentment of Chinese contacts with local Communists seems to have weighed heavily with the Sudanese government.[74]

Although Chou's scheduled visits to Kenya, Tanganyika, and Uganda were cancelled, he received an invitation to visit Ethiopia (January 30–February 1). His reception was rather cool, presumably because of Emperor Haile Selassie's objections to several of the CPR's policies, including its support for Somalia, its general revolutionary activities in Africa, and its hostility toward India.[75]

In Somalia (February 1–4), the relatively ungrateful government seemed mainly interested in further Chinese economic aid, which Chou promised to give.[76] Just before leaving Somalia, he briefly assumed the role

---

69 *Ibid.*, pp. 175–176.
70 Adie, *loc. cit.*, pp. 187–189.
71 *Ibid.*, pp. 189–190; Scalapino, *loc. cit.*, pp. 641–642.
72 *Christian Science Monitor*, January 23, 1964.
73 Adie, *loc. cit.*, pp. 190–191.
74 *Ibid.*, p. 192.
75 *Ibid.*, pp. 192–193.
76 *Ibid.*, pp. 193–194.

of revolutionary instead of diplomat and said that "revolutionary prospects are excellent throughout the African continent."[77] This remark was interpreted as denying the independence of at least some African nations and provoked much criticism. The CPC was forced to make some embarrassed efforts to explain away what Chou had said.[78]

In assessing the CPR's progress in Africa, as in many other fields, much depends on whether one emphasizes what has been accomplished or what remains to be accomplished. Those governments that have not recognized the CPR generally seem to be in no hurry to do so, partly because they know what opportunities for revolutionary activity a Communist Chinese embassy possesses. For the same reason, some governments that have recognized the CPR have tended to lose much of their enthusiasm for it. As elsewhere, the CPR's most enduring appeal is to extreme leftists. North Vietnam is operating fairly extensively in Africa in support of the CPR.[79] In the majority of African states, the CPR seems to have no more than a fair chance, for several years at least, of effecting any basic change in the fundamentally neutral orientation of the indigenous governments, or of competing successfully at least in the vital economic sphere with Soviet, American, and European influences. In some, however, severe local and external tensions offer opportunities that the CPR may be able to translate into significant revolutionary gains. These are probably the countries in which residual European influence is the greatest.

■ **COMMUNIST CHINA AND LATIN AMERICA**

Latin America holds a number of attractions for the CPR, although it must be remembered that attractiveness is not the same thing as accessibility. The region contains raw materials that are important to the American economy and are of some interest to the Chinese. Latin America is relatively close to the United States, contains about one-third of all American foreign investments, and has long been under American influence, so that it is a region in which the United States is theoretically vulnerable to major political setbacks. Latin America is politically restless and unstable, and although the recognized Communist Parties are generally small and weak there is a great deal of active leftist feeling and opposition to "Yankee imperialism" on the part of students and intellectuals. An additional incentive for Communist Chinese interest in Latin America is the obvious fact that it contains some twenty governments that might conceivably be brought to transfer diplomatic recognition from Taipei to Peking and vote

[77] *The Washington Post and Times Herald,* February 4, 1964.

[78] *Christian Science Monitor,* February 20, 1964. A CPC editorial on Chou's trip was careful to limit its definition of the "revolutionary situation" in Africa to "those countries yet to attain independence," as distinct from the "newly emerging countries" (*People's Daily,* February 6, 1964).

[79] *Christian Science Monitor,* July 14, 1964.

for the latter's seating at the United Nations. Apart from Cuba, this is of course a remote possibility at present; even the Soviet Union has succeeded in establishing diplomatic relations with only a few Latin American countries.

Apart from some early contacts with Chinese living in Latin America, the relations with the region appear to have begun when some Latin American leftists visited Peking at the time of the World Federation of Trade Unions conference there (November, 1949). There were further such contacts at a number of other international conferences, and again in Peking at the "peace conference" in October, 1952. Over and above such contacts as these, some Latin Americans felt interested in the CPR bcause of its anti-Americanism and its approach to economic development and "agrarian reform." This was not generally true of Latin American Communists, who were for the most part unimaginative Stalinists subservient to the CPSU.[80]

The beginnings of a change in this situation can probably be traced to Guatemala in 1954. Here the Soviet was in the process of providing, through some of the East European countries, arms for a regime that was rapidly being taken over from within by the Communists. When that regime was overthrown in June, 1954, by an opposition movement supported by the United States, however, the Soviet Union did nothing. A Latin American leftist, Communist or not, might reasonably draw from this episode, as well as from Soviet behavior in Hungary two years later, the inference that the Soviet Union would take serious risks only on behalf of another member of the "socialist camp" or some other regime to which it recognized a special tie. The problem then was one of involving the Soviet Union in the fate of a leftist regime once it had seized power. Another problem was that the "peaceful" path to power that the CPSU increasingly recommended to foreign Communists after the mid-1950's offered few prospects to any in Latin America.[81] On the other hand, some Latin American leftists were encouraged by the Soviet Union's acquisition of ICBMs to believe that at last the Soviet Union had the ability, and would therefore probably have the will, to deter the United States from intervening against leftist revolutions in the Western Hemisphere. This illusion of course died with the Cuban missile crisis, which tended to increase the interest felt by Latin American leftists in the CPC's revolutionary strategy.

It was probably considerations such as these, as well as the Chinese economy's growing need for imported raw materials, that led the CPR to increase its economic, political, and cultural activity in Latin America in

---

[80] Shen-yu Dai, "Peking and Latin America, 1949–1960," paper presented at annual meeting of the Association for Asian Studies, Chicago, March, 1961; Victor Alba, "The Chinese in Latin America," *The China Quarterly*, no. 5 (January–March, 1961), pp. 53–61.

[81] The Soviet approach is known in Latin America as *operacion durmiente*, "laying the railway sleepers" for a future smooth advance. (W. A. C. Adie, "China, Russia, and the Third World," *The China Quarterly*, no. 11 [July–September, 1962], p. 208.)

1956, and again after Vice President Nixon's stormy visit to the region in the spring of 1958.[82] In 1957 the CPC added to its short-wave broadcasts in Spanish some aimed avowedly at Latin America. During this period the CPC's political hopes for Latin America seem to have centered on Mexico, where the former revolutionary and president Lazaro Cardenas was outspokenly favorable to it.[83]

The focus of attention rapidly shifted to Cuba after Castro's seizure of power there at the beginning of 1959. This is not the place for a detailed analysis of Castro's revolution. Suffice it to say that he was (and is) a romantic, idealistic, non-Communist revolutionary who came to power through guerrilla warfare supplemented by political action in a country prosperous by Latin American standards and offering no apparent basis for a leftist revolution except a tradition of American domination and an unpopular police state. The Moscow-oriented Popular Socialist Party (Communist Party) regarded Castro at first with considerable reservations, which he reciprocated, and has never successfully challenged his personal, charismatic leadership of the revolution. Castro's radical domestic program and his determination to foment similar revolutions elsewhere in Latin America have necessarily tended to bring him into conflict with the United States. This in turn has helped to drive him into a close relationship with the Soviet Union, which evidently with Guatemala in mind he regards as his best defense against American pressures.[84]

Castro's revolution bears some obvious resemblances to Mao's, with the important difference that Castro has operated outside the Communist fold and Mao within it. Each revived the stagnant fortunes of Communism, largely by means of guerrilla warfare and political activism, in an important region of the underdeveloped world, in competition with and to some extent in defiance of the more orthodox Communist leaderships, who preferred the futile procedures prescribed by Moscow. Each has ambitions for regional leadership and has been warmly received by the most leftist elements within and outside the regional Communist Parties.[85]

The CPC established contact with the Popular Socialist Party at least as early as 1956,[86] but it evidently found Castro so much more important and congenial that it promptly gave preference to him after he came to power. The CPC press commented favorably on his triumph over Batista, and Mao Tse-tung is said to have told a delegation of Latin American Com-

---

[82] Daniel Tretiak, letter in *The China Quarterly*, no. 7 (July–September, 1961), pp. 148–153.

[83] Cf. *The New York Times*, October 18, 1959.

[84] Cf. Boris Goldenberg, "The Cuban Revolution: An Analysis," *Problems of Communism*, vol. xii, no. 5 (September–October, 1963), pp. 1–9.

[85] Cf. Ernst Halperin, "Castroism—Challenge to the Latin American Communists," *Problems of Communism*, vol. xii, no. 5 (September–October 1963), pp. 9–18.

[86] Andres Suarez, "Castro Between Moscow and Peking," *Problems of Communism*, vol. xii, no. 5 (September–October, 1963), p. 21.

munists who visited Peking after attending the CPSU's Twenty-first Congress (January, 1959) that the Castro revolution offered an excellent opportunity to intensify the anti-American struggle in Latin America. A China-Latin America Friendship Association was established in Peking in March, 1960. Khrushchev showed no comparable enthusiasm for Castro until after the collapse of his détente policy and of the Paris summit conference (May, 1960), and until after the cancellation by the United States of sugar imports from Cuba (July, 1960). It is likely that the Soviet economic and military aid and vague declarations of military support for Cuba that were forthcoming after that were motivated at least partly by the possibility of increasing Chinese influence in Cuba. In other words, Castro has probably used his political connections with the CPC to get what he wants from the CPSU, without in any way accepting Chinese leadership or control. The Russians and Chinese seem to have felt that, for various political reasons, they had no choice but to acquiesce in this game. A specific gain to the CPC from playing it, and also from extending economic aid, was the establishment of a New China News Agency office in Havana in 1959 and Cuban diplomatic recognition of the CPR in September, 1960.[87]

In December, 1960, "Che" Guevara visited Peking and evidently persuaded the CPC to treat Castro alone, and not the Popular Socialist Party as well, as the leader of the Cuban revolution. Not until early 1962, after Castro's declaration that he was a "Marxist-Leninist" and after his successful disciplining of the Cuban Communist leadership, did the CPC begin to concede that his revolution contained some elements of "socialism."[88]

The Cuban missile crisis, in which the CPC gave loud verbal support to Castro and criticized Khrushchev for his "Munich" policy, seems to have increased his ability to extract aid, if not necessarily more than token protection, from the Soviet Union. In April, 1963, shortly before Castro was to visit the Soviet Union, the latter listed Cuba for the first time as a "socialist" country and therefore one entitled to Soviet protection — something that Castro had wanted for at least three years, even if its value seemed doubtful after the missile crisis. The CPC did the same three months later. It should not be assumed that Castro has thrown in his lot completely with the CPSU in the Sino-Soviet dispute, however. His game still appears to be to use the political support of the CPC, for which he probably also feels some genuine admiration, as a means of getting economic and military aid and support from the CPSU. Whether he can continue to play this game successfully it is of course impossible to predict.[89]

Certainly the CPSU has not welcomed the Chinese intrusion in Latin America, either before or since Castro's coming to power. At the celebration of the tenth anniversary of the founding of the CPR (October, 1959),

[87] Cf. *ibid*, pp. 18–22.
[88] *Ibid.*, pp. 22–23.
[89] Cf. *ibid.*, pp. 23–26.

all Moscow-oriented speakers refrained from mentioning Latin America in the same breath with Asia and Africa, whereas the CPC generally brackets all three.[90] The CPSU also appears to have objected to a resolution of the Moshi Conference (February, 1963), favored by the CPC, calling for a conference of delegates from all anti-"imperialist" organizations in Latin America, as well as Asia and Africa.[91]

The CPR has naturally shown a special interest in Brazil, in view of its size and importance. This interest quickened somewhat when Vice President Goulart, who later became President, visited the CPR in August, 1961. Under his administration a number of leftists entered the government, although apparently not in such numbers as to present a serious threat.[92] The official attitude toward the CPR was moderately friendly. The CPC was greatly angered by the military coup that overthrew Goulart early in 1964 and objected vigorously to the arrest of some Chinese alleged to be its agents.[93]

Significant relations between the CPR and Argentina seem to have been confined to the importing of grain.[94]

The CPC has shown an interest in the persistent rural unrest in Bolivia and Colombia and seems to have some influence on extreme leftists in those countries.[95] The same is true in Peru, where early in 1964 pro-CPC and pro-Castro elements gained control of the Communist Party. The Chilean Communist Party, on the other hand, which stands a chance of coming to power by parliamentary means, has understandably shown little sympathy with the CPC.

In Central America the CPC has focused its attention on Panama, because of that country's unique relationship with the United States. At the time of the crisis in Panamanian relations with the United States, in January, 1964, the CPR gave vociferous support to Panama, even though the latter recognizes the Republic of China.

In spite of widespread sympathy in Latin American leftist circles for the CPC, it does not seem likely to realize its own objectives in Latin America in the near future to any significant degree. Probably nothing less than some massive failure in American policy could make Chinese influence in Latin America a major problem. Castro's prospects, on the other hand, look considerably brighter, although probably less so than before the missile crisis. It may be for this reason that the CPC has seemed ready to tolerate Castro's gyrations and treat his cause essentially as its own.

---

[90] Thomas Perry Thornton, "Peking, Moscow, and the Underdeveloped Areas," *World Politics*, vol. xiii, no. 4 (July, 1961), p. 496, n. 10.

[91] Cf. Lowenthal in Brzezinski, *op. cit.*, p. 198.

[92] *The Washington Post and Times Herald*, April 25 and 27, 1964.

[93] *Christian Science Monitor*, May 14, 1964.

[94] Cf. *Christian Science Monitor*, March 9, 1964.

[95] Cf. *The New York Times*, December 16, 1963; Adie, "China, Russia, and the Third World," *loc. cit.*, pp. 207–208.

PART THREE

Communist China as an Asian Power

- ☐ The Korean War
- ☐ The Indochina Crisis I
- ☐ Taiwan and the Offshore Islands
- ☐ Border Problems and Policy I
- ☐ Border Problems and Policy II
- ☐ The Indochina Crisis II
- ☐ Communist China and Northeast Asia
- ☐ Communist China and Southeast Asia
- ☐ Communist China and South Asia

PART THREE

Communist China as an Asian Power

The Korean War

The Korean War was the most serious threat to world peace since 1945, except perhaps for the Cuban missile crisis. It gave rise to the earliest, and to date probably the gravest, threat to which the security of the CPR has been subjected. On the other hand, it also made the CPR a major Asian power.

■ ORIGINS OF THE WAR

Soviet influence in North Korea, down to the outbreak of war in 1950, was dominant; Communist Chinese influence was recessive, although not nonexistent.[1] There is no reason, therefore, to assume that North Korea started the war without Stalin's knowledge, still less over his veto.[2] On the other hand, the common view that Stalin ordered the North Koreans to attack South Korea, primarily for his own reasons, has little to recommend it. Stalin was notoriously cautious in military matters, and one looks in vain at his behavior elsewhere for the sort of direct challenge to "imperialism" that North Korea flung down in 1950. The token nuclear capability, far inferior to its American counterpart, that Stalin possessed at that time was certainly not enough to tempt him to adventures of a kind that he ordinarily avoided. Finally, his interests in the postwar period centered on Europe, and it is most unlikely that he would have taken such a grave risk solely on his own initiative in an area of secondary concern to him.

None of these considerations, however, meant much to the North Korean regime itself. With the emergence of the Republic of Korea in the south under United Nations auspices, in 1948, Korea became the first

---

[1] *North Korea: A Case Study in the Techniques of Takeover*, Washington: Department of State, 1961, pp. 100–121.
[2] This assumption is the theme of Wilbur W. Hitchcock, "North Korea Jumps the Gun," *Current History*, vol. 20, no. 115 (March, 1951), pp. 136–144.

country to experience something resembling a de jure division into a Communist and a non-Communist half. The withdrawal of Soviet and American forces occurred at the end of 1948. Already the North had begun to supplement its political efforts toward reunification with military pressures stopping short, but only just short, of invasion.[3] These efforts were unsuccessful. North Korean agents in South Korea appear to have assured their leaders, however, that a full-scale invasion from the north, but nothing less, would touch off mass revolts against the Rhee government in the south; many American observers in Korea would have considered them too pessimistic.[4] An invasion would obviously require more outside aid and support than North Korea had yet received.

It seems likely that, perhaps after an initial unsuccessful approach to Stalin, the North Koreans took their problem to the CPR. This may well have occurred at the World Federation of Trade Unions meeting in Peking in November, 1949.[5] From later developments it appears that the CPC agreed that Mao should present the North Korean case to Stalin, and during the winter Korean units eventually totaling about 40,000 men began to be transferred from Chinese (in Manchuria) to North Korean control.[6]

To the south, President Syngman Rhee was aware of his government's military inferiority and anxious for reunification on his own, not Communist, terms. It began to appear that he had at least one powerful friend. In his message to the Japanese people on New Year's Day, 1950, General MacArthur, who four years before had inserted into the Japanese constitution the famous Article IX renouncing war and the maintenance of even defensive armed forces, virtually reversed himself by indicating that Japan might have to be rearmed.[7] The following month, Rhee visited MacArthur in Tokyo and on his return said that Korea would soon be unified and that the Republic of Korea would have allies in the process.

These developments occurred during the very important period from mid-December, 1949, to mid-February, 1950, when Mao Tse-tung was in Moscow. The Japanese and Korean questions undoubtedly figured among the long list of topics that the two men discussed. General MacArthur's statement seems to have had an electric effect by arousing fears of a recurrence of Japanese expansion, from which Russia had already suffered something and China a great deal, under American auspices.[8] As usual in

---

[3] Glenn D. Paige in Cyril E. Black and Thomas P. Thornton, eds., *Communist and Revolution: The Strategic Uses of Political Violence*, Princeton University Press, 1964, pp. 220–227.

[4] Cf. *ibid.*, p. 227.

[5] Cf. "The movement of the Korean people against Syngman Rhee, puppet of American imperialism, and for the establishment of a unified people's democratic republic of Korea cannot be halted" (Lui Shao-ch'i, speech of November 16, 1949, released by New China News Agency, November 23, 1949).

[6] *North Korea . . .*, *op. cit.*, p. 117.

[7] Text in *The New York Times*, January 1, 1950.

[8] It will be recalled that the Sino-Soviet alliance concluded on February 14, 1950, was directed against Japan or any power allied with it directly or indirectly.

such cases, the local Communist Party was regarded as the first line of defense, and if necessary an expendable one. On January 6, 1950, the Cominform organ,[9] with Chinese support, began to prod the Japanese Communist Party into abandoning its previous mildness toward the American occupational regime and adopting a much more militant line, which in the spring of 1950 erupted into violence only just short of guerrilla war.

In Moscow, Mao probably urged Stalin to give the North Koreans the permission and logistical support necessary for a formal invasion of South Korea. Mao may have argued that a Communist-controlled South Korea would provide a valuable buffer in the future against a resurgent Japan. Stalin, who was certainly aware of the weak condition of the American forces in Japan and therefore of the limited ability of the United States to respond promptly on the scene to an invasion of South Korea, probably insisted, nevertheless, that he must have convincing evidence that the United States had no intention of defending South Korea. This evidence he very shortly received.

On January 12, in a speech carrying more weight than similar earlier statements by other prominent Americans, Secretary of State Acheson defined the United States' defensive perimeter in the Pacific as one running through Japan, the Ryukyus, and the Philippines; the defense of areas to the west of this line was to be the responsibility of the United Nations. To this seemingly frail shelter he thus committed not only South Korea but Taiwan and Vietnam, all of them areas where a militant Communist Party was then trying to complete the conquest or unification of its country.[10]

Events now began to move in even more rapid and dramatic sequence. On January 13, following the predictable defeat of its resolution demanding replacement of the Republic of China by the CPR in the United Nations, the Soviet Union began to boycott the proceedings of the Security Council. The usual interpretation, and the one for which Stalin probably hoped, has been that the Soviet boycott was motivated by the Soviet defeat on the Chinese representation question; another view holds that Stalin mistakenly believed that his abstention would prevent effective response by the Security Council to the invasion of South Korea. These interpretations, of which the second seems the closer to the truth, are both subject to the crucial objection that Stalin can hardly have felt certain that abstention would be as effective as the veto power, for which he had fought so hard in the negotiations leading to the formation of the United Nations Organization, and which he

---

[9] For a Lasting peace, for a People's Democracy, published in Bucharest.

[10] In fairness to Mr. Acheson, it should be pointed out that of all high American officials he was apparently the most insistent that the United States must resist the attack on South Korea, when it actually came in June (see former Secretary of Defense Louis Johnson's testimony at the MacArthur hearings). Presumably he was aware of his involuntary role in precipitating the invasion and was determined to make amends. It is also worth noting that Secretary Dulles made his famous "massive retaliation" speech on January 12, 1954, the fourth anniversary of the Acheson speech, to discourage a similar Communist underestimate of American firmness in the context of the Indochinese crisis.

would not have abdicated for the sake of a consideration no more important to him than Communist Chinese sensibilities. One must assume the existence of a consideration of enough weight to transform the Soviet presence in the Security Council, with a veto, from a highly desirable situation in Stalin's eyes into an undesirable one.

Secretary Acheson had just stated that the defense of South Korea was the responsibility of the United Nations, and it was clear that one of the first American reactions to the invasion would be to demand action on it by the Security Council, as well perhaps as to bring highly credible charges of Soviet collusion in the invasion. This was a situation full of risks that might have been necessary, and even tolerable, were a genuine Soviet interest to be served, but not in a case where the main interest was a North Korean one. The risks to the Soviet Union of being caught in a crossfire at the Security Council at such a time would be even greater if the crisis in Korea should reproduce itself in other parts of Asia at the same time.

On January 15 (Far Eastern time) the Communist-controlled Democratic Republic of Vietnam (DRV) appealed for international recognition as the government of the whole of Vietnam.[11] The first foreign power to respond was the CPR, which granted recognition on January 18; the Soviet Union did not recognize the DRV until January 30.[12] On January 20, Premier Chou En-lai left Peking for Moscow to take part in the critical concluding weeks of the Sino-Soviet negotiations then in progress.[13]

Among the arrangements completed at that time, I believe there was one to which Stalin gave a highly nervous assent, and to whose implementation he would commit nothing more than logistical support. In a roughly coordinated fashion, so as to divide and weaken whatever American response might occur, the North Koreans were to attack South Korea, the Chinese Communist were to attack Taiwan, and the Vietnamese Communists were to launch an offensive aimed at Hanoi.[14] Before we consider in some detail the aftermath of the first part of this presumed arrangement, the aftermath of the last two may be briefly discussed.

President Truman had announced on January 5, 1950, that the United States would not intervene further in the Chinese civil war and had thereby

---

[11] Text in *Pravda*, January 31, 1950; and Allan B. Cole, ed., *Conflict in Indochina and International Repercussions: A Documentary History, 1945–1955*, Cornell University Press, 1956, pp. 95–96.

[12] *Ibid.*, pp. 121–122. North Korea recognized the DRV on January 31.

[13] Max Beloff, *Soviet Policy in the Far East, 1944–1951*, Oxford University Press, 1953, p. 73.

[14] It is possible that a Chinese military "liberation" of Tibet was also planned as part of this coordinated operation. The CPC gave its first clear indication of an intent to invade Tibet on January 1, 1950, launched the invasion without fanfare in the spring, and announced it at the time of the beginning of the overt Chinese intervention in Korea on October 25 (Robert Ford, *Captured in Tibet*, London: Pan Books, 1958, pp. 43, 63; George N. Patterson, "China and Tibet: Background to the Revolt," *The China Quarterly*, No. 1 [January–March, 1960], pp. 91–93.

conceded Taiwan to the Communists if they could take it. On the 8th, the CPR had demanded the Republic of China's expulsion from the United Nations and its own admission. Things soon began to go wrong with the projected "liberation" of Taiwan, however. Units of the Third Field Army training for the operation were struck by an epidemic of liver fluke. The Nationalists seem to have frustrated a pro-Communist plot on Taiwan on which the CPC was relying. Chiang Kai-shek formally resumed the Presidency of the Republic of China, from which he had "retired" a year earlier, on March 1, 1950. Following the "liberation" of Hainan in April, units of the Fourth Field Army began to move toward Manchuria, presumably as a routine precaution in connection with the forthcoming hostilities in Korea. The Third Field Army remained in position, for the most part opposite Taiwan, until after President Truman's famous and fateful order of June 27, 1950, which in addition to indicating a determination to intervene directly in Korea and indirectly in Indochina saved Taiwan by interposing the Seventh Fleet between it and the mainland.[15] Thereafter only political and not military methods were left to the CPC for the "liberation" of Taiwan, and some units of the Third Field Army also began to move northward.[16]

Unannounced Communist Chinese military aid to the DRV apparently began in the spring of 1950, in the form of equipment, a limited number of "volunteer" technicians, and possibly an agreement for support by Chinese combat units in case of need. In October of the same year the "Vietnam People's Army" (VPA) virtually cleared the French from the mountainous area along the Chinese frontier. Late in December it launched an offensive, apparently aimed at Hanoi, in the Red River delta. In open terrain, however, superior French firepower and energetic counteraction directed by General de Lattre inflicted a major defeat on the VPA in the early months of 1951. The VPA then began to concentrate its efforts on completing the conquest of the mountainous areas.[17]

■ THE OUTBREAK OF WAR

During the spring of 1950 Soviet military equipment flowed in large quantities to North Korea, although not yet to the CPR. Most of this equipment moved across Manchuria, a fact that points to Chinese knowledge

[15] The linking of these three areas in the presidential order indicates that the United States government was aware that all three were threatened at that time and tends to support the hypothesis advanced here, that a coordinated attack in all three areas was planned by the Communist side.

[16] Allen S. Whiting, *China Crosses the Yalu: The Decision to Enter the Korean War*, New York: Macmillan, 1960, pp. 20–23, 64–65.

[17] *Survey of International Affairs, 1949–1950*, pp. 431–435; *1951*, pp. 453–455; Bernard B. Fall, *The Two Viet-Nams: A Political and Military Analysis*, New York: Praeger, 1963, pp. 108–111, 116–117; Jean Marchand, *L'Indochine en guerre*, Paris: Presses modernes, 1954, pp. 187–221.

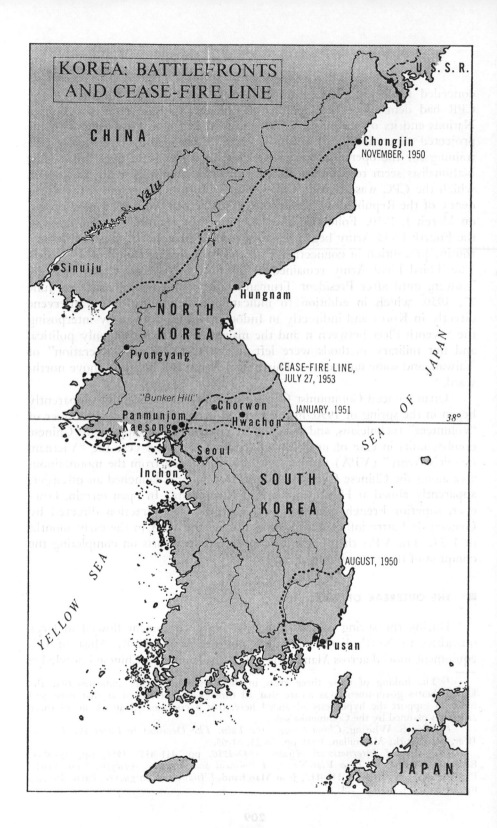

KOREA: BATTLEFRONTS
AND CEASE-FIRE LINE

CHINA

Yalu

•Chongjin
NOVEMBER, 1950

U. S. S. R.

•Sinuiju

NORTH
KOREA

•Hungnam

Pyongyang

CEASE-FIRE LINE,
JULY 27, 1953

JAPAN

"Bunker Hill"   •Chorwon
Panmunjom•   •Hwachon   JANUARY, 1951
Kaesong

Seoul•

Inchon•

SOUTH
KOREA

SEA   *OF*

38°

YELLOW

SEA

AUGUST, 1950

•Pusan

JAPAN

if not actual consent and cooperation.[18] Chinese troop movements to Manchuria continued.

The North Korean attack on June 25 achieved complete tactical surprise and by the beginning of August had driven the far weaker South Korean forces back behind the perimeter formed by the Naktong River, in the extreme southeastern corner of the country. The attack also produced at least one serious complication not anticipated by those who had planned the operation — namely, American counterintervention, not only in the United Nations but on the field of battle. In this unexpectedly difficult situation, a Soviet return to the Security Council offered fewer drawbacks than continuation of the boycott, and an Indian proposal of July 13 offered a face-saving way for the Soviet Union to resume its seat.[19] This it did on August 1. Three days later it introduced a resolution (ultimately voted down, on September 6) calling for both the Korean regimes and the CPR to discuss the Korean question with the Security Council. Since this arrangement would have made Nationalist China a party to the discussions and would not have affected Taiwan, it is not surprising that the CPR's endorsement (on August 7) of the Soviet proposal was lukewarm.[20] The Soviet interest in a negotiated settlement, masked to be sure by much bluster, was reinforced in mid-August, when the North Koreans suffered serious defeats along the Naktong perimeter, by fear that the United States might not only seek a clear-cut victory in Korea but take some sort of revenge against those whom it considered accessories before the fact in the North Korean aggression. Accordingly, the formidable propaganda facilities of the Soviet-inspired "peace movement" were promptly turned loose against the United Nations operations in Korea.[21] During the following months, the Soviet Union's efforts to cope with the challenge posed by the rapid northward advance of the United Nations forces in Korea were confined substantially to warnings and diplomatic maneuvers. The CPR also tried this approach, but when its possibilities had been exhausted Chinese, unlike Soviet, policy quickly took the form of armed intervention.

■ THE CHINESE INTERVENTION

The American decision to protect Taiwan, announced by President Truman on June 27, threatened not only to disturb the termination of the Chinese civil war on Communist terms but also to throw the coordinated

[18] *North Korea . . ., op. cit.*, p. 117.

[19] The Indian proposal was to the effect that the Soviet Union return, and the CPR be admitted, to the Security Council as the best means of reaching a settlement of the Korean crisis. The CPR showed much less interest, at that time, in this proposal or in the Korean situation than in the American decision to defend Taiwan (Whiting, *op. cit.*, pp. 53–62).

[20] *Ibid.*, pp. 72–77, 79.

[21] Marshall D. Shulman, *Stalin's Foreign Policy Reappraised*, Harvard University Press, 1963, p. 154.

Communist offensive, which then appeared to be progressing well in Korea and Indochina, badly off balance. Worse still, the CPR soon began to see signs of what it evidently thought were plans for a coordinated American counteroffensive, and even an "imperialist" intervention against the CPR, led by General MacArthur and employing Chinese Nationalist and South Korean as well as American forces. On July 7, the anniversary incidentally of the beginning of the Japanese invasion of China in 1937, the Security Council adopted in the absence of the Soviet Union a resolution requesting the United States to appoint a commander of the United Nations forces in Korea, who was announced the following day as General MacArthur. At the end of July (the visit had been planned before the outbreak of war in Korea, but had been postponed on that account) General MacArthur held talks on Taiwan with Nationalist officials, after which he began publicly to praise Chiang Kai-shek and call for offensive employment of Nationalist troops against the China coast in support of United Nations operations in Korea.[22]

Important though the Taiwan issue seemed to the CPC, the Korean crisis rapidly assumed even more critical proportions. Statements by Ambassador Warren Austin in the Security Council, on August 10 and 17, seemed to show that the United States government had decided to reunify Korea by force, an act that would bring American troops to the doorstep of Manchuria. On August 13, the first Communist Chinese ambassador arrived in Pyongyang, the North Korean capital, and it is likely that Chinese contingency planning for an intervention in Korea and the arrival of Chinese advance parties in North Korea date from this period. But Peking had not yet exhausted its nonviolent resources. On August 20, in a message to the Security Council, Chou En-lai indicated for the first time that Korea had replaced Taiwan as the CPR's most pressing external concern and demanded that the CPR be represented in any discussions on Korea in the Security Council. On August 26 the CPR named Chang Wen-t'ien as its hypothetical "delegate" to the forthcoming session of the General Assembly.[23] On August 27, the CPR launched a long series of protests at alleged violations of Chinese airspace by American aircraft.[24] The Security Council and even the Soviet Union, however, showed no further interest in inviting the CPR to take part in discussions on Korea. Instead, the Security Council invited Peking on September 29 to discuss Taiwan, an invitation that was not accepted until October 23, and even then perhaps only out of fear that it might otherwise soon be withdrawn as a result of the impending Chinese intervention in Korea. In other words, at a time when the CPR cared most about Taiwan it was invited (by the Soviet Union, at any rate) to discuss

---

[22] The news of this visit was suppressed for a time in the Communist Chinese press (Whiting, *op. cit.*, pp. 81–82), a probable indication of genuine fear.

[23] Cf. *ibid.*, pp. 77–87.

[24] *Ibid.*, p. 98.

Korea, and at a time when it cared most about Korea it was invited to discuss Taiwan.

The approach of United Nations forces to the 38th parallel at the end of September, in pursuit of the beaten North Koreans, confronted the CPC with what seemed to it to be an increasingly serious threat to its security. The United States was supposedly the head of the "imperialist camp" and had intervened in the Chinese civil war on the anti-Communist side. The hostility of General MacArthur and his entourage to the CPR was well known. For an analogy, one need only imagine American reaction if a large Soviet army, under an especially anti-American commander, were to move up the Lower California peninsula toward the California frontier. The analogy is improved if one further imagines that southern California is the main heavy industrial region in the United States, as Manchuria was (and is) in the CPR.

The CPC has generally cited, as its major reasons for intervening in Korea, concern for its own security and a desire to prevent the extinction of North Korea as a "fraternal" Communist state.[25] It seems fairly clear, however, that the second reason ranked far behind the first in Peking's scheme of priorities, and that in its famous slogan, "Resist America, Aid Korea," the first element greatly outweighed the second. In fact, the CPR intimated (in conversations with the Indian ambassador) a willingness to tolerate if necessary the conquest of North Korea by South Korean troops alone, by defining the condition of Chinese entry into the war as the crossing of the 38th parallel by American forces.[26] After American troops actually crossed the parallel with United Nations authorization, however, the CPC continued to demand the withdrawal of all foreign troops from Korea (again indicating something less than intense concern for the fate of North Korea as such), but it gave some signs of being willing to accept a rump North Korean state as a buffer, with its southern boundary in the vicinity of the neck of the Korean peninsula (approximately 39° 30′ north latitude), provided the United States withdrew diplomatic recognition, aid, and military protection from the Republic of China.[27] It may have been with the aim of reaching and holding such a line that Chinese troops secretly began to cross the Yalu River into North Korea, apparently on the night of October 15–16.[28]

If, as seems very likely, the CPR's initial military objectives in Korea were highly limited, its hand was soon to be increasingly forced. For General MacArthur, ignoring the reservations of his own government, its allies, and the Joint Chiefs of Staff, to say nothing of those of the CPR, plunged onward toward the Yalu. On October 24, without prior notice to

[25] E.g., "The Eight Years of the Chinese People's Volunteers in Korea," New China News Agency dispatch, October 25, 1958.

[26] Whiting, *op. cit.*, 108.

[27] *The Manchester Guardian*, November 18, 1950.

[28] Cf. Whiting, *op. cit.*, p. 115.

Washington, he abolished the last "restraining line" that up to that time had prohibited the advance of American, as distinct from South Korean, troops to the Manchurian border.[29] Since that time, the CPR has given the following day, October 25, as the date of the official formation of the "Chinese People's Volunteers" (CPV), which began to engage in limited actions against United Nations forces on October 26. On November 7, a North Korean communiqué admitted the presence of the Chinese "volunteers," who on the same day broke off contact with United Nations forces, presumably in the hope that the latter would retreat to a line acceptable to the CPR.[30] The exact opposite happened, however. On November 24, General MacArthur announced a major offensive to "end the war," and two days later the CPV launched a vigorous and spectacular attack against the dangerously extended United Nations forces.

It seems clear, then, that the CPR's entry into the Korean War was motivated overwhelmingly by concern for its own security, and only very secondarily by concern for North Korean survival. Still less important, apparently, was a desire to reduce American and enhance Chinese influence in the Far East,[31] although there was probably some hope that an act of assumed strategic necessity might also yield some political benefits, such as an improved position with respect to Taiwan and an increase of Chinese at the expense of Soviet influence in Manchuria and North Korea. It is one of the main themes of this study that when the CPR has employed overt violence toward outsiders, as it did in Korea, it has generally done so mainly in order to protect its security rather than to enhance its influence. The latter, after all, can usually be promoted more safely and more effectively by political means.

In spite of the impression of optimism conveyed by its propaganda, the CPC seems to have entered the Korean War in a cautious and even reluctant mood. The CPC was certainly aware of the military risks it was incurring, and in particular of the chance that the United States might use atomic weapons against it either in Korea or in China, the Sino-Soviet alliance notwithstanding.[32] It has been credibly reported that Mao Tse-tung paced the floor for three days and nights before reaching the final decision to intervene in Korea.[33] Accordingly, the CPC maintained that its troops in Korea were volunteers, probably not with any serious expectation of

[29] Tang Tsou, *America's Failure in China, 1941–50*, University of Chicago Press, 1963, pp. 580–582; note the map (p. 581).

[30] Cf. Whiting, *op. cit.*, pp. 116–117.

[31] Cf. *ibid.*, pp. 157–158.

[32] Cf. the blackout of references to atomic weapons in the Chinese press following President Truman's statement of November 30, 1950, on this possibility (Alice L. Hsieh, *Communist China's Strategy in the Nuclear Era*, Englewood Cliffs, N.J.: Prentice-Hall, 1962, p. 3).

[33] Chow Ching-wen, *Ten Years of Storm: The True Story of the Communist Regime in China*, New York: Holt, Rinehart and Winston, 1960, pp. 116–117. Chow was a "democratic personage" (prominent non-Communist) in the CPR at the time.

being believed, but in the hope of providing the United States with a face-saving pretext, in view of the implicit threat of Soviet involvement, for nonretaliation against the mainland of China.

It is widely believed that Stalin agreed to, urged, or even ordered the Chinese intervention. The available evidence suggests that Stalin at most gave reluctant assent. No influx of Soviet weapons preceded the Chinese intervention, such as had preceded the North Korean attack; the CPR began to receive Soviet weapons after, not before, its intrusion into Korea.[34] Stalin certainly sent "volunteer" pilots to help the North Koreans and Chinese, without admitting it, but it is unlikely that he welcomed the inevitably increased risk of escalation entailed by an overt intervention by Chinese ground combat units. Ratifications of the Sino-Soviet treaty of alliance of February 14, 1950, were not exchanged (in Peking) until September 30, shortly before the Chinese intervention.[35] At no time during the Korean crisis did either the Chinese or the Russians state publicly that the situation might require Soviet action under the terms of the alliance. The Soviet Union did not go beyond hinting (for example, in *Pravda*, on December 3, 1950) that the Chinese forces in Korea might not be "volunteers" and citing foreign speculation about the possibility of a Russo-American war in the Far East, while insisting that the CPR was intervening in Korea on its own initiative.[36] Stalin would probably have tolerated reluctantly, without military counteraction, an American and/or South Korean conquest of North Korea, as he had tolerated the liquidation of the leftist regime in Iranian Azerbaijan in 1946 and Tito's defiance of him beginning in 1948.

If such was in fact Stalin's attitude, it can hardly have been Kim Il-song's. Although even when disaster loomed on the Naktong the North Koreans had shown no overt interest in Chinese intervention,[37] such an interest must certainly have developed as the United Nations forces crossed the 38th parallel and entered North Korea. It was obvious that, just as American sea and air activity had not sufficed to save South Korea in June, so Soviet "volunteer" pilots could not prevent the overrunning of North Korea in October. Powerful ground units were needed, and it was clear that while both the Soviet Union and the CPR might have the ability to provide such units, only the CPR had the will to do so. Urgent need probably more than outweighed in Pyongyang, for a time at least, any fear that the presence of Chinese troops might lead to Chinese political control, as the Soviet occupation of 1945 had led to Soviet control.[38] In fact, Chinese

---

[34] Whiting, *op. cit.*, p. 90.

[35] Chinese International Service broadcast, Peking, October 18, 1950.

[36] Beloff, *op. cit.*, pp. 194–195.

[37] "The determination of the Chinese people for the liberation of Formosa is encouraging the Korean people more than anything else," Radio Pyongyang, August 16, 1950 (Quoted in Whiting, *op. cit.*, p. 81).

[38] Cf. Glenn D. Paige and Dong Jun Lee, "The Post-War Politics of Communist Korea," *The China Quarterly*, No. 14 (April–June, 1963), pp. 18–19.

intervention does seem to have increased Chinese influence in North Korea, especially at the local level.

■ DEFEAT FROM THE JAWS OF VICTORY

Having driven the United Nations forces headlong from North Korea, the CPV crossed the 38th parallel on December 26 (Mao Tse-tung's birthday) and launched its second major offensive on New Year's Day, apparently in order to drive United Nations forces out of Korea.[39] It soon suffered heavy losses, however, at the hands of a revitalized Eighth Army under General Ridgway, which then began to roll the Chinese back to the north of Seoul in the celebrated Operation Killer.

Just before the dimensions of its military failure had become clear, and at a time, therefore, when it may have hoped to end the war on a victorious note, the CPR announced its terms for a settlement. On January 17, 1951, it rejected a United Nations truce proposal; repeated its earlier demands that all foreign troops be withdrawn from Korea, that American military protection of Taiwan cease, and that the CPR assume its "rightful place" in the United Nations; refused a ceasefire until after the acceptance of its terms; and insisted on the prompt convening in China of a Seven-Nation Conference (the CPR, the Soviet Union, the United Kingdom, the United States, France, India, and Egypt) to work out a settlement along the lines indicated by the CPR.[40] The CPR's terms would have removed international discussion of the Korean and Taiwanese questions from the halls of the United Nations (located, after all, in the United States) and would have eliminated the Republic of China from the talks. The choice of participants was also interesting. India had already demonstrated receptiveness to the Communist viewpoint on the Korean crisis and other matters; Egypt, even under King Farouk, seethed with anti-Western feeling. The CPR presumably counted on a majority of four, and perhaps support on some points from Britain, at the conference that it was demanding.

The main effect of these demands, however, was to lead the United States immediately to work for the condemnation of the CPR as an aggressor by the General Assembly. In response to Indian inquiries, the CPR then provided some relatively conciliatory clarifications of its demands of January 17; the CPR would "advise" the CPV to return home as part of the overall withdrawal of foreign troops, and a ceasefire could be arranged at the beginning of the conference.[41] This slight easing of the CPR's stand may have reflected both its deteriorating military position in Korea and a

---

[39] David Rees, *Korea: The Limited War*, New York: St. Martin's Press, 1964, p. 177.

[40] Text in *The New York Times*, January 18, 1951.

[41] *The New York Times*, January 23, 1951.

hope of avoiding condemnation as an aggressor by the United Nations, in which it was seeking representation. In any case, over Communist and some neutral (India and Burma) opposition, and with nine neutral abstentions, the General Assembly voted on February 1 to condemn the CPR as an aggressor and to begin studying the application of sanctions.

Developments in the early months of 1951 were not wholly adverse to the CPR, however. As United Nations forces again approached the 38th parallel, it became increasingly clear that the United States and the United Nations would not try to unify Korea by force once more.[42] This decision, plus the possibility of political agreements adverse to the Republic of China and the Republic of Korea, in turn was too much for General MacArthur, who proceeded to risk and incur his own relief from command. In his letter of March 20 to Congressman Martin and his statement of March 24, which implied that the war would be extended to the China mainland unless the enemy command opened negotiations, he publicly revived proposals that had already been advanced and rejected in the dark days of the previous December: a blockade of the China coast, aerial reconnaissance (and presumably bombardment) of Manchuria and the China coast, and employment of Chinese Nationalist forces against the China coast (and perhaps in Korea).[43] Regardless of the merits of this proposal as a way of dealing with the CPR and the Korean War — and the passage of time has tended to make them seem greater rather than less — the way in which it was put forward jeopardized American foreign policy and the principle of civilian control of the armed forces sufficiently to require General MacArthur's relief, which occurred on April 11.

The dismissal of General MacArthur made it clear that the United States and the United Nations were substantially ready for a stalemate truce on the basis of the nearest defensible line to the north of the 38th parallel. The same idea was apparently acceptable to the Soviet Union, which since August, 1950, had been attempting the difficult feat of limiting and ending the Korean hostilities without entirely dropping its support for the CPR's claims.[44] But, although the proposal for a stalemate truce followed by the withdrawal of foreign troops satisfied the basic security objectives for which the CPR had originally entered the war, it did not deal with the considerations of influence that the CPR had later attached to the security motive — in particular, the withdrawal of American protection from Taiwan and the admission of the CPR to the United Nations. The latter objective had been made still more difficult to attain by the General Assembly's condemnation of Communist China as an aggressor. The CPR, apparently in a rare instance

---

[42] Cf. *The New York Times*, March 14, 1951.

[43] Trumbull Higgins, *Korea and the Fall of MacArthur: A Précis in Limited War*, Oxford University Press, 1960, pp. 91–92, 103–114.

[44] Cf. the publication in full in the Soviet press of Senator Edwin C. Johnson's resolution of May 17, 1951, urging an armistice along the 38th parallel, the exchange of prisoners, and the withdrawal of foreign troops.

of using overt violence out of considerations of influence rather than of security, decided on a third offensive, probably with the idea of trading South Korean territory for the satisfaction of at least some of its political demands. The decision proved to be a monumental miscalculation.

On April 22, and again on May 16, after a rapid buildup, the CPV launched heavy but unsuccessful attacks on United Nations forces north of Seoul. These were thrown back with very heavy losses and serious demoralization to the CPV, and the United Nations forces promptly began a limited advance.[45] The CPV's offensive was not only a military catastrophe but precipitated the passage by the General Assembly on May 18, again over Communist and some neutral objections, of a resolution urging the imposition by United Nations members of an embargo on the shipment of strategic materials to North Korea and the mainland of China.

■ THE ARMISTICE NEGOTIATIONS

Although the spring offensive by the CPV did not significantly harden the position of the United States and the United Nations, its failure softened the CPR's position somewhat.[46] On June 23 Jacob Malik made public in New York a Soviet proposal that had been circulating privately for a month; it called for a stalemate truce in Korea and said nothing about Taiwan or the CPR's entry into the United Nations.[47] A proposal of June 30 by General Ridgway for truce talks was accepted by the North Korean and Chinese commands on July 2. Although both North Korea and the CPR must have objected intensely to the idea of agreeing to an armistice without achieving their political objectives — in the former case, the "liberation" of South Korea — there was no realistic alternative.[48]

It is unnecessary to treat in detail the tedious two years of armistice negotiations that began in July, 1951, the Communists' efforts to gain by political means things that they had been unable to gain by military means,

---

[45] Cf. General Almond's description in *Interlocking Subversion in Government Departments, Hearing . . . of the Committee on the Judiciary, United States Senate*, Part 25, November 23, 1954, pp. 2071–2073; and maps, pp. 2117–2120. It has been reported that Marshal P'eng Te-huai, who was then commanding the CPV, was accused at the time he was purged in 1959 of having ordered this attack on his own initiative (David A. Charles, "The Dismissal of Marshal P'eng Te-huai," *The China Quarterly*, No. 8 [October–December, 1961] p. 72). Even if such a charge was made, it is unlikely to have been valid, although it is apparently true that P'eng served as his own political officer in Korea and hence had a relatively free hand.

[46] Cf. the conciliatory article by Soong Ching-ling, "On Peaceful Coexistence," *People's China*, June 1, 1951.

[47] The CPR's endorsement of the Malik proposal raised its political demands once more but did not appear to make their acceptance a condition of the opening of armistice negotiations (*The New York Times*, June 26, 1951).

[48] One of the indications of strain within the North Korean regime over this question may have been the fall of the powerful Ho Kai, First Secretary of the Korean Workers Party, who was purged and committed suicide in 1951 (Paige and Lee, *loc. cit.*, p. 20), although his death was not announced until after the armistice (*The New York Times*, August 12, 1953).

or the bitter but localized military operations that paralleled the negotiations. Neither side attempted a decisive offensive. The Communist negotiators, among whom the Chinese General Hsieh Fang was the most important, after much wrangling dropped their demand for the immediate withdrawal of all foreign troops from Korea, and then abandoned their original insistence on the 38th parallel as the ceasefire line in favor of a line proposed by the United Nations side that left the latter in control of the more highly defensible high ground to the north of the parallel in the eastern sector of the front.[49] In December, 1951, the Communist side finally agreed to provide a list of the prisoners it was holding. It seemed that an armistice was imminent.

Early in January, 1952, however, the United Nations injected into the negotiations an issue of enormous political importance to the Communist side — the issue of voluntary rather than compulsory repatriation of prisoners of war. The implication of course was that a substantial proportion of the Chinese and North Korean prisoners held by the United Nations would refuse to return home and that the United Nations might acquiesce in their refusal. Tension immediately rose as it appeared that the Communists might decline to sign an armistice agreement, and that the United Nations might retaliate. Churchill and Eden visited Washington in January. In February, there were disorders in Hong Kong, loud charges that the United States had waged "germ warfare" against the CPR and North Korea, and obviously Communist-inspired riots among the prisoners under United Nations control that continued into the spring before being effectively subdued. These were all characteristic methods of applying pressures to the opposition, deterring it by political means from unacceptable military retaliation (in particular, resort to nuclear weapons), and if possible giving the worst appearance to whatever course of action the opposition might take.[50]

Nevertheless, the Communist side did not break off talks on the prisoner question. The American hydrogen bomb tests held during March may have helped to remind the Communists of the military odds facing them. In any case a series of eighteen secret talks on the prisoner question was held at Panmunjom from March 25 to April 4. A compromise was reached under which the Communists modified their insistence on compulsory repatriation by agreeing that not more than 116,000 of 132,000 prisoners who were to be screened need be repatriated. The United Nations side, which was genuinely concerned for the prisoners' wishes and rights but did not want the issue to obstruct the conclusion of an armistice, agreed that it would repatriate all prisoners except those who declared explicitly that they would resist repatriation by force. The screening began on April 5 and was applied to 170,000 rather than 132,000, prisoners. Of the 170,000, approximately 100,000 (including 15,000 Chinese out of the 20,000 taken) refused repatria-

---

[49] Much of the action by United Nations forces after the beginning of the armistice negotiations was aimed at gaining and defending this terrain.

[50] It appears that the Soviet Union was heavily involved in orchestrating the "germ warfare" propaganda campaign (Rees, *op. cit.*, p. 359). This would be logical, in view of the Soviet Union's interest in preventing an enlargement of the Korean War.

tion. When the talks recommenced on April 19, the Communist side quickly rejected this result as wholly unacceptable.[51]

The armistice negotiations were not broken off, but they were at an impasse, and tension rose again. The worst disorders among the prisoners on Koje Island occurred in May. On June 23, the anniversary of Malik's proposal for truce talks, American aircraft bombed the Suiho Dam on the Yalu River in the heaviest raid of the war to date, and similar raids followed. Soviet Ambassador Roshchin left Peking for Moscow on July 1, and it seems safe to assume that there were urgent consultations between the two capitals at this time. The CPR may well have demanded action by the Soviet Union, or at least a strong declaration of support, under the terms of the Sino-Soviet alliance.[52] The CPR may also have asked the Soviet Union for the transfer of nuclear weapons and delivery systems, and it certainly reinforced its troops in Korea heavily, probably as a defensive rather than an offensive measure.

Stalin, however, responded only in subdued tones for the time being to the crisis then confronting the CPR and to the demands that the latter must have been making on him. During the important Sino-Soviet political, military, and economic negotiations that began in Moscow in mid-August, 1952, Stalin agreed to a greatly increased program of conventional military aid to the CPR but evidently refused to turn over nuclear weapons or make threatening declarations in support of the CPR. Under an arrangement announced on September 16, he agreed to prolong the presence of Soviet forces in Port Arthur (in Manchuria) beyond the end of 1952, when they had originally been scheduled to withdraw, and until the Communist bloc concluded a peace treaty with Japan. Presumably the purpose of this move was to continue in being at least a symbolic deterrent to an American attack on Manchuria. The CPR had already (in July) begun to moderate the tone of its press on the subject of war and revolutionary violence. Faced with highly limited Soviet support, it again attempted political deterrence of military action by the opponent through convening an "Asian and Pacific Peace Conference," attended by some 400 leftists from thirty-seven countries in various parts of the world including the United States, in Peking in early October.[53]

■ THE FINAL CRISIS

During October the Panmunjom talks were recessed and the scene shifted to the United Nations. A Polish proposal of October 17 for an

[51] *The New York Times,* April 26, 1952.

[52] It will be recalled that the alliance applied against Japan or any power allied with Japan; the security treaty between the United States and Japan had entered into force on April 28, 1952.

[53] See the materials on this conference in *People's China* for September–November, 1952.

armistice along the line already agreed upon, the repatriation of all prisoners, the withdrawal of all foreign troops, and the ultimate unification of Korea was promptly endorsed by the Soviet delegate (Vyshinsky). When these proposals proved unacceptable to the United States, the Indian government began to look for a way out of the deadlock. According to Prime Minister Nehru's later account (made public on December 15), Indian Ambassador Panikkar presented certain proposals to Deputy Foreign Minister Chang Han-fu in Peking on November 16. Since he raised no objection to them, they were presented to the General Assembly on the following day by Krishna Menon. It is not difficult to see why the Indian proposal was acceptable to the Communist side. It stressed throughout the principle of repatriation, rather than the right not to be repatriated against one's will. Its last paragraph seemed to envisage the indefinite retention of prisoners who refused to go home in the custody of the Repatriation Commission (to be composed of representatives of Czechoslovakia, Poland, Sweden, and Switzerland), rather than their release, until their ultimate fate was decided by a political conference to be convened under the terms of Article 60 of the draft armistice agreement.[54] In deference to American objections, however, the Indian resolution was reintroduced on November 23 with the crucial amendment that within 120 days after the signature of the armistice any prisoners who had not been repatriated should be transferred to the custody of the United Nations, which could obviously be expected to release them.[55] This resolution, which was adopted by the General Assembly on December 1, was anathema to the Communist side, because it would deprive them of any power to affect the disposition of prisoners who refused to be repatriated. Vyshinsky denounced the amended Indian proposal in unmeasured terms, and (again according to Nehru's later account) the CPR notified the Indian government privately on November 24 that the proposal was unacceptable.

Once again the tension rose. President-elect Eisenhower visited Korea early in December and conferred with General MacArthur after his return.[56] A new Soviet ambassador, Panyushkin, one of Stalin's favorite trouble shooters and a former ambassador to the United States, arrived in Peking on December 9. Riots broke out once more among the prisoners on Koje Island on December 14.[57] Liu Shao-ch'i, who had been in Moscow since early October, returned to Peking on January 11, 1953, with no public indication of the results of his mission.[58] On February 2, President Eisen-

---

[54] Text in *The New York Times*, November 18, 1952.

[55] Text in *The New York Times*, December 2, 1952.

[56] For the text of MacArthur's recommendations, unpublished at the time, see *Life*, July 24, 1964, pp. 52B–53.

[57] *The New York Times*, December 17, 1952.

[58] Chronology on the Chinese side may be verified from American Consulate General, Hong Kong, "Chronology of Events in Communist China, January–April 1953," *Current Background*, No. 321 (March 15, 1955).

hower announced the famous "unleashing of Chiang Kai-shek" (i.e., the nominal removal of the prohibition on Nationalist offensive operations across the Taiwan Strait that had been imposed by President Truman on June 27, 1950), in the hope of putting enough pressure on the CPR to make it capitulate on the prisoner issue and agree to an armistice. This move had very little effect, however, because the Nationalist Chinese forces were still in no condition to undertake major operations against the mainland. Mao Tse-tung made a defiant speech on February 7, giving no hint of surrender.[59] At about this time, the United States began to apply pressure of a far more effective kind, in the form of a threat to extend the war to the China mainland and use nuclear weapons. At about the same time, the United States also extended an olive branch in the form of a proposal by General Clark on February 22 that both sides agree to exchange sick and wounded prisoners.[60]

The threat naturally produced dramatic results in Peking. The CPC characteristically began to try a number of forms of political deterrence, including loud affirmation of complete solidarity between itself and the Soviet Union. On February 22 and 23 (the latter being Soviet Army Day), Chou En-lai paid an unusual and loudly publicized visit to the Soviet garrison at Port Arthur in the company of Ambassador Panyushkin. At the same time, the CPR released the texts of "confessions" by some American prisoners that they had been guilty of "germ warfare" in Korea. It also appears that Chinese approaches to the Soviet Union went beyond declarations of solidarity. On February 24, a Chinese scientific delegation headed by Ch'ien San-ch'iang, China's leading nuclear physicist, left for Moscow, probably to seek nuclear weapons.

Obviously, much depended on the Soviet response, if any, to the Chinese pleas for aid, support, and perhaps intervention that must have underlain these overt gestures. It may be objected that if Stalin had not taken the main initiative in starting the Korean War, this fact would have

---

[59] Chow Ching-wen (*op. cit.*, p. 82) describes another, unpublished speech by Mao at about the same time as follows: "He declared vehemently, raising his right hand high in the air, 'Everyone of the Chinese officers and soldiers captured in Korea must be repatriated!' We, the members of the conference and the high-ranking cadres who were also present, were greatly impressed. We thought that Mao was angry and that if this was not done, the Korean War would break out again."

[60] Dwight D. Eisenhower, *Mandate for Change, 1953–1956*, New York: Doubleday, 1963, p. 181. General Eisenhower makes it clear that the nuclear threat was made before General Clark's letter was written on February 22. This is an important point, because there seems to be a widespread and erroneous impression that the threat was first conveyed to the Indian government, and then by it to the CPR, during a visit by Secretary Dulles and Harold Stassen to New Delhi on May 20 (Fletcher Knebel, "We Nearly Went to War Three Times Last Year," *Look*, February 8, 1955, p. 27; James Shepley, "How Dulles Averted War," *Life*, January 16, 1956, p. 71). The Truman administration had earlier considered and rejected the use of atomic weapons in Korea, on the basis of General Vandenberg's opinion that the concealment and dispersal employed by the enemy presented no profitable targets (Jack Anderson, "What Really Happened in Korea," *Parade*, September 22, 1963).

reinforced his usual caution, and he would have done nothing. There are powerful arguments, however, for believing the opposite, even if one does not assume that Stalin's psychological state during the last months of his life was any more abnormal than usual. In the first place, he knew that the United States, although in a belligerent mood toward the CPR, was very apprehensive of overt Soviet involvement in the Korean War; threats might be sufficient, therefore, to bring the United States to withdraw its quasi-ultimatum to the CPR, which in any case had not been publicly announced. Secondly, Stalin understood the depth of feeling in Peking on the prisoner issue, and the seriousness of the political setback that his Chinese ally would suffer if it had to retreat on this issue; he himself had shown an obsessive determination to regain control of Soviet citizens who had left the Soviet Union during the Second World War, and he had had Vyshinsky denounce the revised Indian resolution on the prisoner question in abusive language. Thirdly, Stalin might have agreed with a recent Chinese statement that "We ourselves preferred to shoulder the heavy sacrifices necessary [during the Korean War and the Taiwan Strait crises] so that the Soviet Union might stay in the second line";[61] in spite of the continued strengthening of NATO, the Korean War had drawn primary American attention to the Far East and away from the Soviet Union and from Stalin's rapid buildup of his nuclear and delivery capabilities.[62] Finally, although a flare-up in the Far East would obviously involve risks for the Soviet Union, it might also enable Stalin to act more freely elsewhere.

What actions or threats in support of the CPR may Stalin have been considering early in 1953? There is of course the remote possibility that he favored granting the request for the immediate transfer of nuclear weapons and delivery systems that Ch'ien San-ch'iang's delegation may have brought. More realistically speaking, Stalin also had the ability, of which the United States government was very much afraid at that time, to bomb cities and American bases in Japan.[63] Stalin may also have contemplated rushing the hydrogen bomb into operational readiness and using the threat of its use to deter an American attack on the CPR for refusing to capitulate on the prisoner issue, or to deter American retaliation against the CPR in the less likely event that the latter initiated large-scale hostilities in Korea.[64]

To the obvious and valid question of why Stalin might have been willing to take action of this kind at the end of 1952 when he had shown

---

[61] "Two Different Lines on the Question of War and Peace," *People's Daily* and *Red Flag*, November 19, 1963.

[62] Cf. W. W. Rostow, *The United States in the World Arena*, New York: Harper, 1960, pp. 246–247.

[63] Eisenhower, *op. cit.*, p. 180.

[64] The first announcement of Soviet acquisition and testing of the hydrogen bomb was made in August, 1953, after Stalin's death and after the Korean armistice. The event, or at least the announcement of it, may have been timed so as not to jeopardize the conclusion of the armistice.

no such willingness earlier, there is at least a possible answer. To Stalin's way of thinking, his own interest was now involved more deeply than before, but for reasons having less to do with the Far East than with Eastern Europe.

Yugoslavia had begun to buy arms from Western countries in the spring of 1951 and had signed a military aid agreement with the United States in November of the same year. In July, 1952, the United States had promised to deliver heavy artillery, tanks, and jet aircraft. As if this were not bad enough from Stalin's point of view, it soon began to appear that Yugoslav collaboration with the West was going well beyond the buying of arms. In mid-November, 1952, Tito received a visit from the American General Thomas T. Handy, Deputy Commander-in-Chief of the European Command.[65] *Pravda* announced ominously on December 9, the same day that Ambassador Panyushkin arrived in Peking, that it was common knowledge that Yugoslavia was planning "a military attack on her Socialist neighbors,"[66] and soon afterward it was reported that the Yugoslav government was seeking Western aid and cooperation in the defense of the strategic Ljubljana Gap.[67]

It is impossible to be sure how Stalin viewed his Yugoslav problem at that time, although there can be little doubt that he was seriously concerned. Being a perennially suspicious man, with a demonstrated allergy to situations that seemed to threaten a two-front war,[68] he may have been genuinely afraid that the United States was about to launch hostilities, aimed initially at his allies but ultimately at him, simultaneously in the Balkans and the Far East.

It seems more likely, however, that Stalin intended a preemptive attack against Yugoslavia before it became too strong, and before the incoming Eisenhower administration had time to get a firm grip on affairs. Although a Soviet or satellite attack on Yugoslavia would have created a serious crisis that would have tended to distract Western attention from the Far East, it would not have evoked an automatic military response by the United States or NATO, which had no such formal obligation to Yugoslavia, and it would have enabled Stalin to pay off an old score and to eliminate a possible source of future trouble. An entirely possible variant of this analysis is that Stalin may have regarded the Yugoslav situation, and its potential implications for the security of his dearly won defensive buffer in Eastern Europe, as his most pressing concern, and that he may have viewed the

---

[65] *The New York Times,* November 16, 1952.

[66] *The New York Times,* December 10, 1952; note that this was shortly after the crucial Sino-Soviet decision to reject the revised Indian resolution on the Korean prisoner question.

[67] *The New York Times,* December 17, 1952.

[68] Stalin had made his nonaggression pact with Hitler in August, 1939, when he was involved in a serious although undeclared war with Japan in Outer Mongolia; he had signed a neutrality pact with Japan in April, 1941, when the Germans were invading the Balkans in an obvious preliminary to an attack on the Soviet Union.

simultaneous American preoccupation with the crisis in the Far East as a valuable asset.

If Stalin had in fact taken, or had time to take, action along the lines that have just been suggested, it is obvious that he would have incurred serious risks to Soviet security. There are indications that he understood this. On February 17, 1953, he suddenly summoned the Indian ambassador, K. P. S. Menon, for what was to prove his last conversation with a foreigner. The interview was held in Moscow, where contrary to his usual practice Stalin had spent the entire winter. Stalin said a number of agreeable things about India, one of his main purposes obviously being to counteract the expected effort by Secretary Dulles to woo India away from neutrality and onto the Western side when he visited New Delhi in the spring. Stalin was uncommunicative on Korea, but he accused the United States of wanting war over the Taiwan issue[69] and denied that it could be restrained merely by the political pressures of its allies. In this context, he went on to say that when a peasant is attacked by a wolf, "he does not attempt to teach it morals, but tries to kill it. And the wolf knows this and behaves accordingly."[70] Probably Stalin was trying in this characteristically cryptic way to convey to the United States through Indian channels, which the United States was also using to communicate its threat to the CPR, the idea that the Soviet Union was prepared to use force if necessary on behalf of the CPR.

It is clear that if Stalin was contemplating drastic military action of some sort, the fact must have been known to his colleagues and must have greatly aggravated the already tense atmosphere in Moscow. Since about the time of the Nineteenth Congress in October, 1952, Stalin had almost certainly been preparing a vast purge that was to extend into the ranks of his colleagues (although apparently not to Khrushchev). In view of the tense external situation, however, it is not surprising that there is no evidence that Stalin intended to apply the purge to the armed forces at that time.[71] In fact, Marshal Zhukov, in disgrace since 1946, had been secretly recalled at the end of 1952 to become Deputy Minister of War (under Marshal Vasilevsky) and Commander-in-Chief of the Ground Forces. Stalin did not go so far, however, as to rehabilitate Zhukov publicly, for example by listing him among the intended victims of the "Doctors' Plot."[72] Obviously the recall of Zhukov is consistent with the hypothesis that Stalin was expect-

---

[69] Stalin had probably been startled by the Eisenhower administration's "unleashing of Chiang Kai-shek" into fearing that the United States was about to support a Chinese Nationalist attack on the CPR, as it was allegedly about to support a Yugoslav attack on Eastern Europe.

[70] K.P.S. Menon, *The Flying Troika*, London: Oxford University Press, 1963, pp. 26–29.

[71] Wolfgang Leonhard, *Kreml ohne Stalin*, Cologne: Verlag für Politik und Wirtschaft, 1959, pp. 67–79; Leonard Schapiro, *The Communist Party of the Soviet Union*, New York: Random House, 1959, pp. 543–546; Robert Conquest, *Power and Policy in the U.S.S.R.: The Study of Soviet Dynastics*, New York: St. Martin's Press, 1961, pp. 154–191.

[72] Raymond L. Garthoff, *Soviet Strategy in the Nuclear Age*, New York: Praeger, 1958, p. 20.

ing a military crisis at the time and therefore wanted his best field commander in charge. On the other hand, it is also reasonable to suppose that Zhukov and others of the less politically minded Soviet commanders objected to the idea of another major purge, even if they were not to be among its initial victims, and still more to moves that would involve a serious risk of war with the United States. In that case, it would also be reasonable to suppose that they took preventive action. To be effective, such action would have required the cooperation of some of Stalin's civilian colleagues, and it would also have required the elimination of Stalin himself.

During the days following Stalin's interview with Menon on February 17, events in Moscow moved with dramatic rapidity. On February 21, it was announced that Marshal Sokolovsky, who had not been listed as an intended victim of the "Doctors' Plot" and was therefore evidently not in favor with Stalin and perhaps even in his bad graces, had replaced General Shtemenko, who had been listed as a victim, as Chief of the General Staff.[73] On the next day, the "vigilance" campaign, which had filled the Soviet press for some months and had constituted one of the main indications of an imminent purge, abruptly stopped.[74]

On March 3 (the anniversary of the emancipation of the serfs, in 1861), Stalin's colleagues announced that he had suffered a stroke on the night of March 1–2, and two days later that he had died at 9:50 P.M. on March 5.[75] On March 6, with Beria's MVD troops in occupation of Moscow, Stalin's successors effected a major reorganization of the party and governmental leadership, in the course of which Zhukov was announced for the first time as Deputy Minister of War (under Bulganin). In view of the external crisis then confronting the Soviet Union, it is not surprising that the new leadership showed some signs of the "disorder and panic" against which it warned the Soviet people when publicizing the reorganization.[76]

It is highly probable that Stalin's death did not occur at the time, or under the circumstances, given in the official announcement. The well-informed and pro-CPC American leftist, Anna Louise Strong, has stated flatly, but without elaboration, that Stalin died in "late February, 1953."[77]

---

[73] Conquest, op. cit., p. 168. The actual replacement may have occurred somewhat earlier. It is interesting and probably significant that whereas Sokolovsky remained in favor with Stalin's successors, Shtemenko fell fairly rapidly if temporarily into obscurity (ibid., pp. 70, 330, 336).

[74] Leonhard, op. cit., p. 81. This was the eve of Soviet Army Day.

[75] Text in Current Soviet Policies: The Documentary Record of the 19th Communist Party Congress and the Reorganization After Stalin's Death, New York: Praeger, 1953, pp. 246–247. March 5 was the thirtieth anniversary of a letter in which Lenin threatened to break relations with Stalin because of the latter's rudeness to his (Lenin's) wife (see Khrushchev's Secret Speech).

[76] Current Soviet Policies . . ., op. cit., pp. 247–248.

[77] Anna Louise Strong, The Stalin Era, Altadena, California: Today's Press, 1956, p. 116. This book is intended as a refutation along Chinese Communist lines of Khrushchev's Secret Speech. The writer would guess that Stalin died on February 25, the date on which Khrushchev delivered the Secret Speech (in 1956). Leonhard (op. cit., p. 58) is prepared to believe that Stalin died earlier than the alleged date.

If so, the delay in announcing his death was presumably designed to give his successors time to reorganize themselves and take steps to ensure their own security. As for the circumstances of Stalin's death, the original bulletin on his alleged stroke listed loss of consciousness before loss of speech; this would be a medically impossible order, and in any case it would normally be unnecessary to specify loss of speech since it is obvious that an unconscious person cannot speak. It is a reasonable inference that the reference to loss of speech, and perhaps the entire medical bulletin, was concocted by a nonmedical hand with the purpose among others of re-assuring its readers, or those of them who needed reassurance, that Stalin had completely lost touch with his surroundings and was unlikely to re-cover.[78]

To recapitulate: There is at least a strong possibility that never since 1945 (except perhaps in October, 1962) has the world stood as close to general war as it did in February, 1953; that much of this danger stemmed from an apparent willingness on Stalin's part to take drastic action, partly on behalf of the CPR and in connection with the Korean War; and that Stalin was therefore killed on the initiative of elements in the Soviet military high command and civilian leadership.[79]

In view of the new Soviet leadership's obvious concern over the state of its relations with the CPR, it probably felt some disappointment at the fact that the Chinese delegation to Stalin's funeral was led, not by Mao Tse-tung or Liu Shao-ch'i, but by Premier Chou En-lai. This choice tended to emphasize the aloof and superior position that Mao and Liu considered themselves as occupying vis-a-vis the new Soviet leadership and to give the negotiations that followed the funeral a governmental rather than an ideological or party character. Only one member of the delegation, Wu Hsiu-ch'uan, could be considered a specialist in party affairs, and it will be recalled that it had been he who had presented the CPR's case on the Korean and Taiwanese issues before the United Nations Security Council in Novem-ber, 1950. The other "mourners" included the nuclear physicist Ch'ien San-ch'iang (already in the Soviet Union); the then Minister of Public Security, Lo Jui-Ch'ing, whose Soviet opposite number Beria had charge of the Soviet nuclear weapons program; General Chang Tsung-hsun (now Deputy Chief of the "People's Liberation Army" General Staff); General Wang Ping-chang (now Deputy Commander of the Air Force); and Admiral Lo Shun-chu (now Deputy Commander of the Navy).[80] Regard-less of its composition the delegation, and Chou En-lai in particular, was given red carpet treatment; at Stalin's funeral (on March 9) he walked in the front rank of the "mourners."

[78] *Ibid.*, p. 57.
[79] Most Sovietologists seem to be willing to admit at least the possibility that Stalin met a violent end (e.g., Conquest, *op. cit.*, pp. 172, 174).
[80] New China News Agency dispatch, March 7, 1953.

On the following day, there began to appear a number of indications that the new Soviet leadership was trying both to placate the CPC, without conceding its most important demands, and to give face to Malenkov, who to all outward appearances was then "more equal" than the other members of the "collective leadership," by implying Chinese approval of his ascendancy. On March 10, *Pravda* and *Izvestia* announced that Panyushkin was being replaced as ambassador to the CPR by V. V. Kuznetsov.[81] The same issue of *Pravda* carried on page 3 the text of Mao Tse-tung's glowing tribute to Stalin, entitled "The Greatest Friendship," and immediately above it a now celebrated cropped photograph of the signing of the Sino-Soviet treaty of February 14, 1950; four men appearing in the original photograph in front of or between Mao and Malenkov had been obliterated, and Malenkov and Mao had been brought side by side, with Stalin standing (as in the original) immediately on the other side of Mao.[82] This may well have been too much both for some of Malenkov's colleagues and for the CPC. In any case, on the next day *Pravda* stopped mentioning Malenkov's name alone and began to bracket it with those of Beria and Molotov, in that order.[83] On March 14, at a plenary session of the Soviets Party's Central Committee, Malenkov was "released," allegedly but improbably at his own request, from the powerful Secretariat; he remained, however, at the head of the government, in his capacity as premier (officially, Chairman of the Council of Ministers).[84]

Regardless of the exact locus of power within the new Soviet leadership, one of the most pressing things that it had to do was to negotiate with the Chinese mission on the Korean War, which whatever Stalin may have thought was of far greater urgency than the Yugoslav situation. From a knowledge of the nature of the crisis and the composition of the Chinese delegation, a reasonable reconstruction of the negotiations can be made. The Chinese, faced with a clear and present danger and probably convinced that Stalin had been contemplating at least diversionary action on their behalf, almost certainly demanded as much from his successors. They very likely had in mind overt Soviet threats, based on the alliance of 1950, to retaliate against the United States if the latter extended the war to the Chinese mainland and used nuclear weapons. In addition, the Chinese probably pressed for the immediate transfer of operational nuclear weapons and delivery systems, with the necessary instruction in their use, as well as long-term aid in the creation of a Chinese nuclear weapons program. On

---

[81] *Current Soviet Policies* . . ., *op. cit.*, p. 248. Panyushkin returned to the Soviet Union, declined thereafter in his party standing, and never again held a high diplomatic appointment.

[82] *Ibid.*, p. 252. It is worth noting that a photograph (albeit cropped) of a governmental occasion was being published in a party newspaper, and hence presumably in an effort to give face to Malenkov in his party capacity, that of senior member of the Secretariat.

[83] Leonhard, *op. cit.*, p. 97.

[84] Text of announcement in *Current Soviet Policies*. . ., *op. cit., p.* 258.

March 12, a *People's Daily* editorial entitled "Resolutely Oppose the Illegal United Nations Resolution on the Korean Question" again denounced the revised Indian resolution as illegal and urged the United Nations to "take effective measure to curb the schemes of the American aggressors to continue and extend the war," barring which "the Chinese people are resolved to fight alongside the Korean people until American imperialism is ready to quit, until complete victory is won by the Chinese and Korean peoples."

Brave words, but the sequel was much less impressive. The shaky and nervous Soviet leadership made no overt moves and uttered no threats. It did not turn over nuclear weapons, nor did it make any commitment to help the CPR develop its own nuclear weapons program, except perhaps for an agreement to train some Chinese nuclear scientists. In effect, the CPR was left to sink or swim on its own, and it had no choice but to capitulate. Characteristically, it did its best to disguise and minimize this unpleasant fact.

■ THE ARMISTICE AND ITS AFTERMATH

Chou En-lai and most members of his delegation returned to Peking on March 26. Two days later, the Chinese and North Korean military commands in Korea announced acceptance in principle of General Clark's proposal of February 22, made before Stalin's death but ignored up to this time, for an exchange of sick and wounded prisoners.[85] On March 30, Chou En-lai issued an important statement on the Korean negotiations whose most striking feature was perhaps its conciliatory tone. While explicitly not abandoning the principle of the CPR's demand that all prisoners be turned over to a "neutral state" rather than to the United Nations, and making no reference either to the original or the revised Indian proposal, Chou nevertheless insisted on the need for an armistice and for "mutual compromise" (a term rare in Communist pronouncements).[86] At the very least, Chou's statement offered, and was obviously intended to offer, a basis for resuming negotiations at Panmunjom. More realistically speaking, it constituted a veiled, but thinly veiled, Chinese intimation of willingness to surrender, in the face of American threats and Soviet nonsupport, on the crucial question of the nonreturning prisoners.

On this basis, negotiations promptly resumed, and an agreement was reached with little difficulty on the exchange of sick and wounded prisoners ("Little Switch") on April 11. The exchange of the other prisoners ("Big Switch") still presented a much more difficult problem, however, since the current Communist position, as stated by Chou En-lai and others, bore a fairly close resemblance to the original Indian resolution, which had

[85] Text in *The New York Times*, March 29, 1953.
[86] Text in *Documents on International Affairs, 1953*, pp. 359–362.

been unacceptable to the United States. The formal Communist proposal demanded that while in neutral custody the unwilling prisoners should listen to explanations by representatives of the CPR or North Korea designed "to eliminate their apprehensions and to inform them of all matters related to their return to their homeland, particularly of their full right to return home to lead a peaceful life" (i.e., without reprisals). Prisoners who changed their minds and accepted these explanations were to be repatriated promptly. The disposition of any prisoners who still refused to go home would then be referred to the political conference visualized in the draft armistice agreement.[87] These terms were unacceptable on a number of grounds to the United Nations Command, which had to cope with obstruction not only from the Communist side, which (except perhaps for the North Koreans) basically wanted an armistice, but also from the South Korean government, which did not. A set of counterproposals by each side was rejected by the other early in May. After an interlude during which it seems possible that Secretary Dulles conveyed renewed threats against the CPR through the Indian government[88] and that the British government pressed the United States to moderate its position, agreement began to materialize. The United Nations Command defied President Rhee by dropping its insistence on the release of all nonreturning Korean prisoners immediately after the signing of the armistice, and the Communist side agreed that nonreturning prisoners need not be removed from South Korea while in neutral custody. On this basis an exchange agreement was signed on June 8.

Ten days later the South Korean government, which made no secret of its passionate opposition to the terms of the draft armistice agreement, released some 25,000 nonreturning North Korean prisoners in an obvious effort to prevent the signing of the agreement.

The United States government, greatly embarrassed by this action, responded by applying strong diplomatic pressure to President Rhee, who issued a conciliatory statement on July 11 but failed to promise categorically to abide by the armistice agreement. The Communist response was strong but highly selective. After receiving assurances that the United Nations Command had not connived at the prisoners' release, and after seeing that President Rhee was not yielding fully to American pressures, the Communist side evidently decided to teach Rhee a lesson and prevent him from disrupting the armistice arrangement further. On the night of July 13–14, in its last offensive of the war, the CPV heavily attacked the Capital Division, the pride of the South Korean army, while avoiding combat with the nearby United States Third Division. With President Rhee still sputtering, but in a position of demonstrated weakness, the armistice agreement was then signed on July 27. At that time the sixteen members of the United Nations with forces in Korea issued a declaration to the effect that if the

---

[87] Text in *The New York Times*, April 27, 1953.
[88] Cf. Knebel, *loc. cit.*, p. 27; Shepley, *loc. cit.*, p. 71; Rees, *op. cit.*, pp. 419–420.

Communist side again attacked South Korea, in violation of the armistice, "in all probability, it would not be possible to confine hostilities within the frontiers of Korea." The declaration added, hopefully but overoptimistically, that "the armistice must not result in jeopardizing the restoration or the safeguarding of peace in any other part of Asia."[89] Another move designed to minimize the chances of a repetition of Communist aggression against South Korea was the initialing by Secretary Dulles and President Rhee, on August 8, of a mutual defense treaty.[90] At the same time the North Korean regime, which received no comparable overt commitment from its allies, demonstrated its frustration at the inconclusive ending of the war by announcing a major purge, aimed mainly at party leaders who might be suspected of having predicted in 1950 that an invasion of South Korea would lead to pro-Communist popular risings and victory.

Of the numerous repercussions of the Korean armistice, only those few that concern the CPR need be mentioned.[91]

On January 23, 1954, the United Nations Command released those of its prisoners who, after listening to the required explanations by the Communist side, still refused repatriation. These included some 14,000 Chinese (out of a total of about 20,000), who were then sent to Taiwan. We have already seen the lengths to which the CPR had been willing to go to prevent such an outcome. There can be little doubt that the refusal of 70 per cent of the Chinese prisoners taken in Korea to be repatriated was the most serious political setback in the eyes of the world suffered by the CPC down to the spring of 1957, when Mao Tse-tung's ill-considered invitation to the Chinese public to "bloom and contend" resulted in another impressive demonstration of popular dissatisfaction. At the Geneva Conference on Korea that met concurrently with the one on Indochina in the spring of 1954, but without making significant progress toward the reunification of Korea or the withdrawal of foreign troops, Chou En-lai once more revealed the CPC's sensitivity on the prisoner issue by accusing the United States and South Korea of having coerced the prisoners into refusing repatriation. Neither he nor the other Communist delegates made any threat to reopen hostilities in Korea, however.

Early in 1954, relying probably on the threat of "massive retaliation" to deter further Communist aggression, the United States withdrew two of its eight divisions from Korea. In August, in spite of strong objections from

[89] Eisenhower, *op. cit.*, pp. 181–191; *Survey of International Affairs, 1953*, pp. 192–213.

[90] This treaty was approved by the United States Senate in January, 1954, with the explicit understanding, appended to no other such treaty, that it was purely defensive in purpose. The aim of this understanding was to avoid committing the United States to support President Rhee's projected "march to the north."

[91] Except where otherwise indicated, the following interpretation of events since the armistice is based on the chronological account in the appropriate volumes of the *Survey of International Affairs*.

South Korea, it was announced that four more would be withdrawn by mid-1955. Whether because it saw in this a genuine reduction in the potential threat to the security of itself and North Korea, or because it felt itself under political pressure to reciprocate, or both (as seems probable), the CPR announced on September 5, that seven divisions of the CPV would soon be withdrawn from Korea. By October, 1955, a total of nineteen Chinese divisions were said to have been withdrawn.[92] Although the alleged Chinese withdrawals were not properly inspected by the Neutral Nations Supervisory Commission, it is very likely that a substantial reduction in Chinese troop strength in Korea actually took place.

In any case, the maintenance of a large Chinese force in Korea became increasingly unnecessary as military equipment from the Soviet Union and the CPR flowed into North Korea, in violation of the armistice agreement, to rebuild and expand the North Korean army. This process, which was a matter of common knowledge, enraged among others the Swedish and Swiss governments, whose representatives on the Neutral Nations Supervisory Commission in Korea were unable to prevent or even observe it. With a pretense of redressing the Swedish and Swiss grievances by eliminating the need for the Commission's existence, the CPR proposed on April 9, 1956, another conference to discuss the withdrawal of foreign troops and the "peaceful unification" of Korea. The proposal was rejected, and the United Nations Command suspended the operations of the Commission in South Korea "during the time that your side continues in default" in its observance of the armistice agreement.[93]

The Communist side naturally continued in default. Accordingly, on June 21, 1957, simultaneously with the making of a commitment by President Eisenhower to Premier Kishi to begin withdrawing American ground forces from Japan, the United Nations Command announced that, in view of Communist violations of the armistice agreement, it would no longer consider itself bound by the prohibition in the agreement on the introduction of more modern weapons into Korea. The Communist side not unreasonably interpreted this as a threat to introduce nuclear weapons and protested accordingly, although it had apparently been expecting such a step.[94] North Korea promptly repeated the Communist demand for a political conference to achieve withdrawal of foreign troops and unification.[95]

After beginning with the introduction of up-to-date conventional weapons, the United Nations Command announced in late January, 1958, that it had brought in heavy artillery capable of firing atomic shells but refused to say whether the shells had been introduced as well.[96] The effect

---

[92] "The Eight Years of the Chinese People's Volunteers in Korea," *loc. cit.*
[93] Text of both statements in *The New York Times*, June 1, 1956.
[94] Texts in *The New York Times*, June 22, 1957.
[95] *The New York Times*, June 23, 1957.
[96] *The New York Times*, January 29, 1958.

of this announcement on the Communist side was dramatic. On February 5, North Korea repeated the demand for withdrawal of foreign troops and reunification. Two days later, on the eve of North Korean Army Day, the CPR took an initiative that evidently went beyond what North Korea had in mind and was probably distasteful to it;[97] the Chinese proposal stated that the CPR was "prepared to discuss" with North Korea the withdrawal of the CPV and implied that a withdrawal of American forces from South Korea was not a necessary precondition for such a step. At the same time, it was announced that a Chinese delegation headed by Chou En-lai would visit North Korea in mid-February.[98] During his visit Chou paid lip service to the North Korean demand for an American withdrawal. It was far more significant, however, that the joint statement included an announcement to the effect that "the Chinese Government . . . , after consultations with the Korean Government, has further proposed to the Chinese People's Volunteers that they take the initiative in withdrawing from Korea." The withdrawal was to be completed before the end of 1958.[99] In point of fact, it was completed by October 25, the eighth anniversary of the formation of the CPV.[100] It is apparently true that most of the units thus withdrawn merely crossed the frontier into Manchuria, from which they could presumably return if needed. What is more important, however, is that by their withdrawal from Korea they ceased to offer a potential target or trigger for the tactical nuclear weapons that the United States had recently introduced into South Korea.

The CPR naturally continued to give overt political support to its North Korean ally. On September 9, 1958, Chou En-lai issued a threatening statement: "We sternly warn the Syngman Rhee clique: Withdrawal of the Chinese People's volunteers from Korea on their own initiative does not mean that the Chinese people [a vague word implying no governmental obligations] have forsaken their internationalist duty to the Korean people."[101] On December 8, 1958, during a visit to the CPR by North Korean Premier Kim Il-song, the CPR and North Korea jointly issued another demand for the withdrawal of foreign troops and unification of Korea.[102] It was obvious, however, that neither the CPR nor, for that matter, the Soviet Union was prepared at that time to resort to anything

---

[97] A North Korean comment on the CPR's statement said that "the question of withdrawal of foreign troops from Korea is fully dependent upon the withdrawal of the forces of the United States and its followers" ("Manifestation of Consistent Efforts of the Chinese Government for Korea's Peaceful Unification," *Nodong Sinmun*, February 8, 1958).

[98] New China News Agency dispatch, February 7, 1958. The Chinese proposal was reiterated shortly afterward in Chou's speech to the National People's Congress (New China News Agency dispatch, February 10, 1958).

[99] New China News Agency dispatch, February 19, 1958.

[100] "The Eight Years of the Chinese People's Volunteers in Korea," *loc. cit.*

[101] *The New York Times*, September 10, 1958.

[102] *The New York Times*, December 9, 1958.

more than political ploys to achieve those objectives. President Rhee's was evidently not the only regime in Korea that felt entitled to consider itself let down by its allies.

It seems reasonable to end our analysis of the Korean crisis at this point. Many important and instructive lessons can be learned from a careful study of the crisis. From the standpoint of Communist Chinese foreign policy, probably the most important is the conclusion that the CPR treats threats to its security with the greatest alertness and caution. This caution is not always of a passive kind, however. When the CPR thinks it sees a serious but local threat to a vital interest, for example to the safety of its border, it may respond with retaliatory or even preemptive violence on a scale commensurate with the threat. If, however, the threat is a generalized one involving serious danger to the survival of the CPR as a national entity under Communist control, and if the CPR sees no other way of avoiding disaster, it is prepared to compromise on any issue but that of survival itself. Although as much could be said of many other regimes, it must also be pointed out that, short of the brink of disaster, the CPR is more energetic than most in trying to enhance its influence in ways that bear little relation to its security and may even endanger it.

□ 9

The Indochina Crisis I

Chronologically speaking, the war in Indochina was the second major external crisis in which the CPR was involved. The situation in Indochina differed in several ways from that in Korea, and the Chinese response to the two crises differed correspondingly.

■ **KOREA AND INDOCHINA**

Korea and Indochina are both of great strategic importance. Korea lies approximately in the center of the rough triangle formed by Japan, the Soviet Far East, and Manchuria-North China. It served as Japan's main base on the Asian continent prior to the seizure of Manchuria in the 1930's, and had its southern half been allowed to pass under North Korean control in 1950 Japan's security would have been seriously affected. Indochina served France not only as a source of raw materials but as a point of departure for commercial penetration of Southwest China. Conversely, for a strong power based in South China and seeking to extend its influence into Southeast Asia, Indochina offers an excellent springboard. It was Japan's occupation of southern Indochina that led to the American freezing of Japanese assets on July 26, 1941, which in turn proved to be the point of no return on the "road to Pearl Harbor."[1]

---

[1] Japan was seeking to monopolize the rubber, tin, and rice of Indochina, to the exclusion of the Western powers. In addition, the Japanese military had in mind, even before the freezing of Japanese assets by the United States, using Indochina as a springboard for an attack on Malaya and Indonesia (Herbert Feis, *The Road to Pearl Harbor*, Princeton University Press, 1950, p. 234, nn. 16–17). This fact made the Japanese occupation of southern Indochina a much more serious matter to the Western powers than the Japanese occupation of northern Indochina in September, 1940, had been; the latter move had been aimed at China, not Southeast Asia. "It was realized that her [i.e., Japan's] occupation of southern Indo-China would virtually complete the encirclement of the

As for the differences between Korea and Indochina, the terrain is relatively favorable to conventional warfare in the former, and to unconventional warfare in the latter. Hence Korea offered a far more favorable theater for the employment of conventionally oriented Western armies, regardless of nationality, and one in which they could usually bring their superior firepower to bear against their Communist adversaries with devastating effect. Korea also had the important characteristic of being close to the American logistical facilities in Japan. The mountains and jungle that cover the greater part of Indochina, on the other hand, are ideally suited to guerrilla warfare.

Political realities also contributed heavily to making Communist prospects for the conquest of Indochina, or at least of Vietnam, vastly more favorable than those for the forcible unification of Korea.

South Korea was an independent country, sponsored by the United Nations. It had a vigorous if difficult leader (Syngman Rhee) and succeeded in developing a strong national army with the aid and support of the United States, which was anxious to reduce its own involvement in the Korean situation as soon as possible. North Korea's ultimate dependence on the Soviet Union was well known, its act of aggression was blatant, and it was never able to generate significant political support among the South Koreans.

In Vietnam, on the other hand, the French were obviously anxious to delay rather than accelerate their own departure from the scene. Not until 1949, after three years of war, did the French seriously begin the creation of an autonomous Vietnamese state and a Vietnamese national army.[2] Not until mid-1954 did a vigorous if difficult non-Communist leader, Ngo Dinh Diem, emerge in Vietnam. The effect of all this was to confer enormous political and military advantages on the Vietnamese Communists, as compared with both their non-Communist enemies and rivals, French and Vietnamese, and their North Korean colleagues. The Vietnamese Communists' external ties were not particularly obvious; they quickly assumed the role of the leading champion of Vietnamese nationalism; and to match their

---

Philippines and place Japanese armed forces within striking distance of areas and trade routes vital to Britain and America. The occupation would be an act directly menacing to both Powers, and would create a situation in which it would no longer be a question of Britain and America merely avoiding the risk of war, but of their preventing the complete undermining of their security" (Maj.-Gen. S. Woodburn Kirby, *The War Against Japan*, vol. i, *The Loss of Singapore*, London: Her Majesty's Stationery Office, 1957, pp. 68–70). In the light of contemporary events in Vietnam, it is interesting that on July 2, 1941, President Roosevelt proposed the neutralization of Indochina, as well as a guarantee of continued Japanese access to its resources (*ibid.*, p. 70; Feis, *op. cit.*, p. 238). There is an obvious and important difference between the situations then and now: at that time neutralization, in the sense of the withdrawal of foreign troops, might have tended to restore tranquility; at the present time it would not, since the main threat is an indigenous one.

[2] Donald Lancaster, *The Emancipation of French Indochina*, Oxford University Press, 1961, pp. 200ff.

growing military strength they threw up an exceedingly able and prestigious leader, Ho Chi Minh.

This is not to say that the Vietnamese Communists came to power entirely on their own. On the contrary, the CPR made a valuable and perhaps indispensable, but largely covert and indirect, contribution.

A number of considerations argued in favor of an active Chinese role in the Indochina war, apart from the obvious one of territorial contiguity. The CPR clearly has aspirations for a sphere of influence in Southeast Asia, as well as a particular interest in the railway connecting Yunnan, via the mineral-rich region along the Sino-Vietnamese border, with the Hanoi-Haiphong area. The CPC has had historic contacts with the Vietnamese, as well as with the Korean, Communist movement. The CPR gave some military aid to both in connection with their unsuccessful offensives of 1950. The CPR presumably wished the military success of the Vietnamese Communist movement and was certainly not affected at that time by any particular desire for good relations with France, such as has always tended to restrain Soviet policy toward Indochina.[3]

On the other hand, there were powerful arguments against an over-active Chinese role, as is indicated by the fact that, whereas the CPR intervened in the Korean War with its own forces at the end of 1950, following the failure of the North Korea offensive, nothing comparable happened in Indochina. Obviously, the situations in Korea and Indochina differed significantly. There was no serious threat by the French to the Chinese frontier or to Chinese territory, nor did the portion of China bordering on Indochina contain a substantial industrial network. In fact, the poor state of communications in the area even allowing for the Yunnan railway, which was out of commission, was a serious obstacle to any large-scale movements of military equipment, whereas the rail systems of Manchuria and North Korea are relatively well developed. In spite of its defeats in 1950–1951, the DRV and its army were never in serious danger of destruction and never lost the ability to wage at least guerrilla war on a formidable scale. In fact, they soon began to win victories of such proportions that overt Chinese intervention became increasingly unnecessary. That being the case, there was no particular reason why either the CPR or the DRV, which certainly had no desire to become a Chinese satellite, should have favored such intervention. American combat units were not involved, and it was therefore neither necessary for the CPR to repel or deter them nor possible for the CPR to use military pressure in Indochina as a means of promoting its influence objectives with respect to Taiwan and the United Nations, as it attempted to do in Korea. Finally, the very fact of the CPR's large-scale involvement in Korea after the fall of 1950 minimized the chances of its contemplating a comparable involvement in Indochina. It was one thing to

---

[3] It is worth noting that Chinese Nationalist troops occupied Vietnam, down to about the 16th parallel, from September, 1945, to the spring of 1946.

try to divide American attention among three theaters by means of operations conducted by three separate Communist regimes; it would have been quite another for one of those regimes to undertake such operations in more than one of those theaters at the same time. To do this would have been to divide the attention of the Communist regime in question at least as much as that of the United States, and to increase to a dangerous level the chances of American retaliation against the offending regime.

All this was true in general, and it argued on balance against an overt and massive Chinese intervention in the Indochina crisis such as occurred in the Korean War. These general considerations, however, were subject to modification by the exigencies of time and circumstance.

■ THE CHINESE ROLE IN THE INDOCHINA WAR

Even before coming to power in 1949, the CPC expressed its sympathy for the DRV as a brother Communist movement also waging war against "imperialist" intervention and domestic "reaction."[4] In November, 1949, shortly before Chinese Communist troops reached the Vietnamese frontier, Liu Shao-ch'i made a celebrated speech at a World Federation of Trade Unions conference in Peking, in which he stated that "The war of national liberation in Vietnam has liberated 90 per cent of her territory. . . ."[5] It may well have been at this conference that the preliminary plans for the roughly coordinated offensives against South Korea, Taiwan, and the Hanoi area, hypothesized in the previous chapter, were made. The same is probably true of plans for Chinese aid to the DRV. While the conference was still in progress, Mao Tse-tung and Ho Chi Minh exchanged telegrams; Mao's included the statement that "China and Vietnam are meeting on the front line of an [anti-] imperialist struggle. With the victorious development of our struggles for liberation of the two peoples, the friendship between our two peoples will surely become closer day by day. . . ."[6]

The approach of Chinese Communist forces to the Vietnamese frontier at the end of 1949 revolutionized and internationalized the struggle in Vietnam. The French began to take serious steps toward the formation of independent governments in Vietnam, Laos, and Cambodia, and of a Vietnamese national army. The war assumed the appearance of a struggle against

---

[4] There is a favorable reference to the DRV and Ho Chi Minh in the CPC's message of greeting to the important Calcutta Youth Conference ("Congratulations on the Opening of the Southeast Asia Youth Conference," New China News Agency dispatch, North Shensi, February 16, 1948).

[5] New China News Agency dispatch, November 23, 1949.

[6] Quoted in Milton Sacks, "The Strategy of Communism in Southeast Asia," *Pacific Affairs*, vol. 23, no. 3 (September, 1950), p. 240. Although the term "peoples" does not strictly imply obligations or action at the governmental level, it does not exclude them. Context provides the clue, and the context here suggests that plans for covert Chinese aid to the DRV were being formulated at about this time.

international Communism, instead of merely one against local leftist guerrillas. The United States, which had shown little interest in the area since
the Second World War, initiated military aid to the French effort in
Indochina. The DRV, for its part, showed a new confidence in victory,
especially after the conference in Peking just mentioned,[7] and took steps to
establish control over certain dissident Laotian and Cambodian leftists who
had hitherto been making their headquarters in Thailand.[8] Ho Chi Minh,
who had been speaking until recently of keeping the DRV within the French
Union, ceased to do so. Presumably the approach of Chinese power and
the prospect of Chinese military and economic aid both enabled and compelled him to repudiate all ties with France.

Chinese intentions toward Indochina at this time certainly included
the sending of aid to the DRV, but apparently not the commitment of
combat forces in support of the DRV except in the unlikely event that they
should be required to prevent its annihilation. As with respect to some other
Southeast Asian countries, however, the CPR was extremely sensitive to two
issues in Vietnam: the actual or alleged mistreatment of overseas Chinese
and the possibly entry of Chinese Nationalist troops fleeing from the
"People's Liberation Army," but also capable presumably of reentering
Chinese territory at some later time. On November 29, 1949, Premier Chou
En-lai warned all neighboring countries not to harbor Nationalist troops
and other refugees; on January 18, 1950, he protested against alleged French
violence to overseas Chinese. In neither case did he explicitly threaten
military intervention.[9]

Even in the absence of overt threats, the possibility of Chinese intervention was bound to have an effect on the French and the DRV. Both
may have remembered that the flight of the Russian White General Ungern
Sternberg into Outer Mongolia in 1921 had eliminated Chinese influence in
the area and had also led to an invasion by the Red Army that transformed
Outer Mongolia into a Soviet satellite. They unquestionably remembered
the Chinese Nationalist occupation of northern Vietnam in 1945–46. The
French promptly interned the 30,000 or more Chinese Nationalist troops
who crossed into Vietnam in December, 1949, and the early months of
1950.[10] The DRV, which apparently was no more anxious than the CPR
for Chinese Communists to enter Vietnam and fight the French unless abso-

---

[7] *Ibid.*, pp. 238–239.

[8] Thailand had annexed some Laotian and Cambodian territory during the Second
World War but was forced to retrocede it in 1946. This probably helps to explain why
Thai Premier Pridi, who was leftist in any case and allowed the DRV to maintain an
agency in Bangkok and established diplomatic relations with the Soviet Union, also
granted asylum to the Lao Issara and Khmer Issarak leaders in 1946. The leftist elements among them tended to gravitate to North Vietnam after 1949 (cf. Lancaster, *op.
cit.*, pp. 134–135, 198–199).

[9] *A Chronicle of Principal Events Relating to the Indo-China Question, 1940–1954,*
Peking: World Culture, 1954, pp. 27, 29.

[10] Sacks, *loc. cit.*, p. 240; Lancaster, *op, cit.*, pp. 202–203.

lutely necessary, seems to have wanted the French to intern the Nationalist troops so as not to give the CPR a pretext for an invasion whose consequences were unpredictable and probably uncontrollable.[11] The DRV also took pains to proclaim that, whatever the lot of overseas Chinese in the French-occupied areas might be, they were being well treated in the territory under the control of the DRV.[12]

According to a seemingly credible report from French sources, an agreement for Chinese military aid to the DRV was signed in April, 1950. It was in this month that the "People's Liberation Army" captured Hainan, a large and strategically located Chinese island 200 miles southeast of Hanoi. At about the same time, the DRV transferred its main bases to the mountainous areas near the Chinese frontier. Soon afterward some 20,000 Vietnamese began to cross the frontier to receive arms and training, and weapons and supplies began to reach the DRV by junk, from Hainan.[13]

In August the French published a captured document, allegedly dating from early June and indicating a Sino-Vietnamese agreement that, in case of a major French offensive in the border areas, Chinese troops, disguised either as volunteers or as Vietnamese, would enter Vietnam in support of the VPA but withdraw after the end of hostilities.[14] The effect of such a document, assuming the French believed it to be authentic, on French thinking about operations in the border areas can easily be imagined. The only consolation was that the prospect of loss of control over the border and large-scale Chinese military aid to the DRV lent great cogency to French appeals for American military aid. During the successful Vietnamese campaign for control of the border in October, and the ultimately disastrous offensive against the Hanoi area that began at the end of December, the CPR repeatedly accused the French of violating Chinese territory and airspace.[15] These charges closely paralleled the allegations of American violations of Manchurian airspace that the CPR made at about the same time. Presumably the purpose was the same: to demonstrate the CPR's sensitivity to the movements near its frontiers of armies considered to be hostile and its readiness to defend those frontiers if necessary.

Following its defeats in early 1951, the VPA retreated into the mountains to lick its wounds. Chinese aid continued, covertly as before so as not to create unpleasant complications, and it would not be surprising if Chinese advice found a readier market. It is generally believed that it was

---

[11] Cf. the DRV statements in Sacks, *loc. cit.*, p. 241, which were probably designed to startle the French into coping promptly with the Nationalist troops.

[12] *Ibid.*, pp. 241–242.

[13] Edward L. Katzenbach, Jr., "Indo-China: a Military-Political Appreciation," *World Politics*, vol. 4, no. 2 (January, 1952), p. 206. The Japanese captured Hainan in 1939 and used it as a means of applying pressure to northern Indochina and as a training ground and base for the conquest of the rest of Southeast Asia.

[14] *Survey of International Affairs, 1949–1950*, p. 434.

[15] This charge was made, for example, by Wu Hsi-ch'uan in his speech before the United Security Council on November 28, 1950 (*ibid.*, p. 441).

on Chinese advice that an overt Marxist-Leninist party was constituted, for the first time in Vietnam since 1945, in February, 1951. This was the Vietnam Lao Dong (or Workers Party). This party's manifesto and platform were published in *People's China*, then the CPR's leading foreign propaganda organ, on May 1. Shortly afterward the new party proclaimed an alliance with the leftist Laotian and Cambodian movements that it was sponsoring.[16] Rumors of impending intervention by Chinese combat troops continued to circulate, but no such intervention materialized. The VPA resumed the offensive early in 1952, immediately after General de Lattre's death, perhaps with the purpose among others of diverting Western attention from Korea. Again no overt Chinese intervention materialized, both because it was militarily unnecessary, as well as difficult, and probably because the CPR could not afford to increase the risks of American retaliation by adding offensive operations in Vietnam to its already provocative behavior in Korea. In June, 1952, Ho Chi Minh announced that a general offensive would be launched "without counting on anyone other than ourselves."[17] The unadmitted flow of Chinese arms and military technicians to Vietnam, the improvement of communications between Southwest China and northern Vietnam, and the training of Vietnamese military and civilian personnel on Chinese soil continued.[18] Until about the time of the Chinese decision of March, 1953, to sign an armistice in Korea, however, Chinese aid to the DRV was not on a scale large enough to enable the latter to force the French out of the Hanoi area and out of the war. There are two likely reasons for this. In the first place, the CPR probably did not dare divert large stocks of weapons from the Korean front while conditions there still required a high state of readiness. Secondly, the CPR's intervention in Korea had already produced seemingly serious danger of American retaliation. If the CPR had allowed this danger to be augmented by additional American anger at an intensified Chinese intervention in Indochina, the result might have been disaster.[19]

■ **THE CRISIS (1953–54)**

At the beginning of 1953, Laos began to be significantly involved in the Indochinese war. In retrospect, the first sign of this development seems to be the CPR's proclamation, on January 23, of the so-called Hsi-

---

[16] Lancaster, *op. cit.*, pp. 229–230.

[17] *Survey of International Affairs*, 1952, p. 418.

[18] Cf. the Handbook for Political Workers Going to Vietnam, issued by the CPR on December 15, 1952 (text in Allan B. Cole, ed., *Conflict in Indo-China and International Repercussions: A Documentary History, 1945–55*, Cornell University Press, 1956, pp. 125–130).

[19] For example, John Foster Dulles, when not yet Secretary of State, said that the United States should retaliate against the CPR if it intervened in Indochina (*The New York Times*, April 7, 1954).

shuang Pan-na Autonomous Chou, inhabited largely by primitive tribes of Thai extraction and located next to the trijunction of the Chinese, Burmese, and Laotian frontiers, and only about a hundred miles distant from the northern tip of Thailand. This development, it will be recalled, occurred at a time of great tension in the Korean War, and only three days after the inauguration of the Eisenhower administration, and there was probably some connection.[20]

In those days "autonomous" areas along the CPR's frontiers were generally regarded, in rather too alarmist a fashion as it later seemed, as bases for penetration of areas across the frontier inhabited by minorities of similar ethnic stock. It is pertinent to point out that there is a major geographical and cultural watershed in the peninsula of continental Southeast Asia, the Annam Cordillera, which runs roughly along the frontier between Vietnam and Laos. Very generally speaking, to the east of this divide the dominant people are the Vietnamese, whose culture is to a large extent of Chinese origin. To the west, there are a few civilized peoples (mainly the Burmans, the Lao, the Cambodians, and the lowland Thai), and a great many tribal groups in the mountains that are largely of Thai extraction. The civilized peoples west of the Annam Cordillera, as well as the Malay peoples to the south and the Tibetans and related peoples of the Himalayas, owe a much greater cultural debt to India than to China. This fact helps greatly to explain India's keen interest in these regions and its sensitivity to alien intrusions into them, such as it demonstrated in the case of Tibet in 1950. Clearly the new Thai "autonomous" area in Yunnan, located in a salient of Chinese territory jutting into the Indian cultural sphere west of the Annam Cordillera, was bound to be a matter of concern to India. It seems possible that the CPR's immediate object was to exert a degree of pressure on India, which from the beginning had played a crucial middleman's role in the East-West maneuvering over Korea, so as to bring India to try to prevent the Eisenhower administration from enlarging the Korean War.

Another consideration possibly relevant to the formation of the Thai "autonomous" area was the fact that the Burmese army was beginning an offensive against the "KMT irregulars" in Burma; the main road through Cheli, the capital of the area, runs to the Burmese frontier.

There was probably another, more long-range, consideration as well. Although the CPR would unquestionably like to see the DRV control South Vietnam, it is far from certain that it also endorses the DRV's ambition to control the whole of what was once French Indochina. The CPR seems to have ambitions of its own with respect to both the civilized and the tribal portions of the non-Vietnamese territories of Indochina, although it

---

[20] The CPR had proclaimed a comparable Korean "autonomous" area adjacent to the trijunction of the Manchurian, North Korean, and Soviet frontiers on September 2, 1952, in a move probably related to Sino-Soviet bargaining over the Korean War.

has never stated publicly what they are or made an overt issue of them with the DRV. The proclamation of the Thai "autonomous" area in Yunnan may well have been an indirect way of staking a Chinese claim of sorts to Laos, in competition with the DRV, at a time when an invasion of Laos by the DRV had long been expected[21] but had not yet materialized.

In early April, 1953, the DRV launched its first invasion of Laos, which was accompanied by troops of the Pathet Lao (Free Lao) movement that it was sponsoring. The Pathet Lao promptly proclaimed a "resistance government" with headquarters at Sam Neua, near the DRV border. This move was believed at the time to have some connection with the creation of the Thai "autonomous" area in Yunnan.[22] As the invasion began, the DRV radio announced that "The Workers Party and the Vietminh people have the mission of creating a revolution in Cambodia and Laos" and a "union of Vietnam, Cambodia, and Laos." Apparently this was the first occasion on which the DRV's ambition to control the whole of Indochina had been stated so openly and flatly.[23] The invasion lasted only until May, but this was long enough to expose the vulnerability of Laos, to entrench the Pathet Lao in the border province of Sam Neua, and to contribute to the fall of the French government under Premier René Mayer (on May 21), who was succeeded after a prolonged political crisis by Joseph Laniel.[24]

By this time the volume of Chinese military deliveries to the DRV had begun to increase sharply, and the French military position in Indochina threatened to become desperate unless something drastic were done. This would be especially true after the imminent signing of an armistice in Korea. The only hope was to mount enough of a military effort, with sufficient American aid, to make it possible to negotiate with the Communist side a settlement that would leave as much of Indochina as possible free of Communist control. There seems to have been no desire for direct American intervention. There may have been some hope that with good luck France might retain something of a political as well as an economic position in Indochina after the settlement. If not, the French army was in any case coming to think that the main stand against Afro-Asian left-wing nationalism should be made in Algeria, which was close to home and rich in oil. As was indicated in the Navarre Plan, drawn up in July, 1953, by the newly appointed French commander in Indochina, the military prerequisite for the success of this plan for Indochina was increased American aid and the training of additional indigenous troops, and the political pre-

---

[21] Cf. *The New York Times*, April 14, 1953.

[22] *The New York Times*, April 20, 1953.

[23] Quoted in *The New York Times*, April 14, 1953.

[24] One of those who unsuccessfully tried to form a government during the interim was Pierre Mendès-France, who described the war in Indochina as a "crushing burden" that might allow West Germany to overshadow France in Europe and indicated reservations about the European Defense Community—attitudes that were undoubtedly shared by many Frenchmen (*The New York Times*, June 4, 1953).

requisite was independence for the Associated States of Indochina.[25] Independence was accordingly promised to the Associated States early in July.[26]

The French strategy in dealing with the United States was to use the possibility of direct Chinese participation in the war, which was actually very remote even after the signing of the armistice in Korea, as a means of extracting American economic and military aid. The French did not want American intervention, which would probably have led to a pyrrhic victory or perhaps to full-scale Chinese intervention, neither of which the French wanted. On the other hand, the French seem to have used the possibility of American intervention, which was kept alive by a series of threats that began in the autumn of 1953,[27] to deter a Chinese intervention in the unlikely case that one was contemplated. More realistically, American threats against the CPR had a possible utility in encouraging the CPR to restrain the DRV, which within limits it was in a position to do.

This strategy worked fairly well for a time, and if it had been pursued long enough without drastic counteraction by the opposition it might have enabled the French to emerge with a stalemate settlement. At the end of September, 1953, the United States agreed to deliver an additional $385 million in aid to the French in Indochina in exchange for an increased French military effort and an acceleration of the process of granting independence to the Associated States.[28] Soon afterward the Foreign Ministers of the Big Three issued a statement expressing the hope that the Soviet Foreign Minister would join them in a conference on Germany and Austria, and perhaps on Korea and Indochina as well.[29]

These maneuvers presented a difficult problem for Ho Chi Minh, who had controlled most of Vietnam in the late summer of 1945, had soon lost much of what he then held, and has never since regained an equally favorable position. Even his major ally seemed to favor negotiations rather than a fight to total victory. On September 2, 1953 (the eighth anniversary of the founding of the DRV) the *People's Daily* recommended negotiations to the French, and by obvious implication also to the DRV. In November, Ho in a vague reply to some questions put to him by a Swedish newspaper

25 Cf. Henri Navarre, *Agonie de l'Indochine* (1953–1954), Paris: Librarie Plon, 1956, pp. 62–88.

26 Lancaster, *op. cit.,* p. 275. King (later Prince) Norodom Sihanouk of Cambodia had helped to accelerate the process by fleeing briefly to Thailand shortly before (*ibid.,* p. 274).

27 Secretary Dulles said on September 2, 1953, that "There is the risk that, as in Korea, Red China might send its own army into Indo-China. The Chinese Communist regime should realize that such a second aggression could not occur without grave consequences which might not be confined to Indo-China" (*The New York Times,* September 3, 1953). The United States had considered giving such warnings to the CPR at least as early as May, 1952 (Anthony Eden, *Full Circle,* Boston: Houghton Mifflin, 1960, p. 92).

28 *The New York Times,* October 1, 1953.

29 *The New York Times,* October 19, 1953.

implied that he would agree to a ceasefire in exchange for control of all of Vietnam; nothing was said about Cambodia and Laos, or about Vietnam's remaining within the French Union. Ho indicated a strong preference for bilateral talks between France and the DRV, without interference by third parties. Apparently he believed, then as later, that provided his allies deterred an escalation of the conflict "imperialism" would eventually tire of the struggle and abandon Vietnam, if not the whole of Indochina. A hostile reference to the European Defense Community indicated, however, Ho's awareness that issues other than Indochina were involved.[30]

Indeed they were. These were issues too broad to be solved merely by the DRV and France, or on the basis of the DRV's current military position, favorable though it was. As we have seen, the CPR had tried to use first the possibility and then the actuality of its involvement in the Korean War as a means of extracting concessions on other issues, notably Taiwan and the United Nations. Indochina, the main current point of pressure on "imperialism," was now to be used, by the Soviet Union as well as the CPR, to extract concessions on other issues. For the Soviet Union these were the neutralization of West Germany, the dismantling of the European Defense Community, and if possible the elimination of American forces and alliance systems from Europe. For the CPR, the main issues were the same as before: Korea, Taiwan, and the United Nations. Extensive political and diplomatic coordination between the Soviet Union and the CPR seems to have been achieved during the winter of 1953–54. On December 12, a new Soviet ambassador to the CPR, Pavel F. Yudin, a specialist in theoretical and party matters, arrived in Peking; he was to hold the post until 1959, when effective Sino-Soviet political cooperation was wrecked on the reefs of Khrushchev's effort at a détente with the West.

The crescendo of American threats, such as the one contained in Secretary Dulles' "massive retaliation" speech of January 12, 1954, made it unsafe for the CPR to involve itself in the Indochinese war directly. The CPR unquestionably wanted the DRV to improve its bargaining position and above all that of its allies by a final spectacular victory, however. This must be done quickly, before accelerated shipments of American weapons and the expansion of the non-Communist Vietnamese army had time to take effect. The CPR had tried to do the same in Korea, in the spring of 1951, but had failed disastrously because of the enemy's superior firepower. The result had been two years of negotiations, a stalemated armistice, and a failure to bring about the general political conference on Far Eastern problems through which the CPR hoped to gain at the conference table at least some of what it had failed to gain on the battlefield. There is a widespread

[30] Text in Cole, op. cit., pp. 148–149. In connection with my analysis of the last stages of the war and the Geneva settlement I am indebted to Mr. John T. McAlister, Jr., of Yale University, and Mr. David T. Kenney of the School of Advanced International Studies, The Johns Hopkins University.

belief that the DRV did not want to try for a final spectacular victory, which would be costly in Vietnamese lives, but that the CPR insisted.[31] The attainment of the broader Sino-Soviet objectives required more leverage than would be available without such a victory. This meant that the CPR had to supply the DRV with the wherewithal, mainly additional firepower, to make the victory possible.

In December and January, the "Vietnam People's Army" (VPA) invaded central and southern Laos.[32] A movement of other VPA troops into northwestern Vietnam, in the direction of Laos, aroused French fears for the security of northern Laos. The French feeling of political commitment to Laos was understandable; the choice of the place on which to base its defense was not. This was Dienbienphu, just east of the Lao border in Vietnam; French troops occupied this post on November 20, and General Navarre decided two weeks later to make it into a strongpoint for the defense of northern Laos. Dienbienphu is in a valley and the French did not control the surrounding hills, but they believed that the CPR could not or would not supply the VPA with enough artillery to enable it to make the fort untenable.[33] In an equally mistaken judgment, an American team of antiaircraft specialists brought in to inspect the fort assured the French that VPA antiaircraft artillery would be unable to prevent resupply by air.[34]

These estimates were confounded by large new shipments of weapons and supplies by the CPR to the DRV. Special roads were built leading into the hills overlooking Dienbienphu, and field and antiaircraft artillery was brought in from the CPR and manhandled into position without the French being aware of it.[35]

Meanwhile, the Foreign Ministers of the Big Four met at Berlin (January 25–February 19, 1954). The French were so eager for a conference on Indochina, which they believed required Soviet participation and Soviet approaches to the Chinese and North Vietnamese, that they showed some receptivity to Soviet suggestions that they should not join the European Defense Community. No agreement was reached on Germany, however. The main British concern in the Southeast Asian situation, as always during this period, was for the security of Malaya and Singapore.

---

[31] Robert Guillain, La fin des illusions: notes d'Indochine (février-juillet) 1954, Paris: Centre d'Etudes de Politique Etrangère, 1954, p. 71.

[32] Bernard B. Fall, The Two Viet-Nams, New York: Praeger, 1963, p. 125.

[33] Cf. Dwight D. Eisenhower, Mandate for Change, 1953–1956, Garden City, N.Y.: Doubleday, 1963, p. 339.

[34] Bernard B. Fall, Street Without Joy: Insurgency in Indochina, 1946–63, 3rd rev. ed., Harrisburg, Pa.: Stackpole, 1963, p. 312.

[35] A map of the supply routes leading from the CPR to Dienbienphu may be found in Jean Lacouture and Philippe Devillers, La fin d'une guerre: Indochine 1954; Paris: Editions du Seuil, 1960, pp. 56–57. These routes ran southwestward from Kwangsi, rather than southward from Yunnan. One ran within forty miles of Hanoi, the main French center in northern Vietnam. The book just cited, although sometimes inaccurate, is an important source based in part on unpublished archival material.

The United States objected to the Soviet proposal for a five-power conference on Korea and Indochina in which the CPR should be not only a participant but a convenor but finally accepted the British compromise proposal for an enlarged conference in which the CPR should be represented and there should be no indication as to which were the convening powers. The conference was scheduled for April 26, at Geneva.[36] The CPR obviously valued the prospect of its first representation at a major diplomatic conference as a means of getting, if not American diplomatic recognition, then concessions, enhanced international respectability, and a satisfactory settlement of the Indochinese crisis.

There remained the need for a final major victory. On March 13 the VPA launched a savage and costly attack on Dienbienphu, which pulverized the defenders with unexpected artillery fire and gradually strangled their airlift with antiaircraft fire. The psychological impact of this operation, coming as it did at a time when every one else seemed ready for negotiations, was much greater than the military impact. It startled Secretary Dulles into beginning the negotiations that led, later in the year, to the formation of SEATO.[37] One of his purposes was to provide a political basis for American military intervention in Indochina, if it should prove necessary. By this time there was some enthusiasm in French political and military circles and American military circles for American air strikes against the forces attacking Dienbienphu, and for retaliation against the CPR in the event that it should respond by intervening in the war. This idea was opposed, however, by President Eisenhower, Army Chief of Staff Ridgway, most American congressional and public opinion, and by the United States' allies, Britain in particular. After a trip by Secretary Dulles to Europe in April, and further indications of British disapproval at the end of the month, the idea of military intervention, although not of a collective security agreement covering Southeast Asia, was dropped, for the time being at least.[38]

In all probability the CPR had calculated the situation correctly, somewhat along these lines. The United States was not bluffing; it did in fact fear that the fall of Indochina might set in motion a process of "falling dominoes" that might bring Chinese influence deep into Southeast Asia. The United States would fight in Indochina, and perhaps retaliate against

---

[36] Eden, op. cit., pp. 97–100; Lancaster, op. cit., pp. 290–292; Eisenhower, op. cit., pp. 342–344.

[37] The first hint of this came in a speech by Secretary Dulles on March 29, in which he referred to "united action" to save Southeast Asia (The New York Times, March 30, 1954). A few days later, it was announced that the State Department had proposed to Britain, France, Australia, New Zealand, the Philippines, and Thailand that they "join in a common warning against further aggression by Communist China in any part of Southeast Asia" (The New York Times, April 7, 1954).

[38] Lacouture and Devillers, op. cit., pp. 71ff.; Eisenhower, op. cit., pp. 344–351; Fall, The Two Viet-Nams, op. cit., pp. 226–229; Lancaster, op. cit., pp. 298–302. Vice President Nixon said on April 16 that the United States might have to send troops to Indochina (The New York Times, April 18, 1964).

the mainland of China, but only if the CPR intervened directly in the war. Short of that, the United States would be restrained from fighting by a combination of domestic and international pressures. In addition to those already mentioned, the United States would of course take account of the military power of the Soviet Union, where Khrushchev was making belligerent noises by way of reply to the "massive retaliation" doctrine.[39] In addition, the British were anxious for India to join in guaranteeing an Indochinese settlement.[40] Thus it was possible for the CPR, by working through India, to exert pressure on Britain and through Britain on the United States for a favorable settlement in Indochina. This was one of the most important aspects of the complex Sino-Indian bargaining that seems to have begun about the end of 1953, when an Indian delegation arrived in the CPR for the ostensible purpose of negotiating an agreement on Tibet. India may be assumed to have been concerned over the DRV's incursion into Laos in December, 1953.

■ THE GENEVA CONFERENCE

No amount of fighting in Indochina or maneuvering at the conference table could gain much for the Communist powers with respect to Germany or the Far East other than Indochina, partly because France was not a decisive factor in these situations. It was such a factor, however, in the negotiations for the prospective European Defense Community, which already seemed moribund but which the Soviet Union was anxious to do nothing to revive, and in Indochina, an issue needless to say of the greatest importance to the CPR and the DRV. The Communists played skillfully on French fears that a continuation of the war in Indochina would cost France its position in Southeast Asia and bring Western Europe, through the European Defense Community, under German leadership.

Dienbienphu fell on May 7, the day before the Geneva Conference began its discussions on the Indochina question. The psychological effect of the disaster on the negotiations was considerable. Another cloud hovering over the conference was the hydrogen bomb and the fear of a Third World War.[41] This fear was kept alive by menacing American statements and gestures during the conference, which although they irritated and alarmed the Western participants as well as the Communists undoubtedly helped to secure an eventual settlement less favorable to the "socialist camp" than might have been expected. India, although not a formal participant, was actively represented at Geneva by Krishna Menon.

Molotov successfully demanded that the DRV be admitted to the conference as a participant. He and Chou En-lai, who was clearly not sub-

---

[39] This was all the more necessary because Malenkov made his celebrated statement that another world war "would mean the end of world civilization," not merely of "imperialism," on March 12, 1954, the eve of the attack on Dienbienphu.

[40] Eden, *op. cit.*, p. 97.

[41] *Ibid.*, pp. 132, 139.

servient to Molotov and was much the more hostile of the two toward the West, failed to gain representation for the DRV-sponsored "free" Lao and Cambodian movements, however. Both Molotov and Chou supported the DRV's demand that all three of the Indochinese states be treated in substantially the same way, so that the DRV's military victory in Vietnam would make itself felt in Laos and Cambodia too. The essence of the DRV's original demands was that France recognize the DRV's control over the whole of Vietnam and withdraw its troops from all three countries, and that "free" elections be held in each of them as soon as possible.[42] The effect of these demands, if they had been accepted, would have been to bring Vietnam almost immediately, and the other two countries later, under Communist control.

The French government was very anxious for a ceasefire, but not anxious enough to accept these terms. All the Western powers, as well as India and Thailand,[43] were seriously concerned for the security of Laos and Cambodia, as well as Burma and Thailand to a lesser extent. In order to save them the Western powers, the British in particular, were prepared to accept a partitioning of Vietnam, with the DRV in control of the northern portion. Under the influence perhaps of a number of hints of American military intervention, the DRV implied a willingness to accept a partition of Vietnam, rather than holding out for control over the entire country, on May 25.[44] Molotov had already conceded an important Western demand that the observance of the ceasefire be supervised by neutrals.[45]

These concessions still left so many differences, especially over Laos and Cambodia, unresolved that the conference was virtually deadlocked in early June.

On June 8 Molotov, just returned from Moscow, delivered a strong attack on French Foreign Minister Bidault, who was opposed to the partitioning of Vietnam and was suspected of favoring American military intervention.[46] Chou made a tough speech the following day, in which he reiterated his frequent accusation that the United States was trying to use Indochina as a base for military action against the CPR.[47] These stern performances, and Molotov's in particular, contributed greatly to the fall of the Laniel government on June 12.

On June 11, Secretary Dulles made a speech at Los Angeles in which he said that a clash between the CPR and the United States, although not desired by the latter, might occur if there were "open military aggression by the Chinese Communist regime." Even in the absence of such aggression, American military intervention in Indochina might occur as part of a "col-

---

[42] Text in *Documents on International Affairs, 1954*, pp. 127–128.

[43] On India see Eden, *op. cit.*, p. 140; on Thailand cf. Lacouture and Devillers, *op. cit.*, p. 145.

[44] *Survey of International Affairs*, 1954, p. 48.

[45] Lancaster, *op. cit.*, pp. 320–321.

[46] Lacouture and Devillers, *op. cit.*, p. 215.

[47] Excerpts in *Documents on International Affairs, 1954*, pp. 131–135.

lective effort of some of the other nations of the area," under four conditions: "An invitation from the present lawful authorities to come in. Clear assurance of complete independence to Laos, Cambodia and Vietnam. Evidence of concern by the United Nations. Assurance that France will not itself withdraw from the battle until it is won."[48] Events of the next several days apparently suggested to the nervous Communist powers that the United States might see reason to consider these conditions fulfilled.

As for the first and third conditions, Australian Foreign Minister Casey implied soon afterward that the governments of Laos and Cambodia were about to take their cases to the United Nations with Australian support, a move that might lead to United Nations approval for American action in Indochina as it had in Korea. Casey had just had talks with the Indian and Pakistani governments.[49] In Vietnam, the premier resigned on June 16 and was succeeded by the firmly anti-Communist Ngo Dinh Diem. On June 16, the Republic of China drew the attention of the Security Council to the alleged existence of a "Free Thailand" regime based in the Thai "autonomous" area in Yunnan. The Thai government introduced a resolution for the creation of a United Nations peace mission empowered to go not only to Thailand but to Laos and Cambodia.[50] When the Soviet Union vetoed the resolution (on June 18), Ambassador Lodge promptly announced that the United States would bring the issue before the General Assembly.

As for the second condition, France and (non-Communist) Vietnam initialed on June 4 a treaty granting independence to Vietnam within the French Union.[51]

As for the fourth condition, the new French premier, the dynamic Pierre Mendès-France, said at and after his investiture on June 17 that France intended to remain in the Far East, and that he would recommend the sending of French conscripts to Indochina for the first time and then resign if no acceptable Indochinese settlement had been reached by July 20.[52]

Nor was Indochina the only area with respect to which the Communist powers were failing to attain their objectives at Geneva. On June 15, the Western powers broke off the deadlocked negotiations on Korea. President Rhee promptly announced that the armistice in Korea was now invalid and said he was ready to send Korean troops to Indochina.[53] It was announced on June 15 that Prime Minister Churchill and Foreign Minister Eden would visit Washington on June 25, the anniversary as it happened of the beginning of the Korean War.[54]

48 *The New York Times,* June 12, 1954. Text in *Department of State Bulletin,* vol. 30, no. 783 (June 28, 1954), pp. 971–973.
49 *The New York Times,* June 14, 1954.
50 *The New York Times,* June 17, 1954.
51 Text in *Documents on International Affairs, 1954,* pp. 135–137.
52 *Survey of International Affairs, 1954,* p. 51.
53 *The New York Times,* June 16, 1954.
54 *Survey of International Affairs, 1954,* p. 52.

Whatever the extent of the calculation and coordination of these moves may have been, their cumulative effect on the Communist side seems to have been dramatic. On June 14 Molotov, with Chou En-lai's support, agreed that the proposed International Supervisory and Control Commissions (usually known as the ICC) in the three Indochinese countries could decide to make an investigation, although not to recommend action, by a majority vote.[55] A much more important concession came from Chou En-lai on June 16, in a talk with Eden. Chou indicated a willingness to treat Laos and Cambodia on a different footing from Vietnam, to see DRV as well as French troops withdrawn from the two countries, and to give diplomatic recognition to the Laotian and Cambodian royal governments. Molotov and Pham Van Dong, the DRV's chief delegate, gave approval to this proposal, the latter rather ambiguously.[56] This major concession so improved the outlook for a settlement that the leaders of most of the delegations turned over the negotiations to subordinates and left temporarily for home.

On June 23, the third anniversary of the public Soviet proposal for armistice talks in Korea, Chou En-lai met the new French premier at Bern. Chou repeated his concessions with respect to Laos and Cambodia, agreed that there was no urgency about holding an election in Vietnam, and suggested bilateral talks between France and the DRV on the terms of the Vietnamese settlement.[57]

Chou then visited India on June 25–28, probably as the result of arrangements concluded through Krishna Menon at Geneva. One of his aims was probably to insure against the unlikely possibility that Britain might succeed in drawing the Asian members of the Commonwealth (India, Pakistan, and Ceylon), and perhaps the other Colombo powers (Burma and Indonesia) as well, into the collective security arrangement that the United States was proposing for Southeast Asia.[58] Another was probably to arrange for India to be not only a member of the three ICC's for the three Indochinese countries, as it was generally agreed India would be, but the chairman. This would involve India in the strongest possible way in the Indochinese settlement and help to insure against American retaliation for covert violations, of the "salami-slicing" variety, by the DRV of the Geneva agreements. It would also mean additional support for the CPR's insistence that the settlement must not permit American bases in Indochina. In return, India evidently demanded and got a reaffirmation of the "Five Principles of Peaceful Coexistence" and a pledge that the CPR would not commit aggression or subversion against the non-Communist Asian countries. Obviously India had Burma and Thailand most immediately in mind, but Nehru prob-

---

[55] *The New York Times*, June 15, 1954.
[56] *The New York Times*, June 17, 1954.
[57] Eisenhower, *op. cit.*, p. 369; Lacouture and Devillers, *op. cit.*, pp. 231–233.
[58] Cf. Eden, *op. cit.*, pp. 107, 161.

ably also indicated to Chou that he expected the CPR to restrain the DRV from putting pressure on Laos and Cambodia.[59]

From India, evidently at Nehru's suggestion,[60] Chou flew to Burma (June 28–29), where he gave U Nu similar reassurances. Chou then talked with Ho Chi Minh (July 2–3) somewhere near the Sino-Vietnamese frontier. According to the communiqué, the two men had a "full exchange of views" on the Geneva Conference, about which Ho had had little to say and apparently very little enthusiasm.[61] A few days later he made a conciliatory statement, which was given little publicity in the DRV.[62] It is hard to resist the conclusion that he objected to his military victory being made the football of other powers, and that strong Chinese pressure or inducements, or both, were required to secure his acquiescence.

The last and crucial phase of the Geneva Conference, which began in mid-July, was marked by extremely hard bargaining between France and the DRV, the reluctance of the United States to associate itself with the settlement, and the CPR's determination that the United States should do so.

Mendès-France made skillful use of French control of the Red River delta and of threats to continue the war as a means of getting concessions from the DRV. All the negotiators were acutely aware of his self-imposed deadline, and no one seems to have been willing to take the risks and uncertainties that his resignation would entail. The DRV was presumably anxious to inherit Hanoi intact, as the CPR had inherited Peking, and therefore not to have to besiege it. The DRV probably also remembered that the CPR had fought for Peking's port, Tientsin, with serious damage to the city, and was anxious that the same thing should not happen to Haiphong.[63] As against the 18th parallel, which Mendès-France had been demanding as the dividing line in Vietnam, the DRV had been insisting on the 13th or 14th parallel, which as a matter of fact would have corresponded fairly closely with the actual military situation. Now the DRV with Molotov's support suddenly proposed the 16th parallel, which had been the demarcation line in 1945 between the Chinese Nationalist and British occupation zones. This would still have given the DRV a common frontier with Cambodia and control over the naval base at Tourane (Danang) and a major highway leading westward from Vietnam into central Laos, both of which lie between the 16th and 17th parallels. On another vital issue, that of a time limit for general elections in Vietnam, Mendès-France was agreeing to them within eighteen months; the DRV was demanding them within six months. The deadlock was broken at the last minute by Molotov, who was obviously very tired and anxious for a settlement. He proposed the 17th parallel, thus leaving Tourane and the highway to Laos outside

[59] See statements by Chou and Nehru in supplement to *People's China*, July 16, 1954.
[60] Rosemary Brissenden in George Modelski, ed., *SEATO: Six Studies*, Melbourne: F. W. Cheshire, 1962, p. 213.
[61] New China News Agency dispatch, July 7, 1954.
[62] New China News Agency dispatch, July 11, 1954.
[63] Cf. Lacouture and Devillers, *op. cit.*, p. 257.

the DRV's control, and elections within two years. The DRV was very unhappy but could only acquiesce.[64]

For his part, Chou En-lai appeared to be less concerned with these details than with excluding any American military presence from Indochina and ensuring that the three non-Communist Indochinese states did not join or affiliate themselves in any way with SEATO.[65] The United States was agreeable to this, but it rejected a last-minute demand by Chou En-lai that it sign the Geneva agreements. Rather than risk the failure of the conference, Chou then accepted a unilateral declaration by the United States that it would not "disturb" the agreements.[66] Ho Chi Minh, for his part, indicated that his victory had been merely postponed by announcing that he expected "the unification of the nation by means of general elections."[67]

The DRV had already abandoned its claim that its Cambodian puppet, the Khmer Issarak, be granted legality and territorial bases. As Mendès-France's deadline approached, however, the DRV was insisting by way of compensation on an autonomous government controlled by the Pathet Lao in the Laotian border provinces of Sam Neua and Phong Saly. On July 18, Mendès-France argued Chou En-lai into abandoning the DRV's claim, which therefore had to be dropped. Pham Van Dong is reported to have been infuriated at Chou.[68]

Under the Geneva agreements, none of the Indochina countries was to join any military alliances. Neither Vietnamese regime was allowed to receive outside military aid, except on a replacement basis. Laos was allowed to retain a small French military mission. The DRV was to withdraw its forces from Vietnam south of the 17th parallel, from Laos, and from Cambodia. These military arrangements were to be supervised by three ICC's, each with India as chairman and Poland and Canada as the other members. Vietnam was partitioned, in fact although not in name, at the 17th parallel, but it was generally expected that the general elections scheduled for July, 1956, would give the entire country to the Communists. Cambodia, which had seen little fighting and bargained energetically at Geneva, secured the withdrawal of all Communist forces from its territory. In Laos, the forces of the Pathet Lao, a Communist front organization controlled by the DRV, were to concentrate in the two border provinces of Sam Neua and Phong Saly, and general elections were to be held in 1955 to integrate these two provinces into the political life of the country as a whole.[69]

---

[64] *Ibid.,* p. 268.

[65] Cf. *The New York Times,* July 18, 1954.

[66] *The New York Times,* July 20, 1954. Text of the United States declaration in *Documents on International Affairs, 1954,* pp. 140–141.

[67] *The New York Times,* July 25, 1954.

[68] Lancaster, *op. cit.,* p. 334.

[69] Cf. the official British summary of the agreements in Cole, *op. cit.,* pp. 164–165. For the CPR's commentary on the agreements see "Peaceful Negotiations Score Another Great Victory," *People's Daily,* July 22, 1954 (reprinted in *People's China,* August 1, 1954, pp. 3–5).

The CPR had attained at Geneva what seems to have been its main security objective at the time, the exclusion of American bases and alliance systems from Indochina. Presumably it was worried by some vague remarks by Secretary Dulles about a possible "three-pronged attack" on the CPR based on Korea, the Taiwan Strait, and Indochina.[70]

The CPR had enormously enhanced its international prestige, especially with the neutrals, by its role in the Geneva Conference, which had been more important than that of any other participant except perhaps Britain. This was of course the first international conference that it had attended, and the impression that it made was enhanced by the glamor of the unknown. The handsome and urbane Chou En-lai was given a more enthusiastic reception by the press and the public than was any other delegate when he arrived at Geneva.[71] There is no doubt that he performed very ably and effectively at the conference. On the other hand, the CPR made no measurable progress at Geneva toward its basic objectives with respect to Korea, Taiwan, and the United Nations, unless one assumes that the partial withdrawal of American and Chinese forces from Korea in the autumn of 1954 was the result of an unannounced arrangement concluded at or shortly after the Geneva Conference. Since the CPR did not have American recognition or a seat on the United Nations Security Council, there was no assurance that it would be invited to future conferences, in spite of its insistence that it should have a say in the settlement of all major international questions.

Nevertheless, the CPR had reason to feel satisfied on balance with the results of the Geneva Conference, and for this satisfaction a feeling of irritation and frustration on the part of the DRV was not too high a price to pay. The DRV could be squared with economic and military aid, and although its position had been seriously truncated at Geneva it still seemed strong with respect to its most important objective, South Vietnam — because of the guarantee of elections within two years — if less so with respect to Laos and much less so with respect to Cambodia.[72]

■   **AFTER GENEVA**

Although it is related much more closely to the Soviet than to the Chinese role in the Geneva Conference, the fate of the European Defense Community has been mentioned often enough so that it might be well to conclude the subject here. In August, 1954, the French National Assembly put it out of its misery, the main finger on the trigger being that of Mendès-

---

[70] Cf. A. M. Halpern, "Communist China and Peaceful Co-existence," *The China Quarterly*, no. 3 (July–September, 1960), p. 25.

[71] Lacouture and Devillers, *op. cit.*, p. 112.

[72] The partitioning of Vietnam at the 17th parallel had deprived the DRV of a common frontier with Cambodia.

France. He has denied charges that this act was performed in exchange for Soviet moderation at Geneva, and it probably was not. If there was a deal, it was probably with the Gaullists, who supported Mendès-France and provided the Defense Minister in his cabinet. The most that can fairly be said is that Molotov probably took a moderate line at Geneva partly because to do otherwise would have risked the fall of Mendès-France and the coming to power of some one more favorably disposed toward the European Defense Community.[73]

One of the signs of the CPR's enhanced international status as a result of the Geneva Conference was the establishment of closer relations with Britain. The CPR began to treat the British mission in Peking as having diplomatic status and agreed to send one of its own to London. Ambassadors were not exchanged, however. A British Labor Party delegation visited the CPR in August, 1954. The main reason on the Chinese side for an interest in improved Anglo-Chinese relations was a realization, probably gained or at least confirmed at Geneva, that Britain was a useful indirect channel for exerting pressure on the United States.[74]

A direct channel might be even more useful, of course. Here the CPR had a valuable bargaining asset, which it did not hesitate to exploit, in seventy-six Americans whom it admitted to holding prisoner, and it was also anxious for the return of seventy Chinese students then being detained in the United States. On June 5, 1954, two members of the American and Chinese delegations to the Geneva Conference, U. Alexis Johnson and Wang Ping-nan, began talks on these and other questions of common interest. After the Bandung Conference, Nehru and U Nu urged that the talks be conducted at the ambassadorial level. Such were the origins of the Sino-American ambassadorial talks that began at Geneva in August, 1955.[75]

The situation created by the Geneva agreements was one that the Communist side was not likely to disturb by overt invasion, for some time at least. The main problem was one of subversion through and among the primitive Thai peoples who inhabit the remote areas of all the Southeast Asian countries north of Malaya. This was the threat that the United States had mainly in mind when, in September, 1954, representatives of eight states (the United States, Britain, France, Australia, New Zealand, Pakistan, the Philippines, and Thailand) met to discuss collective defense arrangements for Southeast Asia. Accordingly, the United States proposed that SEATO, as it came to be called, should be directed against "Communist aggression," whether invasion or subversion. At the other extreme Pakistan, the only one of the Asian countries invited by Britain that attended the conference, wanted no qualification on the word "aggression," since it

[73] Cf. Lancaster, op. cit., pp. 336–337; Survey of International Affairs, 1954, pp. 141–142.

[74] Cf. ibid., pp. 247–250.

[75] The New York Times, April 22, 1964.

wanted protection mainly against India. The result was a compromise: the wording preferred by Pakistan was adopted, although the other signatories did not consider that possible Indian aggression against Pakistan was covered by the treaty, and the United States appended a reservation to the Manila Pact indicating that it applied only to Communist aggression. The northern boundary of the region to which the treaty applied was drawn just to the south of Taiwan, Hong Kong, and Macao. Thailand was the main country intended to benefit from the treaty's protection. Any of the three non-Communist Indochinese states, although they are of course not signatories to the Manila Pact, may be extended protection under a protocol to the treaty if its government so requests, and they are therefore known as the protocol states. None of them has yet asked for such protection. Major actions by SEATO must be by unanimous vote. In practice this has meant that the British and still more the French have been able to prevent, by at least the implicit threat of a veto, any military intervention by SEATO as such in the Indochina area.[76]

At first, the CPR seems to have accelerated its shipments of arms to the DRV somewhat, but not greatly, beyond the replacement levels permitted under the Geneva agreements.[77] The reasons may have been partly logistical: a new railway connecting Hanoi and Nanning, in Kwangsi, was not completed until early 1955, and at that time the reconstruction of the old railway between Haiphong and Kunming, in Yunnan, was still in its early stages.[78] Political considerations were probably even more important. The CPR and the DRV still evidently hoped that Britain and the Soviet Union, the cochairmen of the Geneva Conference, and the countries represented on the ICC would bring enough pressure at the appropriate time on the United States and South Vietnam to hold the elections promised in the Geneva agreements. In the meantime, large-scale overt violations of the agreements by the Communist side would have been inadvisable.

On June 25, 1955, the fifth anniversary of the beginning of the Korean War, Ho Chi Minh arrived in Peking on an important mission. On July 7, the anniversary of the Japanese attack on China in 1937, the two sides issued a joint communiqué stressing the need for general elections in Vietnam by July, 1956, and announcing that the CPR would grant the DRV 800 million yuan (approximately $338 million) in economic and industrial aid.[79] Ho then moved on to Moscow, where he got comparable political and economic commitments, including a grant of 400 million roubles (approximately $100 million).[80] On his way back to the DRV he stopped briefly at Peking again and then left on July 21, the anniversary

[76] Cf. *Survey of International Affairs, 1954*, pp. 73–82; Eden, *op. cit.*, pp. 161–162. For text of the Manila Pact see *Documents on International Affairs, 1954*, pp. 153–156.

[77] *The New York Times*, October 20 and November 20, 1954.

[78] *Christian Science Monitor*, March 3, 1955.

[79] New China News Agency dispatch, July 8, 1955; text in Cole, *op. cit.*, pp. 238–241.

[80] *Ibid.*, pp. 241–244.

of the signing of the Geneva agreements.[81] The protocol surrounding the trip suggests that for obvious geographical and historical reasons the DRV regarded the CPR rather than the Soviet Union as its main external source of aid and its main hope of political support for the holding of the elections.

It is interesting to compare the behavior of North Korea some two years before toward the two major Communist powers. In September, 1953, North Korea had been promised a grant of one billion roubles (approximately $250 million) in economic aid by the Soviet Union. Two months later North Korea was promised a grant of 8 trillion yuan (equivalent to 800 million of the new yuan in use after March, 1955, and therefore to about $338 million, the same amount later promised to the DRV) by the CPR.[82] The protocol surrounding these commitments suggests that Soviet influence somewhat exceeded Chinese in North Korea, whereas it was much less in North Vietnam.

Perhaps on Chinese advice and obviously in the hope that South Vietnam would fall on schedule without fighting, the DRV formed a "Fatherland Front" in September, 1955, to promote talks between the North and South Vietnamese regimes and the unification of Vietnam through general elections. It was clear that Ngo Dinh Diem was in no mood for elections, however. Accordingly, in April, 1956, Britain was able to secure Soviet agreement to the proposition that the holding of elections in Vietnam was less important than the maintenance of peace.[83] It appeared that the main concession made to the DRV at Geneva in exchange for the setbacks inflicted on it there stood a good chance of vanishing.

---

[81] New China News Agency dispatch, July 21, 1955.
[82] *Survey of International Affairs, 1953*, pp. 240–241.
[83] *Survey of International Affairs, 1955–1956*, pp. 272–273.

10

Taiwan and the Offshore Islands

In its early years, the CPR was confronted with three major problems or crises along its borders: Taiwan, Korea, and Indochina. We have seen that after its efforts to deal with the first of these were frustrated by the extension of American protection to Taiwan on June 27, 1950, the CPR promptly shifted its attention to the second area, Korea. No sooner had the CPR decided, in March, 1953, that it must sign an armistice in Korea than it began to shift its attention to Indochina. Promptly after the signing of the Geneva agreements, it shifted its primary attention to Taiwan again. This was done, of course, with the realization that Taiwan was still under American protection.

■ THE FIRST TAIWAN STRAIT CRISIS (1954–55)

The CPC evidently considered the devoting of major attention to the Taiwan Strait after the Geneva Conference not only feasible but necessary.

In the first place, control of several groups of offshore islands — notably the Tachens, about two hundred miles south of Shanghai; the Matsus, off the port of Foochow and opposite the northern end of Taiwan; and Quemoy, off the port of Amoy — was helping the Nationalists to maintain a fairly effective blockade of the China coast, from Shanghai to Canton.[1] At a time when the CPR was beginning to expand its exports to the non-Communist world and shift its priorities for new industrial investment from the interior to the coastal region, as was the case in 1954, the blockade was more of a nuisance than ever.

---

[1] Cf. *The New York Times,* September 26, 1954.

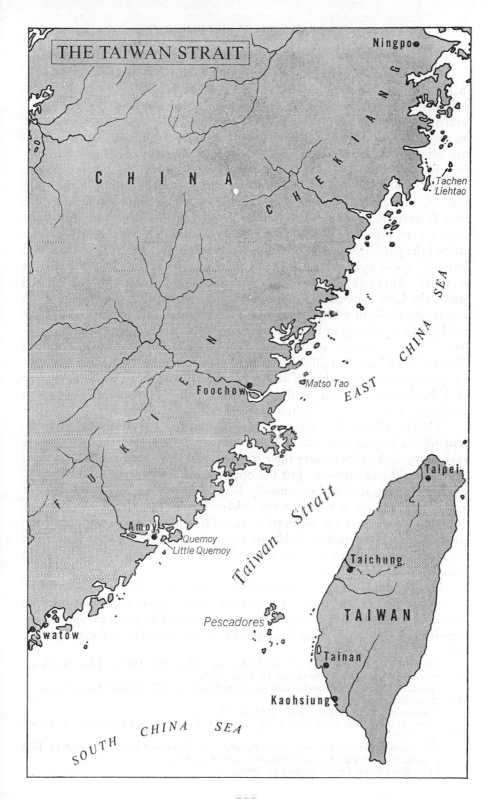

THE TAIWAN STRAIT

Ningpo

CHINA

CHEKIANG

Tachen
Liehtao

EAST   CHINA   SEA

Foochow

Matso Tao

F U K I E N

Taipei

Amoy

Quemoy
Little Quemoy

Taiwan Strait

Taichung

TAIWAN

Pescadores

Tainan

Swatow

Kaohsiung

SOUTH   CHINA   SEA

Secondly, an active threat to the CPR's security seemed to be looming in the Taiwan Strait, at a time when the CPR was involved in a serious political crisis (the purge of Kao Kang and the strains of the early collectivization campaign), and when the modernization and centralization of its armed forces were still in their early stages. In 1954, with American aid and support, the Nationalists began to occupy the offshore islands in force for the first time.[2] The organization as well as the equipment of the Nationalist armed forces was considerably modernized during 1954.[3] On July 26, a small armed clash occurred between Communist and American aircraft over the Taiwan Strait.[4] Two days later, President Syngman Rhee made a very bellicose speech before a joint session of Congress in which he offered the participation of the South Korean and Chinese Nationalist armed forces in a war against the CPR, and if necessary against the Soviet Union as well.[5] Although this proposal was not well received in the United States, the CPR claimed to believe during this period that the United States was trying to form a Northeast Asia Treaty Organization as a counterpart to SEATO, consisting of the United States itself, Japan (then under the pro-American government of Premier Yoshida Shigeru), South Korea, and Nationalist China.[6] In mid-August, Nationalist Premier O. K. Yui said that the propaganda furor already being created by the CPR was due to fear of a Nationalist invasion of the mainland. Other Nationalist leaders also made statements that contributed to the atmosphere of crisis.[7]

Thirdly, Chiang Kai-shek was inaugurated for a second term as President of the Republic of China in the spring of 1954, and the Nationalists gave every sign of increasing their strength and their hold on Taiwan with American aid and support. Just the opposite, of course, was what the CPC wanted. In fact, it would presumably have liked to complete the process of national unification in time for the celebration of the fifth anniversary of the founding of the CPR on October 1, 1954. Although this was out of the question, it still seemed desirable to try to prevent the Nationalists from further entrenching themselves not only on Taiwan but on the offshore islands.

Finally, the Korean and Indochinese settlements left the Taiwan Strait as the only area in which the CPR, realistically speaking, could put pressure on the United States. This was all the more possible because except for the Republic of China few American allies felt any enthusiasm for the policy

---

[2] Stewart Alsop, "The Story Behind Quemoy: How We Drifted Close to War," *The Saturday Evening Post*, December 13, 1958, p. 87.

[3] Joyce Kallgren, "Nationalist China's Armed Forces," *The China Quarterly*, no. 15 (July–September, 1963), pp. 35–36.

[4] *Survey of International Affairs, 1954*, p. 251.

[5] Text in *The New York Times*, July 29, 1954. Cf. *Survey of International Affairs, 1954*, pp. 278–280.

[6] Cf. Chou En-lai, report to Central People's Government Council, August 11, 1954 (in supplement to *People's China*, September 1, 1954, p. 10).

[7] *The New York Times*, August 15, 1954.

of the United States toward Taiwan and the offshore islands, which were excluded in September, 1954, from the coverage of the Manila Pact. It was not clear whether the United States would defend the offshore islands against a Communist attack. If it did, serious strains would be created in its relations with the neutrals and many of its allies, Britain in particular. If it did not, serious strains would be created in its relations with the Republic of China and perhaps with other Asian allies as well, notably Thailand.

On August 1, 1954, Chou En-lai returned triumphally to the CPR from Geneva via Eastern Europe and the Soviet Union. This was Chinese Red Army Day, and the speeches contained more than the usual talk about the "liberation" of Taiwan. On August 11, Chou inserted in an important speech on foreign relations a long passage accusing the United States and the Republic of China of plotting to attack the CPR. One of the "tasks now before us," he said, was "to take determined action on the liberation of Taiwan so as to safeguard China's sovereignty and territorial integrity. . . ."[8] The last phrase may well have been chosen in the hope of throwing upon the United States the onus of violating its own principle of the Open Door by allegedly interfering in China's internal affairs. Chou's pronouncement was echoed a few days later in a manifesto issued by the political parties and major mass organizations of the CPR, including the Taiwan Democratic Self-Government League.[9]

On September 3, Communist artillery began a heavy shelling of Quemoy. On September 7 the Nationalists retaliated with large-scale air attacks against the mainland but discontinued them about a month later, evidently at American request.[10] In December the Communists began to blockade the Tachens, the northernmost of the offshore island groups held by the Nationalists. At this time there was a considerable difference of opinion within the United States government as to what to do. General Ridgway, who believed that the Communist dispositions were more probably defensive than offensive in purpose, opposed any commitment of American forces to the defense of the offshore islands, as did some others.[11]

The outcome was that in December the United States and the Republic of China signed a mutual defense agreement covering Taiwan and any other Nationalist-controlled areas (meaning the offshore islands) to which coverage might later be extended by common agreement. The Nationalists evidently thought they were being offered a guarantee of the defense of the remaining offshore islands in exchange for an evacuation of the vulnera-

---

[8] Chou, *loc. cit.*, p. 4.

[9] "On the Liberation of Taiwan: Joint Declaration of All Democratic Parties and People's Organizations of the People's Republic of China," August 22, 1954 (in supplement to *People's China*, September 1, 1954).

[10] *The New York Times*, September 8; October 8, 9, 1954.

[11] Matthew B. Ridgway, *Soldier: The Memoirs of Matthew B. Ridgway*, New York: Harper, 1956, pp. 278–279.

ble Tachens.[12] This turned out not to be necessarily the case; the so-called Formosa Resolution, passed by both houses of Congress late in January, 1955, authorized the President to defend the offshore islands only if he judged a Communist attack on them to be part of an attack on Taiwan. This was perhaps not a very significant proviso, since the CPC has never admitted publicly that operations against the offshore islands have any meaning except as part of the effort to "liberate" Taiwan. In any case, the Nationalists evacuated the Tachens in February, with the aid of the Seventh Fleet.

Meanwhile, on October 10, 1954, the CPR had sent a message to the United Nations alleging American aggression against Taiwan and asking that the General Assembly urge the Security Council to call for a complete American withdrawal from the Taiwan area.[13] The plea was made slightly more persuasive two days later, when it was announced that the Soviet Union would soon withdraw its last troops remaining on Chinese soil, the garrison at Port Arthur. The CPR's maneuver produced nothing more than an invitation, sponsored by New Zealand and passed by the Security Council, to the CPR to send a delegation to the United Nations to take part in the discussion of the situation in the Taiwan Straits. Although the CPR had accepted a comparable invitation in 1950, it declined this one on the ground that the United Nations had never seated the CPR or taken any action on its numerous complaints of American aggression.[14] Instead, the General Assembly voted in December, 1954, to ask Dag Hammarskjold to seek the release of all United Nations personnel still being held prisoner in the CPR. He visited the CPR in January, 1955, but without much effect beyond conferring an increment of prestige on it.

The Nationalist evacuation of the Tachens did little to ease the tension in the Taiwan Strait. In fact, there was a growing expectation that the CPR would attack the Matsus and Quemoy in the spring. On March 8, Secretary Dulles, just returned from a SEATO Council meeting, warned that "if the Chinese Communists engage in open armed aggression this would probably mean that they have decided on general war in Asia."[15] Although this was an inaccurate analysis, its implications were clear and its deterrent value was probably considerable. Furthermore, the Soviet Union, preoccupied with events in Europe and the formation of the Warsaw Pact, was not even giving much verbal support to the CPR. Although the United States was in no mood to tolerate provocation, it had also made it clear that, the CPR's propaganda notwithstanding, it did not favor offensive action by the Nationalists against the mainland. The approach of the Bandung Conference was probably an additional factor in what seems to have been a decision taken in Peking late in March to ease the military pressure on the

[12] Alsop, *loc. cit.*, p. 87.
[13] Text in supplement to *People's China*, November 1, 1954.
[14] Chou En-lai, message of January 31, 1955, to Secretary General Dag Hammarskjold (New China News Agency dispatch, February 3, 1955).
[15] Text in *The New York Times*, March 9, 1955.

offshore islands.[16] This decision was not communicated to the world, any more than a comparable decision on Korea two years earlier had been. In fact, the United States apparently continued to expect an attack on the offshore islands down to the eve of the Bandung Conference,[17] even though there had been no major change in the disposition of Communist ground forces since the previous September.[18]

On April 23, at Bandung, Chou En-lai made his famous offer to negotiate with the United States on the relaxation of tension in the Far East, and in the Taiwan area in particular. Two days later Admiral Arthur W. Radford, Chairman of the Joint Chiefs of Staff and Assistant Secretary of State Walter S. Robertson arrived in Taipei, evidently with the mission of persuading the Nationalists to evacuate the remaining offshore islands that they controlled.[19] This President Chiang adamantly refused to do, probably because the Nationalist presence on the offshore islands is the best guarantee that both Peking and Taipei have against a "two Chinas" solution.[20] The mission left on April 26.

■ THE PEACEFUL APPROACH (1955–58)

After the Taiwan Strait crisis the Nationalists reinforced and fortified the offshore islands,[21] and the Communists began to build up their bases opposite Taiwan, with emphasis on airfield construction.[22] Nevertheless, there were no hostilities for a time, presumably not only for military reasons but also for political ones.[23] Not until the end of 1955 was the CPR certain that it could make no significant gains with respect to Taiwan through the Sino-American ambassadorial talks that began in August. In the meantime, the CPR launched a letter-writing campaign to high Nationalist officials and circulated rumors that a political deal was in the making.[24]

Toward the end of 1956 the Nationalist blockade of the coast, already shaken by the loss of the Tachens, was further undermined by the opening of a new port, Tsamkong or Chankiang, far to the south and out of reach of the blockade, and the extension of a rail line to Amoy, the port otherwise virtually blockaded by Quemoy.

Against this background, Communist political overtures to the Nation-

16 Cf. Alice Langley Hsieh, *Communist China's Strategy in the Nuclear Era*, Englewood Cliffs, N.J.: Prentice-Hall, 1962, p. 33.

17 Cf. *The New York Times*, March 26, April 18, 1955.

18 *The New York Times*, April 19, 1955.

19 *The New York Times*, April 26, 1955.

20 Alsop, *loc. cit.*, p. 88.

21 *The New York Times*, December 13, 1955.

22 *The New York Times*, November 15, 1955.

23 Cf. *The New York Times*, May 18, 1955.

24 Cf. Lewis Gilbert, "Peking and Taipei," *The China Quarterly*, no. 15 (July–September 1963), p. 61.

alists seemed to offer some chance of success. To lend force to its arguments, the CPR gave Quemoy on January 19, 1956, its heaviest shelling since September, 1954.[25] At the end of the same month, Chou En-lai in the course of an important speech said that, just as had happened in parts of the mainland, "there exists also the possibility of liberating Taiwan by peaceful means," although there was still the alternative of "liberation by means of war if necessary." "In China's history," he went on, "the Chinese Communist Party twice cooperated with the Kuomintang." He promised anyone from Taiwan who came back to the mainland amnesty and employment.[26] He did not add that such an individual could return to Taiwan if he wished; this important point was made shortly afterward in a speech by General Fu Tso-i, who had surrendered Peking to the Communists and had since served as Minister of Water Conservancy under them.[27] Other prominent non-Communists made similar statements at the same time.

At the beginning of June, Chou En-lai spoke optimistically of the chances for a peaceful "liberation" of Taiwan.[28] Later in the month he formally declared the CPR's willingness to negotiate on the question and invited the "Taiwan authorities" to send a delegation to any appropriate place to discuss "specific steps and conditions for the peaceful liberation of Taiwan."[29] Chou's tone was highly conciliatory; the only criticisms he made were of the United States, not the Kuomintang.[30]

Similar invitations, friendly remarks about Chiang Kai-shek, and perhaps specific unpublished proposals to the Kuomintang, continued into 1957. The CPC suggested that the United States might treat the Republic of China as it had treated Britain and France at the time of the Suez crisis.[31] These overtures were unaffected by numerous public Nationalist denials of interest or by the publication of Chiang Kai-shek's memoirs, which said in effect that the historical record proved the untrustworthiness of both the Soviet Union and the CPC.[32] The original, unpublished version of an important speech by Mao Tse-tung of February 27, 1957, on "contradictions" said that Chiang Kai-shek's works, presumably including his memoirs, would be published on the mainland and indicated some hope for an agreement between the CPC and the Kuomintang.[33] The speech was delivered on the tenth anniversary of an unsuccessful rising by Taiwanese against Nationalist control, Mao's implication probably being that if the Kuomintang did not come to terms with the CPC it would be overthrown or at least challenged by the Taiwanese.

---

25 Cf. *The New York Times*, January 22, February 7, 1956.

26 New China News Agency dispatch, January 30, 1956.

27 New China News Agency dispatch, February 3, 1956.

28 *The New York Times*, June 2, 1956.

29 Text in *The New York Times*, June 29, 1956.

30 Cf. *Christian Science Monitor*, June 30, 1956.

31 Cf. *The New York Times*, February 8, 1957.

32 Chiang Kai-shek, *Soviet Russia in China: A Summing-Up at Seventy*, New York: Farrar, Straus and Cudahy, 1957. The preface is dated December 1, 1956.

33 Cf. *The New York Times*, June 13, 1957.

On May 7, 1957, the United States and the Republic of China signed an agreement for the emplacement on Taiwan of Matador missiles, surface-to-surface missiles with a range of about six hundred miles and capable of carrying either nuclear or conventional warheads.[34] Here was a military threat against which the CPC could employ only political counteraction. It had several assets to work with: the nagging Nationalist suspicion that at the ambassadorial talks in Geneva the United States might make concessions to the disadvantage of the Republic of China, such as some sort of "two Chinas" agreement; American statements that the Nationalist armed forces were being equipped solely for defensive missions, or in other words not for a "return to the mainland";[35] the fact that although the United States had signed a status-of-forces agreement with Japan, a former enemy, it had not done so with the Republic of China; and the consequent acquittal by an American military court in May, 1957, of an American sergeant who had killed a Chinese on Taiwan. From these last two developments grew the famous Black Friday riots of May 24, 1957, in Taipei, in the course of which the American Embassy was systematically sacked. There is no reason to believe, however, that the Nationalists were seriously contemplating a deal with the Communists, and in any case the "anti-rightist struggle" that erupted immediately afterward on the mainland created a most unpropitious atmosphere for such a deal. Communist overtures to the Nationalists continued, nevertheless.

■ THE SECOND TAIWAN STRAIT CRISIS (1958)

In 1958, when the Soviet Union's foreign policy seemed to be calling its reliability as an ally increasingly into question, the CPR was faced with another security crisis in the Taiwan Strait. The situation was especially disturbing because it was known that the CPR was trying to develop nuclear weapons, which when acquired would make a Nationalist landing virtually impossible, but that it had not yet developed them. During this transitional period, the Nationalists' incentive to attack would be at a maximum. It began to look in 1958 as though the Nationalists, perhaps as the result of pressures exerted on the United States the previous year, were acquiring for the first time the ability to invade the mainland in force. This "Forward Look," as it was called, was the result of a greatly expanded American program of military aid to the Republic of China.[36] The Nationalist garrisons on the offshore islands had been heavily reinforced since 1955. To the perennially suspicious CPC, the situation seemed even more menacing because in the early months of 1958 the United States reduced its representation at the Geneva talks below the ambassadorial level. The CPC may have thought

---

[34] *Survey of International Affairs, 1956–1958*, p. 339.
[35] Cf. *Christian Science Monitor*, March 28, 1957.
[36] Cf. Kallgren, *loc. cit.*, p. 38.

that this was a step designed to provoke it into breaking off the talks; in any case, it did so. The CPC may also have suspected that President Chiang Kai-shek was anxious to "return to the mainland" before the expiration in 1960 of his second term, the last allowed to him under the Republic of China's constitution. The spectre haunting the CPC at this time was probably that of a Nationalist landing supported by American tactical nuclear weapons, a consideration that would seem to help explain the establishment of "backyard furnaces" and the expansion of the militia in the summer of 1958. In addition to security considerations, there were probably political ones as well, as usual. By exerting pressure at the main point available to it, the Taiwan Strait, the CPR might improve its chances of being included in discussions of such important international questions as disarmament and the Middle East.

Immediately after the conclusion of an important and unprecedented conference convened by the Military Committee of the CPC's Central Committee (May 27–July 22, 1958), the CPC launched a propaganda campaign proclaiming its readiness to "liberate" Taiwan "at any moment."[37] The CPC also began for the first time to base combat aircraft, including jets, on the airfields that it had constructed opposite Taiwan since 1955.[38] At no time during the crisis, however, was an invasion fleet or amphibious force concentrated in the vicinity of the Taiwan Strait. In mid-August *Red Flag* carried a militant article predicting the inevitable victory of the Chinese "people" in their struggle against "imperialism."[39]

It was against this menacing background that Khrushchev and Marshal Malinovsky flew secretly to Peking at the end of July. One of their main purposes was unquestionably to restrain what appeared to be the CPR's eagerness for a preemptive blow against the offshore islands. Obviously they did not succeed in dissuading the Chinese completely. They probably convinced them that the Soviet Union could give the CPR no more than token or propaganda support in a Taiwan Strait crisis and, in exchange perhaps for a pledge by the CPC that it would exercise even more than its usual tactical caution, offered the CPR defensive missiles to deter or repel Nationalist air attacks.[40]

The Communists launched a heavy artillery bombardment of Quemoy on August 23, the anniversary of the Hitler-Stalin pact and a date probably chosen to remind Khrushchev of the consequences of compromising with

---

[37] E.g., New China News Agency dispatch, July 23, 1958.

[38] Cf. *The New York Times*, August 18, 1958.

[39] Yü Chao-li, "The Forces of the New are Bound to Defeat the Forces of Decay," *Red Flag*, August 16, 1958 (in Richard L. Walker, *The Continuing Struggle: Communist China and the Free World*, New York: Athene Press, 1958, pp. 117–130).

[40] Cf. *The New York Times*, August 7, 1958, which is based on Polish sources. A later, much less credible Polish report (*The New York Times*, August 18, 1958) stated that the Soviet Union had agreed to supply the CPR with nuclear weapons and offensive missiles, as well as four more nuclear reactors.

"imperialism."[41] Five days later the CPR's "Fukien Front Command," a source selected to avoid involving the prestige of Peking, broadcast a message to the Nationalist commanders on Quemoy demanding their surrender, on penalty of an "imminent landing." Nothing was said in the message about any attack on Taiwan, so as not to give the United States a basis for invoking the Formosa Resolution as justification for coming to the defense of the offshore islands. The State Department, which was of course following the crisis with close attention and much anxiety, promptly issued a statement reminding the CPR and the world that the United States considered that the defense of the offshore islands was closely related to that of Taiwan, without indicating that the United States necessarily intended to commit its own forces to the defense of the offshore islands.[42]

By this time American vessels were preparing to convoy Nationalist ships as far as points only three miles from Quemoy, which the United States considered to be the limit of Chinese territorial waters. In the hope of obstructing this convoying, the CPR announced on September 4 that its territorial waters extended to a depth of twelve miles. This announcement was probably what evoked an important statement by Secretary Dulles, also on September 4. He said that "the securing and protecting of Quemoy and Matsu have become increasingly related to the defense of Taiwan" and strongly implied that, as other indications at the time also suggested, the United States would defend the offshore islands if the Nationalists proved unable to do so.[43] Since the Nationalists could only defend the offshore islands if they could keep them resupplied, Secretary Dulles was in effect warning the CPR not to interfere with American ships convoying Nationalist ships between the three- and twelve-mile limits. On the following day an early typhoon struck the Taiwan Strait and a Supreme State Conference convened in Peking. On September 6 Chou En-lai issued a statement that, while superficially taking a strong line with respect to the crisis, offered to resume ambassadorial talks with the United States.[44] This offer was promptly accepted by the United States,[45] and at that point any serious danger of a Sino-American conflict virtually disappeared.

Up to this time the CPR, in its statements regarding the crisis, had neither stressed the risk of nuclear war nor mentioned the Sino-Soviet alliance. In exchange for this display of tactical caution, the Soviet Union for its part had responded with statements of support for the CPR, but in a rather subdued vein and from anonymous or low-ranking sources; nothing

---

[41] The New York Times, August 24, 1958.

[42] Texts in The New York Times, August 29, 1958. The Communists issued a second warning a day later (The New York Times, August 30, 1958).

[43] Text in The New York Times, September 5, 1958.

[44] New China News Agency dispatch, September 6, 1958; text in The New York Times, September 7, 1958.

[45] The New York Times, September 7, 1958. Sino-American ambassadorial talks began at Warsaw on September 15.

was said about the claim to a twelve-mile limit, although the Soviet Union claimed an equal limit for its own territorial waters.[46] On September 7, after the danger of a Sino-American war and therefore of Soviet involvement in one had effectively passed, Khrushchev addressed a bellicose letter to President Eisenhower, in which he said among other things that "An attack on the People's Republic of China . . . is an attack on the Soviet Union."[47] On September 19 Khrushchev sent an even more bellicose letter, in which he rejected American suggestions that he try to restrain the Chinese Communists, accused the United States of interfering in Chinese affairs and of trying to create "two Chinas," warned that an atomic attack on the CPR would bring a "rebuff by the same means," stressed Soviet loyalty to the Sino-Soviet alliance, and urged the United States to stop supporting the Nationalists and recognize the CPR.[48] The United States returned this letter unanswered on the ground that it was offensive and out of order, and Soviet statements on the Taiwan Strait crisis promptly became more subdued.[49]

By this time the United States had sent eight-inch howitzers capable of firing atomic shells to Quemoy,[50] in addition to sending some $90 million worth of additional military aid to Taiwan.[51] Nevertheless, aerial fighting and artillery bombardment of Quemoy continued, and on September 22 Nationalist Premier Ch'en Ch'eng said that the Nationalists might launch attacks against Communist shore batteries unless the bombardment eased within two weeks.[52]

On October 5, the day before this deadline expired, Khrushchev issued a "clarification" of his position in which he said that the Soviet Union would involve itself in the conflict only in the event of an American, but not in the event of a Chinese Nationalist, attack on the CPR.[53] On the following day, Defense Minister P'eng Te-huai announced a one-week suspension of the bombardment, which in any case had tapered off considerably since early September, in order to allow resupply of Quemoy, provided there was no American convoying. In a further obvious effort to divide the Nationalists and the United States, he commented that "The day will certainly come when the Americans will abandon you."[54]

---

[46] John R. Thomas, "Soviet Behavior in the Quemoy Crisis of 1958," *Orbis*, vol. vi, no. 1 (spring, 1962), pp. 41–49.

[47] Text in *The New York Times*, September 9, 1958.

[48] Text in *The New York Times*, September 20, 1958.

[49] Thomas, *loc. cit.*, pp. 53–56.

[50] *The New York Times*, September 19, 1958.

[51] *The New York Times*, September 19, 1958.

[52] Tang Tsou, "The Quemoy Imbroglio: Chiang Kai-shek and the United States," *The Western Political Quarterly*, vol. xii, no. 4 (December, 1959), p. 1084. Note his valuable companion piece, "Mao's Limited War in the Taiwan Strait," *Orbis*, vol. iii, no. 3 (fall, 1959), pp. 332–350.

[53] Thomas, *loc. cit.*, pp. 57–58. At no time during the crisis did any Soviet military figure utter any threats (*ibid.*, pp. 58–61).

[54] Text in *The New York Times*, October 6, 1958.

A week later, evidently after some debate in Peking, the ceasefire was extended for an additional two weeks. P'eng Te-huai in announcing the extension remarked that "some Communists" might not understand it.[55] His reference was probably to Chief of Staff Su Yü, a capable soldier and artillery specialist who was transferred at this time to the post of Vice Minister of Defense, where he presumably could be kept under closer control. It seems reasonable to suppose that Su had predicted that artillery could interdict Quemoy and starve it out, and that he objected to the ceasefire as a political ending to what had probably been too political an operation for his taste from the beginning. On October 20 shelling was resumed, on the ground that American vessels were being used as escorts, but on October 25, the anniversary of the formation of the "Chinese People's Volunteers" in Korea, P'eng Te-huai announced that Quemoy would be shelled only on odd-numbered dates. Anna Louise Strong, a frequent spokesman for the CPC, explained its higher wisdom in the following way for the benefit of Soviet readers:[56]

> To take Tsinmentao [i.e., Quemoy] at present would isolate Taiwan and thus assist Dulles in his policy of building "two Chinas." It would deprive the Chinese on Taiwan of their hope of "return to the mainland," hopes that Peking will realize for them, but in its own way. It would throw Taiwan on the mercy of Washington. Hence Peking strengthens Tsinmentao and attaches it firmly to Taiwan, hoping later to take them both in a "package deal."

Miss Strong added that Communist capture of the offshore islands alone might lead to a United Nations trusteeship over Taiwan, and that the CPC intended to expel the United States from the Far East and the Western Pacific "by political and moral pressure, mixed with occasional 'shooting and not shooting,' by pressure within the lands of the Pacific and from all the world's people, without permitting the pressure to develop into a major war."

Although the CPC had not especially improved its political position with respect to the Nationalists, the United States, or the Soviet Union, and although it had suffered some tactical defeats and humiliations, it had demonstrated its willingness to take preemptive action when it feared a Nationalist attack. This demonstration was not without effect.

The United States did not try to persuade the Nationalists to evacuate the offshore islands after the second Taiwan Strait crisis, as it had after the first. In fact, the Nationalists proceeded to strengthen their defenses on the islands far beyond the level that had been achieved by 1958. On the other hand, after a visit by Secretary Dulles to Taiwan he and President Chiang Kai-shek issued a statement on October 23 reaffirming the purely defensive nature of the American military commitment to the Republic

---

[55] New China News Agency dispatch, October 13, 1958.

[56] Anna Louise Strong, "Chinese Strategy in the Taiwan Strait," *New Times* (Moscow), no. 46 (November, 1958), pp. 8–11; quoted in Hsieh, *op. cit.*, p. 128.

of China and saying that the basis for a liberation of the mainland from Communist rule lay in "the minds and the hearts of the Chinese people," not "the use of force."[57] Although high Nationalist officials promptly denied that the Republic of China had abdicated its right to invade the mainland, these words appeared to mean that it would not do so except in the event of large-scale popular risings against the CPC, and that the United States had no obligation to support any kind of Nationalist "return to the mainland." From the CPC's standpoint this represented a gain, or at least a clarification of the situation.

■ THE THIRD TAIWAN STRAIT CRISIS (1962)

The situation in the Taiwan Strait at the end of 1958 represented an impasse from the standpoint of both the Communists and the Nationalists. Only political means remained to the CPC, but even a "peaceful liberation" of Taiwan seemed out of the question as long as Mao Tse-tung and Chiang Kai-shek, who had made a career of fighting each other for three decades, remained at the helm. It was probably with this mainly in mind that the CPR announced early in December, 1958, that Mao would not be a candidate to succeed himself as Chairman of the CPR when his first term expired at the next National People's Congress. The hope presumably was that Chiang would reciprocate when his second (and last constitutional) term as President of the Republic of China expired in the spring of 1960, and that thereby at least two of the obstacles to an accommodation would be removed. As a matter of fact, Chiang did say, a few days after the announcement on the mainland, that he would not be a candidate for a third term, but when the time came he was nevertheless reelected after the appropriate constitutional provision had been voted into abeyance.

Both sides continued to strengthen their military positions in the Taiwan Strait after the crisis of 1958, and the shelling on alternate days continued — it was in fact intensified and the partial ceasefire suspended during President Eisenhower's visit to Taiwan in June, 1960. There was a period of tension in the Taiwan Strait, but no serious fighting, in mid-1959, during the Tibetan and Sino-Indian border crises. The CPR may have suspected the Nationalists of contemplating an attack, and Khrushchev's threatening statement to Governor Averell Harriman at that time in support of the CPR may have been intended partly to deter such an attack.

On the whole, however, the CPC reverted to political tactics after the crisis of 1958. It apparently made some overtures to the Nationalists shortly after the crisis.[58] During the next two or three years there were a number of statements by high CPC officials indicating that the CPC still

---

[57] Text in *The New York Times,* October 24 1958.
[58] *The New York Times,* November 23, 1958.

wanted the United States to withdraw from the Taiwan Strait but proposed to "liberate" Taiwan, not by force, but by some long-term political arrangement.[59]

The years 1961–62 had a symbolic significance for Taiwan, and to a lesser extent for West Irian (Dutch New Guinea) because they were the tercentennial of the "liberation" of Taiwan from Dutch "imperialism" by the Chinese pirate-admiral, Koxinga (Cheng Ch'eng-kung). This suggested the obvious possibility that the CPR might try to imitate Koxinga's example.

Even more obvious, however, was the opposite possibility. The CPR reached its lowest economic ebb in the early months of 1962, but it was clear that the effects of the improved 1961 harvest would soon make themselves felt. Food shortages and unrest were acute in the Canton area, which continued to export large amounts of nongrain foodstuffs to Hong Kong to earn foreign exchange. In May, 1962, some 100,000 persons from that area flooded into Hong Kong, although most of them were soon rounded up and shipped back to the CPR.[60] It seemed that the Republic of China might see reason to find that "the minds and the hearts of the Chinese people" had returned a verdict of guilty against the Chinese Communist regime and to attempt a "return to the mainland" before economic conditions began to improve. Furthermore, the CPR was preoccupied with tensions over its Soviet and Indian borders and over Indochina. Beginning with President Chiang Kai-shek's New Year's Day message to the Chinese people for 1962, a series of more than usually bellicose statements by high Nationalist officials predicted an imminent "return to the mainland." Additional manpower was conscripted into the armed forces, and on May 1 a special new tax was imposed to support the "return to the mainland."[61] A number of high American officials, including Averell Harriman and Allen Dulles, visited Taiwan in the early months of 1962.[62] Their purpose was presumably to restrain rather than encourage Nationalist eagerness for an attack on the mainland and a strong American policy in Indochina,[63] but the always suspicious CPC may have believed just the opposite. The same applies to the appointment in May of a new American ambassador to the Republic of China, Admiral Alan G. Kirk, who had had extensive experience with amphibious operations during the Second World War.[64]

During June, the CPR heavily reinforced its troops opposite Taiwan.[65] On June 23, the CPR issued a statement accusing the "Chiang Kai-shek

---

[59] Gilbert, *loc. cit.,* p. 62.
[60] Frank Robertson, "Refugees and Troop Moves—A Report from Hong Kong," *The China Quarterly,* no. 11 (July–September, 1962), pp. 11–114.
[61] *Ibid.,* p. 114.
[62] Cf. *The New York Times,* March 15, 1962.
[63] Cf. *The New York Times,* March 30, 1962.
[64] Cf. *The New York Times,* May 5, 1962.
[65] Robertson, *loc. cit.,* pp. 114–115; *The New York Times,* June 21, 1962.

gang" of "preparing, with the support and encouragement of U.S. imperialism, for a large-scale military adventure, an invasion of the coastal areas of the mainland" and assuring its opponents that if they attempted an invasion they would be crushed.[66] On the same day, at Chinese request, the Communist Chinese and American ambassadors met at Warsaw to discuss the crisis. In reply to Chinese charges of American support for an impending Nationalist invasion of the mainland, Ambassador John M. Cabot denied that the United States had given or would give any such support.[67] At his next press conference, President Kennedy in effect confirmed this assurance by stressing the defensive character of American commitments to the Republic of China.[68] On July 2 Khrushchev announced, with less emphasis than in 1958, that "Anyone who dares to attack the People's Republic of China will meet a crushing rebuff from the great Chinese people and the peoples of the Soviet Union and the whole socialist camp."[69]

After that the crisis subsided, the CPR having evidently scotched whatever plans the Nationalists may have had for an invasion. The military situation was substantially stalemated as far as major operations were concerned, and the Nationalists turned to intensified guerrilla and commando operations,[70] without of course renouncing their right to "return to the mainland" or their hopes for popular risings against the Communists.[71] The CPC for its part apparently found an atmosphere of moderate tension, which it helped to keep alive by such things as shooting down a Nationalist U-2 on September 9, 1962,[72] useful in keeping pressure on the Nationalists and on domestic and foreign opinion.[73]

On the whole, however, the CPC reverted to political maneuvers. In the summer of 1962, for example, elaborate rumors circulated of a secret political accommodation between the CPC and the Kuomintang, to take effect after President Chiang's death.[74] It seems likely, in fact, that the next major development in the situation may occur after the death of the one or the other top Chinese leader, and that it may make a substantial difference which one dies first.

---

[66] New China News Agency dispatch, June 23, 1962.

[67] The New York Times, June 27, 1962.

[68] The New York Times, June 28, 1962.

[69] The New York Times, July 3, 1962.

[70] Cf. "Guerrilla War Hits Red China," U.S. News and World Report, March 4, 1963, pp. 40–44, which includes an interview with Chiang Ching-kuo.

[71] Cf. The New York Times, July 13, 1963.

[72] The New York Times, September 10, 1962.

[73] Cf. The New York Times, August 22, 1962.

[74] Gilbert, loc. cit., p. 63.

11

Border Problems and Policy I

The two-thousand year history of the Chinese empire is unique, among other respects, in that it was an empire that expanded and contracted its frontiers in a more or less cyclical fashion but never wholly collapsed. The traditional frontiers were often not lines but zones of intermixture between Chinese settlement and the customary habitats of nomadic peoples owing a vague allegiance to the Chinese emperor. Much as no Chinese government since 1911 has conceded the right of Chinese to give up Chinese nationality — until the CPR did so in 1954 — so the Chinese seem traditionally to have been unwilling to concede that territory once gained by the Chinese empire could ever be permanently lost, even if it was formally ceded to a foreign power.[1] The CPC has recently indicated that it regards most or all of the nineteenth-century treaties ceding territory of the Manchu empire to "imperialist" countries, including Russia, as invalid and has implied that it might try to renegotiate those treaties.[2] Even though it is obvious that such statements are more a bargaining device than a serious statement of intent, there can be no doubt that the CPR's border policy is an important subject that causes its neighbors and the world much concern.

■ **THE SINO-INDIAN BORDER: THE BACKGROUND**

The Sino-Indian border has been by far the most important and controversial sector of the CPR's land frontier, at least until very recently.

The northern states and territories of the Indian subcontinent border on two regions of Greater China, Sinkiang and Tibet. The northern frontier of Kashmir with Sinkiang, as far east as the vicinity of the Karakoram Pass,

---

[1] For this idea I am indebted to Mr. O. Edmund Clubb of Columbia University.
[2] "A Comment on the Statement of the CPUSA," *People's Daily*, March 9, 1963.

COMMUNIST CHINA'S SOUTH ASIA BORDER

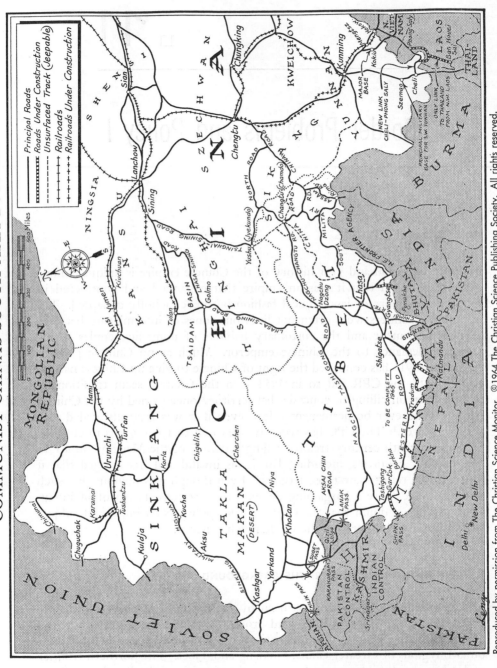

has never been clearly and satisfactorily defined in an international agreement.[3] There are three relevant lines west of the Karakoram Pass. One is the frontier claimed by the British and still accepted by much of the rest of the world, which runs roughly northwest and southeast about fifty miles north of the pass. The CPR claims a frontier running roughly parallel with the British one but forty to fifty miles farther to the south and west, and including a number of passes. The frontier claimed by India sags southward from the British as it proceeds to the east, although it includes the passes just mentioned, until it approaches the frontier claimed by the CPR in the vicinity of the Karakoram Pass. Whichever of these lines one considers to be the true frontier, it separates Sinkiang from territory that, although claimed by India as well as Pakistan, lies on the Pakistani side of the Kashmir ceasefire line. It is therefore more a theoretical than an actual object of controversy between India and the CPR. There does not appear to be much basis for an abstract judgment among these three lines. It may be relevant, however, to point out that the authority of the Manchus was extended to Sinkiang almost a century before that of the British was extended to Kashmir, although the Manchus did not make Sinkiang into a Chinese-style province of their empire until 1884.

Not far east of the Karakoram Pass the boundary becomes one with Tibet rather than with Sinkiang. Tibet had a vassal relationship with successive Chinese dynasties from the thirteenth century and was under fairly effective Manchu control from the mid-eighteenth century, long before British power was extended to the Himalayan region, until about the middle of the nineteenth century. The spiritual authority of the Dalai Lama in Lhasa was recognized, at least vaguely, not only by the Tibetans north of the Himalayan ridgeline but by many of the peoples living to the south of it in Ladakh, Nepal, Sikkim, Bhutan, and the northern edges of the Northeast Frontier Agency. These peoples practiced lamaist Buddhism, like the Tibetans, and were related to them. The yak, the characteristic and indispensable Tibetan animal, prefers not to go below 12,000 feet, and this contour marks roughly the southern limit of Tibetan habitation on the slopes of the Himalayan system to the south of the main ridgeline.

Obviously Tibetan, lamaist peoples to the south of the ridgeline were vulnerable to conquest or domination by stronger peoples living closer to the Northern Indian Plain. One of these was the Hindu Gurkhas, who occupied what is now Nepal shortly after the middle of the eighteenth

---

[3] Alfred P. Rubin, "The Sino-Indian Border Disputes," *The International and Comparative Law Quarterly*, vol. 9 (January, 1960), pp. 103–104. This is by far the most detailed and objective account of the historical and legal aspects of the dispute of which I am aware. L. C. Green, "Legal Aspects of the Sino-Indian Border Dispute," *The China Quarterly*, no. 3 (July–September, 1960), pp. 42–58 (see also the correspondence in ensuing numbers) is useful but not as good. Other accounts tend to be uncritically unfavorable to one side or the other. For the official Indian and Chinese cases, see *Report of the Officials of the Governments of India and the People's Republic of China on the Boundary Question*, New Delhi: Ministry of External Affairs, 1961.

century and extended their authority approximately to the Himalayan ridgeline. When they crossed the ridgeline and invaded Tibet in 1790–92, they were defeated and driven out by the Tibetans and the Manchus.[4] They then became vassals of the Manchus. After some defeats by the still stronger British, the Nepalese also accepted British protection about two decades later. Farther to the west, by 1842 Ladakh had been conquered by the Dogra dynasty of Kashmir, which gave its allegiance to the British soon afterward.[5]

As the British advanced gradually into the Himalayan region in the nineteenth century, they had two main interests in the territory beyond the ridgeline: they wanted to trade, and they wanted their Indian subjects to be able to trade, with Sinkiang and Tibet; and they wanted to protect their territories and the passes leading into them against possible threats from the Russians and Afghans in the northwest and from the Chinese (or Manchus) in the northeast. The Manchus were in an advanced state of decline during the second half of the nineteenth century, however, and offered no particular threat. Accordingly, Lord Curzon, the masterful Viceroy of India (1898–1905) tried through the Younghusband Expedition (1903–04) to eliminate not only Manchu but a degree of Russian influence from Tibet and make it into a virtual British protectorate.[6] The main result was that in 1910 the dying Manchu dynasty strongly reasserted its authority as against the Dalai Lama, who now appeared to be a British puppet, and occupied Lhasa with troops.[7]

Apart from some small areas, mainly passes, in the sector between Kashmir and Nepal, there are two main regions in dispute between the CPR and India, as distinct from the other Himalayan states. One is an area that India claims as part of Ladakh, consisting mainly of the barren Aksai Chin plateau. The other is the area known in British and Indian terminology as the Northeast Frontier Agency and lying between the Himalayan ridgeline east of Bhutan and the southern edge of the foothills overlooking the Brahmaputra Valley. Since it is not seriously disputed by any government that Tibet has never been fully independent in modern times and has always been under Chinese (or Manchu) suzerainty if not outright sovereignty, the only basis for rejecting the Chinese claim to the two areas just mentioned would be an argument that they had never been part of Tibet or had been detached from it by valid international agreements.

The British first occupied Aksai Chin and nearby portions of Ladakh

---

[4] Camille Imbault-Huart, "Histoire de la conquête du Nepal par les Chinois sous le règne de Tc'ie Long (1792), *Journal asiatique*, 7th series, vol. xii (1878), pp. 348–377.

[5] Margaret W. Fisher, Leo E. Rose, and Robert A. Huttenback, *Himalayan Battleground: Sino-Indian Rivalry in Ladakh*, New York: Praeger, 1963, pp. 44–59. This study contains much valuable information but must be used with great care, since the interpretation is uncritically pro-Indian at most points.

[6] Alastair Lamb, *Britain and Chinese Central Asia: The Road to Lhasa, 1767 to 1905*, London: Routledge and Kegan Paul, 1960, pp. 327–330.

[7] *Ibid.*, pp. 330–331.

about 1870. The question of whether they considered that the Manchu dynasty and Tibet had any rights to the area is uncertain and academic. At that time the British were interested in establishing contact with and sending aid to Yakoob Beg, a Turkish adventurer then in control of western Sinkiang and in revolt against the Manchus, and at odds with the Russians. The British hoped to maintain Yakoob Beg as a buffer between themselves and the Russians and the Manchus, but the latter crushed him a few years later.[8] By the end of the century, Anglo-Russian tension had made the British anxious to clarify what they knew to be an obscure situation and to delimit the entire Sino-Kashmiri border for the first time. In 1899, therefore, the British proposed to the Manchus (not to the Tibetan authorities) a frontier that to the west of the Karakoram Pass was similar to the one claimed by India today, but that to the east of the pass dropped down to concede to the Manchus about half of the area currently in dispute. The letter was never acknowledged.[9] In the same year, a customary tributary mission seems to have been sent from Ladakh to Lhasa, presumably with British knowledge and consent. Since no subsequent attempts were made, prior to the coming to power of the present Indian and Chinese regimes, to define this portion of the frontier, it appears that the CPR's claim that the entire Sino-Indian border has never been defined (meaning, apparently, neither delimited nor demarcated) is substantially true with respect to the Sino-Kashmiri frontier. In particular, the Manchus appear to have had some valid claims, through Tibet, in Ladakh, claims that co-existed with other British claims, and neither the Manchus nor any later Chinese government has ever abandoned those claims.[10]

In the eastern sector, British influence began to make itself felt in the late nineteenth century. The area was treated essentially as an unadministered tribal territory until about 1944, when the British occupied it in force for the first time because of Japanese offensives along the Indo-Burmese frontier and in South China. As late as 1922, a map included in the papers prepared for the use of the American delegation to the Washington Conference showed the area as falling within the administrative frontiers of Tibet.[11]

The first serious effort to define the Indo-Tibetan frontier in this area was made shortly after the fall of the Manchu dynasty, the expulsion of its agents by the Tibetans, and the establishment of the Chinese Republic, all of which occurred in 1912. The Chinese Republic was anxious to extend its authority to Tibet. The British preferred to keep Chinese power as far as possible from the Indian frontier and therefore wanted to partition Tibet,

---

[8] Cf. Fisher, Rose, and Huttenback, *op. cit.,* p. 64.

[9] R. A. Huttenback, "A Historical Note on the Sino-Indian Dispute over the Aksai Chin," *The China Quarterly,* no. 18 (April–June, 1964), pp. 201–207.

[10] Cf. Rubin, *loc. cit.,* pp. 120–125.

[11] *Ibid.,* pp. 105–109. The Republic of China protested the entry of British troops into the Northeast Frontier Agency in 1944.

as Mongolia was then being partitioned by agreement between the Chinese and the Russians, into an inner zone (from the standpoint of China) under Chinese administration and an outer zone under Chinese suzerainty — although aspiring to independence — but under indigenous administration. The outer zone would be open respectively to Russian and British influence.

Accordingly the British convened the Simla Conference (1913–14), to which the Tibetans and the Chinese Republic each sent a delegation, the latter rather reluctantly. At the conference the British tried to settle two main issues of interest to them: the frontier between inner and outer Tibet, and the frontier between Tibet and India to the east of Nepal. The first frontier was settled by negotiations among the three delegations. The second was settled solely between the British and the Tibetans, the justification presumably being that only outer Tibet was involved. In return for British efforts to keep as much of Tibet as possible autonomous with respect to China, the Tibetans allowed the British to draw the Indo-Tibetan frontier as they pleased. This was the famous McMahon Line, which was drawn roughly along the Himalayan ridgeline and had its eastern terminus at the point considered by the British to mark the trijunction of the Tibetan, Burmese, and Northeast Frontier Agency frontiers. This point was to the north of an important pass, Diphu Pass, which was therefore considered to be on the frontier between Burma and the Northeast Frontier Agency. The Chinese government promptly protested that it would recognize no agreements on Tibet concluded solely between the British and the Tibetans. The Chinese delegate nevertheless signed some of the maps and documents that issued from the conference, but the Chinese government refused to ratify the Simla Convention. Although the only reason it gave for its refusal was that it objected to the frontier between inner and outer Tibet as being too far to the east and north, there can be little doubt that it also objected to the way in which the McMahon Line had been decided on, even if not to the actual location of the line. No Chinese government has ever ratified the Simla Convention or formally recognized the McMahon Line as a valid boundary.[12] The British did not publish the text of the Simla Convention until 1936 in the hope that the Chinese would decide to ratify it. The attached maps were published for the first time by the Government of India in 1960,[13] and then by the CPR in 1962.[14]

---

[12] Cf. Fisher, Rose, and Huttenback, *op. cit.*, pp. 75–77, which however is misleading as to the Chinese position. A more nearly accurate version of the latter has been presented by the CPR in *Report of the Officials . . ., op. cit.*, pp. CR-20–CR-24. In the Anglo-Russian Convention of 1907 both sides had agreed not to negotiate with Tibet except through the Chinese government (then still controlled by the Manchu dynasty).

[13] *Atlas of the Northern Frontier of India*, New Delhi: Ministry of External Affairs, January 15, 1960, Maps 21–24.

[14] *The Sino-Indian Boundary Question* (*Enlarged Edition*), Peking: Foreign Languages Press, 1962, Reference Map 6 (two sheets). The two differ in that the Chinese

The maps used at the Simla Conference were based on inaccurate surveys. The CPR claims, apparently with justification, that at some time after 1914 the McMahon Line was moved three minutes of latitude farther north at its western end.[15] If so, it was done because the ridge at the higher latitude proved to be higher than the ridge at the lower latitude, not lower as was thought in 1914; in general, the McMahon Line followed the highest ridgeline, which in that area is known as the Thangla Ridge. On the other hand, at some time after 1914 the McMahon Line was dropped slightly to the south at a point on its central sector, so as to put the village of Migyitun within Tibet.[16] It may be that these changes were made shortly after October, 1947, when the Tibetan authorities startled the newly independent Government of India by asking for a vast but rather vague rectification of the boundary in favor of Tibet.[17] The changes do not appear to have been communicated to China at the time.

As far as the customary and legal aspects of the Sino-Indian boundary question are concerned, it seems fair to say that we are confronted with a complex array of overlapping claims, and that there is no adequate basis for a clearcut choice between claims to a number of the areas in dispute, let alone to the entire frontier. In some areas, both claims seem to have roughly equal validity; in other areas, it is possible that neither side has a valid claim.[18] The confusion arises largely because of the imposition by the British, and later by others, of modern concepts of international law and territorial sovereignty on areas where they had never been known before, and where they cut across a complex tangle of customary relationships and obligations operating, to a degree at least, across the Himalayan ridgeline in both directions. The whole issue has never been particularly important or controversial except at times when, and to the extent that, a military threat in one or both directions was thought to exist in the Himalayas. This has obviously been the case since 1950.

A good index to the general confusion is the contradictory maps published by both sides. The fluctuations in the Chinese claim, as shown on various official and semiofficial Chinese maps, have been pointed out by the Indians[19] and are fairly widely known; the latest one occurred in 1960,

---

version shows the signatures and seals of the British and Tibetan plenipotentiaries and some of the place names in Tibetan writing, whereas the Indian version does not. If the CPR added these touches itself, it presumably did so to emphasize the fact that the McMahon Line was agreed on solely between the British and the Tibetans, without Chinese participation.

[15] Cf. *ibid.*, Reference Map 5.

[16] Nehru letter of September 26, 1959, to Chou En-lai (text in Indian White Paper I, p. 44).

[17] Cf. *ibid.*, p. 39.

[18] Cf. Rubin, *loc. cit.*, pp. 108, 117, 120.

[19] E.g., *Atlas of the Northern Frontier* . . . , *op. cit.*, Maps 17, 29, 30, 32, 33, 34, 35, and 38.

when the CPR advanced somewhat the frontier it was claiming in the Ladakh area, apparently to protect a newly built military highway.[20]

Much less widely known are the fluctuations in the Indian maps. In the autumn of 1963, I examined all the official maps of India that had been published both before and after 1947 and were then available in the Map Reading Room of the Library of Congress. No map published before 1954, the year in which the Government of India realized that it had a serious frontier dispute on its hands, shows without any reservations the entire boundary now claimed by India. The details of the British (pre-1947) maps need not be discussed, since they are of less interest than the Indian (post-1947) maps. A map dated 1948 shows the McMahon Line, but with the same symbols as the border between India and Pakistan, which is labeled "not demarcated as an international boundary." No line at all is shown for the outer border of Kashmir, which is labeled "Boundary Undefined." No border is shown in the area just to the southeast of Kashmir and down to Nepal, between Uttar Pradesh and Tibet. A map published in 1950 shows the outer border of Kashmir and the rest of the border down to Nepal as a color wash, without a line, and also labels it as "Boundary Undefined." It is not surprising that none of these maps appears in the atlas on the border dispute published by the Government of India.[21]

There seems to be ample justification, therefore, for the statement[22] that

> While the Chinese claims seem in some cases to be based on unclear grounds, an examination of the incidents which have occurred so far [i.e., down to 1959] between China and India appears to confirm the assertion that on the whole the claims conform to colourable views of legal right which have not perhaps always been given due weight by the Indian Government or the world Press.

This is not to say that an impartial observer can condone the ways in which, or the reasons for which, the CPR has pressed its boundary claims.

As already suggested, the main significance of the Sino-Indian border dispute is strategic. Until 1947, the dominant influence in the Himalayan region was of course that of the British raj. The ability of a power based in the Indian peninsula to exert influence on and to the north of the Himalayas, in a direction exactly the opposite of the one in which such influence had usually been exerted in the traditional past, is to be explained by the comparative absence of strong powers north of the mountains — apart from Russia or the Soviet Union, which after 1900 was generally preoccupied elsewhere — and the fact that Britain was a sea power with vast economic and military resources outside India that could to a degree be brought to bear in the Himalayas when necessary.

---

[20] Cf. map in Huttenback, *loc. cit.*, p. 207.
[21] *Atlas of the Northern Frontier . . .*, *op. cit.*
[22] Rubin, *loc. cit.*, p. 125.

The withdrawal of British power from the Indian subcontinent naturally tended to change the power balance in Asia. The emergence of a strong Communist regime in China in 1949 and its invasion of Tibet in 1950–51 changed the balance even further. The advantage now lay north, not south, of the Himalayas.

To some extent, the Sino-Indian border dispute is one over the control of strategic passes. Control of a pass can of course be used to facilitate invasion, as well as peaceful penetration, of the area beyond. On the other hand, control of a pass can also be used to deny someone on the other side access to one's own territory.

It seems most unlikely that either India or the CPR has any serious intent to invade, in any formal, overt way, what it concedes to be the territory of the other. Each side, however, undoubtedly fears subversive activity by the other: the Chinese by the Indians in Tibet, the Indians by the Chinese in the small Himalayan states and the northern fringes of India. The portions of the Himalayan region claimed by the CPR and India are inhabited largely by minority peoples over whom the hold of the CPR or India, as the case may be, is none too secure. In such a situation, subversive activity by an outside power could have a marked effect. The extent to which this sort of activity has actually been a problem will be commented on later. In short, the Sino Indian border dispute is essentially a struggle for political and military ascendancy in the Himalayas.

In addition to the strategic aspect, the prestige of both countries, on an Asian and even worldwide scale, has become increasingly involved in the dispute. On the Indian side, this is doubly so in the western sector because Indians consider the territory in dispute to be part of the state of Kashmir, the general title to which is in dispute between India and Pakistan. To concede any of this territory to the CPR would involve the risk of ceding even more of it to Pakistan in a permanent partition of Kashmir, which Pakistan seems willing to accept but India does not, or at least did not under Nehru.

■ **THE SINO-INDIAN BORDER TO 1962**

When the Chinese Communist invasion of Tibet became known in October, 1950, the Government of India protested at what it considered a wrongful and unnecessary use of force. The CPR replied rudely that the Indian attitude was "affected by foreign influences hostile to China in Tibet." India replied with an amazed repudiation of the charge.[23]

Realizing that the balance of power in the Himalayas was being upset and that for the first time in many years its northern border might be in danger, India began to strengthen its political and military defenses in the

---

[23] Texts of notes in *The New York Times*, November 3, 1950.

area. It took measures to increase its influence in Nepal and to bring Bhutan and Sikkim under more effective protection. In some cases, such as the Nagas in the hills of Assam, this forward policy tended to stir up trouble. A number of devices were employed, including reminders to the Lamaist peoples of the Himalayan region that Buddhism was of Indian origin. India's limited military capabilities naturally kept the effectiveness of these measures from being complete.[24]

As far as the two major disputed regions were concerned, India occupied the Northeast Frontier Agency, although not quite up to the McMahon Line. Nehru reaffirmed India's position that the line was the border in this area. Chinese troops did not cross the line at that time. In the west, it was another story. Chinese troops entering western Tibet from Sinkiang used Aksai Chin as the only passable route.[25] Chinese troops remained in at least intermittent control of the area without any serious Indian challenge on the ground. In fact, India did not learn of the partial Chinese occupation of Aksai Chin until 1958. Neither Chinese nor Indian troops advanced to the border claimed by the CPR in this sector. In short, generally speaking the Indians occupied the easternmost of the major disputed areas, and the Chinese the westernmost, and in both sectors there was a no man's land between the troops of the two sides.

The following years were ones of mounting tension in the Himalayan region. Bad relations between India and Pakistan, especially over Kashmir, contributed to a turn by Pakistan toward the United States, beginning in 1951. This reorientation, which began to show results after the coming into office of the Eisenhower administration in the form of American military aid to Pakistan, so preoccupied India that it neither could nor would do much about the Sino-Indian border question.

There were many problems relating directly or indirectly to that question. The CPR published maps showing boundaries at variance with those claimed by India; to the Indians, this was "cartographic imperialism."

In eastern Tibet, the Chinese were building roads and bringing in large number of troops and civilian personnel, who after 1952 were fed partly with grain imported from India. This growth of Chinese influence was inevitably accompanied by numerous infringements of the autonomy that the CPR had promised Tibet when the latter's "liberation" was proclaimed in 1951. In the spring of 1952 the Chinese imported their tame Panchen Lama into Tibet Proper (the Lhasa area), where he had never been before, obviously as a counterweight to the pro-Indian and pro-Western Dalai Lama. These measures touched off a revolt in eastern Tibet in 1952–53.[26] The CPR established the Chinese Buddhist Association in the spring of

[24] Cf. A. R. Field, "Bhutan, Kham, and the Upper Assam Line," *Orbis*, vol. iii, no. 2 (summer, 1959), pp. 92–100.
[25] Chinese note to India, December 26, 1959 (text in Indian White Paper III, p. 67).
[26] George N. Patterson, *Peking Versus Delhi*, New York: Praeger, 1964, pp. 157–158.

1953, to control lamaists as well as other kinds of Buddhists. Not only was the CPR propagandizing the Tibetans, but some Tibetans seem to have been used as Chinese agents in Himalayan areas outside Tibet. On September 15, 1952, at Chinese request, India changed its mission in Lhasa, which was a political one inherited from the British and accredited to the Tibetan authorities, into a consulate general accredited to the central government in Peking. This was a considerable loss of face for India in its rather ineffective efforts to protect its own security by maintaining a presence in Tibet and exerting some sort of restraint on Chinese policies there.[27]

We have already seen that in early 1953 the CPR intensified its involvement in the Indochinese war and became active along its frontiers with Burma and Laos. Farther to the west, there were other situations that, while apparently not of Chinese origin, offered possibilities for Chinese troublemaking at India's expense. There were growing revolts against India among the Nagas, beginning in 1952.[28] There were also revolts early in 1952 in Nepal in which one K. I. Singh was prominently involved. When defeated, Singh fled to the CPR by way of Tibet.[29]

India's approach to the Chinese aspect of its Himalayan problems was to treat the CPR with reasonableness and moderation, in the hope of reciprocity. India also wanted to put trade and pilgrimages between India and Tibet on a more regular and satisfactory footing. A mission arrived in the CPR with these purposes in mind at the end of 1953. It was a fairly favorable time for negotiations. The approaching termination of the disposition of the prisoners taken in Korea, in which process India was heavily involved, was about to deprive India of some of its usefulness to the CPR. On the other hand, the CPR's shift to a foreign policy of "peaceful coexistence" and its desire for a favorable Indian attitude on the Indochinese question gave the Indians some bargaining power.

The result was an agreement signed on April 29, 1954, regulating trade and travel between India and "the Tibet region of China." The Indians were given a pledge of nonaggression, in the form of the "Five Principles of Peaceful Coexistence." Since both sides realized that there was a boundary dispute of sorts between them but preferred not to discuss it at that time, the agreement merely named six passes near the middle sector of the frontier (west of Nepal) as routes for trade and pilgrimages, without specifying in whose territory they lay.[30] At the same time, the Indians agreed to withdraw their military escorts from two Tibetan towns where they had been stationed and to turn over their postal, telegraph, and telephone services and rest houses in Tibet to the CPR.[31]

---

[27] Fisher, Rose, and Huttenback, *op. cit.*, p. 83; C. H. Alexandrowicz, "India and the Tibetan Tragedy," *Foreign Affairs*, vol. 31, no. 3 (April, 1953), pp. 499–500.

[28] Patterson, *op. cit.*, pp. 183ff.

[29] *Ibid.*, pp. 140–142.

[30] Text of agreement in Indian White Paper I, pp. 98–101.

[31] *Ibid.*, pp. 102–105.

The fact that neither side had yet adequately explored the frontier area and the growing realization that a boundary dispute existed led to increased patrolling and exploration by both sides from the middle of 1954. In June, troops of both sides met on a disputed area in the middle sector known to the Indians as Bara Hoti and to the Chinese as Wuje. Two years later, after some further incidents in the same area, it was temporarily neutralized by common agreement, without either side abandoning its claim to the area.[32]

Meanwhile, Nehru had visited Peking in October, 1954. He raised the question of the border shown on Chinese maps but according to his own account was assured by Chou En-lai that the question was of no importance.[33]

At this time the CPC began to put increased pressure of several kinds on Tibet, under the guise of preparing it for "autonomy." This policy stirred up increasing discontent among the turbulent Khamba tribesmen in eastern Tibet. The Dalai Lama was in full sympathy with the Khambas, who went into revolt late in 1955, but he was not in a position to take action, especially since he had not yet passed the final examinations required by lamaism of a person in his position and therefore might have been deposed by his own church under Chinese pressure. While visiting India from November, 1956, to March, 1957, he asked for asylum, and it took the combined efforts of Nehru and Chou En-lai, who also was in India at the time, to persuade him to return to Tibet. Nehru promised to use his good offices to moderate Chinese policy in Tibet. According to Nehru, Chou told him that the CPR recognized the eastern end of the McMahon Line as the point of departure for its frontier with Burma and would recognize the line as its frontier with India.

Early in 1957, the CPC announced that "democratic reforms" (such as redistribution of monastic property and abolition of "feudal" labor obligations) would not be introduced into Tibet before 1962, and that most Chinese civilian cadres (but not troops) would be withdrawn. These promises applied only to Tibet Proper; it appears that most of the transferred cadres went to eastern Tibet, where they made life more difficult than ever for the Khambas. By the middle of 1958 the Khamba revolt and Chinese military counteraction had assumed major proportions, and the fighting had begun to spread to Tibet Proper.[34] The situation in Tibet was not only serious and important in its own right but had a virtually determining effect on the future course of the Sino-Indian border dispute. Until the fighting in Tibet became serious, it was the Indians who were the

---

[32] *Ibid.*, pp. 1–16.

[33] Cf. *Leading Events in India-China Relations, 1947–1962,* New Delhi: Ministry of External Affairs (?), 1962, pp. 4–5.

[34] George N. Patterson, "China and Tibet: Background to the Revolt," *The China Quarterly,* no. 1 (January–March, 1960), pp. 97–99.

more nervous; afterwards, it was the Chinese. To the CPC, the disputed and largely uncontrolled nature of the Sino-Indian frontier and the presence of units of the Indian Army near it seemed to offer all sorts of possibilities for collusion between the Tibetan insurgents and Indian "reactionaries," and perhaps others as well.[35]

Military action by the Khambas jeopardized Chinese communications with Tibet from the east as early as 1955 or 1956. Probably for this reason, the "People's Liberation Army" built a military highway across the Indian-claimed Aksai Chin Plateau, between western Sinkiang and Western Tibet, in 1956–57.[36] The Chinese do not appear to have established outposts to the south and west of the road, however, or at least none that were anywhere near the frontier claimed by the CPR. The Government of India seems to have learned of the definite existence of the new road from a Chinese map published in July, 1958.[37] It then protested on the ground that no applications had been received for visas for the personnel working on or using the road.[38] Two Indian patrols sent to reconnoiter in the vicinity of the road were detained by the Chinese for a month.[39] Obviously the security of the highway was a sensitive matter for the CPC in much the same way as the security of Tibet itself.

On December 14, 1958, Nehru initiated what was to prove an important, and to the student an enlightening, correspondence with Chou En-lai on the boundary question. Without referring to the highway, he gave in brief the Indian position on the boundary, which he described as "well-known and fixed." The points he made need not be summarized, since they have already been mentioned.[40]

Chou's reply of January 23, 1959, becomes relatively comprehensible if considered in the light of the fighting in Tibet, which he did not mention. He insisted that "the Sino-Indian boundary has never been formally delimitated" and said that the Aksai Chin highway (or, as the Chinese call it, the Sinkiang-Tibet highway) ran solely across Chinese territory. He denounced the McMahon Line as a "product of the British policy of aggression against the Tibet Region of China" and as illegal. He implied, nevertheless, that the CPR would stay on its own side of the line for the time being and not make a major issue of it, especially since Burmese interests were also involved. As for the boundary question as a whole, he proposed

---

[35] Cf. Chinese note to India of July 10, 1958, which alleges "subversive and disruptive activities against China's Tibetan region carried out in Kalimpong [in India, near Darjeeling] by American and Chiang Kai-shek clique special agents, Tibetan reactionaries and local special agents" (text in Indian White Paper I, pp. 60–62). The Government of India denied the charge (ibid., pp. 63–65).

[36] Shown in Atlas of the Northern Frontier . . . , op. cit., Map. 1.

[37] In China Pictorial, no. 95 (July, 1958), pp. 20–21; cf. Indian White Paper I, p. 46.

[38] Ibid., pp. 26–27.

[39] Ibid., p. 28.

[40] Text in ibid., pp. 48–56.

that, "as a provisional measure, the two sides temporarily maintain the status quo." He claimed to favor a settlement of the dispute through negotiations but said that the CPR could not alter its version of the boundary "without having made surveys and without having consulted the countries concerned." This apparently hinted at a Chinese intention to make the settlement a subject of discussion not only by India and the CPR but also by Burma and the other Himalayan states, all of which border on restless tribal areas in Tibet or Sinkiang. Of these, Pakistan was on bad terms with India and the others, including Burma, could be pressured by the CPR more easily than could India.[41] This in fact is roughly what the CPR has tried to do.

On March 22, when the Tibetan situation had reached the proportions of an open crisis, Nehru replied protesting Chou's assertion that the frontier was undelimited and rehearsing briefly the historical basis of the Indian position on the boundary. He implied that the CPR must evacuate any areas it might occupy on the Indian side of the frontier claimed by India (". . . if any possession has been secured recently, the position should be rectified.").[42] Thereafter the correspondence lapsed for several months.

Late in February, 1959, shortly before he was scheduled to pay what otherwise might have been a still riskier visit to Peking, the Dalai Lama took and passed his final examinations.[43] His position in Tibetan eyes was now secure, and it is significant that the CPC has never tried to engineer his deposition and replacement by someone else. On March 10, the increasingly unruly populace of Lhasa demonstrated in an effort to prevent the Dalai Lama's departure. On March 17, Chinese troops began to fire on the demonstrators, and the Dalai Lama fled with a bodyguard of Khambas. The CPC has insisted until recently that he was kidnaped, presumably in order to leave the way open for a reconciliation and his return. On March 19, heavy fighting broke out in Lhasa.[44] The Dalai Lama crossed the McMahon Line on March 31 and requested asylum, which was granted. Although the Indian government did not treat him as the head of a government in exile or support his pleas to the United Nations, since it did not recognize the independence of Tibet, it showed him every other mark of courtesy and sympathy. Indian public opinion was even more pro-Tibetan, and in Bombay on April 20 a picture of Mao Tse-tung was pelted with tomatoes and eggs.[45]

These developments as a whole shattered the façade of Sino-Indian

---

[41] Text in *ibid.*, pp. 52–54.

[42] Text in *ibid.*, pp. 55–57.

[43] *The New York Times*, March 1, 1959.

[44] Cf. Patterson, *loc. cit.*, p. 99, which is based on later statements by the Dalai Lama; the Chinese account (in *Concerning the Question of Tibet*; Peking: Foreign Languages Press, 1959, especially pp. 8–9) agrees on the basic facts but of course not on the interpretation.

[45] See Chinese protest and Indian reply in Indian White Paper I, pp. 70–72.

friendship that had been carefully maintained since 1954. The CPR evidently suspected that the Tibetan revolt was aided and supported by Indians, and it was convinced that American and Chinese Nationalist agents operating from bases in India were involved. The situation in Tibet, the CPR asserted, "is entirely an internal affair of China and we shall never permit interference from outside."[46] The CPC also insisted, in an editorial of May 6, that Nehru was wrong in the sympathy he had shown for the Tibetan insurgents, who were described as feudal reactionaries trying to impede an inevitable and beneficial revolution introduced by the CPC.[47] At that time, in reality, the CPC was tightening its control, repressing the insurrection with great brutality, and reintroducing "democratic reforms" with much vigor.

On May 16, the CPR's ambassador to India, P'an Tzu-li, made an important and interesting statement to the Indian Foreign Secretary. He began by repeating the CPC's version of the Tibetan fighting and insisted that Tibet was an "inalienable part of China's territory" and that no foreign power had a right to "make Tibet semi-independent or even to turn it into a sphere of influence of a foreign country or buffer zone." Assuming that these remarks reflected a genuine attitude, P'an may have feared that the Indian Army was thinking of taking advantage of the confusion in Tibet to try a repetition of the Younghusband Exposition of 1903. P'an went on to denounce the behavior of the Indian government and public opinion toward the Tibetan crisis and the flight of the Dalai Lama, in whose alleged abduction he implied India was involved. "The facts themselves," he said, "have completely overthrown the allegation that there is no Indian interference in China's internal affairs." He ended with a plea that India, for its own sake as well as the CPR's, do nothing to spoil what he described as the previously good relations between them:[48]

> The enemy of the Chinese people lies in the East — the U.S. imperialists have many military bases in Taiwan, in South Korea, Japan and in the Philippines which are all directed against China. China's main attention and policy of struggle are directed to the east, to the west Pacific region, to the vicious and aggressive U.S. imperialism, and not to India or any other country in the southeast Asia and south Asia. Although the Philippines, Thailand and Pakistan have joined the SEATO which is designed to oppose China, we have not treated those three countries as our principal enemy; our principal enemy is U.S. imperialism. India has not taken part in the Southeast Asia Treaty; it is not an opponent,

---

[46] Chinese note of March 22, 1959 (*ibid.*, p. 67).

[47] "The Revolution in Tibet and Nehru's Philosophy," *People's Daily*, May 6, 1959 (in *Concerning the Question of Tibet, op. cit.*, pp. 239–276). To some extent the CPR was attacking Nehru's work, *The Basic Approach*, which had already been criticized more politely by Pavel F. Yudin, the Soviet ambassador to the CPR, in *World Marxist Review*, vol. 1, no. 4 (December, 1958), pp. 38–54.

[48] Text in Indian White Paper I, pp. 73–76.

but a friend to our country. China will not be so foolish as to antagonize the United States in the east and again to antagonize India in the
West. The putting down of the rebellion and the carrying out of
democratic reforms in Tibet will not in the least endanger India. . . .
We cannot have two centres of attention, nor can we take friend for
foe. . . . Will you be agreeing to our thinking regarding the view that
China can only concentrate its main attention eastward of China, but
not south-westward of China, nor is it necessary for it to do so. . . . It
seems to us that you too cannot have two fronts. . . .

Despite its quaint English, the drift of this statement is clear enough. It
gives a good summary of Chinese declaratory policy at that time, and if
properly interpreted considerable insight into the actual policy. What was
evidently worrying the CPR the most was the possibility that it might be
faced with a more or less coordinated set of pressures on the Tibetan
frontier and in the Taiwan Strait, and it was pleading with India to withdraw or not to take part.

The CPR certainly had reason to be concerned about the situation in
Tibet. After the flareup of fighting in March, 1959, many thousands of
Tibetans, including a large number of male Khambas, escaped into Nepal
and India. There many of them mysteriously acquired arms and disappeared
back into Tibet.[49] From the CPC's standpoint, it was obviously necessary
to close the frontier and deprive the Tibetan insurgents of possible external
sources of aid and support. Chinese troops began to move forward in the
border region, and Indian troops began to do the same in areas where there
was a frontier with Tibet. This process, which continued into 1962, nar-
rowed without quite eliminating the no man's land between the two sides,
and at some points it produced significant contacts between the two armies
for the first time. In the west, the Chinese advanced approximately to the
line they then claimed, built a second highway just inside it (in 1959–60),
and then (in 1960) began to claim a frontier farther forward than the first
so as to give the new road additional protection.[50] In the east, Indian
border police began (in 1959) to establish checkposts along the McMahon
Line, including some at the western end in the area between the original
and adjusted locations of the line; these posts were turned over to the Indian
Army later in the year. In the overheated atmosphere in Peking, these
Indian moves apparently seemed to be a challenge to the CPR's right to
seal the border and a threat to aid the Tibetan insurgents.

On August 7, a minor clash occurred at Khinzemane, which lies in the
western sector of the frontier between the Northeast Frontier Agency and
Tibet and between the two versions of the McMahon Line.[51] A week

[49] George N. Patterson, "The Himalayan Frontier," *Survival*, vol. 5, no. 5
(September–October, 1963), pp. 207–208.
[50] Cf. map in Huttenback, *loc. cit.*, p. 207.
[51] Indian White Paper II, pp. 1–2.

before, incidentally, the Indian government had confirmed its "reactionary" character in the eyes of the CPC by ousting the Communist government of the state of Kerala the day after receiving a large economic aid commitment from the Soviet Union. A more serious clash took place at Longju, a point near the middle of this sector of the frontier and just south of Migyitun. After the fighting the Indian border police evacuated Longju, which was then occupied by Chinese troops. Each side claimed that Longju lay on its side of the McMahon Line. The Chinese claim does not appear to be valid, however, and the supposition that it was not seriously advanced is suggested by the fact that the Chinese evacuated Longju about a year afterward, allegedly on account of plague in the area. The Chinese occupation of Longju may have been aimed at deterring the Indians from moving up to the McMahon Line, and the claim that it was on the Chinese side of the McMahon Line may have been aimed at justifying both the Chinese occupation and a possible future Chinese crossing of the line in force, if it should seem necessary or useful. Another possible purpose was to get the Indians to fall back to the original McMahon Line at its western end.

These incidents naturally produced an uproar in both countries, differing accounts of what had happened, and mutual protests.[52] On September 8, Chou En-lai sent a belated reply to Nehru's letter of March 22. He repeated the general Chinese position on the frontier, including the generalization that it had never been delimited. He affirmed that "the Chinese Government absolutely does not recognize the so-called McMahon Line, but Chinese troops have never crossed that line." The Sino-Indian boundary problem as a whole he described as "a complicated question left over by history," and produced specifically by the fact that "Britain conducted extensive territorial expansion into China's Tibet region, and even the Sinkiang region." He said that Chinese troop movements near the frontier were "merely for the purpose of preventing remnant armed Tibetan rebels from crossing the border back and forth . . ." and pronounced the corresponding Indian movements unnecessary and provocative.[53] The idea that a frontier is invalid if originally fixed by "imperialism" is one with disturbing general implications, and it is perhaps not surprising that the Soviet Union issued the next day its celebrated statement of pained neutrality on the border question. The Sino-Soviet frontier, after all, is a product of tsarist "imperialism." A few days later Nehru flew to Afghanistan, where he later said he talked not only with Afghan officials but the Soviet ambassador.

Nehru apparently considered, not necessarily correctly, that this was the first time that Chou En-lai had put forward a clear and irreversible claim that the McMahon Line was invalid and the Northeast Frontier Agency belonged to China. His reply, on September 26, protested this position

---

[52] *Ibid.*, pp. 3–10.

[53] Text in *ibid.*, pp. 27–33; *Documents on the Sino-Indian Boundary Question*, Peking: Foreign Languages Press, 1960, pp. 1–13.

and went at great length into the history and geography of the frontier question and the recent clashes. He admitted that India had evacuated a post at Tamaden near the western end of the McMahon Line, because it was found to be north of even the revised line, and he requested a similar Chinese withdrawal from Longju. In one sentence he implied what was later to become the explicit Indian position, that no settlement could be reached or even discussed unless the Chinese first withdrew from all territory claimed by India, including of course the area of the two military highways in Aksai Chin: "No discussions can be fruitful unless the posts on the Indian side of the traditional frontier now held by the Chinese forces are first evacuated by them and further threats and intimidations immediately cease."[54]

Almost immediately after receiving this letter the Chinese also received a visit from Khrushchev, in the course of which he publicly urged them not to "test by force the stability of the capitalist system," and in private undoubtedly said much more. It is unlikely that he made much of an impression, and in any case the Chinese were certainly not willing to abandon or jeopardize their existing military highway across Aksai Chin or the second one, farther forward, which they were then apparently in the process of building. On October 20–21 occurred the most serious shooting incident to date. A party of Indians patrolling near the Kongka Pass, which lies near the trijunction between Tibet, Sinkiang, and Ladakh, and through which runs the second Chinese military highway, were fired on by Chinese troops. Nine Indians were killed, and ten were taken prisoner; the latter were released in mid-November, after being harshly treated.[55]

This episode of course created a greater furor than ever, both in the two countries involved and abroad. On November 4, not of course as a result of the Kongka Pass incident, it was announced that President Eisenhower would shortly visit eleven Asian and African countries, including India and Pakistan. To the CPR, it probably began to appear possible that the border dispute was bringing not only the Soviet Union but the United States closer to India, a very undesirable situation from the Chinese standpoint. There was a need for the CPR to give at least the appearance of being reasonable.

On November 7, Chou En-lai wrote another letter to Nehru. This was briefer and milder than his letter of September 8. He pretended that Nehru's letter of September 26 had proposed the maintenance of the status quo along the border, whereas what Nehru had actually said, or at least implied, was that the Chinese must evacuate all territory claimed by India as a precondition for negotiations. Having set up this straw man, Chou then expressed agreement with it. He further proposed that both sides withdraw their troops, but not their civilian personnel, twenty kilometers

---

[54] Text in *ibid.*, pp. 77–113; Indian White Paper II, pp. 34–52.
[55] *Ibid.*, pp. 13ff.

from "the so-called McMahon Line in the east, and from the line up to which each side exercises actual control in the west." He did not define this line or indicate whether it corresponded with the frontier claimed by the CPR. The tactical effect of this reasonable-sounding proposal would have been to eject the Indian Army from its outposts along the McMahon Line but to leave Chinese control of the two highways in Aksai Chin unchanged. On the other hand, the strategic effect would have been to set in motion a strong and perhaps decisive trend toward a compromise settlement of the dispute along at least de facto lines, much like the informal partition of Kashmir between India and Pakistan: India would keep the Northeast Frontier Agency, and the CPR most of Aksai Chin and the other territory it claimed in Ladakh. Although Chou was obviously not complying with Nehru's demand for evacuation of Indian-claimed territory as a prerequisite for talks, he proposed that the two men hold such talks "in the immediate future."[56]

Nehru's reply, on November 16, shows that he was aware that Chou had made an important if somewhat ambiguous proposal, one that he could neither accept nor reject out of hand. He ruled out the idea of a withdrawal from the McMahon Line and proposed instead that each side merely refrain from sending patrols forward. This of course would tend to stabilize and perpetuate the existing Indian control of the Northeast Frontier Agency. As for Aksai Chin, he proposed that each side withdraw behind the frontier claimed by the other. This would have necessitated no significant withdrawals by the Indians but would have deprived the Chinese of their two military highways. He implied that Chinese acceptance of these proposals, which would in effect have brought about a Chinese withdrawal from all territory claimed by India, was a prerequisite for talks between himself and Chou. It was the earlier demand in a slightly different guise.[57] The considerations that prompted Nehru to refuse to discuss what he must have known was the best Chinese offer he was likely to get without war probably included the atmosphere created by the Kongka Pass incident, a reluctance to create a precedent that might affect the Kashmir dispute with Pakistan, and of course a reluctance to back down from his earlier clearly implied position.

Chou En-lai's reply, on December 17, naturally painted the CPR's border policy in a more favorable light than it deserved. In addition, however, it made the important statement that since the Kongka Pass incident the Chinese side had stopped sending out patrols along the entire frontier, and not merely in the eastern sector as proposed by Nehru. He pointed out the one-sided character of Nehru's proposal and urged that the two premiers meet on December 26, Mao Tse-tung's birthday, either in the CPR or at

---

[56] Text in *ibid.*, pp. 45–46; *Documents on the Sino-Indian Boundary Question,* *op. cit.*, pp. 14–17.
    [57] Text in *ibid.*, pp. 129–138; Indian White Paper III, pp. 47–51.

Rangoon. He delivered a Parthian shot by asking whether India would apply Nehru's proposal on the western sector, for a withdrawal by each side behind the boundary claimed by the other, to the eastern sector as well; for the Indians to do so would of course mean to evacuate the Northeast Frontier Agency.[58]

Nehru's reply of December 21 was brief and curt. Understandably, he declined to hold talks with Chou on such short notice, but he proposed no alternate date. Nor did he comment on Chou's Parthian shot. He implied an unwillingness to negotiate at all: "How can we, Mr. Prime Minister, reach an agreement on principles when there is such complete disagreement about the facts?"[59]

On the day Chou had proposed for the talks, the CPR submitted in response to earlier Indian requests a statement of the historical basis of the Chinese case, as well as of the Chinese view of the location of the boundary, which the statement repeated had never been delimited. The statement pleaded once more for negotiations, but without specifying a date.[60]

On February 12, 1960, the Indian government replied with a comparable statement of its position on the boundary.[61] A week before, Nehru had written another letter to Chou En-lai. In it he said, with reference to the Chinese contention that the frontier had never been delimited, "On that basis there can be no negotiations." He added that "for the moment, I do not see any common ground between our respective viewpoints." Nevertheless, he suggested talks between the two premiers at New Delhi in the second half of March.[62] After some further correspondence, Chou agreed to come to New Delhi from April 19 to 25, that is to say immediately after the fifth anniversary of the opening of the Bandung Conference; this is of some significance because the CPR was trying to prove to the world that its at least declared willingness to negotiate was more in accord with the spirit of Bandung than was the Indian attitude.[63] Specifically, the CPR was probably trying to make it appear, when the predictable failure of the two premiers to agree occurred, that it was Nehru and not Chou who had been responsible.

The talks were a total failure. Neither side seems to have changed its position at all, insofar as one can judge from the press conferences held after the conclusion of the talks; the documents have never been published. It is clear that the Indians continued to reject Chinese efforts to take the

---

[58] Text in *ibid.*, pp. 52–57; *Documents on the Sino-Indian Boundary Question, op. cit.*, pp. 18–28.

[59] Text in *ibid.*, pp. 139–141; Indian White Paper III, pp. 58–59.

[60] Text in *ibid.*, pp. 60–82; *Documents on the Sino-Indian Boundary Question, op. cit.*, pp. 29–72.

[61] Text in Indian White Paper III, pp. 85–98.

[62] Text in *ibid.*, pp. 83–84; *Documents on the Sino-Indian Boundary Question, op. cit.*, pp. 142–144.

[63] Chou En-lai, letter to Nehru of March 19, 1960 (text in Indian White Paper IV, p. 6).

de facto situation, which was one in which broadly speaking the Indians controlled the eastern disputed sector and the Chinese the western, as a basis for negotiations, especially since Chou continued to deny the validity of the McMahon Line. Chou denied any knowledge of the existence of the second highway in Aksai Chin.[64] By this time the CPR had begun to build up political and psychological pressure on India for a compromise settlement, by making a preliminary compromise settlement with Burma (in January) and Nepal (in April), both countries far weaker than India and less able and willing to hold out for their full demands. The Indian government was enraged and worried to learn, at the end of 1960, that the northern end of the Sino-Burmese boundary as agreed on between the CPR and Burma at that time apparently began, not at the end of the McMahon Line as had been expected, but at a point about eight miles farther south. Thus the eastern approaches to the strategic Diphu Pass, leading into the eastern regions of Assam and the Northeast Frontier Agency, now lay in Chinese rather than Burmese territory. The CPR replied that the pass lay on, but not at the western end of, the Sino-Burmese border; the western end was also the eastern end of the Sino-Indian border, which had yet to be agreed on.[65] Nevertheless, the maps of the new Sino-Burmese frontier published in the CPR showed the Diphu Pass at the western end, and one is left with the suspicion that the CPR was using the uncertainty to build up pressure on India for concessions to the CPR on the boundary question.

The only thing on which Nehru and Chou seem to have agreed at New Delhi was that officials of both governments should begin talks designed to clarify in the mind of each side the exact nature and basis of the other's claim. The talks took place at New Delhi and Rangoon in the second half of 1960 and resulted in complete disagreement and the publication of two incompatible reports, one by each side. [66] The Chinese advanced somewhat the border they had previously been claiming in the western sector. They refused to discuss their border with Bhutan and Sikkim, even though those states were under Indian protection and therefore could not conduct their own foreign relations; they also refused to discuss the border west of the Karakoram Pass, with the part of Kashmir held by Pakistan. Evidently the CPR did not want India to come between it and the other Himalayan states in this matter. The Indian documentation presented at the talks was fuller and better prepared than the Chinese.[67] The failure of this elaborate documentation to shake the Chinese depressed and worried the Indians greatly. Speaking on November 23, Nehru referred to the possibility of a war between India and the CPR that might last for a generation.[68] For their part

---

[64] Fisher, Rose, and Huttenback, *op. cit.*, pp. 89–90.
[65] Cf. Indian White Paper V, pp. 20–26, 31–35, 37.
[66] *Report of the Officials . . .* , *op. cit.*
[67] Fisher, Rose, and Huttenback, *op. cit.*, pp. 91–97.
[68] *Prime Minister on Sino-Indian Relations*, Vol. I: In Parliament, New Delhi: Ministry of External Affairs (?), p. 370.

the Chinese, as they indicated in a note of May 4, 1961, claimed to feel that they had offered to compromise and been rejected, and that until the Indians too agreed to compromise no progress could be made: "so long as the Indian Government does not give up its attitude of refusing to negotiate and trying to impose its views on others, the Chinese Government will absolutely not retreat an inch from its stand. . . ."[69] Yet the Chinese obviously had far less reason than the Indians to be dissatisfied; they actually controlled most of the western disputed sector, about which they cared greatly, and did not care much about the eastern sector, which they did not control. The Indians, on the other hand, cared about both sectors and were therefore unwilling to leave the Chinese in uncontested possession of Aksai Chin. Numerous military, and especially logistical, problems, however, had to be solved before there was any hope of recovering Aksai Chin.

India had already begun to strengthen its military position in the Northeast Frontier Agency since the hostilities in 1959.[70] In the western sector, the terrain, climate, and poor state of communications made a comparable buildup impossible without extensive preparations. Roads began to be built from Kashmir into Ladakh early in 1960.[71] Improved air transport was also necessary, and in mid-1960 India began to buy transport aircraft and high altitude helicopters from the United States.[72] In the autumn, India began to buy larger amounts of similar equipment, as well as roadbuilding equipment, from the Soviet Union.[73] With the aid of this material, Indian troops began to move forward in the western sector in the spring of 1961, and by the autumn of 1962 they had established a total of 43 outposts in territory claimed by the CPR; none was on the Chinese side of the ridge marking the edge of the Aksai Chin plateau. The Indian outposts were generally in a line roughly parallel to the first Chinese military highway across Aksai Chin and about 100 miles from it; three, however, were fairly near the Kongka Pass and therefore were in the vicinity of the second, more advanced, highway.[74]

This process naturally brought a series of angry protests from the Chinese, the first important one being sent on August 12, 1961.[75] The basic

---

[69] *Indian White Paper V*, p. 26.

[70] Cf. *The New York Times*, January 8, 1960.

[71] *The New York Times*, February 6, August 30, 1960.

[72] *The New York Times*, June 10, September 12, 1960.

[73] *The New York Times*, October 5, November 15, 1960. The Indian purchase of Soviet MIG fighters was related mainly to Indo-Pakistani relations and only indirectly if at all to the Sino-Indian border dispute, and will not be discussed here; for a good account, see Ian C. C. Graham, "The Indo-Soviet MIG Deal and Its International Repercussions," *Asian Survey*, vol. iv, no. 5 (May, 1964), pp. 823–832.

[74] Compare maps in *The Sino-Indian Boundary Question (Enlarged Edition)*, *op. cit.*, Reference Map 4; and Huttenback, *loc. cit.*, p. 207. For further details on Indian troop movements, see "Light on Ladakh," *The Economist*, July 28, 1962, pp. 343–344; *The New York Times*, July 25, 1962.

[75] Text in Indian White Paper V, pp. 48–49; for Indian reply see *ibid.*, pp. 51–54.

argument, of course, was over whose was the territory on which the incidents were occurring.

As to their purpose, Nehru made no secret of the fact that it was to "vacate the aggression [by the Chinese] by whatever means are feasible to us. . . . I do not see any kind of peace in the frontier so long as all recognised aggression is not vacated."[76] He denied that Indian troops had orders not to fire unless fired on: "Where we want to fight, we fight; the posts fight and others fight."[77] He of course preferred to bring about a Chinese withdrawal by peaceful means, but he did not rule out stronger measures: "How do we get that aggression vacated? By diplomatic means, by various measures, and ultimately, if you like, by war."[78] He seemed to be pleased with the progress being achieved: ". . . progressively the situation has been changing from the military point of view and from other points of view in our favor and we shall continue to take steps to build up these things so that ultimately we may be in a position to take action to recover such territory as in their possession."[79]

The statements just quoted were made shortly after Nehru returned from a visit to the United States. To its mounting irritation with Indian policy along the border, the CPR added a belief, or at least the accusation, that India was adopting a more pro-Western orientation; what the CPR did not say publicly was that India was also drawing closer to the Soviet Union. Other irritants were what seemed to the CPR Nehru's essentially pro-Western stand on Laos, the Congo, and Berlin; his behavior at the neutral summit conference at Belgrade in the summer of 1961; and his visit to Japanese Premier Ikeda.[80] Still another irritant was that the Sino-Indian agreement on trade between India and Tibet, signed in 1954 and useful as a means of supplying the growing Chinese garrison in Tibet, was due to expire on June 3, 1962. When the six-month period required to give notice of termination approached at the beginning of December, 1961, the Indians made it fairly clear that they had no intention of renewing the treaty, unless the CPR evacuated all territory claimed by India.[81] All these grievances, as well as the increasingly serious border dispute, were reflected in an editorial denunciation of Nehru by the *People's Daily* on December 7.[82] A week

---

[76] Speech of December 6, 1961, in Parliament (*Prime Minister on Sino-Indian Relations*, Vol. I: Indian Parliament: Part II, New Delhi: Ministry of External Affairs (?), 1963 (?), p. 59).

[77] Speech of December 5, 1961 (*ibid.*, p. 47).

[78] Speech of December, 1961 (in *Indiagram*, Washington: Embassy of India, no. 229 [December 6, 1961], p. 2); this passage is not in the version cited in note 77.

[79] Speech of November 28, 1961, in Parliament (quoted in Klaus H. Pringsheim, "China, India, and Their Himalayan Border (1961–1963)," *Asian Survey*, vol. iii, no. 10 [September, 1963], p. 474).

[80] Cf. *ibid.*, p. 475.

[81] *Ibid.*, p. 476.

[82] "The Truth About the Anti-Chinese Campaign Launched by Nehru in India," *People's Daily*, December 7, 1961.

before, the CPR had implicitly warned India that if it persisted in forward movements near the frontier, the CPR might decide to invade the Northeast Frontier Agency, to which of course it had never abandoned its legal claim.[83]

■ THE SINO-INDIAN BORDER SINCE 1962

For the CPR the spring of 1962 was a time not only of economic crisis but of external problems as well; there was tension in Southeast Asia and the Taiwan Strait, as well as on the Sino-Soviet and Sino-Indian borders. Of these the Taiwan Strait situation seemed the most dangerous to the CPR, and as long as it continued to seem dangerous the CPR confined its policy toward the Sino-Indian frontier to protests, backed probably by unannounced troop movements in Tibet. The CPR was especially concerned to establish two points: that it did not want war with India, but that its position in the western sector was a rightful one and would be maintained.[84]

From the Chinese military point of view, it had to be maintained. In addition to tribal restlessness in Sinkiang, the insurgents in Tibet had never been fully suppressed, and in fact were becoming more rather than less of a problem in the spring of 1962. As always, the CPR was afraid that the Indian Army might try to establish contact with the Tibetans, in one or both of the disputed sectors, and to give them aid. This situation was probably one reason why in the spring of 1962 the CPR eased its pressures on the Tibetan populace somewhat.[85]

In April, a month when Nehru fell ill, the CPR seems to have decided on certain strictly limited measures aimed at deterring further Indian advances. In the middle of the month, it published its version of the report of the officials of the two governments in 1960 and published the texts of twenty-two notes exchanged with India since December, 1961; these were distributed to the delegates to the National People's Congress.[86] In a note of April 30 alleging numerous Indian intrusions in the western sector during the second half of April, the CPR announced that it had ordered its "frontier guards to resume border patrols in the sector from Karakoram Pass to Kongka Pass." It threatened that "if India continues to invade and occupy China's territory and expand the area of its intrusion and harassment on China's border, the Chinese Government will be compelled to consider the further step of resuming border patrols along the entire Sino-Indian boundary."[87] In reply, India repeated its demand, known to be unacceptable to

---

[83] Chinese note of November 30, 1961 (in Indian White Paper VI, p. 4).

[84] Cf. Chinese note of March 22, 1962 (text in Indian White Paper VI, pp. 21–25). For Indian reply see *ibid.*, pp. 32–36.

[85] Cf. George N. Patterson, "Recent Chinese Policies in Tibet and Towards the Himalayan Border States," *The China Quarterly*, no. 12 (October–December, 1962), pp. 191–193.

[86] Pringsheim, *loc. cit.*, pp. 476–477.

[87] Indian White Paper VI, p. 39.

the CPR, for a withdrawal by each side behind the line claimed by the other in the western sector; it added, as a modest inducement, that "The Government of India are prepared, in the interest of a peaceful settlement, to permit, pending negotiations and settlement of the boundary question, the continued use of the Aksai Chin road for Chinese civilian traffic."[88] This was of course rejected, with or without the inducement, and the CPR reaffirmed that it was satisfied with the status quo along the border, pending an overall settlement through negotiation, even if India was not.[89]

Mutual accusations of intrusions continued during May. On June 6, an Indian note said that "Carefully verified reports from . . . Ladakh also show that Chinese troops are daily intruding into Indian territory, pushing forward on trucks and jeeps, blasting the mountainside with heavy explosives, constructing new military bases and extending military bases already set up."[90] All this, of course, did not constitute war, or even local hostilities. For one thing, the CPR was still primarily preoccupied with the situation in the Taiwan Strait. This eased toward the end of June, however, and the CPR was then free to turn its main attention to the Indian frontier.[91] A decision to pass from political pressures and military buildup to actual military pressures in dealing with the Indians in the western sector seems to have been taken at a meeting held in Peking on July 6–13.[92] On July 9, the *People's Daily* warned that "It is still not too late for India to rein in on the brink of the precipice."[93]

On July 10, according to the Indian account, Chinese troops began to surround an Indian outpost in the western sector on three sides, obviously in an effort to bring its garrison to abandon it.[94] The attempt was unsuccessful, and Indian troops continued to move forward to the accompaniment of Chinese protests.[95] On July 21, Chinese troops fired on an Indian patrol for the first time since 1959.[96] On August 4 the CPR began to accuse Indian troops of violating the McMahon Line, probably in order to remind the Indians of the vulnerability of the Northeast Frontier Agency in the

---

[88] Indian note of May 14, 1962 (text in *ibid.*, pp. 41–43).

[89] Chinese note of June 2, 1962 (text in *ibid.*, pp. 56–58).

[90] *Ibid.*, p. 60. Chinese patrolling never seems to have stopped completely after 1959. The Indian White Papers contain charges of only four intrusions by Chinese troops down to the spring of 1962, however, and of two new checkposts established in 1961. Chinese activity of this kind was greatly intensified in the spring of 1962.

[91] John Wilson Lewis, "Communist China's Invasion of the Indian Frontier: The Framework of Motivation," *Current Scene* (Hong Kong), vol. ii, no. 7 (January 2, 1963), in an interesting but impressionistic analysis, sees the CPR's turning on India as an outlet for a continuum of frustrations and self-induced tensions (a "war mood"). He does not allude to the consideration just mentioned or to the meticulously controlled nature of the Chinese military action when it finally came.

[92] "The Perilous Course: Communist China Plunges into 1963," *Current Scene* (Hong Kong), vol. ii, no. 10 (March 15, 1963), p. 8.

[93] Quoted in Pringsheim, *loc. cit.*, p. 482.

[94] Indian White Paper VI, p. 81.

[95] Cf. *The New York Times*, July 25, 1962.

[96] Indian White Paper, p. 92. The CPR accused the Indians of firing first (Indian White Paper VII, p. 1).

hope of deterring further advances in the west. The CPR also repeated its demand for negotiations and insisted that "if only the Indian side stop advancing into Chinese territory, a relaxation of the border situation will be effected at once."[97]

These limited pressures were ineffective. On August 14, Nehru told Parliament that India had three times as many outposts in the disputed western sector as the CPR and demanded a free hand to deal with the situation, which he got.[98] Eight days later the Indian government told the CPR once more that there could be no relaxation of tension on the frontier and no negotiations in the absence of a Chinese withdrawal from all territory claimed by India.[99] The CPR replied on September 13 proposing that talks on the boundary question begin on October 15, without "preconditions"; in other words, the Indians were to drop their insistence on prior Chinese evacuation of all territory claimed by India.[100] This was of course unacceptable to India.

On September 8, what seems to have been a fairly serious clash occurred near the western end of the McMahon Line, in the interval between the two versions of the line. Each side naturally held the other responsible. As in Korea on November 7, 1950, the Chinese may have been trying to bring the opponent either to fall back or to launch a premature offensive for which they were prepared. The CPR had now turned the McMahon Line at both ends, in the west and at the Diphu Pass.

There were other clashes near the western end of the McMahon Line during the next few weeks.[101] The Chinese announced on September 20 the resumption of patrolling along the entire Sino-Indian border.[102] On October 5, Indian Defense Minister Krishna Menon announced the creation of a new border command under Lieutenant General B. M. Kaul in the Northeast Frontier Agency.[103] On the following day, the Indian government sent a note which the CPR evidently interpreted as finally slamming the door on the possibility of negotiations without "preconditions."[104] On October 14, after several days of increasingly serious local fighting and a statement by Nehru on October 12 that Indian troops had been ordered to launch an offensive to drive the Chinese out, Krishna Menon made a speech in which he vowed that "We will fight to the last man, the last gun."[105] On the same day, the *People's Daily* announced that "A massive invasion of Chinese

---

[97] *Ibid.*, pp. 14–18.

[98] *Prime Minister* . . . , Vol. I: Indian Parliament: Part II, *op. cit.*, pp. 103–121; *The New York Times*, August 15, 1962.

[99] Indian note of August 22, 1962 (text in Indian White Paper VII, pp. 36–37).

[100] Chinese note of September 13, 1962 (text in Indian White Paper VII, pp. 71–73).

[101] Cf. *ibid.*, pp. 84ff.

[102] Chinese note of September 20, 1962 (text in Indian White Paper VII, pp. 80–81).

[103] *The New York Times*, October 6, 1962.

[104] Text in Indian White Paper VII, pp. 110–111.

[105] *Christian Science Monitor*, October 15, 1962; *The New York Times*, October 15, 1962. For the Nehru statement see *The New York Times*, October 13, 1962.

territory by Indian troops in the eastern sector of the Sino-Indian boundary seems imminent" and exhorted the "People's Liberation Army" to be ready.[106]

In this way India precipitated war with a stronger enemy, on whose dispositions it had no adequate intelligence, and who had evidently made considerable efforts from the autumn of 1959 to the spring of 1962 to avoid hostilities, but who had watched the steady advance of Indian troops in the western sector with growing concern. Presumably India hoped either that the CPR would now give way or that its other preoccupations, and perhaps Soviet pressures, would enable India to win a local victory. Whatever the Indian thinking may have been, it turned out — to use an expression employed by Gandhi in another context — to be a Himalayan miscalculation.

After some further fighting in the eastern sector, Chinese troops launched a major offensive at several points on both sectors on October 20. A Chinese note of the same date accused the Indians of having attacked first and said that "the Chinese frontier guards were compelled to strike back in self-defense."[107] Throughout the ensuing fighting, the CPR usually continued to refer to its troops involved in the action, who were well prepared regular units of the "People's Liberation Army," as "frontier guards." This was not quite as great an evasion as it would have been to call them "volunteers," but the purpose was presumably about the same.

The first major stage of the Chinese offensive lasted for roughly four days and was a fairly limited affair as compared with the second.[108] It did not penetrate into Indian territory not claimed by the CPR. One of its main accomplishments was the taking of Tawang, in the eastern sector, on October 23. On the following day the CPR proposed a ceasefire, each side to withdraw 20 kilometers from the "line of actual control." Talks between the two premiers were again proposed. In addition, "The Chinese Government appeals to the governments of Asian and African countries for an effort to bring about the materialization of these three proposals." Nothing was said, however, about neutral supervision of the ceasefire, or about participation by any third party in a final settlement of the border dispute.[109] Evidently the CPR was hoping that a limited defeat would prevent the Indians from attempting further advances in the disputed western region, without enraging and humiliating the Indians to the point where they would refuse to negotiate or appeal for international aid and support. *Pravda* endorsed the Chinese proposal, which it called constructive, the day after it was made. It implicitly called on the Indian Communists to support the

---

[106] "Mr. Nehru, It is High Time for You to Pull Back from the Brink of the Precipice," *People's Daily*, October 14, 1962.

[107] Text in Indian White Paper VII, pp. 123–124. See Indian reply in protest in *ibid.*, pp. 125–127.

[108] A convenient and apparently accurate Indian chronological summary of the fighting is given in Indian White Paper VIII, pp. 67–69.

[109] Text in *ibid.*, pp. 2–4.

CPR, or at least to restrain the Indian government. Its tone was also friendly to India, however.[110] The Soviet Union, then impaled on the horns of the Cuban missile crisis, was in no position to add another confrontation to its agenda.

Fighting slackened somewhat after the Chinese offer, but it by no means stopped. Evidently the CPR did not want to give the Indians time to recover under the pretext of thinking over the Chinese proposal. A letter from Nehru of October 27 urged that both sides revert to the positions held on September 8, without rejecting the Chinese proposal outright. An annex to his letter asked the pertinent question, "What is this 'line of actual control'?" In other words, was it the line of November 7, 1959, which as a matter of fact the CPR had never defined, or was it the line created by the recent Chinese offensive?[111]

By the time it received this letter, the CPC had evidently decided that the Soviet endorsement of October 25 was too lukewarm, and furthermore the Soviet Union began on October 26 to show signs of "blinking first" in the Cuban missile crisis. Once more, Khrushchev needed a talking to, and so did the Indian Communists. On October 27, accordingly, the *People's Daily* published another editorial attacking Nehru and demanding by the clearest implication that the Soviet Union and the Indian Communists, as well as others, repudiate him as a "reactionary nationalist." By far the most interesting part of the editorial was its references to the crisis of 1929–30, in which the Soviet Union had invaded Manchuria in order to restore its control over the Chinese Eastern Railway, linking the Lake Baikal area with Vladivostok. The Indian Communists were reminded that during this crisis the CPC had supported the Soviet Union; the implications for the Indian Communists in the present crisis were obvious. The message to the Soviet Union, although expressed more indirectly, was even more interesting and important. It was roughly this: The Chinese Eastern Railway, an artery vital to the Soviet Union, was liable to harassment and seizure by foreign troops precisely because the soil across which it ran was admitted not to be Soviet. The CPR proposed to run no such risks with the Aksai Chin highway; regardless of the legal niceties, the CPR intended to hold this territory and treat it as its own.[112]

Chou En-lai's next letter to Nehru, dated November 4, denied that the CPR was trying to define the "line of actual control" as the one now attained rather than the one of November 7, 1959, and said that "the Chinese armed forces will have to withdraw much more than 20 kilometers from

---

110 "In the Interest of the Peoples, in the Name of Universal Peace," *Pravda*, October 25, 1962.

111 Text in Indian White Paper VIII, pp. 4–7.

112 "More on Nehru's Philosophy in the Light of the Sino-Indian Boundary Question," *People's Daily*, October 27, 1962 (text in *The Sino-Indian Boundary Question (Enlarged Edition)*, *op. cit.*, pp. 93–134).

their present position in the eastern sector." On the other hand, he seemed to leave the way open for Chinese retention of the newly taken ground in the west by saying that "The 'line of actual control' mentioned in the proposal is basically still the line of actual control as existed between the Chinese and Indian sides on November 7, 1959," and that "in the western and middle sectors it coincides in the main with the traditional customary line. . . ," or in other words with the CPR's current boundary claim. He of course rejected the Indian demand for a return to the positions of September 8, 1962.[113] From the Indian standpoint, it was not very reassuring.

Nor was it reassuring, apparently, to the Soviet Union, which in any case had been infuriated by Chinese efforts to brand Soviet policy in the Cuban missile crisis as "another Munich" at Castro's expense. On November 5, *Pravda* published another editorial on the Sino-Indian border crisis. Unlike the first, which was mildly but clearly pro-Chinese, this one was neutral in favor of India. It did not repeat the earlier editorial's endorsement of the CPR's ceasefire proposal, and in fact urged a ceasefire and negotiations "without setting any terms."[114]

Far from accepting the CPR's proposal of October 24, the Indian government had proclaimed a state of national emergency. On November 8, the lower house of the Indian Parliament adopted a resolution moved by Prime Minister Nehru to the effect that "this House affirms the firm resolve of the Indian people to drive out the aggressor from the sacred soil of India, however long and hard the struggle may be."[115] Still the CPR refrained from escalating the fighting then in progress into another major offensive. On November 14, Nehru wrote another letter to Chou in which he definitely rejected the proposal of October 24. His letter and an important annex accompanying it insisted that the CPR was trying to pretend that in the west the line of November 7, 1959, was the same as the line claimed as the boundary since 1960.[116] This charge appears to be valid; in any event, the CPR appended to a letter written by Chou En-lai on November 15 to the heads of the Afro-Asian states a map in which the "line of actual control" of November 7, 1959 was shown as being identical except in a few places with the boundary the CPR had been claiming since 1960.[117]

The CPR had more than enough evidence that its proposal of October 24 had been rejected, and that more pressure would be needed if India were to be forced to accept its terms. In addition, the conflict had already begun to take on the proportions of an Afro-Asian issue, and it probably seemed desirable to deflate India's prestige by a further blow. On November 16

---

[113] Text in Indian White Paper VIII, pp. 7–10.
[114] "Negotiations are the Road to Settling the Conflict," *Pravda*, November 5, 1962.
[115] Text in *Prime Minister. . . . ,* Vol. I: Indian Parliament: Vol. II, *op. cit.,* pp. 138–139.
[116] Text in Indian White Paper VIII, pp. 10–17.
[117] Compare *The Sino-Indian Boundary Question (Enlarged Edition), op. cit.,* Reference Map 5; and map in Huttenback, *loc. cit.,* p. 207.

Chinese forces took Walong, near the eastern end of the Northeast Frontier Agency, which they evidently reached by using the Diphu Pass, and at about the same time launched another major offensive at several points on both sectors. To the West, the town of Bomdila, about halfway between the McMahon Line and the southern border of the Northeast Frontier Agency and near the western end, was taken on November 18. In the west, the action included a Chinese shelling of the airfield at Chushul, which even the CPR does not claim to be on Chinese territory. Since this was the only case in which the Chinese attacked territory not claimed by the CPR, it was an embarrassing episode, and the CPR later denied that it had occurred at all.[118] It might also be pointed out that, under the CPR's proposal, the Indians would have had to evacuate the airfield.

On November 18, India appealed urgently to the United States and Britain for increased military aid. Two days later, the United States lifted the Cuban quarantine, and with the easing of the Cuban crisis presumably found itself freer to turn its attention to the Sino-Indian border. Whether the Soviet Union exerted any pressure on the CPR at this point cannot be determined, but the possibility should not be excluded. In any case, there were plenty of practical reasons why the CPR should not have wanted to continue its offensive. To have done so would have imposed increasing strain on its already overburdened logistics and would have brought Chinese troops onto soil admitted by the CPR to be Indian. The approaching winter would soon make the Himalayan passes behind the CPR's lines all but impassable. Afro-Asian opinion was thoroughly aroused, and except for some of the Asian countries, was already generally tending to side with India.

Another, more positive, argument for calling a halt was that the CPR had already accomplished a great deal. It had demonstrated at least a strong possibility that at some future time it could, if it chose, invade Assam proper, where tea plantations and oil fields earning about one-third of India's foreign exchange are located. It had humbled the Indian Army and placed it on the defensive for the indefinite future. It had resoundingly won a round over India in their struggle for ascendancy in the Himalayas. It had undoubtedly increased the respect and fear, if not necessarily the affection, in which it was held in Afro-Asian and other circles. To any one able and willing to read the evidence, it had shown once more, as it had in 1950, that it will not tolerate the advance of avowedly hostile armies up to its borders.

On November 21, the CPR repeated its proposal of October 24 and announced that its "frontier guards" would cease fire the next day. On December 1, they, although not the local Chinese "civil police," would withdraw 20 kilometers behind the "line of actual control" of November

---

[118] For the denial see Chinese note of December 31, 1962 (text in Indian White Paper VIII, pp. 71–73).

7, 1959. To refute Indian charges that this line was in reality the CPR's version of the frontier, it was said that the withdrawal would leave the Chinese "frontier guards . . . far behind their positions prior to September 8, 1962." The Indians were threatened with another attack if they refused to cooperate. Again the CPR called on the Afro-Asian countries to induce India to negotiate on Chinese terms.[119] Chou En-lai followed this up with another letter on November 28.[120] Nehru's reply, on December 1, still insisted that the CPR was trying to palm off the line it had reached after its first-stage offensive as the line of November 7, 1959.[121] An Indian note of December 19 went so far as to imply that Chinese acceptance of the Indian interpretation of the location of the line of November 7, 1959, was a pre-condition for negotiations.[122] Following a lengthy Chinese note denying the factual accuracy of the Indian interpretation,[123] Chou wrote in a letter to Nehru on December 30 that "the Indian troops should stay in their present positions along the entire Sino-Indian border. . . ." This can be interpreted either as a dropping of the pretense that the "line of actual control" represented something other than the line attained by the CPR in its first or even its second offensive, or a raising of the Chinese terms in view of Indian stubbornness. Both could be correct. In addition, Chou proposed that talks begin in January either in Peking, Delhi, or the capital of a "friendly" Asian or African country.[124] Nehru rejected all this and proposed referring the dispute to the International Court of Justice.[125] By January 9, 1963 however, things had progressed to the point where the Indians had dropped their demands for a return to the September 8, 1962, line, let alone a complete "vacation of the aggression," and had agreed in principle to talks without preconditions, although they continued to insist that "the Chinese were nowhere in 1959 along the line at present referred to by them as 'the 7th November line of actual control.'"[126] Meanwhile the Chinese had ceased firing and pulled back roughly on schedule, at least in the eastern sector.[127] The Chinese had not lost a single prisoner but had taken some 3,000 Indian prisoners, who were released by the spring of 1963 after a largely unsuccessful effort had been made to indoctrinate them.[128]

The Sino-Indian border conflict was of course an important issue in international, and especially Afro-Asian, politics from the beginning. Within a month after the fighting began, peace proposals and offers of mediation

[119] Text in Indian White Paper VIII, pp. 17–21.
[120] Text in *ibid.*, pp. 24–26.
[121] Text in *ibid.*, pp. 28–31.
[122] Text in *ibid.*, pp. 35–38.
[123] Chinese note of December 29, 1962 (text in *ibid.*, pp. 39–46).
[124] Text in *ibid.*, pp. 46–47.
[125] Letter of January 1, 1963 (text in *ibid.*, pp. 48–51).
[126] Indian note of January 9, 1963 (text in *ibid.*, pp. 53–58).
[127] Cf. *The New York Times*, December 15, 1962.
[128] Cf. *Christian Science Monitor*, June 17, 1963.

of various sorts had been made by the United Arab Republic, Ghana, Tanganyika, and Indonesia. Feeling in Africa in general was strongly pro-Indian; in Asia, there was a cautious pro-Chinese tendency, mainly on account of the widespread reluctance to antagonize the CPR. On December 10, 1962, the government of Ceylon organized a conference at Colombo of six Afro-Asian nations (Burma, Cambodia, Ceylon, Ghana, Indonesia, and the United Arab Republic) to discuss mediation of the border dispute. Since the CPR had already made it clear that it was interested only in Afro-Asian pressures on India to accept the Chinese terms, not in Afro-Asian mediation, it regarded the activities at Colombo with serious reservations. India, for its part, was greatly disappointed that of the six countries only the United Arab Republic took a completely pro-Indian stand, and that the communiqué issued after the conference did not describe the Chinese action as aggression or endorse the Indian demand for a return to the line of September 8.[129]

The proposals of the Colombo Conference were communicated to India and the CPR on December 15. They were a vague compromise outline of a ceasefire on the border, which it was hoped would provide a favorable atmosphere for the beginning of direct Sino-Indian negotiations on the substantive issues involved. The proposals urged that the Chinese withdraw twenty kilometers from the "line of actual control," as they had allegedly already begun to do, without entering into the controversial question of where that line actually ought to lie. The proposals urged that Indian troops remain where they were; in other words, they did not necessarily have to withdraw twenty kilometers from the "line of actual control." On the other hand, neither could they regain the forty-three outposts established between 1959 and 1962 in the western sector. The demilitarized zone created by the Chinese withdrawal was to be administered by civilian personnel of both sides.[130]

The Ceylonese Premier, Mme Bandaranaike, then led a delegation to the CPR (January 1–9, 1963) to explain these proposals to the CPC and try to secure their acceptance. The joint communiqué said that "The Chinese Government gave a positive response to the proposals of the Colombo Conference."[131] In fact, the CPR objected to the Colombo proposals and reserved its position with regard to two main points, the lack of provision for an Indian withdrawal and the proposal for civilian posts of both sides to operate in the demilitarized zone. The CPR did not, however, make its reservations a condition for the opening of Sino-Indian talks, which was its main interest.[132]

---

[129] *The New York Times*, December 14, 1962.
[130] Text in Indian White Paper IX, pp. 184–185.
[131] New China News Agency dispatch, January 8, 1963.
[132] Cf. Chou En-lai letter of March 3, 1963, to Nehru (text in Indian White Paper IX, pp. 3–5).

When Mme Bandaranaike came to India (January 10–14), the Indian government requested some "clarifications" of the Colombo proposals. Mme Bandaranaike and her colleagues on the mission then interpreted the proposals as envisaging a Chinese withdrawal from the "line of actual control" of November 7, 1959, as defined by the CPR in the maps attached to Chou En-lai's letter of November 15, 1962, to the Afro-Asian heads of state. The Indians could retain existing military posts up to that time. The number and location of civilian posts to be maintained by both sides in the demilitarized zone would be agreed between them, but the basic point was that the Colombo powers definitely envisaged Indian as well as Chinese posts in the zone. In the east, each side could move up to the McMahon Line except in the two areas (the western end and Longju) where there was a dispute as to the location of the line; these two areas were to be demilitarized.[133] On the basis of these "clarifications" India accepted the Colombo proposals and announced its willingness to begin negotiations with the CPR on that basis.[134] The "clarifications" naturally made the Colombo proposals more unacceptable to the CPR than ever, since it regarded them as an effort to deprive it of the fruits of its victory. There was therefore no agreement and no negotiations, since India in effect made the CPR's acceptance of the "clarifications" of the Colombo proposals a precondition for the beginning of negotiations on the basis of the proposals, and no other basis for negotiations could be agreed on.

As might be expected, both sides continued to play to the Afro-Asian galleries and to denounce each other for the absence of negotiations.[135] The Soviet Union contributed to the debate a statement that, while not going so far as to accuse the CPR of aggression, blamed it for not accepting the Colombo proposals without reservations, as India was said to have done; nothing was said about the "clarifications" requested and received by India.[136] The CPR reprinted this article in the *People's Daily* (on September 25, 1963) and a few weeks later published a furious denunciation of the Soviet Union's essentially pro-Indian policy toward the Sino-Indian border dispute.[137] The Colombo powers were naturally concerned by the lack of progress toward a settlement, and they tended to blame the CPR because India had skillfully maneuvered itself into a public position of having accepted the Colombo proposals without reservations, although with "clarifications." Early in October, President Nkrumah proposed another meeting of the Colombo powers. Instead, President Nasser and Mme Bandaranaike

---

[133] Text in *ibid.*, pp. 185–186.

[134] Nehru letter of January 26, 1963, to Mme Bandaranaike (text in *ibid.*, pp. 186–187).

[135] Cf. Chinese note of October 9, 1963 (New China News Agency dispatch, October 12, 1963).

[136] "Serious Hotbed of Tension in Asia," *Pravda*, September 19, 1963.

[137] "The Truth About How the Leaders of the CPSU Have Allied Themselves with India against China," *People's Daily*, November 1, 1963.

proposed on October 14 another conference of nonaligned countries, such as the one that had met at Belgrade in September, 1961. The CPR would of course not be represented at such a conference, and India would, and one of the main items of business would obviously be the Sino-Indian border dispute. It is easy to see why the CPR so objected to the idea, and why the Nasser-Bandaranaike proposal had much to do with Chou En-lai's visit to Africa at the end of the year.[138]

By early 1964 it appeared that General Ne Win of Burma was trying to mediate the dispute.[139] Soon after he returned from a trip to India, he received a visit from Chou En-lai, and their joint communiqué noted vaguely but encouragingly that "the situation along the Sino-Indian border has eased."[140] The following day L. B. Shastri, who was soon to succeed Nehru as Prime Minister, made some equally vague but conciliatory remarks.[141] On the other hand, India was apparently not prepared to make any substantive concessions,[142] whereas the CPR was reported a few days after the Chou–Ne Win communiqué to have agreed for the first time to allow some Indian civilian checkposts in the demilitarized zone.[143] A few days before his death, Nehru made some remarks implying a willingness to ease India's demands for Chinese acceptance of the "clarifications" of the Colombo proposal if the CPR would respect the demilitarized zone, as it allegedly had not.[144]

Meanwhile, each side had repeatedly accused the other of sending troops into the demilitarized zone and into its territory. Each side continued to strengthen its military position in the Himalayas, although it seems likely that proportionally speaking the Indian buildup was the more rapid of the two. The basic reason for this was also one of the main reasons why, in spite of occasional alarming statements to the contrary, the Indian government did not appear seriously worried about the possibility of another major Chinese attack: the ferocious logistical difficulties facing the CPR in the Himalayas. Another probable consideration was the growing tension along the Sino-Soviet border. There were a number of reports, some of them of Indian origin, of Chinese troops moving away from the Himalayas toward the Soviet frontier.[145] Whether these reports were well founded or not, it seems very likely that the Sino-Soviet border dispute began to seem more serious than the Sino-Indian dispute to the CPC during

---

[138] Cf. K. Krishna Moorthy, "The Fatal Clarification," *Far Eastern Economic Review*, November 14, 1963, pp. 351–352.

[139] Cf. *The New York Times*, February 9, 1964.

[140] New China News Agency dispatch, February 18, 1964.

[141] *The New York Times*, February 20, 1964.

[142] Cf. *Christian Science Monitor*, March 3, 1964.

[143] *The Washington Post and Times Herald*, March 2, 1964.

[144] *The New York Times*, May 18, 1964. A few weeks earlier, Nehru had said that India would negotiate only "on the basis of our own claims" (*The New York Times*, April 7, 1964).

[145] E.g., *Christian Science Monitor*, February 28, 1963.

1963, if not earlier. In fact, one of the considerations behind the Chinese attack on the Indian Army in October and November, 1962, may have been a suspicion that India was acting partly on Soviet encouragement, and that only a short time remained for major military effort in the Himalayas before primary attention had to be focused on the Sino-Soviet frontier. If this hypothesis has any validity, it is clear that another Chinese attack in the Himalayas would require greater Indian provocation than the CPR had been offered by 1962. And a fair-minded observer in possession of the facts would have to concede that it was offered some provocation.

□ 12

Border Problems and Policy II

Although the Sino-Indian border is the most important and controversial sector of Communist China's frontier with non-Communist Asia, it is by no means the only sector over which there has been a dispute since 1949. This chapter deals with the rest of the CPR's frontier, beginning with the Sino-Burmese border. (For map, see endpapers.)

■ **THE SINO-BURMESE BORDER**

Regardless of the exact location of the boundary, the area through which the Sino-Burmese border runs can be divided for convenience into two geographically distinct sectors. The northern sector is mountainous and almost inaccessible; it begins at whatever point one chooses to take as the eastern end of the Sino-Indian boundary, runs roughly southward in the vicinity of the watershed between the Irrawaddy and Salween rivers, and terminates near Bhamo, south of which lies a relatively passable and cultivable gap through which trade has long flowed between Burma and Yunnan. From Bhamo the border runs in a roughly southeasterly direction across hills, plateaus, and narrow valleys, which are difficult but far from impassable, until it reaches the northwestern corner of Laos at the Mekong River.

Before the nineteenth century, as in most parts of Asia, this border was really a zone of intermingled political systems and cultures, rather than a firm line. The people on both sides of the central and southern sectors of the line were and are mostly of Shan (primitive Thai) extraction, and there have been intervals in Burmese history when they dominated most of the country. The Burmans (the people making up the majority of the population of Burma and concentrated in the lowland areas) had intermittent tributary relations with the Chinese empire from medieval times and were invaded successfully by the Mongols in the thirteenth century and unsuccessfully by the Manchus in the eighteenth.

One of the main reasons for the British conquest of Burma during the nineteenth century and its annexation to the Indian Empire was a British desire to reach the supposedly vast resources and markets of Southwest China in competition with the French, who were trying the same thing from the direction of Indochina. The question of the Sino-Burmese frontier became a serious one, at least in the minds of the British, with their destruction of the old Burmese kingdom, which had been a vassal of the Manchus, through the conquest of Upper (northern) Burma in 1885–86. In exchange for a token British concession, soon repudiated, to the effect that the Burmese should continue to send a tributary mission to Peking every ten years, the Manchus ceded whatever sovereignty or other rights they had over Burma to Britain by a convention signed in 1886, which provided that the boundary would be delimited and demarcated by joint agreement.[1] This was first attempted in a convention signed in 1894, which left the wild and unadministered area north of Myitkyina (more precisely, north of a "high conical peak" at 25°35′ north latitude) to be fixed in the future but delimited the entire frontier from that point to the Mekong (the Laotian border).[2] In this agreement the British inadvertently ceded some important passes to China, however, and they therefore revised the agreement in their own favor by another convention signed in 1897. Among the most important features of this convention was an arrangement whereby a small passable and cultivable area, usually known as the Namwan Assigned Tract (not far southeast of Bhamo, at the tip of a salient of Chinese territory jutting into Burma), was perpetually leased to Britain by China.[3]

After this the demarcation of the frontier south of the "high conical peak" got under way, and by 1900 all of it had been demarcated except for a stretch about 200 miles long separating the Wa State (in Burma) from Yunnan. Here it was found that the convention and the maps did not correspond with the terrain, and disagreements developed. Since the area was wild and then considered to be of no importance, nothing further was done. By 1935, however, the dispute became an active one because silver had been discovered in the area. A League of Nations commission under Colonel Frederic Iselin, a Swiss, surveyed and demarcated between 1935 and 1937 a boundary in this area that represented an approximate compromise between the British and Chinese claims. This border, known as the

---

[1] Text in *British and Foreign State Papers 1885–86,* London: Her Majesty's Stationery Office, 1893, pp. 80–81.

[2] Text in *British and Foreign State Papers 1894–95,* London: Her Majesty's Stationery Office, 1900, p. 1311.

[3] Text in *British and Foreign State Papers 1896–97,* London: Her Majesty's Stationery Office, 1901, p. 25.

Iselin Line (or, by the CPR, as the 1941 line) was accepted by Britain in 1937, and by China in 1941. The CPR now claims that the British took advantage of China's involvement in the war with Japan to extract consent to this line.[4]

The British did not bring the area of Burma to the north of Myitkyina and the "high conical peak" under their administration until 1913, when they apparently did so in response to the same Chinese pressures on the Tibetan area that led to the Simla Convention. Even then the extreme northern tip, known as the Triangle, was left unadministered until 1934, although claimed by Britain. The British apparently considered that at the Simla Conference they extended the McMahon Line southeastward along the Sino-Burmese border as far as the "high conical peak," although this extension does not show on the maps that have been published from the conference and seems to have even less standing than the rest of the line. Chinese nonratification of the Simla Convention of course implied non-recognition of the Burmese as well as the Indian sector of the McMahon Line.[5]

The Nationalist Chinese by no means regarded the Sino-Burmese frontier question as closed, and the British were understandably nervous about the presence of Nationalist Chinese troops in Burma in the first and last phases of the Pacific War. After the British withdrawal from India and Pakistan in 1947, and as a similar withdrawal from Burma approached, the Republic of China published a map that revived the Chinese claim to the whole area north of Myitkyina.[6] The following year, the Republic of China refused to accept the annual installment of rent on the Namwan Assigned Tract from the newly independent Burmese government.

Going even farther, a Communist Chinese atlas published in 1950 claimed everything north of Bhamo.[7] An atlas appearing in 1953 moved the line north to Myitkyina, but a note to the map in question said that "These problems [i.e., the Sino-Burmese border dispute, including the allegedly forced acceptance of the Iselin Line by China in 1941] await the establishment of a people's Burma and the final victory of the Asian people's revolution; then they can receive a complete and reasonable solution."[8] Two years later, when the Bandung phase of the CPR's foreign policy was in

---

[4] Cf. Chou En-lai, report to National People's Congress on Sino-Burmese boundary (in *A Victory for the Five Principles of Peaceful Co-Existence*, Peking: Foreign Languages Press, 1960, p. 19).

[5] For a survey of the history of the Sino-Burmese boundary question see Alvin R. Field, "Das Problem der Grenze zwischen Birma und China," *Zeitschrift für Geopolitik*, vol. 30, no. 11 (November, 1959, pp. 7–29).

[6] *Atlas of the Northern Frontier of India*, New Delhi: Ministry of External Affairs, January 15, 1960, Map 34.

[7] Guy Searls, "Communist China's Border Policy: Dragon Throne Imperialism?" *Current Scene* (Hong Kong), vol. ii, no. 12 (April 15, 1962).

[8] *Chung-hua jen-min kung-ho kuo fen-sheng ti-t'u* (Provincial Atlas of the CPR), Shanghai: Shanghai Map Publishers, 1953, note to map 46.

effect, another atlas left the boundary just north of Myitkyina but still rejected the Iselin Line and claimed a portion of what the Burmese considered to be the territory of the Wa State.[9]

During the "armed struggle" phase of the CPC's external policy, roughly from 1948 to 1952, Burma was the only country bordering on the CPR, except for Vietnam, in which an active Communist insurrection was in progress. The significance of this point is complicated, but not cancelled, by the fact that the Burmese government was even more troubled by insurrections by various ethnic minorities, some of whom occasionally collaborated with the Communists, than by the Communists themselves. The CPC presumably hoped that the Burmese Communists could come to power with Chinese support, but without direct Chinese intervention, by taking advantage of the tensions between the Burman-dominated Burmese government and the minorities. Unfortunately for this hope, the Burmese Communists soon split into quarrelling factions, of which the two most important at that time were the "Trotskyite" Red Flags and the orthodox or "Stalinist" White Flags, both of whom were actively in revolt against the government. Although the details are uncertain, there can be little doubt that the CPC provided some arms and training on Chinese soil for White Flag units during the early 1950s, in addition to giving asylum and perhaps arms and training to a non-Communist Kachin insurrectionary named Naw Seng.[10] Chinese aid to the White Flags seems to have tapered off in 1955, reportedly because the CPC made a reunification of the Burmese Communist movement and the stopping of surrenders to government forces a prerequisite for further aid, but probably also because such aid was obviously inconsistent with the Bandung policy.[11]

Following the establishment of "autonomous" areas for minority peoples along the CPR's southern frontier in 1953, the CPR began to woo the Kachins and Shan on the Burmese side of the border, and especially the Kachins. They were urged, for example, to cross over into Yunnan, where they were promised jobs and medical care. Interestingly enough, the leaflets making these promises emanated from the CPR's Ministry of National Defense, a fact indicating that considerations of Chinese security as well as of expanding Chinese and Communist influence in Burma were involved. It also shows that Chinese border guards were probably the main disseminators of the propaganda.[12] The Burmese government, naturally concerned over this propaganda, took what measures it could to counteract it. These included calling a special conference with Kachin leaders at Lweje, in the

[9] *Tsui-chin Chung-kuo fen-sheng ti-t'u* (Latest Provincial Atlas of China), Hong Kong: Dah Chung Book Company, 1955, see map 34.
[10] Richard Butwell, "Communist Liaison in Southeast Asia," *United Asia* (Bombay), vol. 6, no. 2 (June, 1954), pp. 148–149; William C. Johnstone, *Burma's Foreign Policy: A Study in Neutralism*, Harvard University Press, 1963, pp. 181–184.
[11] Cf. *The Nation* (Rangoon), September 13, 1955.
[12] *The Nation*, April 20 and 26, October 22, 1955.

Kachin State, in February, 1956. Communist Chinese observers attended the conference without saying anything. After it was over it was only with obvious reluctance that the local Chinese authorities gave permission for a small party of Burmese to cross the frontier for what they intended as a friendly visit. There they found instead extreme security precautions and an atmosphere of suspicion.[13]

There may have been valid reasons why the Chinese were unusually concerned at that time over the security of their Burma frontier. In fact, from the CPR's standpoint this area was always an object of concern during this period. For one thing, the Kachin State borders on a part of the CPR that is inhabited predominantly by Tibetans, including Khambas. As we have seen, some of the Khambas have been in revolt against the Chinese Communists since at least as early as 1955. Northern Burma offered the nearest, although still difficult, access from outside to the area in which, at least until about 1958, the major fighting between Khambas and Chinese took place.

To discuss more fully the possible relationship of the Sino-Burmese border question and the CPR's security, at least as interpreted by itself, it is necessary to go back a few years. There have been reports that as early as November, 1950, Communist Chinese troops entered the Kachin State for a short time, allegedly to see if the United States was building an air base in the area.[14] Although the answer to this question was obviously no, it does not follow that Chinese Communist concern over what might be going on in the area was entirely ridiculous. The "liberation" of Tibet was then in progress, and it was known that Gyalo Thondup, a younger brother of the Dalai Lama, was in Taiwan in touch with the Chinese Nationalists.[15] In the Shan States, to the south of the Kachin State, several thousand Nationalist troops under General Li Mi had entered Burma in mid-1950, and about a year later they seem to have launched an unsuccessful offensive into Yunnan from bases in Burma. At the end of the year, it was reported that Li Mi had gone to Taiwan, but what was left of his forces were still active in the Burma border territories.[16]

The Burmese government and people not only resented the depredations of these "KMT irregulars," as they were called, in Burma but were afraid that the Chinese Communists might use their activities as a pretext for an invasion. The problem became even more acute, at least in the minds of the Burmese and the CPR, with the "unleashing of Chiang Kai-shek" early in 1953. It seemed possible that Li Mi's men might be scheduled for

---

[13] Eyewitness account in *The Nation*, February 13–14, 1956. For a contrasting Chinese account see New China News Agency dispatch, February 24, 1956.

[14] *The New York Times*, February 1 and 16, 1951.

[15] A. R. Field, "Bhutan, Kham and the Upper Assam Line," *Orbis*, vol. iii, no. 2 (summer, 1959), p. 186.

[16] *Survey of International Affairs, 1951*, pp. 474–475.

an active role in a general Nationalist "return to the mainland." In February, 1953, the Burmese army launched a major offensive against the "KMT irregulars."[17] In March Burma took the issue to the United Nations and terminated the American economic aid program, apparently under the impression that the CPR considered the United States to be involved in the alleged aid being given by the Republic of China to the "KMT irregulars." Under the auspices of the United Nations and with the cooperation of the governments of the United States, the Republic of China, Burma, and Thailand, some 7,000 of the "KMT irregulars" and their dependents were removed to Taiwan by air by July, 1954. Others remained in the vicinity of the border between Burma and Thailand, however. The Republic of China disclaimed any connection with or responsibility for them.[18]

It was probably the presence of the "KMT irregulars" in the border areas and the consequent threat to the security of the CPR that account for the intrusions of Communist Chinese troops into the Shan and Wa States that were frequently reported, although always denied by the Burmese government, from 1952 on. The situation was especially disturbing because the CPR had rejected a number of Burmese overtures for negotiations on the border dispute. In July 1956, the Rangoon *Nation* first brought the problem out into the open with a series of detailed articles on Communist Chinese military incursions, including very recent ones that were said to have occurred in the Wa State and in the vicinity of Myitkyina.[19] Assuming that these reports were substantially accurate, as seems probable, the most likely explanation would run roughly as follows. The Khambas had gone into revolt in eastern Tibet, and it was as important to the CPR then to prevent outside aid from reaching them from the nearest source, northern Burma, as it later became to prevent aid reaching them from northern India when the center of the fighting shifted farther west in 1958. Furthermore, the CPR was by now (1956) in the Bandung phase of its foreign policy, a fact that argued against further manipulation of the border dispute with the idea of acquiring large tracts of territory claimed by Burma. In fact, the uncertainty and resulting instability of the situation along the Sino-Burmese border, to which the border dispute contributed, had probably come to seem to the CPR a liability, in view of the unrest in Tibet. A border settlement therefore was indicated, but it must be one that would not only tend to safeguard the CPR against any threat to its security from the direction of Burma but also leave it in a position to move into Burma if necessary in order to bypass the Khamba areas in eastern Tibet, or conceivably to move against India or Burma itself. Chinese incursions in 1956 may have been designed in part to coerce Burma into agreeing to a compromise border

[17] *The New York Times*, March 27, 1953.

[18] Johnstone, *op. cit.*, pp. 225–233.

[19] *Ibid.*, pp. 191–192; John Seabury Thomson, "Burma: A Neutral in China's Shadow," *The Review of Politics*, vol. 19, no. 3 (July, 1957), p. 332.

settlement in which the CPR got what it wanted the most, much as Chinese military pressures on India a few years later were intended partly to do the same thing. This hypothesis seems to be supported by the fact that at the end of July, 1956, the CPR proposed that the forces of both countries maintain the status quo in the disputed border areas pending a settlement of the issue by negotiations.[20] Premier Ba Swe insisted, however, that negotiations could not begin until Chinese troops withdrew from all territory claimed by Burma.[21] The parallel with what happened between the CPR and India three years later is obvious.

Another issue relating to the Sino-Burmese border is that of the Chinese community in Burma, which is the only one in Southeast Asia to have grown significantly by immigration as well as natural increase since the Second World War. Many Chinese refugees came over from Yunnan during the Chinese civil war; the influx continued after 1949 and seems to have increased after 1956, to the point where the towns of northern Burma were beginning to acquire a distinctly Chinese flavor. At least some of the refugees do not seem to have been genuine, since they came with exit papers from the CPR and therefore apparently with the cooperation of the Communist Chinese authorities. The Burmese side of the frontier was too poorly patrolled to make it possible to stop this influx, but at least a border settlement would be a step in that direction.[22]

In October–November, 1956, U Nu, although not then premier, went to the CPR to negotiate on the border issue. The joint communiqué stated that Burma would consider a "fair and reasonable proposal" made by the CPR, and that by the end of the year Chinese troops would have withdrawn to the east of the Iselin Line and Burmese troops would have withdrawn to the west of three villages near the Hpimaw Pass, which leads into the Kachin State.[23] In December Chou En-lai visited Burma and held talks on the border issue, as well as other things, with Premier Ba Swe.[24] In July, 1957, Chou En-lai made a speech on the border issue to the National People's Congress in which he indicated for the first time in public the official Chinese position, although it had been known for some time through statements by U Nu. In general, the CPR was willing to accept the Anglo-Burmese version of the frontier, whose northern section Chou referred to as the "customary boundary line;" this raised hopes in India that the CPR would also accept the McMahon Line as the boundary between the Northeast Frontier Agency and Tibet. There were, however, two exceptions to Chinese acceptance of the Anglo-Burmese version of the frontier. The CPR would insist on sovereignty over the three villages near the Hpimaw Pass,

---

20 *The New York Times*, August 5, 1956.
21 *The New York Times*, August 8, 1956.
22 Cf. Thomson, *loc. cit.*, pp. 334–335.
23 Text in *A Victory . . .* , *op. cit.*, pp. 6–7.
24 Joint statement in *ibid*, pp. 14–15.

which the Burmese Kachins were very reluctant to part with, and over the Namwan Assigned Tract.[25] U Nu, who returned to power early in 1957, was in favor of this arrangement, which was a fairly reasonable one from the Burmese standpoint, but public opinion in Burma would not allow the Burmese government formally to consent to it.[26] The CPR also showed no anxiety to conclude a definitive agreement, perhaps because the deteriorating political situation in Burma made it hope that it might get better terms by holding out.[27]

The Sino-Indian border clashes in 1959 made a Sino-Burmese boundary settlement a matter of some urgency to both sides: Burma wanted protection against incursions, and the government of General Ne Win was in a better position to settle the question than the indecisive Nu government had been; the CPR wanted a settlement with Burma as part of its diplomatic campaign to isolate India from the CPR's other neighbors. In January, 1960, accordingly, Ne Win went to Peking and signed a preliminary border agreement that was the same as the arrangement tentatively agreed on in 1956, with two exceptions: the CPR ceded the Namwan Assigned Tract to Burma in exchange for some apparently unimportant tribal territories farther to the south, and as the attached maps indicated the northern end of the frontier was so defined as to include the eastern approaches to the Diphu Pass within China rather than Burma.[28] At the same time, Ne Win signed a treaty of friendship that pledged each party not to commit aggression against the other and not "to take part in any military alliance directed against the other Contracting Party."[29] This seems harmless enough, but it has been interpreted by an eminent authority as opening the way to a Chinese veto over Burmese defense and foreign policy.[30] This is a difficult hypothesis to evaluate; the CPR would presumably like this to be the case, but it is doubtful whether it expects a clause in a treaty to lead to such a situation. A similar clause is found in two of the other treaties of friendship that the CPR has signed (those with Cambodia and Afghanistan), but not in five others (those with Yemen, Indonesia, Ghana, Guinea, and Nepal). The most obvious explanation is that the CPR was taking out extra insurance against adherence by Burma or Cambodia to SEATO, or by Afghanistan to CENTO.

U Nu resumed the premiership of Burma shortly after the signing of the two agreements with the CPR and was therefore responsible for implementing them. Surveying of the border, where necessary, began in July, 1960. U Nu went to Peking in October to sign the final boundary treaty,

---

[25] Text in *ibid.*, pp. 16–27.
[26] Cf. Thomson, *loc. cit.*, p. 33.
[27] Cf. Richard J. Kozicki, "The Sino-Burmese Frontier Problem," *Far Eastern Survey*, vol. xxvi, no. 3 (March, 1957), p. 37.
[28] Text in *A Victory* . . . , *op. cit.*, pp. 33–37.
[29] Text in *ibid.*, pp. 30–32.
[30] Johnstone, *op. cit.*, p. 196.

which was identical in substance with the preliminary one, and a year later he and Ne Win both went to the CPR to celebrate the completion of the demarcation process.[31]

In addition, U Nu visited some of the southwestern border areas of the CPR in the spring of 1961 and then went to Peking for further negotiations. The joint communiqué included the statement that [32]

> The two premiers also discussed the question of remnant Kuomintang troops in Burma. Because these remnant Kuomintang troops constitute a great danger, not only to the Union of Burma, but also to the CPR, the two premiers have agreed that the Government of the CPR and the Government of the Union of Burma will, when necessary, act in co-ordination and cooperation to solve the problem of the remnant Kuomintang troops.

As nearly as the controversial episode that evoked this statement can be reconstructed from the available information, it began late in 1960, when a boundary survey team uncovered a concentration of "KMT irregulars" in Burmese territory near the Chinese and Thai borders. In spite of official Burmese denials, it appears that Chinese Nationalist sources, including President Chiang Kai-shek, are correct in saying that Communist Chinese troops then entered Burmese territory and engaged the "KMT irregulars" for a short time before withdawing. The Burmese army then began an offensive of its own. In March, 1961, aircraft of the Republic of China airlifted some 4,000 "KMT irregulars" to Taiwan, and the remainder seem to have dispersed in various directions, some of them entering Thailand and others Laos.[33]

Since that time there has been little news from the Sino-Burmese border. At the price of a boundary settlement that was acceptable although not ideal from the Burmese standpoint, and after the exertion of some pressures, the CPR has established a border that appears to be reasonably secure and across which it is in a position to exert pressures of a subversive variety on its neighbor, without overtly rupturing their alleged friendship.

■ THE BORDERS WITH PAKISTAN AND AFGHANISTAN

The Sino-Pakistani border is unusual in that there has been disagreement not only over where it is, but over whether it exists at all. A Sino-Pakistani common border exists only if one concedes that Pakistan has some sort of claim to Kashmir, or at least to that part of Kashmir on the Pakistani side of the ceasefire line. Since India claims a clear title to the whole of

---

[31] *Ibid.*, p. 197.

[32] New China News Agency dispatch, April 17, 1961.

[33] *The New York Times*, December 29–30, 1960; February 26, March 25, May 23, 1961; *The Washington Post and Times Herald*, January 13, 1961.

Kashmir, it of course denies that a Sino-Pakistani border, a Sino-Pakistani border dispute, or the need for or possibility of a Sino-Pakistani boundary settlement, exists. This study will ignore the metaphysics and legal niceties of this question and confine itself to more manageable problems.

Although Chinese officials have occasionally made informal statements that allowed India to gain the impression that the CPR recognized India's title to Kashmir, the CPR has never committed itself formally on this question. Its stand is in marked contrast with that of the Soviet Union, which endorsed the Indian position in 1955. On the other hand, the CPR has never endorsed the Pakistani position either. Presumably the CPR has wanted to maintain maximum flexibility to deal with a situation in which it has been claiming certain territories that are claimed by not one but two other states.

For its part, Pakistan has been so preoccupied with its disputes with India and Afghanistan that for several years it evidently did not consider the question of the frontier between the CPR and the Pakistani-held part of Kashmir to be a serious problem. The Sino-Indian border hostilities of 1959 seem to have changed this attitude, and they may also have given Pakistan a feeling of additional leverage on India. Early in 1960, President Ayub publicly proposed a joint border defense arrangement with India, so that the subcontinent's entire northern border would be adequately protected. India rejected the offer, presumably not only because of Nehru's general hostility toward Pakistan but because of dislike of any arrangement that might tend to consolidate further the Pakistani position to the west of the ceasefire line in Kashmir.[34] Pakistan's annoyance at this rebuff was evidently reinforced a year later by indications that the Kennedy administration would take an attitude somewhat more favorable to India, and somewhat less so to Pakistan, than its predecessor had done. In any event, Pakistan began early in 1961 to sound out the CPR on the possibility of a border agreement and on March 28 sent a diplomatic note to that effect. The CPR did not reply until February, 1962, when the Sino-Indian border dispute had begun to warm up again after two years of relative quiet.[35] On May 3, it was announced in Peking that the two governments had agreed to negotiate on the frontier between the CPR and "the contiguous areas, the defense of which is under the control of Pakistan," and that "after the settlement of the dispute over Kashmir between Pakistan and India, the sovereign

[34] Cf. Nasim Ahmed, "China's Himalayan Frontiers II: Pakistan's Attitude," *International Affairs* (London), vol. 38, no. 4 (October, 1962), pp. 481–482. Pakistan was probably concerned not only over the territorial dispute with the CPR but over a highway that the CPR had been constructing since 1957 from Kashgar southward toward the northwest corner of Kashmir (cf. A. R. Field, "Strategic Development in Sinkiang," *Foreign Affairs*, vol. 39, no. 2 [January, 1961], pp. 317–318).

[35] Statement by Prime Minister Nehru in Parliament, March 5, 1963 (text in *Sino-Pakistan "Agreement," March 2, 1963: Some Facts*, New Delhi: Ministry of External Affairs, 1963, pp. 32–34).

authorities concerned shall reopen negotiations with the Chinese Government regarding the boundary of Kashmir, so as to sign a formal boundary treaty to replace this provisional agreement."[36]

India of course protested this announcement. Its first note on the subject, sent on May 10, included the remarkable statement that the Sino-Indian frontier extended from the trijunction of the frontiers of India, the CPR, and Afghanistan in the west to the trijunction of the frontiers of India, the CPR, and Burma in the east.[37] If taken at face value, this would deny the independence not only of Bhutan and Sikkim, which are generally recognized to be Indian protectorates, but of Nepal, which is considered an independent kingdom. Even though the CPR of course seized on this statement with glee, India never formally disavowed it, although it did affirm its recognition of Nepal's independence.[38] On the merits of the Sino-Pakistani border negotiations, the CPR replied to India that such negotiations were necessary "to settle the question of the actually existing common boundary so as to maintain tranquillity on the border and amity between the two countries." The reply continued with a barbed question summarizing the CPR's declaratory policy on its border disputes since about the beginning of 1959:[39]

> Since the Burmese and Nepalese Governments can settle their boundary questions with China in a friendly way through negotiations and since the Government of Pakistan has also agreed with the Chinese Government to negotiate a boundary settlement, why is it that the Indian Government cannot negotiate and settle its boundary question with the Chinese Government?

The reference in the Chinese note to maintaining "tranquillity on the border" probably explains why the CPR responded to the Pakistani overtures for border negotiations in the spring of 1962 and not earlier. By that time not only was the Sino-Indian border dispute becoming increasingly serious, but so was the Sino-Soviet border dispute, and the Soviet Union was evidently trying to exploit unrest among Kazakh tribesmen in Sinkiang. Just as the revolt in Tibet seemingly made the CPR willing to concede the Northeast Frontier Agency to India in exchange for a boundary settlement that would aid CPR in coping with the Tibetans, so the unrest in Sinkiang seems to have affected the CPR's attitude on the frontier between Sinkiang and Kashmir and Soviet Central Asia.[40]

Sino-Pakistani negotiations on the border question began on October 12, 1962,[41] the same day that Nehru announced an impending offensive by

---

[36] New China News Agency dispatch, May 3, 1962.
[37] Text in Sino-Pakistan "Agreement". . . , op. cit., pp. 8–9.
[38] Indian note of June 30, 1962 (text in ibid., pp. 14–17).
[39] Chinese note of May 31, 1962 (text in ibid., pp. 10–13).
[40] Cf. The Washington Post and Times Herald, March 16, 1963, citing Indian sources.
[41] New China News Agency dispatch, October 12, 1962.

the Indian army to clear Indian-claimed soil of Chinese troops. On December 28, 1962, it was announced that on December 26 (Mao Tse-tung's birthday), "an agreement in principle has been reached on the location and alignment of the boundary actually existing between the two countries."[42] Detailed negotiations were then held and an agreement signed and published on March 2, 1963.[43] The agreement was technically a provisional one pending the final resolution of the status of Kashmir, not subject to ratification, and, as Article Six indicated, the most favorable one that Pakistan could hope to get even if it eventually gained undisputed title to the whole of Kashmir:

> The two parties have agreed that after the settlement of the Kashmir dispute between Pakistan and India, the sovereign authority concerned will reopen negotiations with the Government of the People's Republic of China on the boundary, as described in Article Two of the present agreement, so as to sign a formal boundary treaty to replace the present agreement, provided that in the event of that sovereign authority being Pakistan, the provisions of the present agreement and of the aforesaid protocol shall be maintained in the formal boundary treaty to be signed between the People's Republic of China and Pakistan.

India of course protested against the agreement and refused to be bound by it in any way.[44] In its analysis of the agreement, India pointed out that the Sino-Pakistani agreement did not define the provisional border in some areas but merely stated the two versions of the border and left the issue to be resolved by surveys on the ground. The Indian analysis also claimed, on the basis of a map supplied by Pakistan at Indian request, that the difference between the CPR's border claim of 1960 and the Pakistani claim (based apparently on what Pakistan claimed as its de facto border in 1961 and running south of what India has claimed since 1947 as the traditional boundary) was about 2,100 square miles, not 3,400 as stated by the Chinese and Pakistani. The area between the Chinese claim of 1960 and the Pakistani de facto 1961 border, as interpreted by India, was divided about equally between the two, whereas it had been stated by Pakistan and the CPR that of 3,400 square miles in dispute 1,350 had been awarded to Pakistan and 2,050 to the CPR. Again according to the Indian analysis, if the boundary shown on Pakistani maps as late as 1962 were taken as the point of departure, Pakistan had provisionally ceded more than 13,000 square miles to the CPR.[45] What the Indian analysis failed to say was that

---

[42] New China News Agency dispatch, December 28, 1962.

[43] New China News Agency dispatch, March 2, 1963; text also in *Sino-Pakistan "Agreement"* . . . , *op. cit.*, pp. 24–28.

[44] Indian notes of March 2, 1963 (to the CPR) and March 5, 1963 (to Pakistan) (texts in *ibid.*, pp. 29–31).

[45] See note 35; also Appendices XIII–XV in work cited.

the 1962 Pakistani frontier corresponded with the one usually shown on British and other western maps, and that the "traditional frontier" shown on Indian maps was a retreat from that line. By this logic, India could be said to have quietly ceded some 11,000 square miles of territory belonging to the British Indian Empire to the CPR.

By mid-1964, the demarcation of the Sino-Pakistani "provisional" frontier was said to be complete, and it was expected that a highway would soon be opened between western Sinkiang and northwestern Kashmir.[46]

In the Sino-Pakistani agreement, unlike the Sino-Burmese boundary treaty, the western end of the line was fixed (at a peak at approximately 74°34' east longitude, 37°03' south latitude). This implied the fixing of one end of the short Sino-Afghan frontier along the end of the so-called Wakhan Corridor, established by British and Russian "imperialism" to separate their holdings in South and Central Asia. The CPR's maps had conceded the existence of this corridor since the mid-1950s, after a few years of claiming virtually the whole of the Pamir Mountains.[47] There can be no doubt that Afghanistan was concerned about this situation and about the CPR's way of pursuing its border dispute with India. Prince Naim, the Afghan Foreign Minister, visited the CPR in September, 1959, shortly after the first Sino-Indian border clashes. The joint communiqué stated rather vaguely that he and his Chinese hosts had "exchanged views on matters of direct interest to China and Afghanistan, Asian problems of major significance, as well as important problems of general concern to the world community."[48] It is almost inconceivable that both the Sino-Afghan and the Sino-Indian borders were not discussed.

On March 2, 1963, the day of the signing of the "provisional" Sino-Pakistani boundary agreement, it was announced that the CPR and Afghanistan "have agreed to conduct negotiations for the purpose of formally delimiting the boundary existing between the countries and signing a boundary treaty."[49] At the first session of the negotiations, which began in June, the chief Chinese delegate said that "the settlement of the Chinese-Afghan boundary question will be another example to all neighboring countries for the peaceful settlement of questions between them through negotiations."[50] Agreement on the very short boundary was reached by August 2 and an announcement issued on that day.[51] The final treaty was signed and its text published on November 22. It was not subject to ratification and went into effect immediately.[52] Since the line is only about twenty miles long, its

---

46 *The New York Times*, August 7, 1964.
47 Compare *Atlas of the Northern Frontier* . . . , *op. cit.*, Maps 33, 34, 36, 37, 38, and 39.
48 New China News Agency dispatch, September 13, 1959.
49 New China News Agency dispatch, March 2, 1963.
50 New China News Agency dispatch, June 18, 1963.
51 New China News Agency dispatch, August 2, 1963.
52 New China News Agency dispatch, November 22, 1963.

exact location does not appear to be very important. The main significance of the Sino-Afghan boundary settlement seems to be that the CPR made its recognition of the Wakhan Corridor formal and took another step toward the diplomatic isolation of India on the border question. It is also possible that the CPR took the opportunity to suggest to the new Afghan government, which had come to power in March, 1963, that it improve its relations with Pakistan, as it seems to have wanted to do in any case.

■ **THE BORDERS WITH THE SMALL HIMALAYAN STATES**

The discrepancies between the Chinese and Nepalese versions of the Sino-Nepalese boundary are small and not very important in themselves. They are given some extrinsic significance, however, by two things. One of course is the CPR's desire to settle its border disputes with as many of its other non-Communist neighbors as possible so as to isolate India. The other is the fact that the Khambas of Tibet are related to the Sherpas (or Sharpas) of Nepal, and that some Khambas have used Nepal as a refuge at various times during the fighting in Tibet.[53]

In March, 1960, shortly before he was to visit India to discuss the Sino-Indian border dispute, Chou En-lai received a visit from Prime Minister B. P. Koirala of Nepal. They signed a boundary agreement that provided in effect, since the differences were not large or very controversial, that they should be settled on the ground by teams of both sides. It also provided that each side should demilitarize a zone twenty kilometers deep on its side of the boundary.[54] It later developed that by the time the agreement was signed the CPR had already agreed in principle that the boundary should run through the summit of Mt. Everest, rather than to the south of it as on earlier Chinese maps. The Nepalese, however, continued to hold out for the entire mountain, on the theory that it had never been climbed to the summit except from the Nepalese side. Thereupon the CPR claimed that on May 25, 1960, two Chinese and one Tibetan mountaineer had reached the summit from the northern side for the first time in history. This claim is regarded with the greatest skepticism by non-Chinese mountaineers, and it had little effect. The final boundary treaty, which was signed during a visit by King Mahendra of Nepal to the CPR in October, 1961, and published on October 13, merely described the boundary as "passing through" Mt. Everest, without specifying the location of the boundary with respect to the summit.[55] The problem was left unresolved

---

[53] Field, "Bhutan, Kham . . . ," *loc. cit.*, pp. 184–185.
[54] Text in *New Developments in Friendly Relations Between China and Nepal*, Peking: Foreign Languages Press, 1960, pp. 21–24.
[55] New China News Agency dispatch, October 13, 1961; cf. Searls, *loc. cit.*, pp. 12–13.

in the public mind by the announcement in January, 1963, that a protocol had been signed specifying the location of the boundary markers, which had already been erected.[56] Any one anxious to settle the question in his mind would presumably have to go to the mountain himself.

On June 26, 1960, the CPR informed the Nepalese government that it intended temporarily to ignore the demilitarized zone on its side of the boundary in order to conduct operations against some Tibetan insurgents in it. Two days later Chinese troops fired on Nepalese troops in the area and of course created a great furor in Nepal. On July 2 the CPR apologized and later paid a small indemnity, but it insisted that the incident had occurred on Chinese territory; in other words, it accused the Nepalese troops involved of violating not only their own demilitarized zone but the frontier itself.[57]

During King Mahendra's visit to the CPR in 1961, an agreement was signed for the construction of a highway between Lhasa and Katmandu, the capital of Nepal. The agreement was negotiated at Chinese initiative, and the CPR completed its section of the highway in 1963 and provided technicians to supervise the building of the Nepalese section, which is scheduled for completion in 1966. The obvious image of a Chinese invasion of Nepal aimed at Katmandu of course cannot be ruled out of court, and the mere possibility of it will presumably make the Nepalese more pliable in dealing with the CPR, but it seems less realistic than the image of a Chinese desire for food imports from Nepal into Tibet to offset those from India that were lost as the result of the Sino-Indian border dispute.[58] Furthermore, the Nepalese are keenly interested in increasing their contacts with the CPR to offset the country's traditional semidependence on India.

In the case of Bhutan, it is India that is building the connecting roads. Bhutan is under Indian protection and allows India to conduct its foreign relations, and yet the only traditional route between Bhutan and India ran through Tibet. In addition, Bhutan has had a boundary dispute with the CPR, the territory involved lying along the northern edge of Bhutan and at its southeastern corner, adjacent to the Northeast Frontier Agency. It seems that Chinese troops crossed territory claimed by Bhutan during both the 1959 and 1962 border hostilities with India. Since 1962, on the other hand, the CPR has issued maps showing the Sino-Bhutanese boundary as the Bhutanese would have it.[59] It has been plausibly suggested that this is the result of a border treaty, probably concluded in secret in 1961 since India theoretically has the right to conduct Bhutan's foreign relations, and that in exchange for a favorable boundary settlement Bhutan has granted

---

[56] Cf. *ibid.*, p. 13.
[57] *Ibid.*, p. 12.
[58] Cf. Dev R. Kumar, "Nepal's Road to China," *Far Eastern Economic Review*, February 20, 1964, pp. 419–421.
[59] Searls, *loc. cit.*, pp. 9–11.

Chinese troops transit rights across its territory.[60] This suggestion is reinforced by the fact that when the CPR lists the boundary agreements it has signed it never mentions Bhutan but always implies that the list is incomplete.

Sikkim, which lies between Nepal and Bhutan, is under even greater Indian influence than Bhutan and is more important to India, because the strategic Chumbi Valley leads through it. The CPR concedes, however, that the Sino-Sikkimese frontier has been delimited since 1890 and demarcated since 1895. There appears therefore to be no border dispute, although Chinese patrols have evidently intruded into Sikkim on several occasions.[61]

■ THE SINO-SOVIET BORDER

During the heyday of "imperialism," the two powers responsible for the greatest losses of Chinese territory, including some areas claimed on only a very vague basis, and influence in Inner Asia were Britain and Russia. Since the British withdrew from their main base in the Indian subcontinent in 1947, the Chinese have been rectifying to a degree the situation that they had created. The question of Russian encroachments is complicated by two important factors: Russia is now a "friendly socialist state"; and the Russians, unlike the British, are still there.

The Sino-Soviet border is divided into a western and an eastern sector by the long interruption of Outer Mongolia, rather as the Sino-Indian border is interrupted by Nepal, Sikkim, and Bhutan. In the west, Communist Chinese maps from 1950 to 1953 showed most of the Pamir Mountain region, or in other words a large part of what the Soviet Union regards as Tadzhikistan, within the CPR. Chinese maps were then adjusted to conform roughly with the Soviet version of the boundary.[62] The rest of the western sector has never appeared in a significantly different way on the maps of the two regimes. In the east, there has been a cartographic dispute over some small areas along the Manchurian border, in particular some islands near the confluence of the Amur and Ussuri Rivers.[63]

The Sino-Soviet dispute seems to have lain largely dormant until 1962, apart from the likelihood that there were some frontier clashes in 1960

---

[60] A. R. Field, letter to *The Washington Post and Times Herald*, January 11, 1963; George N. Patterson, "Recent Chinese Policies in Tibet and Towards the Himalayan Border States," *The China Quarterly*, no. 12 (October–December, 1962), p. 199.

[61] Searls, *loc. cit.*, pp. 9–10.

[62] "Russian Annexations in the Far East and the Sino-Soviet Dispute," *Special Information Note* (Washington), no. 21 (October 11, 1963), p. 1. This study contains an excellent historical survey of this subject. See also Geoffrey Wheeler, "Sinkiang and the Soviet Union," *The China Quarterly*, no. 16 (October–December, 1963), pp. 56–61.

[63] Searls, *loc. cit.*, pp. 15–16; *The New York Times*, February 26, 1961.

caused by movements of nomadic herdsmen back and forth across the frontier. In the spring of 1962, according to the later Chinese account, a substantial number of dissidents in Sinkiang, mainly Kazakhs, fled across the border into the Soviet Union. The CPR has accused the Soviet Union of inciting and organizing this movement, and the Soviet consulates in Sinkiang, at Urumchi and Kuldja, were closed in July, 1962.[64] This episode was not publicized at the time, however, and the first definite indication of the fact that the CPR considered that it had a major territorial dispute with the Soviet Union came in early 1963. On March 8, the CPC published a blast against the American Communist Party in the course of which it said that

> In the hundred years or so prior to the victory of the Chinese revolu-
> tion [i.e., prior to 1949], the imperialist and colonial powers — the
> United States, Britain, France, Tsarist Russia, Germany, Japan, Italy,
> Austria, Belgium, The Netherlands, Spain, and Portugal — carried out
> unbridled aggression against China. They compelled the governments
> of old China to sign a large number of unequal treaties — the treaty of
> Nanking of 1842, the treaty of Aigun of 1858, the treaty of Tientsin
> of 1858, the treaty of Peking of 1860, the treaty of Ili of 1881, the
> protocol of Lisbon of 1887, the treaty of Shimonoseki of 1895, the con-
> vention for the extension of Hong Kong of 1898, the treaty of 1901,
> and so on. By virtue of these unequal treaties, they annexed Chinese
> territory in the north, south, east, and west, and held leased territories
> on the seaboard and in the hinterland of China. Some seized Taiwan
> and the Penghu Islands, some occupied Hong Kong and forcibly leased
> Kowloon, some put Macao under perpetual occupation, and so on and
> so forth.

With regard to the Chinese boundary claims implicit in this catalogue, the statement continued by saying that "when we deal with various imperialist countries, we take differing circumstances into consideration and make distinctions in our policy." As for the "socialist" countries, the interested reader has to content himself with noting the remark that "our policy toward the socialist countries is fundamentally different from our policy toward the imperialist countries."[65] This is a point of some importance, because of the treaties given in the list those of Aigun, Peking, and Ili involved the cession by the Manchus of large areas in the Far East and Central Asia to tsarist Russia.

The Russians remained silent under this goading until shortly after the

---

[64] "The Origin and Development of the Differences Between the Soviet Union and Ourselves," *Red Flag* and *People's Daily*, September 6, 1963. It was reported that American analysts were skeptical of the charge of Soviet involvement (*The New York Times*, September 7, 1963), although there is a long history of Soviet involvement in Sinkiang down to about 1954. On the closing of the Soviet consulates see Daniel Tretiak, "Peking's Policy Toward Sinkiang: Trouble on the 'New Frontier'," *Current Scene* (Hong Kong), vol. ii, no. 24 (November 15, 1963), p. 11.

[65] "A Comment on the Statement of the CPUSA," *People's Daily*, March 8, 1963.

CPC published, on September 6, 1963, its version of the border incidents of 1962. On September 20, *Pravda* began to publish alleged eyewitness statements by Kazakhs who had fled to the Soviet Union from Sinkiang. On the same day, the Soviet government issued a long statement rebuking the CPR for its stand on the test ban treaty. In the course of this statement, it was charged that

> Beginning in 1960, Chinese servicemen and civilians have been systematically violating the Soviet border. In the single year of 1962, more than 5,000 violations of the Soviet border from the Chinese side were registered. Attempts are also being made to "develop" some parts of Soviet territory without permission. [It was then indicated that this charge related mainly to the disputed islands in the Amur and Ussuri Rivers.]
>
> The Soviet Government has a number of times offered to the CPR Government that consultations be held on the question of ascertaining separate sections of the border so as to exclude any possibility of misunderstanding. However, the Chinese side evades such consultations, at the same time continuing to violate the border. This cannot but make us wary, especially in view of the fact that Chinese propaganda is making definite hints at the unjust demarcation of some of the sections of the Soviet-Chinese border allegedly made in the past.
>
> However, the artificial creation today of any territorial problems, especially between socialist countries, would be tantamount to embarking on a very dangerous path. . . .

Then, grandly sweeping the whole issue and any others like it under the rug, the statement added that "The Soviet Union has no frontier conflicts with any of its neighboring states."[66] Conveniently forgotten was the fact that since 1917 the Soviet Union has made territorial gains at the expense of, or annexed, practically every country on which it borders.[67]

During 1963 there were repeated reports that Chinese troops were fighting Kazakh insurgents in Sinkiang, although evidently not on the same scale as in Tibet, and that both the CPR and the Soviet Union were reinforcing their border garrisons.[68] Early in 1964, high Soviet officials were said to have referred to the Sino-Soviet frontier as "the most unquiet border in the world."[69] It was probably this consideration, as well as the continuing tension along the Sino-Indian frontier, that moved Khrushchev to make his proposal of December 31, 1963, that all countries renounce force as a means of settling territorial disputes, although he conspicuously refrained from mentioning either the Sino-Soviet or the Sino-Indian border disputes.[70]

---

66 *Izvestia*, September 21, 1963 (text in *The New York Times*, September 23, 1963).

67 Cf. "Russian Annexations . . . ," *loc. cit.*, p. 8.

68 E.g., *The New York Times*, November 17, December 26, 1963; *Christian Science Monitor*, September 29, October 2, 1963.

69 *Christian Science Monitor*, January 9, 1964.

70 Text in *Pravda* and *Izvestia*, January 4, 1964.

A month later, Chou En-lai told Edgar Snow that "We have reached an agreement with the Soviet Union that negotiations be held on the Sino-Soviet boundary question."[71] A Soviet delegation is reported to have arrived in Peking to discuss the border on February 23, Soviet Army Day, a possible indication of how seriously the Soviet Union regards the problems for its own security created by the situation.[72] In these discussions, the Russians reportedly insisted on confining the agenda to possible minor adjustments of the frontier, whereas the Chinese wanted a comprehensive review of the entire question of the Sino-Soviet border.[73] A few days later, a Soviet official said in India that a joint boundary commission had been established to delimit and demarcate certain sections of the frontier.[74]

Whatever the outcome of these discussions, it is clear that the Sino-Soviet border dispute is still very much alive, at least as a political stick with which each tries to beat the other. In April, 1964, a Soviet jurist, Fedor Kozhevnikov, stated that[75]

> It is known that no territorial questions exist between the Soviet Union and the CPR and that the Soviet-Chinese frontier has taken shape historically. The only question can be of separate clarifications of it, which are necessary. But the Chinese side has for some time been continually and systematically violating the Soviet-Chinese frontier, and furthermore frequently in a crude and provocative manner.

In reality, the issue is much more than a political stick. Both the Soviet Union and the CPR are engaged in a long-term program of developing their Inner Asian regions, a process in which the Russians have a headstart of about a generation. These regions are rich in natural resources, especially minerals (including in the case of Sinkiang petroleum and uranium). They are strategic in several ways: in the context of overall Sino-Soviet relations, as regions in which revolts by restless minorities could spread along or across the frontier, and as areas containing deserts suitable for nuclear testing or space launchings and at least partly out of range of Polaris submarines. Since the indigenous inhabitants are few in number and politically unreliable and technologically backward, there has been substantial organized immigration of Russians and Chinese in recent years into Soviet Asia and into Sinkiang and northern Manchuria, respectively.[76]

---

71 Text of interview in *The New York Times*, February 3, 1964.

72 Tanyug International Service dispatch, Belgrade, February 27, 1964.

73 *The New York Times*, February 26, 1964.

74 *The Washington Post and Times Herald*, March 10, 1964.

75 Tass dispatch, April 8, 1964. A few weeks later, it was said that "Particularly alarming are the incidents provoked by Chinese authorities on the Soviet-Chinese border, which at times take the form of gross provocations" ("On the Nature of the Relations Between Socialist Countries," *Izvestia*, May 30, 1964).

76 On the development of Sinkiang see Field, "Strategic Development . . . ," *loc. cit.*, Tretiak, *loc. cit.*; J. P. Lo, "Five Years of the Sinkiang-Uighur Autonomous Region, 1955–1960," *The China Quarterly*, no. 8 (October–December, 1961), pp. 92–105. For a

The only sector of the Sino-Soviet frontier region where either has maintained forces adequate to do more than hold the local minorities down, at least until recently, is the Far Eastern end. Even there the substantial Soviet forces in the Soviet Far East and the Chinese forces in Manchuria seem to have been maintained primarily against the eventuality of an American attack, perhaps in combination with Japan as visualized in the Sino-Soviet alliance, rather than with an eye to Sino-Soviet friction.[77]

Developments since 1962, however, make it clear that the Sino-Soviet frontier can no longer be considered as militarily quiescent. It seems to be a reasonable generalization that in any border dispute that persists over a period of time, the motives of each side are likely to be mainly defensive: each is afraid of the other. If not, the dispute would ordinarily cease in short order to be a border dispute and escalate to the level of formal war, probably accompanied by an invasion of one country by the other. Unless and until such a Sino-Soviet war begins to appear a practical possibility, it seems wisest to think of the attitude of each side as essentially defensive. If so, what might they be afraid of?

It seems most unlikely that the Soviet Union is seriously afraid of the immigration of ethnic Chinese colonists into Soviet Asia. To mention only one of the many practical obstacles to such immigration, Chinese peasants lack the mobility of nomads and would find it very difficult, even if they could be brought to the frontier, to cross it and evade the Soviet border guards. It is only a little less unlikely that the Russians are afraid, at least for the near future, of serious Chinese efforts to renegotiate the nineteenth century treaties or otherwise lay claim to substantial areas of Soviet Asia. If the Chinese make gestures in that direction, it is likely to be with the purpose of putting pressure on the Soviet Union to get concessions on other matters, or of blackening it as an "imperialist" in the eyes of the Afro-Asian world so as to exclude it from the second Asian-African Conference.

It seems much more reasonable to suppose that for the time being the Soviet Union is more afraid that the influx of dissident Kazakhs from Sinkiang will cause sympathetic unrest among Soviet Kazakhs and might lead the "People's Liberation Army" not only to strengthen and perhaps advance its border posts in critical areas but even to make incursions into Soviet territory to break up or recapture concentrations of Kazakhs. Realistically speaking, if such incidents occurred they would probably not en-

---

good historical introduction to the subject of Communist Chinese Inner Asian policy see Howard L. Boorman in Howard L. Boorman and others, *Moscow-Peking Axis: Strengths and Strains*, New York: Harper, 1957, pp. 142–197. See also W. A. Douglas Jackson, *Russo-Chinese Borderlands: Zone of Peaceful Contact or Potential Conflict?* Princeton, N.J.: Van Nostrand, 1962.

[77] Cf. Malcolm Mackintosh, "Soviet Generals Look at China," *The New Statesman*, October 4, 1963 (reprinted in *Survival*, vol. 5, no. 6 [November–December, 1963], pp. 269–272).

danger the Soviet hold over Soviet Central Asia. Nevertheless, we are speaking of apprehensions, and regimes tend to err on the side of caution when dealing with problems of this kind. The Russians undoubtedly remember that about 1930 many Kazakhs fled from Soviet Central Asia into Sinkiang to escape from Stalin's collectivization and industrialization program, much as Kazakhs are now fleeing in the opposite direction from Communist Chinese policies. In Sinkiang they contributed to revolts by local Kazakhs against Chinese authority, and these revolts in turn gave the Soviet Union an opportunity to send troops to Sinkiang, intervene in its political affairs, and make it into a virtual Soviet satellite for a decade.[78] The Soviet Union is certainly not anxious to run even the slightest risk of seeing something similar happen in reverse.

The basic Chinese fear is almost certainly of a resumption of the historic Soviet pressures on Chinese Inner Asia that were suspended about 1954 with the dissolution of the Sino-Soviet joint stock companies. Such a process would be an especially serious problem for the CPR if it coincided with a period of internal difficulties such as it appears actually faces the Communist Chinese regime in the near future. There are a number of indications of Chinese fears of the reassertion of Soviet influence in Sinkiang. One is the decision in 1958–59 to use the Latin rather than the Cyrillic (Russian) alphabet for the non-Chinese peoples of Sinkiang.[79] Another is the fact that although the Russians have completed their section of the proposed trans-Sinkiang railway as far as the Sino-Soviet border at the Dzungarian Gate, the Chinese have not carried their section beyond the oilfield at Tushantzu, one hundred miles west of Urumchi, although they apparently plan to run a spur northward from Tushantzu to another oilfield at Karamai.[80] It is also possible that the Russians have insisted that their broad gauge be continued into Sinkiang, as it has been continued through Outer Mongolia and into Inner Mongolia, as a measure of protection for Kazakhstan. The CPR certainly does not want Sinkiang Kazakhs and others to be able to escape across the Soviet frontier, take refuge there, and perhaps with Soviet support recross the frontier. Even short of such an eventuality, the CPR probably is afraid that the Soviet Union may smuggle Kazakh agents across the frontiers or otherwise give support to dissidents in Sinkiang. The analogy with the CPR's attitude toward Tibet and the Sino-Indian frontier is obvious. The CPR may also be afraid that the Soviet Union will encourage Outer Mongolia to put pressure on Sinkiang, as happened in 1947, or that the Soviet Union may put pressures on the Sino-

---

[78] Cf. "Russian Annexations . . . ," *loc. cit.,* p. 6.

[79] Allen S. Whiting, "Sinkiang and Sino-Soviet Relations," *The China Quarterly,* no. 3 (July–September, 1960), pp. 36–37.

[80] *Christian Science Monitor,* February 8, 1964; Herold J. Wiens, "The Historical and Geographical Role of Urumchi, Capital of Chinese Central Asia," *Annals of the Association of American Geographers,* vol. 53, no. 4 (December, 1963), pp. 460, 463.

Soviet frontier to relieve Chinese pressures on India, as may in fact have happened already, or to distract the Chinese from some other undertaking.

■ THE BORDERS WITH THE OTHER COMMUNIST NEIGHBORS

The Chinese Communists came into control over the mountainous frontier between Manchuria and North Korea even before taking Mukden in October, 1948. During 1948 the Chinese obstructed North Korean efforts to reconstruct the Supong Dam on the Yalu, about forty miles from Antung. The dispute eased in 1949, perhaps after Soviet mediation and evidently in return for a North Korean agreement to supply power to Manchurian industry.[81] There is a difference between the Chinese and North Korean versions of the frontier in the vicinity of the Changpai (Long White) Peak, the watershed between the Yalu and Tumen rivers. Chinese maps show the entire mountain as Chinese, whereas North Korean maps show the border running through the summit.[82] This difference probably reflects nothing more serious than a controversy over a matter of prestige much like the Sino-Nepalese controversy over Mt. Everest.

The CPR does not seem ever to have disputed the accepted fact that the frontier between China and Vietnam and Laos was delimited and demarcated at the end of the nineteenth century, nor do Chinese maps of this sector of the border differ from any others. The CPR did not list the Sino-French territories detaching Vietnam from Chinese suzerainty among the nineteenth century treaties it mentioned in 1963 as possibly requiring revision. North Vietnam is of course a Communist regime with which the CPR enjoys reasonably good relations, and the Sino-Vietnamese frontier does not run near any prominent peak that might give rise to a controversy for the sake of prestige. The Sino-Laotian frontier is probably also covered by the Chinese desire for good relations with North Vietnam, as well as by a desire not to sharpen unnecessarily the already serious crisis in Laos. As will be shown in the next chapter, however, this has not prevented the CPR from establishing what appears to be a virtual unannounced satellite or buffer zone in Phong Saly, the adjacent province of Laos, and building roads into Phong Saly that increase the Chinese capability for taking military action in the area if necessary.[83]

The only Communist neighbor with which the CPR has so far signed a boundary treaty is Outer Mongolia. Until 1962, Communist Chinese maps showed the entire Outer Mongolian frontier with Sinkiang and the

---

[81] *North Korea: A Case Study in the Techniques of Takeover*, Washington: Department of State, 1961, pp. 116–117.

[82] Searls, *loc. cit.*, p. 17.

[83] Cf. *ibid.*, p. 5.

Inner Mongolian Autonomous Region (which includes western Manchuria) as undelimited and undemarcated. The line shown as the tentative boundary included within the CPR several thousand square miles of territory assigned on most non-Chinese maps to Outer Mongolia. Since the Mongols seem to fear nothing so much as Chinese domination, this discrepancy must have worried them a great deal. They were helped, however, by the Chinese determination to bring political pressure to bear on India and the Soviet Union by settling less difficult border disputes with other countries. Unpublicized Sino-Mongolian boundary talks evidently began in the autumn of 1962, as the fighting on the Sino-Indian border was going on. Chou En-lai invited Outer Mongolian Premier Tsedenbal on December 16 to come to Peking to sign a treaty. Tsedenbal promptly accepted, although he was careful to make it clear that Outer Mongolia was not abandoning its support for the Soviet Union in the Sino-Soviet dispute. The treaty was signed on December 26, 1962 (Mao Tse-tung's birthday, and the date of the agreement in principle on the Sino-Pakistani border) and published on March 26, 1963, the day after the exchange of ratifications.[84]

The maps attached to the treaty are not available, and no one who did not have a detailed knowledge of the topography of the area would be able to trace the agreed boundary without them even from the lengthy description of it in the treaty. Thus it is impossible for an outsider without specialized knowledge to say where the agreed frontier runs, and therefore how the disputed territory was divided between the two claimants. There are a number of indications, however, that the Mongols were dissatisfied with the treaty and that they therefore probably believed that they had gotten the worst of the bargain. These indications include the fact that the treaty was given much more publicity in the CPR than in Outer Mongolia, the three-month delay in the exchange of ratifications (Article Four of the treaty provides that ratifications shall be exchanged "as speedily as possible"), and the fact that a change of Foreign Ministers was announced by Outer Mongolia two days after the exchange of ratifications.[85] Furthermore, a reorganization and strengthening of the Outer Mongolian armed forces that had begun in 1961, apparently with Soviet support, continued.[86] In the spring of 1964 it was reported that security measures had been tightened along the Sino-Mongolian border and that Outer Mongolia was expelling all Chinese technicians and workers, allegedly in fear of a coup.[87] The Outer Mongolian case casts some doubt on the CPR's statement in

[84] *Ibid.*, pp. 16–17. Text of treaty released by New China News Agency, March 26, 1963.

[85] P. Shagdarsuren was "released from his duties in connection with his transfer to other work" and succeeded as Foreign Minister by M. Dugersuren (Montsame dispatch, Ulan Bator, March 27, 1963).

[86] Robert A. Rupen, "Mongolia in the Sino-Soviet Dispute," *The China Quarterly*, no. 16 (October–December, 1963), pp. 76–77.

[87] *The New York Times*, May 22, 1964.

1963 that "our policy toward the socialist countries is fundamentally different from our policy toward the imperialist countries."

■ SOME INFERENCES ON COMMUNIST CHINESE BORDER POLICY

From the analysis of Communist China's border problems and policy that has been presented in the last two chapters, it should be clear that as usual the extreme possible interpretations are untenable.

One of these is that the CPR merely wants boundary settlements and neutral or friendly neighbors, in short tranquillity, presumably in order to devote itself undisturbed to its internal problems. Neither the analysis given here nor the fear of the CPR felt by most if not all of its immediate neighbors supports this view.

At the other extreme is the view that the CPR would like to invade and presumably annex or satellitize as many of its neighbors, or at any rate its non-Communist neighbors, as possible, for national or ideological reasons or both, and that it is deterred from doing so solely by logistical difficulties and military risks. There are many objections to this view, although it must be conceded that logistical difficulties and military limitations and risks would probably operate to deter invasion even if no other disincentives existed. Such additional disincentives definitely exist, however. The most important is the enormous political setbacks, both at home and abroad, that resort to invasion would inflict on a regime to which politics is the breath of life. The CPR's goal seems to be not Chinese provinces but friendly and effective Communist regimes in the neighboring countries, and it knows the great political price that the Soviet Union has paid for its heavy-handed satellitization of Eastern Europe. If one understands the word aggression to mean only direct or overt aggression, and not reprisals or indirect aggression (subversion), the following passage from an interview with an unnamed high Communist Chinese official, evidently Chou En-lai, seems reasonably accurate:[88]

> We are altogether against any kind of aggression. We would never commit aggression. It is not just that we lack for this purpose such important weapons as long-range planes and a big navy; this is only one side of it. The other is our people. We cannot win [the support of our people] for aggression. They would not go along. . . .
> What do we want in Southeast Asia or India? What can we find there? Only more people, jungle, swamps, mosquitoes and snakes, all things which we Chinese cannot stand. What Chinese would want to go there?
> Anyone committing aggression has already lost. Aggression cannot bring anything good, above all it cannot bring victory, but only defeat.

[88] Unattributed interview with the Vienna *Kurier*, July 24, 1964 (text in *The New York Times*, August 7, 1964).

The highways that the CPR has built and is building to and sometimes beyond its frontiers are undoubtedly intended not only to help develop the Chinese border areas and provide additional security for the frontier, but also to help project Chinese influence beyond the frontier. Invasion is only one of the ways in which this could be done, however, and one of the least likely.[89] The CPR's armed forces have always been concentrated heavily in the coastal regions, and even the Sino-Indian and Sino-Soviet border disputes do not seem to have made a radical change in this situation as yet.

Another alarming hypothesis is that the CPR hopes or intends eventually to gain or recover, presumably more by political than military means, vast areas in Asia outside its present borders, over and above the disputed areas along those borders that have been discussed in the last two chapters. The CPC has certainly done some things that seem to lend substance to this suspicion.

In 1960, an Indian student brought home from the CPR a manual published in 1954 and entitled *A Brief History of Modern China*. A map in this book showed Outer Mongolia, Hong Kong, and Macao as integral parts of China and indicated the following as "Chinese territories taken by the imperialists during the Old Democratic Revolutionary Era (1840–1919)": the southeastern part of Kazakhstan and the eastern parts of Kirghizia and Tadzhikistan, although not the cities of Tashkent and Samarkand ("1864: Tashkent falls into the hands of tsarist Russia"); the Soviet Far East north of the Amur River ("1858: Territory ceded to tsarist Russia by the Treaty of Aigun"); the Soviet Maritime Province ("1860: Territory ceded to tsarist Russia by the Treaty of Peking"); the island of Sakhalin ("Territory divided up between Japan and tsarist Russia"); Korea ("Korea, independent [of China] since 1895, was occupied by Japanese imperialists in 1910"); the Ryukyu Islands ("1879: The Ryukyu Islands pass under Japanese domination"); Taiwan ("1895: By the Treaty of Shimonoseki, Taiwan and the Penghu [or Pescadores] Islands fall into the hands of the Japanese"); the Sulu Islands in the Philippine archipelago ("The Sulu Archipelago, under British domination"); Malaya ("1895: Indochina becomes French territory"); Thailand ("1904: Under the joint pressure of French and British imperialism, Thailand proclaims its independence [presumably of China]"); Burma ("1886: Burma falls under British control"); the Andaman Islands, but not the Nicobars ("The Andaman Islands are annexed by the British"); Assam and the Northeast Frontier Agency ("1820: Territory seized from Burma by Britain"); Bhutan ("1865: Bhutan falls under British domination"); Sikkim ("1889: The British invade Chemung [i.e., Sikkim]"); Nepal ("After 1898, Nepal claims that it is independent, whereas in reality it is under British control"); and Ladakh ("1896: The cession of this terri-

---

[89] Cf. Denis Warner, "China's New Roads: Where Do They Lead?" *The Reporter*, September 26, 1963, p. 33.

tory was imposed by a treaty signed with Britain"). The CPR later denied that this map was official, as strictly speaking it was not, but not that it continued to circulate or that it represented the CPC's general thinking.[90] In reality however, this map need be taken no more seriously than American talk in the mid-nineteenth century about Manifest Destiny, whose results were certainly far less impressive than the propaganda.

More authoritative and better known, although vaguer, is the passage already quoted from the CPC's editorial of March 8, 1963. This in turn harks back, with some differences, to a passage in the original version of Mao Tse-tung's *The Chinese Revolution and the Chinese Communist Party* (1939), which has been drastically softened in versions published since 1949:[91]

> In defeating China in war, the imperialist states have taken away many Chinese dependent states and a part of her territories. Japan took away Korea, Taiwan, the Ryukyu Islands, the Pescadores, and Port Arthur; Britain seized Burma, Bhutan, Nepal, and Hong Kong; France occupied Annam [i.e., Vietnam], and even an insignificant country like Portugal took Macao.

Evidently Mao did not consider it politic at that time to mention tsarist Russia's encroachments. It will have been noticed that Soviet encroachments since 1919 were not mentioned even in the editorial of March 8, 1963.

All this may qualify as "cartographic imperialism," but it does not necessarily indicate a serious official intent, still less the ability, to recover any significant part of the areas in question in what is laughingly called the foreseeable future, with or without war. It must be remembered that "imperialism," in the Marxist-Leninist sense, is the main devil in the Chinese Communist demonology, and that the recalling and exaggerating of its misdeeds is a political stock-in-trade with the CPC for both domestic and foreign purposes. In the context of the nineteenth century, the stress is naturally on European and Japanese imperialism; in that of the twentieth, on Japanese and American. Territorial seizures, real or alleged, by "imperialism" at Chinese expense are a primary feature of the demonology.

Turning to what the CPR's border policy is rather than to what it is not, we can infer from two major crises already discussed, the Korean War and the Sino-Indian border dispute, that the CPR will not tolerate the advance to its frontiers of what it regards as hostile armies. It will display caution in dealing with such a problem, especially since 1951 and if the foreign troops are American, and will try to deter a further advance first by threats and political maneuvers and then by limited probing attacks. Then,

---

[90] Searls, *loc. cit.*, p. 3; Jacques Jacquet-Francillon, "The Borders of China: Mao's Bold Challenge to Khrushchev," *The New Republic*, April 20, 1963, pp. 18–22, which reproduces the map on p. 19.

[91] Quoted in Searls, *loc. cit.*, p. 4.

if the hostile advance continues, the CPR will attack (or counterattack, according to one's point of view) to the best of its ability, while still trying to inject an element of political ambiguity into the situation sufficient to minimize the chances of unpleasant complications. The CPR has a similar, although less acute, allergy to foreign irregular operations and air attacks in areas immediately adjacent to its frontiers.

The CPR obviously wants and is trying to seal its borders against the flight or reentry of insurgents or the entry of foreign agents, and above all to prevent extensive contacts between domestic dissidents and actual or potential foreign supporters. This is a difficult problem, both because of the nature of the terrain and because of the fact that the CPR's most martial and rebellious minorities live generally in the vicinity of its inland frontiers. Boundary settlements where indicated, if necessary on a compromise basis, are helpful in dealing with the problem. These considerations go far to explain the CPR's conduct of its various border disputes.

Beyond its frontiers and their immediate vicinity, the CPR clearly believes its security to be best served by having as neighbors countries that are at least neutral and preferably friendly. Such areas, in the frequently invoked Chinese simile, are to China as the lips to the teeth and serve it as buffers against "imperialism." It does not necessarily follow that the CPR wants or is trying to create a full-fledged chain of satellites around its periphery, at least to the south. The CPR's ideal, to which North Vietnam probably approximates the best, is very likely a viable, effective, autonomous, and friendly Communist state on its borders. Where this is not possible, as in the Himalayas and Laos, the CPR may think it best to work toward creating satellites. Where Burma fits is not clear, and the situation there is so confused and unstable that the CPR's policy may not have taken shape yet; if it has, it may be to create a satellite in the long run. In this context, the term satellite must not be understood in the crude sense familiar from Stalin's treatment of Eastern Europe, Outer Mongolia, and North Korea. What is meant is a somewhat subtler relationship in which influence, bordering on control, would be exerted more through party than through state channels, and therefore with a minimum of outward manifestations.

We have seen that the CPR will not tolerate either direct or indirect aggression against itself across its borders, and that the CPR does not appear to intend to use direct aggression as a major means of enlarging its own power and influence. Just the opposite is true, however, of indirect aggression, or subversion. This is a major means of Communist Chinese policy in many countries of the world, and one very difficult to counter. It is probably easiest to practice, and hardest to counter, in countries contiguous to the CPR. The Communist Chinese appear to regard their borders, or at least those that do not touch countries with which they are on friendly terms, as one way streets across which they must have at least the ability to conduct whatever subversive activities they choose. Such an attitude can obviously lead to serious situations, even if one discounts the alarmist theories of invasion or massive territorial claims.

The CPR clearly regards Tibet as the key not only to the security but also to the influence aspects of its Himalayan border policy. In the spring of 1962, the CPR announced something of a moderation of its Tibetan policy. One of the probable reasons for this shift is that at about the same time it began to propagate, quietly on the ground rather than in authoritative published pronouncements, a proposal for a "Confederation of Himalayan States" to include Nepal, Sikkim, Bhutan, the Northeast Frontier Agency, and Nagaland (in Assam). Aksai Chin is obviously not included because it is to be treated as an integral part of the CPR. Tibet is evidently to serve as the model and magnet for this confederation. Although this scheme has not been endorsed by any of the governments of the region and has aroused a good deal of alarm there and elsewhere, it seems to have generated at least some positive response in each of the areas concerned, mainly because of India's unpopularity in the Himalayas.[92] If this plan were ever put into effect, it could lead to the satellitization of the Himalayan states by the CPR.

Apart from problems arising from the movements of dissident tribesmen back and forth, the CPR's long frontier with the Soviet Union and Outer Mongolia seems to be affected mainly by the general course of the Sino-Soviet dispute, historic Mongol fears of Chinese domination, and Chinese fears of a possible resumption of Soviet pressures on Chinese Inner Asia. Although little is known of the actual situation along the CPR's inland frontier with its Communist neighbors, it appears that the CPR has more to lose than to gain by a forward policy if pursued at the strategic, rather than merely at the tactical, level. It seems very likely that, as in so many situations, bumptious behavior by the CPR is largely a sign of fear, in this case of the Soviet Union. It would be rash to say that if such fear actually exists it has no basis.

The CPR's policy toward its long, essentially maritime frontier from Korea to the Taiwan Strait and the Gulf of Tonkin is clearly dominated by fear of the United States, combined with an unwillingness to abandon the CPR's objectives in the area merely because of that fear. The CPR tries to deter American attack, with or without Chinese Nationalist participation, by keeping most of its forces in the coastal areas. Beyond that, it tries to keep American bases and forces as far away from its shores as possible, more by political than by military means. An excellent example is the fact that, since the CPR announced on September 4, 1958, that its territorial waters extended to a depth of twelve miles, it has given a "serious warning" each time an American vessel or aircraft came within that limit.

---

[92] Patterson, *loc. cit.*, pp. 191–193, 197–199, 202. See also Searls, *loc. cit.*, p. 11.

Ultimately the CPR of course hopes to see American bases and forces eliminated from the Far East and the western Pacific altogether, again more by political than by military means. Then and only then does the CPR apparently expect to be able to attain its influence objectives, notably the "liberation" of Taiwan — unless this can be achieved earlier by means of a political agreement with the Nationalists.

□ 13

The Indochina Crisis II

This chapter is an attempt to analyze those aspects of the second phase of the Indochina crisis, since 1954, that have some relevance to Communist Chinese foreign policy. The crisis as a whole, which of course is still very much in progress at the time of writing, is an extremely complicated affair, and considerations of space as well the limitations of my knowledge forbid any effort at a complete analysis. On the other hand, the Chinese aspect of the crisis would be unintelligible without some brief commentary on the course of the crisis as a whole, which therefore is included.

The first phase of the Indochina crisis, down to 1954, showed that North Vietnam (the DRV), rather than the CPR, was the main actor on the Communist side. Within the limits dictated by military security and political advantage, the CPR appeared wholly committed to the "liberation" of South Vietnam by the DRV, but in Laos and Cambodia the CPR seemed to have interests independent of the DRV and to be restraining the latter to some degree. For its part, the DRV had seen itself deprived at the Geneva Conference of most of the footholds it had gained in South Vietnam, Laos, and Cambodia, in exchange for a promise that general elections, which it stood a strong chance of winning, would be held in Vietnam within two years. The recovery of South Vietnam under Ngo Dinh Diem's leadership was so unexpectedly rapid, however, that no outside agency except perhaps the United States would have been able to force it to hold such an election against its will when the appointed time came, and the United States was unwilling to exert the pressure that would have been necessary. Instead, it gave aid and support to Diem's army and political system. British and Soviet recognition, early in 1956, that an all-Vietnamese election as envisaged at Geneva was impossible or at least undesirable under these circumstances in effect deprived the DRV of its last hope of gaining control of South Vietnam without resort to force.

■ **THE RENEWAL OF INSURGENCY IN
SOUTH VIETNAM (1956–59)**

Even Khrushchev had agreed (in his report to the Twentieth Congress) that in such circumstances Communists must use force:

> In the countries where capitalism is still strong and has a huge military and police apparatus at its disposal, the reactionary forces will, of course, inevitably offer serious resistance [to the political program of the "proletariat"]. There the transition to socialism will be attended by a sharp class, revolutionary struggle.

He did not promise Soviet support for this struggle, however. In fact, although he continued the Soviet economic and military aid program to the DRV, he went so far at the beginning of 1957 as to propose the admission to the United Nations of both North and South Vietnam.[1]

As usual in the Indochina crisis, whatever else may be said of the CPR's policy it was at least more actively favorable to the DRV than was that of the Soviet Union. It is likely, for one thing, that the Soviet Union's passivity in the face of the absence of all-Vietnamese elections was one of the main reasons why the CPR objected from the beginning to Khrushchev's proclamation of the "parliamentary path."

Although the East European situation probably outranked the Vietnamese situation in the CPC's scheme of priorities in the latter part of 1956, the first stop (November 18–22) on Chou En-lai's important trip taken at that time was North Vietnam. The joint communiqué issued at the end of his visit indicated, without giving details, that the question of Vietnamese reunification had been one of the most important ones discussed:[2]

> The implementation of the Geneva Agreements in Vietnam is being gravely sabotaged. The South Vietnam regime still refuses to carry out the political clauses of these agreements regarding the peaceful reunification of Vietnam. The United States of America has used all possible means to hinder Vietnam's reunification, in an attempt to turn South Vietnam into its colony and military base, and to prolong indefinitely the division of Vietnam. The two prime ministers [i.e., those of the CPR and the DRV] noted that the countries participating in the 1954 Geneva Conference had the irrefutable responsibility to stop the development of such a situation, and that they should take effective joint measures to ensure full implementation of the Geneva Agreements.

Although it is clear that this message was addressed primarily to the Soviet Union, the two premiers may have hoped that the other cochairman of the Geneva Conference, Britain, which was then on extremely bad terms with

[1] Philippe Devillers, "The Struggle for the Unification of Vietnam," *The China Quarterly*, no. 9 (January–March, 1962), p. 11 n. 3. This article must be used with great care because of its strong anti-Diem and pro-DRV bias.

[2] Vietnam News Agency dispatch, November 22, 1956.

the United States on account of the Suez crisis, might be persuaded to reverse its earlier stand on the issue of elections in Vietnam.

There was of course no significant response to this appeal, and Communist electoral victories in Kerala and Java early in 1957 made it less likely than ever that the Soviet Union would take risky actions over difficult situations when the "parliamentary path" seemed to be working so well in less difficult ones.

As already suggested, the situation as seen by the DRV, and undoubtedly also by the CPR, clearly called for the application of force. An overt invasion of South Vietnam by the powerful "Vietnam People's Army" (VPA), similar to the North Korean invasion of South Korea in 1950, was out of the question. The United States military aid program in South Vietnam at that time was oriented entirely toward giving the South Vietnamese army the ability to oppose such an invasion, and if it had proved unable to do so the South Vietnamese government would unquestionably have called for support from SEATO, and if that proved impossible then from the United States alone. The DRV would then probably have had to invoke Chinese support, which would have entailed both military risks for the CPR and political and military risks for the DRV. The CPR was not formally allied to the DRV in 1957, but then it had not been formally allied to North Korea in 1950. The scenario looked entirely too much like Korea all over again.

There remained of course the alternative of revolutionary or guerrilla warfare of the kind that the CPR and the DRV both already knew so well. Under favorable conditions, such as existed or could be created in South Vietnam, this strategy has been proved repeatedly to be less risky and more effective in the long run than overt invasion, or any form of conventional warfare. Furthermore, the DRV had kept this option open from the beginning; many of its irregular units had gone underground in South Vietnam after 1954, rather than withdrawing to the north of the 17th parallel as required under the Geneva Agreements. The course that evidently seemed most promising to the DRV was to use terrorism and unconventional warfare, largely in the rural areas, to bypass South Vietnam's conventional military buildup, wreck its seeming political consolidation, and aggravate its serious economic weaknesses. The public political rationale for this policy would be that the Diem regime was a "lackey" of American "imperialism" and therefore deserved to be overthrown by those over whom it was attempting to rule. The DRV's effort to engineer a seemingly indigenous overthrow of the Diem government began in about the middle of 1957 with a wave of terrorism directed mainly against village leaders.[3]

At the risk of repetition, it must be stressed that this campaign was

---

[3] Bernard B. Fall, "South Viet-Nam's Internal Problems," *Pacific Affairs*, vol. xxxi, no. 3 (September, 1958), pp. 255–258.

directed by the DRV, not the CPR, even though the latter undoubtedly gave it approval and at least indirect support, in the form of economic and military aid. As in the year preceding the Geneva Conference, it would have been risky for the CPR to involve itself too directly in the struggle, and in any case there was no reason to think that such involvement would be necessary as long as the DRV did not become unduly impatient for victory. There were also political disincentives to excessive Chinese involvement, the basic one being the deep distrust and fear felt by all Vietnamese, regardless of political affiliation, for Chinese power, of whatever political affiliation. Truong Chinh, generally considered to be closer to the CPC than any other major leader in the DRV, had been made the scapegoat in 1956 for the excesses of the land reform program and seemed to be in the background for the time being. Politically speaking, the CPC's problem was to act in such a way as to increase the influence of pro-Chinese individuals like Truong Chinh, as against the pro-Soviet faction in the DRV leadership reputedly led by Vo Nguyen Giap, the Commander-in-Chief of the VPA. Such an increase would be most likely to be achieved by a policy of support for the DRV's objectives, without direct intervention or attempted domination.

It seems that the CPC had some success in enhancing its own political standing and that of its supporters in the DRV in the latter months of 1957, after the beginning of the campaign of terrorism in South Vietnam. In August Ho Chi Minh, who is widely believed to favor not committing the DRV entirely to either the Soviet Union or the CPR, visited the CPR twice in the course of a tour that took him to every country in the Communist bloc. In November he took Le Duan, who was to succeed him as Secretary General of the Vietnam Dang Lao Dong (Labor, or Communist, Party) in 1960, to Moscow with him to attend the meetings held in conjunction with the fortieth anniversary of the October Revolution. He did not return to the DRV until late in December, and during this period there were indications that Truong Chinh and the rest of the pro-CPC faction in the Lao Dong had gained in influence at the expense of the pro-Soviet faction.[4] On December 11, the CPR appointed as its new ambassador to the DRV Ho Wei, who was to hold the post until 1962 and play an important role in Laos as well. Among his other qualifications, Ho had had extensive experience in guerrilla warfare prior to 1949.[5] The possible implications of this appointment for Chinese aid and support to the DRV in connection with its effort to build up the Viet Cong, or Communist-controlled guerrillas, in South Vietnam are obvious.

The level of Viet Cong activity rose steadily during 1958, and yet

---

[4] P. J. Honey, "The Position of the DRV Leadership and the Succession to Ho Chi Minh," *The China Quarterly*, no. 9 (January–March, 1962), pp. 32–33.

[5] Brian Crozier, "Peking and the Laotian Crisis: A Further Appraisal," *The China Quarterly*, no. 11 (July–September, 1962), p. 121.

when the fifth anniversary of the Geneva Agreements approached in 1959 much remained to be done. In the political field, the Diem government had only just begun to behave in the senselessly dictatorial fashion that was eventually to cost it the support of its people and its army. In the military field, the DRV had only a limited presence in Laos and was not yet in a position to use that country as a major route to South Vietnam and thus bypass the heavily defended 17th parallel. In 1959, therefore, it would have been hard to predict the materialization of the two main trends that at the time of writing threaten to tip the balance in South Vietnam in favor of the DRV: the political (more than military) failures of the South Vietnamese governments of Ngo Dinh Diem and his successors, and the DRV's control of the highlands of Laos bordering on South Vietnam.

■ THE CRISIS IN LAOS (1958–61)

As early as 1955, political workers for the Pathet Lao, which is largely controlled by the DRV, began to infiltrate extensively into areas of Laos outside the two border provinces, Sam Neua and Phong Saly, that had been assigned to the Pathet Lao as regrouping areas under the Geneva Agreements. Meanwhile, political negotiations for the integration of these two provinces into the political life of the rest of the country, again as provided by the Geneva Agreements, got under way between the Pathet Lao and a succession of Laotian governments. After several false starts, the government of the neutralist Prince Souvanna Phouma succeeded in November, 1957, in reaching an agreement with the Pathet Lao providing for the formation of a new, legal, parliamentary party, to be controlled by the Pathet Lao and known as the Neo Lao Hak Xat; and for the integration of two battalions of the Pathet Lao army into the Laotian army. In addition, two members of the Pathet Lao, including its nominal (but not actual) leader Prince Souphanouvong, were to be given cabinet ministries. This agreement, which was considered a setback for Western interests in Laos even though it did not specify that Laos was to be neutral, began to be implemented soon afterward, although the military aspect of the integration process remained purely nominal. In May, 1958, elections were held to fill twenty-one seats in the National Assembly, most of them to represent the two provinces still controlled by the Pathet Lao. Of these the Neo Lao Hak Xat and a friendly party together won thirteen, and these combined with eight already held made a total of twenty-one seats in a National Assembly of fifty-nine.

This startling result produced a wave of anti-Communist nationalism in Vientiane. Premier Souvanna Phouma promptly asked the ICC to leave the country, which it did, and thereby eliminated the main means — the Polish veto in the ICC — by which the ICC had enforced a pro-Communist interpretation of the Geneva Agreements on the Royal Laotian Government. Two months later he resigned, so as to permit a new cabinet to be formed without participation by the Neo Lao Hak Xat. This was done by Phoui Sananikone in August. With American support, the Sananikone government then began a vigorous program of political and economic reform. It also took over at least partial control of the two provinces of Phong Saly and Sam Neua, up to now controlled by the Pathet Lao, and began to patrol the poorly demarcated frontier with the DRV.[6] An unannounced incursion by VPA units near the 17th parallel on January 5, 1959, merely drove Sananikone to reorganize his cabinet and get increased powers from the National Assembly. On January 20, Ho Chi Minh visited Peking on his way to attend the Soviet party's Twenty-first Congress in Moscow. He presumably explained that control of at least the highlands of Laos was essential to the subverting of South Vietnam, and that Sananikone's program was therefore a threat to the Communist position not only in Laos but in South Vietnam as well. Chinese editorials and other forms of propaganda promptly began to endorse this view; in fact, the CPR tended to handle most of the diplomacy and international propaganda relating to the Laotian crisis, while leaving the DRV to deal with the situation on the ground, probably along lines mutually agreed on. About January 21, VPA troops quietly occupied some of the high ground overlooking the important road between Savannakhet, on the Mekong in Laos, and Tourane in South Vietnam.[7] On February 18, a day when the CPR signed a trade agreement with the DRV and extended further development aid to it, Foreign Minister Chen Yi accused Sananikone of tearing up the Geneva Agreements on Laos by preventing the return of the ICC and cooperating in an alleged American plan to turn Laos into a military base for "aggression against Indochina," presumably meaning the DRV.[8] Undeterred, Sananikone proceeded in mid-May to try to eliminate the DRV's main local agents by disarming and dissolving the two remaining battalions of Pathet Lao troops; he was successful with the first, but the second escaped and made for the North Vietnamese frontier, which it seems to have crossed.[9]

The CPR issued an official statement on May 18 accusing the Laotian government of provoking civil war. This interpretation, in addition to denying Sananikone's charges that the DRV was aiding and supporting the Pathet Lao, was quite possibly intended as a warning to the DRV that it should minimize its own role in the crisis, and that if it did not it could not expect the CPR to stand behind it to the extent of incurring real risks. In

---

[6] Cf. A. M. Halpern and H. B. Fredman, *Communist Strategy in Laos*, The RAND Corporation, June 14, 1960, pp. 5–13.

[7] *Ibid.*, p. 27.

[8] Text in *Concerning the Situation in Laos*, Peking: Foreign Languages Press, 1959, pp. 1–4.

[9] Halpern and Fredman, *op. cit.*, pp. 55–56.

addition, the statement rehearsed charges already made against the Sanani-kone government, to the effect that it had acquiesced in the exclusion of the ICC, established consular relations with the Republic of China, begun to let the United States make Laos into a strategic base, and allowed "KMT ir-regulars" to use Laotian soil as a base for raids into the CPR.[10] A week later Chen Yi wrote a letter to the cochairmen of the Geneva Conference (i.e., the British and Soviet Foreign Ministers) accusing the Sananikone government of disrupting the Geneva Agreements and demanding officially that the ICC be restored.[11]

Behind the CPR's exaggerated propaganda lay a genuine worry. The CPR's prestige had been damaged and its sense of insecurity heightened by the fiasco at Quemoy, the fighting in Tibet, and the open and rapid deteri-oration of relations with India. The CPR believed, apparently with justifi-cation, that since Sananikone's coming to power the Eisenhower administra-tion had decided to try to make Laos an anti-Communist bastion in Southeast Asia, rather than merely a neutral backwater as implied in the Geneva Agreements. The CPR was no doubt following with concern the rise to influence of J. Graham Parsons, who had been American Ambassador to Laos during the period (1956-57) when Souvanna Phouma was working out his coalition agreement with the Pathet Lao, had become a Deputy Assistant Secretary of State at the beginning of 1958, and in the spring of 1959 had become Assistant Secretary of State for Far Eastern Affairs in succession to Walter S. Robertson, who resigned shortly after the death of John Foster Dulles. It can hardly be a coincidence that Mr. Parsons' rise to be the highest American official concerned specifically with formulating Far Eastern policy occurred during the period when the Eisenhower ad-ministration was trying to make Laos into an anti-Communist bastion, or that he was transferred to Sweden as ambassador at the beginning of 1961, when the Kennedy administration decided to drop the bastion concept and agree to the neutralization of Laos. Thus to the CPR Parsons became the symbol if not the architect of an alleged American effort to deneutralize Laos, arm it, link it with South Vietnam in some sort of relationship with SEATO, and perhaps use it as a base for intensified operations by "KMT irregulars" against the CPR and by American Special Forces against both the CPR and the DRV. If such a program materialized, it would mean at the least a setback to the DRV's effort to seize power in South Vietnam, an effort to which the CPR was politically committed.

During August, 1959, the Sananikone government coped fairly success-fully with some rather feeble attempts by the Pathet Lao to restore the military situation that had existed prior to May, and on August 11 it decided to appeal to the United Nations. From the Communist point of view, if the

[10] Text in *Concerning the Situation in Laos, op. cit.*, pp. 34–36.
[11] Text in *ibid.*, pp. 43–45.

Laotian government was to appeal to anyone outside the country it should have appealed to the cochairmen of the Geneva Conference, who could have been relied on to do what they usually did: nothing. Furthermore, although the Sananikone government had not gone so far as to appeal to SEATO, a step that would have raised the old nightmare of American bases and forces throughout the Indochina area (except for the DRV, of course), the appeal to the United Nations might conceivably lead to international sanction for intervention (or counterintervention) by SEATO and the United States in Laos similar to what had happened in Korea. The CPR promptly denounced the Laotian appeal to the United Nations.[12] As might have been predicted, however, the issue was talked to death in the United Nations, and a factfinding mission sent to Laos in September was unable to find any evidence of direct involvement by the DRV, which had in fact been rather slight.[13]

In November, Secretary General Hammarskjold went to Laos and arranged a compromise whereby the government was to assume a more nearly neutral stance than it had since the summer of 1958, and the Pathet Lao was to refrain from hostilities. It was apparently understood that a violation by the government might bring on action by the DRV on a much larger scale than any so far taken. Sananikone's efforts to implement this compromise brought him into conflict with his more nationalist colleagues, who ousted him in December and formed a government more to their own liking. The non-neutral behavior of this government, including its rigging of an election held in April, 1960, in such a way as to ensure that no Neo Lao Hak Xat candidates were elected, contributed to a growing alarm and anger in Communist quarters over the rightward trend in Laos. The joint communiqué issued at the end of a visit by Chou En-lai to the DRV (May 9–14, 1960) dealt with Laos first among the Indochina countries. It warned that "continuation of the current situation in Laos would be dangerous" and insisted "that the leaders of the Neo Lao Hak Xat Party headed by Prince Souphanouvong should regain freedom, that the International [Control] Commission should resume its activities, that the civil war in Laos should stop, and that the Geneva Agreements should be truly respected and scrupulously implemented."[14] In short, the Pathet Lao must be allowed freedom gradually to subvert Laos with the minimum necessary, covert, support of the DRV and the CPR, without interference by the West or Thailand on behalf of the Laotian anti-Communists. If this should happen, Laos might become a *locus classicus* of the CPC's model of Communist-led "armed struggle," to the confounding of the "parliamentary path." Not only would threats to the CPR's security from the direction

---

[12] Text in *ibid.*, pp. 65–68.
[13] Halpern and Fredman, *op. cit.*, pp. 101–146.
[14] New China News Agency dispatch, Hanoi, May 14, 1960.

of Laos be eliminated, but Laos would become an avenue for the exertion of Chinese and North Vietnamese pressures on South Vietnam, Cambodia, Thailand, and conceivably Burma.

The first significant step toward this goal would obviously be a reversal of the existing trend in Laos in favor of one toward greater neutrality. Such a reversal soon occurred, although not necessarily as a result of the wishes or actions of the CPR or the DRV. In August, 1960, a patriotic, left neutralist paratroop captain named Kong Le (or Kong Lae) seized control of Vientiane and invited Prince Souvanna Phouma, the symbol of Laotian neutrality, to become premier once more. He did so and tried to establish a political situation somewhat resembling the one that had existed in the months prior to the election of May, 1958. He sought the cooperation, or at least the benevolent neutrality, of both the Pathet Lao and the nationalists led by General Phoumi. The latter refused to cooperate, however, and went to Savannakhet, in southern Laos, where he began to create an anti-Communist political and military base.

A situation rapidly developed in which American military aid went mainly to Phoumi in Savannakhet and Souvanna Phouma in Vientiane moved closer to the Pathet Lao, established diplomatic relations with the Soviet Union (a cochairman, it should be remembered, of the Geneva Conference), and began to receive limited amounts of Soviet aid, first economic and then also military, by airlift. Phoumi soon began to move on Vientiane, which he took in mid December. This act drove Souvanna Phouma temporarily to Cambodia, which had already begun to demand internationally supervised neutralization not only of Laos but also of Cambodia itself, and his followers including Kong Le into still closer association with the Pathet Lao. The neutralists and pro-Communists made their headquarters on the strategic Plain of Jars, north of Vientiane, and there both began to receive an increased flow of Soviet arms, airlifted in Soviet transport aircraft across the CPR and the DRV. With this aid the Pathet Lao, which received more external support and was far stronger than Kong Le's neutralist forces, rapidly expanded its control of the Laotian highlands, including those in southern Laos.

Serious defeats suffered by the inept forces of General Phoumi in the spring of 1961 convinced the newly installed Kennedy administration that Laos could not be made into a "situation of strength" or an anti-Communist bastion and that internationally supervised neutralization was the least undesirable solution. To prevent a further deterioration of Phoumi's position, or perhaps even a major disaster like Dienbienphu, the United States pressed for a ceasefire and abandoned its previous lack of interest in the question of reactivating the ICC. A number of threats of intervention by SEATO were used to counter the Communists' understandable lack of enthusiasm for measures tending to hamper their efforts to win a clear-cut victory before the beginning of negotiations.[15] The CPR's main reply to the American gestures and threats came in the form of a statement by Chen Yi, in the course of a press conference held in Djakarta: "If SEATO really does send troops of the SEATO member nations to take part in the civil war in Laos, and if the Chinese Government is requested by the legal government headed by Prince Phouma, we will not remain idle."[16] Obviously this threat was not only vague but conditional on an invitation from Souvanna Phouma, which he had shown no inclination to extend. Furthermore, the threat was directed against intervention by SEATO, not by the United States alone, and it was already clear that SEATO would not take action, if only because of French opposition.

It is possible that the American decision, whether known to the CPR at the time of Chen Yi's statement or not, to negotiate on the Laotian crisis rather than escalate it marked over the long term the psychological and military turning point in the DRV's struggle for control over South Vietnam and at least a large part of Laos.[17]

The repercussions of this episode were serious. In neutral circles, and especially in Cambodia, it was felt that the United States had brought this disaster on itself by its earlier effort to make Laos into an anti-Communist bastion, and that the only possible course was a formalization of the neutrality of Laos implicit in the Geneva Agreements of 1954.[18] In pro-Western circles, and especially in Thailand, the American decision not to escalate confirmed a suspicion that had been gaining ground since 1959, that when the chips were down the United States would balk at risky actions to check the advance of Communism in continental Southeast Asia. Thailand was acutely aware of the vulnerability of its impoverished northern region to Communist infiltration based on Laos.[19]

On the Communist side, the crisis in Laos unquestionably entered into the Sino-Soviet dispute, and in particular into the DRV's attitude toward it. The rigged Laotian election of April, 1960, was certainly not much of an advertisement for Khrushchev's "parliamentary path," and the next several months witnessed what appears to have been a partial eclipse of the presumed pro-Soviet faction under Vo Nguyen Giap and an increase in the influence of Truong Chinh and the pro-CPC faction. The North Vietnamese took a generally, but not strongly, pro-CPC stand at the various Sino-Soviet ideological confrontations of 1960, culminating with the Mos-

[15] George Modelski, ed., *SEATO: Six Studies*, Melbourne: F. W. Cheshire, 1962, pp. 14–15, 177.

[16] New China News Agency dispatch, Djakarta, April 4, 1961.

[17] Cf. Roger M. Smith, "Laos in Perspective," *Asian Survey*, vol. iii, no. 1 (January, 1963), pp. 64–65.

[18] Cf. Roger M. Smith, "Cambodia's Neutrality and the Laotian Crisis," *Asian Survey*, vol. i, no. 5 (July, 1961), pp. 17–24.

[19] Cf. David A. Wilson, "Thailand: Old Leaders and New Directions," *Asian Survey*, vol. iii, no. 2 (February, 1963), pp. 83–87.

cow meetings in November and December. On the other hand, at its Third Congress in September, the Lao Dong followed Ho Chi Minh's customary and essentially neutral course of not burning its bridges with either of the two major Communist powers, seeking aid and support from both, and playing them against each other to the extent possible. At the congress the Secretary Generalship passed from Ho to Le Duan, who probably shares Ho's views on this important question, rather than to a major known adherent of either the Soviet Union or the CPR.[20]

To the CPR the crisis in Laos presented a characteristic mixture of military danger and potential political gains. The danger resulted mainly from the possibility, remote though it was, that the fighting might bring forces of General Phoumi, Thailand, or the United States, or even all three, into Phong Saly province on the Chinese border, where "KMT irregulars" appear to have been already operating. The CPR's cooperation in the air-lift of Soviet arms to the Pathet Lao and Kong Le's troops was presumably designed in part to ward off this contingency, as well as to promote the cause of revolution at minimal risk to itself. The potential political gains would accrue mainly from the usually exaggerated fears held by non-Communists with respect to what the CPR might do in or about Indochina. This fear could and did serve as a useful lever for the extraction of political advantage.

From December 15 to 26, 1960, Prince Sihanouk visited the CPR. Among the documents that he — or rather his premier, Pho Procung — signed was a treaty of friendship and nonaggression providing that neither signatory should join an alliance directed against the other. Insofar as possible, the CPR and DRV were guaranteed in this way against the possibility that Communist pressures on the Indochina area might drive Cambodia to join SEATO or at least appeal for its protection. Two days after the end of Sihanouk's visit, Chen Yi sent a note to the British and Soviet governments denouncing alleged American intervention in Laos and Phoumi's attack on the Souvanna Phouma government and demanding the reactivation of the ICC, provided that it dealt only with Souvanna Phouma and not with Phoumi's regime, which was recognized by the United States as the legal government of Laos. If reactivation under these conditions was not feasible, the Geneva Conference should reconvene. Chen Yi's position was very similar to that already taken by the Soviet Union, except that the Russians were somewhat more insistent on the reconvening of the Geneva

[20] Cf. Honey, loc. cit., p. 34; William E. Griffith, Albania and the Sino-Soviet Rift, M.I.T. Press, 1963, pp. 37, 44–45, 49, 57, 144n.; Donald S. Zagoria, The Sino-Soviet Conflict, 1956–1961, Princeton University Press, 1962, pp. 336–337. Bernard B. Fall, "Power and Pressure Groups in North Vietnam," The China Quarterly, no. 9 (January–March, 1962), p. 40, seems to be mistaken in interpreting the congress as a victory for the pro-CPC faction; P. J. Honey, "North Vietnam's Party Congress," The China Quarterly. no. 4 (October–December, 1960), pp. 66–75, seems to be equally mistaken in interpreting it as a victory for the pro-Soviet faction.

Conference.[21] When Prince Sihanouk proposed on January 1 the convening of a broader conference representing not only the participants in the 1954 Geneva Conference but also the members of the ICC (India, Canada, and Poland), and the other countries having a common frontier with Laos (Burma, Thailand, and South Vietnam), making fourteen countries in all, the Russians and the Chinese promptly endorsed this alternative proposal.

■ THE GENEVA CONFERENCE ON LAOS AND ITS AFTERMATH (1961–64)

At the fourteen-nation Geneva Conference on Laos, which met intermittently from May, 1961, to July, 1962, the Communist participants displayed a degree of agreement so high as to indicate careful prior coordination and to permit the Soviet Union to act as their spokesman on most basic issues. There was general Communist agreement that SEATO protection must be withdrawn from Laos; that all foreign troops, including advisers, must also be withdrawn (no Communist bloc forces need be withdrawn, since none were admitted to be in Laos); that Laos must not be partitioned; and that a coalition government under the premiership of the neutral Prince Souvanna Phouma must be created by the Laotians themselves and placed under a minimum of international supervision. Such a solution, if achieved, would permit the gradual subversion of Laos by the Pathet Lao, with covert support from the DRV and the CPR, to proceed with the least possible risk of international complications. In essence the Communist proposals were adopted (in July, 1962), although the non-Communist participants succeeded in strengthening somewhat the degree of international supervision, and in particular the powers of the restored ICC.

Although in general agreement with the other Communist participants, the CPR, which sent a larger delegation than any other participant, was predictably more intransigent than the Soviet Union and concerned with certain interests of its own. The latter included two that stood out as the most important: the total abolition of SEATO, and not merely the withdrawal of its protection from Laos; and the elimination of all "KMT irregulars" from Laos.

Both these points were dealt with by Chen Yi in his first speech to the conference (on May 16). On the first point, he said that

> The aggressive SEATO military bloc has become the principal tool of the United States for encroaching on the sovereignty of different countries, interfering in their internal affairs and incessantly creating turmoil in Southeast Asia. This bloc is the root of tension not only in

---

[21] Cf. Brian Crozier, "Peking and the Laotian Crisis: An Interim Appraisal," *The China Quarterly*, no. 7 (July–September, 1961), pp. 129–130.

Laos but also in the whole of Southeast Asia. Only by abolishing this bloc can peace and security in Southeast Asia, including Laos, be preserved and consolidated.

He naturally failed to add that the SEATO countersubversion program offered a serious obstacle to the communization of continental Southeast Asia, Thailand in particular. On the second point, Chen insisted that "the remnant Kuomintang troops in Laos must be disarmed and sent out of Laos."[22]

The CPR took an active part in the Geneva Conference from the beginning and was a member of the powerful Drafting Committee.[23] As usual in such cases, it insisted that all decisions taken by the conference must be unanimous, and it therefore had to make some concessions on relatively minor points in order to secure unanimous consent to its major ones.[24] Although the CPR sponsored the Pathet Lao for membership in the Laotian delegation to the conference rather than Souvanna Phouma, who was sponsored by the Soviet Union,[25] the Chinese were if anything more insistent than the Russians that Souvanna Phouma was the only acceptable premier for a neutral Laotian coalition government.[26] The reason for this was to become clear later. The CPR was loud in its demands that foreign troops (other than those of the Communist bloc, who were not admitted to be present) must be withdrawn, and yet it also insisted that international supervision, including the powers of the ICC, must be minimized, allegedly in order not to infringe the sovereignty of Laos.[27] In his second major speech to the conference (on May 24), Chen Yi cited the relatively unsupervised neutrality of Cambodia as the best model for Laos.[28]

One of the major landmarks in the Geneva Conference on Laos was the talks between President Kennedy and Premier Khrushchev at Vienna (June 3–4, 1961), which committed both governments to Laotian neutrality, and the Soviet government to acceptance of the American demand for an "effective ceasefire" as a precondition for negotiations.[29] A few days later

---

[22] New China News Agency dispatch, Geneva, May 16, 1961 (text in "Chronology of Communist Reports on Laos, May 1–July 31, 1961," *Current Background* [Hong Kong: American Consulate General], no. 661 [September 13, 1961], pp. 26–30). Malcolm Macdonald, one of the British delegates, scored a telling point by saying that no Communist power had ever lodged a complaint of aggression against SEATO before the United Nations (Modelski, *op. cit.*, p. 104). The probable reason is that since the Korean War the CPR has disliked having problems relating to its national interests argued before the United Nations, in which it is not represented; it may also hope that a desire to be able to deal more effectively with such problems will lead the United Nations to vote the CPR in.

[23] *Ibid.*, p. 20.

[24] Crozier, "An Interim Appraisal," *loc. cit.*, pp. 116–117.

[25] Modelski, *op. cit.*, p. 15.

[26] Crozier, "An Interim Appraisal," *loc. cit.*, p. 134.

[27] Modelski, *op. cit.*, p. 29.

[28] New China News Agency dispatch, May 24, 1961 (text in "Chronology. . . ," *loc. cit.*, pp. 43–46).

[29] Text of joint communiqué in Modelski, *op. cit.*, p. 60.

(June 10–16), North Vietnamese Premier Pham Van Dong visited the CPR, evidently with the purpose among others of coordinating strategy on Laos and South Vietnam.[30]

In April, 1961, some fourteen months before the actual formation of a coalition government headed by himself, Souvanna Phouma visited the Soviet Union, the CPR, and the DRV in the company of Prince Souphanouvong; originally he was also scheduled to visit the United States, but this part of the trip was cancelled. The main concrete result of the visit to the CPR, so far as is known, was a commitment by the CPR to build a motor road linking the two countries.[31] Six months later, it was agreed that the Souvanna Phouma-Pathet Lao regime would establish a consulate general at Kunming, in Yunnan, and that the CPR would establish one at Phong Saly, the capital of the Laotian province of the same name bordering on the CPR.[32] Soon afterward the CPR created an "economic and cultural mission" in Laos under Ho Wei, its ambassador to the DRV.[13] This mission evidently played an important part in the formulation and execution of Chinese Laotian policy and in its coordination with the DRV, the Pathet Lao, and Souvanna Phouma.[34] On January 13, 1962, the CPR and the Souvanna Phouma–Pathet Lao regime signed agreements establishing civil air communications between them and providing for the CPR to build, without charge to the Laotians, a highway linking the town of Phong Saly with Mengla, the nearest town of any size in Yunnan.[35]

One of the main reasons for the long delay in forming a tripartite coalition government in Laos was the objections of Thailand, which had considerable influence over General Phoumi. Thai objections eased after the United States promised in March, 1962, to give unilateral protection to Thailand in the event of a crisis, which the trend of events in Laos made increasingly likely, even if SEATO as a whole failed to act. Thereupon Phoumi rashly committed a large proportion of his forces to action in Nam Tha, the northwestern province of Laos, which borders on both Burma and the CPR, perhaps in a last ditch effort to obstruct a settlement along the lines envisaged at Geneva. The CPR was alarmed by this development, especially since "KMT irregulars" were allegedly in the area and General Phoumi and Prince Boun Oum were in Taiwan, and by the announcement in mid-May that American troops would be sent to Thailand. For its part the Phoumi regime charged that Communist Chinese troops were in Nam Tha. Whatever the facts of this obscure episode, the result was another defeat for Phoumi by the Pathet Lao, with or without Chinese participa-

[30] Cf. joint communiqué released by New China News Agency, June 16, 1961.
[31] Text of joint communiqué released by New China News Agency, April 25, 1961.
[32] New China News Agency dispatch, October 7, 1961.
[33] New China News Agency dispatch, November 6, 1961.
[34] Cf. Crozier, "A Further Appraisal," *loc. cit.*, pp. 120–122.
[35] New China News Agency dispatch, January 13, 1962.

tion. The tripartite coalition government was finally formed in June and soon established diplomatic relations with the CPR. It was probably the CPR, rather than the DRV, that was mainly responsible for supplying and advising the Pathet Lao in the Nam Tha and Phong Saly areas. If so, the CPR was evidently in the process of establishing a buffer and sphere of influence beyond its border with Laos and perhaps as much as one hundred miles deep.[36]

The Geneva agreements on Laos, signed in July, 1962, gave the Soviet Union approximately what it seems to have wanted for China sixteen years earlier: a superficial stability presided over by a coalition government, whose existence would tend to inhibit "imperialist" intervention and yet would give the local Communists a reasonable chance of coming to power in time by means of salami-slicing tactics. Accordingly, the Soviet Union terminated its airlift to Laos in the spring of 1962 and placed its main reliance on the settlement that it had been instrumental in working out at Geneva.

As it turned out, events in Laos since the settlement of 1962 have moved rather more rapidly than the Soviet Union would probably prefer, and yet it has had no choice but to give at least verbal support to what its fellow-Communists were doing. Prince Souphanouvong has boycotted the coalition government, which supposedly can make major decisions only by unanimous vote, since the spring of 1963, presumably in the hope of hamstringing it. The rightist forces of General Phoumi have remained generally in the Mekong Valley and have not seriously contested control of the highlands with the Pathet Lao. The latter, with Chinese and North Vietnamese political and logistical support, has split and repeatedly attacked Kong Le's neutralist forces, with the effect of driving Kong Le and Souvanna Phouma politically closer to Phoumi and the West.[37] In disgust at this situation, a group of rightist generals staged a coup in Vientiane on April 19, 1964, whose main effects seem to have been to pull Souvanna Phouma still further to the right and widen the gulf between him and the leftist elements, and to increase the tension in and about Laos to a level higher than had existed at any other time since the signing of the agreements of 1962.

Since 1962 the CPR has not confined itself to aiding and supporting the efforts of the DRV and the Pathet Lao in Laos but has pursued its own objectives as well. In December, 1962, it received a rather surprising visitor in the form of General Phoumi Nosavan, now serving as Vice Premier and Minister of Finance in Souvanna Phouma's coalition government. The joint communiqué issued at the end of the visit stated cryptically that the Lao-

---

[36] Cf. Crozier, "A Further Appraisal," *loc. cit.*, pp. 117–119.

[37] Cf. Stuart Simmonds, "Laos: A Renewal of Crisis," *Asian Survey*, vol. iv, no. 1 (January, 1964), pp. 680–685; Stanley Karnow, "Laos: The Settlement That Settled Nothing," *The Reporter*, April 25, 1963, pp. 34–37; Eric Pace, "Laos: Continuing Crisis," *Foreign Affairs*, vol. 43, no. 1 (October, 1964), pp. 64–74.

tians had asked the CPR to "expand" the road it was building from Mengla to Phong Saly so as to make it terminate at Ban Houei Sai in Nam Tha province, just across the Mekong from the northern tip of Thailand. "The Chinese party stated that it would consider this request."[38] This episode makes little sense unless one assumes that the Vientiane government's hold on Nam Tha was so tenuous that Phoumi had no choice but to accede to a Chinese declaration of intent to build such a road, and that the CPR intended to build the road from Mengla rather than from Phong Saly or some other point. The construction of such a road would give the CPR access to the northern part of Thailand and would be essential for this purpose inasmuch as the roads that its technicians were building in the border regions of Burma as part of the Chinese aid program were not connected with the Chinese road net. There have been reports since that time that the CPR has actually been working on a highway from Mengla to Ban Houei Sai.[39]

A further element of confusion and uncertainty was added when a more exalted Laotian delegation, led by King Savang Vatthana and including Souvanna Phouma and several of his ministers, visited the CPR in March, 1963, a few days after the CPR had created (on March 4) a China-Laos Friendship Association. This time the joint communiqué, in addition to routinely pledging both sides to observe the Geneva Agreements of 1962, announced that the CPR would complete the highway between Mengla and Phong Saly the following month, withdraw "all its personnel engaged in road construction" immediately thereafter, and turn the road over to the Laotian government.[40] Nothing was said about the fact that the writ of the Laotian government did not run in Phong Saly province, or about a second road to Ban Houei Sai. Presumably Souvanna Phouma had refused to confirm Phoumi's concession.

Nevertheless, while the political situation in Laos continued to deteriorate, the CPR followed its policy of giving verbal support to Souvanna Phouma and both verbal and actual support to the Pathet Lao. Presumably in an effort to secure more than verbal Chinese support for his efforts to restore something like the situation envisaged in the 1962 agreements, Souvanna Phouma visited the CPR once more in April, 1964. He got a benevolent joint communiqué, but apparently little more.[41] A few days later occurred the rightist coup in Vientiane already mentioned. The CPR denounced the coup and demanded that its leaders restore Souvanna Phouma's freedom of action and that the leaders of the three recognized Laotian factions (Souvanna Phouma, Phoumi, and Souphanouvong) hold

[38] Text released by New China News Agency, December 4, 1962.
[39] Denis Warner, "China's New Roads: Where Do They Lead?" *The Reporter*, September 26, 1963, p. 33; *The New York Times*, April 21, 1964.
[40] Text released by New China News Agency, March 10, 1963.
[41] Text released by New China News Agency, April 8, 1963.

talks on the restoration of political stability, failing which the powers that had participated in the Geneva Conference of 1961–62 should "hold consultations without delay and take effective measures to check the criminal activities of United States imperialism and its lackeys, resolutely uphold the Geneva Agreements and the Laotian Government of National Union and firmly preserve peace in Laos and Indochina."[42]

There was no significant response to this appeal, and in mid-May the Pathet Lao and its so-called "true neutralist" allies opened an offensive against Kong Le's forces in the Plain of Jars, presumably with Chinese acquiescence. Meanwhile two of the Chinese troops and technicians who had been in Phong Saly province for the past few years had been captured by tribesmen on May 8 and turned over to the Vientiane government, which charged soon afterward that Chinese troops had joined Pathet Lao and North Vietnamese forces in committing some atrocities against villages in Phong Saly by way of reprisal.[43]

On May 26 the CPR rejected a British request that it use its influence to restrain the Pathet Lao and proposed, in a letter to the nations that had taken part in the Geneva Conference, that the conference reconvene at Phnom Penh, in Cambodia, to discuss the Laotian crisis. The letter indicated alarm at air action already taken by the United States in support of Souvanna Phouma and Kong Le and at the possibility of further American escalation.[44] Another Chinese statement, on June 9, called the situation in Laos "most dangerous," rebuked the British explicitly and the Poles implicitly for their efforts to find some diplomatic solution to the crisis short of a reconvening of the Geneva Conference, and called for a reconvening of the conference either at Phnom Penh or at Geneva.[45] By this time it seemed to be the CPR, rather than the Soviet Union as at the Geneva Conference, that was speaking for the DRV and the Pathet Lao.

American air action against Khang Kay, the Pathet Lao headquarters in Xieng Khouang province, which resulted in damage to the CPR's "cultural mission" there, was protested by the People's Daily on June 10[46] and in a governmental statement issued on June 13.[47] The latter demanded once

---

[42] CPR Foreign Ministry statement, April 22, 1964 (New China News Agency dispatch, same date). This was the 94th anniversary of Lenin's birth, and the statement was probably intended as a reminder of the Soviet Union's alleged revolutionary duty to take action to nullify the Vientiane coup and create more favorable conditions for the salami-slicing tactics of the Pathet Lao.

[43] The New York Times, May 24, 27, 1964.

[44] New China News Agency dispatch, May 26, 1964.

[45] New China News Agency dispatch, June 9, 1964; for commentary see The New York Times, June 10, 1964.

[46] "Another Serious Step Taken by the United States in Extending Armed Intervention in Laos," People's Daily, June 10, 1964; for commentary see The New York Times, June 11, 1964.

[47] New China News Agency dispatch, June 13, 1964; for commentary see The New York Times, June 14, 1964.

more the reconvening of the Geneva Conference and threatened, not very convincingly, that otherwise "the flames of war in Indochia may spread." Soon afterward the *People's Daily* proclaimed that "peace in Indochina and Southeast Asia is hanging by a thread."[48] The lack of any major overt Chinese act made it appear that these prophecies of doom were designed mainly to startle the other powers into reconvening the Geneva Conference. The same was probably true of a special military review and a "working conference" of party officials held in the CPR in mid-June.[89]

Clearly worried by the refusal of the United States to be deterred by such warnings, Chen Yi stated on June 24 that[50]

> The situation in Indochina has become increasingly grave in the past few days. In disregard of the serious protests of the Laotian and Chinese people, the United States is continuing its wanton bombing in Laos and stepping up its preparations for new military adventures in southern Vietnam. It openly vaunted that it would extend the war in Indochina and completely tear up the two sets of Geneva agreements.
>
> It must be pointed out that Indochina is situated by China and not by the United States. China is a signatory to the two sets of Geneva agreements. Nobody should have any misunderstandings. The Chinese people absolutely will not sit idly by while the Geneva agreements are completely torn up and the flames of war spread to their side [i.e., apparently, to their border]. We have advocated the convening of the Geneva Conference to seek first of all a peaceful settlement of the Laotian question. However, should any people mistake this for a sign of weakness and think they can do whatever they please in Indochina, they would repent too late.

The rather synthetic Sino-American military confrontation over Laos soon eased sufficiently, although not necessarily as a result of Chen's warning, for the CPR to be able to turn its main attention to political matters. It had been growing more and more disgusted with Souvanna Phouma for his increasingly anti-Communist attitude, and on July 6 the *People's Daily* strongly implied that the CPR no longer recognized him as a neutral or as the premier of Laos; it also denied his charge, which was supported by considerable evidence, that the CPR was actually building the highway from Mengla to Ban Houei Sai.[51] This rebuke was understandably interpreted as a threat to transfer Chinese diplomatic recognition from the Souvanna Phouma government to a government to be created by the Pathet

---

48 "Serious Provocation by U.S. Imperialists," *People's Daily*, June 15, 1964; for commentary see *The New York Times*, June 16, 1964.

49 Cf. *The New York Times*, June 19 and 21, 1964.

50 New China News Agency dispatch, June 24, 1964; for commentary see *The New York Times*, June 26, 1964.

51 "Serious Advice for Prince Souvanna," *People's Daily*, July 6, 1964; for commentary see *The New York Times*, July 7, 1964.

Lao-dominated "true neutralists,"[52] but this step had not been taken by the time of writing.

A Chinese note of August 2 to the Soviet Union welcomed the latter's support for the reconvening of the Geneva Conference and reminded it politely of its duty to promote the leftist cause in Laos:[53]

> The Chinese Government hopes that the Soviet Government will truly shoulder its responsibilities as a cochairman of the Geneva Conference and, together with the other socialist countries, make continued efforts to stop the U.S. imperialist aggression and intervention in the Indochinese states, safeguard the Geneva agreements, and defend the peace of Indochina.

In a weak and highly fluid country bordering on the CPR, such as Laos, there seem to be three main components to Chinese policy. One is to create if possible an unannounced buffer zone and sphere of influence in the border area, so as to provide security — for example, by creating the facilities to give warning of any possible hostile movements — and to facilitate contact with local leftists and the ultimate subversion of the country as a whole. Another is pressures on the government, through diplomatic channels if available, among others, so as to influence its composition and policies. The third is contact and cooperation with the local leftists, and perhaps with the overseas Chinese community. Border disputes and the actual or alleged presence of "KMT irregulars," although genuine issues to some extent, have been skillfully used where possible to give the CPR leverage on the country in question. In the case of Laos and perhaps the border regions of Burma, possibly the most important single Chinese purpose is to gain covert access to the border regions of Thailand, so as to add subversion to the concert of pressures that the CPR hopes will ultimately push Thailand out of SEATO and so deprive the latter of its only significant base in continental Southeast Asia. The DRV's main interest in Laos also seems to be an extrinsic one, namely access to South Vietnam. These considerations help to explain why the obvious possibility of serious Sino-Vietnamese friction over comparative influence in Laos does not seem to have materialized so far. Nor is there any reason why the Pathet Lao should not cooperate in Chinese subversion of Thailand and North Vietnamese subversion of South Vietnam as the price of indispensable aid and support in its own quest for power.

■ **THE VIETNAMESE CRISIS (1959–64)**

In the spring of 1959, at the time the Laotian crisis assumed serious proportions, the North Vietnamese regime evidently decided to intensify

---

[52] *Christian Science Monitor*, July 8, 1964.

[53] New China News Agency dispatch, August 2, 1964; for commentary see *The New York Times*, August 3, 1964.

its terrorism and subversion in South Vietnam; by the end of the year this activity had become a major problem for the Diem government.[54] The CPC was then in a militant mood on account of such things as the crisis in Tibet and its growing controversy with Khrushchev over the "national liberation movement," and there is no reason to doubt that it was wholly in favor of the DRV's step, as long as it did not tend to increase unduly North Vietnamese influence on Laos and Cambodia. One of the main objectives of Asian Communist guerrilla warfare, and one that is only too often achieved, is to provoke the government in power into politically suicidal mass reprisals against civilians, in the hope of annihilating some terrorists in the process. The Diem government obligingly fell into this trap, and its domestic political standing rapidly declined to the point where there was a major, although unsuccessful, army revolt against it in November, 1960.

In the latter months of 1960, Laos rather than South Vietnam was the main focus of attention in the Indochina area. In the summer and autumn of 1960 Prince Sihanouk began to propose an international guarantee of the neutrality of his own country and of Laos, which was then presided over by Souvanna Phouma and Kong Le. When they were driven out of Vientiane by Phoumi's forces, Sihanouk went almost immediately (December 15–26) to the CPR, where he got a "treaty of friendship and nonaggression" and probably some sort of assurance that as long as he behaved himself his country would not suffer in the course of the impending escalation of the Laotian struggle by the DRV, presumably with the support of the CPR.

The DRV's response to the Laotian crisis, as well as to the military revolt in South Vietnam, was to have its agents in South Vietnam proclaim the creation of a National Front for the Liberation of South Vietnam (NFLSV) on December 20.[55] The NFLSV's program described its foreign policy as one of "peace and neutrality" and announced that it intended to "develop free relations with the nations of Southeast Asia, in particular with Cambodia and Laos."[56] This was the germ of the NFLSV's later, more explicit, demand for a coalition government, the withdrawal of foreign troops, a confederated "peace zone" embracing Laos and Cambodia as well as South Vietnam, and the subsequent reunification of Vietnam by "peaceful" means. As in 1954, at the Geneva Conference, the DRV was trying to use a victory, actual or potential, in one of the Indochinese states as a lever for communizing the others. Also as in 1954, the CPR was to show only a very limited partiality for this idea.

---

[54] Cf. Secretary Rusk's news conference of May 4, 1961 (*The New York Times*, May 5, 1961).

[55] Radio Hanoi, January 29, 1961.

[56] Text in Bernard B. Fall, *The Two Viet-Nams: A Political and Military Analysis*, New York: Praeger, 1963, pp. 439–443.

By the spring of 1961, the rapid expansion of Communist bases in the highlands of Laos posed a mortal threat to South Vietnam. Realizing this, the United States accelerated its aid to the Diem government, the culminating step being the mission of General Maxwell D. Taylor to Saigon in October. This raising of the level of American involvement in South Vietnam was naturally anathema to both the DRV and the CPR. On October 30, the North Vietnamese Foreign Minister sent a message of protest to the United Nations Secretary General.[57] When the CPR "endorsed" this appeal, on November 29, it refrained from mentioning that it had been addressed to the United Nations and thus indicated once more the allergy that it had developed since 1951 to having matters in which it considered its security to be involved handled by the United Nations.[58] To counter the Taylor mission, the CPR sent a military mission of its own to the DRV (December 15–31), under Marshal Yeh Chien-Ying. Apparently this mission agreed to increase the flow of Chinese equipment and training for the VPA. It may also have offered the DRV some sort of military alliance, such as the CPR had concluded with North Korea a few months earlier, but if so the DRV evidently did not accept.

Parallel with this military escalation went a political escalation, to which added point was given by an attack on the South Vietnamese presidential palace in February, 1962, by two mutinous fighter aircraft, which then sought asylum in Cambodia. Presumably to maximize its own external support, or at least to avoid being forced to commit itself totally to either party to the Sino-Soviet dispute, the DRV tried with some slight success to mediate the dispute in the early months of 1962. On January 16, a joint statement by a labor group affiliated with the NFLSV and by the All-China Federation of Trade Unions committed the "Chinese workers and people" to support neutrality for South Vietnam, but nothing was said about a "peace zone."[59] Two days later Radio Hanoi announced that "during the last days of 1961 Marxist-Leninists in South Vietnam met and decided to set up the Vietnamese People's Revolutionary Party." The party's platform endorsed the idea of a "broad democratic coalition government" and "national reunification by peaceful means," but not neutrality for South Vietnam or a "peace zone."[60] There is convincing evidence that, as the term Marxist-Leninist, probably modeled on Fidel Castro's famous confession of faith a few weeks earlier, suggests, this was a crypto-Communist party created by the DRV, probably in order to control the NFLSV and to direct on the ground the politico-military campaign planned in Hanoi against the Diem government and its American ally.[61] The NFLSV, for its

[57] Text released by Vietnam News Agency, October 30, 1961.
[58] New China News Agency dispatch, November 29, 1961.
[59] New China News Agency dispatch, January 16, 1962.
[60] Radio Hanoi, January 18, 1962.
[61] Cf. P. J. Honey, "North Vietnam's Workers' Party and South Vietnam's People's Revolutionary Party," *Pacific Affairs*, vol. xxxv, no. 4 (winter, 1962–63), pp. 381–383.

part, continued to agitate for a foreign policy of "peace and neutrality" for South Vietnam.[62] Neither the CPR nor the DRV said much about the concept of neutrality for South Vietnam as a rule, the former probably because the idea had become entangled with that of a "peace zone," to which it objected, and the latter because it wanted to make it appear that the demand for neutrality was entirely a spontaneous one originating in South Vietnam itself.[63]

The Communist position in South Vietnam was somewhat complicated when on June 2, partly no doubt because of the deterioration in its own relations with the CPR, India voted with Canada in the ICC for Vietnam, over Polish objections, to accuse the DRV of "acts of aggression and subversion" against South Vietnam. The DRV and the CPR of course denied the charge, which was made only after five years of terrorism in South Vietnam, on June 4 and 9 respectively. This embarrassing accusation was more than offset, however, by the fact that an agreement on Laos was coming into existence along lines highly acceptable to the Communist side. The Laotian settlement was now to be cited by the Communists as the prototype for South Vietnam. Speaking before the World Conference for General Disarmament and Peace in Moscow the following month, Nguyen Van Hieu, Secretary General of the NFLSV, demanded that Indochina be made a "peace zone."[64] A few days later, he falsely attributed the proposal for a neutral "peace zone" embracing South Vietnam, Laos, and Cambodia to Prince Sihanouk.[65] On July 20, the anniversary of the signing of the Geneva agreements of 1954 and a few days before the signing of the Geneva agreements on Laos, the NFSLV announced "four emergency policies"; these included the following demands:[66]

> Form a national coalition government composed of representatives of political parties having different political tendencies. . . . This government is to be responsible for achieving and ensuring peace, holding free general elections. . . , releasing all political prisoners. . . .
> South Vietnam will pursue a foreign policy of peace and neutrality, establish friendly relations with all countries, first and foremost the neighbor countries.

Shortly afterward the NFLSV issued a "fourteen-point policy of independence and neutrality," which contained the statement that "South

[62] Cf. statement of January 17, 1962, released by Vietnam News Agency, January 24, 1962.

[63] Cf. Ho Chi Minh's Interview with London *Daily Express*, in which he said that "It is up to the people of South Vietnam to decide whether South Vietnam is to have a neutral regime or any other regime; nobody can go counter to the people's aspirations" (Vietnam News Agency dispatch, March 27, 1962).

[64] Tass dispatch, July 10, 1962.

[65] Vietnam News Agency dispatch, July 16, 1962. The DRV shortly felt compelled to publish Sihanouk's denial of paternity of the idea (Vietnam News Agency dispatch, July 25, 1962).

[66] Vietnam News Agency dispatch, July 22, 1962.

Vietnam is ready to form with the kingdoms of Cambodia and Laos a peaceful and neutral zone in Southeast Asia, in which each member enjoys full sovereignty."[67]

Nguyen Van Hieu took his case to the CPR in September–October and received a rare Chinese endorsement of the NFLSV's interpretation of South Vietnamese neutrality. The joint communiqué affirmed that[68]

A national, democratic coalition government embracing all political tendencies must be established [in South Vietnam], a foreign policy of peace and neutrality must be realized. South Vietnam must be prepared to form a neutral zone together with Cambodia and Laos, in which their respective sovereignty is fully retained.

These demands were repeated in an editorial in the *People's Daily* the following day.[69] Later events were to show that this Chinese endorsement of the NFLSV's concept of South Vietnamese neutrality had either been given with tongue in cheek or was withdrawn soon afterward, presumably because it seemed to threaten a great increase of North Vietnamese influence in Laos and Cambodia, the other components of the "peace zone." The temporary endorsement may have been evoked by the hope of North Vietnamese support in the escalating Sino-Indian border crisis, and such support was forthcoming in November.

Against a background of deteriorating conditions, from the anti-Communist standpoint, in Laos and South Vietnam, Prince Sihanouk spent nearly the whole month of March, 1963, in the CPR, and it was announced on April 27 that Liu Shao-ch'i, Chairman of the CPR, would shortly visit Cambodia and the DRV. On May 8, while Liu was briefly back in the CPR after visiting Cambodia and before visiting the DRV, there began the conflict between the South Vietnamese Buddhists and the Diem government that was to contribute so heavily to the latter's downfall. Sihanouk was enraged by Diem's treatment of his Vietnamese fellow-Buddhists, and it was probably with at least Sihanouk's passive cooperation that the flow of arms to the Viet Cong, or Communist guerrillas, from the DRV and the CPR was greatly accelerated after the middle of 1963, an estimated three-fourths of them passing through Cambodia.[70] The decision to intensify the pressures on the Diem government in this way was probably taken during Liu Shao-ch'i's visit to the DRV (May 10–16, 1963). The joint communiqué naturally made no mention of this but merely endorsed

---

67 Vietnam News Agency dispatch, August 18, 1962.
68 New China News Agency dispatch, October 5, 1962.
69 "Heroic People, Shining Example," *People's Daily*, October 6, 1962.
70 Cf. *The New York Times*, January 5, May 20, 1964; *Christian Science Monitor*, September 9, 1964; Secretary McNamara's news conference of March 5, 1964 (text in *The New York Times*, March 6, 1964). On the Buddhist crisis see Charles A. Joiner, "South Vietnam's Buddhist Crisis: Organization for Charity, Dissidence, and Unity," *Asian Survey*, vol. iv, no. 7 (July, 1964), pp. 915–928.

neutrality for South Vietnam, without referring to the "peace zone."[71] After Ngo Dinh Nhu's famous military raid on the Buddhist temples on August 21, both Ho Chi Minh (on August 28) and Mao Tse-tung (on August 29) issued personal statements protesting the raid and attributing ultimate responsibility for it to the United States. Also on August 29, President de Gaulle further complicated an already confused situation by saying that Vietnam should be able to live "in independence from exterior influences, in internal peace and unity, and in concord with its neighbors." He made it clear that he was referring to "all of Vietnam."[72] Since this vague proposal obviously bore some resemblance to the NFLSV's proposals for a neutral South Vietnam, a "peace zone," and ultimate reunification of Vietnam, and since it clearly called for an American withdrawal, it was welcomed, although not necessarily with any great enthusiasm, in the DRV. The main drawback of de Gaulle's oracular utterance from the Communist standpoint was that it was evidently meant to imply an end to the Chinese presence in North Vietnam, as well as to the American presence in South Vietnam; furthermore, it gave no indication that the French government would welcome an increase of North Vietnamese influence in Laos and Cambodia. The CPR evidently found de Gaulle's statement ambiguous and puzzling and said little about it.

After the overthrow of the Diem government on November 1, the NFLSV published "six urgent demands," of which the sixth specified a neutral coalition government for South Vietnam and the formation of a neutral "peace zone" together with Laos and Cambodia, prior to the ultimate "peaceful" reunification of Vietnam.[73] On at least two occasions during the next several weeks, the CPR gave an indication of what it really thought of these proposals by going through the motions of "endorsing" the "six urgent demands" in some detail, but without mentioning the concept of neutrality or that of the "peace zone."[74]

The coming to power of General Nguyen Khanh in South Vietnam at the end of January, 1964, followed by some threatening remarks on the Vietnamese situation by President Johnson in February, naturally caused some concern in the DRV and the CPR. A North Vietnamese delegation journeyed to Moscow at the end of January, but apparently without getting any significant Soviet commitments; the bland joint communiqué barely mentioned the situation in South Vietnam.[75] It was clear that effective external support for the DRV in the event of American escalation, if any, would have to come from the CPR, which had received no deliveries of

---

[71] Text released by New China News Agency, May 16, 1963.

[72] *The New York Times*, August 30, 1963.

[73] Text released by Vietnam News Agency, November 17, 1963.

[74] "Oppose the Intensified U.S. Imperialist Aggression in South Vietnam," *People's Daily*, December 2, 1963; Liu Ning-i, speech of December 21, 1963 (Peking radio, December 21, 1963).

[75] Text released by Vietnam News Agency, February 15, 1964.

military equipment from the Soviet Union since 1960 and had shown itself since the Korean War to be very reluctant to run serious risks over situations in which the United States was involved. In addition to Vietnamese nationalism and traditional sinophobia, one of the considerations that inhibit the DRV from taking the Chinese side unreservedly in the Sino-Soviet dispute is probably the fact that the CPR has deprived itself, by its political pressures on the Soviet Union, of any hope of acquiring in the near future the sort of weapons it would have to have to deter the United States from escalating the conflict to the level of a major attack on North Vietnam, if it should decide to do so. Furthermore, the Soviet Union seems no more willing to make such weapons available to the DRV than to the CPR.

A number of developments in the first weeks of 1964 emphasized both the DRV's need for external support and the uncertainty of its prospects of getting it. On February 12, the newspaper *Nhan Dan* rejected President de Gaulle's proposal that North as well as South Vietnam be neutralized. The January number of the periodical *Hoc Tap*, which was released on February 11, carried an important article listing the options open to the United States regarding South Vietnam as withdrawal, greatly increased aid, and an attack on the DRV, perhaps with nuclear weapons. The last possibility, which obviously disturbs the DRV greatly, was rated as unlikely because the United States would have to "cope" with the CPR, "or eventually the socialist camp as a whole." The actual outcome predicted was an eventual American withdrawal after "some years" of "heavier and heavier defeats," but only following a "general counteroffensive" by the United States and the South Vietnamese government in 1964.[76] The New China News Agency's summary of the article, which was not published until February 28, omitted the passage dealing with possible aid to the DRV by the CPR and other members of the "socialist camp." Nor did a note of March 3, from Chen Yi to the North Vietnamese Foreign Minister, and a *People's Daily* editorial of March 4 on the Vietnamese situation, make any mention of possible Chinese intervention on behalf of the DRV. The editorial assured the North Vietnamese, and others who might find themselves in a similar situation, that the political situation in the world as a whole would deter the United States from attacking North Vietnam, and that in the absence of such an attack the existing conditions of the struggle in South Vietnam favored the Communist side in the long run:[77]

> The decisive factor in war is man, and the role played by man in a war is determined by its nature. . . . All unjust wars inevitably meet with the opposition of the people, whereas all just wars enjoy their support. . . .

[76] See the excellent analysis in "Hanoi Foresees Victory in South Vietnam But Only After Long Guerrilla War," *Special Information Note* (Washington), no. 39 (April 7, 1964).

[77] For commentary see *The New York Times*, February 14 and 29, March 5, 1964.

The victories of the South Vietnamese people have encouraged and supported all the oppressed nations and peoples of the world. . . .

At the same time, the struggles of the Asian, African, and Latin American peoples have also assisted the South Vietnamese people by harassing U.S. imperialism on all fronts and thus preventing it from throwing its all against the South Vietnamese people.

It is likely that the CPR's obvious reluctance to run any serious risks over the Indochinese crisis was due not only to the inadequacy and obsolescence of its armed forces, and its usual caution in situations where the United States is involved, but also to its preoccupation with the Sino-Soviet border dispute. In any event, the DRV clearly had no choice but to proceed with great care. In an interview with the Australian pro-Communist journalist Wilfred Burchett, on April 13, Ho Chi Minh went so far as to show a polite interest in President de Gaulle's proposals:[78]

> At the present juncture, I think that President de Gaulle's suggestions on the neutralization of this part of Southeast Asia including South Vietnam — meaning also by this word the liquidation of military bases and foreign interference — deserves serious attention.

Ho then indicated that he would insist on France's supporting the "peaceful unification" of Vietnam.

The spring and summer of 1964 witnessed the tenth anniversary of the Dienbienphu battle and the Geneva Conference and agreements. Clearly the DRV wanted to lend luster to the occasion by further victories, and the CPR was of the same mind provided the risks to itself were not excessive and North Vietnamese influence in Laos and Cambodia were not unduly increased. On July 1, on the occasion of the CPC's forty-third birthday and the 300th "serious warning" by the CPR to the United States over intrusions by American ships and aircraft within the twelve-mile zone of territorial waters claimed by the CPR, the *People's Daily* warned once more that American military power would not deter the CPR from defending itself and pursuing its objectives. At about the same time, the DRV increased the rate at which its regular troops were infiltrating into South Vietnam, to supplement the efforts of the local Viet Cong.[79] Obviously this was the kind of step that the CPR and the DRV considered most likely to accelerate victory in South Vietnam with the least risk of American escalation.

Such escalation remained a possibility, however, and the CPR set about trying to deter it by a carefully graded series of threats and gestures. The DRV and the world were assured, in a note from Chen Yi on July 6 and an editorial in the *People's Daily* on July 9, that the CPR recognized the DRV as a fellow-member of the "socialist camp," and as the "lips" to its

---

[78] Vietnam News Agency dispatch, April 24, 1964.
[79] *The Washington Post and Times Herald*, August 15, 1964.

own "teeth," and that the Chinese "people" would never allow the United States to "play with fire" with impunity.[80] Although these statements were less strong than they were intended to appear, they did contain a hint that the Chinese "people" might decide to send "volunteers" to help the DRV if the need arose. A similar note was struck in a governmental statement of July 19 and a *People's Daily* editorial of July 20.

In a news conference held on July 23, President de Gaulle made another attempt to be helpful. He proposed the convening of another conference on Indochina with the same membership as the one held in 1954. He advocated the termination of intervention in Indochina by the "powers bearing direct responsibility for what was and what is the fate of Vietnam." He named as those powers France, China, the Soviet Union, and the United States; the omission of Britain, a major architect of the 1954 settlement and a cochairman of both Geneva Conferences, was characteristic of de Gaulle's diplomacy. He also advocated "massive" and disinterested economic and technical aid to Indochina.[81]

In spite of occasional threats and warnings emanating from Moscow, it was fairly clear that the Soviet Union was most reluctant to be involved by its nominal allies in the Indochinese crisis, and that reponsibility for deterring possible American escalation rested with the CPR. By the end of July there were reports of the massing of Chinese troops and aircraft in the area bordering on North Vietnam.[82] Words also remained an important element of deterrence, however, On August 1 the Viennese newspaper, *Der Kurier*, published two interviews recently given in Shanghai to one of its editors, Dr. Hugo Portisch, one by Chen Yi and the other by an unnamed high official, evidently Chou En-lai. The interview with Chen Yi added nothing of importance to previous Chinese statements on Indochina and other subjects. The other interview, however, was an interesting and important one.[83]

Its main theme was a denial of any aggressive intent on the part of the CPR toward the rest of Asia, on both political and military grounds. The military grounds stated were the inadequacy of Chinese military power for offensive combat against a first class enemy, not the fear of retaliation against the mainland of China; in fact, it was explicitly affirmed that a nuclear attack on the CPR could not bring victory to the United States. In view of the CPR's obvious fear of such an attack if it should actually occur, and its equally obvious belief that it is unlikely to occur, this last statement was probably intended as additional insurance against the already improbable.

As for Indochina, the CPR's objective was defined as the familiar one

---

[80] For commentary see *The New York Times,* July 10, 1964.
[81] Excerpts in *The New York Times,* July 24, 1964.
[82] Cf. *The Washington Post and Times Herald,* July 26, 1964.
[83] Text of unattributed interview in *The New York Times,* August 7, 1964.

of "peace and neutrality," which was described as the only situation that would be acceptable to both the United States and the CPR and was defined as consisting essentially of the withdrawal of "all foreign troops," a term that would presumably not include Chinese "volunteers." Following this withdrawal, North and South Vietnam and the three factions in Laos should settle their political future among themselves "without being influenced from without." Nothing was said about a "peace zone" linking Vietnam, or at least South Vietnam, to Laos and Cambodia. The DRV was referred to simply as North Vietnam, and nothing was said about its membership in the "socialist camp" or about any Chinese obligation to defend it for its own sake.

The conditions under which the CPR might intervene in Indochina were defined solely in terms of Chinese national interest:

> We would feel threatened only if, perhaps, the United States would send up their "special warfare" [forces] toward the north, if they attacked North Vietnam. . . . This would directly endanger the stability of our border and of the neighboring provinces. In such a case we would intervene. . . . Our army is . . . mobile and can be committed to action any time along our borders. . . . this will not be a second Korea. . . . A very wide and a very broad front can be set up there [i.e., in Southeast Asia]. Such a war would not remain isolated in a narrow space. It would also involve Vietnam [i.e., presumably, South Vietnam], Laos, and Cambodia, and perhaps also Thailand. . . . In this area the Americans can achieve nothing with even the most up-to-date weapons.

This statement seemed to imply that North as well as South Vietnam should be neutralized, that the CPR recognized no overriding obligations to the DRV, that only the entry of American ground forces into North Vietnam would pose a threat to Chinese security grave enough to produce Chinese intervention, and that this intervention would take the form of a Chinese invasion of the whole of Indochina. Such an invasion would probably be most distasteful to the DRV except as a last resort, since it would tend to reduce it to the status of a Chinese satellite. In less extreme situations, such as a limited American sea or air attack on the DRV, the latter seemed to be promised nothing in particular in the way of direct Chinese support. The inferiority of Chinese to American sea and air forces would make this reluctance understandable, but not necessarily acceptable, to the DRV, which probably considers that except for Chinese pressures on the Soviet Union the CPR might now possess the means of dealing in kind with possible American sea and air action in the South China Sea and the Tonkin Gulf.

The next act in the Vietnamese crisis may well have represented an attempt by the DRV to test the CPR's reluctance, clearly implicit in the unattributed interview published in Der Kurier, to respond militarily to anything short of an entry into North Vietnam by American ground forces or special forces. On August 2, three North Vietnamese torpedo boats attacked the American destroyer *Maddox*, which was patrolling about thirty miles offshore. The *Maddox* fired on the torpedo boats, apparently sinking one and damaging the others. This episode evoked no further American retaliation and no known significant response from the CPR. On the night of August 4, there were further attacks by North Vietnamese torpedo boats on the destroyers *Maddox* and *C. Turner Joy*. In retaliation, American carrier aircraft heavily attacked the bases of the DRV's torpedo boat fleet on August 5.[84]

Both the DRV and the CPR protested, promptly and loudly, that the American air attack was an unprovoked act of aggression, because there had been no attack by North Vietnamese torpedo boats on the night of August 4; it was not denied that there had been an engagement on August 2. The CPR's governmental statement, issued on August 6, affirmed, as neither of the interviews published in *Der Kurier* had done, that

> The DRV is a member of the socialist camp, and no socialist country can sit idly by while it is being subjected to aggression. The DRV and China are neighbors closely related to each other like the lips and the teeth, and the Vietnamese people are intimate brothers of the Chinese people.
>
> Aggression by the United States against the DRV means aggression against China. The Chinese people will absolutely not sit idly by without lending a helping hand. The debt of blood incurred by the United States to the Vietnamese people must be repaid.

Obviously this statement, superficially threatening though it was, did not commit the CPR, as distinct from the Chinese "people," to any specific action to help collect the "debt of blood" owed to the Vietnamese "people," and yet the possibility of Chinese "volunteers" was hinted at once more.[85] An editorial in the *People's Daily* took approximately the same line.[86] A slightly more threatening note was struck, but primarily for domestic consumption, in a speech delivered by a second-rank official, Liao Ch'eng-chih, before a rally on August 9:[87]

> It is even necessary to take practical action and volunteer our support for the struggle of the Vietnamese people in their struggle against U.S. aggression in defense of their homeland. . . .
>
> The DRV is our fraternal neighboring country which is as close to us as our lips and teeth. . . . The Chinese people can never permit

[84] Useful chronologies in *The New York Times*, August 9, 1964; *Christian Science Monitor*, August 11, 1964.

[85] Text in *The New York Times*, August 7, 1964.

[86] "The U.S. Aggressors Cannot Cover up Their Ugly Countenance," *People's Daily*, August 7, 1964.

[87] Peking radio, August 9, 1964.

themselves to sit with folded arms without lending a helping hand to the fraternal Vietnamese people when they are subjected to U.S. ruthless aggression.

Here the threat to send "volunteers" was raised to a somewhat higher, but still not very credible, level. The sending of "volunteers," whether rationalized as a step in defense of the DRV or as one in defense of Chinese security, would be risky. Less risky, and of more practical help to the DRV in its immediate situation, would be the provision of a measure of air cover, which would have the advantage of tending to deter further American air attacks and thus minimize the need for more drastic measures by the CPR. If unacknowledged, such a step would be only slightly more risky for the CPR than the similar step that Stalin had taken in sending unacknowledged "volunteer" pilots to help North Korea. On August 11 the United States Department of Defense announced that the CPR had moved an unspecified number of jet fighters into North Vietnam,[88] and a few days later the CPR stated that it was holding large-scale maneuvers throughout South China.[89] Some sort of incident occurred in the Tonkin Gulf on September 18 without evoking another American air attack on the DRV.

The air attack on August 5 seems to have surprised both the DRV and the CPR by its speed and intensity. It also seems to have caused the CPR to abandon its previous lack of interest in actively deterring anything short of an American ground attack on North Vietnam and to do what the DRV had probably wanted when it created the first torpedo boat incident: to provide some air cover for the DRV. If this proved effective, the United States might find itself stymied in the Vietnamese crisis. It already seemed unable to reverse the unfavorable trend of the struggle in South Vietnam, which could therefore continue on its way toward a Communist victory. At the intermediate level, American air attacks on North Vietnam might be deterred or at least hindered by Chinese air cover, and an American ground attack by the Chinese threats to send in troops or at least "volunteers." Direct retaliation against the CPR might be deterred by general political considerations and, in spite of the state of Sino-Soviet relations, by fear of the possible Soviet response. As long as the United States let itself be deterred by these considerations, there could be reasonable confidence in Peking and Hanoi that the DRV would succeed in reunifying Vietnam and in enhancing Chinese security by removing a potential foothold for SEATO in continental Southeast Asia.

Probably emboldened by the continued political instability of the South Vietnamese government, and perhaps by the Communist Chinese nuclear test, the Viet Cong intensified its attacks against American personnel and the South Vietnamese army in November, 1964, with the result

---

[88] *The New York Times*, August 12, 1964.
[89] *The New York Times*, August 14, 1964.

that in the following February the United States resumed air attacks on North Vietnam. The mission of Soviet Premier Kosygin to Hanoi in the same month appeared to indicate that the Soviet Union was trying to compete with the CPR and restrain it and the United States by giving at least somewhat greater support to the DRV and implying that President Johnson would have to ease the pressure on North Vietnam if he wanted to see a fulfillment of his expressed desire for better Soviet-American relations. The CPR, for its part, still seemed reluctant to incur serious risks by passing from threats to action, although it was obviously under pressure to make a contribution to the defense of North Vietnam against any further American attacks.

□ 14

Communist China and Northeast Asia

For nearly a century before the Second World War, northeastern Asia (Japan, Korea, Manchuria, and what is now the Soviet Far East) was the focus of intense if intermittent rivalry between Japan and Russia, with China generally in a passive role. Since the war, it is Japan that has so far been forced into the passive role, and the main rivalry appears to be that between a resurgent China and the Soviet Union, with of course the addition of the vastly complicating factor of the presence of overwhelming American sea and air power in Japan and other nearby areas. This chapter will confine itself to those aspects of this situation that relate to Communist China's policy toward Japan and Korea.

■ SINO-JAPANESE RELATIONS: SOME UNDERLYING CONSIDERATIONS

In the CPR's quest for security, Japan figures in the first place as a power that invaded China with devastating effect in 1937 and was ultimately defeated, not by China, but by the United States in the Pacific. A resurgence of expansionist Japanese militarism does not seem likely at the present time, but if it should occur and especially if it were supported by the United States, it would be a serious threat to the CPR. There is an obvious analogy here with the Soviet fear of a possibly rampant West Germany, or still more of a reunited non-Communist Germany backed by the United States.

Even in the absence of a recurrence of Japanese militarism, the American military presence in and near Japan is regarded by the CPR as a serious threat. In addition to its obvious potential for an attack on the CPR, it enables the United States to intervene when necessary in Korea, the Taiwan Strait, and Southeast Asia. Since the CPR is not a naval power and the Japanese are not afraid of it, partly for that reason, the defensive mission of American forces stationed in and near Japan is essentially one of protecting Japan against the Soviet Union, of which the Japanese most certainly are afraid. They have therefore accepted American bases that give them protection against the Soviet Union but that also give the United States great leverage on the CPR in the areas mentioned. In addition, the Japanese have in effect purchased American protection against the Soviet Union by adopting a China policy fairly close to that of the United States. The net effect of all this is that Japan, and above all Japan's alignment with the United States, appear to the CPR as a major threat to Chinese security, as well as to other aspects of the CPR's foreign policy.

It is worth adding that, presumably because of its greater power, the large forces that it has long maintained in the Far East, its lesser interest in expansion, and the relative remoteness of its major centers from the Far East, the Soviet Union seems to take a much less serious view of the threat posed by the American position in Japan than does the CPR. At present the Soviet Union has no need or desire to invade Japan, and presumably nothing short of general war would bring American forces in Japan into action against the Soviet Union. The CPR, on the other hand, is almost constantly exerting pressure on various parts of Asia, and it is therefore concerned with the capability of counterintervention and retaliation possessed by American forces based in and near Japan.

National power, the second of the CPR's main objectives, might be enhanced by trading with, and perhaps receiving technical assistance from, Japan, the nearest industrialized country to the CPR. The CPR might even go so far as to adopt an approach to economic development somewhat resembling that of Japan prior to World War II, which would be far better suited to China's needs than the obsolescent Stalinist pattern that it borrowed from the Soviet Union after 1950. The present state of Sino-Soviet relations makes such a possibility less remote than it would have seemed a few years ago.

Sino-Japanese relations also bear on the problem of the territorial unification of China. The CPR repudiates as invalid the San Francisco peace treaty of 1951, by which Japan renounced title to Taiwan without specifying to whom sovereignty over it was being transferred, and the treaty of 1952 by which Japan made peace with the Republic of China and implicitly recognized its title to Taiwan. The CPR bases its own claim to Taiwan largely on the Cairo Declaration of 1943 promising Taiwan to China, of which the CPR of course claims to be the legitimate government in succession to the Kuomintang-controlled Republic of China. The CPR's position would be somewhat strengthened if a Japanese government, presumably Socialist rather than Communist, were to endorse it.

The CPR has great respect for Japan's dynamism, and in particular for its postwar economic and technological achievements. An alignment with such a power would greatly increase the CPR's influence, in Asia in particular. It is probable that the CPR would like to invert the Japanese Co-Prosperity Sphere of a generation ago and see a Sino-Japanese partnership in which the CPR provided the political leadership and Japan provided the main economic sinews, and conceivably naval power as well. This would be vastly preferable from the CPR's standpoint to the Sino-Indian partnership that Nehru visualized until about 1959. To play this role, Japan would have to be politically reliable from the CPR's standpoint. Ideally, it should be Communist. The Japanese Communist Party, however, has almost no chance of coming to power, mainly because unlike Communist Parties in some other Asian countries it has never been able to gain the support of indigenous nationalism. In fact, since Japan was never a colony, regards the Soviet Union as its main enemy, and has attained reasonable political stability since the Second World War, the Japanese Communists have generally been suspect in the eyes of Japanese nationalists, although less so than before the war. The Communists' Soviet connections have told against them, and largely because of a generally enlightened American policy toward Japan Japanese nationalism has not generated enough anti-American animus to find the Communists a thoroughly congenial ally. Even the Japanese Socialists, many of whom agree with the Communists on some things, have never shown much interest in concrete political collaboration with the Communists.[1] It seems, then, that the most that the CPR could hope for would be a Socialist government that would take an anti-American line on those issues on which the policies of the United States and the CPR clash. This line might then lead to conflicts with American "imperialism," which in turn would drive the Socialists into closer collaboration with the CPR and the Japanese Communists and perhaps ultimately permit the latter to come to power.

Even in the absence of any such situation, the CPR evidently hopes that the widespread objections in Japan to American China policy, and to the way in which the United States has maneuvered Japan into pursuing a parallel policy, will accelerate what the CPR evidently regards as the inevitable progression of American policy through three stages: sole recognition of the Republic of China, a "two China" policy (which the CPR has claimed for several years that the United States was trying to bring into being), and sole recognition of the CPR.[2]

---

[1] Paul F. Langer in A. Doak Barnett, ed., *Communist Strategies in Asia: A Comparative Analysis of Governments and Parties*, New York: Praeger, 1963, pp. 66–67, 69.

[2] Paul F. Langer in Kurt London, ed., *Unity and Contradiction: Major Aspects of Sino-Soviet Relations*, New York: Praeger, 1962, p. 221.

The CPR has many assets in the form of favorable attitudes that are widespread in Japan, especially but by no means exclusively among the left. The most important of these attitudes are a sense of the ethnic and cultural kinship between the Chinese and Japanese; an absence of fear of the CPR combined with widespread respect and admiration for such Communist Chinese achievements as fighting the United States to a draw in Korea and building at least the rudiments of a heavy industrial system; a feeling of guilt for past acts of aggression against China; a belief that the Japanese alone understand China and can deal with it successfully; a desire to push Sino-Japanese trade at least to its prewar level, and higher if possible; a resentment at Japan's partial dependence on the United States and a longing to escape from it; and a hope that by showing friendship to the CPR Japan might secure the modification of the provision of the Sino-Soviet alliance dealing with Japan.[3]

The CPR's initial objective with respect to Japan is to bring it to detach itself from the United States and adopt what the CPR describes as a policy of "independence, democracy, peace, and neutrality." To this end Chinese propaganda plays on the Japanese attitudes already mentioned, on the widespread Marxist tendencies in Japanese intellectual and public life, and on the Japanese horror of nuclear war (as brought home by the bombings of Hiroshima and Nagasaki in 1945) and of nuclear testing (as brought home by injuries to the crew of a Japanese fishing vessel by fallout from an American thermonuclear test in 1954).

■ SINO-JAPANESE RELATIONS TO 1957[4]

In 1949, shortly before the founding of the CPR, the United States decided to move toward a peace treaty with Japan without reference to the attitude of the Soviet Union, which was demanding that the treaty be worked out in the veto-ridden Council of Foreign Ministers. The CPC injected itself into the question, in mid-1949, with a demand for a preparatory conference of "four nations, with the full representation of the Republic of New Democratic China, for eradicating Japanese militarism and for materializing the democratization of Japan."[5] This appeal had no effect on the situation. The aiming of the Sino-Soviet alliance of February 14, 1950, at Japan was probably designed in part to help prevent Japan from

[3] Cf. C. Martin Wilbur in Hugh Borton and others, *Japan Between East and West*, New York: Harper, 1957, pp. 199–203, 224–239; Shao Chuan Leng, *Japan and Communist China*, Kyoto: Doshisha University Press, 1958, pp. 106–125.

[4] This section draws heavily on a valuable unpublished study by Alice Langley Hsieh, *The Strategy and Tactics of Communist China's Foreign Policy Toward Japan*, RAND Corporation, September 7, 1956.

[5] "Prepare Promptly a Peace Treaty with Japan," New China News Agency statement, June 20, 1949.

signing a separate peace with the Western powers without the participation of the "socialist camp," something that Japan was reluctant to do in any case.[6] The main concern of the Communist regimes was to eliminate American bases from Japan if possible. The imminence of the Korean War made this problem particularly urgent.

It was probably considerations such as these that lay behind the Cominform's orders to the Japanese Communist Party, in January, 1950, to stop trying to make itself "lovable" and wage a "resolute struggle" against American influence in Japan.[7] Although the CPC endorsed these instructions,[8] the likelihood that they were really Stalin's rather than Mao's is suggested by the CPC's evident belief that the violence in which the Japanese Communists proceeded to engage was excessive and was tending to isolate them from other elements of the Japanese political scene.[9]

Beginning in 1950, the CPR spelled out what it regarded as suitable terms for a Japanese peace settlement. They included cession of the Ryukyus and southern Sakhalin to the Soviet Union, which was already in possession, and of Taiwan to the CPR, which was not. In other words, the Soviet Union was to use its influence on Japan and the Western powers to gain Taiwan for the CPR. In addition, the United States was to evacuate its Pacific trust territories and all foreign troops were to withdraw from Japan. The CPR was also insistent on the principle that Japan must be permitted no armed forces at all, a situation that would not only prevent it from being an independent threat to the CPR but would offer the maximum opportunity for a Japanese Communist seizure of power. By May, 1951, however, the CPR had accepted the Soviet position that Japan could be allowed to maintain some limited defense forces provided that it had no military ties with the United States. Soviet demands at the San Francisco Conference in September, 1951, to which neither the CPR nor the Republic of China was invited, were therefore very similar to the CPR's own.[10]

In reality, the treaty that emerged from the San Francisco Conference neither ceded Taiwan to the CPR nor placed any limits on Japanese rearmament, reliance for the latter purpose being placed on Article Nine of the Japanese constitution. These considerations, as well as the CPR's exclusion from the conference, led Chou En-lai, in a statement issued on September 18, 1951, to denounce the treaty as invalid. The CPR was even more enraged by the arrangement worked out during the next few months, under which Japan permitted the continuation of American bases and signed

---

[6] Cf. "New Era of Sino-Soviet Friendship," *People's China*, March 1, 1950, pp. 30–32.

[7] *For a Lasting Peace, for a People's Democracy!* January 6, 1950.

[8] "The Japanese People's Road to Liberation," *People's Daily*, January 17, 1950.

[9] Cf. "The Present Situation in the Struggles of the Japanese People," *People's Daily*, July 7, 1950.

[10] Cf. James William Morley, *Soviet and Communist Chinese Policies Toward Japan, 1950–1957: A Comparison*, New York: Institute of Pacific Relations, 1958, pp. 1–2.

a peace treaty with the Republic of China in return for American protection against foreign aggression or internal subversion.

As the Korean War entered its phase of greatest tension in early 1952, the Soviet Union and the CPR opened a political and economic offensive apparently aimed at counteracting the effects of the San Francisco settlement and reducing Japan's value to the United States as a logistical base and ally. Following the American lead, the Japanese government had imposed a total embargo on trade with the CPR at the end of 1950, and this step was known to be widely unpopular in Japan. Following an economic conference held in Moscow in April, 1952, with the purpose of finding ways to undermine the strategic trade controls that had been imposed against the Communist bloc, the CPR began to negotiate a series of "unofficial" trade agreements with a variety of private Japanese organizations and delegations. As usual in Communist Chinese foreign trading practice in those days, the agreements called for barter deals, in which the commodities most desired by Japan, such as coal, were to be traded against those most desired by the CPR, mostly metallurgical products, some of which were embargoed by the Japanese government. Thus the CPR hoped to build up pressure in Japan for a drastic modification or elimination of the embargo. In fact, the Japanese government did make certain modifications in the embargo list, but they were not as sweeping as the CPR, or the Japanese interests anxious to trade with it, desired.[11]

The spring of 1952 also saw an increase in Communist Chinese information-gathering on and propaganda to Japan. By this time the thousands of Japanese technicians stranded in China by the end of the Second World War, who had been helping in postwar reconstruction, had almost exhausted their usefulness, and the CPR was preparing to launch its First Five Year Plan with Soviet rather than Japanese technical aid. Economic as well as political considerations, then, pointed to the use of Japanese personnel, including prisoners of war, as bargaining counters and propaganda devices. In mid-December, 1952, accordingly, the CPR announced that it would repatriate the 30,000 Japanese said to be still in China, under certain conditions. These were designed so as to increase the political pressures on the Japanese government to grant at least de facto recognition to the CPR. Repatriation of these Japanese, who had been thoroughly indoctrinated, began in the spring of 1953. The program had a favorable effect on Japanese public opinion, from the CPR's standpoint, and opened channels of communication between the CPR and various Japanese private organizations.[12] In October, 1953, the CPR created some consternation in Japan by announcing, after 26,000 Japanese had been repatriated, that the program was completed; thousands of Japanese believed in Japan to be still alive and in

---

[11] *Ibid.*, pp. 3–7.

[12] Cf. A. Doak Barnett, *Communist China and Asia: Challenge to American Policy*, New York: Harper, 1960, pp. 261–262.

China were unaccounted for. The uncertainty on this subject, combined with gratitude for the return of the 26,000, left the CPR in a strong bargaining position with respect to Japan.[13]

Japan was one of the Asian countries over which a growing divergence between Soviet and Communist Chinese policies appeared after the death of Stalin. Both the Soviet Union and the CPR wished to establish diplomatic relations with Japan, mainly in order to erode its alignment with the United States, and to establish more nearly "normal" commercial relations with it. In the case of the CPR, however, such a "normalization" was rendered very difficult by the relations between Japan and the Republic of China. The basic question was whether the Soviet Union, which had no such problem, would wait for an appropriate time to use its leverage on Japan so as to make the establishment of Soviet-Japanese relations conditional on the establishment of "normal" relations between Japan and the CPR.

The first clear indication that the Soviet Union might not be prepared to act in this way came on September 11, 1954, when Molotov indicated a readiness to "normalize" Soviet relations with Japan without saying anything about Sino-Japanese relations.[14] This statement came shortly after the beginning of the Taiwan Strait crisis and only three days after the signing of the Manila Pact; the Soviet Union was probably afraid that tension in these areas might lead the United States to form a Northeast Asia Treaty Organization, including Japan, and anxious to do what it could to head off such an eventuality. In addition, there began about 1954 an unadmitted contest between the CPR and the Soviet Union for influence in non-Communist Asia, one of whose outward signs was the admission of the CPR to and the exclusion of the Soviet Union from the Bandung Conference. Because of its importance and its proximity to both contestants, Japan was bound to figure prominently in this competition.

The subject of policy toward Japan was undoubtedly discussed during Khrushchev's visit to the CPR in October, 1954. A joint declaration, issued on October 12 by the two delegations, invited Japan to "normalize" its relations with both the Soviet Union and the CPR, but it did not indicate whether these were two separate problems or whether "normalization" with the CPR was a prerequisite for "normalization" with the Soviet Union.[15] Presumably this vagueness reflected a compromise between the probable Soviet preference for separating the two questions and the probable Chinese preference for joining them.

In mid-December, after the fall of the pro-American Yoshida government and the inauguration of a government under Hatoyama pledged to improve Japan's relations with the Communist powers, the Soviet Union

---

[13] *Ibid.*, p. 264.
[14] Morley, *op. cit.*, p. 9.
[15] Text in *ibid.*, pp. 35–36.

began to indicate serious interest in a settlement of specific issues with Japan, without a peace treaty, and without making an issue of either the San Francisco treaty or the security treaty between Japan and the United States. After much hard bargaining, a settlement was concluded along these lines in October, 1956, and the Soviet Union acquired the valuable asset of an embassy in Tokyo.[16]

Although the CPR did not express irritation at being left astern by the Soviet Union, it gave some indications at the end of 1954 that it would continue to insist on the abrogation of Japan's relations with the Republic of China and of its security treaty with the United States as the minimum price for the "normalization" of relations between Tokyo and Peking.[17] On the other hand, the CPR also increased its efforts to establish contact with unofficial elements in Japan that might put pressure on the government to "normalize" its relations with the CPR, at least to the extent of de facto recognition. At the end of October, 1954, the first major delegation from the CPR, one representing the Chinese Red Cross, visited Japan, and at about the same time Chou En-lai told a Japanese delegation that if Japan abrogated its security treaty with the United States it would be possible for the CPR and Japan to sign a nonaggression treaty.[18] After the Bandung Conference the flow of Japanese visitors to the CPR rapidly increased and became greater than the flow from any other country.[19]

The devices employed to build up pressure on the Japanese government were numerous. In a report to the National People's Congress in 1955, Chou En-lai accused the Japanese government of obstructing the "normalization" of Sino-Japanese relations and of holding "large numbers of Chinese who were taken to Japan by force during the war." More important, he broadened the assault on the American-Japanese security treaty and SEATO with the following proposal:[20]

> The Chinese people hope that the countries of Asia and the Pacific Region, including the United States, will sign a pact of collective peace to replace the antagonistic military blocs now existing in this part of the world, so that the collective peace first advocated by the Indian Government may be realized.

In an interview with Japanese reporters on August 17, Chou repeated this proposal and indicated that the San Francisco treaty need not stand in the way of "normalization" of Sino-Japanese relations, but he insisted that Japan must cut its ties with the Republic of China and indicated that it

---

[16] *Ibid.*, pp. 10–13; William J. Jordan in Borton and others, *op. cit.*, pp. 257–261.

[17] Morley, *op. cit.*, pp. 13–17.

[18] Barnett, *Communist China and Asia, op. cit.*, pp. 264–265.

[19] Cf. Herbert Passin, *China's Cultural Diplomacy*, New York: Praeger. 1963, pp. 41–54.

[20] New China News Agency dispatch, July 30, 1955.

might have to pay reparations to China.[21] This statement, and a similar one on November 4, were clearly designed to inveigle the Japanese government into conducting negotiations with the CPR and thus giving it de facto recognition, something that it declined to do. During 1956 the CPR continued to exploit the Japanese desire for peace, trade, and return of Japanese nationals still in China as means of moving toward "normalization," but with indifferent success.

The coming to power of the conservative, American-oriented Kishi government in February, 1957, seems to have convinced the CPR that a more intensive exploitation of the available leverage would be required and that by far the best instrumentality for the purpose would be the Japanese Socialist Party, which for some months had been showing an increasingly friendly attitude toward the Japanese Communist Party.[22]

■ SINO-JAPANESE RELATIONS SINCE 1957

In April, 1957, Secretary General Asanuma Inejiro of the Japanese Socialist Party led a goodwill mission to the CPR. The joint statement issued by Asanuma and Chang Hsi-jo, President of the Chinese People's Institute of Foreign Affairs, indicated that the discussion had covered all actual or possible aspects of Sino-Japanese relations, and stated in particular that[23]

... the time has come for the governments of Japan and the People's Republic of China to restore diplomatic relations as soon as possible, formally and completely . . . the establishment of long-term and positive cooperation between China and Japan is the basis of the friendly settlement of various outstanding issues. . . . the right of representation at the United Nations Organization should belong to the People's Republic of China. . . .

Certain existing agreements between the people's organizations of the two countries, together with matters on which agreement might be reached, should be developed into agreements between the two governments at the earliest possible date. . . .

It is hoped that antagonistic military blocs in Asia will be abolished and that an agreement will be signed to ensure collective peace among the Pacific or Far Eastern countries, including China, Japan, the Soviet Union and the United States. . . .

It is especially necessary to prohibit the manufacture, stockpiling, and use of nuclear and thermonuclear weapons. Therefore, agreements

[21] Leng, *op. cit.*, pp. 91–92.
[22] Cf. Paul F. Langer in Borton and others, *op. cit.*, p. 76.
[23] Text released by New China News Agency, April 22, 1957. For additional details see Leng, *op. cit.*, pp. 96–101.

to this effect should be concluded as soon as possible between the United States, the Soviet Union, and Britain, which have nuclear weapons; and prior to the signing of such an agreement, an agreement must be concluded to place a ban on the testing of these weapons.

The CPC's endorsement in this statement of a test ban without nuclear disarmament, an idea to which it has generally objected, shows how greatly it wished to make an impression on Japanese leftist opinion and how eager it was to promote the still more important objective of the elimination of American nuclear striking power from its bases near the CPR. Mao Tsetung allegedly told the Asanuma delegation that the Sino-Soviet alliance could be revised to eliminate the reference to Japan if a "pact of collective peace" could be established in the Pacific region.[24] Mao also told the delegation a flat lie to the effect that the CPR had no intention of developing nuclear weapons of its own.[25] Statements of this kind were probably designed to give the Japanese Socialists a stronger case for advocating the abrogation of the security treaty with the United States.[26]

In the spring of 1957, in the hope of increasing its trade with the CPR, Britain lowered its restrictions on such trade to the same level as those applied against the Soviet Union, a process known as abolishing the "China differential." Soon afterward Premier Kishi visited the United States and Taiwan, partly in order to secure a reluctant consent to Japan's taking the same step, which it did in July. On the other hand, Kishi maintained his pro-American attitude on political questions and showed no inclination to grant any sort of recognition to the CPR. Worse still, from the Communist Chinese standpoint, he began to negotiate a revision and renewal of the security treaty with the United States. If Sino-Japanese relations were to be "normalized," Kishi had to go, and the approach of a Japanese general election in May, 1958, seemed to offer an opportunity. During the ensuing months the CPR grew increasingly difficult in its dealings with unofficial Japanese trade missions. A few days before the election, it made an issue of the Japanese government's refusal to let the CPR's trade mission in Japan fly the Communist Chinese flag and proceeded to repudiate all existing Sino-Japanese trade agreements, suspend trade, seize some Japanese fishermen, and loudly denounce Kishi and all his works. At the same time the CPR sharply increased its exports to Southeast Asia. This step probably harmed Japanese interests, but the main purpose was in all likelihood more basic: in its trade with Japan, the CPR had taken care to maintain a favorable balance, the foreign exchange accumulated in this way being needed to meet the CPR's loan repayments to the Soviet Union. Trade with Japan being suspended, the lost earnings must be replaced, and Southeast Asia was

---

[24] Barnett, *Communist China and Asia, op. cit.,* p. 273.
[25] Tokyo *Yomiuri,* April 22, 1957.
[26] Wilbur in Borton and others, *op. cit.,* p. 211.

the obvious area in which to replace them. It is worth noting that the Soviet Union did not follow the Chinese lead by interrupting commercial relations with Japan.[27]

The CPR had miscalculated. Its behavior probably harmed the Socialists and helped Kishi, who emerged triumphant from the elections. This setback merely served, however, to intensify the CPR's efforts to work with the Socialists to discredit and overthrow him. In March, 1959, shortly after a visit by Secretary General Miyamoto Kenji of the Japanese Communist Party,[28] Asanuma returned to the CPR at the head of another Socialist delegation. On March 17 he and Chang Hsi-jo issued a celebrated joint statement affirming that[29]

> Both sides reiterate emphatically that, in view of the current international situation and the situation in Asia, it is necessary to bring about an overall and unconditional prohibition of the testing, manufacture, stockpiling, and use of nuclear weapons of any description. . . . Both sides have reached unanimity of views on setting up an area free from nuclear weapons in the Far East and the Pacific and exerting efforts together with all the countries concerned. . . . the governments of China and Japan should immediately proceed into a stage of negotiating the formal and overall resumption of diplomatic relations. . . .
>
> The Chinese side deems it necessary to put into effect the following three principles. The Kishi government must: first, immediately stop its hostile policy toward China; second, stop taking part in the two Chinas scheme; third, stop obstructing the restoration of normal relations between China and Japan; and take corresponding measures in these respects, so as to break the present deadlock. Otherwise, it will be impossible to resume Sino-Japanese trade.
>
> The Japanese Socialist Party . . . not only fully agrees with the above three principles put forward by the Chinese side but clearly advocates nonrecognition of the existence of "two Chinas" and asserts that the liberation of Taiwan is China's internal affair. It advocates recognition of the representation of the Chinese People's Republic in the United Nations and maintains that, to normalize the relations between China and Japan, the "Japan–Chiang Kai-shek Peace Treaty" must first be abolished and a peace treaty must be signed with the People's Republic of China.
>
> The Chinese side welcomes these viewpoints of the Japanese Socialist Party. The Chinese side further points out that the questions of politics and economics between the two countries cannot be separated; the questions of economics and politics must be negotiated simultaneously and must be settled simultaneously. At the present moment, the ques-

---

[27] Barnett, *Communist China and Asia, op. cit.*, pp. 273–276; Leng, *op. cit.*, pp. 102–104, 167–169.
[28] Joint statement released by New China News Agency, March 4, 1959.
[29] Text released by New China News Agency, March 17, 1959.

tion of politics must be given preference. The Japanese Socialist Party expressed agreement with this. . . . After Japan smashes the Japan-U.S. "security treaty," achieves complete independence, and concludes mutual nonaggression pacts with China and the Soviet Union, then it can be expected that the military clauses against Japan in the Sino-Soviet treaty, directed against Japanese militarism, will naturally become null and void.

After a peace pact between the Asian and Pacific countries — first of all, a collective security pact between China, Japan, the Soviet Union, and the United States — is concluded, the neutral position of Japan will be further insured.

The Japanese Socialist Party delegation stresses that although diplomatic relations between Japan and China have not yet been resumed and contracts between the two countries have reached an almost complete break since spring last year, nevertheless, to foster the friendship between the peoples of the two countries, people's diplomacy, such as friendly contacts and cultural exchange, should be promoted as practical circumstances warrant. . . .

As if this classic specimen of "people's diplomacy" were not enough, Asanuma was reported by the Chinese as having said a few days earlier that "U.S. imperialism is the common enemy of the peoples of Japan and China."[30] This remark created a strong adverse reaction in Japan, except on the extreme left, and this reaction in turn contributed to Asanuma's assassination in October, 1960, by a right-wing fanatic.

By the time of the Asanuma visit, the negotiations on the revision of the Japanese-American security treaty were already well under way and the CPR was anxious to bring about its abrogation by Japan if possible. The fact that the revised treaty made certain concessions to Japan was far more than outweighed, in the eyes of the CPR and the Japanese left, by the fact that it retained American bases in Japan and of course continued to commit Japan to the side of the free world, without allowing it to assume some sort of neutral posture. On January 14, 1960, five days before the revised treaty was to be signed, the CPR's Foreign Ministry issued a statement of protest.[31] Four days after the signing, a rally was held in Peking whose main feature was a speech by Kuo Mo-jo, a leading "peace partisan," who insisted that the main menace to Japanese security was not the Communist powers but the United States.[32] Since one of the main reasons for Communist objections to the presence of American forces in Japan is the fact that it enables the United States to protect South Korea from invasion or absorption from the north, additional point was given to the agitation against the revised American-Japanese security treaty, at least in extreme leftist

[30] New China News Agency dispatch, March 12, 1959.
[31] New China News Agency dispatch, January 14, 1960.
[32] New China News Agency dispatch, January 23, 1960.

eyes, by the disorders in South Korea that accompanied the fall of Syngman Rhee on April 27. In a speech given at a rally held in Peking on the following day, Liu Ning-yi rejoiced that "While the just patriotic struggle of the South Korean people against the fascist rule of the U.S.-Rhee clique is surging onward, a new mounting upsurge has emerged in the Japanese people's struggle against the Japan-U.S. military alliance."[33]

The revised security treaty was regarded with deep misgivings by many in Japan, including some who were not especially leftist, for reasons reflecting tensions in the social and political institutions that had emerged in Japan since the Second World War.[34] The discontent exploded into wild demonstrations after Premier Kishi abruptly pushed the ratification of the treaty through the Diet on May 19. The CPR had already warned him not to do so, on the ground that the U-2 episode had just shown how dangerous it was for a country to become a base for American activity directed against the "socialist camp."[35] The CPR was of course delighted with the cancellation of President Eisenhower's projected visit to Japan as a result of the demonstrations,[36] and at Kishi's resignation in July.

Kishi's successor, Ikeda Hayato, was less distasteful to the CPR, since he was far less openly pro-American and adopted a moderate, "low posture" line both at home and abroad. On the other hand, he of course abided by the security treaty, whereas the CPR felt that its own strong stand on this question had been amply vindicated by the demonstrations and Kishi's resignation. When a Chinese mission led by Liu Ning-yi attended the Sixth World Conference Against Atomic and Hydrogen Bombs in Tokyo in August, therefore, it took a very hostile line toward the Ikeda government; this was the first important Chinese mission to Japan in nearly three years.[37] Liu made it clear, for example, that the CPR still upheld the "three principles" first enunciated in the Asanuma-Chang Hsi-jo statement of March 17, 1959. On the other hand, the economic disaster that overtook the CPR in the summer of 1960 interested it much more than before in resuming large-scale trade with Japan, although not to the point of abandoning its political objectives. On August 27, Chou made a statement to a Japanese trade delegation in which he put forward three commercial principles to parallel the three political ones just mentioned. These were, "government agreements, private contracts, and special consideration in individual cases." Under these conditions, Chou said, "Sino-Japanese trade could be gradually

---

[33] New China News Agency dispatch, April 28, 1960. There was another rally against the treaty in Peking on May 9.

[34] For an excellent discussion see Edwin O. Reischauer, "The Broken Dialogue with Japan," *Foreign Affairs*, vol. 39, no. 1 (October, 1960), pp. 11–26.

[35] "Warning to Nobusuke Kishi," Peking *Ta Kung Pao*, May 13, 1960.

[36] Cf. documents in *Support the Just Struggle of the Japanese People Against the Japan-U.S. Treaty of Military Alliance*, Peking: Foreign Languages Press, 1960.

[37] Speech by Liu Ning-yi released by New China News Agency, August 2, 1960. Cf. Langer in London, *op. cit.*, pp. 218–219.

resumed." For good measure he attacked the American-Japanese security treaty, which he described as a "menace to Southeast Asia."[38]

Beginning about 1961, Chinese interest in increasing trade and improving relations with Japan grew noticeably greater. This trend was probably due not only to the condition of the Chinese economy but also to a parallel Soviet effort to increase trade with Japan that began early in 1961.

It would be tedious and unnecessary to mention more than a few of the countless informal talks between Communist Chinese and Japanese delegations that occurred during the next few years. In January, 1962, another Japanese Socialist delegation, led this time by Suzuki Mosaburo, visited the CPR and issued a joint statement that repeated the essential points of the Asanuma-Chang Hsi-jo statement of 1959, in addition to endorsing Asanuma's obiter dictum that the United States is the "common enemy" of the Chinese and Japanese peoples.[39]

The security crisis that confronted the CPR during the next few months, indications of improving Japanese relations with South Korea and the Republic of China, and the occurrence on July 7 of the twenty-fifth anniversary of the beginning of the Japanese invasion of China, produced an outpouring of editorials and interviews with Japanese reporters. At the beginning of August, the Eighth World Conference Against Atomic and Hydrogen Bombs met in Tokyo, and on August 5 the Soviet Union thoughtfully detonated a hydrogen bomb in the atmosphere. This created an uproar in Japan and a problem for the Chinese delegation, which had been assuring the conference that the United States was the only real enemy of the peoples of the world.[40] The CPR's decision was to persist in its stand of damning only "imperialist" torpedoes, as though "socialist" fallout was not harmful. After some noisy scenes at the conference between the Chinese and Japanese Communists on the one hand and some Japanese Socialists on the other, a declaration emerged that conceded something to the Communists by failing to condemn past Soviet or future Chinese nuclear testing, and something to the Socialists by failing to condemn the American-Japanese security treaty or to name the United States as the "chief enemy of peace."[41] This episode drastically worsened the relations of the Japanese and Chinese Communists with the Japanese Socialists. The situation was not improved when Chen Yi, in an interview on September 19, stated flatly that the CPR was working to acquire nuclear weapons. In spite of the adverse reaction created by the CPR's nuclear policy and its economic difficulties, Chen continued to insist on the inseparability of

---

[38] "Minute" of Chou's statement released by New China News Agency, September 12, 1960.

[39] New China News Agency dispatch, January 13, 1962.

[40] See speech by Chinese delegate Pa Chin (New China News Agency dispatch, August 1, 1962).

[41] Text of declaration released by New China News Agency, August 7, 1962.

politics and economics in Sino-Japanese relations and on the necessity for the CPR's admission to the United Nations and for complete nuclear disarmament.[42]

In spite of this unpleasant interlude, the CPR continued to do its best to woo any and all elements in Japan that were not wholly committed to the official Japanese policy toward the United States and the CPR.[43] On the other hand, the CPR also made it clear that it considered the Japanese Communist Party to be the "leader of the Japanese people's movement."[44] Evidently it was thought necessary to give this assurance to the increasingly isolated and ineffectual Japanese Communists in order to strengthen their tendency to align themselves with the CPC in the Sino-Soviet dispute and to counteract the influence of a faction in the party that was espousing Togliatti's doctrine of "structural reform" in lieu of violent revolution.

The Ninth World Conference Against Atomic and Hydrogen Bombs met at Hiroshima on August 5, 1963, the day of the signing of the nuclear test ban treaty. It, and to a lesser extent a formal Chinese counterproposal for complete nuclear disarmament, became the King Charles' head of the conference. There was a noisy dispute between the Japanese and Chinese Communists, the left Socialists, and some delegations from third countries on the one hand, and the right Socialists, the Soviet delegation, and their foreign supporters on the other. The conference was virtually paralyzed, and its declaration omitted to mention either the treaty or the Chinese counterproposal.[45]

Probably to counteract the unfavorable impression produced on all sections of Japanese public opinion except the extreme left by Chinese assertiveness, and in particular Chinese opposition to the test ban treaty, the CPR established a China-Japan Friendship Association on October 4, 1963, with the mission of expanding informal relations between the two countries and promoting an early "normalization" of official relations.[46] Although it might seem surprising that the CPR waited so long to take such an obvious step with respect to the country that was probably the most im-

---

[42] Tokyo *Yomiuri* and Tokyo *Kyodo*, September 20, 1962. In earlier interviews, Chen had not mentioned the CPR's nuclear program (interview of June 13, New China News Agency dispatch, October 1, 1962; interview of May 29, Tokyo *Journalist*, June 26, 1962).

[43] Cf. joint statement on cultural exchange by Chinese People's Association for Cultural Relations with Foreign Countries and delegation of the Japan-China Friendship Association (New China News Agency dispatch, October 12, 1962); memorandum on Sino-Japanese trade signed by Liao Ch'eng-chih and Takasaki Tatsunosuke (New China News Agency dispatch, November 9, 1962); trade protocol of December 27, 1962 (New China News Agency dispatch, same date); fisheries agreement of January 23, 1963 (New China News Agency dispatch, same date); statement by Chinese and Japanese relief organizations, May 28, 1963 (New China News Agency dispatch, same date).

[44] Chang Hsiang-shan, "Japanese People's Struggles and the Japanese Communist Party," *Red Flag*, October 16, 1962.

[45] Cf. William E. Griffith, *The Sino-Soviet Rift*, M.I.T. Press, 1964, pp. 202–203.

[46] New China News Agency dispatch, October 4, 1963.

portant single object of its "people's diplomacy," it should be realized that Japan became in this way the first country for which the CPR has established a Friendship Association without having also established diplomatic relations.

A significant, although unofficial, step toward "normalization" of Sino-Japanese relations was taken with the signing on November 9, 1963, of a Sino-Japanese fisheries agreement. It imposed certain restrictions on the activities of Japanese fishermen in the waters near the China coast for the valid purpose of preventing excessive depletion of the fish population, and it specifically excluded Japanese fishing boats from three militarily sensitive areas: the Gulf of Chihli (the northwestward extension of the Yellow Sea), the island group lying to the southwest of Shanghai and the mouth of the Yangtze River, and the entire Taiwan Strait.[47]

The French recognition of the CPR in January, 1964, markedly increased the psychological and political pressure on the Ikeda government to "normalize" relations with the CPR. By a fairly narrow margin, the Japanese government decided that a proposal by Chou En-lai for Sino-Japanese ambassadorial talks should be ignored and that the considerations that had originally determined Japan's China policy, the attitude of the United States in particular, should continue to govern.[48] Sino-Japanese trade had begun to climb in 1963, however,[49] and it continued to do so during 1964, with the result that trade both ways during the first eight months of 1964 reached $192 million, a level unmatched since the Second World War.[50] The CPR established a commercial mission in Tokyo and intensified its efforts to broaden trade contacts with Japan even after the Tonkin Gulf crisis of August. This seemed to show both that the CPR did not expect a major war and that its various overtures to Japan were partly designed, as usual, to draw Japan ultimately away from its alliance with the United States, an alliance that so greatly facilitated American military operations in the Pacific and the Far East.[51] In September, it was announced in Japan that after eight years of intermittent talks China and Japan had concluded an informal agreement to exchange correspondents.[52]

Since the noisy Ninth World Conference Against Atomic and Hydrogen Bombs of August, 1963, the convening organization, the Japan Council Against Atomic and Hydrogen Bombs (Gensuikyo), had split through the withdrawal of its moderate elements. The Tenth World Conference, held

---

[47] "Fishery Agreement for the Yellow Sea and East [China] Sea Between China Fishery Association and the Japan-China Fishery Council," *Current Background* (Hong Kong: American Consulate General), no. 724 (December 6, 1963).

[48] Cf. *The Washington Post and Times Herald*, February 16, 1964. On the Chou proposal see Tokyo *Kyodo*, May 22, 1964.

[49] Cf. *Christian Science Monitor*, March 31, 1964.

[50] *The New York Times*, October 13, 1964.

[51] *Christian Science Monitor*, August 19, 1964.

[52] *The New York Times*, September 27, 1964.

at Tokyo in August, 1964, was controlled by the Chinese and Japanese Communists and their supporters in Japan and other countries, some of whom were alleged to be residents of the CPR specially brought to Japan to "represent" their countries of origin at the conference. By this time the Japanese Communist Party had begun to exchange increasingly irritated letters with the Soviet party as a result of the Japanese party's strong tendency to side with the Chinese on such major aspects of the Sino-Soviet dispute as Khrushchev's proposal to convene a twenty-six-party conference. Unable either to shake or accept the dominance of their opponents at the Tokyo conference, the Soviet delegation and its supporters walked out and held a separate conference at Hiroshima and Nagasaki.[53]

Although the Sino-Soviet dispute has divided and weakened the Japanese left, it has also given Japan at least a modest opportunity to play the CPR against the Soviet Union, or perhaps more accurately to take advantage of the CPR's anxiety for good relations with Japan to extract support from it on the main issues outstanding between the Soviet Union and Japan. Of these issues one, apart from the overriding one of the real or assumed threat to Japanese security and survival posed by the Soviet Union, stands out. This is the Soviet seizure from Japan, in 1945, of the southern half of the island of Sakhalin and the Kurile Islands. Japan has been demanding the return of the two small islands of Habomai and Shikotan, off the coast of Hokkaido, which it says with apparent justification have never been considered part of the Kuriles, and of the two southernmost islands of the Kurile group, Kunashiri and Etorofu. The Soviet Union has agreed in principle to return the first two of these as part of a Soviet-Japanese peace settlement but has made no commitment regarding the last two. This issue, which is a lively one in Japan, has inevitably given the CPR a point of leverage, and in particular a possible means of disrupting the tendency of the right wing of the Japanese Socialist Party to be driven by its growing distrust of the CPR into a closer relationship with the Soviet Union.

From July 6 to 15, 1964, a Japanese Socialist delegation led by Secretary General Narita Tomomi visited the Soviet Union for talks with its leaders. Both sides agreed that preparations for a Soviet-Japanese peace settlement and a "normalization" of Sino-Japanese relations would be desirable. Khrushchev agreed once more to return Habomai and Shikotan but talked only vaguely about Kunashiri and Etorofu.[54] In the middle of this visit, Mao Tse-tung gave an interesting interview on July 10 to another Japanese Socialist delegation led by Sasaki Kozo. In addition to repeating some old and familiar points, Mao said some things that were not only new but sensational. He flatly supported Japan's claim for the return of all four

---

[53] "Communist Quarrels," *Special Information Note* (Washington), no. 62 (September 15, 1964).

[54] Tokyo *Kyodo*, July 15, 1964.

islands and said that the Soviet Union had taken too much territory in Mongolia and Manchuria, evidently from China, and too much in Eastern Europe from Rumania, Germany, Poland, and Finland.[55] The interview created an immediate sensation in Japan, but not in the world at large until the Soviet Union published it with some deletions in *Pravda* on September 2 (VJ-Day), partly with the intention of accusing Mao of inciting Japan to resume the kind of aggression that had been so disastrously terminated in 1945. The accompanying editorial compared Mao with Hitler in his alleged desire for additional *Lebensraum*.[56] The gist of the editorial was repeated in an interview held by Khrushchev with a Japanese parliamentary delegation on September 15, and according to some versions of the interview he went so far as implicitly to threaten the CPR with a "doomsday machine."[57]

This obvious Sino-Soviet competition for influence on Japan seems to stem partly from the Soviet Union's attempt to use its power to harm or help Japan as a means of counteracting Communist Chinese political approaches to Japan, and in particular the Chinese efforts to gain Japan's support for the Chinese position on disarmament: complete nuclear disarmament, without conventional disarmament.

■ COMMUNIST CHINA AND KOREA

During the years before 1945, there developed four factions within the Korean Communist movement: the domestic faction, which stayed in Korea under the Japanese occupation and was never able to make a serious bid for power in the party afterward; the Manchurian faction, composed of anti-Japanese guerrilla fighters most of whom were driven by the Japanese army into the Soviet Far East after 1940; the Soviet faction, consisting of members of the Korean community that Stalin had abruptly transferred from the Soviet Far East to Soviet Central Asia when the danger from Japan became acute, about 1937; and the Yenan faction, whose members had worked with and were oriented toward the CPC. After the Soviet entry into North Korea in 1945, the occupation authorities picked a member of the Manchurian faction, who has since gone by the name of Kim Il-song, as the puppet ruler of their emerging satellite.[58] Like some other puppets, Kim was later to show a remarkable capacity to outgrow his humiliating status.

An early indication that the Yenan faction could not be discounted appeared when a member of that faction, Kim Tu-bong, was elected chairman of the Korean Workers Party, which was formed in mid-1946 as a

[55] Tokyo *Asahi Shimbun*, July 12, 1964; *Tokyo Shimbun*, July 14, 1964.

[56] "In Connection with Mao Tse-tung's Talk with a Group of Japanese Socialists," *Pravda*, September 2, 1964.

[57] Official text of interview released by Tass, September 19, 1964.

[58] Chong-Sik Lee, "Politics in North Korea: Pre-Korean War Stage," *The China Quarterly*, no. 14 (April–June, 1963), pp. 3–9.

first major step toward uniting the four factions.[59] Chinese Communist successes in neighboring Manchuria led to the beginning of economic and quasi-diplomatic relations between the CPC headquarters in Manchuria and the Soviet-North Korean regime in Pyongyang in 1947. In the spring of 1948, a joint military headquarters was established at Pyongyang on which the CPC, as well as the Soviet and North Korean military authorities, was represented.[60] Despite the persistence of some Chinese influence, however, North Korea remained essentially a Soviet satellite, at any rate down to the proclamation of the Democratic People's Republic of Korea (DPRK) on September 8, 1948, and the withdrawal of the Soviet occupation force shortly afterward. Stalin's behavior suggested confidence that even after the withdrawal of his troops he could control the DPRK, that the latter could defend itself against any likely attacks from the South, and that in fact it could ultimately reunite the country.

Efforts to subvert the non-Communist South Korean regime that emerged at the same time as the DPRK began in 1947 and were intensified in 1948.[61] The South Korean army proved itself able to cope with this sort of threat, however, so that an invasion appeared necessary if South Korea was to be "liberated" from the north. The result of course was the Korean War, an interpretation of which has already been presented in Chapter 8.

During at least the first two years following the beginning of the Chinese intervention in the Korean War, the CPR seems to have made no serious effort to satellitize North Korea. There were a number of reasons, from the CPR's standpoint, why satellitization would have been neither practically possible nor desirable. The Yenan faction in the Korean Communist movement, through which Chinese control would have had to be exercised, was strongest in the North Korean army, and its power position was badly weakened by the catastrophic North Korean defeats in the autumn of 1950; one of the leading North Korean generals belonging to the Yenan faction, Mu Chong, was purged by Kim Il-song at the end of 1950.[62] The defeats suffered in turn by the "Chinese People's Volunteers" in the spring of 1951 must have further weakened the CPR's capacity to establish control over the North Korean regime. Furthermore, after those defeats the CPR probably felt no desire to assume responsibility for unifying Korea in the face of American opposition, especially in view of its pressing preoccupation with the confrontation in the Taiwan Strait. To have tried to replace Soviet with preponderant Chinese influence in North Korea

---

[59] *Ibid.,* p. 10.

[60] Kiwon Chung, "The North Korean People's Army and the Party," *The China Quarterly*, no. 14 (April–June, 1963), p. 109.

[61] Glenn D. Paige in Cyril E. Black and Thomas P. Thornton, eds., *Communist Revolution: The Strategic Uses of Political Violence*, Princeton University Press, 1964, pp. 221–227.

[62] Glenn D. Paige in Barnett, *Communist Strategies in Asia, op. cit.*, pp. 235–236.

would have produced a serious controversy with Stalin that the CPR could hardly afford at that time, especially since its abrupt "liberation" of Tibet must have already irritated Stalin by implying that the CPR did not trust him to keep his hands off Tibet while it intervened in Korea. Something had to be conceded to the Soviet Union as the acknowledged "leader of the socialist camp," of which North Korea was of course a member. The CPC also seems to believe in principle, partly no doubt on the basis of its own experiences with Stalin, in the internal autonomy of Communist Parties and regimes. The CPC was probably pleased to see that Kim Il-song not only showed no interest in accepting Chinese control but was showing signs of asserting his autonomy with respect to Stalin; in 1951 he purged Ho Kai, a leading Soviet Korean.[63] This step may have been a reaction to the Soviet Union's insistence on opening armistice negotiations. Since the CPR's main motive in intervening in the Korean War was to protect its own security by denying the United States the power to occupy North Korea, it followed that the orientation of the North Korean regime was a secondary consideration as long as it stayed in the "socialist camp." To the extent that the CPR showed an interest in influencing Pyongyang's behavior, it seems to have emphasized the cultivation of long-term goodwill rather than the establishment of direct control; the behavior of the Chinese "volunteers" toward the North Korean population was notably better than that of the Soviet occupation army had been during the period from 1945 to 1948.[64] The Chinese "volunteers" went so far as to accept Kim Il-song's nominal command, although probably little more.[65]

These considerations do not seem to have been radically affected even by the tension resulting from the CPR's decision in 1952, despite its defeats of the year before, not to sign an armistice that would deny it control over the majority of the prisoners it had lost. The creation of the Yenpien Korean Autonomous Chou adjacent to the trijunction of the Manchurian, North Korean, and Soviet frontiers on September 3, 1952, at a time when the CPR was heavily reinforcing its troops in Korea, was probably intended as a means of putting pressure on Stalin for additional support by implying a threat to satellitize North Korea, rather than as an actual step toward satellitization. In any case, the CPR was soon forced to capitulate in Korea, and the decision to do so undoubtedly cost it much of its influence on Kim Il-song. Soviet influence on Kim was presumably reduced at the same time by the death of Stalin and the fall of Beria. The partial withdrawal of the Chinese "volunteers," beginning in late 1954, parallel with a partial American withdrawal from South Korea, emphasized once more

---

[63] Glenn D. Paige and Dong Jun Lee, "The Post-War Politics of Communist Korea," *The China Quarterly*, no. 14 (April–June, 1963), p. 20.

[64] *Ibid.*, p. 19; Robert A. Scalapino, "The Foreign Policy of North Korea," *The China Quarterly*, no. 14 (April–June, 1963), p. 45.

[65] Cf. Chung, *loc. cit.*, p. 112.

that Chinese security, rather than the orientation of the North Korean regime, was the CPR's main concern.

Although Kim Il-song was clearly in the process of enlarging his political freedom of action, the shattered condition of his economy rendered him dependent for aid on the Soviet Union and the CPR. His ability to extract such aid was enhanced by the massive aid granted to South Korea by the United States during and after the Korean War. On September 19, 1953, the Soviet Union agreed to make a grant of one billion (old) roubles ($250 million at the official Soviet exchange rate) to North Korea for reconstruction. On November 24, the CPR promised North Korea a comparable grant of 8 trillion (old) yuan (about $338 million).[66] As a result of these and later similar commitments, made in roughly equal amounts by the Soviet Union and the CPR, North Korea has been able to develop the industrial sector of its economy to the point where its per capita industrial output exceeds that of the CPR.

Even after the armistice, the main political preoccupation of the North Korean regime continued to be reunification. The outlook was not encouraging. In May, 1956, Syngman Rhee was elected to a third term as President of the Republic of Korea, even though his handpicked running mate, Lee Ki-pong, was defeated by an opposition candidate, John M. Chang. Under these circumstances political approaches to reunification offered little prospect, and the main hope of reversing the military verdict of 1953 seemed to lie in energetic Soviet support. The Twentieth Congress (February, 1956) had showed, however, that the Soviet Union had not the slightest intention of providing such support. Khrushchev's attack on Stalin at that time also tended to undermine the personal position of Kim Il-song, who had originally been Stalin's creature. At the end of August, accordingly, the leaders of the Yenan faction tried to overthrow Kim but failed, perhaps because Kim had already shown that he was no longer a puppet of Moscow. For their pains most of the insurgents were soon purged and fled to the CPR.[67] In late 1957 the purge was extended to the army, and in the spring of 1958 the remnants of the Yenan faction attempted an unsuccessful military coup.[68] The attempt may have been evoked not only by internal developments but by a belief that the approaching withdrawal of the "Chinese People's Volunteers" would soon deprive the Yenan faction of its last source of support. It is of course interesting and significant that the CPR does not seem to have intervened to protect its friends, or that if it did, it was unsuccessful.

It has already been suggested that acceptance of a foreign "model" by a Communist Party or other political movement need not imply acceptance

---

[66] *The New York Times*, November 24, 1953.

[67] Paige and Lee, *loc. cit.*, p. 22; Paige in Barnett, *Communist Strategies in Asia, op. cit.*, p. 239.

[68] Chung, *loc. cit.*, pp. 121–122.

of leadership or control from the source of the "model." It also seems that rejection of the leadership or control of a foreign power need not imply rejection of its "model." The excitement attending the launching of the Great Leap Forward in the CPR, in 1958, led to a vague feeling in some foreign countries, including the Soviet Union, that the CPR might conceivably have found the key to rapid economic growth and therefore to increased power. It followed that, if so, then what seemed to be good for the CPR might also be good for other countries, such as North Korea, that considered themselves to be in a similar situation. Such seems to have been the thinking of Kim Il-song at the very time when he was completing the process of liquidating the remnants of the Yenan faction. In mid-1958 he launched his own version of the Great Leap Forward, which in September he designated the Flying Horse Movement (a winged horse was also the symbol of the Great Leap Forward). He did not go so far, however, as to imitate all the features of the "people's communes." In December, 1959, apparently as a result of Soviet pressures, North Korea decided to slow the pace of economic activity and to designate 1960 as a "buffer period."[69]

On April 27, 1960, at a time when the agitation in Japan against the revised American-Japanese security treaty had already begun to gather headway, Syngman Rhee fell from power in South Korea. His fall was the result of widespread opposition, especially on the part of students, to his increasingly highhanded behavior, and it was accomplished with the tacit support of the South Korean army. In spite of the fact that the United States was also pleased by Rhee's fall, and that South Korean Communists had little to do with it, the event seems to have aroused great expectations in Pyongyang and Peking. From their point of view, it was a sign that, ten years after the outbreak of the Korean War, the day of reunification might be coming closer.[70] Kim Il-song considered that the time had come to intensify his efforts on all fronts. In August he announced an ambitious Seven Year Plan for the development of the North Korean economy and proposed a "federation" of North and South Korea as a preliminary to "the complete peaceful unification of the fatherland" through "free general elections."[71] Kim had to be careful in his political maneuvers, since the population of South Korea is about twice that of North Korea.

---

[69] John Bradbury, "Sino-Soviet Competition in North Korea," *The China Quarterly*, no. 6 (April–June, 1961), pp. 15–22; Paige in Barnett, *Communist Strategies in Asia, op. cit.*, pp. 242–247; communiqué of December 1–4 plenary session of Central Committee of Korean Workers Party (North Korean Home Service broadcast, December 5, 1959). Kim Il-song visited the CPR in December, 1958, mainly in order to observe the Great Leap Forward at first hand.

[70] Cf. Paige in Black and Thornton, *op. cit.*, pp. 232–234.

[71] Cf. Kim's speech of August 14, 1960 (Korean Central News Agency dispatch, same date); Bradbury, *loc. cit.*, pp. 23–26.

The main obstacle to the reunification of Korea on Communist terms was of course American "imperialism." It is therefore not surprising that North Korea has tended to lean increasingly to the Chinese side in the Sino-Soviet dispute that came out into the open in the spring of 1960, since one of the main issues in the dispute was the extent to which international Communism should struggle actively against "imperialism." The Chinese no more than the Russians were in a position to support another invasion of South Korea, but at least their international strategy offered the hope that worldwide politico-military pressures on American "imperialism" might compel it to withdraw from its exposed beachhead in South Korea. This is roughly the line that seems to have been taken by the predominantly military Chinese delegation that visited North Korea to help celebrate the tenth anniversary of the formation of the "Chinese People's Volunteers" (October 25, 1960).[72] Providentially from the Chinese standpoint, this anniversary fell shortly before the important Eighty-One Party Conference in Moscow, which Mao Tse-tung and Kim Il-song alone among Communist Party leaders failed to attend, and at which the North Koreans seem to have taken an essentially pro-Chinese line.[73] Certainly the later North Korean interpretations of the Moscow meetings followed the Chinese line closely.[74]

The regime of Premier John M. Chang, who succeeded Syngman Rhee as the leading political personality in South Korea, was a mixed bag from the Communist point of view. On the one hand, he was American-oriented and showed some interest in joining Japan, the Republic of China, and the Philippines in a Northeast Asia Treaty Organization.[75] Such a development would of course have been anathema from the Communist Chinese as well as from the North Korean standpoint. On the other hand, Chang was a weak and ineffectual leader. He did nothing to promote reunification, whereas there had been a widespread hope in South Korea that the fall of Rhee might bring reunification closer, although not on Communist terms. Disappointment in Chang was reflected, among other things, in a certain amount of agitation in South Korea in favor of a "neutral, unified" Korea. When therefore Chang was overthrown, to the expressed displeasure of the United States, on May 16, 1961, in a military coup planned by officers some of whom had had left-wing associations in the past, Pyongyang and Peking seem to have been momentarily encouraged. It soon became clear, however, that the new South Korean leadership was unwilling or at least unable to

---

[72] Cf. *ibid.*, pp. 26–27.

[73] The North Korean party had been one of the twenty-six that had held a preparatory conference to draft the Moscow Statement.

[74] A. M. Halpern, "The Emergence of an Asian Communist Coalition," *The Annals of the American Academy of Political and Social Science*, vol. 349 (September, 1963), pp. 118–119.

[75] Cf. *The New York Times*, May 7, 1960.

show any interest in Communist proposals for reunification, and the Communist line toward the junta shifted to one of at least outward hostility. The North Koreans continued to insist, nevertheless, that although the South Korean junta was struggling to resist reunification the prospects for it were becoming brighter, presumably as a result of the unstable situation in South Korea and North Korean propaganda.[76] The CPR took a very similar line.[77]

The military coup of May 16 in South Korea, which was carried out without the knowledge and contrary to the wishes of the United States, seriously damaged the relations between the South Korean army and the American-controlled United Nations Command, one of whose main reasons for existence was to restrain any tendency on the part of the South Korean army to "march to the north" to reunite the country. In spite of an agreement finally reached by the South Koreans and Americans on May 26 regarding control over the South Korean forces, the military coup therefore was probably interpreted in Pyongyang as somewhat increasing the chances of a "march to the north." Some such thought was presumably in Kim Il-song's mind when he arrived in the Soviet Union on June 29, some three weeks behind President Sukarno and two days behind North Vietnamese Premier Pham Van Dong. On July 4, General Pak Chong-hui, who had been one of the main engineers of the May 16 coup, assumed sole power within the junta ruling South Korea. Two days later, without prior public notice, the Soviet Union and North Korea signed and published a treaty of "friendship, cooperation, and mutual assistance." It was valid for ten years and bound each party to give military aid and support "with all means at its disposal" if the other were "the object of an armed attack by some state or a coalition of states."[78]

From Moscow the North Korean delegation moved on to Peking, where it got a noticeably warmer welcome and another treaty of "friendship, cooperation, and mutual assistance." The Chinese treaty was somewhat more positive in tone than the Soviet; for instance, it pledged both parties to "adopt all measures to prevent aggression against either of the contracting parties by any state." Furthermore, the Chinese treaty was to remain in force indefinitely.[79]

Defensive alliances were of little help to Kim Il-song in his efforts to reunify the country, and for this purpose he was left largely to his own devices. His answer was further to intensify the propaganda in favor of his political proposals addressed to South Korea. His belief in the Soviet Union's concern for the interests of small Communist regimes was probably

---

[76] Cf. Paige in Black and Thornton, *op. cit.*, pp. 234–236.
[77] Cf. "The Peaceful Unification of Korea Will Surely Be Realized," *People's Daily*, June 25, 1961.
[78] Text released by Tass, July 6, 1961.
[79] Text released by New China News Agency, July 11, 1961.

shaken by Khrushchev's treatment of Albania, with which North Korea continued to maintain friendly relations after Khrushchev's denunciation of Hoxha at the Twenty-second Congress (October, 1961). North Korea's political and economic relations with the CPR grew closer during 1962, and those with the Soviet Union evidently less so.[80] At the same time the North Koreans began to stress the Chinese line of self-reliance in economic matters, which implied that a reduction in economic relations with the Soviet Union, at whose initiative is not clear, was in progress.[81]

The Cuban and Sino-Indian border crises and the test ban treaty further depreciated Soviet and enhanced Chinese stock in Kim Il-song's eyes, and he took an unreservedly pro-Chinese line toward all three. Unlike Ho Chi Minh, who kept his pro-Chinese leanings within rigid bounds and even tried to mediate the Sino-Soviet dispute, Kim increasingly and outspokenly took the Chinese side. This was made abundantly clear by the pronouncements at the time of a visit by Choe Yong-kon, Chairman of the Praesidium of the North Korean Supreme People's Assembly, to the CPR in June, 1963,[82] and to a lesser degree at the time of a visit by Liu Shao-ch'i to the DPRK in September, 1963.[83]

There were probably two main reasons for this difference. One is that, by virtue of its intervention in the Korean War and its signing of a defensive alliance with North Korea, the CPR has taken a somewhat more active interest in Korean than in Vietnamese unification, let alone Indochinese unification. The second is that North Korea borders on the Soviet Union as well as on the CPR, is therefore in a better position to play them against each other, and can if necessary replace its present pro-Chinese orientation with a pro-Soviet one, whereas the DRV, which borders on the CPR but not on the Soviet Union, might set in motion an irreversible trend toward Chinese control if it went too far in aligning itself with the CPR.

Probably the determining factor in relations between the CPR and the DPRK is the extent to which Kim Il-song considers Peking to be sympathetic and helpful in connection with its attempt to unify the country by means less dangerous than those employed in 1950. Since about 1960, he has seemed to believe that the CPR at least deserved higher marks on this score than the Soviet Union. He also probably sees reason to believe that the collapse and "liberation" of South Korea is drawing closer. After General Pak's narrow victory in the presidential election of October, 1963,

---

[80] Cf. Halpern, *loc. cit.,* pp. 121–122.

[81] E.g. Kim Il-song's speech to Supreme People's Assembly, October 23, 1962 (Korean Central News Agency dispatch, same date); "Self-Reliance and the Construction of a Self-Supporting National Economy," *Nodong Sinmun,* June 12, 1963.

[82] Cf. joint statement by Liu Shao-ch'i and Choe Yong-kon released by New China News Agency, June 23, 1963.

[83] There was no joint communiqué on this occasion, merely a press communiqué. It is also interesting that Liu arrived too late (September 15) to take part in the celebration of the fifteenth anniversary of the establishment of the DPRK (September 8).

political disorders, including student demonstrations, assumed proportions serious enough to compel the resignation of Kim Chong-pil, a close collaborator of Pak's, as chairman of the ruling Democratic Republican Party in June, 1964. The CPR, as might be expected, expressed enthusiastic support for the opposition to General Pak.[84] It remains to be seen, however, how long Kim Il-song's confidence in the CPR could survive a failure to achieve the unification of Korea.

---

[84] "The Storm That Cannot Be Quelled," *People's Daily*, June 5, 1964.

15

Communist China
and Southeast Asia

If we may judge by current trends, it seems likely that Southeast Asia will be the area where the CPR will win its greatest extramural successes during the next few decades.

Historical considerations lend additional weight to this supposition. When the Chinese began to expand out of their home in the Yellow River Valley in the first millennium before Christ, their main direction of advance was southward. There they encountered peoples most of whom were either Thai or Austronesian (Malay) by race, and therefore related to peoples whom today we consider to be indigenous to Southeast Asia. Most of these peoples were either annihilated, assimilated, or herded back into mountainous areas while Chinese took over the valleys of what thus became South China. The southward expansion of the Chinese was checked partly by geographic factors and partly by the emergence to the south of them of civilized states. Three of the peoples controlling these states — the Vietnamese, the Thai, and the Burmese — had earlier been partially displaced southward from China and its peripheral regions by Chinese and other pressures (Mongol in the case of the Thai, Tibetan in the case of the Burmese). As the main center of power and civilization in eastern Asia, traditional China when strong always exerted some influence on Southeast Asia, and many Southeast Asian rulers acknowledged themselves for varying periods to be more or less nominal vassals of the Chinese empire.[1] This influence naturally declined during the nineteenth and early twentieth cen-

---

[1] Cf. Herold J. Wiens, *China's March Toward the Tropics*, Hamden, Conn.: Shoe String Press, 1954.

turies, when China was generally in a state of chaos and most of Southeast Asia was firmly under the control of the principal Western powers.

■ COMMUNIST CHINA'S POLICY TOWARD SOUTHEAST ASIA

As we have seen, the CPR is always sensitive to real or assumed threats to its security, and in particular to the security of its frontiers. Its leaders remember that for nearly a century before they came to power various powers established their authority over regions peripheral to China and then proceeded to extend their influence, sometimes to the point of satellitization, into the adjacent regions of China itself. The CPR is determined that this process will not be repeated, and it has shown no willingness to tolerate any other strong land power on the continent of eastern Asia except, for reasons of expediency even more than for reasons of ideology, the Soviet Union.

When the CPR looks at Southeast Asia from the standpoint of its own security, it thinks first and foremost of the security of Southwest China. The British and the French in their bad old colonial days regarded continental Southeast Asia as important mainly because it seemed to offer the best access to Southwest China, and it was primarily for this reason that they occupied Burma and Indochina respectively. The French succeeded in establishing a virtual sphere of influence in much of Southwest China, which China was forced to recognize in 1898. The Japanese occupation of northern Indochina in 1940 was mainly aimed at cutting Southwest China, where the Chinese Nationalists were then making their headquarters, off from one of its few remaining outlets to the outside world, the narrow-gauge railway running from Kunming to Hanoi and Haiphong.

As for the security of contemporary Southwest China, it like other more or less peripheral regions of the CPR is populated to a large extent by minority peoples to whom the CPC has become increasingly objectionable both because it is Chinese and because it is Communist. We have already seen something of the lengths to which a somewhat similar situation in Tibet has made the CPC willing to go in dealing with its Himalayan frontiers. Since the rise of a feeling of concern for China's security, including that of its border regions, on the CPC's part does not wait until the actual arrival of a hostile army at one of the borders, the CPC naturally looks with misgivings on two major military base complexes in Southeast Asia that are available to "imperialist" forces in time of crisis. One centers on Bangkok, the other on Singapore. Bangkok is the funnel through which any major military intervention in continental Southeast Asia by the United States or SEATO would occur. Singapore performs the same function with respect to the Malaysian and Indonesian region. From the CPC's viewpoint, these two base complexes must go, by political means, since military means are impractical at least for the present. The CPC also regards as obnoxious the idea of any Southeast Asian country, and in particular any such country near the Chinese frontier, entering into any sort of military alliance with a Western power; in point of fact, none in continental Southeast Asia except Thailand has done so.

From the standpoint of power, which I have defined as the second of the major objectives of Communist Chinese foreign policy, Southeast Asia obviously contains many valuable industrial raw materials and has an exportable surplus of rice, a fact of increasing possible interest to the CPR since it began to import significant quantities of food in 1961. To date the CPR has not become a major importer of industrial raw materials from Southeast Asia, its main imports of this kind having consisted of rubber from Indonesia and Malaya, some petroleum from Indonesia, and coal, bauxite, wolfram, and uranium from North Vietnam. It is conceivable that the CPR might also interest itself in the future in iron from the Philippines. It must be remembered, however, that Japan and the industrial countries of the West are also in the market for Southeast Asian raw materials.

It is widely believed that the CPR's food and population problem will drive it sooner or later to colonize Southeast Asia, with or without invasion, in order to develop its agricultural potential more fully. There are a number of powerful arguments against this theory. In the first place, and not necessarily conclusive, Chou En-lai has recently denied any intent to do such a thing.[2] Other, more persuasive, arguments are the serious military risks that would be entailed unless and until the United States disengaged itself from the region, the colossal cost of such an undertaking, and the disadvantageous political tensions that would be generated. It seems more likely that the CPR's food problem will be solved, if at all, essentially within its present borders, with Southeast Asia, whether under Communist control or not, playing at most the part of a major exporter of grain to China.

As for influence, it is the general opinion, and one that I share, that the CPC regards Southeast Asia basically as a Chinese sphere of influence, from which obviously other major external powers are to be excluded sooner or later to make way for Chinese hegemony. Bangkok and Singapore are important in this context as well as in that of Chinese security. I have already suggested, by way of qualification, that geographic and military realities severely limit the extent to which the CPR is able to exert pressure on Indonesia, as distinct from the continental Southeast Asian countries, and that the CPR may therefore be willing to tolerate an autonomous but friendly Indonesia, even if non-Communist, for a long time to come. Even in Indonesia, however, and certainly in the other countries

---

[2] Unattributed interview in the Vienna *Kurier*, August 1, 1964 (text in *The New York Times*, August 7, 1964).

as well, the CPC is eager to see the local Communist Parties come to power as soon as possible, and wherever possible. Such a situation presumably seems to the CPC to promise the greatest contribution by Southeast Asia to Chinese security and influence. It does not follow, however, that the CPC necessarily believes that such seizures of power can occur in all the countries of Southeast Asia in the near future. Local conditions are obviously the main determinant in this matter, and local conditions vary greatly.

■ COMMUNIST CHINA AND THE OVERSEAS CHINESE

The term overseas Chinese, as used here, refers to persons of predominantly Chinese culture living in Southeast Asia. In this sense, the number of overseas Chinese lies somewhere between ten and fifteen million, probably nearer to the upper than to the lower limit. The number of persons in Southeast Asia with a significant proportion of Chinese blood is much larger, but except in the case of those whose culture is still essentially Chinese this fact does not appear to be significant. The number of overseas Chinese who are actively involved, as Chinese, in the politics of their countries of residence, or of either of the "two Chinas," is considerably smaller than the total number of overseas Chinese. Thailand, Indonesia, and Malaya have the largest overseas Chinese communities; the proportion of Chinese in the total population is highest in Singapore and Malaya. Although immigration from China has greatly declined in recent years, there is still a large number of immigrant or first generation Chinese in Southeast Asia, but it is impossible to say what percentage of the total they constitute. The ancestors of the others immigrated for the most part in the second half of the nineteenth century or the first few decades of the twentieth. The great majority of both groups hail originally from one of two Chinese coastal provinces, Fukien and Kwangtung.

At first assimilation of these immigrants proceeded fairly rapidly, especially in the predominantly Buddhist countries of continental Southeast Asia, and intermarriage was common because of a shortage of women among the immigrants. In the early twentieth century, however, this process was abruptly checked by the arrival of larger numbers of Chinese women, and still more by the upsurge of nationalism, often with a distinct anti-Chinese tinge, among the indigenous elites, and among the overseas Chinese themselves after the Chinese Revolution of 1911. The main reason for indigenous resentment of the overseas Chinese, apart from their resistance to assimilation, has been the strong and sometimes overwhelming position that they have gained in the economies of all the Southeast Asian countries except the most backward one, Laos. This position enabled them to remit approximately $100 million annually to China, largely to relatives, in prewar years. Another problem is the fact that, as China has grown stronger or at least more assertive since 1911, the overseas Chinese have come to be regarded in some quarters as potential fifth columnists, in spite of the fact that the vast majority consider Southeast Asia and not China as their home and lead peaceable lives dedicated mainly to preserving what they regard, not always accurately, as traditional Chinese culture and to making money. As a result of these attitudes, which were generally shared by the prewar colonial governments even though they welcomed the skills and energy contributed by the overseas Chinese, it has been difficult for overseas Chinese to acquire local citizenship and take part in local politics outside their own communities, nor have many wished to do so until recently. Still another problem is the fact that since shortly before 1911 the various governments of China have usually taken the line that all overseas Chinese, even those not born in China, retain and always will retain Chinese citizenship.

The most stringent prewar measures against the overseas Chinese were taken not by the colonial governments but by Thailand, the only country in Southeast Asia to escape colonization. These restrictions became increasingly severe as the Thai military rose to power during the 1930s, and they were reimposed after essentially the same group returned to power in 1948. Thai legislation has seriously restricted Chinese economic activity and Chinese schools, the latter being the main means by which Chinese culture is perpetuated among the overseas Chinese. Chinese middle (i.e., high) schools have been virtually eliminated and serious inroads made even at the elementary level. The Thai government has also made no real effort to integrate its overseas Chinese into the political life of the country, has denied them Thai citizenship, and has discriminated against them as noncitizens. The Republic of China, with which Thailand has maintained diplomatic relations since 1948, has been unable to give the overseas Chinese in Thailand, or anywhere else, effective protection. The overseas Chinese in the Philippines have fared only slightly better than those in Thailand. In 1956 the Diem government of South Vietnam granted compulsory Vietnamese citizenship to all overseas Chinese born in Vietnam, except a few who were repatriated to Taiwan, imposed severe restrictions on all Chinese born abroad, and closed many occupations to aliens. The resulting disruption of the economy was so great, however, that the government soon had to modify its economic restrictions against the overseas Chinese.

The states whose policies toward the overseas Chinese have been mentioned so far have had their hands strengthened, to a degree at least, by the fact of their American alignment. This does not hold true, of course, of neutral Indonesia, but Indonesia has the advantages, in its overseas Chinese policy as in other respects, of being by far the largest and most populous country in Southeast Asia and of being essentially unafraid of the CPR, because of its insular location and the CPR's comparative lack of naval power. Indonesia has therefore taken a rather harsh line with its overseas

Chinese, which the CPR for political reasons has generally elected not to contest. Indonesia has excluded foreign-born overseas Chinese from citizenship and granted it only to those among the locally born Chinese who were willing explicitly to renounce Chinese and opt for Indonesian citizenship. Aliens, and the overseas Chinese in particular, have been barred from many lines of economic activity. Chinese schools have been drastically reduced in number. Those Chinese who have acquired Indonesian citizenship have been allowed to take part in local (not national) political life, but they still encounter widespread economic discrimination.

Although neutral like Indonesia, Cambodia shares none of its advantages in dealing with the problem of the overseas Chinese. Nevertheless, it has had considerable latitude in practice because of the CPR's decision to woo it. In 1956, after declaring his country's independence of France (September, 1955) and making visits to Taiwan (December, 1955) and the CPR (February, 1956), Prince Sihanouk debarred aliens from sixteen occupations and simultaneously made citizenship much easier for Chinese to acquire. When many of them applied for Cambodian citizenship, however, the requirements were raised again. Since that time, careful handling of the situation by Cambodia and the CPR appears to have kept it within the limits of tolerance.

In Malaya, the Chinese population so nearly equals the Malay that the government, although largely Malay, is in no position to apply stringent sanctions against overseas Chinese unless they are suspected of subversive activity. On the whole, the government's program since the attainment of independence in 1957 has been one of creating a common Malayan citizenship, available to Chinese on relatively easy terms, rather than one of coercing the Chinese. The latter, however, are expected to modify their cultural exclusiveness somewhat, and their schools are being brought within the national school system. Malaya has insulated its Chinese problem as far as possible from outside pressures by refraining from recognizing and having diplomatic relations with either China.

Relations between the overseas Chinese and the indigenous population are probably better in Burma than in any other Southeast Asian country. The two peoples get on well in their personal relations, and because of competition from the Burmese Indian community the Chinese are less prominent in commerce than in most other countries in the region. For these reasons and because of Burma's very great vulnerability to Communist Chinese pressures and the fact that the government of independent Burma has generally been weak and unstable even by Southeast Asian standards, no coherent policy toward the overseas Chinese seems to have been formulated, and matters have essentially been allowed to drift.[3]

---

[3] The foregoing background information on the overseas Chinese is based largely on two excellent brief surveys: G. William Skinner, "Overseas Chinese in Southeast Asia," *The Annals of the American Academy of Political and Social Science*, vol. 321

The majority of the overseas Chinese, even though largely unassimilated, do not present a serious problem to their countries of residence or actively serve the cause of Communist China. There is, however, a minority who do, for one or more of the following reasons: alienation from the local indigenous societies and a resulting ghetto mentality; resentment of discrimination experienced at the hands of Western colonial and indigenous independent governments; the poor career prospects for young educated Chinese in Southeast Asia; the appeal of Leninist and Maoist techniques of political action; incitement and organization by the CPC, some of it dating from before the Second World War; pride in the first strong Chinese regime, regardless of political orientation, to emerge in many decades; an image of the CPR as the main custodian of Chinese culture and the place of origin of the overseas Chinese or their ancestors; the hope of protection by the CPR from local discrimination; and an expectation of eventual Chinese hegemony in Southeast Asia. There is evidently a hard core of supporters of the CPR among the overseas Chinese who are moved by most or even all of these considerations and are not likely to change their views. There is a much larger number of overseas Chinese who, although basically favorable to the CPR, have been periodically repelled by its excesses, notably the land reform campaign and the Great Leap Forward. It is an interesting fact that most of the overseas Chinese who are active on behalf of Chinese Communist causes hail originally from Fukien and Hainan, rather than Kwangtung (apart from Hainan); feelings between the CPC and the Cantonese have never been good, and Kwangtung is markedly underrepresented in the upper levels of the CPC.[4] Another important point is that active pro-CPC feeling is more widespread among younger than among older overseas Chinese. This fact is explained not only by such obvious considerations as the universal tendency toward radicalism on the part of the young but by the fact that a knowledge of standard Mandarin Chinese, conveyed through the schools in the Southeast Asian Chinese communities as well as on the mainland of China and Taiwan, is much more common among the young than among the old. Knowledge of Mandarin readily becomes a manifestation of Chinese nationalism and also opens up easier channels of access for Chinese Communist propaganda.

Both Communist China's Common Program of 1949 (Article 58) and its constitution of 1954 (Article 98) promise protection to the rights and interests of overseas Chinese, without stating whether they are regarded as

(January, 1959), pp. 136–147; A. Doak Barnett, *Communist China and Asia: Challenge to American Policy,* New York: Harper, 1960, Chapter 8. For a longer study see G. William Skinner, *Report on the Chinese in Southeast Asia,* Cornell University: Southeast Asia Program, 1951. See also Douglas P. Murray, "Chinese Education in South-East Asia," *The China Quarterly,* no. 20 (October–December, 1964), pp. 67–95.

[4] On this point and some others in this section I am indebted to A. Sabin Chase, who has had long experience in China as a Foreign Service Officer and has made studies of the overseas Chinese and of the ethnic minorities in China.

retaining Chinese citizenship. The strong presumption that they are normally so regarded is strengthened by the fact that they are represented in the Chinese People's Political Consultative Conference, an unwieldly advisory body with no real constitutional standing, and under the Electoral Law are entitled to elect thirty delegates to the National People's Congress, the majority of the thirty representing the Chinese communities in Southeast Asia.

Chinese Communist policy toward the overseas Chinese is presumably formulated in the first instance by the CPC's Politburo, or its Standing Committee. Implementation of the more formal and overt aspects of the policy is the responsibility of the Commission on Overseas Chinese Affairs of the State Council (or cabinet). The Commission supervises the work of some local agencies in Kwangtung and Fukien that handle such specialized problems as remittances by overseas Chinese and the resettlement of returned overseas Chinese.[5] Implementation of the more informal and covert aspects of overseas Chinese policy appears to be the responsibility mainly of the United Front Work Department of the CPC's Central Committee, which handles relations with other Chinese groups and organizations.

From the CPC's standpoint, the overseas Chinese represent a number of important assets, or potential assets. They can be used to provide bargaining leverage in dealing with Southeast Asian governments, by conveying the impression that fair treatment of the overseas Chinese is a prerequisite for good relations with the CPR. The overseas Chinese can help the CPC to maintain contact with, finance, and influence local Communist Parties. The overseas Chinese have some potential for subversive activities on their own, without regard to local Communist Parties controlled by indigenes; to date such activity has been conducted mainly in Malaya, Singapore, and Sarawak. Overseas Chinese mercantile interests obviously provide valuable outlets for Chinese exports and sources of import. The overseas Chinese community provides welcome remittances. It also provides a modest supply of skilled manpower for the CPR, in the form of overseas Chinese who return to the CPR to live and students who go there to study.

To capitalize on these potential assets represented by the overseas Chinese the CPC makes three main types of appeal to them. It offers, or claims to offer, protection against local oppression and discrimination. Through its voluminous propaganda addressed to the overseas Chinese, it constantly stresses its alleged legitimacy as the government of China and the custodian of the Chinese cultural tradition and appeals to their pride in its achievements. It promises, and to some extent grants, special privileges to dependents of overseas Chinese and to returned overseas Chinese, the main purpose being to keep the flow of remittances from their friends and relatives in Southeast Asia up.[6]

---

[5] Skinner, *op. cit.*, p. 81.
[6] Skinner, *loc. cit.*, p. 144.

On the other hand, the overseas Chinese also represent some serious liabilities to the CPC. They are in a state of comparative cultural and political isolation from, and antipathy toward, the indigenous populations, and they are a fertile source of tensions between the CPR and the governments of Southeast Asia. Most of the overseas Chinese do not give the CPR active or effective political support. The Chinese communities, even if they were considerably more favorable to the CPR than they are, would not be in a position to seize power except perhaps in Singapore and conceivably in Malaya, and if they did they would create a first class crisis in the CPR's relations with the area and confront it with embarrassing and possibly dangerous responsibilities for providing support and protection. In fact, it is difficult if not impossible for the CPR to give effective protection to the overseas Chinese even under present conditions; in this connection, it should be borne in mind that the great majority of the overseas Chinese are concentrated in the most productive and prosperous regions of Southeast Asia, which happen to be comparatively remote from the Chinese frontier. Finally, as we have seen a large amount of feeling hostile to the CPR has been generated among the overseas Chinese by some of the policies and trends on the mainland of China.

Malaya and Singapore, which have the highest proportion of Chinese, have always been the main theater of Chinese Communist activity among the overseas Chinese. In 1925, under the auspices of the Comintern, the CPC and the Indonesian Communist Party inaugurated a joint effort in Malaya; a natural division of labor was soon arrived at whereby the Indonesian party concentrated on the Malay community and the CPC on the Chinese. Only the second of these aspects of the effort had any real importance, since the Malays were politically apathetic. During the lifetime of its alliance with the Kuomintang, the CPC did much of its political work among the Chinese in Malaya and elsewhere in Southeast Asia through the Kuomintang apparatus, without establishing a formal and separate organization of its own. In 1927, however, after the break between the CPC and the Kuomintang, the CPC organized with the evident approval of the Comintern the Southeast Asia Communist Party (Nan Yang Kungch'an-tang),[7] which had at least a degree of supervisory authority over all Communist activities in the region. Understandable friction soon developed, however, between the CPC and the Comintern, which evidently felt that the existence of the Southeast Asia Communist Party was tending to give the CPC too much influence in the area.[8] Partly as a result of this tension, the Comintern dissolved the Southeast Asia Communist Party in the spring of 1930 and shifted to the idea of developing a more conventional Com-

---

[7] In Chinese, Nan Yang means literally South Seas, but it is used simply to mean Southeast Asia.

[8] Gene Z. Hanrahan, *The Communist Struggle in Malaya*, New York: Institute of Pacific Relations, 1954, pp. 6–8.

munist Party for each of the major colonial territories, which Chinese could presumably join but which would generally be dominated by indigenes. Almost immediately after the dissolution of the Southeast Asia Communist Party, an important Comintern agent, Joseph Ducroux, was arrested by the British in Singapore; the suspicion inevitably arises that he may have been informed on by a Chinese. In any case, on the basis of his revealing confession British and Chinese police soon struck heavy although not quite crippling blows at the main East Asian centers of the Comintern network, in Singapore, Malaya, Hong Kong, and Shanghai.[9] Nevertheless, a Malayan Communist Party dominated by overseas Chinese, and presumably by the CPC, was promptly formed, and it soon became the most effective Communist Party in Southeast Asia during the interval remaining before the outbreak of war.

As is well known, the Malayan Communist Party formed with some British help what was probably the most effective guerrilla organization to emerge anywhere in Southeast Asia during the period of the Japanese occupation; it directed its activities impartially against the Japanese and against unsympathetic Chinese. In mid-1948 the MCP went into open revolt against the British authorities and launched a jungle-based guerrilla war that was not officially declared by the Malayan government to have been suppressed until 1960. Although some arms and personnel from the CPR entered Malaya early in 1950, the Malayan guerrillas lacked an "active sanctuary" and were rendered increasingly ineffective by energetic British military and political counteraction. As early as 1951 they felt compelled to curtail their military activities somewhat, and about 1954 the MCP shifted its emphasis from jungle warfare to political action in the "white" areas, even though a force of a few hundred guerrillas remained in being astride the frontier between Malaya and Thailand. There can be no serious doubt that the MCP has always been and is still under Communist Chinese (not Soviet) influence, if not outright control.[10]

As might be expected, the most energetic Chinese Communist attempts to date to manipulate and exploit the overseas Chinese for political advantage were made during the early years after 1949, when the CPC was unsparing in its denunciation of the governments and non-Communist leaders of Southeast Asia. At the overt level, the CPC in effect promised protection for overseas Chinese in exchange for support. Its strident propaganda also accused the Southeast Asian governments of barbarously persecuting the overseas Chinese, presumably in a characteristic attempt simultaneously to engender and associate itself with powerful negative emotions.[11] At the covert level, and during 1950 and 1951 in particular, the CPC used

9 *Ibid.*, pp. 11–13.
10 Cf. *ibid.*, pp. 79–80.
11 Skinner, *op. cit.*, p. 83.

crude threats against relatives living in China as a means of blackmailing Chinese living abroad, including of course Chinese in Southeast Asia, into sending remittances. Covert branches of the CPC were formed among overseas Chinese communities. Apart from those Southeast Asian Communist Parties (in Malaya and Thailand) that were overwhelmingly Chinese in ethnic composition, the CPC encouraged Southeast Asian Chinese Communists to become active in local Communist Parties dominated by indigenes. This accordingly happened, but there were inevitable frictions, with the seeming result that in two parties (those of the Philippines and Indonesia, both immunized against extreme Chinese Communist pressures by ocean barriers) Chinese elements were actively curbed by the indigenes.[12] Overseas Chinese businessmen were encouraged to contribute to the war-chests of local Communist movements, whether Chinese or indigenous.

By about 1953, the CPC came to the inescapable conclusion that, as in its general policy toward Southeast Asia, it had overreached itself. The fortunes of the Communist revolts in Southeast Asia, except for the one in Vietnam, were waning rapidly, and the CPR was beginning to make its peace with Asian nationalism and neutralism to the extent that seemed necessary to its foreign policy objectives. The CPC's active efforts to exploit the overseas Chinese had aroused the governments and indigenous peoples of Southeast Asia against both the CPR and the overseas Chinese, who acquired a reputation for being a fifth column that they have not yet shaken off. The CPC's policy inevitably tended to get the overseas Chinese into trouble, from which the CPC had no effective means of rescuing them. The overseas Chinese themselves, except for the most leftist, were understandably angered at the CPC because of its policy toward them and also because of its land reform program, in the course of which many relatives of overseas Chinese suffered. This was an especially material point because the CPC was planning to launch, and did in fact launch in 1954, a major export drive, not only for the general purpose of promoting industrialization but also specifically in order to accumulate foreign exchange against the time, at the end of 1954, when it would have to begin repaying the Soviet credit that had been extended to it in 1950. If the CPR's exports to Southeast Asia were to be expanded, if the overseas Chinese merchants were to play an active part by importing Chinese goods, and if overseas Chinese remittances were to be kept at a desirable level, greater good will toward the CPR on the part of both the governments and the Chinese communities of Southeast Asia would be required.

The first major public indication of a shift in policy came in a speech by Chou En-lai in September, 1954, in which he promised that the CPR

---

[12] Cf. U. Alexis Johnson in C. Grove Haines, ed., *The Threat of Soviet Imperialism*, Baltimore: The Johns Hopkins University, 1954, p. 360. Ambassador Johnson's discussion is somewhat unclear, and he appears to be mistaken in referring to the party of Malaya rather than of Indonesia.

would encourage the overseas Chinese to respect the laws and customs of the countries in which they lived and was prepared to "settle" the question of their citizenship.[13] Chou discussed the question with Nehru when he visited Peking in October, and the CPR began negotiations with Indonesia about the same time for a mutually satisfactory solution to the citizenship problem. The subject of the overseas Chinese was widely discussed at the Bandung Conference, and the CPR must have become more convinced than ever of the advisability of moderating its policy on this score. Prime Minister Kotelawala of Ceylon proposed that the CPC dissolve its branches among the overseas Chinese, only to be told by the *People's Daily* that to do so would be an act of interference in the internal affairs of other countries.[14]

There was one outstanding exception to the general trend toward comparative moderation in the CPR's overseas Chinese policy, along the lines suggested by Chou En-lai's statement of September, 1954. This was the situation in Singapore, which was a special case and is discussed in the next section. It should not be thought that the CPR's espousal of the Bandung line meant a complete cessation of efforts to manipulate the overseas Chinese, any more than it meant a complete cessation of political activities directed against the neutral Asian governments, even though a marked shift of tactical emphasis occurred on both fronts. Liu Shao-ch'i told the CPC's Eighth National Congress in 1956 that "We must continue to unite with patriotic Chinese living in various places abroad; they too are a component part of the United Front."[15] The CPC continues to recognize as overseas Chinese all cultural Chinese living abroad who have not formally adopted the citizenship of their country of residence and given up that of the CPR. The CPC also insists that overseas Chinese must not be coerced into making this choice, and it would presumably consider invalid any choice of local citizenship that it believed, rightly or wrongly, to have been extorted by force or pressure. The CPC insists that those whom it continues to regard as overseas Chinese must take as active a part in the political life of the CPR as a minimum necessary regard for the laws and customs of their countries of residence will permit. Nor is it at all clear that the CPC has really given up all political interest even in those overseas Chinese who have taken out local citizenship, in spite of its opportunistic claims to have done so.[16] The question of citizenship probably does not strike the CPC as being of prime importance in the long run, since it expects eventually to see the Communist Parties of the area in power and itself

---

13 New China News Agency dispatch, September 24, 1954.

14 *The New York Times*. April 25, 1955.

15 New China News Agency dispatch, September 16, 1956.

16 Cf. Ho Hsiang-ning (Chairman of Overseas Chinese Affairs Commission), "Overseas Chinese Support the Government," *People's Daily*, April 25, 1959 (a report to the National People's Congress).

dominant in some sense over them, except perhaps for Indonesia and the Philippines.

The Great Leap Forward, Chinese suppression of the Buddhist Tibetans, and the corresponding adoption of a somewhat harder foreign policy line about 1958 were not accompanied by any drastic intensification of Chinese Communist efforts at manipulating the overseas Chinese, with the exception of the special situation in Indonesia that will be considered later. In 1958, however, there was a marked increase in Chinese exports, mainly textiles, to Southeast Asia, and much of it was distributed through overseas Chinese channels. Malaya and Singapore responded by imposing temporary restrictions on imports of this kind, and Malaya closed the local branch of the Bank of China in 1959. An even more sweeping restriction on imports from the CPR was imposed by Thailand.[17]

Since 1949 several hundred thousand overseas Chinese have returned to the CPR, either on a permanent or a temporary basis. There was a sizeable influx of repatriates from Indonesia after 1960 and a smaller one from India after 1962. The returned overseas Chinese may be divided into two main categories, students and residents. Both categories, together with the dependents of overseas Chinese still abroad, have presented the CPC with some difficult problems of management. On the one hand, to show the returned overseas Chinese and overseas Chinese dependents no special consideration would adversely affect the CPR's image in the eyes of the overseas Chinese and the flow of their remittances to the mainland of China. On the other hand, too much consideration would create resentment and disaffection on the part of ordinary Chinese and perhaps even hinder the CPC's general domestic program. The result has inevitably been that the CPC has tried to steer something of a middle course between extremes. From the land reform campaign to the Great Leap Forward, it tended to treat the returned overseas Chinese and overseas Chinese dependents with much consideration; during the Great Leap Forward, they were treated almost like anyone else; since the collapse of the Great Leap Forward, they have once more been shown somewhat greater consideration than has been shown to ordinary Chinese. In the early years after 1949, returned overseas Chinese residents were generally resettled in the vicinity of Canton. More recently the majority seem to have been resettled in extreme South and Southwest China, where many of them raise tropical crops similar to those of Southeast Asia.[18] It is clear that the returned overseas Chinese, like many if not most ordinary Chinese, have tended to become increasingly disillusioned and discontented with their lot under Chinese Communist rule. This is true not only of residents but also of overseas Chinese students, who in

---

[17] Foreign Agricultural Service, United States Department of Agriculture, *Communist China's Cotton Textile Exports: Their Growth and Their Effect on World Markets*, FAS-M-52, Washington, 1959, especially pp. 17–20.

[18] Cf. source cited in note 16.

most cases have not been permitted by either the CPR or their previous country of residence to return home, and some of whom were active in the demonstrations that occurred in 1957 in the course of the Hundred Flowers campaign.[19]

Remittances by overseas Chinese to the mainland of China, most of which pass through governmental and private Chinese banks in Hong Kong, may be divided into two main categories, remittances to dependents and investments. The distinction is not a neat one, since overseas Chinese who invest money in the CPR often use the dividends to support dependents in China. From 1949 to the beginning of the Great Leap Forward, total overseas Chinese remittances averaged about $30 million per year. The Great Leap Forward, in the course of which returned overseas Chinese were herded into "people's communes" like everyone else, lowered the figure to an estimated $17 million in 1959 and $15 million in 1960.[20]

The most ambitious effort by the CPC to encourage investment by overseas Chinese was probably the establishment of the Overseas Chinese Investment Corporation in February, 1955, with a capital equivalent to about $50 million. It was a "joint state-private enterprise" of a type characteristic of the CPR, in which private investment is permitted but the state retains full control. The Overseas Chinese Investment Corporation absorbed a number of smaller organizations that had been set up earlier for similar purposes. Overseas Chinese were officially promised that their investments would bring a return of 8 per cent per annum.[21] The purposes for which overseas Chinese investment was to be encouraged were semi-officially described as the "development of forests, uncultivated land, and agriculture, construction of houses, and founding of cultural and educational enterprises."[22] That the CPC was willing to pay dividends at the rate of 8 per cent on money invested in activities of such low profitability suggest both the acute shortage of capital in the CPR and the CPC's preoccupation with activities not related to public welfare.

The collapse of the Great Leap Forward in 1960 increased the importance in the CPC's eyes of the question of overseas Chinese remittances. In 1961 it began to encourage overseas Chinese to send food parcels to relatives on the mainland, and Chinese with relatives overseas wrote to them to the same effect. Gift parcels were guaranteed prompt delivery, and it was promised that an equivalent amount of food would not be deducted from the recipients' regular rations. In 1962, when the food situation began to improve, the CPC encouraged remittances in the form of funds, which

[19] Robert S. Elegant, The Dragon's Seed: Peking and the Overseas Chinese, New York: St. Martin's Press, 1959, p. 36.
[20] Edward F. Szczepanik in Edward F. Szczepanik, ed., Symposium on Economic and Social Problems in the Far East, Hong Kong University Press, 1962, pp. 117, 129.
[21] Hong Kong Ta Kung Pao, February 15, 1955.
[22] Hong Kong Ta Kung Pao, November 28, 1954.

could be used for extra food, rather than food parcels. The following year the CPC began to restrict the number of parcels from abroad to one per person per month.[23]

■ COMMUNIST CHINA AND SOUTHEAST ASIAN COMMUNISM

North Vietnam is of course the only area in Southeast Asia to date that is controlled by a Communist regime claiming to belong to the "socialist camp." The relationship between the CPR and the DRV is an obscure and controversial one, but in view of the situation in Indochina it is a relationship of great importance. Most of what it seems pertinent to say about this relationship has already been said, mainly in Chapters 9 and 13, and a brief recapitulation is all that is needed here.

The CPR played an important if not decisive role in bringing the North Vietnamese Communists to power. It gives them political and military support in connection with their effort to subvert South Vietnam, but it also maintains direct contact with the South Vietnam Communist guerrillas. The CPR seems to have grave reservations about North Vietnamese designs on Laos and Cambodia, which it evidently regards as at least partly its own sphere and as an access route to Thailand. Practically speaking, the CPR is in no position to dictate to the DRV even if it wished to do so, although it certainly exercises a great deal of influence on the DRV. Nor has the CPR shown itself willing to run any serious risk of a military confrontation with the United States on behalf of the DRV: risks of this order it generally assumes only if its own security seems so to require. On the whole, it is probable that the relationship between the CPR and the DRV is about as smooth as either party could reasonably hope for, and that the CPR would be happy to see Communist regimes of a similar vitality in control of all Southeast Asian countries, provided that they could be brought to power in a way that would assure at least a degree of Chinese leadership.

The North Vietnamese Communists, generally speaking, seem to feel a strong sense of cultural affinity with their Chinese neighbors, as well as a greater degree of ideological affinity than they feel with the Russians. In particular, the North Vietnamese share the militant anti-Americanism of the CPC, for analogous reasons, and they probably believe that the CPC's worldwide revolutionary strategy and its approach to relations among Communist states and parties are the most likely to produce results favorable to their own interests. The North Vietnamese are also aware of their dependence on Chinese aid and support and are certainly anxious to have Chinese protection in case of need. On the other hand, the Vietnamese

---

[23] "The China Market: 1962," *Current Scene* (Hong Kong), vol. ii, no. 14 (June 1, 1963), pp. 9–10.

have a long history of resistance to Chinese political domination, and the North Vietnamese leadership is unquestionably determined not to become a Chinese satellite or to allow a situation to arise in which Chinese armies invaded North Vietnam, even if they came nominally as friends. The North Vietnamese are probably annoyed at Chinese maneuvering in Laos and Cambodia and certainly distressed at the CPR's obvious reluctance to take any genuine risks on their behalf. To the Chinese plea that the CPR lacks the weapons necessary to take such risks, the North Vietnamese probably make the answer that the CPR might be in a better position on this score if it had not provoked the Soviet Union into terminating military deliveries in 1960. For these reasons, or something like them, Ho Chi Minh has shown a strong reluctance to endorse wholeheartedly the Chinese side in the Sino-Soviet dispute. Like the East Europeans, Ho may fear that a complete Sino-Soviet split would lead his giant neighbor to increase its pressures on him, instead of having as now to bid for his support against its opponent. Furthermore, North Vietnam is geographically too remote from the Soviet Union to receive much help from it, either in the unlikely event that a serious dispute developed between the CPR and the DRV, or in the less unlikely event that the DRV committed itself completely to the Chinese side, found the Chinese embrace suffocating, and tried to disengage itself. Much the best thing from North Vietnam's standpoint is to try to preserve as much freedom of action as possible with respect to both the Soviet Union and the CPR consistent with a basically pro-Chinese orientation, and this is what Ho Chi Minh seems to have done and to want his successors to do. It is entirely possible that after the death of Ho, who has been a major figure in international communism for a generation, North Vietnam may draw closer to the CPR, assuming always that the latter does not try to push its influence to the point of outright domination.

Next to that of Vietnam, the Communist movement in Southeast Asia that is of greatest importance to the CPR is that of Malaya and Singapore, which is overwhelmingly Chinese in ethnic composition. There can be little doubt that Communist activities in both territories are directed by the Malayan Communist Party; when Ch'in P'eng, the MCP's Secretary General, proposed truce talks in 1955, the invitation went to the Chief Ministers of both Malaya and Singapore, and both in fact talked with him in December of that year. Prior to 1955, when both territories attained partial self-government, the MCP was unable to throw down any major challenge to the British administration in Singapore, which is small and accessible. In the jungles of Malaya it was of course another story. The CPC undoubtedly sympathized with, and probably directed, the guerrilla war that the MCP carried on there for about six years, before withdrawing fom the unequal contest and establishing its main base astride the border between Malaya and Thailand. Presumably the CPC's and the MCP's objective in the initial phase of the struggle was to wage a "protracted war" that would diminish the value of Malaya to the British economy, draw in an increasingly large proportion of Malaya's numerous Chinese population and preferably some of the Malays as well, and produce in time a Communist seizure of power. At that point Singapore would presumably be subdued and amalgamated by pressures from the direction of Malaya, as happened during the Japanese invasion in 1942. But the British proved to be politically resourceful and militarily superior, and most of the Chinese population did not rally to the MCP. Furthermore, the MCP had no nearby "active sanctuary" from which large quantities of arms and advisers could flow in, as the North Vietnamese had in China, nor (after 1945) the helpful presence of a powerful foreign army engaged in conflict with the government to be overthrown, as was the case in China from 1937 to 1945.

After 1954 the MCP virtually ceased guerrilla warfare in favor of political struggle, which obviously would be greatly facilitated if the MCP were legalized. Accordingly, Chief Minister Tengku Abdul Rahman of Malaya and Chief Minister David Marshall of Singapore met and talked with Ch'in P'eng, at his original suggestion, in December, 1955. Ch'in demanded complete legalization of the MCP. Although he said that the party would lay down its arms once Malaya took over responsibility for its own internal security from the British, it appeared that he meant it would cache its weapons in the jungle, as it had for a time after 1945, rather than turning them in to the government. No agreement was possible on this basis, and the talks were soon broken off.[24] As another way of promoting its political fortunes, the MCP promptly effected a nominal reorganization that installed as token Chairman a Malay and as a token Vice Chairman an Indian, while Ch'in P'eng retained the crucial post of Secretary General.[25] In 1959, official documents were published in Malaya[26] and Singapore[27] showing that the MCP was engaged in extensive agitation, propaganda, and organizational activity among the Chinese in the two territories, especially students and workers.

Once it had become clear that the guerrilla war in Malaya was going to fail, and that Malaya was beginning (in 1955) to pass under the control of a strongly anti-Communist indigenous government with excellent security services and the will to use them, it became mandatory for the time being for the CPC and the MCP to prevent the merger of Singapore with Malaya, which would place the Chinese majority in Singapore, on which Communist influence was very strong and among which anti-British feeling ran high, under the domination of the Federation of Malaya. For after

---

[24] *The New York Times*, December 29, 1955. On January 5, 1956, the CPR published a manifesto just issued by the MCP and embodying its political demands.

[25] *The New York Times*, January 6, 1956.

[26] *The Communist Threat to the Federation of Malaya*, Kuala Lumpur: Government Press, 1959. For commentary see *The New York Times*, March 28, 1959.

[27] *Communist Literature in Singapore*, Singapore Legislative Assembly sessional paper, 1959.

about 1954 it was probably in the schools and factories of Singapore, rather than in the jungles of Malaya, that the main hope for the ultimate communization of both lay. In addition, the CPC and the MCP wanted *merdeka* (independence from Britain) for Singapore, for the time being under a non-Communist government since a Communist seizure of power in the near future would dry up Singapore's trade and subject the CPR to increased responsibilities and risks. Another important objective was to get all British bases out of Singapore.

The CPC and the MCP had some promising material with which to work, in the shape of the leftist, pro-CPR, ethnocentrism rampant among the younger Chinese of Singapore, their anti-British feelings, and a number of local issues that naturally arose out of these attitudes, such as an attempt by the government of Singapore in 1954 to impose conscription.[28] But while young Chinese may have rioted, in the spring of 1954 and the autumn of 1956 in particular, mainly over local issues, the Communist cadres who incited and organized the riots were probably thinking of the growing belief in non-Communist circles that Singapore could only be saved from eventual communization through merger with Malaya. The Malayan government, and the Malay community generally, were reluctant to take Singapore under their wing, since to do so would give the Chinese a plurality, or perhaps even a majority, of the population in the combined state. Every major outbreak of violence in Singapore tended, and was probably intended, to reinforce this reluctance.

Nevertheless, such a merger did offer the best hope of saving Singapore from the MCP, and in December, 1955, just before the talks with Ch'in P'eng, Rahman proposed that Singapore and the British territories in Borneo join the Federation of Malaya.[29] David Marshall was also in favor of a merger of Malaya and Singapore, and the two men held talks on the subject early in 1956.[30] Marshall was a weak and mercurial leader who hesitated to use force against rioters, so that violence tended to increase under his administration. Furthermore, the dissidents may have been encouraged by the violence in Cyprus and still more by the stormy election in Ceylon in the spring of 1956, which brought to power a party committed to the removal of British bases.[31] Marshall's successor, Lim Yew Hock, improved the situation by means of energetic military and police action against Communist-led student groups and unions, taken in the autumn of 1956.

For the next few years, Communist activities in Singapore seem to have been aimed mainly at infiltrating and strengthening the leftist People's Action Party, one of whose leaders, Lim Chin Siong, was evidently also a member

---

[28] Cf. Justus M. van der Kroef, "Nanyang University and the Dilemmas of Overseas Chinese Education," *The China Quarterly*, no. 20 (October–December, 1964), p. 99.

[29] *The New York Times*, December 25, 1955.

[30] *The New York Times*, March 4, 1956.

[31] Cf. *The New York Times*, April 16, 1956.

of the MCP. When, therefore, the People's Action Party won a landslide victory in the elections of May, 1959, there was widespread feeling that Singapore was on its way to becoming the Cuba of Southeast Asia. The new Chief Minister, Lee Kuan Yew, seemed to confirm this fear by insisting on the release of certain of his leftist colleagues, including Lim Chin Siong, who had been in jail for some time. It soon appeared that these fears were exaggerated. The PAP leftists resumed political activity but were not given effective power in the new government. Lee Kuan Yew proved to be a leader of energy and ability. He openly favored a merger of Singapore with Malaya as a prelude to complete independence and, presumably to make this idea more acceptable in Kuala Lumpur, promoted what would otherwise have seemed a rather ludicrous "Malayanization" of his administration.[32]

By the spring of 1961, Lee appeared to be losing ground to the leftists within his own party and to the Communists, who advocated immediate *merdeka* for Singapore, without merger with Malaya. Mainly for this reason, Lee readily fell in with a revival in London and Kuala Lumpur, at about the same time, of Rahman's proposal of 1955 for a Malaysian Federation embracing Malaya, Singapore, and the British Borneo territories. This idea was of course anathema to the extreme left in Singapore, which in July, 1961, broke with the People's Action Party, formed a new party known as the Barisan Sosialis, and endorsed the idea of a "democratic merger" between Malaya and Singapore, without the Borneo territories, as at least preferable to Malaysia.[33]

A referendum held in Singapore at the beginning of September, 1962, gave a strong endorsement to the formation of a Malaysian Federation along lines already worked out by Rahman and Lee Kuan Yew. The Barisan Sosialis' response was to tighten its control over its allies and begin a series of demonstrations, which were met with arrests. An election on September 21, 1963, a few days after the formal inauguration of the Malaysian Federation, resulted in a victory for Lee Kuan Yew. This led in turn to further demonstrations and arrests, and pressure by the Singapore government on the Barisan Sosialis and its allies was intensified after Rahman's victory in the Malayan general election of April, 1964. The consequence of the increasing governmental pressure on the Barisan Sosialis was a split in its ranks between those who continued to favor a militant line against Malaysia, and those who favored a turn toward greater moderation.[34] The CPC's sympathies presumably lay, and lie, with the militants, but obviously their unaided strength was not availing them very much against a government able and determined to cope with them.

———
[32] J. M. van der Kroef, "Singapore's Communist Fronts," *Problems of Communism*, vol. xiii, no. 5 (September–October, 1964), pp. 54–55.
[33] Cf. *ibid.,* p. 55.
[34] *Ibid.,* pp. 60–61.

In July, 1964, serious communal rioting broke out in Singapore between Malay and Chinese extremists. Presumably the Chinese were egged on if not organized by the MCP, and the government of Singapore was convinced that the Malays were incited by Indonesian agents, Communists or otherwise. There are, in fact, indications that an arrangement exists between the CPC and the MCP on the one hand, and the Indonesian Government and the Indonesian Communist Party on the other, to collaborate in stirring up the Chinese and Malay communities of Malaya and Singapore, as well as North Borneo, against the Malaysian Federation.[35]

Next to the DRV and the Chinese Communist movement in Malaysia, by far the most important Communist movement in Southeast Asia, both in fact and in the eyes of the CPC, is the Indonesian Communist Party (PKI). The CPC helped and supported the PKI, mainly through overseas Chinese channels, after the PKI's disastrous rising at Madiun in 1949.[36] As both the CPR and the PKI increasingly conciliated the Sukarno government after the early 1950s, however, the PKI's ties with the CPR and the presence of overseas Chinese in the PKI were reduced, or at least concealed.

D. N. Aidit, who became the leader of the PKI in 1953, steered it into a path of peaceful political activity that greatly enlarged its membership and influence and may have provided Khrushchev with the inspiration for his concept of a "parliamentary path" to power for local Communist Parties. On the other hand the PKI, although it was allowed to participate in national politics at the highest level, found itself partially trapped in a web of restraints that Sukarno skillfully wove about it, mainly between 1955 and 1959.[37] The most important restraint was and is the army, whose leadership, especially at the regional level, is strongly anti-Communist.[38] The Indonesian armed forces, furthermore, have received large quantities of military equipment, some of which is very advanced but much of which would be useful in coping with an insurrection, from the Soviet Union, especially since 1961. Thus the PKI for the time being is in no position at all to try to break out of Sukarno's trap by violent means.

The strange triangle (Sukarno, the army, and the PKI) that has dominated Indonesian politics since about 1959 seems to depend, for the comparative durability it has shown so far, partly on the Japanese tradition of seeking political consensus rather than conflict, but even more on finding external enemies on whom tensions can be vented, so that they need not be

[35] Cf. *The New York Times*, July 27, September 27, 1964; *The Washington Post and Times Herald*, July 26, 1964.

[36] Cf. Justus M. van der Kroef, "Dilemmas of Indonesian Communism," *Pacific Affairs*, vol. xxxv, no. 2 (summer, 1962), p. 148.

[37] Donald Hindley, "President Soekarno and the Communists: The Politics of Domestication," *The American Political Science Review*, vol. lvi, no. 4 (December, 1962), pp. 915–926.

[38] Cf. Daniel S. Lev, "The Political Role of the Army in Indonesia," *Pacific Affairs*, vol. xxxvi, no. 4 (winter, 1963–64), pp. 349–364.

worked off at home. The PKI has been at least as vocal as Sukarno, and more so than the army, in urging "confrontations" with external opponents, and it has a special reason for wanting them: they tend to distract the army's attention from the PKI, and they represent the most practical way in which a state of national emergency could be created and in which the Indonesian army might be weakened to a point that would make a Communist seizure of power possible.

From the political situation in which the PKI finds itself it is not difficult to deduce the probable reasons why, since about 1961, it has tended to side increasingly with the CPR in the Sino-Soviet dispute. Although the CPR is collaborating with Sukarno, it has not armed the Indonesian army, as the Soviet Union has. The CPC's insistence that the Soviet Union, as head of the "socialist camp," has the obligation to lead a militant struggle against "imperialism," and that the Soviet party has the obligation to give priority to the interests of brother Communist Parties over those of bourgeois governments, undoubtedly appeals to the PKI. The CPC offers the only hope of significant aid and advice to the PKI if it should ultimately decide to try to seize power by force. Although the PKI has expressed its overt objections to Soviet policy in Communist theoretical and organizational terms,[39] it seems probable that its main actual objections run somewhat along the lines just suggested. Furthermore, the CPC has wooed and flattered the PKI, as it has Sukarno, and seems to have been instrumental in persuading him to take some actions favorable to the PKI, such as banning two anti-Communist parties, the Body for the Promotion of Sukarnoism (in December, 1964) and the Partai Murba (in January, 1965).[40] The CPC also seems to want the PKI, like the Communist Parties of other Southeast Asian countries with whose governments the CPR is on relatively good terms, to put just enough political pressure on the government to give the CPR some leverage and keep the government in question to the left of center in the hope of forestalling a Communist revolt, without applying enough pressure to bring on reprisals with which the party is not prepared to cope. Presumably this situation is intended to persist until the eventual materialization of conditions favorable to a Communist seizure of power. Thus it is not surprising that the PKI has tended recently to speak more critically than before of some of Sukarno's colleagues, although not yet of Sukarno himself.[41]

Little can be said, because little is known, of the CPC's relations with the lesser Communist movements of Southeast Asia. The CPC undoubtedly maintains its own organization among the overseas Chinese and exerts a

---

[39] Cf. Donald Hindley, "The Indonesian Communist Party and the Conflict in the International Communist Movement," *The China Quarterly*, no. 19 (July–September, 1964), pp. 99–119.

[40] Cf. *The New York Times*, January 8, 1965.

[41] Cf. *Christian Science Monitor*, May 20, 1963.

strong influence, although not necessarily always to the exclusion of the Soviet party, on the indigenous Communist Parties. In the two countries with hostile governments, Thailand and the Philippines, political conditions do not permit much subversive activity by local Communists, with or without the CPC's approval. In Cambodia, where internal security is fairly good so far except in some border regions, but whose government is of course friendly to the CPR, the CPC seems to follow a policy toward the local Communists similar to its policy toward the PKI; it encourages them to keep up a level of opposition to the government sufficient to keep it under some pressure, and yet not enough to provoke serious reprisals or a diplomatic crisis with the CPR.

With Burma, whose government is necessarily friendly to the CPR but is also unstable and essentially anti-Communist in its domestic policies, the CPC has had a more complex problem. During the militant early years after 1949, the CPC gave the Communist Party of Burma, sometimes known as the White Flags, aid and encouragement in connection with their guerrilla war against the government. This aid and encouragement slacked off during the Bandung phase of the CPR's foreign policy, but they were resumed after the adoption of a tougher Chinese line toward the underdeveloped areas in 1957–1958.[42] Since Chinese dealings with the White Flags, as well as with their legal counterpart, a front organization known as the National United Front, were covert, they gave the CPC leverage on the Burmese political scene without provoking a major rupture with the Burmese government, which was and is too much afraid of the CPR to quarrel with it except in extreme situations. Chinese aid and support, which the Soviet Union was in no position to match, also brought the White Flags onto the Chinese side in the Sino-Soviet dispute. This tendency seems to have grown still stronger since the government broke off truce talks with the White Flags and arrested many members of the National United Front in the autumn of 1963, and the White Flag leaders returned to the jungle to resume their long-standing guerrilla war. One of the most cordial messages that the CPR received while celebrating its fifteenth anniversary (October 1, 1964) came from the White Flags. It praised almost every major aspect of Communist Chinese domestic and foreign policy and seemed to urge that the CPR continue its existing policy toward Burma: correct and even friendly relations at the state level, support for subversion at the party level.[43] The CPR rebroadcast this message in both English and Burmese, and there was a great deal of irritation on the part of the Burmese government and press.[44]

The CPC's relations with the Burmese Communist movement is of

[42] Cf. Aleksandr Kaznacheev, *Inside a Soviet Embassy: Experiences of a Russian Diplomat in Burma*, Philadelphia: J. B. Lippincott, 1962, pp. 139, 215.

[43] New China News Agency dispatch, September 30, 1964.

[44] *The New York Times*, November 1, 1964.

course not the only, and not necessarily even the most important, aspect of its relations with Burma. Some other important aspects, relating to the problems of the Sino-Burmese border, have already been discussed (in Chapter 12). But there still remains something to be said on this subject.

■ COMMUNIST CHINA AND BURMA

To the CPR, Burma is of interest first and foremost because the presence of a hostile force on its soil would threaten the security of Yunnan and eastern Tibet. In addition, Burma offers the CPR, as it did to the Chinese Nationalists during the Second World War, the best access route to the Bay of Bengal and the Indian Ocean, although a difficult one. Finally, Burma has an exportable surplus of rice, although this fact has not had much significance until recently, since not until 1961 did the CPR become a major importer of grain. Burma is very vulnerable to Chinese pressures because of its extreme weakness and instability, which since the attainment of independence in 1948 have manifested themselves in continual ethnic and Communist revolts. It is probable that in the long run the CPR hopes to make Burma, like the other countries of at least the mainland portion of eastern Asia, into a virtual dependency of some kind, without annexing it. But there is a long distance between the formulation of such an objective and its realization.

On December 16, 1949, Burma became the first non-Communist country to extend diplomatic recognition to the CPR. Presumably because of the importance of Burmese recognition as a possible precedent, the CPR reciprocated only two days later.[45] The CPC, nevertheless, felt a strong hostility, which it did not try to conceal, toward U Nu's government, as toward other independent, neutral Asian governments. Even during this early unfriendly period, however, the CPR refrained from invading Burma or giving more than modest covert aid to the Burmese Communists. For this self-denial there were several probable reasons. Above all, the CPR was heavily preoccupied with the Taiwan Strait and Korea. Communications on both sides of the Sino-Burmese border are relatively poor. The Burmese Communist movement's effectiveness had been greatly decreased by its fission in 1948 into three guerrilla forces and one legal organization. Partly for this reason, the Burma Army under General Ne Win began to win victories against the Communists, as well as against the ethnic minorities also in revolt, in 1949. Not only was the Burmese government beginning to gain the upper hand against its domestic opponents; it was by no means slavishly pro-Chinese, as it showed when it refused to credit the CPR's

---

[45] "Diplomatic Relations of Communist China," *Current Background* (Hong Kong: American Consulate General), no. 440 (March 12, 1957).

charges that United Nations forces in Korea were guilty of germ warfare. Even though it had left the British Commonwealth, Burma remained relatively pro-British, and it is conceivable that excessive Chinese pressures might have driven it to seek military aid and support from the West.

Burma was naturally more perturbed by the war in Indochina than by the one in Korea. By 1953 Vietnamese and Chinese pressures on Laos began to threaten the security of that country, and therefore indirectly that of Burma as well as Thailand. There were probably two main reasons why Burma did not follow Thailand's example and join SEATO. For one thing, Burma was less seriously threatened by developments in Laos than was Thailand. Secondly, even though it had left the British Commonwealth, Burma maintained close relations with India, and Nehru was passionately convinced that neutrality and good will were better ways of coping with possible Chinese designs on South and Southeast Asia than was adherence to Western military alliances. Burma therefore clung to its neutrality, and when U Nu visited the CPR in December, 1954, he promised the Chinese that Burma would never allow its territory to be used for purposes of military operations or espionage against the CPR. He also offered to mediate between the CPR and the United States, whose mutual hostility he termed the greatest threat to peace in eastern Asia.[46] The CPR, however, has never shown much interest in such mediation by Burma or any other country, although it tries to use third countries as means of putting pressure on the United States.

Burma was alarmed in 1959 by the CPC's treatment of the Tibetans, who are fellow-Buddhists, and by the ensuing Sino-Indian border crisis, which reminded the Burmese that their boundary with the CPR had not been finally settled and had more than once been crossed by Communist Chinese troops in the past. In mid-1959 Aleksandr Kaznacheev, an official of the Soviet Embassy in Rangoon, sought asylum in the American Embassy and publicly denounced Soviet and Communist Chinese subversion against Burma. Probably in part for these reasons, Burma decided in July to reverse a policy it had adopted in 1953 and accept economic aid once more from the United States.[47] In February, 1960, Khrushchev visited Burma; his reception was polite, although reserved, and he promised to increase the flow of economic aid and cultural exchange.[48]

By this time the CPC had already decided that it had overreached itself in adopting the harsh line toward Asian neutrals that it had taken since 1957–58. Its decision evidently was to make a tactical withdrawal to a position from which it could be more selective in its policies. India was to be made an example of the results to which an anti-Chinese policy, even though labeled as neutrality, could lead. Afghanistan, Nepal, Burma, Cam-

---

[46] New China News Agency dispatch, December 10, 1954.
[47] *The New York Times*, July 7, 1959.
[48] Summary of joint communiqué in *The New York Times*, February 19, 1960.

bodia, and Indonesia were to be treated in such a way as to demonstrate the advantages of a policy of "genuine" neutrality and good relations with the CPR, and it will be recalled that by the end of 1961 the CPR had signed treaties of peace and friendship with all five.

Burma was chronologically the first of these to sign a treaty with the CPR. Ne Win was about to retire from power in favor of an elected government. His successor, U Nu, was already committed to a boundary settlement and good relations with the CPR, but the CPR probably wanted to bind the Burma Army through Ne Win while time remained. Furthermore, Khrushchev was about to visit Burma. Before his visit, but after it had been announced, Ne Win flew to Peking, where on January 28 he signed a boundary agreement and a treaty of friendship and nonaggression, whose provisions have been discussed in Chapter 12.

After U Nu's return to power the boundary agreement was made into a formal treaty, which was signed on October 1, 1960, the CPR's National Day; ratifications were exchanged in Rangoon on January 4, 1961, Burma's National Day.[49] At that time Chou En-lai signed an agreement under which the CPR was to make an interest-free loan to Burma of £30 million, the largest it has ever made to any non-Communist country, for purposes of economic development.[50] Credits of this kind to neutral countries have of course been a regular feature of the CPR's foreign policy during periods when it was feeling comparatively well disposed toward the neutrals, but the unique size of the credit to Burma seems to call for some comment. The immediate political purpose of the loan was probably to render the Burmese government as cooperative as possible with respect to a problem then perturbing the CPR: the possibility that the right wing coup of December, 1960, in Vientiane might lead to fighting near the Chinese border and reactivate the problem of the "KMT irregulars," of whom as we have seen there were then some in Burma and Laos. The collaboration of the Burma Army in preventing hostile activities along the CPR's border would be a valuable asset, and it seems to have been forthcoming.

The gratitude inspired in Burma by the CPR's relatively generous behavior, reinforced by traditional Burmese fear of Chinese power, combined to raise the CPR's stock in Burma to unprecedented heights.[51] Issues of course continued to arise, such as the granting by the Burmese government of asylum to two political refugees from the CPR in mid-1961.[52]

General Ne Win seized power from U Nu for the second time on March 2, 1962, for reasons having little or nothing to do with Sino-Burmese relations. One of the first acts of the new military government was to

---

[49] A final protocol to the boundary treaty was signed on October 13, 1961, after demarcation had been completed.

[50] New China News Agency dispatch, January 9, 1961.

[51] Cf. *The New York Times*, June 12, 1961.

[52] *The Washington Post and Times Herald*, June 15, 1961.

express its intention of maintaining good relations with the CPR and to request diplomatic recognition, which was extended on March 6.[53]

The Ne Win government has followed a policy of isolating Burma from the outside world as nearly as possible, and in the process has very nearly isolated itself from its own people. While the CPR can influence the moody and unpredictable Ne Win, it cannot control him, any more than the Soviet Union can control Castro. One of the early acts of the Ne Win government was to nationalize all banks, including those owned by foreigners. This presented a serious problem to the Burmese branches of two of the CPR's banks, the Bank of China and the Bank of Communications, which for years had been making large loans to overseas Chinese businessmen in Burma on condition that they support the CPR. Faced not only with the loss of these two branches but with the disclosure of their records to the government, the CPR announced that it was "voluntarily" giving the branch banks to Burma, without compensation.[54]

The rise of tension along the Sino-Indian frontier, culminating in heavy fighting in October, 1962, naturally gave the Ne Win government much concern. Although U Nu had earlier tried to mediate between the United States and the CPR, Ne Win at first showed no overt interest in mediating between India and the CPR. Instead, Burma preserved what was probably the quietest and most neutral attitude of any of the Colombo powers.[55]

On April 12, 1963, Liu Shao-ch'i stopped briefly at Rangoon on his way to Indonesia,[56] immediately after a visit to Burma by Soviet Defense Minister Malinovsky. Liu returned on April 20 for a six-day visit. The main business discussed was the Sino-Indian border dispute, in which the Burmese government had begun by this time to try to mediate, and some of its byproducts, such as the treatment of Chinese nationals in India.[57]

On February 5, 1964, Chou En-lai made a brief and unpublicized stop at Rangoon on his way home from his foreign tour. Three days later, Ne Win arrived unexpectedly in New Delhi for talks with Nehru.[58] At Chou's suggestion, Ne Win seems to have proposed to Nehru that the two premiers meet once more to discuss the border dispute, but Nehru refused.[59] From February 14 to 18, Chou returned to Burma and was presumably informed of Nehru's attitude.[60] Five months later, Chou En-lai and Chen Yi paid an unexpected "private" visit to Burma shortly after the departure of Soviet Deputy Premier Mikoyan. The joint communiqué expressed primary con-

[53] New China News Agency dispatch, March 7, 1962.
[54] Information from a Burmese friend.
[55] Cf. The New York Times, December 26, 1962.
[56] New China News Agency dispatch, April 12, 1963.
[57] Cf. joint communiqué (New China News Agency dispatch, April 26, 1963).
[58] The New York Times, February 9, 1964.
[59] The New York Times, February 19, 1964.
[60] Text of joint communiqué released by New China News Agency, February 18, 1964.

cern over the "deteriorating situation in Southeast Asia, particularly in South Vietnam and Laos." It also explicitly reaffirmed the validity of Article 3 of the Sino-Burmese treaty of friendship and mutual nonaggression, which in effect pledges the CPR not to commit aggression against Burma and Burma not to join SEATO.[61]

For the time being, the Burmese government seems to be in reasonably good control of its country, which it is pushing rapidly in the direction of an extreme socialist, but non-Communist, regime. It is doubtful, however, whether Burma can stand out alone for long against the increasing pressures that the CPR, in conjunction with the Burmese Communists, appears to be bringing to bear on it. A turn by Burma toward the United States would be out of keeping with Burma's tradition and would be too obvious a defiance of the CPR, and in any case the United States by its performance in Indochina has probably made itself appear in Burmese eyes as too frail a reed to lean on. India also appears too frail, and its relations with Burma have been worsening since about 1962. There remains as the only possible alternative the Soviet Union, whose press has been referring with strong approval to the domestic and foreign policies of the Ne Win government.

■ COMMUNIST CHINA AND THAILAND

It has already been suggested that the CPR does not welcome the idea of undue Vietnamese Communist influence on, let alone control over, Laos and Cambodia. The same applies even more strongly to Thailand, which the CPR appears to regard as exclusively its own sphere. Ever since early 1953, when Vietnamese pressures on Laos began, there have been recurrent rumors, regularly denied from Peking, of the existence of a "Free Thailand" movement in Southwest China; certainly that area has seen the formation of a number of "autonomous" areas inhabited by tribal Thai peoples, which may have been hopefully designed to appeal to similar peoples in nearby countries, including Thailand. The one hundred miles of Burmese and Laotian territory separating the northern tip of Thailand from the Chinese frontier give Thailand some protection, but not enough, against Chinese pressures.

It was of course the situation in Indochina that led to the formation of SEATO in 1954, and the main purpose of that organization has always been to protect Thailand against North Vietnam and the CPR. Bangkok is the headquarters of SEATO and is the center of a substantial complex of bases and facilities through which SEATO, or the United States alone, could move to protect Thailand or intervene in Laos. From the Chinese Communist standpoint, these bases and Thailand's status as the only continental

---

[61] New China News Agency dispatch, July 12, 1964. For commentary see *The New York Times*, July 11, 1964.

Southeast Asian member of SEATO constitute not only an obstacle to political, or conceivably military, expansion, but also a potential menace. The obstacle and the menace must both be removed, and Thailand moved somehow into a neutral position. Military means toward this end being obviously impractical, at least for the present, political means must be employed.

The CPR's response to Thailand's decision to join SEATO was relatively moderate. In July, 1954, Pridi, a leftist former premier of Thailand, made some broadcasts from the CPR, where he had been living in exile for some years, urging the Thai to repudiate the action of their "reactionary" government and promising that they would have good relations with the CPR if they did so.[62] At the Bandung Conference, Chou En-lai went out of his way to assure the Thai delegate, Foreign Minister Prince Wan Waithayakon, that the CPR harbored no aggressive or subversive designs on Thailand and that the broadcasts by Pridi would be discontinued, and invited him to visit Southwest China to see for himself that no "Free Thai" movement was in operation there. The broadcasts were discontinued, but the visit was never made.[63]

These assurances and an overoptimistic hope of large Chinese orders for Thai rice, as well as the general atmosphere generated by the Bandung Conference, had some effect on the Thai government. Premier Pibul relaxed his restrictions against trade with the CPR, which began to increase. He permitted free political discussion and eased some restrictions against the overseas Chinese, and the result was an upsurge of leftist political activity and the appearance of several Communist-oriented Chinese newspapers. Unofficial Thai delegations began to visit the CPR. There was in fact a definite drift toward neutralism in Thailand, even on the part of the government, and this trend grew somewhat stronger after the fall of Pibul in the autumn of 1957 and the ascendancy of the police chief, General Phao.[64] The widespread expectation that a change in Thailand's alignment was impending was strengthened by the revolution of July, 1958, in Iraq, which took that country out of the Baghdad Pact. There is no reason to doubt that the Communist bloc, and the CPR in particular, would be very happy to see Thailand duplicate Iraq's performance.

The drift toward neutralism, and still more the expectation of a further drift, was among the main reasons for the seizure of power by Marshal Sarit in October, 1958. His five-year rule was much more efficient, and more determinedly anti-Communist, than that of his predecessors. Nevertheless, Communist successes in Laos, the Kennedy administration's decision

---

[62] R. Gavin Boyd in George Modelski, ed., *SEATO: Six Studies*, Melbourne: F. W. Cheshire, 1962, p. 170.

[63] Cf. Rosemary Brissenden in *ibid.*, p. 216; *The New York Times*, April 20, 1955.

[64] Cf. Modelski in *ibid.*, pp. 110–111; Boyd in *ibid.*, p. 112; *Christian Science Monitor*, March 14, 1956.

not to fight for Laos, the decision of the Geneva Conference to neutralize it, the increasing paralysis of SEATO by France, and the building of a road from the CPR toward the Thai border, alarmed Marshal Sarit. He accordingly asked and received, in March, 1962, a guarantee that the United States would defend Thailand unilaterally if SEATO should fail to act when needed. This guarantee evoked a predictable denunciation from the CPR.[65] The sending of American troops to Thailand in mid-May, which occurred during a period of tension in the Taiwan Strait, was received in Peking with still greater indignation and expressed alarm. The Chinese line was that the United States was about to intervene in Laos, and that "The Chinese people . . . absolutely cannot tolerate the establishment by United States imperialism in areas close to China of any new military bridgeheads spearheaded against this country."[66]

Although Marshal Sarit preserved Thailand's alliance with the United States, he could not eliminate neutralist and pro-Chinese feeling from his country. An interesting view of Thai attitudes was expressed by Prince Sihanouk in a recent interview published in the French press:[67]

> A few years ago, in Peking, Mao Tse-tung said to me: "Ask us for whatever you like in order to crush Diem and the other American puppets in Saigon, but spare the Thai, do not ask us for anything against them." Why? Because the Chinese know very well that the alignment of Bangkok on the American side is temporary, and that it can reverse itself tomorrow. The Chinese are giving shelter to Pridi, who although not a Communist is the leader of the left opposition [in Thailand].
>
> Perhaps I shall astonish you by saying that I never go to Peking without being contacted there by some semi-official emissary of Bangkok. Peking is full of Thai Edgar Faures. The Americans protest. After their return the emissaries are arrested. They spend a few pampered days in prison, just long enough to calm the Americans. Then they are released.

Although this account may be discounted somewhat as coming from a source very hostile to Sarit, it certainly tends to confirm the belief that neutralist and pro-Chinese feeling in Thailand is far from dead.

The trend toward neutralism grew stronger after Sarit's death in December, 1963, and the emergence of a somewhat weaker although no less anti-Communist successor regime.[68] On November 1, 1964, an organization known as the Independent Thailand Movement was formed and issued a

---

[65] Cf. Ko Hsien-wei, "Thailand on a Dangerous Road," *People's Daily*, April 5, 1962.

[66] "Drive U. S. Aggressors Out of Southeast Asia!" *People's Daily*, May 19, 1962.

[67] "Cambodia, China and S. E. Asia," *Survival*, vol. 6, no. 5 (September–October, 1964), p. 242.

[68] Cf. *The New York Times*, November 14, 1964.

manifesto, which was rebroadcast in Thai by Peking radio on December 13. A few excerpts will give the flavor of the manifesto:

> Our dear fatherland has been transformed into a new-type colony of the United States imperialists. . . . They have used Thai territory as a base for military aggression against neighboring countries.

The manifesto went on to demand a policy of "peace and neutrality" for Thailand and to say that "Following the successful explosion of the Chinese atomic bomb we can see that the world situation has become favorable for us." During the following weeks there was a marked increase in clandestine radio broadcasts beamed to Thailand from somewhere in Laos or North Vietnam, and apparently of infiltration of backward northern Thailand by Communist agents, whether sent by the CPR, the DRV, the Pathet Lao, or by more than one of these is not clear.[69] In any case, Thailand is clearly due to experience increased pressures aimed at undermining its present government and foreign policy and at pushing it into neutralism. If such a trend should materialize, the CPR would obviously be one of the main beneficiaries.

■ COMMUNIST CHINA AND CAMBODIA

An understanding of Sino-Cambodian relations requires some knowledge of Cambodia's peculiar position in Southeast Asia. The Cambodians controlled the greatest empire in Southeast Asia about a thousand years ago, but from approximately 1400 on they came under growing pressure from two more numerous and powerful peoples, the Thai and the Vietnamese. From these pressures French rule over Indochina rescued the Cambodians for almost a century. In 1941 the French set on the Cambodian throne a supposedly malleable young man, Norodom Sihanouk. Under the stimulus of domestic political opposition and Vietnamese Communist pressures, however, he took an active role in the mid-1950s in extracting independence from the French and then, in 1955, abdicated in order to devote his full time to politics rather than ceremonial.

Sihanouk continues to experience domestic political opposition. His principal opponents are in exile, and he suspects them of being supported by Thailand and South Vietnam, and perhaps by the United States. There is some leftist opposition among intellectuals and students, including a small Communist movement, known as the Pracheachon, which is apparently controlled by the DRV. Cambodia has substantial Chinese and Vietnamese minorities, among both of whom Communist influence is fairly strong.

The French departure from Indochina has left Cambodia comparatively

---

[69] *The New York Times,* January 9, 1965.

naked to its enemies, of whom the Thai are regarded with less distaste than the Vietnamese because they are culturally closer, even though the Thai make the larger territorial claims against Cambodia. Interestingly enough, Sihanouk has said that much as he dislikes SEATO he favors the continuation of an American military presence in Thailand. Presumably he believes that this presence tends to restrain both Thai and North Vietnamese aggression against Cambodia. He apparently regards a North Vietnamese "liberation" of South Vietnam as inevitable, although undesirable, and has been highly critical of the American military effort there and of the successive regimes that have emerged in Saigon since 1954. He hopes that a policy of neutrality will help to maintain the independence of Cambodia, and if possible of Laos. Strict neutrality does not seem enough to him, however, to guarantee Cambodia's survival, in view of its bad relations with South Vietnam and Thailand. He needs a protector, and France is no longer available to play this role, although since 1963 it has given Cambodia increasing diplomatic support. Since both Thailand and South Vietnam are aligned with the United States, and since Sihanouk believes that the latter has not done enough to restrain them, there is a certain logic in his looking for a protector to the Communist side, and hence to the CPR. He hopes that by cultivating good relations with the CPR he can counterbalance the combination of the United States, South Vietnam, and Thailand and can persuade the CPR to restrain both the Chinese community in Cambodia and the DRV, which Sihanouk seems to regard as the greatest although not the most immediate threat to Cambodian independence.[70]

The first major stimulus to Cambodian neutrality was probably Thailand's adherence to SEATO in 1954, which automatically alienated Sihanouk from SEATO and rendered him receptive to Nehru's alternative of cultivating good relations with the CPR.[71] The appeal of this alternative was enhanced by Chou En-lai's performance at the Bandung Conference. Relations with Thailand deteriorated sharply in the early months of 1956, and there was a general expectation that all-Vietnamese elections would be held later in the year and would give the DRV control of South Vietnam, and therefore a common frontier with Cambodia. These were probably the main considerations that brought Sihanouk to Peking in February. Apart from the innocuous joint communiqué,[72] Sihanouk apparently assured the Chinese that he would not appeal for protection to SEATO and received in return a pledge that the CPR would restrain the DRV from putting pressure on Cambodia.[73] North Vietnamese anti-Cambodian propaganda

---

[70] Cf. "Cambodia, China and S. E. Asia," *loc. cit.,* p. 243.

[71] Cf. Michael Leifer, "Cambodia and Her Neighbors," *Pacific Affairs,* vol. xxxiv, no. 4 (winter, 1961–62), p. 364.

[72] Text released by New China News Agency, February 18, 1956.

[73] Cf. Leifer, *loc. cit.,* p. 373.

did in fact slacken. Sihanouk further reinforced his international position by establishing diplomatic relations with the Soviet Union in May, 1956.

A Sino-Cambodian trade agreement was signed in April, 1956,[74] and two months later the CPR gave Cambodia a grant without "strings" of £8 million for equipment and technical services in connection with its economic development program.[75] The enterprises set up under this program, especially a plywood factory, encountered some serious technical difficulties,[76] but the presence of an economic mission gave the CPR an important channel of quasi-diplomatic contact with the Cambodian government and a means of getting in touch with the Chinese community.[77]

Chou En-lai helped to keep the CPR's image as a friend and protector of Cambodia alive by visiting it during his foreign tour at the end of 1956.[78] His tumultuous reception by the Cambodian Chinese community alarmed the Cambodian government, but Chou tried to reassure it by telling a group of leading Chinese, at a reception, that all Chinese in Cambodia should observe local laws and customs and try for the best possible relations with the Cambodians.[79] Nevertheless, Communist influence on the Cambodian Chinese community continued to be a problem for the Cambodian government, which in early 1958 took steps to restrict the circulation of Chinese Communist propaganda.[80]

This friction was soon overshadowed, however, by serious border clashes between Cambodia and South Vietnam. Sihanouk threatened to recognize the CPR, which gave loud support to Sihanouk in the dispute, if the United States did not restrain South Vietnam. He may also have been influenced by the growing tension in Laos, the coup of July 14 in Baghdad, Iraq's withdrawal from the Baghdad Pact, and the widespread belief that Thailand might follow Iraq's example. On July 17, accordingly, Cambodia extended diplomatic recognition to the CPR, which promptly reciprocated.[81] This step naturally tended to worsen Cambodia's relations with Thailand and South Vietnam.

In August, 1958, after talks with Nehru in New Delhi, Sihanouk visited the CPR for the second time. He was evidently impressed by his reception, which was a masterpiece of organized enthusiasm. The CPR was then in the throes of the Great Leap Forward and must have conveyed to

---

[74] New China News Agency dispatch, June 1, 1956. Among the items that Cambodia agreed to export was rubber.
[75] New China News Agency dispatch, June 22, 1956.
[76] Cf. P. H. M. Jones, "Cambodia's New Factories," *Far Eastern Economic Review*, May 9, 1963, pp. 319–322.
[77] Cf. Boyd in Modelski, *op. cit.*, p. 175.
[78] Text of joint communiqué released by New China News Agency, November 27, 1956.
[79] New China News Agency dispatch, November 27, 1956.
[80] Boyd in Modelski, *op. cit.*, p. 176.
[81] Text of messages of recognition released by New China News Agency, July 24, 1958.

Sihanouk an impression of boundless dynamism. His hosts took care to show him the CPR's newly installed research reactor.[82] In the joint communiqué the CPR praised Cambodia's policy of "peace and neutrality," promised once more to urge Chinese living in Cambodia to live in harmony with the Cambodians, and offered increased economic aid.[83] Sihanouk seems to have been more than ever convinced that, although in the long run the CPR might be destined to dominate Southeast Asia, in the short run it harbored no aggressive designs on Cambodia and was in fact its best source of external support.

Chou En-lai visited Cambodia in May, 1960, on the occasion of the king's funeral.[84] The effect of his visit, and in particular of a statement he made, that the CPR would come to Cambodia's support if it were threatened from outside, was to raise Chinese prestige in Phnom Penh higher than ever.[85] Several weeks later, three of Sihanouk's sons arrived in Peking to study.[86]

In mid-December, 1960, following a visit to several other Communist bloc countries and immediately after the outbreak of fighting in Vientiane, Sihanouk came to the CPR for the third time. In addition to a "treaty of friendship and mutual nonaggression," Sihanouk got a promise of increased Chinese technical assistance and a reaffirmation of the CPR's peaceful intentions toward Cambodia.[87] The CPR, however, did not explicitly endorse Sihanouk's proposal, which he had made in September before the United Nations General Assembly, for a neutral zone embracing Laos and Cambodia and guaranteed by the major powers and their allies.[88] Probably the CPR believes that it can manage Cambodia more easily if it is kept as isolated as possible from outside influences other than its own. When Sihanouk, on January 1, 1961, proposed a conference to guarantee the neutrality of Laos alone, the CPR supported him.[89] It did the same when, in August, 1962, after the Geneva Conference on Laos, Sihanouk began to propose a similar conference to guarantee the neutrality and integrity of Cambodia.[90]

By this time Cambodia and Thailand had broken off diplomatic relations, and Vietnamese-Cambodian relations had also deteriorated as a result of the conviction in Saigon, which was supported by considerable evidence, that Cambodian territory was being used as a sanctuary by Viet Cong

---

[82] New China News Agency dispatch, August 22, 1958.
[83] Text released by New China News Agency, August 24, 1958.
[84] Text of joint communiqué released by New China News Agency, May 8, 1960.
[85] Cf. *The New York Times*, May 29, 1960.
[86] New China News Agency dispatch, July 20, 1960.
[87] Text of joint communiqué released by New China News Agency, December 21, 1960.
[88] On the proposal see Leifer, *loc. cit.*, p. 373.
[89] New China News Agency dispatch, January 15, 1961.
[90] New China News Agency dispatch, August 29, 1962.

units. Since the West showed little interest in Sihanouk's proposal for another conference, he threatened to invite the CPR to send troops to protect Cambodia.[91]

Sihanouk visited the CPR for the fourth time in February, 1963, mainly in order to discuss the Sino-Indian border dispute, on which his stand was moderately pro-Chinese.[92] Liu Shao-ch'i returned the visit in May; it has already been suggested (in Chapter 13) that this visit was probably related for the most part to the situation in Laos and South Vietnam.[93] The trip was enlivened by the frustration of an attempt to assassinate Liu.

Diplomatic cooperation between Cambodia and the CPR remained close, although Sihanouk was by no means a Chinese puppet. He continued to advocate the CPR's admission to the United Nations, endorsed its position on nuclear disarmament, and took a line on the crises in Laos and South Vietnam that was not very different from that of the CPR. In return, the CPR gave Cambodia vocal support in its conflicts with South Vietnam, Thailand, and the United States, whose aid program in Cambodia was suspended by Sihanouk in November, 1963, on the suspicion that the United States was aiding his domestic opponents.[94] Sihanouk invited France to make up for the lost American aid, a step that was logical in view of Sihanouk's appreciation of France's former role in Indochina and the interest in the Indochina crisis that de Gaulle had been expressing since August.[95] The immediate gain to the CPR from its stand was an air transport agreement, signed with Cambodia on November 25.[96] The CPR also supported Sihanouk's revived proposal for a conference to guarantee Cambodia's neutrality.[97]

In spite of the fall of Ngo Dinh Diem in November, 1963, and the death of Sarit in the following month, Sihanouk continued to be obsessed with the belief that Thailand and South Vietnam were plotting his destruction with Western connivance. He threatened to form an alliance with the CPR.[98] More practically speaking, he sent a mission to the Soviet Union and the CPR in March, 1964, to buy arms.[99] The first shipment of Chinese weapons arrived promptly, to the accompaniment of loud declarations from Peking that the "Chinese people" fully supported the "Cambodian people" in their struggle to maintain their independence.[100]

A visit by Sihanouk on the occasion of the CPR's fifteenth National

[91] *The New York Times*, September 4, 1962.
[92] Joint communiqué released by New China News Agency, February 27, 1963.
[93] Joint communiqué released by New China News Agency, May 5, 1963.
[94] Cf. *The New York Times*, November 21, 1963.
[95] *The New York Times*, November 23, 1963.
[96] *The New York Times*, November 26, 1963.
[97] New China News Agency dispatch, December 18, 1963.
[98] *The New York Times*, December 30, 1963.
[99] *The New York Times*, March 11, 1964.
[100] *The New York Times*, March 15–16, 1964.

Day (October 1, 1964) produced little but fresh indications of common concern over the situation in Indochina and a willingness on the part of each side to give public support to the other's main foreign policy objectives.[101] Sihanouk was evidently disappointed by the CPR's refusal at that time to sign an alliance with him and go beyond the sending of arms and the issuing of windy declarations of support. He was even more worried by the refusal of the DRV and the NFLSV, in informal negotiations conducted in Peking at about the same time, to guarantee the integrity of Cambodia's frontiers.[102]

Although the CPR has never publicly stated its design for Cambodia, it may be inferred from the record just summarized. At first sight, it is a surprising one. The key appears to be the CPR's conviction, already mentioned, that Cambodia (as well as Laos) is its proper sphere, not that of the DRV. Hence, as we have seen, the CPR has given Cambodia helpful, although by no means total, support against pressures from the DRV, as well as from Thailand and South Vietnam. To date the CPR does not seem to have stirred up much opposition to Sihanouk in Cambodia, although it has been strengthening its hold on the overseas Chinese community and probably trying to increase its influence on the Cambodian left. Presumably the CPR does not expect to see for some years the materialization of what must be assumed to be its ultimate objective in Cambodia: a Peking-oriented Communist regime.

■ **COMMUNIST CHINA AND INDONESIA TO 1962**

Because of its size and insular location, and the CPR's lack of naval power, Indonesia has been able to pursue a much more independent and dynamic policy toward the CPR than have the countries of the Asian mainland.

Indonesia did not respond to the CPR's original request for general diplomatic recognition. On March 28, 1950, therefore, the CPR sent a special message asking for Indonesian recognition, which was then accorded on April 13. A Chinese ambassador, Wang Jen-shu, reached Indonesia in August, 1950, but since no Indonesian ambassador came to the CPR Wang went home in 1952 and left the Chinese embassy in Djakarta under a chargé d'affaires. The reasons for the Indonesian delay in exchanging ambassadors are not hard to infer. The Indonesian government was incensed by the overstaffing of the Chinese embassy, by the CPR's establishment of unauthorized consulates, and by flagrant Communist Chinese efforts to manipulate the large overseas Chinese community and to exert influence on the PKI,

---

[101] Joint communiqué released by New China News Agency, October 5, 1964. For commentary see *The New York Times*, October 7, 1964.
[102] Cf. *The New York Times*, November 9, 1964; January 6, 1965.

which until about 1953 was on the worst of terms with the Indonesian government. After the coming into office of the leftist Ali Sastroamidjojo cabinet, Indonesia at last sent an ambassador to Peking in October, 1953, and a year later another Chinese ambassador, Huang Chen, reached Djakarta. During this period, nevertheless, Indonesia ignored the United Nations' restrictions on trade with the CPR and exported rubber to it.[103]

In 1954, as the CPR's external behavior mellowed somewhat and its leaders indicated an interest in settling the status of the overseas Chinese, the Indonesian government began to negotiate with the CPR on the difficult issue of the citizenship of Chinese who had been born in Indonesia and therefore could be considered to possess dual nationality; there was no serious thought of admitting large numbers of foreign-born Chinese to Indonesian citizenship. The Indonesian government had already tried to deal with this question through legislation, but with unsatisfactory results. Indonesia insisted that it would grant citizenship only to those Indonesia-born Chinese who would officially repudiate Chinese nationality. There were two probable reasons for this attitude: Indonesia did not want to grant citizenship to Chinese of doubtful political loyalties, and it felt that it would be easier to restrict and exploit noncitizen than citizen Chinese through economic legislation directed against aliens. The CPR probably objected to this attitude, but it evidently felt that in the interest of its general relations with Indonesia it had no choice but to accede. A treaty was accordingly signed on April 22, 1955, while Chou En-lai was in Indonesia for the Bandung Conference. It incorporated the Indonesian position, with the added proviso that the citizenship of any person of dual Sino-Indonesian nationality who did not opt for one citizenship and repudiate the other within two years after the entering into force of the treaty should be determined by the origin of his father, which in the vast majority of cases would be Chinese. Since it seemed likely that, for reasons of ignorance, indifference, or reluctance, many Indonesian-born Chinese would not make a positive choice within the two-year period, this provision represented a significant victory for the Indonesian position. Another important feature of the treaty was the fact that it allowed Indonesia-born Chinese who might sympathize with the Republic of China only the choice between Indonesian and Communist Chinese citizenship.[104]

The treaty's subsequent history shows why neither the CPR nor, even though the treaty represented a victory for Indonesia, other Asian countries have moved to conclude similar treaties. At first, to be sure, the treaty's reception in Indonesia was enthusiastic, and Premier Sastroamidjojo paid a

---

[103] Cf. "Diplomatic Relations of Communist China," *loc. cit.*; Lea E. Williams, "Sino-Indonesian Diplomacy: A Study of Revolutionary International Politics," *The China Quarterly*, no. 11 (July–September, 1962), pp. 185–186.

[104] Cf. Donald E. Willmott, *The National Status of the Chinese in Indonesia, 1900–1958*, revised edition, Cornell University: Modern Indonesia Project, 1961, pp. 44–48. The text of the treaty may be found in *ibid.*, pp. 130–134.

euphoric visit to the CPR a month after its signature.[105] On second thought, however, a variety of objections to the treaty occurred to various elements of Indonesian public life and to the affected Chinese themselves. In 1956, nevertheless, the second Sastroamidjojo cabinet gave its official endorsement to the treaty, which was approved by the Indonesian parliament on December 17, 1957. The CPR ratified the treaty on December 30. Enough differences of interpretation remained, however, so that Indonesia declined for the time being to exchange ratifications and so bring the treaty into effect.[106]

In spite of the existence of these strains in Sino-Indonesian relations, another important force working in the opposite direction began to make itself felt during the mid-1950s. This was President Sukarno's growing admiration for the CPR, for which there seem to be three grounds. In the first place, Sukarno respects regimes that have been established through armed revolution against "imperialism." Secondly, Sukarno, who soon became disgusted with the futility and instability of parliamentary government and party politics in Indonesia, has evidently been impressed with the CPC's success, or apparent success, in manipulating a seemingly broad domestic political consensus under authoritarian rule, in large part by focusing political tensions on an external enemy, "imperialism," which is created to the extent that it does not actually exist. This approach has seemed to Sukarno to offer valuable lessons for Indonesia. Thirdly, the Indonesian elite has a tendency, on both national and ideological grounds, to want to expand so as to dominate all areas of Southeast Asia inhabited by Malay-speaking peoples.[107] Expansionist tendencies are to some extent an outgrowth of the peculiar and delicate political system, which has already been discussed, that President Sukarno began to construct in Indonesia in 1956 and completed in 1959. Sukarno evidently believes that, if properly approached, the CPR can render him valuable cooperation in the pursuit of his political goals, for example by not inciting the PKI to revolt and by keeping pressure on Western "imperialism" in the Taiwan Strait and Singapore.

The CPC for its part seems to have reasoned that, since Sukarno was in increasingly effective control of Indonesia and since it lacked the means to buy him off or put effective pressure on him either through the PKI or the Indonesian Chinese, it had no choice but to collaborate with him, for the time being at least. If it was to be effective, this collaboration must seem to be as enthusiastic as possible. From it the CPC might hope to gain by deterring Sukarno and the Indonesian army from turning on the PKI, by shielding the overseas Chinese in Indonesia and the Malaysian territories to a

---

[105] Williams, *loc. cit.*, p. 188.
[106] Willmott, *op. cit.*, pp. 48–61.
[107] Cf. Bernard K. Gordon, "The Potential for Indonesian Expansionism," *Pacific Affairs*, vol. xxxvi, no. 4 (winter, 1963–64), pp. 378–393.

degree from the effects of Indonesian expansionism, and by receiving some diversionary value from Indonesian adventures in Southeast Asia.

In 1956, in the course of a tour of Communist bloc countries, Sukarno arrived in the CPR just in time to take part in the celebration of the October 1 holiday. He was greeted by enormous, highly organized, but apparently enthusiastic crowds, which may be presumed to have had an effect on his vanity.[108] He was also presented with a large, handsome set of photographic reproductions, in color, of his own presidential collection of paintings, which the CPR had produced at obviously great expense. Sukarno seems to have been especially impressed with the CPC's formula for handling its potentially troublesome Islamic community: an appearance of great consideration, combined with secular education of the youth, political neutralization, and tight control behind the scenes. At the end of his visit, Sukarno invited Mao to return it, and Mao accepted.[109] Even though the trip was never made, the acceptance by Mao of an invitation to visit a non-Communist country remains an interesting and, as far as I know, unique event.

The impressions gained by Sukarno on his trip to the CPR probably contributed something to his concept of Guided Democracy, which is the name he has given to the political system already described. In mid-1959, during a visit to the CPR, Wilopo, a prominent Indonesian political figure who was serving as chairman of a council appointed to draw up a draft permanent constitution for Indonesia, said that "I almost feel as if I could complete the draft constitution here in China."[110] Soon afterward Sukarno announced that during his stay in the CPR Mao Tse-tung had offered to send arms to Indonesia.[111] On May 15, 1958, after military revolts had broken out against Sukarno but also after the inevitability of their eventual suppression had become clear, the CPR officially repeated its offer to send arms, and by implication "volunteers" as well, to Indonesia.[112]

Partly because of the suspected involvement of the Republic of China in the revolts against Sukarno, and partly because of the need of the shaky governmental sector of the Indonesian economy to subsist on expropriation, the year 1958 saw the Indonesian government seize many of the assets of the pro-Nationalist Chinese in Indonesia, close down their schools and newspapers, and deport some of their leaders. The predictable applause from Peking proved to be premature, because in the following year came the turn of the Indonesian Chinese in general, including the pro-Communists among them. A series of regulations were promulgated making it illegal for aliens, or in other words Chinese, to operate retail businesses in the rural

---

[108] For an eyewitness account of the organizing of this reception, see Robert Loh, "Setting the Stage for Foreigners," *The Atlantic*, vol. 204, no. 6 (December, 1959), pp. 80–81.

[109] New China News Agency dispatch, October 16, 1956.

[110] Chinese International Service broadcast, July 3, 1957.

[111] Agence France Presse dispatch, Djakarta, July 20, 1957.

[112] *The New York Times*, May 16, 1958.

areas after the end of the year. In August, a drastic currency conversion wiped out the fortunes of many Chinese businessmen.[113] The crisis, and particularly the anti-alien economic regulations just referred to, obviously brought to mind the citizenship status of the Indonesian Chinese and the fact that the Sino-Indonesian treaty on this subject was not yet in effect. On June 1, the Indonesian government further involved the treaty by promulgating unilaterally a set of regulations dealing with the manner in which the treaty should be interpreted and enforced, even though it had not yet entered into effect.[114]

The CPR protested vigorously against these regulations, and still more vigorously against the discriminatory economic legislation. Much as it valued good relations with Sukarno, it obviously felt that there were limits to what it could afford to put up with for the sake of those relations. With some ambiguous and troubled support from the PKI, the CPR set out to try to bring about the rescinding of the discriminatory legislation and the exchange of ratifications of the treaty on dual nationality. It was to fail in the first and succeed in the second.

According to Indonesian sources, Chinese diplomatic and consular personnel toured Java, incited Chinese to disobey and evade the discriminatory economic regulations, and even fomented riots. Again according to Indonesian sources, when Foreign Minister Subandrio visited Peking (October 7–11) to discuss the issue, he was outrageously bullied.[115] Nevertheless, the two sides managed to put together a joint communiqué that stated those things on which they could agree, such as the "liberation" of Taiwan and West Irian by the CPR and Indonesia respectively, and added this on the subject of the overseas Chinese:[116]

> Both the foreign ministers take cognizance of the fact that in the process [of moving] toward economic development and stability in Indonesia, the economic position of the Chinese nationals residing there may be affected in some way. . . . Both the foreign ministers agree that the economic resources of those Chinese nationals will still play a useful role in the economic development of Asia.

The impression of agreement conveyed by these platitudes was soon dispelled by further controversy. It was becoming increasingly obvious that the CPR could not effectively protect Indonesian Chinese against discrimination and that its best course was still to wash its hands of as many as possible of them by giving up its claim to their citizenship, even though those Indonesian Chinese who acquired Indonesian citizenship could not realistically expect to escape all further discrimination by so doing. On

113 Williams, *loc. cit.*, pp. 191–194.
114 David Mozingo, "The Sino-Indonesian Dual Nationality Treaty," *Asian Survey*, vol. 1, no. 10 (December, 1961), pp. 25–26.
115 *The New York Times*, November 19, 1959.
116 New China News Agency dispatch, October 11, 1959.

December 9, therefore, Chen Yi wrote a letter to Subandrio in which he proposed that ratifications of the dual nationality treaty be immediately exchanged so that the treaty could go into effect, that the Indonesian government agree not to discriminate against overseas Chinese who did not acquire Indonesian citizenship in return for a pledge by the CPR to encourage them to abide by the laws and customs of Indonesia, and that the CPR repatriate any Chinese in Indonesia who desired to return home.[117] In reply, Subandrio complained of the political and economic behavior of the Chinese in Indonesia and shrewdly pointed out that there was an incompatibility between their joyously capitalistic tendencies and the "socialist" character of the power that was attempting to protect them. He accused the CPR of flagrantly trying to obstruct the implementation of the controversial economic regulations. He insisted that the regulations must be obeyed and that Chinese interference must stop. On the other hand, he agreed to the exchange of ratifications of the dual nationality treaty and to the repatriation of any Chinese so inclined.[118] Ratifications were accordingly exchanged at last on January 20, 1960, during a visit to Djakarta by Chen Yi.[119]

For several months, however, serious friction and disagreements persisted over the implementation of the treaty and over the repatriation of overseas Chinese, many of whom had suffered injury and loss of property. When Khrushchev visited Indonesia in February, he indicated that Indonesia had the right to treat its overseas Chinese in any way it chose.[120] At last, on December 15, 1960, the joint committee that had been established to work out regulations governing the implementation of the treaty reached an agreement. It appears that Sukarno, who was generally regarded by the Indonesian Chinese as being more on their side than most of his officials, personally intervened to make agreement possible by liberalizing somewhat the conditions under which Chinese could acquire Indonesian citizenship.[121] Sukarno probably felt that compromise was needed in the interest of more important matters such as his "confrontation" with the Netherlands over West Irian, which was then beginning to come to a head and in which Chinese support might be useful.

The fact that the CPR and Indonesia had reached a major political understanding by compromising their differences over the Indonesian Chinese was indicated by a triumphal visit paid by Chen Yi to Djakarta at the end of March, 1961. There he signed a treaty of friendship, a cultural agreement, and of course a joint communiqué. The latter proclaimed the usual Indonesian support for the CPR's admission to the United Nations,

[117] New China News Agency dispatch, December 11, 1959.
[118] Indonesian Home Service broadcast, December 13, 1959.
[119] New China News Agency dispatch, January 25, 1960.
[120] *The New York Times*, February 21, 1960.
[121] Mozingo, *loc. cit.*, pp. 26, 29.

indicated agreement on such issues as Laos and the Congo, and firmly supported the signatories' claims to Taiwan and West Irian. Sukarno announced that he had accepted an invitation to visit the CPR again.[122] Ambassador Huang Chen was subsequently recalled to Peking and made a Deputy Foreign Minister.

The CPR was far from being Indonesia's only source of external support. Khrushchev had evidently decided to improve his relations with Indonesia so as to create trouble for the West and forestall an undue increase of Chinese influence. During his visit in February, 1960, he promised Indonesia vastly increased economic and military aid. Specific agreements on military aid were worked out by Indonesian Defense Minister Nasution during two visits to Moscow, in January and June, 1961. Sukarno was also present on the latter occasion, and in fact he celebrated his sixtieth birthday in Moscow.[123]

He then proceeded to the CPR, where ratifications of the treaty of friendship and the cultural agreement concluded shortly before were exchanged. More to the point, Sukarno kept referring during his visit to his determination to "liberate" West Irian and to his support for the "liberation" of Taiwan by the CPR, of South Korea by North Korea, and of South Vietnam by the DRV. He reminded his Chinese listeners that it was exactly three hundred years since the Chinese pirate admiral Koxinga (Cheng Ch'eng-kung) had "liberated" Taiwan from Dutch "imperialist" forces. It must be realized that at this time the Soviet Union was not only sending large amounts of modern military equipment to Indonesia but was actually inciting it to attack West Irian. Although Sukarno undoubtedly realized that the CPR could not send comparable aid, he may have believed that it could and should create a diversion in the Taiwan Strait that would distract the attention of the United States Seventh Fleet, the main ultimate deterrent against such an Indonesian attack on West Irian. This would explain the repeated references to Taiwan. Although the joint communiqué referred to Taiwan and West Irian,[124] it is virtually certain that if Sukarno asked for active Chinese support he was told that the CPR was in no position to give such support and that it disapproved of any full-scale attack on West Irian, which would be dangerous and would tend to drive Indonesia further into the arms of the Soviet Union. It is entirely possible that the method that Indonesia began to adopt about the middle of 1961, the infiltration of small bodies of troops into West Irian, rather than a frontal assault on the Dutch and possibly on the Seventh Fleet, represented acceptance of the Chinese rather than the Soviet proposals for a suitable approach to the

---

122 New China News Agency dispatch, April 3, 1961.
123 Cf. Guy J. Pauker, "The Soviet Challenge in Indonesia," *Foreign Affairs*, vol. 40, no. 4 (July, 1962), pp. 612–626. Pauker overestimates the extent to which the Soviet Union has been using Indonesia, rather than the other way round.
124 New China News Agency dispatch, June 15, 1961.

"liberation" of West Irian, as well as a revival of the Indonesian tradition of guerrilla warfare. In any case, the Dutch soon wearied of the contest and on August 15, 1962, after American mediation, agreed to transfer West Irian to the control of the United Nations for a period of six months, after which it would pass under Indonesian control. Although there is room for doubt as to how much the CPR contributed to this resounding victory for Indonesia, there is no doubt as to which side it was on.

Sino-Indonesian cooperation, which was roughly paralleled by an increasing closeness between the CPC and the PKI, soon reached the point where the Indonesian government was facilitating the convening in Djakarta of meetings of Communist front organizations at which the CPC could carry on its vendetta with Khrushchev. The CPR, for its part, was supporting Sukarno's proposal for a second Asian-African Conference, which like the first one would give the CPR a useful forum for improving its image in the developing countries. In the summer of 1962, the Indonesian government under pressure from the CPR barred a Nationalist Chinese team from taking part in the so-called Asian Games held at Djakarta, and under Arab pressure also barred a team from Israel. The Indian representative objected to the exclusion. In reprisal, and evidently at the instigation of the Indonesian government, a mob invaded and damaged the Indian embassy.[125]

■ COMMUNIST CHINA AND THE "CONFRONTATION" OVER MALAYSIA

The PKI, which was already in close touch with an "independence" movement in Brunei and Sarawak led by A. M. Azahari, began to express ideological and political objections to the formation of Malaysia as early as the last months of 1961.[126] Since its own survival and growth, under present conditions, depend partly on the maintenance of a continuous state of external crisis, the PKI was undoubtedly concerned to find a successor to the West Irian issue when that should be settled, as it was in August, 1962. The Indonesian government, on the other hand, displayed an attitude of benevolent indifference toward Malaysia at first, probably because it was still preoccupied with West Irian. In September, 1962, however, following the agreement with the Dutch and the referendum in Singapore endorsing the formation of Malaysia, the Indonesian government began to express a growing opposition to Malaysia that soon burgeoned into a full-blown "confrontation."

Probably the most important reason for Indonesia's determination to "crush" Malaysia is the peculiar internal Indonesian situation, in which all

---

[125] *The New York Times,* September 7, 1962.
[126] Justus M. van der Kroef, "The Sino-Indonesian Partnership," *Orbis,* vol. viii, no. 2 (summer, 1964), pp. 334–335.

three of the major actors find it useful to seek "confrontations" with external opponents, each for its own reasons but also for some common reasons: the desire to put off grappling with difficult problems, such as military and economic reforms, and above all to postpone a political showdown, at least until after Sukarno's death. Secondly, Indonesia sees Malaysia, especially in view of the presence of British bases in it, as a threat; Malaysia if successful could exert an attraction on Sumatra and Indonesian Borneo and might, if it chose, intervene in internal Indonesian affairs, as Indonesia accuses Malaya and the Western powers of having done at the time of the revolts of 1958. Thirdly, a viable and prosperous Malaysia would obviously constitute a major obstacle to any expansionist designs on the part of Indonesia. Fourthly, on ideological grounds Indonesia finds Malaya, and now Malaysia, distasteful as a capitalist state and one that gained whatever degree of independence it possesses without armed revolution. Fifthly, there is an obvious personal rivalry between the two Malay statesmen, Rahman and Sukarno, for preeminence. Sixthly, Indonesia thinks of itself as the major power of insular Southeast Asia and is enraged at not having been consulted with regard to the formation of Malaysia. Finally, Indonesian sources sometimes hint that Malaysia is likely to come eventually under Communist Chinese control and that Indonesia does not want to coexist, in Borneo at any rate, with such a state. This last objection, however, seems to be intended for Western consumption rather than as a serious consideration; in reality, Sukarno at least seems confident of his ability to preserve a smooth working relationship with the CPR, or if necessary to manage its efforts to play a major role in his part of Southeast Asia.[127]

Although the CPR, for its part, undoubtedly objected to Malaysia from the beginning, it refrained for longer than did either the PKI or the Indonesian government from making a public issue of its opposition. It undoubtedly realized the strong domestic political motivation behind Indonesia's decision to "confront" Malaysia and probably doubted that Indonesia would be able to bring off a victory against the British as it had against the Dutch. The CPC, and still more the MCP, had acquired a healthy respect for British determination and military skill, and probably for the successor governments in Kuala Lumpur and Singapore as well. The CPR was probably reluctant to jeopardize its important trade with Britain and Malaya, or push Britain into increasing its military aid to India. It probably feared military complications from which it might be called on to rescue Indonesia. It was preoccupied with its own "confrontation" with Khrushchev and with its problems in Korea, the Taiwan Strait, and Indochina. It continued to regard the United States, not Britain, as the main enemy. It probably had enough reservations about the way the overseas Chinese in

---

[127] Cf. Donald Hindley, "Indonesia's Confrontation with Malaysia: A Search for Motives," *Asian Survey*, vol. iv, no. 6 (June, 1964), pp. 904–913. For a statement of the anti-Chinese hypothesis see *The New York Times*, September 7, 1964.

Indonesia had been treated not to want to see any more brought under Indonesian rule unless there were no help for it. It undoubtedly objected to Sukarno's fondness for President Kennedy and Tito and his obvious eagerness for Soviet economic and military aid.

On the other hand, the steady progress being made by Rahman and Lee Kuan Yew toward the formation of Malaysia, and in particular the MCP's failure to obstruct the Singapore referendum of September, 1962, made it obvious that neither the CPR nor Indonesia alone would be able to strangle Malaysia in its cradle. The logical result has been a trend toward increasingly close Sino-Indonesian cooperation directed toward "crushing" Malaysia.

On December 8, 1962, the followers of Azahari, who was then in Manila, rose in revolt against Malaysia and proclaimed the "Unitary State of Kalimantan Utara" (i.e., of North Borneo), which allegedly exercised sovereignty over the three territories of Sarawak, Brunei, and British North Borneo (Sabah). The revolt was soon crushed, and the survivors fled to Indonesian Borneo. Whatever the nature of Azahari's connections with Indonesia before the revolt may have been, there is no doubt that after the revolt Indonesia became his patron and probably his master, while denying that it had any intention of absorbing North Kalimantan.[128]

It is uncertain whether the CPC and its numerous sympathizers among the Chinese plurality in the North Borneo territories were aware in advance of Azahari's plans, but it is likely that they were. In any case, by March, 1963, almost certainly with the knowledge and approval of the CPC, several hundred young Chinese from Sarawak were beginning to cross into Indonesian Borneo to receive training in guerrilla warfare from Indonesian army units.[129] The fact that some of these Chinese soon became disillusioned with their treatment by the Indonesians does not affect the generalization that cooperation between the CPR and Indonesia against Malaysia has tended to become increasingly close.

It is conceivable, although of course far from certain, that the CPR and Indonesia have agreed on an ultimate partition of Malaysia into two spheres of influence: a Chinese sphere in Malaya and Singapore and an Indonesian sphere in North Kalimantan. Meanwhile, one can imagine a degree of tactical cooperation that would allow Chinese to fight in Sarawak, as they have, and Indonesian troops to land in small numbers in Malaya, as they have, in an effort to stir up resistance to Malaysia among the Malays.

Sukarno may believe that the salt water that would then separate the Chinese sphere from Indonesia and its sphere, narrow though it would be in places, would be sufficient protection in case of a souring of the Sino-

128 Cf. Justus M. van der Kroef, "Indonesia, Malaya, and the North Borneo Crisis," *Asian Survey*, vol. iii, no. 4 (April, 1963), pp. 177–178.

129 Justus M. van der Kroef, "Communism and Chinese Communalism in Sarawak," *The China Quarterly*, no. 20 (October–December, 1964), pp. 60–64.

Indonesian entente. Since both the CPR and Indonesia have claimed a twelve-mile limit to their territorial waters and since the Strait of Malacca is less than twenty-four miles wide at its lower end, the two powers might be able to deny passage through the strategic Strait of Malacca to foreign warships if they partitioned Malaysia along the lines described and maintained good relations with each other.

The CPC, for its part, probably expects the PKI to come to power in Indonesia within a few years after Sukarno's death, and in that case it probably foresees no difficulty in arriving at an amicable arrangement regarding the partitioning of Malaysia and the status of the overseas Chinese in Indonesia and North Kalimantan. The PKI probably feels much the same. It has taken care to reinsure its relations with the overseas Chinese and the CPC by deploring discrimination against the Indonesian Chinese. As for its obvious problem with the army, it seems to feel that under the cover of the "confrontation" with Malaysia it may be able to persuade Sukarno to order the "arming of workers and peasants," or in other words of Communist-controlled mass organizations, which it urged for example in January, 1965.[130]

One of the most important early links in the chain of Sino-Indonesian cooperation against Malaysia seems to have been forged during a visit by Indonesian Foreign Minister Subandrio to Peking (January 2-7, 1963). He came while Mme Bandaranaike was also in the CPR trying to persuade its leadership to accept the Colombo proposals, and the Sino-Indian border dispute was the main ostensible reason for Subandrio's visit as well. He held his own separate talks with Chinese officials, however, and it is clear that not only the Sino-Indian border dispute but also Malaysia was discussed. There may in fact have been something of a bargain: an essentially, although not vociferously, pro-Chinese attitude on the part of Indonesia with regard to the former, in exchange for increased Chinese support for Indonesia in its "confrontation" with Malaysia.[131] During Subandrio's visit both Chou En-lai and Chen Yi referred publicly and approvingly to the struggle of the "people" of Brunei, but not of North Kalimantan as a whole.[132]

This continued to be the Chinese line into the spring, when as we have seen Chinese from Sarawak began to cross into Indonesian Borneo to receive training for an active role in the "confrontation." Even then Chinese pronouncements continued to refer to the struggle of the "people" of Brunei rather than of North Kalimantan, but they began to denounce Malaysia much more openly and vigorously than before.[133]

---

[130] Cf. *The New York Times,* January 19, 1965.

[131] Text of joint communiqué released by New China News Agency, January 8, 1963.

[132] New China News Agency dispatch, January 4, 1963.

[133] Cf. Pi Wen, "Dissect the 'Federation of Malaysia' Plan," *Shih-chieh Chih-shih* (World Culture), no. 7 (April 10, 1963).

Another major step forward for the Sino-Indonesian partnership was a visit by Liu Shao-ch'i to Indonesia (April 12–20, 1963). In part the visit was designed as a Chinese answer to one by Soviet Defense Minister Malinovsky shortly before. By this time the CPR had evidently decided to give public recognition to the situation in Borneo, without necessarily endorsing Azahari's claims; an editorial that appeared in the *People's Daily* as Liu was beginning his visit referred to the "North Kalimantan people's struggle for independence,"[134] a line which Chinese pronouncements have taken ever since. Liu's visit was not entirely a triumphal procession. He seems to have objected to Indonesia's treatment of its overseas Chinese and to Sukarno's effort at that time to offer Rahman a substitute for British protection in the form of a confederation, originally proposed by President Macapagal, embracing Malaya, the Philippines, and Indonesia. Liu, in an unpublished remark made in Bali, reminded his hosts that the United States, not Britain, was the main enemy.[135] Nevertheless, it is probable that further arrangements for joint operations in North Kalimantan were made; Azahari's forces made their first attack on Sarawak on April 19, while Liu was still in Indonesia.[136] The joint communiqué affirmed Indonesian support for the Chinese position that there should be direct negotiations between the CPR and India on their border dispute and Chinese support for the struggle of Indonesia and the "people" of North Kalimantan against "neocolonialism in the guise of Malaysia."[137]

A few weeks later, following the lifting of martial law on May 1, Indonesian mobs rioted against overseas Chinese in some parts of Java. The CPR protested, but not very vigorously, and Sukarno predictably blamed the riots on his political enemies. Clearly the overseas Chinese remained a serious point of friction in Sino-Indonesian relations, but not serious enough to obstruct cooperation with respect to common problems such as Malaysia.[138]

Malaysia came into existence on September 16, 1963, with no more concession to Indonesia than a sixteen-day delay beyond the inaugural date originally scheduled. The enraged Sukarno ordered an embargo against Malaysia, Indonesian mobs sacked the British and Malayan embassies, and the United States suspended its aid program to Indonesia. Another event of great importance to the Sino-Indonesian partnership was President Johnson's announcement on December 18, 1963, that the United States Seventh Fleet would extend its operations into the Indian (or Indonesian) Ocean. This step obviously had great potential significance in connection with both the

134 "In the Interests of Friendship, Unity, and Peace," *People's Daily*, April 12, 1963.
135 *The Washington Post and Times Herald*, April 26, 1963.
136 *The New York Times*, April 22, 1963.
137 Text released by New China News Agency, April 20, 1963.
138 *The New York Times*, May 20, 24, 1963. Cf. "The Riots in Java," *Far Eastern Economic Review*, May 30, 1963, pp. 463–464.

CPR's plans for South Asia and the Indian Ocean and with the "confrontation" with Malaysia. The CPR naturally denounced the plan.[139] Sukarno promptly said that the Seventh Fleet could not deter Indonesia from "crushing" Malaysia, and other sections of Indonesian opinion echoed his statement.[140]

After the breakdown in the spring of 1964 of a ceasefire arranged by United States Attorney General Robert F. Kennedy, Indonesia asked and was promised another round of Soviet military deliveries, a step not necessarily to the CPR's liking. On the other hand, the CPR was undoubtedly pleased with the line on international affairs, one very close to its own, that Sukarno took at the second conference of nonaligned nations, held at Cairo in October, 1964.[141]

In November, while engaged in a number of political maneuvers designed to mobilize foreign support for his campaign against Malaysia, Sukarno briefly visited Shanghai, where he talked with Chou En-lai. Sukarno did not go on to Peking, and no joint communiqué was issued.[142] It is entirely possible that Sukarno expressed the view that the CPR was not giving him enough support against Malaysia. In any event, a few weeks later (November 27–December 3, 1964) Chen Yi paid another visit to Indonesia. He seems to have offered Indonesia about $50 million in economic aid, which as it turned out was roughly the amount of United Nations aid that Indonesia forfeited by withdrawing from the United Nations in January, 1965, following the election of Malaysia to the Security Council.[143] Chen reportedly advised Sukarno to intensify his guerrilla pressures on North Kalimantan, which up to that time had not been very effective, and it seems that Indonesia was preparing in any case to do exactly that. Chen is said to have offered to try to reactivate guerrilla warfare in Malaya on the basis of the small force of MCP guerrillas that had been kept in being for a decade on the Thai frontier. Chen reportedly urged Sukarno to ban two anti-PKI parties, the Body for the Promotion of Sukarnoism and the Partai Murba, which was soon done. Sukarno and Chen may have agreed that Indonesia would leave the United Nations, the better to promote an alignment between Indonesia and the various Communist regimes in the Far East (the CPR, the DRV, and North Korea) that do not belong to the United Nations.[144]

Further signs of increasingly close Sino-Indonesian cooperation have been the opening of a civil air service,[145] outspoken Chinese support for

---

139 New China News Agency dispatch, December 20, 1963.
140 *The New York Times,* December 20, 1963.
141 Cf. *The New York Times,* October 7, 11, 1964.
142 New China News Agency dispatch, November 4, 1964.
143 This offer was later confirmed by Indonesian sources.
144 *The New York Times,* January 8, 1965. Text of joint press release (not a joint communiqué) released by New China News Agency, December 3, 1964.
145 New China News Agency dispatch, January 6, 1965.

Indonesia's decision to withdraw from the United Nations,[146] and a visit by Subandrio and a delegation of Indonesian military officers to the CPR late in January, 1965.

The cooperation between Sukarno and the CPR is only one of many examples since 1917 of tactical cooperation, sometimes very close, between a leftist nationalist leader and the local Communist Party or a foreign Communist regime. In more cases than not, the nationalist has come out better than the Communists, and there is no compelling reason why Sukarno should suffer at the hands of either the CPR or the PKI as long as his life and political arrangements last. A failure to "crush" Malaysia, which seems likely, would however severely strain Sukarno's relations with the CPR and with the PKI. If Malaysia were to be crushed, there is the obvious likelihood that the Chinese and Indonesian victors would soon quarrel over the spoils. But probably the crucial question that will determine the general course of future Sino-Indonesian relations is the political trend in Indonesia after Sukarno's death. A regime controlled by the PKI would probably preserve good relations with the CPR, but one controlled by the army would be much less likely to do so.[147]

---

[146] Chinese statement of January 10, 1965 (New China News Agency dispatch, same date).

[147] General Nasution has visited the Soviet Union more than once but has never visited the CPR so far as I know.

□ **16**

Communist China
and South Asia

The Indian subcontinent has been a prime target of the international Communist movement since the early 1920s, but until 1947 the British presence foreclosed the possibility of significant Communist penetration. Since 1947, on the other hand, despite the dominant position of the Congress party in Indian politics, the subcontinent has become a somewhat more rewarding objective of Communist policy, Chinese as well as Soviet. From the Chinese standpoint, the geopolitical importance of the region is very great: it contains the only large, populous, non-Communist countries that border directly on the CPR. Clearly the trend of political developments in the Himalayas and beyond is bound to be of the greatest interest to Peking at all times.

■ **COMMUNIST CHINESE POLICY TOWARD SOUTH ASIA**

The Indian subcontinent completely lacks the high degree of racial homogeneity conferred on China by its overwhelming majority of Han (i.e., ethnic) Chinese. Just as ethnic homogeneity in China has been reflected over the centuries in political unity, as a rule, so ethnic heterogeneity in India has normally been reflected in political disunity, only partly counteracted by the widespread acceptance of Hinduism. In modern times, what political unity India has possessed has been largely the result of conquest first by the alien Moguls and then by the alien British. It follows that the subcontinent, especially since its partitioning in 1947, can never be a serious rival, let alone a threat, to the CPR, as long as the latter retains its present degree of unity and dynamism. It also follows that the CPR has never been interested in falling in with Nehru's former dream of an independent India and a resurgent China combining to oust Western influence from eastern Asia and give joint political leadership to the entire region.

Long before the attainment of Indian independence, the leaders of the Indian Congress came to feel a keen interest in what they took to be Stalin's successful solution to the problem of welding the diverse nationalities of the Soviet Union into a political unit without depriving them, outwardly at least, of their cultural autonomy. Stalin reciprocated by doing his best to promote the balkanization and subsequent communization of the Indian subcontinent by playing on what Indians call its "fissiparous tendencies." It was presumably with this in mind that the Indian Communists advocated that the constituent parts of what later became the Indian Union be allowed to secede if they chose. Gandhi and Nehru were anathema to Stalin because of their "bourgeois" origins and their devotion to the cause of Indian unity.[1]

The CPC appears to share the Stalinist objective of balkanization of the South Asian subcontinent, and furthermore to have maintained it since the death of Stalin whereas his successors give every indication of having abandoned it, for a time at least.[2] India was probably one of the areas that Liu Shao-ch'i had in mind when he wrote late in 1948 that[3]

> The proletariat advocates moving step by step toward world unity along various concrete paths of free separation (aiming at breaking the imperialist countries' oppression and bondage of the great majority of the world's nations) and free federation (the various nationalities federating on a completely voluntary basis, after the breaking of imperialist oppression).

On the other hand, the CPC's probable preference for Indian balkanization has always been tempered by two important qualifications: the process must not be allowed to install the Soviet Union as the dominant power in the region, thereby outflanking the CPR to the south, and the fragments must not be allied with the West. To this even the temporary survival of the Nehru government, which the CPC regarded as weak and reactionary, was preferable.

Evidence of Stalin's designs on South Asia was not long in coming to hand. At the beginning of 1948, at a critical juncture in the unfolding of Communist policy toward South and Southeast Asia, the United States Department of State published its sensational compilation of documents on

---

[1] Cf. Selig S. Harrison, *India: The Most Dangerous Decades*, Princeton University Press, 1960, pp. 137–155.

[2] Cf. remark by Chou En-lai in 1952 on the Indian regional press, quoted in *ibid.*, p. 145.

[3] *On Internationalism and Nationalism* (official summary in *China Digest* [Hong Kong], December 14, 1948).

relations between Hitler and Stalin during the short life of their star-crossed nonaggression pact.[4] From these documents the world, presumably including the CPC, learned that in 1940 Hitler, who was prematurely in a mood to partition the supposedly moribund British Empire, had urged Stalin to subscribe to the proposition that "The Soviet Union declares that its territorial aspirations center south of the national territory of the Soviet Union in the direction of the Indian Ocean." Sensing an effort to distract him from the Balkans, Stalin had insisted that the protocol be reworded so as to specify that "the area south of Batum and Baku in the general direction of the Persian Gulf is recognized as the center of the aspirations of the Soviet Union."[5] Nevertheless, he did not disavow an interest in South Asia and in fact implicitly admitted one. Stalin's evident interest in South Asia again became something more than an academic matter after the British withdrawal from the region in 1947–48.

In a number of necessarily limited ways during the next few years, the CPC seems to have tried to ward off undue Soviet influence on the Indian subcontinent and safeguard its own hopes for an ultimate major role in it. Thus the CPR reciprocated Indian diplomatic recognition on January 4, 1950, only five days after it had been extended.[6] The CPR's final decision, in October, 1950, to intervene in the Korean War was accompanied by a marked acceleration of its timetable for the "liberation" of Tibet, probably in the fear that Stalin might take advantage of Chinese preoccupation with Korea to extend his influence through Sinkiang and Tibet toward the borders of the Indian subcontinent. As we have seen, Communist Chinese maps claimed large portions of the Pamir Mountains, where Soviet territory most closely approaches South Asia, until 1953, the year of Stalin's death.

With the death of Stalin, the appearance of a less geopolitically minded leadership in the Kremlin, and the Soviet withdrawal from western Sinkiang in the spring of 1955, the CPR could afford to feel less concerned over possible Soviet power plays in the direction of South Asia. According to a seemingly credible account, the CPC in 1955 or 1956 went through the motions of agreeing to a secret Soviet proposal that it recognize South Asia and the areas to the west of it as a Soviet sphere, in return for a Soviet pledge to treat all of Southeast Asia except for Indonesia as a Chinese sphere.[7] If such an agreement was actually made, it was not respected for long by either side, by the Chinese even less than by the Russians.

The CPR's own design for South Asia has never been openly stated. It

[4] Raymond James Sontag and James Stuart Beddie, eds., *Nazi-Soviet Relations, 1939–1941: Documents from the Archives of The German Foreign Office*, Washington: Department of State, 1948.

[5] *Ibid.*, pp. 257–259.

[6] "Diplomatic Relations of Communist China," *Current Background* (Hong Kong: American Consulate General), no. 440 (March 12, 1957).

[7] Aleksandr Kaznacheev, *Inside a Soviet Embassy: Experiences of a Russian Diplomat in Burma*, Philadelphia: Lippincott, 1962, pp. 142–143.

seems reasonable to suppose, however, that it intends to establish itself as the dominant power in the Himalayas, although not necessarily by means as crude as invasion and annexation. From there it could provide an "active sanctuary" for the political and perhaps military efforts of the Indian Communist Party, or more accurately, probably, for the more militant of the regional fragments of the Indian Communist Party. The CPC seems to favor the balkanization of the subcontinent into its component linguistic and cultural subregions, as an aid to communization and Chinese penetration, and as at least an interim situation pending an ultimate reunification of the subcontinent if this can be accomplished on terms acceptable to the CPC. The death of Nehru is presumably expected to facilitate this process.

■ **COMMUNIST CHINA AND INDIA TO 1959**

In the spring of 1945, Mao Tse-tung said that[8]

> We hope that Britain will be able to grant India independence, because an independent and democratic India is not only the demand of the Indian people but also a necessity of world peace.

At that time Mao had some reason to feel optimistic about the future of India, since the leaders of the Congress were in jail, and the Indian Communists enjoyed British favor and legality because of their support of the war and were still allowed to belong to the Congress. In mid-1945, however, the Congress leaders were released, and at the end of the year they expelled the Communists from their ranks. Accordingly one Indian Communist leader, B. T. Ranadive, began to organize local insurrections against both the British and the Congress in 1946, but he was overruled by his colleagues and the party supported Nehru for a short time.[9]

To Stalin, the British Labor Party's grant of independence to India and Pakistan in August, 1947, was a clever trick designed to preserve British investments and perpetuate British economic control by conceding a meaningless political freedom. The episode had much to do with Stalin's formation of the Cominform the following month and its proclamation of a more militantly anti-"imperialist" line for the entire international Communist movement. There is every reason to believe that the CPC agreed with this analysis. As late as 1953, for example, we see a Chinese writer arguing that "India's industry is totally subservient to Britain's industry. . . . India's economy is still a colonial economy, and not an industrial economy."[10]

---

[8] *On Coalition Government (Mao Tse-tung hsuan-chi*, Manchuria Publishing House, 1948, p. 342). In *Selected Works of Mao Tse-tung*, vol. 4, p. 303, the passage has been amended to read, "We hope that India will be independent. . . ."

[9] M. R. Masani, *The Communist Party of India: A Short History*, New York: Macmillan, 1954, pp. 88–89.

[10] Chi Yun, "How China Proceeds with the Task of Industrialization," *People's Daily*, May 22, 1953.

In response to the granting of independence and the general tone of the Cominform's initial pronouncements, but not necessarily in accordance with any instructions received either from Stalin or the CPC, some of the regional elements of the Indian Communist Party, notably in the princely state of Hyderabad (annexed by India in 1948), went into revolt along Maoist lines. The emphasis was on guerrilla warfare and a "soft" line toward "rich peasants," although not toward landlords. At the Second Congress of the CPI, held shortly after the Calcutta Youth Conference of February, 1948, Ranadive became Secretary General of the Indian party. The type of violence that he favored was essentially urban, and he had no sympathy with the independent rural warfare being practiced by some of the local elements of his party. Accordingly, he decided to strike at the root of the problem; he publicly attacked Mao Tse-tung's theories as "horrible and reactionary," and "such that no communist can accept them."[11] For this he was explicitly told by the Cominform, while Mao was in Moscow conferring with Stalin, that Mao's strategy was the proper model for the Indian Communists as well as for most other Asian Communists.[12] On the other hand, Ranadive had congratulated Mao the previous October on the establishment of the CPR and had received a reply from Mao to the effect that India would soon be "liberated" by its Communist Party from Anglo-American "imperialism" and its Indian "lackeys."[13]

The CPC's relations with the Indian Communist Party had remarkably little influence on the other arm of its "dual policy" toward India, its relations with the Nehru government. Its propaganda notwithstanding, the CPC does not appear to have regarded the remaining British presence in India as more than economic in nature, or Nehru's fundamental sins as amounting to much more than his "bourgeois" origins and his anti-Communist domestic policy. Nehru, for his part, was eager for good relations with the CPR, provided it did not encroach on India's traditional cultural sphere of influence, which he apparently defined to include Tibet and most of Southeast Asia except for Vietnam, in addition to the South Asian subcontinent itself. Nehru's policy during and after the Korean War suggested that he was quite willing to give limited support to the CPR's policies toward what he conceded to be its proper sphere, namely the Far East and Vietnam.

If Nehru was tacitly proposing a gentlemen's agreement to the CPR, as seems probable, he must have felt greatly frustrated at seeing it founder repeatedly on the problem of Tibet. The CPC began its invasion of the Kham area of eastern Tibet on October 7, 1950, and announced it on October 25, the date of the official creation of the "Chinese People's Volun-

---

11 Quoted in Masani, *op. cit.*, p. 101. Cf. John H. Kautsky, *Moscow and the Communist Party of India*, New York: John Wiley, 1956, Chapter 2.
12 *For a Lasting Peace, For a People's Democracy!* January 27, 1950.
13 Masani, *op. cit.*, pp. 96–98.

teers" in Korea. On the following day the Indian government protested at this resort to force, but without disputing Chinese sovereignty over Tibet. Although Chinese propaganda had been defining the "liberation" of Tibet from the "Anglo-American imperialists and their running dog Nehru" as the purpose of the invasion, the Chinese reply to the Indian note took a vaguer stand at one point when it denounced the Indian protest as "having been affected by foreign influences hostile to China in Tibet." This formulation, which India repudiated with "amazement," permitted the inference that Soviet rather than Anglo-American-Indian designs on Tibet might have been the object of the CPC's concern.[14]

Nehru decided not to keep the issue alive, although he began to strengthen India's political and military defenses in the Himalayan region, and the CPR for its part was anxious to retain as much official Indian goodwill as possible because of its involvement in the Korean War, in which friendly neutrality on the part of India was a great help to the Communist side. Accordingly, Mao Tse-tung visited the Indian Embassy in Peking on January 26, 1951, India's national holiday, toasted the friendship of the Chinese and Indian peoples, and referred cordially to Nehru.[15] This opportunistic desire for Indian diplomatic collaboration did not prevent the CPR from closing down the Indian consulates in Sinkiang and expelling Indian like other foreign businessmen from China during the Korean War.[16]

A friendlier era in Sino-Indian relations opened with the signing of the agreement on Tibet in April, 1954. Nehru evidently hoped that, by getting the CPR to subscribe to the "Five Principles of Peaceful Coexistence," taking an active part in the Geneva Conference on Indochina, and assuming the chairmanship of the International Control Commissions for the three Indochinese states, India could shield Burma, and if possible the rest of Southeast Asia except for Vietnam, from the Chinese and the North Vietnamese. Nehru was also furious at SEATO because of the adherence to it of his pet abomination, Pakistan. He persuaded Ceylon not to join SEATO, as it was inclined to do, and Burma to put its trust in the "Five Principles of Peaceful Coexistence" and in his supposed ability to manage the CPR, as he attempted to do during his visit to Peking in October, 1954. Thailand, which was even more concerned than Burma over the danger of Communist aggression and subversion, took the opposite course and joined SEATO. Nehru's approach seemed to be vindicated by Chou En-lai's moderate and reasonable behavior at the Bandung Conference, even though the continued publication of Chinese maps showing a Sino-Indian frontier differing from the Indian version remained a source of irritation and worry in New Delhi.[17] Nehru

---

[14] Texts in *The New York Times*, November 3, 1950.

[15] K. M. Panikkar, *In Two Chinas: Memoirs of a Diplomat*, London: Allen and Unwin, 1955, p. 125.

[16] *The New York Times*, June 23, 1950; *The Times of India*, October 30, 1954.

[17] Cf. Rosemary Brissenden in George Modelski, ed., *SEATO: Six Studies*, Melbourne: F. W. Cheshire, 1962, pp. 205–214, 232.

claimed to believe that the CPR's occasional demonstrations of belligerency were due mainly to concern for the security of its borders, as in the case of the Korean War, a view that makes all the more remarkable the Indian performance along the Sino-Indian border in 1961–62.[18]

The CPR for its part was in a somewhat chastened mood after the Korean War. Its diplomatic interests took precedence over its revolutionary interests for the time being, and Indian goodwill retained a high value. Chinese propaganda harped continually on a mythical two thousand years of Sino-Indian friendship. Chou En-lai began regularly to insert warm references to "our great neighbor India" into his public reports on foreign affairs.

This euphoria could last only as long as no serious issue between China and India arose to wreck it. Of the available possible issues of this kind, Indo-Soviet relations and Tibet proved to be the hardy perennials.

At first, to be sure, the Soviet Union's increasingly friendly policy toward India had more an anti-American than an anti-Chinese purpose. Partly at least in response to the chilly attitude of the Eisenhower administration toward neutralism, the Soviet Union began to show an interest in conciliating India within a few months after Stalin's death. The trend was intensified in 1954 by the strong Indian reaction to the United States alliance with and military aid program in Pakistan. Other landmarks were the beginning of large-scale Soviet economic aid to India, Nehru's visit to the Soviet Union in 1955, Bulganin's and Khrushchev's visit to India at the end of the year and their strong endorsement of the Indian position on Kashmir (something that the CPR has never done), and the dissolution of the Cominform on April 17, 1956 (Khrushchev's birthday), as a gesture to Tito and Nehru. Even the Communist electoral victory in Kerala in 1957 and the chill in relations between Khrushchev and Tito in 1958 did not seriously affect the trend toward closer Indo-Soviet relations.[19]

By about 1957, it seems likely that Nehru was thinking of his good relations with Khrushchev primarily as anti-Chinese insurance, the main reason being his growing concern over the situation in Tibet.

For his part, Khrushchev seems to have been growing increasingly convinced of the wisdom of aiding and supporting Nehru in his efforts to create a unified, secular, developing India. Khrushchev probably thought of his support of Nehru as a holding operation of indefinite but not permanent duration, designed to head off a possible growth of Western or Chinese influence on the subcontinent pending the ultimate materialization of the "parliamentary path" to power for the Indian Communists. The latter eventuality must have been very much in Khrushchev's mind after the Communist victory in Kerala in the Indian general election of 1957. Soviet

---

[18] Ibid., p. 207.
[19] Cf. Arthur Stein, "India's Relations with the USSR, 1953–1963," Orbis, vol. viii, no. 2 (summer, 1964), pp. 358–362.

support for the unity of India would also help to keep the Indian Communists united, even if not always happy over Soviet policy. The unity of the party, rather than a triumph for the luxuriant "fissiparous tendencies" within it, must have seemed desirable in Moscow because Soviet influence was comparatively strong on the central leadership of the party, whereas Chinese influence was comparatively strong in some of the regional components. In short, Khrushchev appears to have been trying both to lay the foundations for an ultimate smooth transition to Communist rule in India, and to build up India under whatever government as a counterweight to the CPR, a massive extension of whose influence into the Indian subcontinent would have serious adverse consequences for the Soviet position not only in Asia but in the entire world.[20] If this is even a reasonable approximation of Khrushchev's attitude, it is little wonder that the CPR displayed a growing exasperation at his Indian policy from the late 1950s on.

Tibet was of even more immediate and acute importance in the promotion of hostility between the CPR and India. Revolts broke out among the Khambas in eastern Tibet late in 1955, and the Dalai Lama's government farther to the west was clearly in sympathy with the Khambas although in no position to take overt action in support of them. At the end of 1956, the Dalai Lama visited India to take part in the celebration of the 2,500th anniversary of the birth of the Buddha. By this time he had almost made up his mind to stay in India until the CPC moderated its Tibetan policy. After a talk with Chou En-lai, who also visited India at the time, Nehru told the Dalai Lama that there would be such changes and advised him to return to Tibet. He did so in February, 1957.[21] Chou told Nehru that the CPC was respecting Tibet's autonomy and would continue to do so.[22] He was evidently angered by Nehru's intervention, however, and of all the stops Chou made during his trip this was the only one that produced no joint communiqué. In July, 1958, the CPR forced Nehru to cancel a proposed visit to Lhasa, which he had promised the Dalai Lama he would make.[23]

■ SINO-INDIAN RELATIONS SINCE 1959

The explosion of fighting in Lhasa on March 10, 1959, the Dalai Lama's flight to India, and his cordial reception there sharply worsened the relationship between the CPR and India, which was already deteriorating. The myths both of traditional and current Sino-Indian friendship were destroyed in the eyes of all but the most leftist of Indians. The others, as well as many

---

[20] Cf. *ibid.*, p. 372.

[21] Dalai Lama's statement of June 20, 1959 (quoted in *The Question of Tibet and the Rule of Law*, Geneva: International Commission of Jurists, 1959, pp. 197–198).

[22] Nehru's statement of April 27, 1959 (in *The New York Times*, April 28, 1959).

[23] George N. Patterson, "China and Tibet: Background to the Revolt," *The China Quarterly*, no. 1 (January–March, 1960), p. 98.

people in other parts of the world, condemned the CPR for its brutal behavior in Tibet. For its part, the CPR seemed to see confirmation of its
suspicions that Indian encouragement, if not outright aid and support, lay
behind the Tibetan resistance. At the very least, the existence of a poorly
controlled frontier with India gave Tibetans a chance to escape, and therefore a greater willingness to resist than they would otherwise have had.

Sino-Indian relations grew still tenser after the border fighting that
occurred in the summer and autumn of 1959. Nor did they recover afterwards, as they had after the exchange of acrimonious notes on Tibet in
1950. The situation was radically different now. The CPR was much more
deeply committed in Tibet than before, and it was not involved in a major
international crisis and therefore had no need of Indian good offices, which
would probably not have been available in any case. By its barbarous behavior toward what, as we have seen, India regarded as a part of its traditional cultural sphere, the CPR had probably jeopardized the chance of
India's continuing to recognize the Far East and Vietnam as a Chinese
sphere, as it had done during the Korean War.

The abrupt worsening of Sino-Indian relations in the spring of 1959, as
a result of the Tibetan crisis, had the predictable effect of drawing India and
the Soviet Union closer together. India seems to have been exploiting its
position skillfully when, on July 30, 1959, it obtained a preliminary Soviet
commitment to a new development credit of approximately $378 million
and then, on the following day, ousted the Communist government in the
state of Kerala. The Soviet Union took little public notice of this action,
kept the credit in effect, and gave increasingly outspoken support to the
Indian side of the Sino-Indian border dispute. Evidently the anti-Chinese
aspect of Khrushchev's entente with Nehru took precedence over his concern for the prospects of the "parliamentary path" in India. The effect of
all this was inevitably to sharpen still further the CPC's anger at both
Khrushchev and Nehru.

By this time Nehru had come to typify in the CPC's eyes the "bourgeois reactionaries" of the underdeveloped world, and its attitude toward
Nehru probably contributed to its growing reservations about the "national
bourgeoisie" as a whole. These reservations were expressed as follows by a
leading Chinese Communist theoretician in the autumn of 1959:[24]

> It is clear to all that the People's Republic of China founded after the
> victory of the new-democratic revolution is fundamentally different
> from the nationally independent countries led by the national bour-
> geoisie which have come into existence in Asia and Africa since World
> War II. On account of specific historical conditions, the proletariat in
> these countries failed to attain hegemony in the national-democratic

---

[24] Wang Chia-hsiang, "The International Significance of the Chinese People's Victory," *Red Flag*, October 1, 1959, reprinted in *Ten Glorious Years*, Peking: Foreign
Languages Press, 1960, pp. 275–279.

revolutionary movements. As a result, state power fell into the hands of the bourgeoisie after independence was achieved. . . . But after all the bourgeoisie is the bourgeoisie. When in power, it does not follow resolute, revolutionary lines, it oscillates and compromises. Therefore it is out of the question for these countries to pass to socialism, nor is it possible for them to accomplish in full the tasks of the national-democratic revolution. What is more, even the national independence they have achieved will not be secure. Under the attack of the reactionaries both at home and abroad, there is often the danger of retrogression and the loss of the national independence already gained. . . . Thus, in the final analysis, they [i.e., the national bourgeoisie] cannot escape the control and clutches of Imperialism.

The CPR's appraisal of Nehru and his "ilk" was considerably harsher than one that had been made in 1958 by Pavel Yudin, Soviet Ambassador to the CPR from 1953 to 1959, in commenting on Nehru's article, "The Basic Approach."[25]

Even apart from the border dispute, which came increasingly to dominate Sino-Indian relations after 1959, the CPC saw more and more reason to object to Nehru's general attitude. He continued to improve his relations with the Soviet Union and to show sympathy for the Dalai Lama and the Tibetan people. After 1960 he diverged from the Communist stand on such important issues as Berlin, the Congo, and Laos. In 1961 he visited the United States and Japan and while at the first conference of nonaligned nations (at Belgrade) expressed displeasure over Soviet nuclear testing. Nevertheless, the CPR congratulated India promptly and warmly on its "liberation" of Goa from Portuguese "imperialism," on December 18, 1961.[26] Beneath the surface, the CPR was probably aware that the Goan operation was in part an effort, successful as it turned out, to ensure the election of Defense Minister Krishna Menon to Parliament over his Socialist opponent, Acharya Kripalani. Although Kripalani was objectionable to the CPR because of his pro-Western leanings, Menon was probably even more so because he was a major link in Nehru's understanding with the Soviet Union and was the architect of the Indian Army's attempt to occupy disputed territory along the Chinese frontier with the aid of Soviet equipment.

Although the idea of an economic competition between India and the CPR, presumably for the hypothetical honor of providing a model for the rest of Asia, has been greatly overworked, it is true that the CPR has always asserted loudly that Nehru's approach to economics would produce neither socialism nor development. In recent years, the CPR has derived a good deal of loudly advertised satisfaction from India's difficulties in such fields

---

[25] Cf. Pavel Yudin, "Can We Accept Pandit Nehru's Approach?" *World Marxist Review*, vol. 1, no. 4 (December, 1958), pp. 42–54.

[26] Chinese government statement of December 19, 1961 (New China News Agency dispatch, same date).

as agriculture and foreign exchange.[27] In fact, those difficulties have been held largely responsible for Nehru's "anti-China" policy.[28]

After the border fighting of 1962, the CPR was of course infuriated by Nehru's skill in evading some of the logical consequences of defeat. In addition, it charged him with persecuting Chinese nationals living in India and with admitting intelligence agents of the Republic of China. In December, India closed its consulates at Shanghai and Lhasa, on the ground that they had been subjected to harassment, and made the CPR close its consulates at Calcutta and Bombay.[29]

Nehru's death on May 27, 1964, deprived India of a leader with world-wide influence, and specifically of the leading spokesman within the Afro-Asian world for the Indian case against the CPR. Although Peking officially condoled with the Indian government on Nehru's death,[30] it probably hoped and may have believed that Asian opinion was right in feeling that a major obstacle to the extension of Chinese influence was gone.[31]

The CPR has watched Nehru's successors with growing disapproval. It denounced the visit of an Indian parliamentary delegation to Taiwan in June, 1964, as symbolizing the adoption of a "two Chinas" policy.[32] The CPR objected strongly to Prime Minister Shastri's performance at the Cairo conference of nonaligned nations (October, 1964), and especially to his proposal that the conference officially request the CPR not to conduct a nuclear test. It also denounced Shastri's continuation of Nehru's policy of seeking and accepting American military aid. According to the CPR, this policy meant that, since at least as long ago as 1962, India was neutral in name only.[33]

■ SINO-PAKISTANI RELATIONS

Pakistan recognized the CPR on January 5, 1950, the day after the CPR had reciprocated Indian recognition;[34] clearly Pakistan did not want to risk leaving the field to India. The CPR did not reciprocate Pakistani recognition until February 4. Like the Soviet Union and the Indian Communists, the CPC had tended to oppose the creation of Pakistan, on the ground that "autonomy" for the Moslems within an Indian federation was to be preferred to a separate Moslem state. The CPR may have feared that Pakistan would exert an attractive force on Chinese Moslems, especially

27 E.g., "What Kind of Stuff is Nehru's Much-Advertised 'Socialism'?" *Red Flag*, April 1, 1963.

28 Cf. "Behind Nehru's Anti-China Policy," *Red Flag*, September 13, 1963.

29 Chinese note of December 8, 1962 (in Indian White Paper VIII, pp. 123–124).

30 New China News Agency dispatch, May 27, 1964.

31 Cf. *The New York Times*, May 29, 1964.

32 New China News Agency dispatch, June 30, 1964.

33 Cf. New China News Agency dispatch, October 9, 1964; for commentary see *The New York Times*, October 11, 1964.

34 "Diplomatic Relations of Communist China," *loc. cit.*

those in Central Asia. Finally, Pakistan had already begun to show some signs of greater interest in American than in Soviet aid.

On the other hand, the CPR must have been reluctant to leave the diplomatic field in Karachi to the Soviet Union, which had recognized Pakistan in the spring of 1948. Pakistani jute and cotton undoubtedly appealed to the CPR, which soon began to import them in exchange for coal.[35] The most important consideration of all in favor of recognition may have been the fact that Pakistan then aspired to play a leading role among the Moslem states of the Middle East, and that the CPR therefore regarded a relationship with it as a prerequisite to a role of its own in the Middle East.

Under some such circumstances as these, Sino-Pakistani diplomatic relations got under way during 1950. Their tendency has been to grow closer with the passage of time, in spite of Pakistan's decision in 1953–54 to accept American economic and military aid and enter the American alliance system. From the Pakistani point of view, the CPR has probably seemed useful almost from the beginning as a counterweight to the increasing tendency of the Soviet Union to aid and support India and Afghanistan, with both of which Pakistan has generally been on bad terms. From the Chinese point of view, Pakistan has seemed useful for its ability to divert India's attention from Aksai Chin and Tibet, which as we have seen Nehru regarded as part of the Indian cultural sphere.

Pakistan at first supported the CPR for admission to the United Nations and then abstained on the United Nations vote condemning the CPR as an aggressor in Korea (February, 1951) and twice (1952 and 1957) on the question of a moratorium on discussion of the question of Chinese representation in the United Nations.[36] The CPR preserved neutrality on the Kashmir dispute, rather than endorsing the Indian position as the Soviet Union came to do. Nor did the CPR condemn Pakistan's adherence to the Baghdad Pact (later CENTO) and to SEATO.[37]

At the Bandung Conference (April, 1955), Chou En-lai went out of his way to conciliate the Pakistani Prime Minister, Mohammed Ali, and invited him to visit the CPR. Relations grew increasingly close during the next few years, roughly in proportion as Soviet aid to and support of India expanded. A China-Pakistan Friendship Association was formed in May, 1956.[38] In October, Prime Minister Suhrawardy visited the CPR, and in December Chou En-lai returned the compliment. The joint communiqué issued on the latter occasion affirmed that there were "no real conflicts of interest between the two countries" and implied that common opposition to the Western role in the Suez crisis had drawn them closer together.[39]

---

[35] S. M. Burke, "Sino-Pakistani Relations," *Orbis*, vol. viii, no. 2 (summer, 1964), p. 392.

[36] *Ibid.*, pp. 391–392.

[37] Cf. Geòrge Modelski in Modelski, *op. cit.*, p. 131.

[38] New China News Agency dispatch, May 27, 1956.

[39] New China News Agency dispatch, December 24, 1956.

In 1958, a year that witnessed military seizures of power in Sudan, Burma, and Thailand, and a revolt by military and Moslem elements in Indonesia, the military section of the Pakistani elite swept aside the civilians, and Field Marshal Mohammed Ayub Khan assumed virtually dictatorial powers. His domestic policies were decidedly more anti-Communist, and his foreign policies somewhat more so, than those of his predecessors. In 1959, when the Tibetan situation and the Sino-Indian border became critical, Ayub launched the first of a series of efforts to use Chinese pressures on India as a means of taking the main weight of the Indian Army off Pakistan and of making progress toward a favorable settlement of the burning Kashmir dispute. He proposed an agreement between India and Pakistan for joint defense of the subcontinent, India to be broadly responsible for the defense of the border with the CPR and Pakistan for the border with the Soviet Union. Since the Chinese military threat to the subcontinent, real or assumed, was obviously more serious, or at least more pressing, than the Soviet, the proposal would have had the main practical effect of deploying the Indian army primarily against the CPR instead of against Pakistan. India showed no interest in this proposal, perhaps because it was counting on the Soviet Union to restrain the CPR so that it could continue to devote its main attention to Pakistan and Kashmir. There was some improvement in Indo-Pakistani relations, but its main landmark was not a joint defense arrangement but an agreement on the division of the waters of the Indus, concluded in September, 1960.[40]

Ayub became increasingly irritated with the Soviet Union for its threatening attitude toward Pakistan and its growing support of India, particularly on the Kashmir issue. After the bringing down of the American U-2 that had taken off from the vicinity of Peshawar in West Pakistan, on May 1, 1960, Khrushchev threatened with rocket retaliation any country that allowed itself to be used in a similar way in the future. By that time, the CPR's relations with both the Soviet Union and India were so bad as to suggest to Ayub the obvious possibility of a limited alignment with the CPR as a means of balancing the Indo-Soviet combination. The basis for such a policy lay in the fact that official Sino-Pakistani relations had always been maintained at a polite, and sometimes at a friendly, level. An additional benefit that might accrue to Pakistan from improving its relations with the CPR, the sworn enemy of the United States, was increased American aid and attention to Pakistan, which was feeling increasingly neglected by the United States, and more so by the Kennedy administration than by the Eisenhower administration.[41]

As we have seen, Pakistan began to make confidential approaches to

[40] Cf. Burke, *loc. cit.*, pp. 393–394.
[41] For an excellent presentation of the Pakistani case see Mohammed Ayub Khan, "The Pakistan-American Alliance: Stresses and Strains," *Foreign Affairs,* vol. 42, no. 2 (January, 1964), pp. 195–209.

the CPR on the subject of their common de facto border early in 1961, and the CPR responded early in the following year. The CPR, for its part, felt an analogous interest in strengthening its hand in dealing with the Indo-Soviet combination by means of a limited understanding with Pakistan, especially since Pakistan had begun in 1961 to support the CPR's admission to the United Nations. On May 3, 1962, as it happened the day after Krishna Menon had firmly declared to the United Nations Security Council that India had never committed itself to a plebiscite in Kashmir, the CPR announced for the first time that it intended to open border negotiations with Pakistan.[42] Soon afterward it was reported that the CPR had offered to sign a treaty of friendship with Pakistan.[43]

The flow of arms from the United States and the British Commonwealth into India, which began during the Sino-Indian border fighting in the autumn of 1962 but continued after the fighting had stopped, aroused grave concern in Pakistan. It appeared to Pakistan that India was exploiting an exaggerated fear of a Chinese invasion of India as a means of extracting military aid from the West on a scale sufficient to alter the military balance in the Indian subcontinent drastically to the disadvantage of India's major opponent, which remained Pakistan rather than the CPR. India seemed to be strengthening its military position opposite the CPR only to a level sufficient to deter another attack, which was unlikely in any event, and positioning most of its new as well as of its old military strength opposite Pakistan. American and British assurances that India would not be permitted to use its Western arms against Pakistan were not accepted in Rawalpindi as credible.[44] In spite of some renewed talks, encouraged by the United States, on Kashmir, Indo-Pakistani relations worsened sharply, and so did Pakistan's relations with the West.

Logically enough, Sino-Pakistani relations grew correspondingly closer. The talks on the border question proceeded fairly rapidly to the signing of an agreement on December 26, 1962. Despite at least one denial by President Ayub,[45] it appears that secret Sino-Pakistani talks on a possible treaty of some sort began soon after the outbreak of fighting on the Sino-Indian border and continued into 1963. It was credibly reported at first that the CPR had offered Pakistan a nonaggression pact, and that Pakistan had replied that this would be acceptable only if accompanied by an agreement to settle all disputes peacefully, by mediation or arbitration if necessary.[46] There were other similar reports during 1963,[47] and Pakistani Foreign Minister Bhutto went so far as to imply publicly that the CPR had con-

---

[42] See Chapter 12, note 36.

[43] *The New York Times*, May 26, 1962.

[44] Cf. Ayub, *loc. cit.*, pp. 200–209; *The New York Times*, November 19, 1962.

[45] Press conference of September 11, 1963 (*The Washington Post and Times Herald*, September 12, 1962).

[46] *The New York Times*, November 26, 1962.

[47] E.g., *Christian Science Monitor*, September 11, 1963.

cluded a tacit alliance with Pakistan against India.[48] It must be emphasized that there is no convincing evidence that Pakistan contemplated moving any closer to the CPR than was necessary to counteract the increase threat to its security that it perceived in the Western and Soviet policies of supporting and arming India.

Of a series of negotiations and agreements between the CPR and Pakistan that began early in 1963, one of the most important was a civil aviation agreement concluded in late August.[49] Prime Minister Nehru promptly announced that Chinese aircraft would not be allowed to fly across Indian territory,[50] and American officials expressed concern over the prospect of improved Chinese access to the Middle East and Africa.[51] In September, 1963, Pakistan endorsed the Chinese proposal for a summit conference of all nations to discuss the abolition of nuclear weapons.[52]

In February, 1964, Chou En-lai visited Pakistan on his way back from Africa. He and President Ayub issued a joint communiqué on February 23 (Soviet Army Day) which supported the CPR's position on nuclear disarmament and on Chinese representation in the United Nations, and in return committed the CPR to observe the principles of peaceful coexistence laid down at the Bandung Conference and, for the first time, to support the Pakistani demand for a plebiscite in Kashmir ("the wishes of the people of Kashmir").[53] In addition, Ayub evidently tried to moderate the CPR's position on Taiwan but was able to secure no more than an informal and obviously not binding assurance that the CPR would be satisfied with an American agreement in principle that Taiwan belonged to the CPR.[54] Shortly after Chou's departure, Ayub said at a press conference that Pakistan would be glad to use its good offices to bring about an easing of tension between the United States and the CPR if it were invited to do so.[55] This trial balloon was promptly shot down by the United States.[56]

During 1964, construction of a highway linking Pakistani-held Kashmir and Sinkiang across the Pamirs proceeded from both ends.[57] At the end of July, Pakistan accepted a Chinese offer of a $60 million interest-free economic credit.[58]

---

[48] "An attack by India on Pakistan involves the territorial integrity and security of the largest state in Asia. . . ." (speech of July 17, 1963, in *Survival*, vol. 5, no. 5 [September–October, 1963], pp. 220–223). For commentary see *The New York Times*, July 18, 1963.

[49] *The New York Times*, August 30, 1963; see also *Christian Science Monitor*, June 14, 1963.

[50] *The New York Times*, September 4, 1963.

[51] *The Washington Post and Times Herald*, June 30, 1963.

[52] *The New York Times*, September 21, 1963.

[53] New China News Agency dispatch, February 24, 1964.

[54] *The New York Times*, February 22, 1964; *The Washington Post and Times Herald*, February 27, 1964.

[55] *Christian Science Monitor*, February 25, 1964.

[56] *The Washington Post and Times Herald*, February 28, 1964.

[57] *The New York Times*, August 7, October 1, 1964.

[58] *The New York Times*, August 1, 1964.

Prime Minister Nehru's death on May 27, 1964, held important implications for Sino-Pakistani relations, as well as for Sino-Indian and Indo-Pakistani relations. Nehru cherished a doctrinaire hatred of Pakistan, but his successors appear to be somewhat less committed on this score. His death was followed by at least a superficial relaxation of Indo-Pakistani tension, and in mid-October Prime Minister Shastri visited Pakistan on his way home from the conference of nonaligned nations at Cairo.[59] If a genuine Indo-Pakistani understanding should materialize, it would obviously eliminate most of the grounds for the Sino-Pakistani rapprochement and would clearly be in the interest of both India and Pakistan. To an outside observer, it may reasonably appear that although India is entitled to insist on a Kashmir settlement of a kind not likely to inflame Hindu extremism in India, the major concessions must come from India. In particular, Pakistan is entitled to receive convincing assurances that India is not trying to destroy it and does not wish to see it destroyed.[60] As for Pakistan's relations with the CPR, it is unlikely that any efforts by Pakistan to use a marriage of convenience to moderate general Chinese intransigence will succeed any better than have analogous attempts by such countries as the Soviet Union, the United Kingdom, and India.

■ **COMMUNIST CHINA AND THE HIMALAYAN STATES**

During the ten-year premiership of Prince Daud (March, 1953–March, 1963), Afghanistan's main preoccupations were hostility to Pakistan over the "Pushtunistan" issue and economic development, mainly through Soviet and American aid. Since the government was in full control of the country and there was no Communist Party, the CPR had virtually no opening for revolutionary activity, except conceivably among the urban intellectuals. In the state field, there was little basis for an active Sino-Afghan relationship except for the short and relatively noncontroversial common frontier and the Afghan hostility to Pakistan. The CPR and Afghanistan exchanged diplomatic recognitions in mid-January, 1950, but actual diplomatic relations were not established until about five years later.[61]

In January, 1957, immediately after his trip to the Soviet Union and Eastern Europe, Chou En-lai visited Afghanistan. It seems likely that the Afghans insisted on their right to accept aid from both the Soviet Union and the United States but agreed not to allow anti-Chinese activities on their soil, and that Chou promised not to carry on subversion in Afghanistan and to discourage any possible Soviet activity of this kind, in addition to

[59] *The New York Times,* October 13, 1964.
[60] Cf. Burke, *loc. cit.,* p. 404.
[61] "Diplomatic Relations of Communist China," *loc. cit.*

trying to moderate Afghan militancy toward Pakistan, which he had visited a few weeks before.[62]

In September, 1959, Afghan Foreign Minister Naim visited the CPR, unquestionably in the hope of receiving assurances that the Chinese would not extend their militancy along the Sino-Indian border to Afghanistan. He received such an assurance, implicitly at least.[63]

The resignation of Premier Daud and the assumption of effective power by King Muhammed Zahir in March, 1963, were followed almost immediately by an easing of Afghan-Pakistani tension and the beginning of the negotiations on the Sino-Afghan border. Although it is certainly not necessary to assume that the CPR used the lure of a boundary settlement and the threat of trouble along the border as a means of easing Afghan pressures on Pakistan, the possibility cannot be excluded that some such consideration entered into Afghan calculations at that time. In November, 1964, the Afghan king visited the CPR, for reasons and with results that are unclear.

It seems probable that the CPR has no active designs on Afghanistan at the present time and will be satisfied to see it retain a non-Communist government for an indefinite period as long as it also remains neutral.

The same cannot necessarily be said of Nepal, which lies directly athwart the Sino-Indian frontier. Until 1954 Nepal had more or less nominal diplomatic relations with the Tibetan government in Lhasa, but none with China itself. In that year, however, Indian recognition of the Communist Chinese "liberation" of Tibet made that situation seem intolerably anomalous, and Nepal began to consider establishing relations with the CPR.[64] A serious complication was the presence in the CPR of the reputedly leftist Nepalese politician K. I. Singh, who had fled to Tibet in 1952 after an unsuccessful attempt to seize Katmandu, the capital of Nepal. Diplomatic recognitions were exchanged between the CPR and Nepal at the beginning of August, 1955,[65] a few months after the accession of King Mahendra, and in September K. I. Singh returned to Nepal, evidently at Chinese request and probably as part of the Sino-Nepalese bargaining centering on the exchange of recognitions.[66] Singh remained active in Nepalese politics and even became premier for a short time, but he is not known to have served Chinese interests in any active way.

In 1956 Nepal became concerned over incursions into its territory by bands of Tibetans, perhaps in connection with the anti-Chinese revolts that began in eastern Tibet, a region not contiguous with Nepal, late in 1955.[67] The Nepalese government evidently hoped to prevent these incursions from

---

[62] Hints of at least some of this appear in the generally innocuous joint communiqué (New China News Agency dispatch, January 23, 1957).
[63] Cf. the joint communiqué (New China News Agency, September 14, 1959).
[64] The New York Times, May 9, 1954.
[65] New China News Agency dispatch, August 1, 1955.
[66] New China News Agency dispatch, September 15, 1955.
[67] The New York Times, February 15, 1956.

becoming a threat either to its internal security or to its relations with the CPR by means of an arrangement with Peking analogous with the one reached by India in April, 1954. An agreement was accordingly reached at Katmandu in September, 1956, the principal negotiators being Nepalese Foreign Minister C. P. Sharma and Chinese Ambassador to Nepal P'an Tzu-li. P'an also served as Ambassador to India, and his concurrent appointment as Ambassador to Nepal symbolized the fact that at that time the CPR claimed to recognize Nepal as part of the Indian sphere. The agreement terminated all previous ones between Nepal and Tibet, and in particular a treaty of 1856, just a hundred years before, under which Tibet and Nepal had formed what amounted to an alliance against the British. Nepal recognized Tibet as part of the CPR. Trade, consular relations, and pilgrimages between Tibet and Nepal were provided for. Adults living in Tibet who held the citizenship of both the CPR and Nepal were enabled to divest themselves of Nepalese citizenship. It was agreed that the ambassador of each signatory to India should continue to serve as its ambassador to the other signatory "for the time being." The agreement was to remain in force for eight years.[68]

In October, 1956, Nepalese Prime Minister Prasad went to the CPR and signed an agreement providing for a Chinese grant of 60 million Indian rupees (about $12 million) to Nepal. No Chinese technicians were to be sent, however, an indication of Nepalese and still more of Indian fears as to the effect that Chinese technicians might have on Nepal's internal security and external orientation. Another indication that the agreement was sensitive was the fact that it was not published for nearly a month.[69] The agreement was probably one of the irritants that marred Chou En-lai's visit to India a few weeks later and resulted in the absence of a joint communiqué.

By this time the CPR had announced that it would begin preparing Tibet to receive "autonomous" status within the CPR, such as has been conferred on Inner Mongolia and some other areas inhabited by minorities. One purpose of this step was probably to enhance the appeal of the Chinese approach to the problems of minorities and small states in the Himalayan region. It was in about 1956 that the CPR, through unpublicized local channels, began to broach in the Himalayan region the idea of some sort of confederation of "autonomous" Himalayan states.[70] Although at first this proposal apparently did not include Nepal, it obviously might be expanded to do so at a later date.

While the CPR was promoting the revolutionary aspect of its policy toward Nepal in this way, it was also pursuing its diplomatic effort to win

[68] New China News Agency dispatch, September 24, 1956.
[69] New China News Agency dispatch, November 3, 1956; this agreement had been signed on October 7.
[70] George N. Patterson, "Recent Chinese Policies in Tibet and Towards the Himalayan Border States," *The China Quarterly*, no. 12 (October–December, 1962), p. 193.

the friendship of the Nepalese government. In January, 1957, after another stop in New Delhi, Chou En-lai visited Katmandu and issued with Prime Minister Acharya a joint communiqué that pledged both countries, meaning in effect the CPR, to observe the Five Principles of Peaceful Coexistence and the spirit of the Bandung Conference.[71]

The crisis in Tibet and along the Sino-Indian border naturally aroused much anxiety in Nepal. Prime Minister B. P. Koirala went to India in October, 1959, and again in January, 1960, and received an assurance from Nehru that India would defend Nepal if necessary. This episode evoked an outburst of anti-Indian feeling, which is always latent in Nepal, and Koirala evidently thought it wise to balance his trips to India with one to the CPR. There, in March, 1960, he secured a border agreement and a grant of 100 million rupees (about $20 million), this time to be accompanied by Chinese technicians. In addition, both sides agreed to establish embassies in Peking and Katmandu; this innovation meant that their ambassadors to each other would no longer be their ambassadors to India and obviously represented a major setback for Indian influence in Nepal.[72] Chou En-lai's visit to Katmandu the following month produced a compromise on the question of the ownership of Mt. Everest and a Sino-Nepalese treaty of peace and friendship.[73]

Growing political unrest in Nepal, and in particular wrangling between the throne and the politicians, led King Mahendra to suspend the constitution and assume personal control of the government in December, 1960. This step was met with a guerrilla resistance that found sanctuary and probably a degree of support in India. In turn the king naturally sought to improve his relations with the CPR, which was only too glad to reciprocate. A state visit by King Mahendra to the CPR in September and October, 1961, produced an agreement, evidently proposed by the CPR, to build a highway between Lhasa and Katmandu and a pledge that "China would never adopt an attitude of great nation chauvinism toward Nepal."[74] Indo-Nepalese relations continued to deteriorate, however,[75] and Chen Yi accordingly announced early in October, 1962, that the CPR would "stand by" Nepal in case of need and attacked "foreign interference and subversion" in Nepal.[76]

Almost immediately afterward, however, Indo-Nepalese tension was completely overshadowed by the outbreak of heavy fighting on the Sino-

---

[71] New China News Agency dispatch, January 29, 1957.

[72] Text of joint communiqué released by New China News Agency, March 25, 1960; cf. Shen-yu Dai, "Peking, Katmandu and New Delhi," *The China Quarterly*, no. 16 (October–December, 1963), pp. 92–93.

[73] Cf. documents in *New Development in Friendly Relations Between China and Nepal*, Peking: Foreign Languages Press, 1960, pp. 92–93.

[74] Text of joint communiqué released by New China News Agency, October 15, 1961.

[75] *The New York Times*, April 21, 1962.

[76] Dai, *loc. cit.*, p. 97.

Indian border. Probably at Indian insistence, the Nepalese insurrectionaries shortly announced that they were suspending their operations against King Mahendra, in order not to provide the CPR with an excuse for invading Nepal.[77] This development, as well as the completion of the demarcation of the Sino-Nepalese border during November, 1962, removed much of the grounds for King Mahendra's hostility to India and his wooing of the CPR. Although Chinese aid programs in Nepal continued in effect, although the highway between Lhasa and Katmandu continued to be built, and although some Nepalese politicians showed an interest in renewed Chinese proposals for a Himalayan confederation, Chinese influence in Nepal apparently declined.[78] The Soviet Union as well as India benefited from this trend, and during 1963 the Soviet presence and Soviet aid programs in Nepal grew much more noticeable.[79] It is probably significant that Chou En-lai did not visit Nepal during his trip through South Asia early in 1964, that the Sino-Nepalese trade agreement of 1956 was apparently allowed to lapse during 1964 even though there was no cessation of Sino-Nepalese trade, and that four large caches of arms evidently of Chinese origin were discovered in Nepal in the autumn of 1964.[80]

The species of protectorate that India has exercised over Bhutan and Sikkim since 1950 has tended to inhibit Chinese political gains in those Himalayan states, although of course the CPR also has assets in the form of fear of its military power and the general dislike of India. As we have seen, the quiet redrawing of Chinese maps during 1962 to bring the Sino-Bhutanese boundary into line with Bhutanese and Indian ideas on this subject suggests that the CPR has made a secret boundary agreement with Bhutan, possibly in exchange for transit rights for Chinese troops in the event of another Sino-Indian clash. In addition, there is evidence that the CPR has offered to extend diplomatic recognition and economic aid to Bhutan, but that India has fended this off by accelerating its own programs in Bhutan.[81]

The Prime Minister of Bhutan, Jigme Dorji, was assassinated on April 5, 1964, apparently as part of an unsuccessful attempt by some army officers to seize power. The assassin stated after his arrest that he had served with the Indian Army and been taken prisoner during the fighting in 1962 and reindoctrinated by the Chinese. He was given the mission of killing Jigme Dorji, apparently because the CPR had failed to win him over to its side and to its proposals for a Himalayan confederation. The assassination was evidently arranged to coincide with the plot just mentioned.[82] Although the CPR strongly denied this version of the episode,[83] there seems to be no

[77] *The New York Times*, November 9, 1962.
[78] Cf. Patterson, "Recent Chinese Policies . . . ," *loc. cit.*, p. 197.
[79] Cf. *The Washington Post and Times Herald*, November 17, 1963.
[80] *The New York Times*, September 30, 1964.
[81] Patterson, "Recent Chinese Policies . . . ," *loc. cit.*, pp. 199–200.
[82] *The Washington Post and Times Herald*, April 7, 28, 1964.
[83] New China News Agency dispatch, May 4, 1964.

reason to doubt that the CPR would be capable of such a plot in the course of its efforts to establish its ascendancy in the Himalayas by methods stopping short, but not always very far short, of a major war.

■ **COMMUNIST CHINA AND CEYLON**

Like the other countries of the British Commonwealth in South Asia, Ceylon recognized the CPR early in 1950. The government of Ceylon at that time was pro-Western, however, and in fact was only barely dissuaded by Nehru from joining SEATO in 1954.[84] Accordingly, the Soviet Union repeatedly vetoed Ceylon's application for admission to the United Nations, and both the Soviet Union and the CPR denied it diplomatic recognition.

These political considerations did not prevent the development of significant economic relations between the CPR and Ceylon, however. Ceylon is a food-deficit area with an exportable surplus of rubber, among other things, and rubber was one of the items that United Nations members were urged under the terms of the sanctions voted against the CPR by the General Assembly in May, 1951, not to export to the mainland of China. Ceylon, not being a member of the United Nations, could ignore the embargo with impunity. In November, 1952, just after the brief boom in raw materials on the world market caused by the Korean War had begun to collapse, the CPR and Ceylon reached an agreement providing for a short-term sale of Chinese rice to Ceylon at £54 a ton, and for a long-term sale at £56 a ton, in exchange for the purchase of Ceylonese rubber by the CPR at a price slightly in excess of the Singapore price. Thus the CPR got its much-needed rubber and Ceylon got a better price for its rubber than it would otherwise have gotten, in addition to the rice. During the next few years the prices charged Ceylon for Chinese rice and those charged the CPR for Ceylonese rubber were both lowered, in keeping with trends in the world market. In 1954, after much hard bargaining, the Ceylonese government persuaded the CPR to accept a proportionately greater reduction in rice than in rubber prices, again in keeping with the trend of the world market.[85]

Meanwhile, the CPR had not been neglecting opportunities to advance Chinese influence and Communist subversion in Ceylon. One reason for this was the fact that Ceylon has a great and obvious importance for naval operations in the Indian Ocean, and that at that time Britain still had a naval base at Trincomalee, on the eastern coast of Ceylon. The most promising avenue seemed to be the influential and numerous Buddhist monks

---

[84] Rosemary Brissenden in Modelski, *op. cit.*, pp. 206–208.
[85] Based on *Keesing's Contemporary Archives*; cf. A. Doak Barnett, *Communist Economic Strategy: The Rise of Mainland China*, Washington: National Planning Association, 1959, p. 68.

of Ceylon. In October, 1952, a member of the small minority of Ceylonese monks who held leftist political views led the Ceylonese delegation to the "peace conference" in Peking. Soon after that Communist sources in Ceylon, both within and outside the Buddhist monastic community, began to distribute pro-Chinese propaganda. Among this there were, by miscalculation, photographs of Chinese soldiers sitting on a famous statue of the Buddha and of former Buddhist temples converted into schools. These photographs naturally produced a strong adverse reaction in Ceylon.[86]

The period following the Geneva Conference of 1954 witnessed an intensification of Sino-Soviet rivalry in Asia. The Soviet Union tended to woo large countries such as India, whereas the CPR showed a preference for small countries, whose affections could be purchased at less cost. One of these was Ceylon, in spite of or perhaps because of its rather pro-Western orientation. At the Bandung Conference, Ceylon was one of the main countries on whose leaders Chou En-lai turned his famous charm. As though not to be outdone, the Soviet Union at last allowed Ceylon to enter the United Nations in December, 1955, as part of a "package deal" involving the admission of sixteen new members.

In the spring of 1956, Ceylon's internal and external orientation was sharply changed in a leftist and neutralist direction by the coming to power of Prime Minister S. W. R. D. Bandaranaike after a hotly contested election. Bandaranaike soon began to demand the withdrawal of British bases, especially the naval base at Trincomalee, from the island, and an agreement to that effect was signed in October, 1957. Ceylon and the Soviet Union agreed to establish diplomatic relations in September, 1956. Shortly afterward Sir Claude Corea, one of Ceylon's most distinguished diplomats, led a mission to the CPR that reached an agreement in principle to establish diplomatic relations and expand trade.[87] The first concrete result of this mission was a rice-for-rubber agreement for 1957, in pursuance of the long-term agreement concluded in 1952.[88] Chou En-lai's visit to Ceylon in January, 1957, resulted in a definite decision to establish diplomatic relations and secured a declaration of support, which had not been forthcoming during his visits to Burma and India, for another Asian-African (Bandung) Conference.[89] In 1957 the CPR insisted on lowering the price it would pay for Ceylonese rubber, but by way of compensation it made a grant of about $15 million to Ceylon for purposes of economic development.[90] The grant was followed a year later by a credit of 50 million rupees (about $10 million), bearing interest at 2.5 per cent.[91]

---

[86] *The New York Times*, August 23, 1953.
[87] Text of joint communiqué released by New China News Agency, September 16, 1956.
[88] New China News Agency dispatch, December 30, 1956.
[89] R. Gavin Boyd in Modelski, *op. cit.*, p. 175.
[90] Barnett, *op. cit.*, p. 75.
[91] New China News Agency dispatch, September 22, 1958.

On the other hand, the CPR was by no means content to confine itself to diplomatic and commercial approaches in its dealings with Ceylon, and the island's acute tensions between its Sinhalese-speaking majority and its Tamil-speaking minority provided points at which revolutionary pressures could profitably be applied. It appears highly probable that both the Soviet and the Chinese embassies were active not only in disseminating propaganda but in financing and inciting the strikes and communal riots that occurred in Ceylon in 1958.[92]

The mounting communal tension in Ceylon led to the assassination of Prime Minister Bandaranaike by a Buddhist monk in 1959, but not before Bandaranaike had pronounced the Tibetan crisis to be an internal affair of the CPR that it might handle as it chose.[93] On the other hand, many Ceylonese less leftist or less diplomatic than the Prime Minister, including many Buddhist monks, were naturally outraged by the CPR's treatment of the Buddhist, or more precisely lamaist, Tibetans. This unpleasant development, however, did not prevent the conclusion of another rice-for-rubber agreement covering 1959.[94]

Although the government of Mme Bandaranaike, who succeeded her late husband as Prime Minister after an interregnum, attempted to mediate the Sino-Indian border dispute at the end of 1962, its stand on the dispute was essentially pro-Indian and naturally tended to strain Sino-Ceylonese relations. On the other hand, the CPR was undoubtedly pleased when Ceylon became involved in a dispute with the United States that began with the nationalization of some American investments and culminated with a suspension of American aid to Ceylon in February, 1963. The CPR was also pleased with the formation of a pro-Chinese splinter party composed of defectors from the pro-Soviet Ceylonese Communist Party, in January, 1964.[95] Still more important, in view of the unfolding of a plan to send ships of the United States Seventh Fleet into the Indian Ocean, was a statement by Mme Bandaranaike on February 24, 1964, two days before Chou En-lai was due in the island, that her government would not permit aircraft or ships armed with or equipped to carry nuclear weapons to land in Ceylon, and that she hoped the United States would abandon its plan.[96] This meant of course that Ceylon had made explicit its commitment, which was implicit in its neutral policy, not to allow the base at Trincomalee to be used by American nuclear submarines.

Chou received a cool welcome on the part of both the government and

---

92 *The New York Times,* July 13, 1958.

93 New China News Agency, April 23, 1959.

94 New China News Agency dispatch, June 13, 1959.

95 Cf. *The New York Times,* January 7, 1964.

96 *The New York Times,* February 24, 1964. The post-Khrushchev Soviet leadership has welcomed this statement (in its memorandum of December 7, 1964, to the United Nations on disarmament).

the people of Ceylon.[97] He was reinforced by Mme Sung Ching-ling (Mme Sun Yat-sen), who flew from the CPR especially for the occasion, presumably in order to talk to Mme Bandaranaike woman to woman. The joint communiqué condemned colonialism in all forms, without mentioning the United States; endorsed complete nuclear disarmament; committed Ceylon to the proposition that "Taiwan is an integral part of China"; reaffirmed and commended Ceylon's decision to refuse entry to nuclear weapons; endorsed both the second Bandung Conference favored by the CPR and the second conference of nonaligned nations favored by Ceylon and pronounced them "not mutually exclusive"; stated that "Ceylon would continue its efforts to promote Sino-Indian reconciliation"; and pledged the CPR to supply Ceylon with badly needed textiles and rice.[98] As it turned out, the CPR waived further interest payments on its credits to Ceylon, whose economy is plagued by an acute shortage of foreign exchange, shortly after Chou's visit.[99]

In sum, Sino-Ceylonese relations offer a rather interesting case study in Chinese policy toward a small, weak, underdeveloped country, lacking a common frontier with the CPR and therefore not vulnerable to direct coercion, capable nevertheless if aroused of providing facilities for the CPR's enemies, and leftist and neutralist in orientation but with a Communist movement so divided and weak as to have few prospects of coming to power in the near future.

---

[97] *The New York Times*, March 1, 1964.
[98] Text released by New China News Agency, March 1, 1964.
[99] *The New York Times*, May 6, 1964.

PART FOUR

In Conclusion

□ 17

The Chinese Nuclear Test and the Fall of Khrushchev

An investigation of the circumstances surrounding an event in the Communist world of the greatest importance and sensitivity, such as the death of Stalin, resembles the act of coming to a clearing in the forest and discovering bark torn from the trees, bloodstains on the ground, confused footprints suggesting a struggle, and an impression the shape and size of a human body, but no body. Merely because subsequent searching does not uncover the body, is one to deny that violence has been done?

So it is with the fall of Khrushchev. It is, in brief, the contention to be advanced here that Khrushchev fell mainly because, in a rather exaggerated mood of desperation over the approach of a Communist Chinese nuclear test and certain related developments, he was pushing the Sino-Soviet dispute, in both its party and its state aspects, beyond what has been described as its previous "patterns and limits."[1] He was, in my opinion, pushing Sino-Soviet relations to the brink of war.

■ SOME INADEQUATE EXPLANATIONS

The initial, official explanation of Khrushchev's fall in mid-October, 1964, was that he had been relieved as First Secretary of the CPSU and Chairman of the Council of Ministers at his own request, "in view of his advanced age and the deterioration in the state of his health."[2] This ex-

---

[1] Cf. Zbigniew Brzezinski, "Patterns and Limits of the Sino-Soviet Dispute," *Problems of Communism*, vol. 9, no. 5 (September–October, 1960), pp. 1–7.

[2] *Pravda* and *Izvestia*, October 16, 1964.

planation, incredible from the start, was all but demolished on the following day, when an editorial in *Pravda*, without naming Khrushchev, denounced him by implication for "hare-brained scheming" (*prozhekterstvo*) and similar errors.[3] Nevertheless, it is true that Khrushchev turned seventy on April 17, 1964, and had been for some time in an evidently deteriorating state of physical and mental health.[4] In fact, it is impossible to credit the behavior ascribed in this book to Stalin before his death, and to Khrushchev before his fall — behavior that seems to be reasonably well established by circumstantial evidence — except on the hypothesis that in each case age, poor health, nervous strain, and too much power induced a frame of mind that was at least partly irrational. It is still true that power tends to corrupt, and absolute power, or even the somewhat less than absolute power possessed by Khrushchev, corrupts absolutely.

The explanation of Khrushchev's fall that seem to be most widely accepted among Soviet specialists is that it was caused by differences with his colleagues over matters of party power and domestic policy. It is certainly true that friction between Khrushchev and some of his colleagues on such questions had been discernible — although not to most academic sovietologists — since 1962, even before the Cuban missile crisis. It seems that Khrushchev may have been planning to bypass normal party procedures and procure the naming of his son-in-law, Aleksei Adzhubei, to whom he had entrusted a number of important diplomatic missions, as Foreign Minister and conceivably even as First Secretary of the CPSU.[5]

In the policy field, it is true that Khrushchev's approach to economics, including his division of the CPSU apparatus in 1962 into an agricultural and an industrial hierarchy and his Virgin Lands program, had not worked well and had become very controversial. It is also true that many of Khrushchev's generals resented his repeated efforts to cut back conventional military expenditures in favor of the missile forces.[6]

These explanations, either separately or together, do not seem to account for a number of features of Khrushchev's ouster, and in particular for the suddenness and (to the outside world) unexpectedness of it, the secrecy surrounding it, or for the fact that since Khrushchev's fall his successors have purged Adzhubei and have effected some reorganization but have made few major substantive changes in Khrushchev's domestic policies. Khrushchev became First Secretary of the CPSU in 1953, and under the party statutes adopted in 1961 he could not have sat on the Praesidium for more than three terms (i.e., twelve years, or until about

---

[3] "The Unshakable Leninist General Line of the CPSU," *Pravda*, October 17, 1964.
[4] This was pointed out by Professor Philip E. Mosely of Columbia University shortly after Khrushchev's fall (*The New York Times*, October 17, 1964).
[5] Cf. *Christian Science Monitor*, October 20, 1964.
[6] Cf. Victor Zorza, "Khrushchev's Losing Fight with His Marshals," *Life*, November 6, 1964, pp. 43, 79–85.

October, 1965, since the statutes also provide that a Party Congress shall be held at least every four years), unless he had been reelected to a fourth term by at least a three-fourths majority of the Central Committee voting by secret ballot.[7] Thus a dissatisfied minority of the Central Committee would have been able to remove Khrushchev from the Praesidium, in any event, within about a year after his fall actually occurred. The conclusion seems inescapable that, whatever long-term disputes may have existed between Khrushchev and his colleagues, something else happened that made it impossible to wait until 1965 to remove him. It has already been suggested that this lay within the realm of things affecting the external security of the Soviet Union, a subject even more sensitive than those just mentioned.

In the following pages, the story as I have come to see it will be told for the most part in the past indicative. This is done mainly in order to avoid endless hedges and circumlocutions and must not be taken as indicating absolute certainty on my part that the hypothesis is completely correct. I claim only that it fits the circumstantial evidence to be given below much better than does any alternate theory that has so far been advanced.

■ KHRUSHCHEV, COMMUNIST CHINA AND EUROPE

There is little doubt that during the months before his fall, Khrushchev, stung by the increasingly bitter Chinese attacks on him, was maneuvering to have the CPC and those parties supporting it read out of the international Communist movement, and that this extreme step was arousing serious misgivings even among parties otherwise sympathetic to Khrushchev's struggle against the CPC. One of the most burning issues in Khrushchev's mind was evidently the CPC's encouragement of the formation of "Marxist-Leninist" splinter parties in countries where the leadership of the existing Communist Party was in pro-Soviet hands.

In a letter of February 29, 1964, to the CPSU Central Committee, the CPC Central Committee proposed that the two Central Committees appoint delegations to hold talks in Peking from October 10 to 25, 1964 — not an unreasonable idea, since the preceding talks of this kind had taken place in Moscow in July, 1963. At some unspecified interval after that, the CPC proposed a preparatory conference to be attended by 17 of the 26 parties that had drafted the Moscow Statement of 1960. Then, after "adequate preparations" had been made, or in other words in the more or less indefinite future, a "meeting of representatives of all Communist and Workers Parties" should be held. Although the proposal was vague on this point, it

---

[7] *Program of the CPSU* (1961), Chapter III, Section 25.

certainly said nothing to indicate that the splinter parties would not be invited to the meeting.

The CPSU Central Committee rejected this proposal on March 7 and advocated instead that the two Central Committee delegations meet in Peking in May rather than October, that a preparatory conference of twenty-six (rather than seventeen) parties be held in June and July, 1964, and that the full international meeting be held in the autumn of 1964. A later letter from the CPSU Central Committee, written on June 15 but not published until July, added that the splinter parties should be excluded.

Although Khrushchev gave some signs during the months immediately before his ouster of stretching out his timetable, probably in view of domestic and foreign opposition, his desire to expel the CPC and its supporters from the international Communist movement remained fairly clear. It appears, however, that the state aspect of his confrontation with the Chinese loomed even larger in his mind than the party aspect.

In the realm of Sino-Soviet state relations, the subject that seems to have given Khrushchev the most immediate concern was the CPR's progress toward a nuclear test and the acquisition of nuclear weapons. As we have seen, Khrushchev had terminated his aid to the CPR's nuclear weapons program in 1959, or at the latest in 1960, and the nuclear test ban treaty of 1963 had been intended by all three original signatories as an antiproliferation device, with special reference to the CPR and West Germany. At the time of the test ban negotiations, however, Khrushchev indicated to Governor Harriman that he was not much worried about the CPR's acquisition of nuclear weapons, an event that he evidently considered to be far in the future.[8] In the latter part of 1963, there were a number of statements by Communist Chinese spokesmen to the effect that it might be years before the CPR could conduct a nuclear test, let alone produce operational nuclear weapons.[9] On September 29, 1964, however, United States Secretary of State Dean Rusk predicted that the CPR would conduct a nuclear test soon, perhaps on October 1, a logical date since it was the fifteenth anniversary of the founding of the CPR.[10] It would appear that something had happened in the meanwhile to speed up the Chinese nuclear program.

It will be recalled that France and the CPR exchanged diplomatic recognitions on January 27, 1964. This event represented a major diplomatic success for the CPR and projected it into world, and especially European, politics as never before. Especially since France was on reasonably good terms with West Germany, although less so than it had been during Adenauer's last years, Khrushchev must have been reminded that, just as Stalin had always feared joint action against him by Germany and

---

[8] *The New York Times,* July 30, 1963.

[9] E.g., Chen Yi interview with Japanese newsmen in Tokyo *Kyodo,* October 28, 1963; also *The Washington Post and Times Herald,* December 8, 1963.

[10] *The New York Times,* September 30, 1964.

Japan, so his own problems would be gravely compounded if his opponents on his Asiatic and European flanks should combine against him. The Sino-Soviet border regions, Berlin, and East Germany would be the areas where he would be most readily vulnerable to pressures by such a combination.

French recognition of the CPR was promptly followed by a marked intensification of the Sino-Soviet dispute that took the form of increasingly bitter attacks from both sides and culminated in the publication in the CPR on October 12, the day on which Khrushchev was overthrown by the Praesidium of his own party, of the second volume of a Chinese edition of his speeches and writings.

A hint of a possibility sufficient to give Khrushchev serious concern was dropped by Maurice Thorez in a speech delivered on March 25. In it he remarked that[11]

> We approve of the recognition of People's China, even if, as they say, de Gaulle has ideas in the back of his mind about it, even if the de facto agreement between de Gaulle and Mao Tse-tung about the dissemination of the nuclear weapon and their common hostility to the Moscow treaty [i.e., the test ban treaty] may surprise us.

Right or wrong, Thorez was talking about opposition to the test ban treaty and an agreement on nuclear dissemination as two different things, not one. He may have meant to allege a secret agreement on French technical assistance to the CPR in the last stages of its effort to conduct an initial nuclear test. It may be significant that on March 28, the day after the publication of this speech, Khrushchev held a two-hour talk with Edgar Faure, on which virtually no information was released except for the fact that the CPR was among the subjects discussed.[12] It will be recalled that it had been Faure's mission to the CPR in October, 1963, that had paved the way for the Sino-French exchange of diplomatic recognitions. It may also be significant that the last foreigner whom Khrushchev saw before his fall was French Minister of Atomic and Space Research Gaston Palewski, who had lunch with him at his Black Sea vacation spot on October 13, just before his departure for Moscow to receive the news of his ouster.

It is of course a fair question why de Gaulle might have felt any interest in helping the CPR with its nuclear weapons program. Both de Gaulle and Mao are anxious to diminish the enormous influence on world affairs exerted by the United States and the Soviet Union, and in particular to shatter the limited collaboration between them that began after the Cuban missile crisis. Obviously one of the most important bases for that influence is the virtual duopoly that the United States and the Soviet hold on strategic nuclear power. Consequently, both French and Chinese nuclear policy calls for the

---

[11] *L'Humanité*, March 27, 1964.
[12] *The Washington Post and Times Herald*, March 29, 1964.

proliferation of national nuclear forces, probably in order to create so much worry for the two superpowers that they will agree to complete nuclear disarmament.

If there was in fact a Franco-Chinese agreement on nuclear collaboration, it must have seriously worried Khrushchev, because it clearly brought closer the day of the first Chinese nuclear test, an event which at the time of the test ban negotiations Khrushchev had evidently regarded as a remote event of no great concern.[13] The reasons for Khrushchev's probably heightened concern over the Chinese nuclear test must be sought not only in the general deterioration of Sino-Soviet relations, and in particular the worsening of the Sino-Soviet border dispute, but in the direction of West Germany.

The Soviet leadership had repeatedly made it clear that one of the main reasons why it opposed a Chinese nuclear capability was that it would tend to promote, somehow or other, the acquisition of nuclear weapons by West Germany. A Soviet statement of August 21, 1963, addressed to the CPR, had said that

> It would be naive, to say the least, to assume that it is possible to conduct one policy in the West and another in the East, to fight with one hand against the arming of West Germany with nuclear weapons, against the spreading of nuclear weapons in the world, and to supply these weapons to China with the other hand.

In an important speech delivered on February 14, 1964 (the anniversary of the Sino-Soviet alliance), and devoted mainly to attacking the CPR, Suslov reiterated that[14]

> The CPSU Central Committee and the Soviet Government have already explained why we do not believe it expedient to help China in the production of nuclear weapons. It would inevitably arouse in return a reaction in the nuclear arming of the states of the imperialist camp, including West Germany and Japan. These countries, being better developed economically, scientifically, and technically, could certainly have produced more bombs than China and could have created a nuclear potential with greater speed. Revanchist tendencies are very strong in these countries.

As for the ways in which West Germany, assuming that it desired to do so and that its appetite were whetted by a Chinese nuclear test, might go about trying to acquire nuclear weapons, Max Reimann, the First Secretary of the Communist Party of (West) Germany, said in March that West Germany was in fact already trying to acquire nuclear weapons from three sources: from the United States through the Multilateral Nuclear Force

---

13 Cf. *The New York Times,* July 30, 1963.
14 *Pravda,* April 3, 1964.

(MLF), which was beginning to seem a practical possibility about that time; from France; and from a research and development program of its own.[15]

Since the present West German government and most of West German public opinion clearly have no intention, with or without nuclear weapons, of attacking Eastern Europe or the Soviet Union, it may reasonably be asked whether the Soviet Union has any basis for its frequently expressed fears of a West German acquisition of nuclear weapons, and therefore of the alleged stimulating effect on West Germany of a Chinese nuclear test. This fear has been expressed so often and in so many contexts, both before and since the fall of Khrushchev, that I cannot dismiss it as mere propaganda. I believe it is genuine, although greatly exaggerated. There appear to be several grounds for it. Soviet public opinion has exerted an increasing influence on Soviet foreign policy since the death of Stalin, and there is no doubt that for obvious historical reasons Soviet public opinion is deeply apprehensive of West Germany, and especially of any possibility however slight that it might acquire nuclear weapons.[16] The Soviet leadership, whose outlook is closer to that of the man in the street than was the case under Stalin, probably shares this attitude to some extent. If France did in fact help the CPR with its nuclear weapons program, it might also help West Germany, so as to give it an alternative to joining the MLF, instead of merely inviting West German support in the creation of an essentially French nuclear force as had been the case heretofore. West Germany might find itself in a position to play the United States and France against each other in the nuclear field. A nuclear West Germany might feel emboldened by the deterioration of Sino-Soviet relations, and in particular by the Sino-Soviet border dispute, to take action that it might otherwise not think of taking. East Germany above all would be vulnerable to West German bargaining from strength on the basis of a nuclear capability. Although the likelihood of these possibilities materializing might seem slight, even in Soviet eyes, it is obvious that if any of them should materialize the results for the Soviet Union might be extremely serious. One should not confuse the two elements of risk: probability and seriousness.

Certainly the Soviet Union has acted since the beginning of 1964 as though it were seriously worried about some such situation, or combination of situations, as has just been suggested. It will be recalled that Khrushchev proposed on December 31, 1963, that all nations renounce the use of force in territorial disputes; he probably had the Sino-Soviet frontier and the eastern frontiers of Germany primarily in mind. Of the similar steps taken by Khrushchev during the following months, it seems necessary to mention

---

[15] Max Reimann, "Against German Militarism and For the Development of France-German Friendship," *L'Humanité*, March 21, 1964.

[16] Cf. *The New York Times*, December 23, 1964.

only the treaty of friendship between the Soviet Union and East Germany, signed in June.[17]

Parallel with this evidence of growing anxiety on the part of the Soviet Union went signs of similar concern on the part of East Germany, which was, except for Outer Mongolia, the most immediately vulnerable of all the actors involved. Again, only a few examples need be given. Speaking on Lenin's birthday (April 22), Hermann Matern, an East German leader, denounced the CPR for trying to poison the relations between East Germany and the Soviet Union and for abandoning East Germany to West Germany by encouraging, through its nuclear policy, the acquisition of nuclear weapons by West Germany.[18] An East German editorial published several weeks later states that[19]

> The attitude of the Chinese leaders concerning the German question, the revival of imperialism and militarism, and the demands for atomic weapons by West German militarists and revanchists is in complete contradiction to their assurances that they support the struggle of the German Democratic Republic.

There were certainly grounds for East German concern over an increasing closeness between the CPR and West Germany, and over what it might lead to. Negotiations to strengthen economic relation between Peking and Bonn were begun in May, and exchange of correspondents was agreed on in June. There were even rumors that diplomatic relations might be established; if that should happen, it would probably mean a break between the CPR and East Germany, since the Soviet Union is the only state to date that each of the Germanies has allowed to have diplomatic relations with the other.[20]

■ **THE CRUNCH**

Sino-Soviet negotiations on the border dispute, an issue at least as sensitive as the question of Chinese nuclear weapons, began on February 23, 1964 (Soviet Army Day), the same day incidentally on which a Chinese chargé d'affaires arrived in Paris. These negotiations evidently broke down early in the summer, and their breakdown was probably what led Mao Tse-tung to make his famous comment on the territorial question in the course of an interview with a Japanese Socialist delegation on July 10. In his comment he appeared to propose joint action by the CPR, Japan, Finland, Poland, East and West Germany, and Rumania to revise, chiefly

---

17 Text in *The New York Times*, June 13, 1964.
18 *Neues Deutschland*, April 23, 1964.
19 *Neues Deutschland*, June 10, 1964.
20 Cf. *The New York Times*, June 6, July 22, 1964; *Christian Science Monitor*, April 27, 1964.

at Soviet expense, the boundaries established at the end of the Second World War.[21]

> There are too many places occupied by the Soviet Union. In keeping with the Yalta Agreement the Soviet Union, under the pretext of insuring Mongolia's independence, actually placed this country under its domination. Mongolia takes up an area which is considerably greater than the Kuriles. In 1954 when Khrushchev and Bulganin were in China we took up this question but they refused to talk to us. They [i.e., the Russians at the end of the Second World War, not Khrushchev and Bulganin] appropriated a part of Rumania. Having separated a portion of East Germany they chased away the local inhabitants to West Germany. They divided a part of Poland and annexed it to the Soviet Union and gave a part of East Germany to Poland as compensation. [This sentence was ommitted from the Soviet version of the interview.] The same thing took place in Finland. They took everything they could.

From the Soviet standpoint, no more sensitive subject could be imagined. The question of Japanese territorial claims against the Soviet Union is especially sensitive because if the Soviet Union were to return the disputed islands to Japan, the United States would come under additional political pressure to return Okinawa to Japanese administration. If that should happen, American nuclear weapons could no longer be kept on Okinawa, and an important element of the American capability to deter and contain the CPR would be eliminated. This the Soviet Union does not seem to want, at least for the time being. On September 2 (VJ-Day), *Pravda* published a vitriolic rebuttal that denounced Mao as the heir to Hitler and the Japanese militarists and accused him of wanting to annex Outer Mongolia.[22]

Five days after the Mao interview, the Republican nomination for President of the United States went to Senator Barry Goldwater, whom the CPR proceeded to hail as "its" favorite candidate, on the stated ground that if elected he would speed up the operation of the "contradictions" between "imperialism" and "socialism." Senator Goldwater's affinity for the West German right wing was well known and was the subject of a good deal of comment by American journalists during that period. In his growing mood of exasperation, Khrushchev may have taken this talk, and Goldwater's chances of being elected, more seriously than was necessary. He may have feared that a Chinese nuclear test would increase Goldwater's chances of election, and that he would then press nuclear weapons on the West Germans. The chances of this happening, in Khrushchev's eyes, would probably be increased if the CPR conducted a nuclear test, with which it would be known to have received some Soviet help in the past.

---

[21] Tokyo *Sekai Syuho*, August 11, 1964.

[22] "In Connection with Mao Tse-tung's Talk with a Group of Japanese Socialists," *Pravda*, September 2, 1964.

For the events that were to happen later, at least a plausible explanation is that Khrushchev decided about this time, probably in July, to knock out the CPR's nuclear weapons installations with a missile strike, probably with nonnuclear warheads. This would be done after the first Chinese nuclear test, so as to have as much justification as possible. It has been reported by a reputable source that Governor Harriman had suggested some such procedure to Khrushchev at the time of the test ban negotiations.[23] Certainly this way of dealing with the problem, which has been described by an American journalist as no more difficult than performing a tonsillectomy, would have been much more effective than another method that Khrushchev was reported to have considered, that of destroying the installations by means of a raid by dissident Kazakhs.[24] If Khrushchev in fact formulated such a plan, it is easy to understand the thinking that lay behind a subsequent charge made by Jacques Grippa, a Belgian Communist very close to the CPC, that Khrushchev had made a "threat of military aggression against the CPR."[25]

As will be indicated later, there is reason to think that some of Khrushchev's colleagues were aware of his plan, objected to it as an example of "harebrained scheming," and conveyed a warning to the CPR. The latter had very few ways of deterring Khrushchev, apart from the obvious but unacceptable option of abandoning any idea of holding a nuclear test. The most obvious form of deterrence was a threat to invade Outer Mongolia, the only one of the Asian Communist countries the dominant faction of whose leadership had consistently supported the Soviet Union in its quarrel with the CPR. The loss of Outer Mongolia, with which the Soviet Union had had an alliance since 1936, would deprive the Soviet Union of much of the credibility of its claim to speak as an Asian power.

Relations between the CPR and Outer Mongolia, as we have seen, had been deteriorating since early 1963. In the spring of 1964, Outer Mongolia ordered the remaining Chinese technicians out.[26] Soon afterward the CPR imposed a boycott on trade with Outer Mongolia,[27] and by September it was being reported from Yugoslav sources that the CPR was concentrating troops along the Sino-Mongolian border.[28] Outer Mongolian sources denied rather unconvincingly that they had any information on such troop concentrations.[29]

---

[23] *The Washington Post and Times Herald,* October 2, 1964. See also *The New York Times,* October 2, 1964.

[24] *The Washington Post and Times Herald,* November 15, 1964.

[25] *People's Daily,* November 21, 1964.

[26] Cf. *The New York Times,* May 22, 1964.

[27] Cf. *The New York Times,* September 1, 1964.

[28] *The New York Times,* September 11, 1964. See also P. H. M. Jones, "Drums Along the Amur," *Far Eastern Economic Review,* October 15, 1964, pp. 137–140; M. T. Haggard, "Mongolia: The Uneasy Buffer," *Asian Survey,* vol. v, no. 1 (January, 1955), pp. 19–21.

[29] *The New York Times,* September 12, 1964.

Yumzhaagin Tsedenbal, the Outer Mongolian leader, who had been a frequent visitor to the Soviet Union for several years past, especially during the summer campaigning season, continued this practice in 1964. He attended the celebration of Khrushchev's seventieth birthday (April 17, 1964) and made a speech in which he said that "our country — Mongolia — is situated on the border of the CPR. We daily see all the pernicious effects of the incorrect line which the Chinese leaders pursue in the international Communist movement."[30] On June 13 Outer Mongolia published a resolution that had been adopted on December 22 by the Central Committee of the Mongolian People's Revolutionary Party (the Outer Mongolian Communist Party); this resolution criticized the "incorrect" Chinese line in some detail.[31] At the end of July the Mongolian Central Committee wrote a letter to the same effect to the CPC Central Committee: "It is perfectly clear that an ancient nationalism bordering upon racism, militant great state chauvinism, and unprincipled attitude toward Marxism-Leninism are the basis of the theory and practice of the Chinese schismatics."[32]

By this time, it will be recalled, Mao had held his interview with the Japanese Socialists. Tsedenbal talked with Mikoyan in Moscow on July 21.[33] On August 23, Tsedenbal held a "friendly and cordial conversation" with Khrushchev in the Crimea.[34] This was the twenty-fifth anniversary of the Hitler-Stalin pact, which Stalin had concluded partly in order to free his hands in the west for the time being and turn his full attention to the Japanese invasion of Outer Mongolia that was then in progress. The analogy with the present is obvious: Tsedenbal probably urged Khrushchev either to put his European concerns on ice for the time being and come to the defense of Outer Mongolia as Stalin had or, better still, to drop his "harebrained scheming" and thereby relieve the Chinese pressure on Outer Mongolia. A few days later, while Khrushchev was in Czechoslovakia, Tsedenbal visited Moscow again and held talks with other Soviet leaders.[35]

A week after the Soviet Union published its attack on Mao's statement to the Japanese Socialists, Outer Mongolia did the same. The Mongolian statement accused the CPR of trying to annex Outer Mongolia and praised the Soviet Union as "our true, unselfish friend and reliable protector."[36]

Meanwhile, Khrushchev was trying to find a way to defuse what he took to be his West German problem. On September 3, the day after *Pravda's* attack on Mao Tse-tung, the West German government announced that Khrushchev had just accepted a long-standing invitation to visit Bonn. In order to make his visit possible, Khrushchev had abandoned all his own

---

30 *Pravda*, April 18, 1964.
31 *Unen*, June 13, 1964.
32 Ulan Bator radio, July 31, 1964.
33 Moscow radio, July 22, 1964.
34 Tass dispatch, August 23, 1964.
35 *Unen*, August 29, 1964.
36 Montsame dispatch, September 9, 1964.

previous conditions for such talks and had accepted the West German conditions, which included the proviso that German unification must be among the subjects discussed.[37] The CPR promptly began to accuse Khrushchev of selling East Germany out in favor of West Germany, but the East Germans themselves defended the prospective visit as a contribution to peace. Although the visit was not to occur for several months, the announcement seems to have evoked a prompt response in Moscow, evidently from some of Khrushchev's colleagues who objected to anything that smacked of appeasement of West Germany. On September 6, a West German official was the object of a gas attack in Moscow. The Bonn government protested and threatened to cancel its invitation to Khrushchev, but no apology was forthcoming from Moscow until October 13, the day after Khrushchev's ouster by the Praesidium, by which time the incident no longer needed to be kept alive since the visit obviously would not occur.

Secretary Rusk's announcement of September 29, which was evidently based on American satellite reconnaissance, that the CPR would soon conduct its first nuclear test, perhaps on October 1, probably brought the tension in Moscow to a peak. But no test occurred on October 1, or for about two weeks thereafter. If Khrushchev was planning to destroy the CPR's atomic installations after the first test, and if the CPR was aware of that fact, it obviously would not have tested while Khrushchev was still in power. On October 2, it was announced in Moscow that a new economic plan had just been decided on in accordance with Khrushchev's preference for stressing investment in agriculture and consumer good, not defense.[38] Evidently Khrushchev believed that with his existing strategic forces he could manage the Chinese nuclear problem, and if necessary the Sino-Soviet border dispute as well, without disrupting his economic planning by large new investments in conventional military forces, such as his ground generals were probably urging him to make in view of the deteriorating state of Sino-Soviet relations.

■ KHRUSHCHEV'S FALL AND THE CHINESE TEST

It is abundantly evident that if Khrushchev was in fact planning to destroy the Chinese nuclear installations, and if the Chinese were threatening to retaliate by invading Outer Mongolia, some at least of those of Khrushchev's colleagues who were aware of the situation must have considered this to be a classic example of "harebrained scheming." The "unity" of the "socialist camp" would be shattered beyond repair. If they protested, as they probably did, it is clear that their protests were to no avail. The

[37] *The New York Times,* October 14, 1964.
[38] *Pravda,* October 2, 1964.

only solution, as with Stalin in February, 1953, was to remove the dangerous leader with the minimum necessary use of force.

The first overt indication that important changes in the Soviet hierarchy might be in the making came on July 13, three days after Mao's interview with the Japanese Socialists, when Leonid I. Brezhnev gave up his time-consuming figurehead position as Chairman of the Praesidium of the Supreme Soviet, probably in order to devote all his time to work within the Praesidium and Secretariat of the CPSU.

On September 30, the eve of the CPR's National Day, Khrushchev left for another vacation in the Crimea. In paying this insult to the CPR he evidently felt sure that his plans were in order, and he can have had no serious suspicion that anything was afoot against him in Moscow.

On October 7, East Germany celebrated the fifteenth anniversary of the inauguration of its Communist regime. The chief Soviet delegate was Brezhnev; the chief Chinese delegate was Ulanfu, a Mongol and the CPR's leading specialist in the affairs of both Inner and Outer Mongolia. The chief Outer Mongolian delegate was of course Tsedenbal, who had stopped in Moscow on his way to East Berlin. After the celebration Tsedenbal had discussions with Ulbricht[39] and rather ostentatiously decorated a Soviet tank unit stationed in East Germany, to the accompaniment of loud talk about the Soviet Union as the protector of Outer Mongolia.[40] It was probably at about this time that the news of the plot to overthrow Khrushchev was disseminated among the handful of Communist leaders, including Tsedenbal, who needed to know.

Khrushchev was evidently ousted from the Praesidium and Secretariat, in his absence, on the night of October 12, and from the Central Committee, by a rump meeting of that body, on October 15. His removal as Chairman of the Council of the Ministers (i.e., Premier) was evidently also arranged on October 15.[41] Those who engineered his ouster were probably aware that October 12 was the tenth anniversary of an agreement by which Khrushchev had promised to give the CPR scientific and technological aid with a supposedly peaceful nuclear program, and that October 15 was the seventh anniversary of his agreement to give the CPR at least token aid with the construction of nuclear weapons, as well as the first anniversary of the coming into force of the test ban treaty. The irony of Khrushchev's relationship to the CPR's nuclear weapons program was this: he had given it valuable, probably indispensable, aid, but he had soon regretted having done so and had pushed his efforts to undo his own mistake, as he now

---

[39] *Neues Deutschland,* October 9, 1964.

[40] Radio Volga, October 12, 1964.

[41] I am not much impressed by the evidence adduced in Petr Kruzhin, "The Technique of the 'Palace Revolution,' " *Bulletin of the Institute for the Study of the USSR,* vol. xi, no. 12 (December, 1964), pp. 4ff., that it was planned at first to remove Khrushchev only from his party, and not from his state, posts.

considered it, to the brink of war. This was certainly an example of "hare-brained scheming."

Once Khrushchev's fall had been accomplished and announced, it was safe for the CPR to conduct its nuclear test. This it did, secure in the knowledge that there would be no tonsillectomy, on October 16.

If there was one Soviet marshal whose cooperation would have been essential to Khrushchev's plans, it was Marshal Sergei S. Biryuzov, whom Khrushchev had made chief of the rocket forces in 1962 and Chief of Staff in 1963. Biryuzov supported Khrushchev's views on the importance of missiles as against ground forces down to the last. On October 19, Biryuzov was killed in a plane crash, together with a number of other Soviet officers, while trying to land at Belgrade in only moderately bad weather, in order to take part in the celebration of the twentieth anniversary of the liberation of Belgrade by the Soviet Army. The Soviet government requested that no Yugoslav officials examine the wreckage, and the official explanation given out for the accident was that the pilot had become confused as to whether landing directions were being given to him in feet or meters.[42] This is obviously fantastic, since feet are invariably used in such cases, and it seems much more likely that the Soviet secret police (KGB) or its Yugoslav counterpart had somehow gotten access to the control tower and guided the aircraft into a mountainside. In this way the principal soldier who had probably been privy to Khrushchev's plans, and one who evidently remained loyal to him, was prevented from talking, or possibly defecting.

One of the most interesting aspects of the aftermath of Khrushchev's fall was the behavior of the Outer Mongolian leaders, who had more reason than most to be pleased with it, even though they had supported Khrushchev almost to the end. The Outer Mongolian commentary on Khrushchev's ouster was the promptest and most enthusiastic of any country in the Communist bloc. Tsedenbal was in Hungary when it was announced. Nevertheless, on October 16 a message went forward over his signature from Ulan Bator to Moscow congratulating Brezhnev and Kosygin on their new offices and addressing them, in a manner highly unusual in such messages, by the familiar and affectionate form: dear Leonid Ilich, dear Aleksey Nikolaevich.[43] Tsedenbal then proceeded with his tour of Hungary and Poland, two countries having great symbolic significance for Communist bloc affairs since 1956. Khrushchev's fall had been received with confusion and reservations in the Communist world, especially in East Germany. The first occasion on which Gomulka publicly expressed his endorsement of Khrushchev's ouster was a rally held during Tsedenbal's visit to Poland.[44]

[42] Cf. *The New York Times*, October 20, 1964.
[43] Montsame dispatch, October 16, 1964. The Outer Mongolian Defense Minister's greeting to Marshal Malinovsky on the occasion of the anniversary of the October Revolution also used this form of address.
[44] Cf. *The New York Times*, October 29, 1964.

It is also interesting that after the fall of Khrushchev the tension in Sino-Mongolian relations appears to have been somewhat reduced, and the Outer Mongolian regime conducted a purge of allegedly nationalist, but very probably pro-Chinese, elements in December.

■ **SINO-SOVIET RELATIONS SINCE THE FALL OF KHRUSHCHEV**

There was also a relaxation of Sino-Soviet tension, and yet the fundamental issues remained. Khrushchev's successors were bound, as he had been, by certain parameters, such as the nuclear superiority of the United States and the needs of a modern economy. The most they could do was to try to break out of the vicious circle in which Khrushchev had found himself caught by adopting a policy of marginally greater friendliness toward the CPR and marginally greater toughness toward the United States. But such adjustments were not likely to be enough to meet the CPC's demands for a radical revision of Khrushchev's policies. With regard to Germany, the new Soviet leadership has continued to show serious concern over the MLF and the possibility that West Germany might acquire nuclear weapons, but the edge seems to have been taken off its concern by the increasing probability that the MLF will not materialize. The new Soviet leadership shows little more enthusiasm for the Chinese nuclear program than Khrushchev did. It refrained from congratulating the CPR on its test, and a number of statements by the Soviet Union and East European regimes have shown that the Chinese test is not regarded as conducive to world peace. It has made it clear that it intends to abide by the test ban treaty and does not intend to abandon India.

The CPR, for its part, had never pretended to believe that Khrushchev alone was responsible for those Soviet policies to which it had objected. It had consistently denounced not only Khrushchev but his "clique." The CPR was clearly delighted with Khrushchev's fall and considered it a major victory, but it knew very well that his successors had been members of his "clique." Now it was up to them to prove themselves in the eyes of Peking, not only by abandoning Khrushchev's extreme hostility toward the CPR but by adopting certain positive policies, such as real toughness toward the United States and a more militant line in the underdeveloped areas.

On November 5, Chou left for Moscow to take part in the celebration of the October Revolution anniversary and hold talks with the new Soviet leadership. His delegation consisted largely of specialists in party rather than state affairs; this was appropriate, since although Khrushchev's fall had taken the immediate danger of war out of the state aspect of the relationship, the new Soviet leadership had already indicated that it intended to proceed with Khrushchev's plan for calling a preliminary conference of 26 Communist Parties, to be followed by a general meeting. It was not yet clear, however, whether the "unity" at which these conferences were allegedly aimed was to be achieved by conciliating the Chinese or by drumming them out of what Moscow recognized as the international Communist movement.

Even though little information was released on the talks that Chou had with the new Soviet leadership, it was clear that they did not go well. Evidently neither side was willing to make any concessions of substance, and the fundamental issues in both the party and state spheres remained. The Soviet version of the joint communiqué issued at the end of the talks merely listed the participants and added that "The talks were held in a frank, comradely atmosphere," which in Communist diplomatic parlance meant that they were rather cool if not worse.[45] The Chinese version of the communiqué did not even include this last sentence.[46] When the Chinese delegation returned to Peking, it was met by Mao Tse-tung among others, although he had not seen the delegation off.[47] This was a clear indication that Mao stood behind his representatives in their refusal to compromise on essentials.

A week later *Red Flag* carried an exultant article on the fall of Khrushchev, a subject on which the CPC had been comparatively reticent up to that time. Khrushchev was said to have fallen because he had espoused "modern revisionism," and by clear implication his successors were warned not to follow his example. Khrushchev had defamed Stalin, collaborated with American "imperialism," obstructed the CPR's nuclear program and its defense capabilities in general, preached peaceful coexistence and the "parliamentary path" to the international Communist movement, fawned on Tito, unjustifiably injured Albania, withdrawn his technicians from the CPR, fostered a Sino-Soviet border crisis, supported India against the CPR, tried to make other "socialist" countries into economic appendages of the Soviet Union, attacked "Marxist-Leninists" who would not follow his line, called an "illegal" meeting of 26 Communist Parties for December 15 "so as to create an open split in the international Communist movement," and tried to restore capitalism in the Soviet Union.[48] This virulent article can hardly have improved the already troubled atmosphere in which Sino-Soviet relations were being conducted.[49]

By the early months of 1965, it had become even clearer that the fall of Khrushchev had brought no fundamental changes in the Sino-Soviet relationship except to put it back, in its state aspect at least, more or less within the "patterns and limits" that had governed down to 1963. The CPC and parties friendly to it were implicitly accusing the new Soviet leadership of

---

[45] Tass dispatch, November 13, 1964.
[46] New China News Agency dispatch, November 13, 1964.
[47] New China News Agency dispatch, November 14, 1964.
[48] "Why Khrushchev Fell," *Red Flag*, November 21, 1964.
[49] Cf. *The New York Times*, November 22, 1964.

"modern revisionism" and refusing to take part in its series of conferences. The Soviet Union was showing signs of competing more actively with the CPR for influence on Asian Communist Parties than had been the case for several years, however. This was especially true of North Vietnam, which seems to have been growing somewhat disenchanted with the CPR because of the obvious limits on the lengths to which the CPR is able and willing to go in managing the Indochinese crisis.[50]

■ THE AFTERMATH OF THE CHINESE NUCLEAR TEST

The Chinese nuclear test, which was conducted in Sinkiang on October 16, was a test of a device, not a weapon, of low yield. On the other hand, the basic fissionable material used was enriched uranium, probably produced in a gaseous diffusion plant, not the less sophisticated plutonium that had been used in the initial tests held by the other nuclear powers.[51] A Japanese nuclear physicist came to the conclusion, after a careful analysis of fallout from the test, that the device had included "tampers" composed of U-238, which suggested that the device was intended as the prototype for a hydrogen, or fusion, bomb.[52] It was clear that it would be several years before the CPR had the ability, even if it had the desire in spite of the obvious danger of retaliation, to deliver any significant number of nuclear or thermonuclear warheads, whether by aircraft or missile, on targets in other Asian countries against modern defenses.[53]

The Chinese statement that announced the test also denounced the test ban treaty, called for complete nuclear disarmament, affirmed that the CPR was developing nuclear weapons only because of the threat posed by American "imperialism," insisted that the CPR would never be the first to use nuclear weapons, and demanded an agreement by all nuclear powers not to use nuclear weapons and a "summit conference of all the countries of the world" to "discuss the question of the complete prohibition and thorough destruction of nuclear weapons." Unlike the Chinese statements at the time of the test ban treaty, this one did not call for the destruction of means of delivery of nuclear weapons, this being one of a number of recent indications that the CPR may intend to make at least a token entry into the space race.[54]

Although the test sent a thrill of pride and excitement through the Communist elite, including scientists, and apparently even through the Chi-

---

[50] Cf. *The New York Times,* January 24, 1965.

[51] *The New York Times,* October 20, 22, 1964; *Christian Science Monitor,* October 26, December 17, 1964.

[52] Tokyo *Kyodo,* November 4, 1964.

[53] Cf. *The New York Times,* October 5, 26, 1964.

[54] New China News Agency dispatch, October 16, 1964; text in *The New York Times,* October 17, 1964.

nese public, the CPR in general avoided loud boasting or other efforts to maximize the psychological effect of the test on other countries.[55] This comparative caution resembled that of Stalin after his first test and probably stemmed at least in part from the same cause: a feeling of extreme vulnerability and a desire not to arouse the United States unduly. Nevertheless, as the CPR was well aware, the Chinese nuclear test made a considerable impression on the world. U Thant proposed that the five nuclear powers, which were the permanent members of the United Nations Security Council if one conceded the CPR's claim to such membership, hold talks on nuclear disarmament. The United States indicated a willingness for the CPR to take part in the eighteen-nation disarmament talks being held at Geneva under United Nations auspices. The CPR scornfully rejected both these proposals and repeated its demands for its own immediate seating in the United Nations, to the exclusion of the Republic of China, and for a general summit conference to discuss complete nuclear disarmament.[56]

Reactions to the Chinese nuclear test and to the proposal for a summit conference on the abolition of nuclear weapons naturally varied with the political sympathies of the respondents. There were prompt congratulations from a variety of leftist unofficial organizations in many countries of the world. Among the governments, regimes, and parties that commented promptly and approvingly on the test and the proposal were North Vietnam, Albania, Cambodia, Pakistan, Guinea, Congo Brazzaville, Mauritania, the Japanese Communist Party, the Communist Party of Indonesia, the "True Neutralists" in Laos, and the National Front for the Liberation of South Vietnam. Among the governments that commented unfavorably or with strong reservations were Ceylon, Afghanistan, Burma, Ethiopia, Senegal, Ghana, Mexico, Kuwait, and France (which insisted on the destruction of delivery vehicles and on controls over nuclear disarmament).

There were no congratulations on the test from the Soviet Union or the pro-Soviet members of the Communist bloc, and their comments on the proposal for a summit conference on nuclear disarmament were fairly slow in coming. The first was the Yugoslav, which was sent on November 21 but not published by the New China News Agency until December 16; it in effect rejected the Chinese proposal by supporting the test ban treaty and the principal of general and complete disarmament, and not merely nuclear disarmament. The Soviet Union, on the other hand, replied on December 28 that it completely supported the Chinese proposal for a summit conference on nuclear disarmament; probably the new Soviet leadership considered the prospects of such a conference so remote that it saw no point in making an issue of the matter. By the time of writing, similar

---

[55] *The New York Times,* October 19, 1964.

[56] "New Starting Point for Strivings for Complete Ban on Nuclear Weapons," *People's Daily,* November 22, 1964. For comment see *The New York Times,* November 23, 1964.

declarations of support had been sent by Bulgaria (January 9, 1965), Outer Mongolia (January 11), and Hungary (January 15).

A few other important reactions to the Chinese nuclear test remain to be noted. President Johnson promptly reaffirmed the "readiness of the United States to respond to requests from Asian nations for help in dealing with Communist Chinese aggression."[57] Shortly afterward, he made a speech in which he deplored the Chinese test and called on the CPR to adhere to the test ban treaty.[58] The United States flatly rejected the Chinese proposal for a summit conference on nuclear disarmament.[59] Soon after the Chinese test, and probably in order to counteract its effects, the United States announced that in the previous March it had stationed a squadron of fifteen B-52 jet bombers on Guam.[60] Shortly after the test, but not necessarily as a result of it, American Polaris submarines began to visit Japan and it became clear that some of them would take up stations in the Indian Ocean.[61]

Probably no government in the world was more directly affected by the Communist Chinese nuclear test than the Republic of China. In his New Year's Day message, President Chiang Kai-shek stated that he felt an obligation to destroy the Communists' nuclear installations as a preventive measure and as an inducement to the people on the mainland to rise in revolt. In the meanwhile, he advised all scientific and technical personnel on the mainland to stay away from the installations for the sake of their own safety.[62] The meaning of this threat, if any, remains to be determined.

The Japanese reaction to the Chinese nuclear test, as might have been expected, was largely negative. The government of Premier Sato Eisaku, which came into office shortly after the test, drew perceptibly closer to the United States and farther from the CPR in political, although not in economic, matters. A delegation of the Socialist Party that happened to be in the CPR at the time of the test criticized it in the presence of some Chinese leaders, apparently to their amazement.[63]

In India there was a heated public debate as to whether to ask for increased support from the West or to begin an Indian nuclear weapons program, as Chairman of the Atomic Energy Commission Homi J. Bhabha seemed to favor. Prime Minister Shastri was opposed, for the time being at any rate, to the production of Indian nuclear weapons, and most of his colleagues agreed. Accordingly, in December the House of the People rejected by a large majority a resolution introduced by the right-wing Jan

[57] Text of statement in *The New York Times,* October 17, 1964.
[58] Text in *The New York Times,* October 19, 1964.
[59] *The New York Times,* October 24, 1964.
[60] *The New York Times,* October 27, 1964.
[61] Cf. *The New York Times,* October 16, 1964.
[62] Central News Agency dispatch, December 31, 1964.
[63] *The Washington Post and Times Herald,* October 19, 1964.

Sangh Party in favor of the production of nuclear weapons.[64] On the other hand, India agreed to the stationing of American Polaris submarines in the Indian Ocean.[65]

The Indonesian reaction was characteristically bizarre. A general announced that Indonesia would soon produce an atomic device of its own.[66] This statement seems incredible, unless one makes the possible but questionable assumption that the CPR has agreed to give nuclear aid to Indonesia.

The short-term effects of the Chinese nuclear test and of the imminent acquisition of nuclear weapons on the CPR's military behavior will probably not be very great; caution is still advisable and will presumably continue to be practiced. In the political field, the CPR may be even bolder than before, for example in giving support and military aid to left-wing movements in connection with local wars and subversive efforts in Asia and elsewhere. The CPR will presumably continue to propagandize in favor its own approach to nuclear disarmament, in the hope of setting a bandwagon in motion among the smaller nations.

The United States will presumably continue to increase its watchfulness and preparedness in the regions bordering on the CPR.

The most immediate short-term effects of the emergent Chinese nuclear capability are likely to be felt on the mainland of Asia. The Communist regimes — North Korea and North Vietnam, and especially the latter — will probably feel and display a somewhat increased confidence and aggressiveness, at any rate unless and until it becomes clear that the behavior of the CPR itself has not been significantly affected. The non-Communist countries on the mainland of Asia will probably feel a vague and not necessarily justified fear of increased Chinese belligerency and a heightened reluctance to invoke American protection, for fear of escalation.

On the long-term future I do not propose to comment. I leave that to those with crystal balls less clouded than mine.

---

[64] *The New York Times*, October 27, November 9, December 13, 1964; January 9, 1965.

[65] *The New York Times*, January 8, 1965.

[66] *Christian Science Monitor*, December 17, 1964.

□ **18**

Some Reflections on Coping With Communist China

Having just disavowed any intention of peering into the long-term future of Communist China's development as a nuclear power, I nevertheless consider it necessary to say something about the general lines along which the CPR is likely to move during the next decade or two, as a basis for some comments on what steps the United States might take to protect its interests in the face of the Chinese challenge.

■ CHINA'S FUTURE

To a great extent the CPC has offered its people and the world bread and circuses, or more accurately ideology and politics, as a substitute for intelligent and energetic grappling with China's real problems. Among these, the race between food and population stands out as by far the most important. Although the CPR will probably succeed in increasing its food supply somewhat over the years ahead, it is unlikely to have much success in controlling the size of its population, a problem whose very existence it has been most reluctant to admit in public. We are likely to see neither a spectacular breakthrough nor a dramatic collapse, but a continual pressing of population upon the means of subsistence accompanied nevertheless by some industrial and military growth. The lot of the peasant, in view of demographic realities and his leaders' penchant for heavy industrial development, will never be an easy one and may often be an acutely difficult one, but the CPC seems to have learned from the disaster of 1959–61 that there

489

are limits beyond which the peasant cannot safely be driven.[1] To date the CPC has exploited for the most part those types of economic resources and activities from which a quick return was possible; future progress is likely to be more dearly won. The situation would probably be eased if the CPC would postpone indefinitely its plans for heavy industry and devote itself to agriculture, light industry, and population control, with Japan rather than the Soviet Union as its main foreign model. The chances of its doing this in the near future, however, seem slight.

The impending death of Mao Tse-tung is almost certain to produce an atmosphere of political uncertainty and insecurity. Sufficiently careful preparations for this event have been made so that the regime will probably survive it without collapsing. What we know of the views of Mao's likely successors suggests that for five or ten years after Mao's death there will not be many changes in basic domestic and foreign policies; if anything, what changes occur may be in the direction of greater toughness and militancy. On the other hand, there is a reasonable chance that ten or fifteen years after Mao's death the new generation of leaders who will be coming to the top will hold views that are significantly less militant and doctrinaire, at any rate in foreign policy.[2] In short, a long-term trend toward "mellowing," such as has occurred in the Soviet Union since the death of Stalin, is a reasonable expectation, although the interval before it sets in may be substantial. As will be suggested later, an American policy of firmness and even toughness is more likely to accelerate such a mellowing process than is a policy of conciliation or appeasement.

As for future foreign policy, it must be remembered that, notwithstanding the roseate view of China and the Chinese that prevailed among Americans from the late nineteenth century until about 1949, China when strong has always been a problem for the rest of Asia. This was true of the Nationalists in the days of their greatest power, in the 1930s and briefly after 1945. It has been still truer, and will remain still truer, of their Communist successors.

On the other hand, as this book has suggested, Chinese efforts to exercise leadership in Asia will not necessarily be of an overt military kind. The CPC learned by about 1951 that, as long as the United States remained a military power in Asia, China could not dominate Asia by force. It then turned to subtler and more political methods, some of which however have been far from peaceful. Chinese incitement and aid to "national liberation

---

[1] Cf. Edwin Jones, "Peking's Economy: Upwards or Downwards?" *Problems of Communism,* vol. xii, no. 1 (January–February, 1963), pp. 17–25; and his letter in *The China Quarterly,* no. 14 (April–June, 1963), pp. 229–234.

[2] Cf. John Wilson Lewis, *Chinese Communist Party Leadership and the Succession to Mao Tse-tung: An Appraisal of Tensions,* U.S. Department of State, January, 1964. A somewhat less optimistic view is expressed in Donald W. Klein, "The 'Next Generation' of Chinese Communist Leaders," *The China Quarterly,* no. 12 (October–December, 1962), pp. 57–74.

movements" and other friendly regimes, in Asia and elsewhere in the under-developed world, has become a serious problem and may become an even more serious one. The most obvious purpose of such activity by the CPR, of course, is to advance the cause of Communism. On the other hand, the Comintern in its early years conducted intensive revolutionary activity in many parts of the world not only to promote Communism but also to safe-guard the security of the infant Soviet state, which the "imperialists" were always suspected of plotting to strangle in its cradle. Similarly, the CPC seems to have decided in 1957 or 1958 that, in view of the nuclear balance of power and Soviet irresolution, it could not rely on the Soviet Union in crisis situations and therefore would do well to encourage revolutionary movements against "imperialism" wherever possible, in order to confuse and tie down "imperialism" and distract its attention from the CPR and the Far East. This policy is likely to continue, and it will not be easy to cope with, since direct retaliation against the CPR for actions of this kind in other areas, especially if they are remote from China, seems a political impossi-bility.

If there is a single taproot of the Sino-Soviet dispute, it is the problem of policy toward "imperialism." By containing the CPR, to an extent that has been greater than even many of the advocates of containment realize, and in particular by denying it Taiwan, the United States has driven the CPR to make unacceptable demands on the Soviet Union, forced the two Communist allies on each other's horns, and brought out the latent incom-patibilities and tensions in the Sino-Soviet relationship. Although this situa-tion seems likely to continue, the possibility of change sufficient to bring about a substantial Sino-Soviet reconciliation should not be excluded.[3] This could come about if the Soviet Union adopted a policy toward the United States sufficiently vigorous to be compatible with Chinese demands, or if the CPR moderated its policy toward the United States either after gaining control of Taiwan by some means or after renouncing its ambition to con-trol Taiwan. On the whole, a Chinese mellowing seems less unlikely than a Soviet toughening.

■ **AMERICAN CHINA POLICY[4]**

Probably the main determinant of American China policy is not so much the efforts of the United States to prevent the CPR from increasing its power and influence in Asia and elsewhere as the CPC's obsessive anti-Americanism. For this feeling there seem to be several causes. One of

---

[3] Cf. John R. Thomas, "Sino-Soviet Relations After Khrushchev and Mao," *Orbis*, vol. vii, no. 3 (fall, 1963), pp. 537–549.

[4] Some references on American China policy (other than the historical aspect) will be found in the Bibliographical Note.

course is the central role that the concept of "imperialism," which is now allegedly led by the United States, plays in Marxist-Leninist thinking. Another is the fact, just alluded to, that the United States tries to contain the CPR, and in particular to deny it Taiwan and thus to keep alive a rival regime. Thirdly, the CPC tries to maintain a seemingly wide, although spurious, domestic consensus partly by projecting as much hostility as possible outward against the most conveniently available target, which since 1945 has happened to be the United States. Fourthly, an anti-American policy helps to isolate Chinese intellectuals from politically dangerous foreign contacts. Finally, there may well be an important personal element: one of Mao Tse-tung's sons seems to have been killed while serving in Korea as a fighter pilot.[5] The United States was considering the establishment of diplomatic relations with the CPR in the autumn of 1949, but the CPR frustrated this intention, almost certainly with full consciousness of what it was doing, by maltreating American diplomatic and consular personnel. American protection of Taiwan and American and later Chinese intervention in Korea after June, 1950, set the seal on Sino-American hostility. In short, the origin of this hostility seems to be attributable more to Chinese than to American policy.

In spite of all this, it is widely believed that the United States can and should try to remove the main grounds for Chinese hostility by a policy of conciliation, short of abandoning Taiwan. This is almost a contradiction in terms; no concessions short of an abandonment of Taiwan and a withdrawal of American military power from the Far East and the Western Pacific would have any appreciable effect on Chinese hostility toward the United States. As some secret Chinese military documents captured by Tibetan guerrillas in 1961 show, the CPR insists on a "package deal" and will accept no halfway measures:[6]

> It is better to keep Sino-American relations frozen and stalemated for many years. All differences must be settled at the same time, if a settlement is expected; that is, the U.S. withdrawal from Taiwan, formal recognition of new China, the exchange of reporters, and so on must be settled together.

It should also be remembered that at least three important nations — the Soviet Union, the United Kingdom, and India — have tried and failed to moderate Chinese truculence by a policy of concessions or aid. The United States, which would start from a much more disadvantageous position in Communist Chinese eyes, could hardly succeed where the others failed unless perhaps it were willing to reverse the course of American foreign

---

[5] This has been rumored for some time and was recently confirmed by Deputy Foreign Minister Wang Ping-nan (formerly Ambassador to Poland) (Edward Behr, "Red China Face to Face," *The Saturday Evening Post*, November 14, 1964, p. 28).

[6] Quoted in Lewis, *op. cit.*, p. 27.

policy for nearly a century by giving up all claim to be a Far Eastern power.

The China problem of the United States is not the same as the China problem of any other country, and there is no reason why the China policy of the United States should be the same as that of any other country or why the United States should design its China policy mainly to please other countries.

American diplomatic recognition of the CPR, for the indefinite future, appears not only unnecessary and undesirable but infeasible, mainly because it would destroy the Republic of China, the oldest ally of the United States in Asia whatever its faults, destroy what is left of the United States' reputation for consistency in policy, make the policy of containment of the CPR substantially more difficult to maintain, and in any event encounter an impossible set of Chinese conditions. Recognition is not necessary to negotiation on substantive questions, where such negotiation is desired on both sides. The United States can hold nearly instantaneous communication with the CPR through the ambassadorial talks in Warsaw, whereas the ambassadors of countries that have recognized the CPR generally have the greatest difficulty in securing an interview with an official of the Foreign Ministry. Nor is recognition necessary from the standpoint of intelligence and information. Foreign diplomats and journalists in the CPR, even those from friendly countries, are tightly restricted and closely watched, and in general they report little of real value to the outside world. The same is even truer of the majority of short-term travelers in the CPR. Most of the best reporting on the CPR is done from Hong Kong.

Analogous considerations apply against the seating of the CPR in the United Nations, although of course this is not a question that can be decided by the United States alone, or even by the United States and the CPR together. The CPR wants to come into the United Nations, but not at the cost of significant political concessions of any kind, because it feels that its eventual admission without conditions is inevitable unless the United Nations should collapse, in which case the problem would obviously lose all significance. In the meanwhile, the CPR tries to use the gradually (not rapidly) growing sentiment in favor of bringing it into the United Nations as a means of applying pressure for the conceding of its main political demands, including if possible control over Taiwan.

Much of the doubt about the containment policy and of the feeling in favor of concessions to the CPR arises out of a very deep-seated and widespread conviction, held by many eminent and intelligent persons, that the use of force in international affairs is not only immoral but ineffective. The question of morality I leave to those who consider themselves competent to determine what is moral and what is immoral, but there is a good deal to say in reply to the charge of ineffectiveness. Force has always been one of the main factors in relations between animals, men, and states, and it will always be unless and until mankind buries its differences in order to go to war with another planet. Force can be effective even if it is not used with political discrimination and in pursuit of a valid objective. The policy of containing the CPR has a valid objective and has generally been applied, and should of course continue to be applied, with political discrimination.

As has been suggested, the American containment of the CPR, and in particular the denial of Taiwan to the CPR, has been a major factor in inflaming the Sino-Soviet dispute and in fact in bringing down both Stalin and Khrushchev. The present, when Mao's death seems fairly imminent and his regime may be due for a political time of troubles, is hardly the moment to abandon or substantially modify a policy that on the whole has produced results advantageous to the United States and the free world. A careful study of the history of the Cold War, I am convinced, would bear out the assertion that Communist "mellowing," following a phase of acute frustration, is best promoted by an American policy of intelligent (not blind or irrational) firmness and even toughness, including threats when necessary. The continued effectiveness of such a policy of course assumes a maintenance of at least the present degree of American strategic superiority over the Soviet Union, which the CPR would like the Soviet Union to eliminate, but which the Soviet Union could not eliminate without reducing its people once more virtually to the subsistence level.

This is not to say that minor, as distinct from substantive, concessions to the CPR could not or should not be attempted. These might include an easing of trade and travel restrictions, for example. It should be made clear to American exporters, however, that any great expectations will be disappointed, and that they cannot expect any effective support from their government in their dealings with the CPR. Such concessions, if they were reciprocated, might have some slight effect, over the long term, in mitigating Chinese hostility. But they would not allow Americans to communicate with the younger generation of Chinese Communist leaders and to influence their views sufficiently to be of much help in the short run. In reality, the CPR would almost certainly reject any such overtures with scorn, or try to use them as means of working toward diplomatic recognition. The most that could realistically be expected, then, is that attempts at minor concessions would tend to improve the widespread, but not necessarily justified, image of American China policy as being negative and rigid.

One of the Communist gains from the Korean War, which on the whole represented a Communist defeat on points, was the widespread conviction in the United States, in the Pentagon and elsewhere, that "never again" must American ground forces be committed to combat, in large numbers at any rate, against Communist forces on the mainland of Asia. Since the threshold above which the use of American nuclear weapons against the CPR or its allies becomes probable is rather high, for political as well as military reasons, the "never again" mood has given considerable

494

aid and comfort to Asian Communists, especially the North Vietnamese. The only place where American combat ground forces are permanently stationed on the mainland of Asia at the present time is South Korea, and it is worth pointing out that South Korea has remained free, although precariously free, of Communist control since 1950 to a large extent because of the presence of such forces. It goes without saying that the United States should continue to protect South Korea.

On the other hand, as the American experience in Korea in 1950 and the Indian experience in the Himalayas in 1962 suggest, the United States should in general avoid sending ground forces into areas contiguous to the CPR: North Korea, North Vietnam (but not South Vietnam), northern (but not necessarily central or southern) Laos, northern Burma (but not necessarily northern Thailand), and the Himalayas.

In Indochina, the North Vietnamese have of course perfected the art of remaining below the nuclear threshold while pursuing their objectives through irregular warfare. This fact, combined with the mistaken American decisions to give virtually unconditional support to Ngo Dinh Diem, and first to make Laos into a bastion and later to neutralize it, obviously threaten the loss of the whole of Indochina to the DRV and the CPR. At the present time, South Vietnam is clearly the critical area. Neutralization would mean the communization of South Vietnam on the installment plan, and a political agreement with the Communists appears possible on no other basis. Down to February, 1965, at any rate the United States has tended to use the excuse that there is no stable government as a way of avoiding unpleasant decisions as to what it should do. In reality, no stable government could possibly exist in the face of American irresolution and a widespread belief that the government is losing the war with the Communists. Military successes seem to be the prerequisite for stable government at the present time, not the other way around, and only the United States is capable of bringing off any major military successses against the Communists in the near future.

While keeping its ground forces out of North Vietnam, the United States should send some into South Vietnam. Even if they were not used, or were not used effectively, against the Viet Cong, their presence would give South Vietnam the same assurance of determined American support that South Korea has had since 1950. As for the question of effectiveness, it is true that American ground forces at the present time have little if any preparation for jungle warfare. The most successful jungle warfare since the Second World War has been fought by the British, and an excellent British training school for jungle warfare still exists in Malaya. It would not seem unreasonable to send as many American Army and Marine units as possible, as soon as possible, through this school. In addition, it might be militarily advisable to send American ground forces into selected areas of Laos, other than near the Chinese frontier. This would be a violation of the Geneva Agreements of 1962, but the Communists have already made a mockery of them. One of the purposes for which a Foreign Service exists is to explain to the world on behalf of its government why such things must be done, when the need arises. In addition, the United States should conduct whatever attacks may seem useful or necessary against supply points and other targets in North Vietnam and Laos. This should not necessarily include attacks against installations that are not being directly used for purposes of fighting the war in Indochina, but such installations could be selectively threatened with attack as a means of deterring the DRV from further escalation and perhaps even of inducing it to bargain. A naval blockade of the North Vietnamese coast, as well as intensified patrolling of the lower Mekong River to intercept as much of the Communist arms traffic as possible, should be seriously considered and probably instituted.

Actions of this kind would stand some chance of providing a necessary, although not a sufficient, condition for the emergence of a stable government in South Vietnam and the winning of the war against the Viet Cong. They might well also bring intensified military intervention by the CPR. This, however, could be managed by whatever threats of retaliation, or actual retaliation, might seem necessary. As long as American ground forces did not enter North Vietnam, it is unlikely that the CPR would commit its own ground forces.

If South Vietnam were to fall to the Communists, its loss would be a heavy blow to the United States and a heavy, although not necessarily fatal, blow to the whole of continental Southeast Asia. The Chinese approach to revolution would probably gain new momentum in the underdeveloped areas, especially Africa. This seems to be the direction in which events are now moving and will continue to move unless the United States escalates its involvement somewhat along the lines suggested. If the United States were to escalate and South Vietnam were nevertheless to go under, the result would still be preferable to an abandonment of South Vietnam or its loss without an increase in the level of American effort. For the outcome of a determined even if unsuccessful struggle would be that Asian Communism would be much more unlikely to try to reproduce the Indochinese crisis somewhere else.

The United States should continue to protect Taiwan and to discourage the Republic of China from invading the mainland, except in the unlikely event of a Communist collapse. The United States should be prepared, however, for the unpleasant but not disastrous possibility that the leaders of the Republic of China may decide some day to reach an accommodation with the CPR. It would be better for the United States to be abandoned by the Republic of China than to abandon it, for instance by adopting a de jure "two Chinas" policy.

In insular Southeast Asia, it obviously important from the standpoint of the United States that Indonesia not be allowed to "crush" Malaysia. If Malaysia and the United Kingdom prove unable to cope with Indonesian pressures and Communist Chinese pressures, the United States should provide whatever aid and support may be necessary.

In the South Asian region, it seems advantageous to both American and Indian interests that units of the United States Seventh Fleet continue to operate in the Indian Ocean. If requested by India, the United States should provide air cover for Indian cities, industrial installations, and even combat units in the unlikely event of another war between India and the CPR. On the other hand, the United States should under no circumstances commit its own ground forces to the Himalayan region. The United States should also review its program of military aid to the Indian ground forces. As suggested earlier, this aid seems to have been used more to strengthen India's position against Pakistan than against the CPR, which India evidently has no intention of trying to dislodge from the Aksai Chin area for a long time to come. The result has been to increase still further India's military superiority over Pakistan, make India somewhat more reluctant to make necessary compromises over Kashmir, and drive Pakistan at least temporarily into the arms of the CPR. It is very questionable, in short, whether the precipitate and unnecessarily large program of American aid to the Indian ground forces was a wise step, and the least that can be said is that it ought to be reconsidered.

The remaining major sector of the Chinese periphery is of course the Sino-Soviet frontier. It is clearly in the interest of the United States that Sino-Soviet relations should be as bad as possible, subject to the qualification that the United States must then be prepared for the contingency of increased Chinese militancy in the underdeveloped areas. The United States can best embroil the CPR and the Soviet Union with each other, in the future as in the past, by containing both of them impartially, not by devious efforts to manipulate one against the other. On no account should the United States assume that the Soviet Union, because it is at present the less militant of the two Communist rivals and is a "white" power, is therefore a lesser threat and should somehow be favored over the CPR. If the CPR may have the greater will to inflict harm on the free world, the Soviet Union clearly has the greater ability to do so. A policy of discriminatingly equal hostility toward both, unless and until they decide to behave as civilized states, seems the best policy.

In the unlikely event of a major war between the United States and the CPR, the United States should avoid committing its ground forces to the mainland of China, but not to peripheral areas that may be judged critical. Air attacks could probably be conducted against the CPR, without involving the Soviet Union to more than a manageable degree, if they did not amount to an unprovoked strategic attack and if they avoided targets located near the Soviet frontier.

Obviously a long-term policy of containing the CPR and competing with it for influence in Asia involves strengthening friendly Asian states, whether neutral or formally aligned with the West. The United States has of course been doing this since about 1950, and its programs designed to promote this objective should certainly be continued. It has become fairly clear, however, in Asia and elsewhere, that the existing economic and military aid programs need rethinking and overhauling, since the rate of progress toward political stability and economic development in the under-developed countries has in general been disappointingly slow, at any rate in view of the urgency of the threats that confront them. Much more attention needs to be paid to population control. The sending of commodity aid, whether in grant form or in exchange for soft local currencies, should in general be discontinued. The main exception would be foodstuffs in cases of real need, by which I do not mean a desire to relieve surpluses in the United States. Technical assistance should be expanded and in general should be conducted in the recipient countries or in somewhat more advanced countries in the same region, not in the United States.

Military aid programs are not as bad as it has become fashionable in some circles to believe. For one thing, they help to make the armed forces of the recipient countries into still more valuable repositories of all too scarce technical and organizational skills. On the other hand, military aid programs should be aimed as much as possible at internal security, nation-building, and defense against aggression where such aggression is a genuine possibility and not merely a propaganda invention. This has not always been the case in the past.

Probably the greatest contribution that the United States and the other industrialized countries could make to the stability and development of the underdeveloped areas would be to work out an effective multilateral method of stabilizing the prices on the world market of the primary products that make up most of the exports of the underdeveloped countries. The fact that such a scheme would be very difficult to achieve does not excuse the countries concerned from trying to achieve it.

To return to the specific subject of China, a significant improvement in the CPR's domestic and foreign policies, and therefore in its relations with the United States, Asia, and the world, would seem to require a change of leadership in Peking sufficient to produce a major reorientation of thinking. Such a change appears most unlikely during Mao's lifetime and during the tenure of his immediate successors. After that, we may at least be permitted the luxury of cautious hope.

Bibliographical Note

The principal sources on which this study is based are given in the notes to the text and will not be listed again here, if only to prevent what is already a rather long book from verging on the unmanageable. What follows is therefore intended as a supplement to, not a recapitulation of, the notes.

Certain background reading may be recommended to those who feel the need of it.

An excellent general history of the Far East is Edwin O. Reischauer and John K. Fairbank, *East Asia*, 2 vols., Boston: Houghton Mifflin, 1960 and 1965. Also useful is Franz Michael and George E. Taylor, *The Far East in the Modern World*, revised edition, New York: Holt, Rinehart and Winston, 1964. A briefer, more readable, and generally excellent introduction to an understanding of China is John K. Fairbank, *The United States and China*, revised edition, Harvard University Press, 1958. On Communist China, the reader may be referred to Harold C. Hinton, "China," in George McT. Kahin, ed., *Major Governments of Asia*, revised edition, Cornell University Press, 1963, pp. 3–149; and John Wilson Lewis, *Major Doctrines of Communist China*, New York: Norton, 1964. Three excellent articles on the "state of the art" of the study of Chinese politics are: Howard L. Boorman, "The Study of Contemporary Chinese Politics: Some Remarks on Retarded Development," *World Politics*, vol. xii, no. 4 (July, 1960), pp. 585–599; A. M. Halpern, "Contemporary China as a Problem for Political Science," *World Politics*, vol. xv, no. 3 (April, 1963), pp. 361–376; Chalmers Johnson, "The Role of Social Science in China Scholarship," *World Politics*, vol. xvii, no. 2 (January, 1965), pp. 256–271.

On Communism, R. N. Carew Hunt, *The Theory and Practice of Communism*, 5th revised edition, New York: Macmillan, 1957; and Alfred Meyer, *Communism*, revised edition, New York: Random House, 1960, are standard and useful.

Since China is obviously one of the underdeveloped countries, although a special case in many ways, a knowledge of the subjects of underdevelopment and development is desirable; probably the best work on this subject is the classic by W. Arthur Lewis, *The Theory of Economic Growth*, Homewood, Ill.: Richard D. Irwin, 1955.

The following discussions of American China policy may be helpful: *United States Foreign Policy: Asia* (the Conlon Report), Washington: U.S. Government Printing Office for Senate Committee on Foreign Relations, 1959; Chester Bowles, "The 'China Problem' Reconsidered," *Foreign Affairs*, vol. 38, no. 3 (April, 1960), pp. 476–486; Harold M. Vinacke, "United States Policy Towards China: An Appraisal," *Far Eastern Survey*, vol. 29, no. 5 (May, 1960), pp. 65–90; John K. Fairbank, "Communist China and Taiwan in United States Foreign Policy," University of Connecticut: The Brien McMahon Lectures, November 21, 1960; Robert P. Newman, *Recognition of Communist China? A Study in Argument*, New York: Macmillan, 1961; John Wilson Lewis, "Quemoy and American China Policy," *Asian Survey*, vol. ii, no. 1 (March, 1962), pp. 12–19; "America and China: Opportunity for New Policies?" *The China Quarterly*, no. 10 (April–June, 162), pp. 45–83; Kung-lee Wang, *Observations on Counterweights to Rising Chinese Communist Power*, Washington: Research Analysis Corporation, Technical Paper RAC-TP-90, June, 1963; Assistant Secretary of State Roger Hilsman, "United States Policy Toward Communist China," speech delivered on December 13, 1963 (excerpts in *The New York Times*, December 14, 1963); Takashi Oka, "Recognition Presses U.S. Policymakers," *Christian Science Monitor*, March 4, 1964; George F. Kennan, "A Fresh Look at Our China Policy," *The New York Times Magazine*, November 22, 1964, pp. 27, 140–147. The Council on Foreign Relations is about to publish a series of volumes dealing with various aspects of American China policy.

A few of the official Communist Chinese documents cited in the text may be found in G. V. Ambekar and V. D. Divekar, eds., *Documents on China's Relations with South and South-East Asia, 1949–1962*, Bombay: Allied Publishers, 1964. Some others may be found in the Chinese periodical *Peking Review* (the successor to *People's China*). Fairly full coverage of the Communist Chinese press is provided by the various series of translations published by the American Consulate General, Hong Kong, and in particular *Survey of the China Mainland Press*, which appears five times a week. The Union Research Institute (Hong Kong) also publishes translations of articles from the Communist Chinese press. The official distributor in the United States for Communist Chinese publications intended for consumption in the English-speaking world is China Books and Periodicals, 2929 Twenty-fourth Street, San Francisco, California 94110. When a New China News Agency release is cited in the text, it should be assumed that the dateline is Peking unless otherwise stated; major New China News Agency releases are generally both broadcast and published in the press.

Although nothing of any real value has been published on the subject of interpreting Communist Chinese documents, a good deal of reflected light is shed by some studies relating to the Soviet Union. Among the most valuable of these are: R. Conquest, *Power and Policy in the U.S.S.R.: The Study of Soviet Dynastics*, New York: St. Martin's Press, 1961, Chapter 3; Donald S. Zagoria, *The Sino-Soviet Conflict, 1956–1961*, Princeton University Press, 1962, pp. 24–35, "A Note on Methodology"; Donald S. Zagoria, *Talmudism and Communist Communications*, The RAND Corporation, P-2631, September, 1962; Myron Rush, "Esoteric Communication in Soviet Politics," *World Politics*, vol. xi, no. 4 (July, 1959), pp. 614–620.

The full title of the valuable Indian documentary collection cited as Indian White Paper is *Notes, Memoranda and Letters Exchanged Between the Governments of India and China*, followed by the terminal dates of the period covered and the number of the volume; all volumes are published by the Ministry of External Affairs, Government of India.

In addition to the scholarly sources cited in the notes, it seems desirable to mention two that came to my attention too late to be utilized fully: Arthur A. Cohen, *The Communism of Mao Tse-tung*, University of Chicago Press, 1964; William E. Griffith, *The Sino-Soviet Rift*, M.I.T. Press, 1964. Neither contains anything that would cause me to modify significantly any of my interpretations or conclusions.

Postscript

Although the main purpose of this postscript is to summarize the principal trends in Communist China's foreign policy and foreign relations since the completion of the manuscript, it may be of interest to mention first two clear indications of Sino-Soviet tension during the period before Khrushchev's fall that have recently come to my attention. I have learned that in mid-1964 Soviet Far Eastern forces took part in large-scale maneuvers to cope with a hypothetical Chinese invasion of the Maritime Province from Manchuria, and that in September, 1964, Soviet scientific delegates to a "Pugwash" conference in Czechoslovakia are reported to have argued for a comprehensive nuclear test ban (i.e., one including underground testing) and for sanctions against any power violating it, whether it had adhered to the agreement or not.

In the field of domestic Chinese affairs, the economic concessions made at the end of 1960 are still basically in effect, but the political atmosphere is one of tension, aggravated by external crises such as the one over Vietnam. Mao Tse-tung is not known to have appeared in public from roughly mid-March to mid-June, and it is likely that he was ill. He and his colleagues have given increasingly frequent indications of fear that the younger generation, and perhaps even their own successors, may turn away from "socialism" and reach some sort of accommodation with "imperialism." Increasing political controls, culminating with the abolition of ranks and insignia effective June 1, have been applied to the armed forces, presumably in the hope of ensuring absolute reliability in the event of a war or succession crisis. In July, Li Tsung-jen, a former Acting President of the Republic of China, returned to the mainland of China after some fifteen years in the United States. His intended role probably relates to the perennial Communist political maneuvers aimed at the Nationalists. Conceivably, it may relate to Vietnam; Li at one time controlled the province of Kwangsi, which borders on Vietnam.

The CPR conducted its second nuclear test on May 14. It apparently represented something of a technical improvement over the first and may even have involved an actual weapon dropped from an aircraft. In June the CPR withdrew forty-seven atomic scientists, who appeared to be the last of its scientists studying at the Soviet Joint Nuclear Research Institute at Dubna. Shortly thereafter, indications, which had been discernible for several years, that the CPR favored nuclear proliferation by "peace loving" countries became clearer and more numerous; they were especially evident in the Chinese statements made to, and in connection with, the annual ban-the-bomb conference in Japan in late July. There have been reports that the CPR is giving Indonesia aid for an Indonesian nuclear test; on the other hand, it has been rumored that the CPR may hold a test of its own somewhere in Indonesia.

Sino-Soviet relations have remained in a highly paradoxical state. The two regimes have evidently decided not to have a complete, formal break with each other, and yet they have made no serious effort to improve their relations with one another. Both have tended to lose influence in some quarters, the Soviet Union among the East European Communist Parties and the Chinese among the Asian Communist states. Partly perhaps because of its weakened position, the Soviet party has suspended its efforts at "collective mobilization" of the international Communist movement against the CPC and its followers. The farthest it has gone was a highly unsuccessful eighteen-party conference convened at Moscow on March 1, from which the revisionist Italians and not the Russians emerged as the victor, and which the CPC not only boycotted and denounced but tried to disrupt, by means of a riotous demonstration of Chinese and North Vietnamese students in front of the American Embassy in Moscow on March 4, followed by loud criticism of the Soviet Union for using police against the students. Since Khrushchev's fall, the Soviet leadership has shown an increased interest in supporting left wing "national liberation movements" and has moved actively and with some success to recapture lost influence in North Korea and North Vietnam. The CPR, for its part, succeeded in excluding the Soviet Union from the preparatory conference held at Djakarta in April for the Afro-Asian (or Second Asian-African) Conference.

Both the Soviet Union and the CPR have been startled and disturbed by the American air attacks on North Vietnam (beginning in February) and the sending of American combat forces to South Vietnam (beginning in March). The effect to date of these actions, and of the marked effect on the military situation in Vietnam that they have produced, has been to cast the Sino-Soviet alliance, and its members individually, further in the light of paper tigers. The Soviet Union has implemented a pledge, apparently made before the beginning of the American escalation, to send antiaircraft missiles and bombers to North Vietnam; the former, which are defensive, have been used in combat, but the latter, which are offensive, have not. The CPR has not yet gone beyond a continuation of the measures it had already begun to take before the escalation: defensive preparations in South China, the sending of jet fighters to North Vietnam, vigorous insistence that the United States must withdraw its troops from Vietnam before any negotiations can begin (North Vietnam, which is suffering more, seems less insistent on this point), offers to send "volunteers" if the "Vietnamese people" so request, and vague threats of a land war in Indochina if the United States escalates further. Both the Chinese and the Russians of course try in every way to make capital of the American policy in Vietnam; each denounces the other for its ineffectiveness in the crisis; and no doubt each has lost some face with Hanoi, the Chinese probably more than the Russians.

In the late summer, Kashmir and the Himalayas replaced Vietnam as the leading crisis area in Asia. Pakistan had for months been growing restless over the refusal of the Shastri government to settle the Kashmir dispute and over its increasing integration of Indian-held Kashmir into the Indian Union. The CPR, which sympathized with Pakistan without necessarily wishing to make any great efforts on its behalf, was at least indirectly involved; it was also concerned about Khamba guerrilla activity in Tibet, in the vicinity of the frontier with Sikkim. For Pakistan, the last straw was the Indian arrest of Sheikh Abdullah, the "lion of Kashmir," on May 8, not long after he had talked with Chou En-lai in Algiers (on March 30). Pakistani military activity in Kashmir intensified in mid-May and culminated when irregular forces crossed the ceasefire line early in August, apparently in the expectation that they would evoke sympathetic popular uprisings. This action, however, did not result in the hoped-for uprisings, but rather in an Indo-Pakistani war, the details of which need not be discussed here.

The incomplete available evidence on the CPR's relationship to this crisis strongly suggests that Peking did not want a major war, either between India and Pakistan or between itself and India. It also indicates that coordination between the CPR and Pakistan before and during the crisis was poor and that although each was disappointed by the other's performance, the CPR did feel some necessity to exert pressure on India to counterbalance the increasing military difficulties in which Pakistan found itself as the fighting progressed. Apart from some threatening troop movements along the frontiers with Ladakh and Sikkim, the CPR's role in the crisis consisted mainly of a warning to India to stop violating the Tibet-Sikkim frontier (August 27), loud charges of Indian aggression against Pakistan (September 7–8), and a three-day "ultimatum" (later extended for another three days) to India to dismantle fifty-six military installations that had allegedly been erected on the Tibetan side of the Tibet-Sikkim border (September 16). These three acts of intervention closely followed, respectively, three major turning points in the Indo-Pakistani fighting: the crossing of the ceasefire line in Kashmir by Indian troops, an Indian invasion of West Pakistan (in the vicinity of Sialkot and Lahore), and indications that India would continue fighting even after President Ayub had shown an interest in a ceasefire. The CPR withheld its withdrawal (September 22) of the "ultimatum," which was withdrawn on the (apparently false) ground that India had complied with it, until it was certain that Pakistan would accept a ceasefire ordered by the United Nations Security Council; presumably the CPR did not want to be accused of taking pressure off India while the crisis was still in progress. At the time of writing, there are reports that the CPR is constructing a wall along the Tibet-Sikkim frontier, which if true suggest that the CPR's main immediate object is to use the crisis as a favorable opportunity to try to isolate the Tibetan guerrillas from Sikkim. Much as the CPR sympathizes with Pakistan in its quarrel with India, and much as the CPR would like to secure Indian agreement to a frontier settlement along Chinese lines, there is as yet no convincing evidence that the CPR is willing to run the risks of another frontier war for these ends, especially at a time when tension over Vietnam is running high.

The summer months also brought fresh evidence of Sino-Indonesian collaboration aimed at "crushing" Malaysia and expelling Western influence from Southeast Asia, and of the CPR's willingness to cater to the self-esteem of an Indonesia still moving rapidly to the left by bolstering its self-proclaimed position as a leader of the "New Emerging Forces." Early in June, Indonesia published a "Manifesto of the Malayan National Liberation League," a body presumably dominated by the Chinese-led Malayan Communist Party. The manifesto was reprinted by the CPC press a month later, and at about the same time some recrudescence of Communist guerrilla activity occurred in the vicinity of the Thai-Malayan frontier. Chinese guerrillas continued active in Sarawak. The expulsion of Singapore from the Malaysian Federation in August, although apparently in no way due to these developments, overjoyed both Peking and Djakarta. The CPR also demonstrated increasing interest in the situation in the Philippines, where relations with the United States were at a low ebb and the Communist-led Huks were once more becoming active.

In its activities in Africa, the CPR continued to enjoy good relations at least with sections of the elites (not always with the highest officials) in the most leftist countries, such as Tanzania, Uganda, and Congo Brazzaville. In other areas, on the other hand, such successes were more than offset by the continued eradication of the leftist-tribal revolt in the Congo, which the CPR had supported, by Premier Tshombe's white mercenaries; by the image increasingly held by moderate Africans of the CPR as a subversive force, an image strengthened by another remark by Chou En-lai, made while in Tanzania during the second of two trips to Africa in 1965, to the effect that Africa was "ripe for revolution"; and by the postponement of the Afro-Asian (or Second Asian-African) Conference, originally scheduled to open at Algiers on June 29. The Algerian regime of Ben Bella had been moving rapidly to the left and had been subject to increasing "licensed infiltration" by the Moscow-oriented Algerian Communists. This trend intensified frictions with the army and its leader, Colonel Houari Boumedienne, who seized power on June 19. Probably pleased at the sight of one more setback for the nonviolent Soviet path to power, and in any case anxious for the conference to be held on schedule, the CPR promptly and opportunistically recognized the Boumedienne government. Together with Boumedienne, the CPR, Indonesia, and their supporters insisted on the convening of the conference as planned, as well as on the exclusion of the Soviet Union and Malaysia. The moderates (led by India, Ceylon, Japan, Thailand, and the Philippines), however, succeeded in engineering a postponement of the conference until November 5, on the ground that conditions in Algiers were too insecure to permit the conference to be held in safety at that time. The net result of this episode was a blow to Chinese prestige.

In Latin America, Chinese influence appears to have suffered as a result of a bargain seemingly struck between the Soviet Union and Castro and his supporters late in 1964. In exchange for some Soviet aid in connection with armed uprisings in selected countries, mainly the Dominican Republic, Venezuela, and Peru, the Castroites have inclined toward the Soviet side in the Sino-Soviet dispute.

The Chinese record in the underdeveloped areas, then, continues to be a mixed one, with the percentage of setbacks seemingly on the increase. Although there is likely to be a great deal of turmoil in the underdeveloped areas over the coming decades, it seems possible that the distinctively Chinese contribution to the turmoil may not be as great as once appeared probable. Asia, rather than Africa or Latin America, will almost certainly continue to be the region where the distinctively Chinese role is the greatest.

October 1, 1965

Index